Fifth Edition

Juvenile Delinquency

A Sociological Approach

Jack E. Bynum
Southern Oregon University

William E. Thompson
Texas A&M University-Commerce

Allyn and Bacon
Boston • London • Toronto • Sydney • Tokyo • Singapore

Series Editor: Jennifer Jacobson
Editor in Chief, Social Sciences: Karen Hanson
Editorial Assistant: Sarah McGaughey
Marketing Manager: Jude Hall
Editorial Production Service: Whitney Acres Editorial
Manufacturing Buyer: Joanne Sweeney
Cover Administrator: Linda Knowles
Electronic Composition: Omegatype Typography, Inc.

Internet: www.ablongman.com

Between the time Website information is gathered and published, some sites may have closed. Also, the transcription of URLs can result in typographical errors. The publisher would appreciate notification where these occur so that they may be corrected in subsequent editions.

Library of Congress Cataloging-in-Publication Data

Bynum, Jack E.
 Juvenile delinquency a sociological approach / Jack E. Bynum, William E. Thompson. — 5th ed.
  p. cm.
 Includes bibliographical references and index.
 ISBN 0-205-32177-1
 1. Juvenile delinquency—United States. I. Thompson, William E. (William Edwin), 1950– II. Title.

HV9104 .B9 2001
364.36'0973—dc21   00-053598

Printed in the United States of America

10 9 8 7 6 5 4 3 2 1   06 05 04 03 02 01

Credits:

Cartoon on page 18 is by Bill De Ore. Originally published in *The Dallas Morning News,* Universal Press Syndicate, April 23, 1999. Reprinted by permission.

Cartoon on page 207 from *Sense and Nonsense About Crime: A Policy Guide* by S. Walker. Copyright © 1985 by Wadsworth Inc. Reprinted by permission of Brooks/Cole Publishing Co., Pacific Grove, CA 93950.

Excerpts on pages 351–352 are from a CBS documentary entitled "Moscow Vice" from the television series *48 Hours.* © 1990. All rights reserved. Originally broadcast on May 31, 1990 over the CBS Television Network.

Photo credits are listed on page xxii, which should be considered an extension of the copyright page.

To the memory of our parents–Jack and Frances Bynum,
and Edwin and Flora Thompson–who through their precepts and examples
helped us become the authors of this book and not the subjects

CONTENTS

LIST OF FIGURES

LIST OF TABLES

PREFACE

Juvenile delinquency is one of the most complex, interesting, and challenging phenomena in the United States. Newspapers, television, and radio bombard us with accounts of juvenile misbehavior and crime that range from truancy to first degree murder. Consequently, youths who violate the law receive considerable attention from law enforcement officials, social agencies, criminologists, and social and behavioral scientists.

This book is guided by the basic premise that juvenile delinquency is inherently social in nature. It is a social concept, part and product of the society in which it occurs. Thus, any meaningful discussion of delinquency must be expressed in a sociological framework that views it in relation to the normative processes and societal responses that define it. More specifically, this book approaches delinquency as it relates to and emerges from the youth's family, neighborhood, school, peer group, social class, and overall cultural and social environment.

Rather than aligning this analysis to any particular theoretical perspective, we used an eclectic sociological approach that integrates elements from a wide spectrum of causal theories. Thus, we have attempted to present delinquency in its broadest sociological context. This approach should give the reader a growing awareness of and sensitivity to the social nature of human behavior, whether it be socially adjudged as conforming or nonconforming, normative or deviant, acceptable or unacceptable, good or bad, or some paradoxical mixture of these seemingly antithetical evaluations.

This sociological work has been enhanced by the inclusion of some important contributions of social workers, criminologists, psychologists, and other specialists who have sought to understand, explain, control, and prevent juvenile delinquency. The reader will note that each section of the book is carefully grounded in knowledge and research and unified by the sociological theme that delinquency must be viewed within its social context.

The book is organized in a format that guides the reader through an unfolding sequence of interrelated dimensions of the study of juvenile delinquency: conformity, causes, collective behavior, and social control. Each part begins with a brief introduction which includes basic sociological concepts and ideas related to the topical theme of that section. For example, Part I Conformity, Deviance, and Juvenile Delinquency, before addressing the problem of juvenile delinquency, incorporates a brief introduction to sociology and the sociological perspective. The normative system of society and the concepts of conformity and deviance are introduced and explained. In Part II Causes of Juvenile Delinquency, students are first introduced to the nature of scientific theory and the theory building process. Then, they are presented with specific theories which attempt to explain the causes of delinquency. Part III Juvenile Delinquency in a Social Context begins by looking at the nature of social groups and their impact upon individuals. It then proceeds to explore the influence of family, schools, youth subculture, and gangs on juvenile behavior. The social control of juvenile behavior is presented in the last two sections of the text. Part IV Social Control: The Juvenile Justice System includes detailed coverage of those arenas of social confrontation encountered by recalcitrant youth: police contacts, juvenile courts, and community correctional agencies. Part V Strategies for Dealing with Juvenile Delinquency begins with a systematic evaluation of the major classic and contemporary programs developed for the prevention and treatment of delinquency in the United States. Part V concludes the book with a challenging call for innovative revisions in the social and legal status of young people and in our approach to the problem of juvenile delinquency.

Each of the five parts is divided into topically related chapters. Again, as in earlier editions of this book, each chapter begins with a list of Reading Objectives for that particular unit of content. These alert the readers in advance to the specific learning expectations for that chapter so that they may identify, extrapolate, and integrate major concepts while proceeding through the chapter. The learning objectives are reemphasized at the end of the chapter through the use of Questions and Topics for Study and Discussion that are designed to help prepare students for examinations and to stimulate class discussion. These teaching and learning aids are reinforced by a comprehensive glossary at the end of the book that includes definitions of key terms and concepts.

We have continued our use of three types of innovative and instructive boxes or sidebars entitled: *Concept Application, Cross-Cultural Focus,* and *Controversial Issue.* Each chapter contains one to three of these boxes, which have proved to be popular with students. The Concept Application boxes apply abstract theoretical concepts to concrete situations facing young people today. Cross-Cultural Focus boxes incorporate an international dimension providing examples of delinquency in other societies, cultures, and subcultures. Controversial Issue boxes address some of the critical juvenile delinquency questions facing society.

Several new and important changes and additions are included in this fifth edition. For example, all data on delinquents and delinquency derived from FBI Uniform Crime Reports and U.S. juvenile courts, plus corresponding statistical analyses, have been updated. Moreover, we have inserted a Department of Justice Internet Website where assiduous scholars may derive the most currently available crime/delinquency data. Also included in Chapter 3 is a "balanced perspective" section that focuses on the vast, underreported majority of youth who generally conform to behavioral expectations of society and do *not* become delinquents.

Since 1994, there has been a significant decline in the number of juvenile arrests for most crime categories. This trend as well as the recent series of violent school assaults committed by teenagers are closely examined in several relevant chapters of this edition. Extensive new material on the motivation, activities, and numbers of gangs and gang members have been incorporated into Chapter 12. Chapters 15 and 16 have been revised and augmented with expanded sections on juvenile probation and aftercare, as well as creative new treatment and prevention strategies for dealing with delinquents and their antisocial conduct.

Rather than compartmentalizing gender and racial involvement in delinquency in isolated chapters, we have chosen to integrate these important topics throughout the book. In sum, this book provides a comprehensive examination of juvenile delinquency in a pedagogical style designed with our readers/students in mind.

While the authors assume final responsibility for the book, as with any other work of this magnitude, many people made significant contributions for which we are indebted. We would like to thank Mica Thompson and Lisa Busby for their "behind the scenes" work. Also, we appreciate the help, support, and encouragement from many friends and colleagues during our exciting fourteen-year journey through the five editions of this book.

Special thanks are extended to those who, through the years, have reviewed the entire manuscript and made helpful and constructive suggestions for revision: Professor John A. Arthur, University of Minnesota–Duluth; Professor Steven R. Cureton, University of North Carolina–Greensboro; Professor Kathleen Heide, University of South Florida; Professor Mark Mantyh, University of Wisconsin–Milwaukee; Professor Stephanie Amedco Marquez, Arizona State University; Professor Wilson R. Palacios, University of South Florida; Professor Jerome Rosonke, Northern State University; Professor Raghu Singh, Texas A&M University–Commerce; and Professor Craig C. White, Fairmont State College.

We are also indebted to the editors, staff, and production affiliates of Allyn and Bacon for their help and technical assistance with this fifth edition, especially Karen Hanson, Sarah McGaughey, Karen Corday, Marjorie Payne, and Faye Whitney-Lussier. Finally, our most heartfelt thanks and love go to Margaret Bynum and Jenny Bynum-Hilton, and to Marilyn, Brandon, and Mica Thompson for their unwavering love, support, and encouragement.

J.E.B.
W.E.T.

PHOTO CREDITS

p. 11, Jonathan Nourok/PhotoEdit; p. 16, © B. Daemmrich/The Image Works; p. 29, Y. Momatiuk & J. Eastcott/Stock Boston; p. 39, Phil MvCarten/PhotoEdit; p. 44, © Ken Lax/ Photo Researchers, Inc.; p. 60, © B. Daemmrich/The Image Works; p. 72, ©Bob Daemmrich/Stock Boston; p. 81, © Jeff Greenberg/PhotoEdit; p. 104, Joseph Szabo/Photo Researchers; p. 110, Elizabeth Crews/Stock Boston; p. 123, Corbis; p. 135, Bob Daemmrich Photo, Inc.; p. 141, © Mark Richards/PhotoEdit; p. 163, Michael Weisbrot/Stock Boston; p. 173, © Hazel Hankin/Stock Boston; p. 185, Peter Southwick/Stock Boston; p. 191, © Bob Strong/The Image Works; p. 194, © M. K. Denny/PhotoEdit; p. 211, © Mary Kay Denny/PhotoEdit; p. 215, © Will Waldron/The Image Works; p. 218, Eugene Richards/ Magnum Photos, Inc.; p. 238, Bob Daemmrich Photo, Inc.; p. 247, Barbara Rios/Photo Researchers, Inc.; p. 249, Paul Fortin/Stock Boston; p. 264, Elizabeth Crews/Stock Boston; p. 274, © Mark Leffingwell/Boulder Daily Camera; p. 289, John Nordell/Index Stock; p. 297, © Syracuse Newspapers/Gary Walts/The Image Works; p. 303, John Maher/Stock Boston; p. 332, © Bob Sietz/Photo Researchers, Inc.; p. 339, Akos Szilvasl/Stock Boston; p. 342, © A. Ramey/PhotoEdit; p. 366, James L. Shaffer; p. 371, © A. Lichtenstein/The Image Works; p. 378, Rachel Epstein/PhotoEdit; p. 389, Billy E. Barnes/Stock Boston; p. 396, Richard Hutchings/Photo Researchers, Inc.; p. 405, AP Wide World/Coshocton Tribune, Dante Smith; p. 414, Blair Sietz/Photo Researchers, Inc.; p. 418, AP/Wide World Photos; p. 434, Corbis; p. 453, Schuyler Photography/Stock Boston; p. 458, © A. Ramey/ Woodfin Camp & Associates; p. 464, © Tony Savino/The Image Works; p. 476, Spencer Grant/Stock Boston; p. 490, Erika Stone/Photo Researchers; p. 493, Nita Winter/The Image Works.

PART

I

CONFORMITY, DEVIANCE, AND JUVENILE DELINQUENCY

Introduction: The Sociological Perspective and Focus on Juvenile Delinquency

There are several reasons why most readers will identify with the subject of this book. For one thing, the book is about young people—in many cases, not much younger than most of the college students who will be reading the book. Moreover, you may experience a powerful empathy for American youths in general as we explore and explain the frustrations and marginality of being adolescent—a situation and status shared by nearly every youth who grows up in the United States.

Additionally, as the thoughtful reader gains insight into the deviant and disruptive behavior of juvenile offenders, personal youthful escapades may be recalled that, if discovered or reported, might have resulted in an adversarial confrontation with society and adjudication as a juvenile delinquent. The reader will probably be surprised to learn that most illegal acts attributed to young people do not apply to adults and violate the law only if the offender happens to be a minor.

Part I explains the **sociological perspective** for the study and understanding of juvenile delinquency. From the sociological viewpoint, delinquency must be viewed and explained as part and product of the social context in which it occurs. Within this general sociological perspective, there are three basic approaches to the study of human society and behavior (each with its cadre of supporting sociologists): the functionalist approach, conflict approach, and the interactionist approach. The **functionalist approach** *views society as a social system comprised of a network of interrelated and interdependent parts.* Consequently, it regards delinquency primarily as the result of some type of breakdown in the overall functioning of basic social institutions in society. The **conflict approach** *views society as being comprised of a variety of heterogeneous groups all competing for the highly valued resources society has to offer (such as wealth, power, and prestige).* Consequently, deviant behavior such as juvenile delinquency tends to be viewed as the result of conflicting values held by members of various social groups who must socially interact with one another. The **interactionist approach** *views society as being a product of the shared expectations held by individuals as they socially interact on a face-to-face daily basis.* Thus, juvenile delinquency is viewed as a matter of social definition that arises out of the course of social interaction. In Part I, and throughout this book, we have chosen not to tie our analysis of juvenile delinquency to any one of these interpretive approaches. Rather, we place delinquency in its broadest sociological context, using relevant concepts, theories, and explanations from the functionalist, conflict, and interactionist approaches as they apply. This eclectic approach supplies a balanced presentation of all theoretical viewpoints, yet leaves the instructor free to emphasize his or her own overriding theoretical preference, unencumbered by the authors' possible choice.

Part I of the book sets the stage and furnishes direction to our unfolding study of juvenile delinquency. Chapter 1 identifies and analyzes various approaches to defining juvenile delinquency. For example, the **legal definition** emphasizes a specific age as the dividing line between juvenile delinquency and adult crime. A different approach utilizes the **role definition,** which discounts the occasional youthful misbehavior and focuses instead on the individual who sustains a consistent pattern of delinquent behavior. Yet a third image of the delinquent and the nonconforming behavior is supplied by the **societal response definition,** which concentrates on the perceptual exchanges between the actor (the alleged delinquent) and the audience (society) that judges the behavior in question and can impute a delinquent identity. In actual practice, and in Chapter 1, all three of these definitions are combined to give us a complete and operational description of what constitutes "juvenile delinquency" in American society.

The Chapter 2 discussion of society, rules of conduct, conformity, and deviance places juvenile delinquency in an overall social context. Thus, the sociological perspective supplies an appropriate foundation and ongoing framework for the careful consideration of juvenile delinquency as a significant social problem in American society.

Chapter 3 explains the various sources of juvenile crime statistics and a catalog of the kinds and incidences of juvenile offenses. The longitudinal national trends in juvenile delinquency are set forth, and some of the weaknesses of data on delinquency are discussed. Chapter 3 concludes with a composite profile of those demographic traits that most nearly characterize the "typical" juvenile delinquent. The reader is cautioned, however, that while such profiles may be helpful in summarizing and pointing out statistical trends in arrests and court referrals, they can also unfairly stereotype those groups identified by the composite profile unless we are acutely aware of certain weaknesses in official crime and delinquency statistics.

As you read Part I, and embark upon your study of juvenile delinquency, we encourage you to approach the subject and this book with an open mind. While common sense can and should play an important role in the attempt to understand any social issue, unfortunately much of what passes for common sense about juvenile delinquency may, in fact, be nothing more than "common nonsense." The astute student involved in sociological inquiry will attempt to avoid some of the common misconceptions and pitfalls related to the study of delinquency by developing critical thinking skills and laying aside personal feelings about the subject.

CHAPTER

1

JUVENILE DELINQUENCY

The Act, the Actor, and the Audience

Reading Objectives

The reading of this chapter will help you achieve the following objectives:

1. Comprehend the legal and social importance of carefully and accurately defined terms such as "juvenile" and "adult."
2. Understand the difference between criminal behavior and juvenile delinquency.
3. Understand the difference between criminal offenders and juvenile delinquents.
4. Conceptualize and compare the legal definition, role definition, and societal response definition of juvenile delinquency.
5. Understand social **status** and social **role** and explain how these concepts can be used to describe a youth's commitment to a delinquent career.
6. See how the identification of an individual or a behavior as delinquent is possible only in a social context, involving the interplay between the actor, a norm, an act, and an audience perception of the act.

Introduction

In this opening chapter, we emphasize the sociological nature of juvenile delinquency and how society defines delinquency by looking at the social dynamics of the act, the actor, and the audience. The terms **"act," "actor,"** and **"audience"** conjure up images of the theater, but can be used effectively as analogs to help us understand much of our behavior in everyday life.

Ever since the comedies and tragedies of life were adapted for the stage by early Greek actors, the theater has held fascinating appeal for performers and spectators alike. One reason for the powerful appeal of the stage, the actors, and the roles they play is that humans are naturally imitative. We can readily identify with many parts and plots that reflect our own real or imaginary lives, in the past, present, or future. William Shakespeare (1623), the seventeenth century dramatist, was alluding to this trait in human nature when he general-ized in Act II of *As You Like It* that all the world is a stage and we are the actors in the drama of life. Sociologist Erving Goffman (1959) artfully appropriated elements of the theater to analyze social life as a carefully orchestrated drama. Similarly, Melvin DeFleur and asso-ciates (1976:175) observed that "deviance involves a complex interplay between a social norm, an actor, an act, and an audience that defines the act as nonconforming..." This dramaturgical analogy offers an excellent sociological framework within which to define and commence our study of juvenile delinquency. More specifically to this chapter, these theatrical metaphors will help us to identify, state, and differentiate the major definitions of juvenile delinquency prevalent among sociologists and criminologists.

What Is Juvenile Delinquency?

In order for any communication to be successful, there must be common language or shared mutual understanding of key words, terms, and concepts. This applies to mass media com-munication, public stage performances, the classroom learning environment occupied by teachers and students, and even to an informal dialogue between two friends:

> *When you tell a friend about a concert you have attended or a movie you have seen, you use a vocabulary that you know your friend will understand. You include all of the background information your friend needs in order to understand what you are talking about; you use an organizational plan that will make it easy for your friend to follow your explanation; and you use grammatical structures that make your meaning clear (Johnson, 1987:134).*

The principle of effective communication is especially important in the academic and sci-entific communities, where the highly specialized and precise terminology of various dis-ciplines must be used liberally to describe complex phenomena. Therefore, it is customary to begin a discussion or discourse with carefully structured definitions in order to promote clarity and comprehension (Johnson, 1987; Lastrucci, 1967).

To begin our study of the phenomenon of juvenile delinquency, two basic questions must be answered: First, what is a juvenile?; and second, what is delinquency? While the two terms "juvenile" and "delinquency" are used frequently by Americans, it is interesting to note that they are relatively new concepts that do not necessarily connote the same mean-ings to all who use them.

What Is a Juvenile?

In 16th and 17th century American society, essentially two lifestages existed: *childhood* and *adulthood*. In traditional agrarian America, the normative expectations for children and for adults were clearly differentiated, and fairly well defined. Very young children were consid-ered helpless and totally dependent upon other family members for survival. However, as soon as a child was physically capable of helping around the house or in the fields, some routine chores were assigned. Children were expected to obey their parents, and the old adage "Children shall be seen, but not heard" was widely practiced. The early American colonists, reflecting the sober child-rearing practices of their European and religious backgrounds, were strict disciplinarians. For example, "the laws of 1660 even made lying by children and failure to observe the Sabbath punishable offenses" (Weisheit and Culbertson, 1990:6). Normative conformity and "godliness" were almost synonymous; and parents, strongly supported by the clergy, considered the punishment and correction of children as largely a family responsibility.

While no American laws explicitly defined "childhood," the practice of exempting young children from legal responsibility for their deviant behavior was widely followed. British common law exempted children under the age of 7 from the criminal courts because they lacked **mens rea,** or *criminal intent,* required for criminal conviction. Since much of American criminal law is based upon British common law, the same practice was traditional in the United States. Children over the age of 7 were considered old enough to know right from wrong and to understand the consequences of their actions, and were considered responsible for their law-violating behavior.

However, the child over the age of 7 was not viewed as an adult. Typically, adulthood was not reached until after the onset of puberty, when expectations of work, marriage, and other "adult" activities were assumed. An adult was perceived as a man or a woman who was physically grown and had reached mature size and strength.

The Industrial Revolution came to the United States in the 19th century with the mechanization of factory production, rapid urbanization, and mass migration of rural people into the large cities—all with historic and often traumatic implications for the children of the United States. Children, especially the children of immigrants and the poor, came to be seen as cheap factory workers until the cruelty of child labor was made public. Finally, near the end of the 19th century, new child labor laws were legislated to protect youths from such exploitation:

> *The awareness of childhood as a distinct period of life is, then, a historical creation. Once this awareness developed, the nature of childhood and what should be done about it became a matter of ideological controversy, and it has remained so down to our time. At some periods and among some groups, the child has been regarded as basically tender and innocent. In opposition to this has been the notion that the child is wild and needs to be tamed. These two images continue to have their respective adherents (Elkin and Handel, 1978:62).*

The rapid social changes associated with the American experience continued to have an impact on attitudes and values related to young people. No longer able to assume meaningful responsibilities as members of farm families, urban youth were required to undergo a much longer period of dependence and extended preparation before entering adulthood and the world of work:

> *The ensuing social reform movement transformed the image of the child from one of cheap factory labor to one of apprentice to factory work. Instead of being sent to the factory, children were sent to school to prepare them to work in factories.*

School bells, like factory whistles, signaled the beginning and the end of the school day. And children, like their parents, carried lunch pails to be opened at the noon whistle (Elkind, 1991:136).

During the twentieth century, the special social status of children was even more clearly defined and the parameters around their place and participation in U.S. society were delimited. The values of extended dependency and formal education, and the absence of fulfilling roles evolved into social realities. What developed in American society was the emergence of a new lifestage to identify the period in life in which a young person was no longer considered a child, but was not yet fully considered an adult. The concept of **adolescence** was socially created to describe *that period of life between childhood and adulthood* (White, 1989).

The creation of adolescence produced a legal dilemma in terms of dealing with the youth who violated the law. In response to society's desire to hold children over the age of 7 legally accountable for their behavior, but not as fully accountable as adults, new laws were enacted to deal with the special problem of law violation by youths. The term **juvenile** began to be used when states passed laws establishing the legal age for adulthood. **Juvenile** referred to *any person under the legal age of majority.* Hence, the term encompasses a broader age range than adolescence, which is generally considered to begin with the onset of puberty. However, most juvenile law violation that comes to the attention of juvenile courts occurs during the period of adolescence. Consequently, in relation to delinquency, the terms juvenile and adolescent are virtually interchangeable. The creation of the social concept of adolescence along with the legal concept of juvenile created a new social problem for the United States: **juvenile delinquency**—which continues as a major challenge into the twenty-first century.

What Is Delinquency?

We may begin to answer this question by examining some recent newspaper headlines gathered from several states:

"TEEN GANG WAR ERUPTS IN CENTRAL CITY!"
"HIGH SCHOOL VANDALIZED AND BURNED BY STUDENTS!"
"HOME INVASION BY TEENAGERS LEAVES ELDERLY COUPLE INJURED!"
"SEVENTEEN-YEAR-OLD YOUTH HELD FOR MURDER PLOT!"
"POLICE BATTLE PROFESSIONAL SHOPLIFTING RING OF JUVENILES!"

Many people at first glance might assume that these news reports announce unquestionable and typical cases of juvenile delinquency. However, consignment to a juvenile court is seldom that simple. The short, attention-grabbing headlines do not supply enough information upon which to base any final conclusions. We know nothing about such important matters as guilt, motives, extenuating circumstances, or the age in each state at which people become legally responsible as adults for their behavior. Moreover, there is nothing typical about these publicized events. Most juvenile behavior conforms to the normative standards of the larger society, and conforming behavior is seldom considered newsworthy. Furthermore, most juvenile delinquency is less sensational, is treated routinely, and re-

During the colonial period of American history, it was customary to publicly punish common criminals, religious nonbelievers, and disobedient
children. (Illustration by Marilyn Thompson)

ceives little public notice. Thus, at the beginning of this inquiry into the nature of juvenile
delinquency, an operational definition is in order.

There are literally hundreds of definitions of juvenile delinquency already in existence.
Their total number probably approximates the sum of the number of scholars, writers, and experts who have addressed the problem. The majority of the definitions contain only minor differences, that is, they use different words to describe the same idea. Many other definitions of
juvenile delinquency vary only in emphasis or approach, according to the academic background, specialty, or interest of their originators. The sociological perspective and the dramaturgical analysis cited earlier suggest a summary of all these definitions into three categories:

1. **The legal definition.** Here the emphasis is almost entirely on *the act,* the norm-
   violating behavior that is legally classified as juvenile delinquency.
2. **The role definition.** In this case, the focus is primarily on *the actor,* the juvenile
   whose role performance is identified as delinquent.

3. **The societal response definition.** This approach concentrates more on *the audience,* the members of the social group or society that reacts to the actor and the act and finally determines whether or not delinquency has actually been committed and if the offender is a true juvenile delinquent.

These definitional categories or approaches are not mutually exclusive. They cannot be completely separated or isolated from one another. Some overlap is inevitable and even desirable. They differ mainly in emphasis. Therefore, they are best understood as three vital dimensions of juvenile delinquency, and all must be considered together in order to formulate a complete definition of this complex social phenomenon. The thorough student of juvenile delinquency utilizes all three of these definitional approaches in determining whether the headlined incidents cited at the beginning of this section, or any other events, represent genuine cases of juvenile delinquency.

The Legal Definition

The oldest and most familiar description of criminal misconduct by a juvenile is the legal definition based upon formally codified laws, which specify offenses, sanctions, and age parameters. As previously mentioned, until the late nineteenth century, less serious deviance on the part of youths was considered to be a family matter. On the other hand, extreme or persistent cases of youthful nonconformity or obstinacy became a matter for community discipline. Public rebuke, whippings, and even capital punishment were administered to children (Reid, 1996).

As the United States developed, major changes in social values and social organization took place. As the population grew and the power of the state was extended, the authority of the family and religious institutions was reduced. For example, stronger feelings emerged and prevailed that the prevention of juvenile crime and the treatment of offenders were community as well as familial responsibilities. The outcome was that more and more troublesome children and youths were subjected to confinement and community-based programs of correction (Schlossman, 1977). Finally, during the last quarter of the nineteenth century, as the concept of adolescence emerged, the nation experienced a growing humanitarian desire to deal differently with the delinquent juvenile than with the criminal adult. Further modification in juvenile corrections soon followed.

The historical development of a formal juvenile justice system in the United States began in 1899. The Illinois state legislature passed a revolutionary bill regarding "juvenile delinquency" and authorized the establishment of the first juvenile court in Cook County (Chicago). From that beginning, similar legislation was successfully enacted in all the other states, creating special legal procedures apart from the older criminal court system for dealing with children and youths accused of violating a state law or municipal ordinance (Mennel, 1982). The historical development of the juvenile court and subsequent developments in juvenile justice are more thoroughly discussed in Chapter 14, Juvenile Courts.

Included within the various laws establishing juvenile courts is a formal, *legal definition* of juvenile delinquency. In general, **juvenile delinquency** is legally defined as *any act which, if committed by an adult, would be a crime.* Such forbidden activities are reflected in the codified criminal statutes of federal, state, and local governments. Both juvenile and adult violators may expect serious sanctions or penalties.

Juvenile delinquency is a large category of illegal conduct acted out by youths younger than the legal age of complete adult responsibility. Such antisocial behavior encompasses all the usual offenses that threaten persons and property.

Each state legislature has also designated a specific age as the dividing line between juvenile and criminal offenders. This arbitrary boundary between childhood and adulthood reaffirms the historical position that most individuals below the "age of majority" or "adult-hood" are presumed to lack the maturity necessary for full legal responsibility. Therefore, their cases are normally processed through the juvenile court where penalties are usually less severe than in the adult criminal court. The legal concept of **mens rea** still prevails in United States jurisprudence and typically sets the minimum age for delinquency at 7 years, when it is assumed that the child is old enough to consciously demonstrate criminal intent (Willing, 2000). The upper chronological boundary line is demarcated by the laws of most states, which declare people to be adults on their eighteenth birthday, and juvenile court jurisdiction ends. In recent years, some states have lowered this maximum age for persons under juvenile court jurisdiction (*Children in Custody,* 1974). Cox and Conrad (1996:88) indicated that three states designated the age of 16 as the maximum age; seven states, 17; one state, 19; and the rest, 18. Persons older than the maximum age under juvenile court jurisdiction in their state are generally considered to be adults and their cases are adjudicated in the criminal court. There are important exceptions to these rules, however, which apply to juveniles re-manded to the criminal court to face trial as adults for particularly serious crimes. In 1996, for instance, nearly 10,000 juveniles' cases nationwide were transferred to adult criminal courts (Snyder and Sickmund, 1999:170).

Most Americans are more or less familiar with the legal definition of juvenile delinquency, especially the chronological demarcation between juvenile delinquency and adult crime. This may be traced to the cultural importance many people place on the attainment of the legal age of 18, when citizens can vote, enlist in a branch of the military, marry without parental consent (in some states), and do many other things that are forbidden before adult status is achieved. The legal definition is also in harmony with the traditional view held by laymen regarding criminals and delinquents. According to Don Gibbons (1976:1), the man on the street tends to divide the world into "the good guys" and "the bad guys"…"The common view is that delinquents, criminals, and other deviants are alien persons among us." It follows that the arbitrary and apparently explicit codification of illegal behavior, and recommended procedures for dealing with it, are supported by the majority of people.

The establishment of a legal definition of juvenile delinquency that differentiated youthful offenders from adult criminals generally has been viewed as a commendable development and step forward in the jurisprudence of this country. It reinforced the normative system of society and simultaneously offered a humane measure of differential treatment for children and youth who ran afoul of the law. A major strength of the legal definition is its practicality and utility for law enforcement officers, who often must make procedural decisions in the field based upon the age of suspects.

Status Offenses

Many other youthful activities, while not criminal in the usual sense, may also come to the attention of law enforcement agencies if they appear to conflict with the best interests of a given community or the youth in question. Such acts as school truancy or the consumption of alcoholic beverages are not illegal when done by adults but are prohibited for juveniles. Thus, because the community forbids such behavior by minors, these acts are *illegal due only to the age status of the juvenile offenders* and are appropriately referred to as **status offenses** (Bernard, 1992; Flowers, 1990). This point is clearly reflected in a broad legal definition of juvenile delinquency supplied by The Children's Bureau, one of the federal agencies that compiles statistics on juvenile delinquency:

> *Juvenile delinquency cases are those referred to courts for acts defined in the statutes of the State as the violation of a state law or municipal ordinance by children or youth of juvenile court age, or for conduct so seriously antisocial as to interfere with the rights of others or to menace the welfare of the delinquent himself or of the community. This broad definition of delinquency includes conduct which violates the law only when committed by children, e.g., truancy, ungovernable behavior, and running away (Juvenile Court Statistics 1974:11).*

What has emerged is a two-dimensional legal definition of delinquency. This definition includes criminal acts by juveniles along with the acknowledgment of the juvenile court's ability to adjudicate children as delinquent if they have committed an act that, while not illegal, is considered inappropriate for juveniles. Consequently, the **legal definition** of delinquency has become *any act which would be a crime if committed by an adult, or any act* *which the juvenile court may deem inappropriate and for which a juvenile can be adjudi-cated delinquent.* (Chapter 3 contains a more detailed discussion of status offenses.)

Problems with the Legal Definition

A recurring complaint about this approach to classifying juvenile misbehavior is that the "explicit" guidelines are often extremely vague. The legal definitions of delinquency used by the various states adequately extend the adult criminal code forbidding such acts as murder and rape to children and youths. However, annual statistical summaries reveal that the largest proportion of juvenile offenses are status offenses and are often included under such imprecise, catch-all phrases in the legal definitions as "ungovernable behavior" and "incorrigible." Rather than defining delinquent conduct with any uniform and objective consistency, these broad descriptions permit much more subjective interpretation by local police and juvenile authorities than is found in adult criminal cases.

As an example of how such wide latitude in interpretation of juvenile laws can lead to capricious adjudication, we note that children can be referred to juvenile courts for "knowingly associating with vicious and immoral persons." In such cases, someone in authority must resolve these ponderous issues: What is an "immoral person?" What are the criteria for immorality? Exactly what is meant by "associating" with such persons? Can guilt by association be imputed to a child? Does "associating with vicious and immoral persons" make one an accomplice to crime? Does "association" mean any contact or is association a matter of degree? It is little wonder that there are great inconsistency and variability in the adjudication of delinquency from state to state, court to court, time to time, and case to case. The problem is compounded when the lack of uniformity in age parameters, vague definitions of delinquency, and subjective dispositions lead to questionable credibility of national delinquency statistics. For how can the incidence of various forms of youthful crime be compiled and compared adequately in the absence of a fairly uniform legal definition?

For decades, criminologists, sociologists, and law enforcement authorities have argued that the measurement of the volume, character, and trends of juvenile delinquency would be greatly improved if the legal definitions were clarified, consistent, and reduced in scope (e.g., Sellin and Wolfgang, 1964:64).

Since 1970, about half of the state legislatures in the United States have passed laws modifying the social identity and treatment of status offenders. Such changes have been encouraged by the Juvenile Justice and Delinquency Act of 1974 which would withhold federal funds for delinquency prevention from states that "place in detention or correctional facilities children who are charged with offenses that would not be criminal if committed by adults" (Diegmueller, 1978:15).

In 1976, the National Advisory Committee on Criminal Justice Standards and Goals strongly urged that the long list of vague and often capricious status offenses be delimited to five specific categories:

1. School truancy
2. Repeated disregard for or misuse of lawful parental authority
3. Repeated running away from home
4. Repeated use of intoxicating beverages
5. Delinquent acts committed by a juvenile younger than 10 years of age (Weis, 1980:9).

A new nomenclature evolved in some states to define status offenders with less stigmatization and more appropriateness to the nature of their offenses. For example, New York passed a "Person in Need of Supervision" (PINS) law, which itself was later declared discriminatory by a New York Court of Appeals. Other states adopted one or more of the following descriptive titles for status offenders and youths who were neglected, abused, or otherwise dependent upon the state: "Juvenile in Need of Supervision" (JINS), "Minor in Need of Supervision" (MINS), "Child in Need of Supervision" (CHINS), and "Children in Need of Assistance" (CHINA). A few states, prompted by a 1973 recommendation from the International Association of Chiefs of Police, have even sought to replace the acrimonious term "juvenile delinquent" with the less damaging designation of "unruly child" (Kobetz and Bosarge, 1973:37).

While these efforts to refine the definition and improve the treatment of status offenders are promising, they fall far short of effective nationwide reforms. The systemic injustices to juveniles in the United States and errors in delinquency data are chronic and continuous. (A more detailed discussion of status offense reforms is presented in the last chapter of this book).

Another problem encountered with the legal definitions of juvenile delinquency is the common practice among young and chronic criminals in big cities to use the juvenile court age limitation as a shelter to avoid criminal prosecution. A magazine report graphically described how society's program for lenient and rehabilitative treatment of juvenile offenders has been misused in some places:

> When he is caught, the courts usually spew him out again. If he is under a certain age, 16 to 18 depending on the state, he is almost always taken to juvenile court, where he is treated as if he were still the child he is supposed to be. Even if he has murdered somebody, he may be put away for only a few months… Small wonder that hardened juveniles laugh, scratch, yawn, mug and even fall asleep while their crimes are revealed in court. A New York teenager explained in a WCBS radio interview how he started at the age of twelve to rob old women: "I was young, and I knew I wasn't gonna get no big time. So, you know, what's to worry? If you're doin' wrong, do it while you're young, because you won't do that much time." (Time, 1977:19) (The common practice of many adult criminals to utilize juveniles in more risky robberies was also reported in the Medford (OR) Mail-Tribune, 1997.)

The Role Definition

The legal definition, if used as the sole criterion for determining delinquent behavior and juvenile status, would make it difficult for law enforcement officers to consider any relevant variables other than age and the specific offense brought to their attention. The role definition of juvenile delinquency, by focusing mainly on the actor rather than on the antisocial or nonconforming act, functions as an important corollary to the legal definition. This definitional approach expands the inquiry from "What is juvenile delinquency?" to include the question: "Who are the juvenile delinquents?"

The role definition partially repudiates the strictly legal definition by rejecting the notion that the casual or occasional experimenter with such behavior as truancy, vandalism, fighting, and running away is a true juvenile delinquent. According to the **role definition,**

BOX 1-1   Controversial Issue

The following anecdote is an experience of one of the authors while he was an assistant principal at a public high school, and illustrates one of the important concepts discussed in this chapter.

"Child or Adult?"

Juvenile is a status in our society—a social position somewhere between "child" and "adult." Like any social status, it is accompanied by a set of role expectations. While the normative role expectations for adults and for children are fairly clear-cut, those for juveniles are much more ambiguous. Told constantly by parents, "You're a young adult now, why don't you act like it?" only to be denied responsibilities and freedom with the phrase "You're too young," juveniles find themselves in a societal "double bind" where they are simultaneously "too old" and "too young" for a realistic and viable role.

I recall an encounter with a ninth-grade student. He had been sent to my office for "acting childishly" in class. He had no doubt been involved in behavior that was disruptive, and the teacher had finally become exasperated and sent him to the office. In my typical assistant-principal-disciplinary tone, I asked, "What seems to be the problem?" With a genuinely confused look, the student replied, "I don't know what the teacher expects out of me…in fact…I don't know what anybody expects out of me!"

Without any coaxing on my part, the student went on to describe the predicament he had experienced in the classroom. He pointed out that since the first day of school, all the teachers had emphasized that he was in high school now; that he was a young adult and would be treated as such; and that he was expected to act like one. He said that even though one particular teacher constantly reminded her students that they were adults, she often treated them like small children. He cited some of the classroom rules that he considered petty and humiliating, including not being allowed to chew gum and having to ask permission to go to the bathroom. "Does that sound like the way to treat adults?" he asked. Before I could answer, he related a brief story about his parents constantly demanding that he "act his age" and show more responsibility and maturity. Yet, when he wanted to stay home one weekend when his parents had planned to be out of town, they flatly refused, reminding him that "he was only fourteen," and that if he insisted on staying home, they would have to hire a *babysitter.*

I tried to interrupt to respond (I probably would have offered some type of defense for both the teacher and his parents), but before I could speak, he recited some examples of contradictory expectations he had recently experienced:

> *After passing a required examination, he was legally licensed to operate a motorcycle, and was expected to obey all traffic laws like an adult—but he could not legally drive a car…If he went to see a Disney movie rated G he was considered an adult and was required to pay adult admission; but if he tried to see an X-rated movie, he was told that it was for adults only, and he was a child.*

These examples reflect some of the obviously inconsistent, confusing, and often contradictory normative expectations faced by adolescents in our society. Between the ages of 12 and 18, the majority of American youth find themselves in a social "no man's land." They are no longer children and childish behavior is not tolerated, yet they are not adults and many adult behaviors are strictly prohibited.

*   *   *   *

Compare and contrast children, adolescents, and adults with regard to legal and social rights and responsibilities. Have you experienced similar circumstances where you were expected to behave as an adult while still being treated like a child? What problems did you experience? What could be done to help reduce some of the problems associated with the ambiguity of the status of adolescence?

the juvenile delinquent is *the individual who sustains a pattern of delinquency over a long period of time, and whose life and identity are organized around a pattern of deviant behavior* (Hirschi, 1969).

With this definition in mind, the ordinarily conforming and law-abiding boys who, on Halloween night, disregarded laws concerning the drinking of alcoholic beverages by minors, disturbing the peace, malicious mischief, assault, and the curfew were not juvenile delinquents even though they violated those norms (see the **Concept Application** at the end of Chapter 2). In fact, the entire community seemed to anticipate and aid the annual Halloween "riot," which functioned as a "release valve," permitting bored and restrained teenagers to "blow off some steam." Thus, the role definition insists that the actor's behavior must reflect a commitment to a delinquent role and life-style before the actor can be realistically identified as a juvenile delinquent.

Two fundamental sociological concepts are inherent in this description of the delinquent: **social status** and **social role. Status** is defined as *the prestige position of a person in relation to other persons in the social group or society.* Any social group or society of people who are together for any length of time will develop a status hierarchy. Those at the top of the social stratification system have more wealth, power, prestige, and authority than those at the bottom. Most of us learn where we and others stand on the "ladder of social status" in our social group and community.

There are two ways by which we may acquire social status in our society. **Ascribed status** is *a status position and level of prestige that is granted some people by virtue of their*

The marginal status of adolescents may lead them to experiment with legal adult behavior such as the consumption of alcoholic beverages. Such conduct is illegal for juveniles and constitutes a status offense.

birth. For example, Queen Elizabeth II of England was fortunate enough to have been born to parents who were members of the royal family, and they passed this high status position on to the present queen. Similarly, some of the descendants of oil magnate John Rockefeller, automobile manufacturer Henry Ford, and other successful industrialists hold high status positions today because of inherited wealth. Ascribed status is also the category of status often imputed to those at the bottom of the stratification system who, because of the poor and lowly circumstances of their birth, may always be relegated to an inferior status as residents of the slums, ghettos, and migrant labor camps.

The second way to acquire social status is through the exercise of individual ability and effort or by undertaking certain status-changing experiences in life such as attending college. This is called **achieved status,** and in our society is *usually based upon educational level and occupation.* Sociologists have found that Americans have a well-defined hierarchy of occupations, each with a designated level of prestige or status attached (Johnson, A., 1992). As each person enters the work force, there is general consensus regarding the appropriate level of the individual's social status based upon occupation, together with concomitant levels of formal education and income (Bynum, 1987). Thus, the unemployed—especially men of working age—have low social status.

The juvenile or adolescent status in our society is a rather precarious one. Neither adult nor child, the adolescent has a *marginal* social status. He or she is often torn between the normative expectations and responsibilities associated with adulthood, and the freedom from accountability afforded children. The marginality experienced by young people is extremely important from a sociological perspective, and will be further explored throughout this book as a major contributing factor to the problem of juvenile delinquency.

Social role is defined as *the behavioral performance expected of a person who holds a certain status in the social group or society.* A role assignment goes with every status and thus becomes an important part of the normative system that organizes society and controls the behavior of its members. Over time, certain statuses and their associated roles become infused with honored tradition, and little deviation is tolerated. For example, in our society, men are expected to be "masculine"—traditionally viewed as being competitive and aggressive, and to stoically refrain from weeping. Women are still often expected to be "feminine"—stereotypically viewed as being nonassertive, and eager for fulfillment as wives and mothers. Soldiers are expected to be brave and not cowardly. Ministers are expected to be devout and less susceptible to the temptations of "the world, the flesh, and the devil." The role expectations for juveniles are much less clear than they are for adult men and women. However, as was indicated in the legal definition of delinquency, certain behaviors by adults that are tolerated clearly violate the normative expectations for youth (e.g., drinking of alcoholic beverages, smoking, and sexual activity). Consequently, society's perception of the juvenile status and its concomitant role expectations are major influences in the process of defining juvenile delinquency.

Like status, some roles are imputed to members of society and can be difficult to change. Generally, people can perform only the roles that are approved and assigned by social consensus. However, occasionally roles can be successfully manipulated or modified. For example, the feminist movement has made substantial gains in weakening the traditional and stereotyped role of women in the United States by promoting contemporary and alternative roles.

Bill DeOre/The Dallas Morning News

Some roles are considered permanently "off limits" to all the members of society. Theoretically, at least, the criminal and delinquent roles are not legal or legitimate alternatives. This is the heart of the role definition of juvenile delinquency. A persistent and consistent pattern of delinquent behavior may be perceived as a valid indicator of the desired and intended role and life-style of the youth in question. Although some role behavior is the result of unconscious socialization and the internalization of social expectations, at other times we consciously and purposely act out roles that afford a dramatized presentation of self-identity (Goffman, 1959, 1967).

Problems with the Role Definition

Attempts have been made to integrate the legal definition with the role definition of juvenile delinquency. The legal definition, with its emphasis on the norm and the act of violation, theoretically merges very well with the role definition stressing the actor's patterned delinquent performance. However, the combined product is, in some instances at least, difficult to operationalize:

> For example, New Mexico rests its definition of delinquency on the word "habitual": A delinquent child is one who, by habitually refusing to obey the reasonable and lawful commands of his parents or other persons of lawful authority, is deemed to be habitually uncontrolled, habitually disobedient, or habitually wayward; or who habitually is a truant from home or school; or who habitually so de-

ports himself as to injure or endanger the morals, health, or welfare of himself or others. (Cavan, 1961:243)

A problem with such laws is that there is no clear definition of what is meant by terms such as incorrigible, habitual, or indecent conduct. As Cavan (1961:243) asked, "How often may a child perform an act before it is considered habitual?" Paradoxically, the search for a committed and consistent pattern of delinquency can sometimes frustrate the effort toward consistent judicial treatment of American youth.

Another criticism of the role definition is that it overlooks the fact that a deviant role seldom occupies all of a person's time, energy, and behavior. Nearly everyone, even a child, has several different roles and is usually able to easily and quickly move from one to another. A juvenile delinquent may alternately be student, part-time employee, brother, son, and gang member, depending upon the circumstances and with whom he is interacting. He spends his time eating, sleeping, working, playing, stealing cars, and doing many other diversified activities. Only one of his roles and a very small portion of his time involve illegal behavior. David Matza (1964), with forceful logic, contended that juvenile delinquents are very much like everyone else; that only intermittently are the social bonds tying them to the mass of conforming society loosened enough to permit an occasional deviation. Obviously, this is a serious contradiction in the role definition, which describes the delinquent as an actor whose life and identity are wholly organized around deviant behavior.

The Societal Response Definition

The emphasis on a social norm, an individual actor, or a norm-violating act, either alone or in combination, does not equate with an adequate and complete definition of juvenile delinquency. While these factors are all relevant and vital to a definitive description and conceptualization of the process and condition of delinquency, something is still lacking.

According to the **societal response definition,** *in order for an act and/or an actor to be defined as deviant or delinquent, an audience must perceive and judge the behavior in question.* The **audience** is *the social group or society to which the actor belongs or aspires to belong.* It is not possible or necessary for all the members of the social group to personally view and evaluate the conforming or nonconforming quality of a person's behavior. In the case of juvenile delinquency, significant and representative members of the social group—parents, teachers, neighbors, police officers, or others—may perform the audience function by having knowledge of or witnessing the act and making the societal conclusion and response. It is even possible for the juveniles committing law-violating behavior to identify their actions as delinquent and, in a sense, to act as their own social audience. The social consequences of delinquency are not experienced, however, unless the deviant perception is shared by authoritative and influential others who can affect one's life.

The major sociological concept of *society* includes the notion of an "audience"—that is, the social group that formulates the rules or norms, and thereby oversees and judges the subsequent behavior of all the members of the group. In this sense, "social groups create deviance by making the rules whose infraction constitutes deviance…" (Becker, 1963:9). In other words, without society there would be no norms; without norms there would be no deviant behavior; without deviant behavior there would be no system of sanctions. Albert

Cohen and James Short applied this idea to juvenile delinquency when they stated, "Just as crime is a creation of the criminal law, so juvenile delinquency is a creation of the statutes establishing the juvenile courts" (cited in Merton and Nisbet, 1971:91). Over time, the process of becoming delinquent develops sequentially from a socially derived norm, to the violation of that norm by an actor, to social definition and adjudication by an audience. A youth is finally and officially defined as a juvenile delinquent when that status is conferred upon the youth by a court. This process is thoroughly discussed in Chapter 14.

We may extend the dramaturgical analogy a bit further by perceiving society as being somewhat more involved than a passive audience of spectators. Society's active audience role is similar to that of the theater audience that scrutinizes each actor's performance. The audience communicates to the actors its estimation of the quality of the performance with appropriate sanctions—applause, hisses, or other expressions of judgment. Societal response to behavior—the official judgment regarding normative expectations and the actor's conforming or deviant act—is the last and determining dimension to be incorporated into a more complete *sociolegal* definition of juvenile delinquency.

Problems with the Societal Response Definition

This definition reflects the labeling approach to juvenile delinquency. The labeling perspective views delinquency as a social "label" placed on juveniles and their actions when those viewing the acts (or who are later apprised of them) judge them to be deviant. The labeling perspective is more thoroughly explained in Chapter 8, Sociological Explanations of Juvenile Delinquency.

Society is an association designed to improve the personal and collective welfare and survival chances of all of its members. A society is endowed with remarkable endurance and usually outlives its individual members. Over time, social norms, values, attitudes, and viewpoints are also manipulated, changed, discarded, or replaced, in harmony with the changing pragmatic needs of the social group. So, while a society may prevail for a relatively long time, the cultural components are not always as permanent and invariable. This adaptability and flexibility have greatly aided the survival of society. For example, every major world religion traces the norm "Thou shalt not kill" to both social and divine origins. Modern nations have institutionalized that canon, and compliance is required of their citizens. The norm is widely and thoroughly internalized so that people are generally shocked and indignant by the disregard for human life manifested in some criminal activities. However, when society perceives it as necessary, that norm can be quickly modified or reduced in importance or relevancy. Medals and public honors are bestowed on military men for their prowess in killing the national enemy. One of the most successful and popular dramatic plots involves a United States Marshal or other "good guys" heroically gunning down the "bad guys" in "winning the West." The point is that an **a priori** definition of the situation can intervene between the definitive norm and its applications which influences the social judgment of a given act.

The societal response definition of juvenile delinquency, while incorporating some elements of other definitional approaches, is not without its problems. The sociolegal focus on the audience, comprised of direct and indirect witnesses, becomes the key variable in determining the delinquent or nondelinquent status of an act or actor. But witnesses do not always agree on what they are seeing. As an example, consider the case of a teenage girl who is caught shoplifting in a department store. Her parents may view this as a single isolated act, totally incompatible with their daughter's usual behavior. If the police are called, the responding officer may see the shoplifting activity as theft and feel obliged to arrest the youth. The perception and reaction of the store manager are also influenced by personal background and circumstances. If continually victimized by widespread shoplifting on the part of high school students, the store manager may decide to "make an example" of the girl, and prosecute her. On the other hand, if her parents are affluent or prominent in the community, the store manager may regard the incident as trivial rather than risk alienating the family and their friends. Audience evaluation of the act and the actor may be further diversified if the youth belongs to a peer group in her school or neighborhood that values such daring and nonconforming escapades and consequently rewards her with higher status within the group. The conflict and varying dominance of these segments of the perceiving and reacting audience often result in differential treatment of many young offenders. This persistent definitional inconsistency is heavily underscored in the discussion of juvenile delinquency statistics presented in Chapter 3.

A Synthesized Definition of Delinquency

The conceptual definition of juvenile delinquency that will be utilized throughout this book combines aspects of all three of the major definitional categories. It includes criminal acts committed by juveniles and the status offenses deemed to be inappropriate behavior for youths. It includes the fulfillment of the delinquent role and also takes into account the complex social processes involved in the societal assessment and response to delinquency. Consequently, when we use the term **juvenile delinquency,** we are referring to *illegal conduct by a juvenile that reflects a persistent delinquent role and results in society regarding the offender as seriously deviant.* This synthesized definition, however, while operational for present consideration, also suggests a variety of problems, such as lack of uniformity in laws, and lack of consistency in what is considered appropriate and inappropriate behavior in society. Resolutions to these problems in defining juvenile delinquency are suggested in Chapter 17 as we rethink the delinquency problem.

SUMMARY

In this chapter, we examined the complex definitions of juvenile delinquency. The definitions of delinquency tend to fall into three broad categories: **legal, role,** and **societal response.**

The legal definition focuses upon the act committed by the youth. Every state has established statutes that define criminal behavior. The legal definition indicates that delinquency occurs when juveniles between a specified age range (usually 7 to 18 years) commit an act that would be considered a crime if committed by an adult. Criminal statutes are norms that have been formally codified by society. These laws usually reflect the prevailing values of a society, and prohibit behaviors viewed as being dysfunctional to the overall stability of society. Murder, rape, robbery, theft, and other criminal offenses clearly threaten the established social order. The legal definition goes beyond this, however, as states also have enacted statutes that make it illegal for juveniles to commit certain acts that would not be considered criminal if committed by an adult. These status

BOX 1-2   Cross-Cultural Focus

**The Cultural and Legal Definitions
of "Child" and "Juvenile Offender"
in Other Nations**

In the United States, juvenile delinquency is legally defined as any act which, if committed by an adult, would be a crime. For example, many states define delinquency as the behavior of children between specific ages (usually between the ages of 7 and 18) that violates state or local criminal statutes (Willing, 2000). With these definitions as a reference point, many interesting comparisons and contrasts can be made with prevailing cultural and legal definitions in a cross section of other nations.

SOUTH AUSTRALIA. Sweeping changes were introduced through the Juvenile Court Courts Act of 1971 and the Community Welfare Act of 1972 for dealing with juveniles in trouble in South Australia. The significant features of the legislation included the following (Nichols, 1980:155, 156, 157):

1. Juvenile Aid Panels were established as an alternative to court proceedings for most 10- to 16-year-old offenders.
2. No conviction is possible for an offender under 16 years of age.
3. Minimum age of criminal responsibility was set at 10 years.

BRAZIL. Since 1921, due to the reforms brought about by a juvenile court judge, Jose Candido de Albuquerque Melo Matos, the illegal behavior of people below 14 years of age was decriminalized and excluded from any process of law. At the same time, it was established that offenders between 14 and 18 should be submitted to legal procedures especially designed for that age group (Cavalieri and Rios, 1980:7).

ISRAEL. Israel has extended the jurisdiction of its juvenile courts from 16 to 18 years and raised the age of criminal responsibility from 9 to 12 years.

The Youth Labour Law of 1953 defines a "child" as a person below 16 years, and an "adolescent" as a person between 16 and 17 inclusive....

The Apprenticeship Law of 1953 defines a "juvenile" as a person who has not yet reached the age of 18 (Reifen, 1980:57, 68).

JAMAICA. The Juvenile Law makes provision for dealing with three categories of children up to the age of 17 years: those in need of care and protection, those beyond control, and those eight years of age and over who commit offenses against the law. It was the responsibility of the juvenile court to determine whether a child brought before it fell into any of these categories....

For offenders the Juvenile Law fixed the age of criminal responsibility at eight years. It stated: "It shall be conclusively presumed that no child under the age of eight years can be guilty of any offense." At 17 the offender passed out of the jurisdiction of the juvenile court (Cumper, 1980:36, 38).

NIGERIA. With regard to juvenile delinquency, and therefore juvenile justice, the Children and Young Persons Law is applied. The law itself is referred to as "An Ordinance to make provision for the welfare of the young and treatment of young offenders and for the establishment of juvenile courts." Under it a "child" means a person under the age of 14 years and a "young person" means a person who has attained the age of 14 years and is under the age of 17 years. Thus, no person under the age of 17 years who is apprehended by the police can be brought before a court of summary jurisdiction (Asuni and Jack, 1980:101).

THE PHILIPPINES. Youth offenders, under Philippine laws, include children over nine and under 15 years who are not delinquents; children under 18 years who are delinquent but are entitled to suspended sentence; and youths under 18 who also are delinquent and are not entitled to suspended sentence; and those 18 to 20 years, who while considered as adult offenders, may be entitled to probation before service of sentence; executive clemency even before the service of sentence; executive clemency even before the service of the minimum sentence; and parole after service of the minimum sentence (De Jesus-Amor, 1980:106).

Continued

BOX 1-2 *Continued*

POLAND. According to Polish penal code, young people are classified into three categories: those under 13 years of age, those between 13 and 17 years of age, and a special category for offenders from 16 to 17 years of age. Children younger than 13 years of age do not bear any criminal responsibility. In their case the judge decrees a 'non-lieu' and prescribes one of the educational measures stipulated in the penal code.

　　The line of conduct in the case of offenders 13 to 17 years of age depends on their mental and moral maturity. Young people 16 to 17 years of age can be held responsible for crime (Zabrodzka, 1980:41).

SAUDI ARABIA. Through the application of Islamic law, the kinds of punishment vary according to the age of the offender. Also, a child is considered to pass through three phases. First, the *unconscious phase* that continues until his seventh year. In this phase he is referred to as a 'kid' and, as such, cannot be condemned for any transgression.... The second phase, called the *unfulfilled conscious phase,* is a pe-

riod from the seventh to the eighteenth year. In it responsibility is limited to what is known as 'punitive responsibility.' Any series or number of crimes is treated and dealt with individually.... Crimes in this phase and any punishment given are not recorded against the offender and consequently have no adverse effect upon his future.... The *fulfilled conscious phase* begins at the end of the eighteenth year. At this age, the youth is held to be fully responsible for any crime he commits; punishment is determined according to Islamic law (Al-Athl, 1980:129–130).

* * * *

　　Based upon your reading of this chapter, how do the cultural and legal definitions of "child," "juvenile delinquent," and "legal responsibility" in the United States compare with those of other countries outlined in this section? In your judgment, do the juvenile laws and penal codes of these other nations seem to favor the legal definition, the role definition, the societal response definition, or some combination of these definitions of juvenile delinquency?

Sources

Most of the references cited in this Cross-cultural Focus were included in the five-volume set entitled *Justice and Troubled Children Around the World,* edited by V. Lorne Stewart. New York: New York University Press. 1980. These author-contributors are listed alphabetically:

Al-Athl, Abdullah Mohammed. "Saudi Arabia." Vol. III, 117–140.

Asuni, Tolani, and Jack, David D. L. "Nigeria." Vol. IV, 91–105.

Cavalieri, Alyrio, and Rios, Jose Arthur. "Brazil." Vol. I, 1–17.

Cumper, Gloria. "Jamaica." Vol. III, 31–48.

De Jesus-Amor, Ester. "The Philippines." Vol. III, 103–116.

Nichols, Helen. "South Australia." Vol. III, 141–165.

Reifen, David. "Israel." Vol. I, 57–86.

Zabrodzka, Halina. "Poland." Vol. V, 33–53.

Also see: Willing, Richard. 2000. When children kill, who takes the blame? *USA Today* (March 3): 3A.

offenses are legally defined as acts of delinquency because they violate the normative role expectations associated with the juvenile status in our society. Thus, while the drinking of alcoholic beverages, smoking, and truancy are not crimes when done by adults, they are viewed as threatening to youths and their successful internalization of society's cultural values and social norms.

　　We also explored the role definition of delinquency. This definition shifts the focus of delinquency away from the specific act and onto the actor. The role

definition tends to overlook the occasional minor transgression against social norms, and views delinquency as being a persistent pattern of law violating behavior by a youth. This definition focuses heavily upon the status accorded juveniles in our society and the social role expected to accompany that status. While there is little argument over the validity of the values reflected in laws forbidding murder, rape, robbery, theft, and other violent and property offenses, the values reflected in the laws creating status offenses are not uniformly supported.

The third major definitional category focuses upon the societal response definition of delinquency. This definition views delinquency primarily as being a result of the reaction of a social audience to a particular actor and act. The observing representatives of society have the power to judge and impute a delinquent label to a youth whose behavior is perceived to warrant such a label.

As the interplay unfolds between the act, the actor, and the audience, different interpretations of what has happened and what is happening confound the implementation of any definition of juvenile delinquency. Thus, efforts to make practical application of the definitions often appear ambiguous. The legal definition of juvenile delinquency is plagued by vague phraseology that permits subjective criteria as to what constitutes a delinquent act. The role definition is weakened by a lack of consensus about exactly how much nonconforming, antisocial behavior is necessary to indicate commitment to a delinquent role and identity. The societal response or sociolegal definition is dependent upon some type of consensus on the part of a social audience that deviance has been committed and that something should be done about it.

Finally, we constructed a synthesized definition to be used for our purposes in studying the problem of juvenile delinquency. This definition encompasses the major elements of all three of the aforementioned definitions. While not without some problems and limitations, this synthesized definition provides a clear conceptual framework for our study of the delinquency problem.

In Chapter 2, we establish a solid sociological foundation for the study of juvenile delinquency. We explore the social nature of humans and discussed the basic social processes involved in establishing norms and defining conformity and deviance. Juvenile delinquency is a serious form of deviant behavior and a social problem about which U.S. society has become greatly concerned.

Concept Integration

Questions and Topics for Study and Discussion

1. Define and explain the following terms and concepts: juvenile, adolescent, adult, mens rea, social role, social status, ascribed status, and achieved status.
2. What is juvenile delinquency?
   - based on the legal definition?
   - based on the role definition?
   - based on the societal response definition?
3. What is a juvenile delinquent? How does a delinquent differ from the adult criminal? How does the delinquent differ from the occasional experimenter with nonconforming or antisocial behavior?
4. Define *status offense*. Should status offenses be part of the legal definition of delinquency? Why? Why not?
5. Use the dramaturgical analogy to help explain the interplay and relationship between the social norm, the act, the actor, and the audience, and some common form of youthful misbehavior such as truancy from school, shoplifting, or something of your choice or from your experience.
6. Outline the problems associated with each definition of juvenile delinquency. In your judgment, can any of these problems be resolved? If so, how?

References

Albanese, J. S. 1993. *Dealing with delinquency: The future of juvenile justice* (3rd ed.). Chicago: Nelson-Hall Publishers.

Becker, H. 1973. *The outsiders.* (Revised ed.). New York: The Free Press of Glencoe.

Bernard, T. J. 1992. *The cycle of juvenile justice.* New York: Oxford University Press.

Bynum, J. 1987. Social status and rites of passage: The social context of death. *Applied sociology.* Acton, MA: Copley, pp. 9–15.

Cavan, R. S. 1961. The concepts of tolerance and contraculture as applied to delinquency. *Sociological Quarterly* 2(Fall):243–258.

Children in Custody. 1974. *A report on the juvenile detention and correctional facility census of 1971.* Washington, DC: National Criminal Justice Information and Statistics Service, LEAA.

Cohen, A., and Short, J. 1971. Crime and juvenile delinquency. In *Contemporary social problems* (3rd ed.) R. K. Merton and R. Nisbet (Eds.). New York: Harcourt, Brace, Jovanovich, pp. 89–146.

Cox, S. M., and Conrad, J. J. 1996. *Juvenile justice: A guide to practice and theory* (4th ed.). Dubuque, IA: Wm. C. Brown.

DeFleur, M., D'Antonio, W. V., and DeFleur, L. B. 1976. *Sociology: Human society* (2nd ed.). Glenview, IL: Scott, Foresman and Co.

Diegmueller, K. 1978. The forgotten juveniles: 'Crimeless' criminals. *Parade.* September 3, 1978. pp. 14–15.

Elkin, F., and Handel, G. 1978. *The child and society: The process of socialization* (3rd ed.). New York: Random House.

Elkind, D. 1991. The child: Yesterday, today, and tomorrow. In *Human development* (19th ed.). L. Fenson and J. Fenson (Eds.). Guilford, Connecticut: The Duskin Publishing Co., pp. 136–141.

Flowers, R. B. 1990. *The adolescent criminal.* Jefferson, NC: McFarland & Company, Inc.

Gibbons, D. 1976. *Delinquent behavior* (2nd ed.). Englewood Cliffs, NJ: Prentice-Hall.

Goffman, E. 1959. *The presentation of self in everyday life.* Garden City, NY: Doubleday and Company (Anchor Books).
1967. *Where the action is.* Garden City, NY: Doubleday and Company.

Hirschi, T. 1969. *Causes of delinquency.* Berkeley: University of California Press.

Johnson, A. G. 1992. *Human arrangements* (3rd ed.). Fort Worth, TX: Harcourt Brace Jovanovich, Inc.

Johnson, J. 1987. *The Bedford guide to the research process.* New York: Bedford/St. Martin's Press.

Juvenile Court Statistics. 1974. DHEW Pub. No. (SRS) 73-03452. Washington, DC: U.S. Department of Health, Education and Welfare.

Kobetz, R. W., and Bosarge, B. B. 1973. *Juvenile justice administration.* Gaithersburg, MD: International Association of Chiefs of Police, Inc.

Krisberg, B., and Austin, J. 1978. *The children of Ishmael.* Palo Alto, CA: Mayfield.

Lastrucci, C. L. 1967. *The scientific approach.* Cambridge, MA: Schenkman.

Matza, D. 1964. *Delinquency and drift.* New York: John Wiley.

Medford Mail-Tribune. 1997. Adult criminals use juveniles. (January 12):5-A.

Mennel, R. M. 1982. Attitudes and policies toward delinquency in the United States. *Crime and Justice* 4 (Chicago: University of Chicago Press), pp. 191–224.

Oates, S. B. 1977. *With malice toward none.* New York: Harper & Row.

Park, R. E. 1928. Human migration and the marginal man. *American Journal of Sociology* 33 (May):893.

Reid, S. T. 1996. *Crime and criminology* (8th ed.). Hightstown, NJ: McGraw-Hill.

Schlossman, S. L. 1977. *Love and the American delinquent.* Chicago: University of Chicago Press.

Sellin, T., and Wolfgang, M. E. 1964. The measurement of delinquency. New York: John Wiley.

Shakespeare, W. 1623. *As You Like It* (Act II. sc. vii, 1. 139).

Snyder, H. N., and Sickmund, M. 1999. *Juvenile offenders and victims: 1999 national report.* Office of Juvenile Justice and Delinquency Prevention. Pittsburgh, PA.

Stonequist, E. H. 1937. *The marginal man: A study in personality and culture conflict.* New York: Charles Scribner's Sons.

Time. 1977. The youth crime plague. *Time* (July 11):18–28.

Weis, J. G. 1980. *Jurisdiction and the elusive status offender: A comparison of involvement in delinquent behavior and status offenses.* Washington, DC: U.S. Government Printing Office.

White, J. L. 1989. *The troubled adolescent.* New York: Pergamon Press.

Willing, R. 2000. When children kill, who takes the blame? *USA Today* (March 3):3A.

A SOCIOLOGICAL OVERVIEW

Society, Norms, Conformity and Deviant Behavior

Reading Objectives

The reading of this chapter will help you achieve the following objectives:

1. Define and understand the Sociological Perspective of human behavior as it applies to the study of juvenile delinquency.
2. Understand how our human need for interaction and interdependence resulted in the development of human society.
3. Trace the origins and purposes of social norms—rules of conduct for members of social groups.
4. Define and give examples of mores and folkways as different kinds of social norms governing our behavior.
5. Explain the concepts of conformity and deviance as alternative responses to the behavioral expectations of society for its members.
6. Understand why societal response to the violation of norms (degree of punishment, reward, or ambivalence) may vary with the culture, time period, social status of the offender, and other factors.
7. Comprehend how some deviant behavior can be beneficial to society.
8. Understand why juvenile delinquency, as a form of deviant behavior, is considered a serious social problem.

Introduction

There are many ways of looking at any phenomenon. You are probably familiar with the old story about the three blind men who encountered an elephant for the first time. One of them ran his hands over the animal's broad side and described the elephant as like a wall. The second blind man, as he felt one of the creature's huge legs, became convinced that the elephant is similar to a tree. Finally, the third blind man, as he handled the beast's flexible trunk, declared that the elephant resembles a large rope. We may be amused at the ludicrous conclusions of the three blind men, but they aptly illustrate that people tend to "see" and interpret things within their own frame of reference, that is, based on limited personal experience and inclination. These diverse viewpoints are called perspectives.

The problem of consistently and accurately describing and explaining what we "see" is even more difficult when we look at human behavior. For humans and their conduct comprise the most perplexing yet interesting set of variables to fall under our scrutiny. Even intelligent and well-intentioned observers of a common act or event do not always agree on what they have seen. A primary task of attorneys and judges in criminal and juvenile court proceedings is to disentangle contradictory versions from eyewitnesses of what actually happened, and why.

For example, in a recent hearing involving a 16-year-old male accused of attempted sexual assault of a female student in a crowded high-school parking lot, his male companions excused their friend's behavior with "He was drunk and didn't know what he was doing." One adult in the neighborhood was even more tolerant and stated: "The kid didn't do anything out of the ordinary. Boys will be boys!" Another observer claimed that the girl had dressed seductively and "asked for it," adding that "a maladjusted and immature boy reacted accordingly."

On the other side in the case, a friend of the victim declared that the alleged offender suddenly attacked and began ripping at the victim's clothing without provocation. Another nearby witness characterized the defendant as "a born criminal and well-known bum in the community who should be put away for a long time!"

All of these conflicting opinions were stated with conviction. Yet the various claims that the accused sexual assailant was somehow unaccountable, moved by a normal hormonal "call of the wild," an emotionally troubled youth unable to resist temptation, or the outraged generality that such individuals "commit the crime because they are slime!" (Downey, 1993), are somewhat unconvincing. They all have oversimplified the issues related to normative conformity and deviant behavior. By themselves, they not only fail to unequivocally establish the innocence or guilt of the alleged juvenile delinquent, but offer superficial explanations of the youth's conduct.

The Sociological Perspective

Sociology may be defined as *the systematic analysis of the social aspects of human life.* As a broad field of study and knowledge, **sociology** has also been described as *the scientific quest to discover, explain, and predict the patterned social behaviors within human groups and between groups and individuals.* Practical applications of sociological knowledge have been made to countless social issues and problems, including the causes and consequences of juvenile delinquency.

In pursuit of sociological insights and research objectives, sociologists have been guided by a unique viewpoint or approach. This *sociological perspective* consistently holds that human behavior is generally an inherent, social act that can be traced to powerful forces in the social environment surrounding each actor. Expanding on this position, Peter Berger suggests that "things are not what they seem" (1963:23) and that the sociologist must have a broader vision that moves away from the particular to the general; from the narrow, familiar, and easy explanations of social life to the larger, interconnected, and more profound social environment.

C. Wright Mills called the sociological perspective a "sociological imagination" (1959). Armed with this view of the social world and approach to human behavior, keen observers are free from the confines of common sense and the apparently obvious. They are finally able to mentally explore all kinds of fascinating factors and variables in the social background of an individual or group that may be related to behavior. Thus, a sociological inquiry into the case described earlier of the youth accused of sexual assault might begin with these probing questions:

1. What is his family background? Are his parents deceased, missing, or divorced? Do they have necessary parenting skills? Are there positive and reliable adult role models in the family and home?
2. What kind of socialization has the youth experienced? Were ideals and values favorable to law-abiding behavior consistently instilled at an early age? On the other hand, has he been exposed to attitudes or examples that could encourage law violation?
3. Has he had a positive school experience? Was there a good relationship with teachers and other students? Does he have any kind of learning disability? Did he drop out of school prior to the incident? If so, why?
4. Has the youth's social class and/or racial identity negatively affected his social acceptability or self esteem? Does he have a fulfilling job? Does he perceive the world as a dangerous and hostile environment that offers him little opportunity for success? Are frustration, poverty, alienation, and crime endemic and a way of life in his neighborhood?
5. Who are his friends and close associates? Does this young man belong to a gang or other group with a record of antisocial behavior? Are there subcultural influences on him that are in conflict with the behavioral expectations of the larger society?
6. What are his attitudes toward women, sex, and violence?

The answers to such questions as these—springing from a sociological approach to understanding juvenile delinquents and delinquency—will unfold throughout this book. Such knowledge regarding the social origins of misbehavior is not intended as an excuse or justification for the offender. Rather, an awareness of possible causal linkages between a person's social milieu and his or her illegal conduct should enhance the remedial and rehabilitative work for juvenile delinquents in the United States.

The Social Nature of Humans

Shortly, we will turn our attention to norms or rules of conduct, the necessity for a large measure of conformity in society, and the seriousness of antisocial deviance. However, these important topics will be more meaningful if their discussion is prefaced by and grounded in a brief overview of the basic social needs and practices of our species.

The Social Imperative

Many young people have expressed a strong desire to disengage from "authoritarian teachers," "abusive and insensitive parents," or some other interpersonal conflict or unpleasant situation in the family, school, or community. However, on second thought, nearly everyone realizes the impracticality of such a course of action. Not only is it virtually impossible to escape permanently from social contact with other humans, but, after reflecting on the loneliness and vulnerability of isolation, few people really desire to totally and irrevocably separate themselves from society. On the contrary, intrinsic to human nature, and resting upon each of us, is an irresistible social imperative that demands our participation in society.

Most species of animals and insects are social creatures. They band together in social groups for companionship and mutual aid as well as in response to the biological urges to propagate their kind and nurture their young. Thus, the bird gravitates to the companionship and security of its flock; the honeybee orients its entire life span to the hive and the swarm; the cow on the hillside lives in proximity to and association with her herd. Men and women are also social creatures, drawn and driven by powerful forces to communicate and cooperate with a social group in order to collectively enhance personal and species survival (Barash, 1982). However, the human social imperative is not solely a biological or genetically programmed response as in the lower forms of animal life. People's compulsion toward sociality also is embedded in the cultural content of every society and consciously transmitted to each new generation as a learned response to our basic needs for social interaction and social interdependence.

Adolescents often demonstrate a particularly powerful social imperative. They enthusiastically seek their peers and congregate gregariously in shopping malls, parking lots, and

Our social interaction and social organization are overt manifestations of an intrinsic and vital social imperative that characterizes most species—including humans. We are drawn together for mutual aid and survival. We form friendships, groups, and societies.

other public places of high visibility that have been designated by the group for informal social interaction. Indeed, teenagers especially, appear to find security and identity in the company of other youths. Studies of juvenile delinquency indicate that even illegal acts are committed mostly in small groups.

Social Interaction

The human need for social interaction with our own kind was dramatically illustrated in the televised news account of a tired, tattered, and aged Japanese soldier who was discovered a few years ago on a remote Pacific island. Forty years earlier, during World War II, he was a young enlisted man in the Japanese garrison on the island. Near the end of the war, after most of the garrison had been killed or captured by invading American troops, this Japanese soldier and several comrades retreated into the jungle. They planned to hide until the tide of war turned again in their favor and Japanese military forces would return to the island. But they did not return. The handful of Japanese hid in caves, foraged for food at night, and carefully avoided detection by the local people and U.S. soldiers. Thus, they effectively were cut off from communication with the outside world and did not know that the war had ended. The days stretched into weeks; the weeks into months; and the years passed. Their weapons rusted and their uniforms turned to rags. They were undernourished and sick. Finally, one by one, the Japanese soldiers died, leaving a lone survivor.

After his discovery and return to Japan, he told of his experiences during those years of self-imposed exile and isolation. He described the loneliness as worse than the swarms of insects, hunger, and sickness. He reported: "In despair I often carried on audible conversations with friends—long since dead. In the evenings I would creep to the edge of the village and secretly watch and listen to the people and vicariously interact with them." Thus, his social needs overruled even his fear of capture or death and ultimately led to his detection. He was finally defeated and captured by one of the greatest enemies of mankind—unrelenting and unnatural loneliness—which reduced him to a forlorn, desperate, shadowy figure, skulking on the periphery of human society.

Many social scientists have argued that our credentials as human beings rest on more than typical biological similarities. They conclude that the normal development of human nature and personality is largely dependent on prolonged and positive interaction with other people. For example, the early focus of Kingsley Davis (1940) and others on feral or "wild" children, who had been deprived of human companionship and socialization, sought to establish causal linkage between social interaction and "becoming human."

More recently, Eric Miller (1978) reported on the discovery of three small rural children, locked in a wire cage in their parents' backyard. County welfare officials described the children as unsocialized and uncivilized—naked, wild, covered with excrement, and unable to talk or feed themselves. In addition, a large number of contemporary researchers have gathered considerable evidence of an association between social isolation, psychological stress, and maladjustment (e.g., Freeman and Giovannoni, 1969).

While very few of America's youth experience the literal isolation of feral children existing in attics, cages, or some other lonely place, many *do* feel a kind of *symbolic isolation*—a desolate alienation from parents and other adults who do not understand them. Such a barrier to meaningful communication and social interaction between the generations has often been cited as a seedbed for serious deviance and delinquency by many youngsters (Erikson, 1956; Perez, 1978).

Social Interdependence

The desire and willingness to participate with other persons in an interdependent social relationship is to acknowledge the vulnerability of the individual in dealing with a difficult and often dangerous environment. Thus, the social imperative that moves us to join forces and collaborate with others immediately expands our intellectual and technological resources for personal and collective survival. At the same time, membership in society improves the accumulation and transmission of cultural knowledge to succeeding generations.

One of the earliest and most convincing statements supporting the necessity for social interdependence among humans came from the zoologist Peter Kropotkin (1914:57) who concluded that "the vast majority of species live in societies and they find in association the best arms for the struggle of life." Kropotkin's classic work on the subject is appropriately titled *Mutual Aid.*

Sociologists, too, have contributed major theoretical insights and empirical findings that support the idea of a social imperative as the compelling force in the formation of interdependent social relationships. Emile Durkheim ([1938] 1947) suggested that humans find resolution to chronic conflict through social organization. For example, if there is a growing density of human population in an area, the struggle for scarce resources is reduced through a division of labor or increased occupational specialization. In this way, Durkheim said, people can coexist and cooperate in a shared environment.

Robert Park (1936) perceived social interdependence as a kind of symbiotic or collaborative relationship between diverse individuals and segments of the population. Their competition is balanced with a pragmatic cooperation for the mutual benefit of all parties and groups involved. Park's conceptualization has had widespread application in explaining the development and social organization of human communities.

A large number of studies have verified that human societies everywhere are characterized by a pervasive and persistent web of social relationships. For example, Arnold Green (1972) reported how preliterate societies have well-established patterns of communal and collective behavior in the procurement of sustenance, religious practices, government, and other dimensions of social life. William Foote Whyte (1943), in his well-known *Street Corner Society,* found extensive social organization, primary group relationships, and social control mechanisms in lower class urban slums that some earlier writers had suggested were lacking in such areas.

The informed consensus of these scholars is that human isolation is contrary to human nature and detrimental to the survival of the species. Consequently, we have gathered ourselves together to form families, tribes, villages, communities, cities, nations, and a wide variety of other social groupings. **Society** is the general term for *people living in social interaction and social interdependence.*

On a smaller scale, involving fewer people and less formal organization, social interdependence also characterizes the many groupings of young people at school or in their neighborhood. For example, the accomplishment of any collective task—whether it be students performing in the school band, children playing games at recess, or street gangs at war with rival groups—all require a strong sense of social interdependence and cooperation.

Social Organization

Social interaction varies in intensity and complexity, depending on the size of the group, the relationship of the participants, the environment, and the objective or purpose of the interaction. In other words, social interaction ranges from the brief and superficial contact between strangers who wait on a street corner for a traffic light to change, to the secondary and instrumental relationship between store clerk and customer, to the more permanent and intimate interrelationships between marriage or business partners. It includes the relatively passive interaction of a theater audience or a class of students, as well as the dynamic collective behavior of a football team or an angry gang fight.

Seldom is social interaction as spontaneous and unstructured as it may seem on the surface. Nearly all of the social interaction between the members and groups that comprise a society is guided by an extensive and detailed network of social organization. Every social group and society organizes its members and their behavior into generally recognized and accepted patterns so as to ensure the smooth operation and continuity of its collective existence. Most people are willing to standardize their behavior in many ways and to relinquish some individuality in order to function effectively as a social unit.

Norms

We have indicated already that most of our human behavior is social in that it takes other people into account, their expected responses to one's actions, and the shared meanings that members of the group place upon these actions. It follows that an important dimension of social organization is the vast array of rules that serve as guidelines for socially acceptable behavior. All of these *rules, standards, laws, regulations, customs, and traditions—the "do's and don'ts" of human conduct and social interaction*—are referred to as **norms** by social scientists. *Behavior that conforms or is in harmony with this code of rules* is said to be **normative.**

Some societal norms are **prescriptive**—that is, *they "prescribe" certain kinds of behavior as acceptable or desirable*—such as the generally accepted practice in our society that men shake hands with each other when they are introduced, and the legal requirements that children must attend school until a certain age and that men must register with Selective Service for possible military conscription when they reach their eighteenth birthday. Another prescriptive norm is that we must wear clothing in public (although the style and amount of clothing may vary widely, for example, whether one is going to the beach or to the senior prom). Other norms are **proscriptive**—that is, *they prohibit certain kinds of behavior as unacceptable to society*—such as our laws forbidding assault and theft, and the less seriously enforced curfew ordinances in some cities that deny minors access to public places after a specific nighttime hour. Other examples of prohibitive norms that govern the behavior of youths in the United States are age restrictions on marriage and the consumption of alcoholic beverages.

Sources of Norms

Where did we get our system of norms? There are several contrasting and controversial theoretical viewpoints regarding the origin of norms that societies utilize to control the behavior of their members. The two most widely discussed and accepted viewpoints are the models of **Social Consensus** and **Social Conflict.**

Social Consensus

The political philosopher Thomas Hobbes ([1651] 1914:63) was convinced that the uncontrollable natural inclination of humans is predatory, that is each person is, "as a wolf to his fellow man." Hobbes believed that in the distant past, people willingly had surrendered much of their independence to a central and absolute government in order to protect themselves from one another and so created an ordered, workable society. This voluntary abdication of a measure of personal autonomy and submission to group norms in exchange for security supplied by a dominant power structure is known as a **Social Contract.**

The theoretical viewpoint that societal norms are founded upon longstanding consensus among the members of a society about how to best organize behavior was more fully developed by Max Weber (1925), William Graham Sumner (1906), Kingsley Davis (1948), and others during this century. These sociologists argued that the major rules of conduct are "traditional" in that they have deep roots in the historic cultural values of a people. Over time, and with continual usage in fulfilling basic needs of the society, these norms become well-established and institutionalized as "the right way to do things." As long as they work and do not become obsolete through advancing technology or social change, these norms tend to remain in what Durkheim ([1938] 1947) called "the collective conscience of the people." Thus, they are passed on successfully from generation to generation through socialization.

Social Conflict

A contrary viewpoint on the origin of social norms was offered by Karl Marx and Friedrich Engels ([1848] 1964), Marx ([1867] 1967), and others who advanced the thesis that a great many norms are founded on the political and economic power of dominant owners of property who comprise a ruling class, rather than on the cultural consensus of the common people. Marx, with his orientation toward social class conflict, viewed the normative system of society as generated by the greed of the ruling capitalistic class in order to consolidate its ownership of the means of production and to control the working classes. This economic exploitation, according to Marx and Engels, would lead to an inevitable war of the classes and the overthrow of the dominant capitalistic system. Then, according to socialistic ideology, the norms of the new classless society would truly reflect the will of the people.

Class conflict as an original source of norms, especially laws, continues to have strong proponents (e.g., Dahrendorf, 1959; Chambliss, 1973; Quinney, 1970). Dahrendorf (1959) focused on the differential distribution of authority and coercive power in social organizations that represent the various social classes. He pointed to the legislative/political generation of law and the selective enforcement of the law as exercises of the upper and middle classes to discriminate against the underclasses. Dahrendorf (1959:165) hypothesized that "the patterns of domination and subjection that exist in social organizational arrangements lead to systematic social conflicts of a type that is germane to class conflicts in the traditional (Marxian) sense of this term." This theme has been developed further by Chambliss (1973) and by Quinney (1970), who have argued that criminal statutes are one of the ways that the powerful in American society inflict their will upon the socially disadvantaged. For example, since statutes regulating the behavior of juveniles are passed by legislatures comprised of adults, and enforced and interpreted by adult police officers, district attorneys, and judges, the conflict model of the origin of norms has been utilized by some to help explain the phenomenon of juvenile delinquency.

Both theoretical explanations concerning the origin of norms—social consensus and social conflict—represent extreme **ideal types.** An **ideal type** is a term coined by Weber (1947:99–100) to describe *a kind of conceptual model, expressing in a pure, and therefore hypothetical, form, the core characteristics of a pattern of conduct.* The usefulness of the ideal type is that it offers a point of reference for comparing actual conditions and deviations. Thus, social consensus and social conflict models represent idealized, unrealistic norm-producing circumstances. More moderate theorists contend that, while there may be some historical instances in which social norms developed exclusively from one or the other of these two sources, most contemporary societies can trace their norms to a combination of these origins.

Folkways and Mores

Sociologists classify norms into two categories on the basis of their importance to the social order and how seriously society regards their violation. William Graham Sumner (1906), by using the societal reaction to nonconformity to measure the value or importance of norms, helped us to distinguish between two types of social norms: **folkways** and **mores.**

Folkways

Folkways are *informal agreements or understandings about what is considered appropriate and inappropriate behavior.* Folkways may be very old and entrenched in the culture, such as our tradition of singing the National Anthem prior to sporting events, or they may be relatively new, and indicate normative conflict with older norms (and older generations), as exemplified by the dress and behavior of some hard rock and punk rock bands. Folkways may change or fluctuate periodically as do fads and fashions in clothing. Some men have been embarrassed by their tardy discovery that the width in neckties and coat lapels of their outdated wardrobes was suddenly inappropriate attire. Similarly, the fashionably prescribed length for a woman's skirt seems to change almost annually. Folkways also include detailed rules of etiquette covering table manners, dating behavior, habits of grooming and cleanliness, language, and many other aspects of daily life. Just a generation or so ago, it was considered improper behavior for a young woman to overtly initiate a romantic contact with a young man, or even ask for a date. It was a widely accepted folkway that "nice girls should avoid appearing forward or flirtatious…" Happily, for many males and females alike, this tradition has been replaced by a more relaxed and tolerant set of rules for social contact between the sexes.

Society does not usually consider the violation of a folkway a serious offense, and severe penalties are seldom administered. However, members of society show their displeasure in unofficial, informal ways. People whose eating habits are judged as uncouth and ill-mannered by society will not be arrested, though they may well find themselves avoided by others and dining alone. Someone who wears a sweatshirt and jeans to a formal church wedding will not be excommunicated, but probably will be the target of direct or indirect ridicule. The social group may be annoyed by such overt challenges to propriety but does not feel particularly threatened. This is precisely the difference, according to sociologists, between folkways and mores.

Mores

The most important and seriously enforced societal norms are called **mores. Mores** are *salient norms in that they are perceived as germane to the overall cohesion and survival of society.* Consequently, their violation is seen as threatening to crucial values. The mores often are reflected in our formal laws and are systematically written down in a legal code that defines their violation as criminal behavior and prescribes the method and degree of punishment. More specifically, the criminal law (and juvenile law) is a codified body of statutes generated by a political authority or government to standardize and regulate the behavior of societal members and to provide for punishment of the violators of the rules. Since these more important and serious rules are "regarded as a conserving force in the life of human beings, protecting what society stands for..." (Birenbaum and Sagarin, 1976:16), the formal law enforcement agencies of the state may be used in their enforcement. Examples of mores are laws forbidding theft and murder, reflected in the Ten Commandments as well as in the criminal codes of the various states.

The patience and permissiveness that often characterize the societal reaction to those who violate folkways are not extended to those who transgress important mores. Historically, society has shown little tolerance for anarchists, traitors, heretics, kidnappers, murderers, looters, terrorists, and others whose norm-violating behaviors were interpreted as a menace to the basic stability and security of society. This kind of extreme deviant behavior is still one of the surest ways for individuals to be declared "Public Enemies" and find their photographs and uncomplimentary descriptions of their conduct in the newspapers and perhaps on the local post office wall.

At the same time, the universal application of all the laws to all the people belonging to a national society like the United States, and the interpretation of all behavior as conforming or deviant in relation to these laws, are not as simple or clearcut as the aforementioned examples suggest. Most of the major social norms, or group-shared expectations, are designed to enhance, preserve, or accomplish those things generally considered to be of great value in the culture of the larger society. When a cultural value does not undergird a social norm or law, it becomes very difficult (if not impossible) to enforce the law consistently or permanently. For example, due to the zeal and political influence of a minority group of social reformers, the prohibition of the manufacture and sale of alcoholic beverages became a national law through the Eighteenth Amendment to the Constitution in 1919. However, it soon became clear that law enforcement officers and agents could not control the illegal manufacture, transportation, and sale of alcoholic beverages. Too many Americans had values contrary to the intent of the prohibition law and finally, in 1933, the Eighteenth Amendment was repealed.

The general application of norms is sometimes made difficult by the population composition of a heterogeneous society. The United States contains many subgroups that are highly differentiated according to age, social class, occupation, religion, politics, and ethnic-cultural backgrounds. These groups often represent different circumstances and orientations and thus do not always share the same values and rules (Lemert, 1964). Becker (1973) cited the example of Italian immigrants who, by continuing to make wine for themselves and their friends during the prohibition era, simultaneously were conforming to the standards of the Italian subculture and breaking the law of their new country.

Robert Park (1928) was one of the influential scholars at the University of Chicago during the formative years of sociology in this country, and was one of the first to identify the plight of certain individuals and groups who experience only marginal and incomplete social assimilation. Stonequist's (1937) *The Marginal Man* pinpointed the second-generation immigrant as the classic example of this phenomenon. He traced this marginality to the abrasive cultural conflict experienced by the new ethnic minorities in the United States. The experience of divergent and often contradictory cultural norms has the potential for generating normative confusion, alienation, and, hence, deviant behavior in some individuals. Park, Stonequist, and others portrayed the **marginal person** as *being caught between two conflicting cultures.* The person's commitment is torn and fragmented between the two, and, consequently, the individual fails to fully identify with either of the groups in question. For example, many children of immigrants are exposed simultaneously to the language and traditions of the "old country" in their homes and ethnic neighborhoods, as well as to the intense socialization of their U.S. school and youthful peer group. Thus, they become marginal in the sense that they lack complete integration into either the larger society or the subculture. The marginal person, with mixed and marginal status and identity, inhabits a frustrating social limbo between two societies and cultures (Arnold, 1970). This unfortunate situation has been considered a contributing factor in causing some juvenile delinquency, and as you will see in Chapter 6, the concept has been incorporated in some explanatory theories. While this cultural conflict between subgroups and the larger society may confound the definition of normative and deviant behavior, every society seriously endeavors to distinguish between behavior that conforms to prevailing norms of social life and behavior that deviates markedly from those norms.

Normative Behavior: Conformity

Earlier in this chapter we discussed the origins and purposes of norms as they affect our personal and collective survival. This point can be further clarified by focusing on the definition of **norms** as *group-shared expectations* for behavior. Every social group operates under some set of fundamental regulations which each member starts learning from the day of birth. Charles Cooley (1922) perceived **conformity** as being *the attempt to maintain a normative standard established by a social group.* His early insight, that compliance and conformity with social expectations can be explained by the human tendency to adopt imitatively the prevailing patterns of behavior around oneself, has been expanded and refined into the contemporary viewpoint among sociologists that the individual internalizes the customs of his or her society through a process called socialization. **Socialization** is *the effective transmission and internalization of culture content* (Benedict, 1934). Thus, it includes learning to respond to social situations in socially acceptable ways. Every person, from earliest infancy, and through continual interaction with parents, siblings, peers, teachers, and many other members of the social group, is exposed to the values, attitudes, and behavioral practices that are expected and acceptable. The idealized objective of this socialization is the social control or conformity of the individual, although it is usually articulated as "getting educated," "being properly raised," or "brought up to be law-abiding." In this way, even the process whereby we "put society in man" (Berger, 1963) becomes an institutionalized norm. Social control is considered most effective when it is manifested as self-control in harmony with what is socially expected from others (Scott, 1971; Mantell, 1974).

Through successful socialization, *most* of us conform *most* of the time to *most* of the important norms of our society. For example, although juvenile crime is widespread, most teenagers are not tempted to assault or rob other people. As very young children, the majority learned to respect the person and property of others. This is not to say that *all* of our conformity is spontaneous and without complaint. Fear of punishment, penalties, and other negative sanctions can elicit a pragmatic conformity as an assist to internalization. For example, not all students refrain from "ditching school," cheating on examinations, and bullying their classmates because they love and respect their teachers and have an unquenchable thirst for knowledge and education! Their temptations along these lines are held in check by the prospect of retribution.

When the socialization of group-shared expectations is ineffectual in producing the desired conformity, society has equipped itself with more direct and coercive techniques that may be applied to the nonconforming individual. These range from informal rebuke and ridicule at one extreme all the way to formal, state-imposed fines, imprisonment, and even capital punishment at the other. Obviously, we are never totally free or independent to determine our own course of action, for the society external to the individual continually monitors and molds the behavior of each member.

In addition to eliciting our personal conformity, what we have learned about norms as group-shared expectations helps us predict much of the behavior of other members of society. For example, the great majority of people learn while very young that the right to use the public streets and sidewalks is balanced with a personal responsibility to abide by certain social norms. We have learned to expect that under ordinary circumstances other individuals will respect us and our property. We may usually participate in public social life without fear of insult or physical assault. Those persons whom we meet also have learned to anticipate the same respect from us. We need not be personally acquainted with everyone who shares our community. Our group-shared social expectations—whether in the form of municipal ordinances, constitutional rights, religious dogma, federal or state laws, or simply tradition—usually function very well to preserve order on our streets and sidewalks, even among strangers.

The ability to control and predict human behavior, based on norms or group-shared expectations, pervades virtually every area of social life. This was the point made in the play *Fiddler on the Roof* when a perceptive old man exclaimed: "It may seem foolish to those unacquainted with our ways, but without our traditions, we would be as unstable as a fiddler on a roof!" (Stein, 1964). And without doubt our dominant cultural values—manifested in norms, traditions, customs, laws, and group-shared expectations—are part of the "glue" that holds society together, contributing major support to its stability and social organization.

Deviant Behavior: Nonconformity

Many persons find it disagreeable, inconvenient, or otherwise unsatisfactory to order their lives in harmony with all of the behavioral norms of their society, and are tempted to deviate. If their socialization experience or other forms of social control do not restrain them, some of these persons will not conform to all of the norms. Realistically, virtually everybody violates some social norm at some time. These nonconforming members of society and their deviant behavior are a major focus of study in sociology.

Deviant behavior is *conduct that is perceived by others as violating institutionalized expectations that are widely shared and recognized as legitimate within the society.* Simply put, deviance is the violation of norms. So, in sociological terms, deviant behavior involves a complex interplay between a social norm, a member of a social group whose actions are considered to be subject to that norm, and other members of the social group who observe the actor and define a particular behavior as nonconforming to a degree exceeding the tolerance limits of the majority (Cohen, 1966; DeFleur, et al., 1976; Ritzer, et al., 1987).

Some people argue that our societal norms or standards of conduct are non-negotiable—that they should be treated as inflexible absolutes. Therefore, they have little patience or tolerance for deviant behavior. By taking the position that deviance is only disruptive and destructive to the social group, it becomes possible to classify everybody into one or the other of two opposing subgroups: the "Insiders" and the "Outsiders." Unfortunately, this kind of dichotomous thinking permits motivation and morality to be quickly and conveniently imputed to those on each side as they are adjudged "good" or "bad," "right" or "wrong," "friend" or "foe," "loyal and law-abiding," or "antisocial and criminal," a "good kid" or a "juvenile delinquent." While this approach is convenient and can be easily applied to almost any person or issue, it oversimplifies the realities of social life. Even though our society is surrounded with a scaffolding of behavioral norms, most of these norms are less rigid than they may seem at first glance. Sociologists have discovered that the members of society display a paradoxical and generous amount of tolerance for much deviant behavior, depending on several important variables.

First, the nature of the offense can determine the level of society's tolerance for norm violation. In many instances, our tolerance for minor norm-breaking requires only that the offender acknowledge the transgression. For example, a breach of etiquette such as a sneeze in a public place generally requires only the phrase "excuse me" from the offender to remedy the situation. Goffman (1965) called this "remedial work." Even some formal laws, such as traffic ordinances, or many of the statutes governing juveniles (such as curfews) can be occasionally violated and, if no accident results, or no harm is perceived, the transgressors can usually pay a fine or receive a warning, and gain the sympathetic understanding of society since such experiences have happened to most of us.

A second factor that determines the level of society's tolerance for deviant behavior is the social status of the offender. The seventeenth century political doctrine known as the

Deviant behavior may be different and even shocking. It may be troublesome and even irritating or intimidating. To many, it may be the opposite of conformity, but only a minor portion of deviant behavior is considered antisocial or criminal.

Divine Right of Kings offers a classic illustration. James I of England and supporting royalists, in order to excuse and boost his shoddy reign, claimed that subjects are required by God not to resist their monarch but passively to obey him, even if, in their view, he is wicked (Figgis, 1922). In this century, Edwin Sutherland (1961) pinpointed the reality of large-scale illegal acts committed by businessmen, corporation executives, and other middle- and upper-class professionals in the course of their occupations. He invented the term "white-collar crime" for such offenses as financial fraud, monopolistic practices, price fixing, and embezzlement, and contended that such professional malpractice enjoyed greater social tolerance. Offenders often go unpunished or are treated leniently because they share the same social class as those with power and authority in society. Similarly, it has been well documented that many communities are often more tolerant of some of the activities and escapades of middle and upper class youngsters that are designated as juvenile delinquency when carried out by lower class youths (Myerhoff and Myerhoff, 1964).

A third element affecting the level of tolerance manifested toward deviant behavior is the cultural context in which it occurs. In other words, there is a paradoxical kind of cultural relativity when it comes to tolerance toward many forms of deviance. *An act that violates the norms of one particular society may represent approved conformity from the point of view of another social group.* This principle of **cultural relativity** is especially helpful in understanding behavior and societal reactions to it in a heterogeneous society such as ours, made up of a number of subgroups with their own distinctive values and norms. Groups such as teenage gangs, homosexuals, drug addicts, and some urban slum dwellers support subcultures whose values, beliefs, normative practices, and shared attitudes run counter to those to which the larger society subscribes. Thus, a given act, and the level of tolerance it receives, must always be interpreted within the framework of the relevant cultural or subcultural system.

Fourth, tolerance for nonconforming behavior often has a temporal dimension. That is, types of behavior that are strongly disapproved of at one time may be tolerated and even encouraged at a later time in the same society. For example, in the 1950s hair extending below the ears on young men was considered deviant and even effeminate. Later, long hair on young men was thought of as stylish or inconsequential by a great many people. Similarly, in colonial America, youths in their early teens were allowed to carry guns and to marry, and were expected to engage in a variety of behaviors that would be considered deviant today.

In one sense, the entire country has become more tolerant of children and their behavior. Prior to the twentieth century, the violation of important laws by American children was considered to be criminal behavior, and children could be incarcerated with hardened adult felons. Today, in what most Americans consider to be a more enlightened society, there are special agencies, courts, and institutions to deal with juvenile delinquents. Our growing sensitivity and concern for the special problems of our youths is detailed in later chapters of this book.

Negative Aspects of Deviance

By the time most individuals reach college age, they are aware of many of the negative consequences of deviant behavior, especially for the person regarded as deviant. The socialization experience of children and adolescents includes enough penalties, punishments, threats, and warnings regarding misconduct that the unpleasant personal "payoff" for many forms of deviance becomes relatively clear. So pervasive is this message that our cultural folklore is replete with familiar proverbs and dire forecasts concerning the certain and ultimate doom for those who pursue a course of willful deviant behavior. The theme is apparent in such common expressions as: "Those who play with fire will get burned"; "Those who live by the sword will die by the sword"; "Chickens always come home to roost"; "You made your bed, now lie in it"; and "They enjoyed the dance, but now must pay the fiddler."

Deviant behavior such as juvenile delinquency also has a number of negative consequences for society. These negative consequences include, but would not necessarily be limited to:

1. Personal Harm. Deviance can hurt people. Violent acts such as murder, rape, assault, and robbery create obvious personal injury for their victims. Property crimes such as theft, auto theft, burglary, and arson, also cause pain, suffering, and financial loss for those who

BOX 2-1   Cross-Cultural Focus

Conformity, Deviance, and Delinquency among Native Americans*

There are less than two million American Indians in the United States and, compared to the other more populous racial groups in the country, their juvenile delinquency is negligible. However, in states such as Arizona and New Mexico where they *do* represent a sizable minority, and where Native American cultural identity is still vigorously preserved, misconduct by Indian youths is of serious importance.

The delinquent acts which usually bring Native American boys to court are similar to those of other boys and are rarely acts of violence against the person. The most prevalent offenses among young Native American males are drunkenness, petty theft, sex offenses, vandalism, and incorrigibility. Among young Native American females, the most common forms of illegal behavior are sex offenses, incorrigibility, and drunkenness. Historically, the percentage of commitments to juvenile institutions in centers of large Native American population shows a marked over-representation of Native Americans. For example, in South Dakota, where Native Americans account for 5 percent of the population, 50 percent of the training school population is composed of them (Robinson, 1960:175).

Alcoholism among some tribes and the illegal consumption of alcohol by many Native American teenagers are chronic social problems. Although drunkenness seems to be associated with many criminal acts (among all racial and ethnic groups), there is no evidence that Native Americans are inherently more susceptible to intoxication or to alcoholism. However, the historical and social experience of American Indians suggests some useful insights regarding their apparent vulnerability to excessive drinking:

> *Drinking was heavy on the American frontier during the nineteenth century among farmers, trappers, and cowboys. It was these groups that the Indians came into contact with and from whom they secured their first alcohol. In addition, most Indians were unfamiliar with the use of alcohol and this inexperience, along with the encouragement of white men, led to excessive drinking....*
>
> *Different tribal groups exhibit great variations in drinking behavior.... The Pueblo of the southwestern United States, for example, are abstainers.... There are some tribes, however, where there is a large proportion of heavy drinkers, such as the Ojibwa where researchers classified 42 percent of the adults as heavy drinkers (defined as being drunk 2–5 times a week) (Clinard and Meier, 1998:287).*

The consensus among both Native Americans and others who have sought to account for the heavy drinking among Indians is that it began and has continued as a consequence of culture conflict, marginality, and anxiety experienced by the indigenous minority as the white man's ways were arbitrarily imposed. "The excessive drinking among Native Americans appears to be related to a breakdown of old institutions and social control techniques" (Reasons, 1972:92).

Similarly, other forms of deviance among American Indians also have been traced to the marginality and loss of self-esteem and social identity of a people whose traditional lands and culture have been threatened by the dominant society. Jack Bynum (1987) compared and analyzed new and unusually high suicide rates among six American Indian tribal nations. Of special concern was the startling increase in suicidal behavior of children, adolescents, and young adults among the Navaho, Cheyenne, Sioux, and Shoshone-Bannock during the 1960s. Bynum concluded that the culture conflict and anomic burden of "the marginal man" were etiologically significant as younger generations of Native Americans often find themselves caught in a precarious social dilemma. Simultaneously socialized to commit themselves to their traditional heritage and values as well as to the culture of the larger society, many young American Indians have found suicide a viable way of escape from an untenable situation.

Continued

BOX 2-1 *Continued*

The use of the hallucinogenic drug, peyote, as part of the ritual and religious experience of the Native American Church offers a classic example of the cultural relativity of conformity and deviance. Cocaine, peyote, and other such hallucinogenic drugs are legally classified as dangerous drugs in the United States and possession and consumption are generally forbidden by law. However, peyote has been used for over 100 years by many American Indian tribes as a cultural residual of the Ghost Dance religious movement.

In the 1870s the prophet Wodziwob told of a vision in which the ancestors of Native Americans came on a train to Earth with explosive force, after which the earth swallowed up the whites. Members of a number of tribes joined in the movement in the hope of salvation from white oppression.... In the late 1880s there was a resurgence; the prophet Wovoka experienced a vision ordering him to found a new Ghost Dance religion. The religious fervor spread through the Plains tribes. Trancelike dances were a central part of the ritual;... Peyotism surfaced

as the Ghost dance movement was being destroyed; it reflected another way of protesting white cultural pressures. Long used by individual practitioners to deal with sickness, peyotism did not become a group religion until 1880. Between 1880 and 1890 it spread throughout the Plains. The new religion reflects an ambivalence toward Christianity. Peyote rituals involved singing and praying, but were distinctive in the eating of peyote and in the visionary experiences this induced. (Feagin, 1989:200)

Although the manufacture, sale, and possession of such hallucinogenic drugs are controlled by federal law, it is interesting to note that when peyote is used in certain religious ceremonies by the Native American Church, the practice is exempt from some of these legal controls. The substance is now generally recognized as contributing to the fulfillment of a basic need in some tribal societies and is accepted and integrated into the norms of those cultures. Our American principle of religious freedom has now proven to be flexible enough to tolerate the use of peyote by particular people under special circumstances.

Sources

Bynum, J. E. 1987. Suicide and the American Indian: An analysis of recent trends. Pp. 367–377. In Howard Bahr, Bruce Chadwick, and Robert Day (Eds.). *Native Americans today.* New York: Harper and Row, Publishers. (1972); and in *Applied Sociology* J. E. Bynum (Ed.). Acton, MA: Copley, pp. 5–8. 1987.

Clinard, M. B., and Meier, R. F. 1998. *Sociology of deviant behavior* (10th ed.). Fort Worth: Harcourt Brace College Publishers.

Feagin, J. R. 1989. *Racial and ethnic relations* (3rd ed.). Englewood Cliffs, NJ: Prentice Hall.

Reasons, C. E. 1972. Crime and the Native American. Pp. 79–95. In Charles Reasons and Jack Kuykendall (Eds.). *Race, crime, and justice.* Pacific Palisades, CA: Goodyear Publishing Company, Inc.

Robinson, S. M. 1960. *Juvenile delinquency: Its nature and control.* New York: Holt, Rinehart, and Winston.

*There are ancient aborigine peoples still residing in many modern nations whose dominant white societies arrived only in recent centuries. The Eskimos, American Indians, Australian aborigines, and other ancient peoples have all shared the problems associated with culture shock as they have struggled to survive the intrusive dominance of newer and technologically advanced societies. A serious residual of this culture conflict has been the surprising and complex deviance of the younger generations of native populations. In the context of this book, this brief focus on Native Americans is representative of all such indigenous societies.

are victimized by them. While the majority of delinquent acts are nonviolent, many of them create physical and emotional harm for the victims, the perpetrators, and their families.

2. Threatens Norms. Any act of deviance involves norm violation, and hence potentially calls into question the norm being violated. When social rules and guidelines are broken, and if no discernible social harm is readily apparent, the norm may be judged to be unimportant. In some cases, when one rule is questioned, rules in general may be questioned. Juveniles, in particular, are likely to question rules that govern their behavior when they occasionally violate one of them and perceive no really harmful consequences. For example, the teenager who has been warned about the serious consequences of smoking marijuana may try it and feel that it caused no readily apparent harm. This may lead the youth to also question the potential harm of drugs such as cocaine and heroin against which similar warnings were received.

3. Costs. Deviance can be extremely expensive for society in both the literal and figurative senses. A tremendous amount of money, time, and energy is spent every year for law enforcement, courts, probation and parole, institutions, programs, and agencies whose sole purpose is to attempt to control, treat, and prevent social deviance. Juvenile delinquency, for example, costs Americans hundreds of millions of dollars each year. Beyond the monetary costs, deviance can take a tremendous psychological, emotional, and social toll on the members of a society. When people are afraid to go out at night, or to live in certain areas of a city, or in other ways feel threatened, deviance is costing a society far more than dollars and cents.

4. Social Disruption. Deviance also can be socially disruptive. When people do not know what to expect of their fellow human beings in a given situation, social interaction can be severely disrupted. Norm violation can lead to fear, anxiety, mistrust, and confusion for the members of society.

5. Social Order is Threatened. Deviant behavior can threaten the stability and social order of a society. As indicated in the consensus model, societal members establish social norms in an effort to create and maintain a sense of social order. The violation of these norms, even in isolated cases, can threaten that order temporarily. Widespread norm violation can create havoc and threaten social stability, as in the cases of mobs, riots, and revolutions.

6. Self-Perpetuation. In some ways, deviance can create more deviance, and hence, be self-perpetuating. The old adage "Give 'em an inch, and they'll take a mile" reflects the widespread assumption that when one norm is broken, it is very likely to lead to other norms being broken. Part of the reason that there are so many norms regulating juvenile behavior stems from the view that youths must learn at an early age that rules exist and that they must not be broken. Otherwise, many believe that the violation of one rule will encourage the violation of others. Similarly, the punitive view of our criminal justice system is based upon the idea that when caught, a law violator must be publicly punished in order to deter others from similar deviance.

Because of the negative consequences of social deviance, most members of society attempt to prevent, limit, and control norm violation as much as possible. When a particular type of deviance, such as juvenile delinquency, is viewed as uncontrolled, or worse yet, uncontrollable, it is likely to be defined as a major social problem, and society will mobilize in an effort to minimize its negative consequences.

Positive Aspects of Deviance

It would be simplistic and unrealistic to terminate our discussion of deviant behavior with the assumption that *all* of the consequences of deviance are socially and personally destructive.

On the contrary, some deviant acts may generate very positive results for the group or society in which they occur.

We can initiate the discussion of the importance of deviance to society by acknowledging that while all deviant behavior is nonconforming, not all deviant behavior is completely antisocial. In fact, sociologists have identified several forms of unorthodox and deviant behavior that, when generally recognized as beneficial to the social group or community, often elicit considerable tolerance. Emile Durkheim (1938) began this line of thought with his thesis of the "Functional Necessity of Crime." Later studies by Robert Dentler and Kai Erikson (1959) and by Lewis Coser (1956) further developed the concept. This discussion is indebted to all of those scholars for the following composite list of positive functions of deviance:

1. Reaffirmation of Norms. Often, the deviant is rejected and the group's norms are reaffirmed. In this way, the occasional violation may revitalize the collective conscience of the people. Just as we mentioned that norms may be threatened when norm violation occurs and no discernible harm is apparent, when deviance clearly causes social harm social norms are likely to be reaffirmed and strengthened. For example, the obvious harm caused by serious forms of juvenile crime lends support to prevailing social norms that regulate juvenile misconduct.

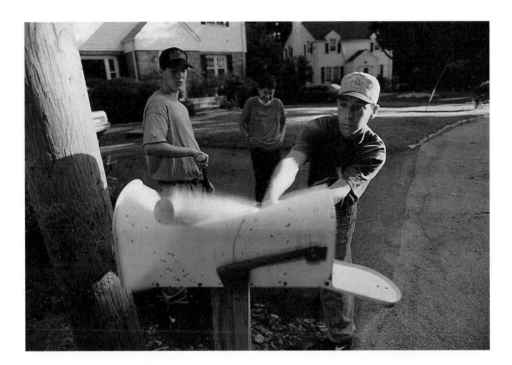

What appears as youthful mischief to participants can be a serious offense to the larger society. Here, several boys damage a mailbox.

2. Social Solidarity. In many cases, the deviant is rejected and the social group is united. Internal enemies, functioning as a built-in "out-group," can bring people together in a common defense of their community in much the same way as do external and hostile enemies. History is replete with tragic examples of crucifixions, lynchings, and witch hunts that united the larger society and enabled people to blame their fear and frustration on selected scapegoats.

3. Unity on Behalf of the Deviant. The reaction of the social group is not always punitive toward the deviant. Juvenile delinquency, for example, provides a variety of instances in which various social groups, agencies, and society as a whole unite not against delinquents, but on their behalf. Many acts of delinquency are viewed as being the result of unfortunate social circumstances experienced by the youths committing them, and individuals and groups often unite in an attempt to alleviate those undesirable situations in order to help the delinquent.

4. Contrast Effect. The deviant offers a convenient and complementary contrast to those who conform. Sometimes the public exposure and chastisement of deviants is one of the means used to make conformity meritorious. Perhaps the unspoken message in some condemnations is: "Our indignation over deviant behavior is evidence of our virtue, and proof that we would never commit such offenses!" More overtly, parents often point their fingers at the youth in serious trouble with the law to warn their own children that if they don't behave, they may face a similar fate some day.

5. "Safety Valve." Some forms of deviance may serve as a kind of safety valve for society. Human society is comparable to a boiler under pressure that might explode from inner social, political, and economic tensions unless some "steam" is periodically drained off. Many forms of nonserious juvenile misconduct are viewed as relatively harmless events of youths "letting off a little steam." Comments like "boys will be boys," or "kids have to sow a few wild oats" represent the view that minor deviance entered into periodically by youths is "normal" and far preferable to following all norms rigidly until the pressure builds and ultimately leads to some serious type of deviant behavior.

6. Leadership. In some cases, deviant behavior can help to develop and promote new social leadership. Group dynamics, ranging from gang fights to social movements, often require and generate leaders who excel in articulating group needs and organizing the efforts of the group to achieve their collective objectives. Occasionally someone on the order of Joan of Arc emerges, whose visionary and deviant behavior ultimately placed the 19-year-old at the head of the French Army! (Later, as Joan fell from favor, she was burned at the stake, thus also sadly fulfilling for her society the second positive aspect of deviance outlined in this list.)

7. Social and Cultural Change. Deviance and deviants may encourage meaningful social and cultural change. This may include the work of innovative administrators who cut through bureaucratic "red tape" to serve fellow workers, eccentric but brilliant inventors, and even revolutionaries like Patrick Henry and George Washington, who helped bring about major social change. On a less dramatic scale, the first to try a new hairstyle, dress style, or other innovative fad or fashion is usually considered deviant.

8. Warning Device. Deviance also may serve as a warning signal. Rising poverty levels, divorce rates, levels of unemployment, and rates of juvenile delinquency—all in the same area of a city—may indicate defects in the social structure or organization of society. Astute political leaders, observing such indicators of impending social erosion, may then take preventive measures.

9. Variety and Excitement. Finally, some forms of social deviance merely reflect the wide variety of personalities, characters, cultural orientations, and behavior manifested by people who dare to be different. Imagine how incredibly dull human society would be if everyone was a total conformist, seemingly cut out by the same predictable, conforming "social cookie cutter."

The section of this chapter that dealt with conformity ended by stating that "norms...and group-shared expectations—are part of the glue that holds society together..." At the same time, and paradoxically, this discussion of nonconformity can be concluded with the statement that deviation from those norms is also part of the glue that holds society together.

Juvenile Delinquency

Deviant behavior can become a social problem when it is continuous, chronic, and widespread, and perceived by a substantial and significant part of the population as nonproductive and threatening to the general well-being of society. Juvenile delinquency is a form of deviant behavior because it involves the violation of norms by children and youths. However, this form of deviant behavior comes to national attention because many of the norms that are violated are deemed to be important enough that they have been codified into criminal and/or juvenile laws. It should be noted that many of the behaviors identified as juvenile delinquency are not criminal acts, but relatively trivial forms of deviance. The various criminal laws and juvenile statutes that are most frequently violated by youths in the United States are detailed in Chapter 3. Nevertheless, juvenile delinquency involves enough of the nation's young people in serious, antisocial behavior that it is perceived by a large segment of our society to be a major social problem. Consequently, it receives a great deal of attention from scholars, civic leaders, law enforcement officers, and the mass media. News articles such as the following arouse citizen concern over the problem of juvenile delinquency:

YOUNGER KIDS ARE KILLING, ROBBING

Orlando, FL (AP)   Children increasingly are committing crimes ranging from armed robbery to murder, say criminal justice experts.

"Ten years ago, it was a shock to see a 7, 8, or 9 year-old come into the system; now it's not," said Danny Dawson, chief of the Orange-Osceola County State Attorney's juvenile division.

Kathleen Heide,...at the University of South Florida...completed a two-year study of adolescent killers.

She characterized about 10 percent of them as "nihilistic"—those who derive pleasure from hurting others. Among six other categories were those who regard crime as a sport and homicide as an unavoidable aspect of robbery.

In another category were abused children, who might kill a parent but who tend more toward suicidal than homicidal behavior, she said. "These are basically good kids," Ms. Heide said. "They go through life with an attitude that life is to endure." (**From:** *Manteca Bulletin,* **Vol. 78, No. 363, Dec. 29, 1986**)

CHILDREN CHARGED IN POISONING PLOT

Lucerne Valley, CA *Four sixth graders were arrested for allegedly planning to kill their teacher by spiking her Gatorade with rat poison.*

Sondra Haile, 54, never drank the poison because a child warned her that someone had put poison in her bottle, said Deputy Cheryl Huff of the San Bernardo County Sheriff's Department. (**From:** *Skagit Valley Herald,* **Sedro Woolley, Washington, February 5, 1997:A2).**

PIZZA DELIVERY MAN SLAIN BY TEENAGE ROBBERS

Pittsburgh, PA *Jay Weiss, a 34-year-old man who worked for Chubby's Pizza, was killed by two teen-agers while delivering a pizza to them. As the man lay dying, the two boys sat on a curb and ate the pizza.* (**Thomas J. DiLorenzo,** *USA Today,* **June 25, 1997:13A).**

One might attempt to rationalize that since juvenile delinquency has some positive consequences for society, such as reinforcing the validity of violated norms, mobilizing society for its control, and generating jobs for the army of law enforcement personnel, the resolution or serious reduction of juvenile delinquency could actually be dysfunctional to society. However, society is not inclined to make these theoretical "tradeoffs" for the sake of the status quo. Juvenile delinquency is perceived to jeopardize the basic social values regarding the safety and security of persons and property.

Large numbers of U.S. citizens feel unsafe in their homes, neighborhoods, or workplaces. Many have even stopped going out at night for fear of violent crime. Sociologists who study the effect of media coverage of crime on the public's fear of crime report that attitudes about the safety of one's neighborhood and about going out at night in the city in which one resides vary directly with the rate of index crimes in that city. The crime reports that are most closely correlated with fear of crime are those describing sensational murders in one's own city—that is, murders that are reported on the front pages of newspapers and on television (Kornblum and Julian, 1992:154).

Richard Fuller and Richard Myers (1941) also helped establish the linkage between deviant behavior such as juvenile delinquency and a national social problem:

Social problems are what people say they are. Two things must be present: (1) an **objective condition** *(crime, poverty, racial tensions, and so forth) the presence and magnitude of which can be observed, verified, and measured by impartial social observers; and (2) a* **subjective definition** *by some members of the society that the objective condition is a "problem" and must be acted upon. Here is where values* *come into play, for when values are perceived as threatened by the existence of the objective condition a social problem is defined. (Cited in McKee, 1974:496)*

Paraphrasing David Dressler and Donald Cams (1973:532), juvenile delinquency is a social problem. It is social in that it has to do with human relationships within society. It involves people, their ethical values, and their relations with one another. Juvenile delinquency is a problem because it is "regarded as involving undesirable dislocations in social patterns and relationships within the society." It represents what is "wrong" or "improper," "dangerous" or "unfair." Society is committed to doing something about these discrepancies between social standards and the actual conduct of so many youthful citizens.

The sociological approach of this book capitalizes on sociologists' practical and demonstrated ability to clarify the underlying nature and causes of social problems such as juvenile delinquency. As Broom and Selznick (1963:4) pointed out, this clarification includes the necessity "to estimate more exactly their dimensions, and to identify aspects that seem most amenable to remedy with the knowledge and skills at hand."

SUMMARY

Chapter 2 began with an explanation of the sociological perspective that links a person's behavior with his or her society or social context. Applying this approach to juvenile delinquency, we may perceive it as a reaction to or reflection of the family, peers, neighborhood, socioeconomic status, and many other dimensions of the offender's social experience.

The discussion of conduct norms, conformity, and deviance was initiated with a brief overview of our compelling social imperative—an inherent need and desire for social interaction and social interdependence with others. Thus, the foundation is laid for the development and organization of human society.

When people come together to form a society, generally acceptable forms of social interaction and patterns of behavior are recognized. This social organization is based upon the establishment of norms, both prescriptive and proscriptive, that serve as guidelines for behavior considered appropriate and/or inappropriate. The norms may arise out of general social consensus, or may emerge out of social conflict. Norms may take the form of folkways, which are informal yet very important guidelines for our everyday behavior. Or they may be more seriously enforced mores, which are considered vital to the survival of society. When these norms are formally codified into legal statutes governing behavior, we refer to them as laws.

The establishment of norms immediately creates the concepts of conformity (adherence to social norms) and deviance (norm violation). Through the process of socialization, societal members are taught to internalize the norms of society as their own and to generally conform to the attitudes, beliefs, and behaviors considered appropriate.

When individuals violate society's norms they are considered deviant and their behavior is often socially sanctioned. Most people view extremely deviant behavior as serious, and perhaps antisocial; and we discussed several negative aspects of social deviance, such as personal harm, threat to norms, costs, disruption, threat to social order, and the encouragement of other forms of deviance. On the other hand, there also are some socially positive aspects of deviance. These include the reaffirmation of norms, promotion of social solidarity, uniting on behalf of (or against) the deviant, contrasting deviance with conformity, providing a "safety valve," establishing leadership, bringing about social and cultural change, acting as a "warning device" to society, and providing variety and excitement. Therefore, just as conformity plays an important role in maintaining society, so does social deviance.

Juvenile delinquency is a specific form of social deviance and is regarded as a major social problem in the United States. Members of our society are concerned, and in many cases alarmed, at the extent of law violation involving American youth. This book treats juvenile delinquency as a social problem, and contends that in order to be more clearly understood, it must be viewed in its broadest sociocultural context.

Concept Integration

Questions and Topics for Study and Discussion

1. What is the sociological perspective of human behavior? How is it applied to the study of juvenile delinquency?
2. What evidence can you cite from your reading of this chapter or from your own experience to support the idea that humans need social interaction and social interdependence?
3. What is social organization? How are social norms related to social organization?
4. Identify and explain the differences between the two subcategories of social norms. Can you give at least one example from your own experience of each of the two kinds of norms?
5. Explain the theoretical origins of our social norms.

BOX 2-2 Concept Application

The many fundamental sociological concepts discussed in this chapter will be a useful foundation for the study of human behavior in general, and juvenile delinquency in particular. The following anecdote relates an experience of one of the authors and provides additional examples and a concrete application of some of these important concepts.

"Deviance or Conformity?"

I grew up in an agricultural valley of Central California and attended a small-town high school. It was a quiet rural environment characterized by close-knit, informal relationships where nearly everyone knew a great deal about everyone else—including such details as family and marriage connections, religious and political persuasions, number of acres owned by each family, and any past scandals.

Nothing really exciting ever seemed to happen in our community. The business district of the town was just three blocks long and included a post office, grocery store, feed store, hardware store, and two gasoline service stations. Church, school, and Grange activities apparently satisfied the social needs of the community (the pool hall having been successfully closed by local ministers as a corrupting influence on the youth). My home town enjoyed a reputation as a very law-abiding place and the one elderly police officer had little difficulty in keeping the peace.

However, there was one night of every year when the high school boys of our town abruptly changed the usual pattern of their behavior, rampaged through the town, and broke a dozen laws. Everyone in the community knew when it was about to happen because considerable preparation always preceded this deviant behavior. During September and October of each year, the high school boys collected surplus and spoiled fruit, vegetables, and eggs. The activity came to a climax on Halloween night, when about 75 youths drove pickup trucks, loaded with their overripe "ammunition," onto the deserted Main Street of the town. Then and there, for several hours, bands of beer-saturated boys fought pitched battles with rotten produce. Other citizens seldom dared venture onto Main Street during this yearly melee. Even the old policeman was strangely absent. Any unwary motorists who did blunder into the area on Halloween night had their automobiles pelted and smeared with tomatoes and eggs.

The boys carried out many mischievous pranks. For example, one year they discovered a loaded manure spreader parked nearby and, after hooking it up to an old car, spread several inches of manure up and down the three blocks of Main Street. As usual, the following day two county sheriff's deputies arrived early at our high school with a truckload of rakes and shovels. All of the boys were dismissed from school for the day to clean up the town. Then our little community returned to its usual pattern of peaceful and predictable behavior—until the next Halloween.

* * * *

In light of the chapter that you just read, were the high school boys violating any social norms? List as many laws and regulations as you can that may have been violated. In your opinion, and in the judgment of their community, were the high school boys "juvenile delinquents"? Explain how their Halloween behavior was conforming to *another* group-shared expectation. Finally, point out how their "deviant behavior" may have had a positive function for the community.

6. What are the purposes or functions of social norms? Try to think of a norm that you have encountered that seems to have no purpose or function for society.

7. What is the difference between conformity and deviance? In your judgment, is it fair for society to restrict some of our individual freedoms in order to achieve a general conformity to social norms?

8. Based on your reading of this chapter, and your own opinion, would it be possible and good for society to outlaw all deviant behavior? Briefly explain or justify your answer.

9. Why is juvenile delinquency considered deviant behavior? Is juvenile delinquency a social problem?

References

Arnold, D. O. (ed.) 1970. *The sociology of subcultures.* Berkeley: The Glendessary Press.

Barash, D. P. 1982. *Sociobiology and behavior* (2nd ed.). New York: Elsevier.

Becker, H. 1973. *The outsiders.* (Revised Ed.). New York: The Free Press of Glencoe.

Benedict, R. 1934. *Patterns of culture.* Boston: Houghton-Mifflin.

Berger, P. 1963. *An invitation to sociology.* Garden City, NY: Doubleday.

Birenbaum, A., and Sagarin, E. 1976. *Norms and human behavior.* New York: Praeger.

Broom, L., and Selznick, P. 1963. *Sociology* (3rd ed.). New York: Harper & Row.

Chambliss, W. J. 1973. *Functional and conflict theories of crime.* New York: MSS Modular Publications.

Cohen, A. 1966. *Deviant behavior.* Englewood Cliffs, NJ: Prentice-Hall.

Cooley, C. H. 1964. *Human nature and the social order.* New York: Schocken Books (Originally published in 1902.).

Coser, L. 1956. *The functions of social conflict.* New York: The Free Press.

Dahrendorf, R. 1959. *Class and class conflict in industrial society.* Palo Alto, CA: Stanford University Press.

Davis, K. 1940. Extreme isolation of a child. *American Journal of Sociology* 45:554–565. 1948. *Human Society.* New York: Macmillan.

DeFleur, M., D'Antonio, W. V., and DeFleur, L. B. 1976. *Sociology: Human society* (2nd ed.). Glenview, IL: Scott, Foresman and Co.

DiLorenzo, T. J. 1997. Pizza driver safety transcends civil rights. *USA Today,* June 25, 1997:13A.

Dentler, R., and Erikson, K. 1959. The functions of deviance in groups. *Social Problems,* 7 (Fall):98–107.

Downey, M. 1993. *The Mort Downey Show.* TV Channel 27, Ft. Worth, TX. September 24.

Dressler, D., and Carns, D. 1973. *Sociology: The study of human interaction* (2nd ed.). New York: Alfred A. Knopf.

Durkheim, E. 1938. *The rules of sociological method.* Translated by Sarah A. Solvay and John H. Mueller. George E. G. Catlin (Ed.) New York: The Free Press of Glencoe.
1947. *Division of labor in society.* Translated by George Simpson. New York: The Free Press.

Erikson, E. 1956. The problem of identity. *Journal of the American Psychiatric Association.* 4, 1 (January):56–121.

Figgis, J. N. 1922. *The divine right of kings.* London: Smith.

Freeman, H. E., and Giovannoni, J. M. 1969. Social psychology of mental health. Pp. 690–719. In Gardner Lindsey and Elliott Aronson (Eds.) *Handbook of social psychology* (2nd ed.). Reading, MA: Addison-Wesley.

Fuller, R., and Myers, R. 1941. Some aspects of a theory of social problems. *American Sociological Review* 6 (February):24–32.

Goffman, E. 1965. *Behavior in public places.* New York: The Free Press.

Green, A. 1972. *Sociology.* New York: McGraw-Hill.

Hobbes, T. 1914. *Leviathan* (Everyman's Library Edition). London: J. M. Dent.

Kammeyer, K. C. W., Ritzer, G., and Yetman, N. R. 1997. *Sociology: experiencing changing societies* (7th ed.). Boston: Allyn & Bacon.

Kornblum, W., and Julian, J. 1992. *Social problems* (7th ed.). Englewood Cliffs, NJ: Prentice-Hall.

Kropotkin, P. 1914. *Mutual aid: A factor in evolution.* Boston: Extending Horizons Books.

Lemert, E. M. 1964. Social structure, social control, and deviation. Pp. 957–971. In Marshall Clinard (Ed.) *Anomie and deviant behavior: A discussion and critique.* New York: The Free Press.

Manteca Bulletin. 1986. More kids are killing, robbing. AP Florida, *Manteca Bulletin,* Vol. 78, No. 363, Dec. 29.

Mantell, D. M. 1974. Doves and hawks: Guess who had the authoritarian parents? *Psychology Today* (September):56–62.

Marx, K., and Engels, F. [1848] 1964. *The communist manifesto.* Translated by Samuel Moore. Joseph Katz (Ed.). New York: Washington Square Press.

Marx, K. [1867] 1967. *Capital.* Friedrich Engels (Ed.). New York: International Publishers.

McKee, J. B. 1974. *Introduction to sociology* (2nd ed.). New York: Holt, Rinehart and Winston.

Miller, E. 1978. We just put them in the cage so they won't get away. *The Dallas Morning News,* July 2, 1978:1.

Mills, C. W. 1959. *The sociological imagination.* New York: Oxford University Press.

Myerhoff, H., and Myerhoff, B. 1964. Field observations of middle-class gangs, *Social Forces* 42 (March):328–336.

Park, R. E. 1928. Human migration and the marginal man. *American Journal of Sociology* 33 (May): 893. 1936. Human ecology. *American Journal of Sociology* 42 (July):1–15.

Perez, J. F., 1978. *The family roots of adolescent delinquency.* New York: Van Nostrand Reinhold Company.

Quinney, R. 1970. *The social reality of crime.* Boston: Little, Brown & Co.

Scott, J. F. 1971. *Internalization of norms: A sociological theory of moral commitment.* Englewood Cliffs, NJ: Prentice-Hall.

Skagit Valley Herald. (Sedro Woolley, WA). 1997. Children charged in poisoning plot. February 5, 1997:A2.

Stein, J. 1964. *Fiddler on the roof.* New York: Crown Publishers.

Stonequist, E. H. 1937. *The marginal man.* New York: Charles Scribner's Sons.

Sumner, W. G. [1906] 1959. *Folkways.* Boston: Ginn.

Sutherland, E. 1961. *White collar crime.* New York: Holt, Rinehart and Winston.

Weber, M. [1925] 1947. *The theory of social and economic organization.* Translated by A. M. Henderson and T. Parsons. New York: The Free Press.

Whyte, W. F. [1943] 1981. *Street corner society* (3rd ed.). Chicago: University of Chicago Press.

3

THE DIMENSIONS OF THE DELINQUENCY PROBLEM

Reading Objectives

The reading of this chapter will help you achieve the following objectives:

1. Define the various kinds of crime according to the common classification and criteria used throughout the United States.
2. Identify the sources of the data and statistical information on juvenile delinquency in the United States.
3. Explain the various data-collecting techniques that are used and the strengths and weaknesses of each methodology.
4. Understand how unreliable and/or invalid data or data-gathering procedures can lead to questionable findings and conclusions regarding the magnitude of juvenile delinquency.
5. Trace the general dimensions of the delinquency problem with official FBI and juvenile court statistics on the incidence and trends of juvenile crime in the various offense categories.
6. Based on arrest statistics, conceptualize the Delinquent Profile as a summary and descriptive statement of many characteristics of the "average" juvenile delinquent.
7. Analyze and critique the data supporting the various traits comprising the composite Delinquent Profile. Explain why the amount and kind of juvenile delinquency vary, or seems to vary, according to the sex, race, place of residence, and other characteristics of the offenders.

Introduction

In 1930, a voluntary national program for the collection of crime statistics was initiated by the International Association of Chiefs of Police (IACP) and the United States Federal Bureau of Investigation (FBI). The resulting annual reports on criminal activity in the United States have revealed serious and consistently high rates of juvenile delinquency. The *First Annual Report of the National Institute of Law Enforcement and Criminal Justice* (1974:15) reported that "during the 1960's, the arrest rate for juveniles increased six times faster than for adults." By 1970, juveniles under the age of 18 accounted for one-fifth of all arrests for violent crime and for more than half of all arrests for burglary. In 1973, The National Advisory Commission on Criminal Justice Standards and Goals identified juvenile delinquency as a critical, high priority, national concern:

> *The highest attention must be given to preventing juvenile delinquency, minimizing the involvement of young offenders in the juvenile and criminal justice system, and reintegrating them into the community.* (Standards and Goals for Juvenile Justice, *1974:3*)

The news media also continually focus on the crimes committed by U.S. youths, especially those crimes of a violent and sensational nature:

> *More and more teenagers, acting individually or in gangs, are running amuck.... Adolescence is often a troubled time of rebellion and rage.... But juvenile crime appears to be more widespread and vicious than ever before.... What is chilling about many of the young criminals is that they show no remorse or conscience, at least initially. Youths brag about their exploits and shrug off victims' pain* (*Toufexis,* Time Magazine, *1989, pp. 52–58*).

It is not surprising, therefore, that the national problem of juvenile delinquency continues to receive constant attention from an army of law enforcement personnel, criminologists, and other scholars in the social and behavioral sciences. Without minimizing the gravity of youthful crime, it should be pointed out that much of what we read or hear on the topic in the news media is selective reporting of those aspects of juvenile delinquency that will quickly capture public attention. Obviously, headline or feature stories of juvenile gang wars raging in the streets or of a maniacal teenager committing mayhem in a school sells more newspapers than a report that the vast majority of juvenile arrests are for property crimes, vandalism, and juvenile status offenses such as the violation of liquor laws (*FBI,* 1991, 1999:220). Equally lacking in sensationalism are the data-based findings that only 7 to 10 percent of delinquents are chronic and violent offenders, and this hard-core group commits up to 63 percent of all serious and violent juvenile crime (Snyder and Sickmund, 1999).

In this chapter, in order to more fully comprehend the magnitude of juvenile delinquency in the United States, we review the methods by which information on crime is acquired, the various kinds and incidence of criminal activity, current trends, and characteristics of offenders as indicated by available statistics.

Juvenile Delinquency Data

Statistical data and quantitative information are regularly collected in order to provide fresh insights regarding juvenile delinquency in the United States. If this social problem is ever to be completely understood, prevented, or controlled, accurate up-to-date information must be available to answer such questions as: How many juvenile offenses and arrests occur each year? What kinds of juvenile misbehavior are most common from year to year? What trends can be extrapolated from the past and the present, and projected for the future? Is there a "typical" juvenile delinquent? If so, what are his or her social, economic, and demographic characteristics?

Validity and Reliability

The methods and procedures used to collect and analyze data determine their accuracy and, from that, the usefulness of the findings. For example, it is impossible to identify all the children and youths who have violated a juvenile statute or whose behavior could be interpreted by others as delinquent. Even if this prodigious task of identification could somehow be accomplished, administering a questionnaire or conducting an interview in every case would be too expensive and impractical. Consequently, most research efforts to measure the amount and kinds of delinquent behavior utilize information collected by law enforcement agencies about known offenders. Conversely, such data are severely limited in informing us about the offenses and traits of delinquent youths who are not apprehended.

Other investigators into juvenile delinquency have implemented sampling strategies in which a relatively small number of known delinquents or other subjects are selected and surveyed on the assumption that they are representative of a much larger population. However, if the respondents who comprise the "sample of representative delinquents," for example, are conveniently gathered from Chicago street gangs, the findings would not give an accurate picture of all of the juvenile delinquency in Chicago. **Validity** and **reliability** are two precise concepts that will help us understand these common problems and errors in research methodology.

Validity

A measure has **validity** when it *in fact measures whatever it is supposed to measure.* A finding or conclusion is valid if it accurately reflects factual evidence. As an example, suppose Professor Smith at University A decides to interview a sample of students about their possible participation in unreported or undetected delinquent activities. The professor may be extremely careful to randomly select subjects so that they are representative of all the students attending the college (this is a very difficult task since every student must have an equal chance of being included in the sample). However, during the interviews, if the professor directly or indirectly, consciously or unconsciously, indicates expected or desired responses to the questions, there is an excellent chance that the students will tell the professor exactly what they think he wants to hear. Consequently, the findings will be invalid. In addition, if the students feel intimidated by the investigator's attitude, questions, or presence, they may be inclined to understate their involvement in delinquent behavior. So, besides a random sample, other factors in the survey instrument, the subjects, and the lack of anonymity in the situation can affect the validity of the results.

Reliability

A measure has **reliability** when *it yields the same results upon repetition of the measuring procedure or replication by other investigators.* For example, suppose that another teacher at a different school—Professor Jones at University B—hears or reads about Professor Smith's research at University A on unreported and undetected delinquency. Professor Jones then decides to conduct a similar investigation to see how many students at her institution committed various kinds of unreported and undetected crime. Jones also wants to see if her findings agree or disagree with Smith's.

In order to make a fair comparison of the findings from the two studies, the survey conditions, methodology, and subjects must be as nearly identical as possible. Professor Jones therefore uses the same survey questionnaire used by Professor Smith at University A. She also carefully selects her subjects with the same random sampling procedures, and makes every effort to ensure that the sample of students at University B is as similar as possible in background to those surveyed by Smith at University A. It follows that if, after replicating Professor Smith's study, Professor Jones discovers that her findings are essentially the same, we may conclude that the survey instrument or measuring procedure is reliable—that is, it can be relied upon to yield similar results when used by different, independent researchers at different places and points in time.

In summary, validity and reliability clearly are related, and both are enhanced if survey questions are structured so that they can be readily understood by the subjects and elicit informative, straightforward answers. Additionally, validity and reliability are reinforced if subjects are systematically and consistently selected in the same way each time data are collected. Comparisons should be made only between the two or more samples, or of a single sample at different points in time, if variables such as age, race, sex, and social class have been **controlled,** or *held reasonably constant and similar,* from group to group, and from time to time.

These general principles of social science research methodology will be useful in our later evaluations of juvenile delinquency data and concomitant findings and conclusions. They are appropriate considerations with regard to truancy, homicide, unreported crimes, or any other statistical report on juvenile delinquency.

Official Sources of Delinquency Information

Two agencies of the federal government, operating independently of each other, collect and summarize juvenile crime statistics on a national scale into annual reports. They are the Federal Bureau of Investigation (FBI) and the Office of Juvenile Justice and Delinquency Prevention.

FBI Uniform Crime Reports

Since 1930, the FBI has compiled data on crime and delinquency from a network of city, county, and state law enforcement agencies across the country. The numbers and kinds of reported offenses, the numbers and kinds of offenses resulting in arrest, and characteristics of offenders such as age, sex, race, and place of residence form the basis of the FBI compilations. Each year the FBI summarizes the data into statistical tables and issues a *Uniform Crime Report* for the information and use of law enforcement officers and others concerned with the national crime problem.

The FBI Uniform Crime Reporting Program is designed to attain three basic objectives:

1. To measure the extent, fluctuation, distribution, and nature of serious crime in the United States...

2. To measure the total volume of serious crime known to police.

3. To show the activity and coverage of law enforcement agencies through arrest counts and police employee strength data (FBI Uniform Crime Reports, 1975:2).

In addition, the division of arrest data into "ages under 18" and "ages 18 and over" categories is of tremendous help to law-enforcement personnel and researchers using FBI *Uniform Crime Report* data to separate juvenile delinquency from adult crime, according to the legal definition of delinquency presented in Chapter 1. The FBI reported that over two million individuals under 18 years of age were arrested in 1998. That is over 18 percent of all arrests that year in the United States (see Table 3-1).[1]

A major strength of the Uniform Crime Reporting Program is that *standardized definitions* of the main kinds of crime are utilized by *all law enforcement agencies* reporting from the various states. This is why the annual FBI compilations are called "*Uniform* Crime Reports." The definitions for the first eight UCR categories follow:

1. Murder and Nonnegligent Manslaughter. The willful (nonnegligent) killing of one human being by another.

2. Forcible Rape. The carnal knowledge of a female forcibly and against her will. Assaults or attempts to commit rape by force or threat of force are also included.

3. Robbery. The taking or attempting to take anything of value from the care, custody, or control of a person or persons by force or threat of force or violence and/or by putting the victim in fear.

4. Aggravated Assault. An unlawful attack by one person upon another for the purpose of inflicting severe or aggravated bodily injury.

5. Burglary. The unlawful entry or attempted entry of a structure to commit a felony or theft. (A felony is any offense punishable by death or imprisonment.)

6. Larceny-theft. The unlawful taking, carrying, leading, or riding away of property from the possession or constructive possession of another. Attempted larcenies are included.

7. Motor Vehicle Theft. The theft or attempted theft of a motor vehicle.

8. Arson. Any willful or malicious burning or attempt to burn, with or without intent to defraud, a dwelling house, public building, motor vehicle or aircraft, personal property of another, etc. (*FBI Uniform Crime Reports, 1998*).

Because of their seriousness, frequency of occurrence, and likelihood of being reported to the police, these eight crime categories were chosen as the basis for the Uniform Crime Report Index, and are referred to as **Index Offenses.** The Index is useful for charting and analyzing changes in the volume of crime in its various and most serious forms from year to year. Table 3-1 is a part of the *1998 Uniform Crime Reports;* the first eight offense categories listed at the top comprise the UCR Index for that year.

---

[1]The unavoidable time lag between FBI collection of arrest data and publication of annual crime reports, plus the necessary delay between an author's preparation of a manuscript and its publication can result in data being up to three or more years old before it gets to the textbook reader. However, an assiduous scholar can acquire the most current arrest data available from the FBI home page address on the Internet: www.fbi.gov (followed by reference to "Uniform Crime Report").

TABLE 3-1   Total Arrests, Distribution by Age and Crime Categories, 1998 (9,505 agencies; 1998 estimated population: 185,964,000)

Offense charged	Total all ages	Ages under 15	Ages under 18	Ages 18 and over
TOTAL	10,295,129	582,661	1,855,002	8,440,127
Percent distribution[1]	100.0	5.7	18.0	82.0
Murder and nonnegligent manslaughter	12,335	139	1,470	10,865
Forcible rape	21,922	1,384	3,769	18,153
Robbery	87,129	5,848	23,400	63,729
Aggravated assault	359,892	17,192	51,360	308,532
Burglary	233,435	30,840	81,894	151,541
Larceny-theft	940,243	122,763	300,033	640,210
Motor vehicle theft	107,003	9,845	38,386	68,617
Arson	12,144	4,199	6,324	5,820
VIOLENT CRIME[2]	481,278	24,563	79,999	401,279
Percent distribution[1]	100.0	5.1	16.6	83.4
PROPERTY CRIME[3]	1,292,825	167,647	426,637	866,188
Percent distribution[1]	100.0	13.0	33.0	67.0
CRIME INDEX TOTAL	1,774,103	192,210	506,636	1,267,467
Percent distribution[1]	100.0	10.8	28.6	71.4
Other assaults	947,596	68,916	168,240	779,356
Forgery; Counterfeiting	81,254	649	5,006	76,248
Fraud	268,351	1,240	7,689	260,662
Embezzlement	12,215	59	1,108	11,107
Stolen property, buying, receiving, possessing	98,466	6,319	24,159	74,307
Vandalism	213,495	39,716	90,156	123,339
Weapons, carrying, possessing, etc.	136,049	10,313	32,232	103,817
Prostitution and commercialized vice	68,536	139	1,019	67,517
Sex offenses (except rape & prostitution)	65,967	5,645	11,208	54,759
Drug abuse violations	1,108,788	22,998	146,394	962,394
Gambling	9,216	162	1,149	8,067
Offenses against the family and children	99,776	2,549	6,945	92,831
Driving under influence	968,868	404	14,501	954,367
Liquor laws	448,187	11,256	111,838	336,349
Drunkenness	510,318	2,215	17,648	492,670
Disorderly conduct	501,866	46,491	132,410	369,456
Vagrancy	22,002	559	2,110	19,892
All other offenses (except traffic)	2,702,882	86,458	320,207	2,382,675
Suspicion	3,812	248	965	2,847
Curfew and loitering law violations	136,293	37,191	136,293	—
Runaways	117,089	46,924	117,089	—

Source: Federal Bureau of Investigation. 1999. *Crime in the United States, 1998: Uniform Crime Reports.* Washington, DC: U.S. Government Printing Office. Table 38, p. 220.

[1]Because of rounding, the percentages may not add to total.
[2]Violent crimes are offenses of murder, forcible rape, robbery, and aggravated assault.
[3]Property crimes are offenses of burglary, larceny-theft, motor vehicle theft, and arson.

Juvenile Arrests for Specific Offenses

The first four Index Offenses—murder, forcible rape, robbery, and aggravated assault—are often grouped together and referred to as "violent crimes." **Violent Crimes** are *those that are directed against a person.* During 1998, persons under 18 years of age accounted for 16.6 percent of the violent crimes in the United States. The last four Index Offenses—burglary, larceny-theft, motor vehicle theft, and arson—are combined under the heading of "property crimes." **Property Crimes** are *non-violent crimes directed against property.* In 1998, persons under age 18 were credited with 33 percent of the 1,292,825 property crimes in the United States.

Table 3-1 indicates that percentages of arrests for violent crimes attributed to persons between ages 15 and 17 and to persons age 18 and over are approximately the same as the proportions of the national population in these two age groupings. At the same time, FBI arrest records in Table 3-1 show that the probability is much higher that youths will be arrested for property crimes than will adults.

Of the eight specific offenses comprising the Crime Index, 14 percent of the 1998 arrests for murder were of youths under age 18. During the same year, 11 percent of the murder victims were also under 18 years of age. Of the total clearances by arrest for forcible rape in 1998, nearly 16 percent involved persons under 18 years of age. Persons under the age of 18 were the offenders in 30 percent of all 1998 robbery clearances, while over 14 percent of the national aggravated assault clearances by arrest involved persons under age 18. Burglary, larceny-theft, and motor vehicle theft are common forms of juvenile crime, with persons under age 18 accounting for 37 percent, 34 percent, and 40 percent respectively of all 1998 arrests for offenses falling in those three categories.

Arson was added to the Crime Index in 1979 in response to national concern over rapidly rising arson rates. Of special significance to our study of juvenile delinquency is the fact that 1998 arrest statistics for arson demonstrate a higher percentage of juvenile involvement than in any other Index crime. Arrestees under age 18 represented over 51 percent of all arson cases cleared by arrest. Wayne Wooden (1985:23–24) warned of an "Arson Epidemic":

> ...*Children are responsible for the majority of arson cases, a share that also appears to be increasing rapidly. And unlike other juvenile crimes, arson is disproportionately a white, middle-class activity.... (Also see: Karchmer, 1984:78–83; Schaaf, 1986:16–19; and Craig, 1996:A1)*

Overall national trends in juvenile delinquency as well as the longitudinal trends for specific juvenile offenses are analyzed in a later section of this chapter.

Status Offenses

A very large proportion of law-violating behavior by U.S. youths falls into those vague areas collectively referred to as "status offenses." In contrast to crimes—specific and punishable offenses whether committed by adults or juveniles—status offenses are violations that are applicable only to juveniles. They cover such behavior as school truancy, the purchase and consumption of alcoholic beverages, knowingly associating with immoral persons, running away from home, being beyond parental control, and curfew violations. While status offenses may vary from place to place and in the consistency and seriousness of law enforcement, they are considered violations of the codified laws of a state or municipality as are traditional crimes such as assault and robbery. The difference is that the conduct described as a "status offense" is illegal only if the offender happens to have the social and legal status of a "juvenile," defined in most jurisdictions as a person under 18 years of age. In New York state, a status offender is defined as a child under 16 who does not attend school or "who is incorrigible or ungovernable or habitually disobedient and beyond the lawful control of parents or other lawful authority" (Diegmueller, 1987:15). Critics argue that such legal definitions and codes of conduct are sufficiently variable and vague as to result in great disparity in law enforcement and thereby attach undeserved criminal stigma to many thousands of young people.

Status offenses, as an appendage to criminal law especially designed for wayward youths, appeared very early in United States jurisprudence, reflective of conservative and traditional concern with child rearing and character development. Such laws, while often appearing today as arbitrary and intrusive, were based on the state's generally accepted role as *parens patriae*. This Latin phrase imputes to the state the ultimate parental authority over citizens who demonstrate a need for protection and direction because of age, infirmity, immaturity, or some other condition that limits personal responsibility. Although idealistic in origin, the widespread application of juvenile status ordinances prior to 1965 resulted in the incarceration of a tremendous number of children and youths. For example,

> *Wisconsin researchers found that nearly 41 percent of the state's detained youths were status offenders. Studies conducted in Arizona, California, Utah, and Delaware produced similar findings. (Diegmueller, 1987:14)*

Since the mid 1960s, through a series of landmark decisions from the United States Supreme Court (detailed in Chapter 14), society has become more aware of children as individuals and more sensitive to their legal rights. Reforms have been instituted that soften the treatment and adjudication of status offenders. There is growing support for the idea that the large majority of status offenders should not be arrested and that their cases should be removed from the juvenile justice system. These advocates contend that the juvenile court should be reserved for youths who commit more serious offenses. Nevertheless, the annual *Uniform Crime Reports* reveal that many thousands of youngsters are arrested for status offenses each year. For example, Table 3-1 enumerates almost 111,838 arrests of persons under age 18 for violation of liquor laws; 136,293 for curfew and loitering law violations; and 117,089 for running away from home in 1998. The differential treatment sought for the youngsters in these categories is epitomized in a sign on the office wall of Doug Gibson, Executive Director of a Youth Crisis Center in Oklahoma City (Manley, 1979:23). The sign is a simple reminder and appeal for understanding of the special and common problems of youth: "HUCK FINN WAS A STATUS OFFENDER." To those who recall Mark Twain's story, Huckleberry Finn as a truant and runaway was indeed a status offender (Manley, 1979:23). Moreover, as is shown in a later section of this chapter, most of us were probably status offenders at one time or another!

Male and Female Involvement in Juvenile Delinquency

Table 3-2 divides the number of arrests of persons under age 18 in 1998 into separate categories for male and female offenders. The *Uniform Crime Reports* reveal that male juveniles are arrested, on average, about three times more often than females. This male/female

Every year hundreds of thousands of American youths are arrested for violating state and federal laws, as well as municipal and county ordinances. These data are collected and published annually as part of the *FBI Uniform Crime Reports.*

disparity continues in those cases that are processed by juvenile courts and among young people who are institutionalized as a consequence of their delinquent behavior. An exception to the pattern of higher arrest percentages for males is the incidence of arrests of females under 18 years of age for the status offense of running away from home. Running away continues to be an especially common recourse of young females in situations that appear untenable to them, and rates and percentages for this offense are relatively stable from one year to the next.

Nationally, between 1994 and 1998, the number of juvenile arrests declined for most offense categories. Surprisingly, however, the *proportional* decrease in arrests of males below age 18 was much larger than the *proportional* decrease in arrests of females in that same age category. For example, while arrests of males for violent crimes decreased over 22 percent, the arrests of their female counterparts decreased just two percent. Similarly, arrests of juvenile males for property crimes declined nearly 21 percent while the number of arrests of juvenile females declined just 7.6 percent.

TABLE 3-2   1998 Juvenile Arrests: Distribution by Sex, Crime Index Offenses, and Other Selected Offense Categories (7,729 agencies; 1998 estimated population: 163,698,000)

Offenses	Number of Arrests Under Age 18	Percent[1] Male	Percent[1] Female
All Offenses	1,631,787	73	27
Crime Index:			
Violent Crimes[2]	70,731	83	17
Property Crimes[3]	382,504	71	29
Other Selected Offense Categories:			
Vandalism	78,930	88	12
Prostitution and commercialized vice	869	47	53
Weapons (carrying, possessing, etc.)	28,702	91	9
Drug abuse violations	125,126	86	14
Liquor law violations	98,508	70	30
Curfew and loitering law violations	127,086	69	31
Running away	104,931	42	58

Source: Federal Bureau of Investigation. 1999. *Crime in the United States, 1998: Uniform Crime Reports.* Washington, DC: U.S. Government Printing Office. Adapted from Table 35, p. 217.

[1]Percentages are rounded to nearest whole number.
[2]Violent crimes are offenses of murder, forcible rape, robbery, and aggravated assault.
[3]Property crimes are offenses of burglary, larceny-theft, motor vehicle theft, and arson.

In contrast to the general trend of fewer arrests of young people between 1994 and 1998, there were major increases in arrests of young people for the three offense categories of drug abuse, liquor law, and curfew and loitering law violations. Here again, a paradoxical pattern emerged of differential proportions of change in criminal involvement for males and females. While arrests of males under 18 years of age for these offenses increased 23 percent, 35 percent, and 44 percent respectively, the arrests of females under 18 years of age increased 43 percent, 47 percent, and 60 percent for the same offenses.

The above data from the *1998 Uniform Crime Reports* seem to suggest that the proportional differences between male and female delinquency is narrowing in some offense categories.

While longitudinal trends in arrests of young females for these specific offenses are still tenuous, they are interpreted by some observers as indicative of a steady breakdown of the double standard for male-female behavior that long dominated western cultures (Adler, 1975). The hypothesis that the proportional upsurge in female participation in delinquency is traceable to the equal opportunities implicit in the feminist movement has been challenged by Josefina Figueira-McDonough's study (1984) that found only a weak and partial link between feminist orientation and delinquency by a sample of girls. At the same time, the conclusion by Meda Chesney-Lind and Randall G. Sheldon (1998) that "female delinquency has changed little in the past two decades…. [and] what changes we have seen in girls' misbehavior have been in minor and traditional female offenses" (1998:239), has been refuted by data presented in the *FBI Uniform Crime Reports* since 1991 (also see Eileen Poe-Yamagata and Jeffrey A. Butts, "Female Offenders in the Juvenile Justice System," OJJDP, U.S. Department of Justice, 1996).

But the role of women in crime is also expanding into traditional male areas…. Apparently, socialization experiences are changing for women. If trends of female crime continue they will represent an increasing segment of total crime. Therefore, the focus on female crime is indeed vindicated and should not be abandoned (Forsyth and Foster, 1993:139).

Male/female participation in juvenile delinquency will be further detailed in Chapters 4 and 12.

The Racial and Ethnic Factor in Juvenile Delinquency

The term **racial group** applies to *"those minorities, and corresponding majorities, that are classified according to obvious physical differences"* (Schaefer, 1979:9). Among the obvious attributes used to differentiate and classify racial groups are skin color, facial features, and hair color and texture.

There are at least four races represented in the population of the United States. Whites, although a numerical majority, may be traced to over a score of different national origins in Europe. The black segment of our population traces its origins to a wide spectrum of ancient African nations. United States citizens of Asian or Pacific Islands backgrounds have roots reaching back to China, Japan, Korea, and many other diverse cultures and nationalities. American Indians and Alaskan Natives are descendants of the original and indigenous populations of the geographical areas now included in the United States. Blacks, Asians/Pacific Islanders, and American Indians/Alaskan Natives are numerically smaller groups than whites and are considered to be racial minorities.

The racial background of juvenile delinquents has received considerable attention from law enforcement agencies and criminologists. This focus was intensified by the discovery that racial minorities do not always manifest the same level of delinquency involvement as do members of the dominant racial group. For example, official FBI Crime Reports consistently show that young blacks are disproportionately overrepresented in juvenile arrest statistics. For example, while black youth comprised only 15 percent of the juvenile population in 1997, they accounted for over half of the arrests for murder, robbery, and gambling under 18 years of age.

As indicated by the FBI data given in Table 3-3, white youths are much more likely than black youths to be arrested for property crimes, accounting for over 70 percent of all property crime arrests of persons under age 18. At the same time, the relative difference in the population sizes of the two racial groups indicates that young black youths account for an unusually high proportion of arrests for violent crimes. The great majority of violent assaults by African Americans are committed against members of their own racial group.

According to Table 3-3, the official tabulation of participation in delinquency by young American Indian/Alaskan Natives and Asian/Pacific Islanders is proportionately insignificant. Their population size, as well as the number of arrests made among them, are very small compared to the much larger white and black populations and the delinquency involvement of youngsters from those two groups.

TABLE 3-3   1998 Juvenile Arrests: Distribution by Racial Groups and Major Crime Index Categories

	White		Black		American Indian/ Alaskan Native		Asian or Pacific Islander	
	Number	Percent	Number	Percent	Number	Percent	Number	Percent
ARREST TOTALS	1,313,524	71.3	478,395	26.0	20,741	1.1	28,546	1.6
Index Crimes	340,674	67.7	146,151	29.1	6,401	1.3	9,702	1.9
Violent Crimes[1]	44,001	55.3	33,703	42.3	740	.9	1,175	1.5
Property Crimes[2]	296,673	70.1	112,448	26.6	5,661	1.3	8,527	2.0
Non-Index Crimes[3]	972,850	72.4	332,244	24.7	14,340	1.0	18,844	1.9

Source: Based on data derived from Federal Bureau of Investigation. 1999. *Crime in the United States, 1998: Uniform Crime Reports.* Washington, DC: U.S. Government Printing Office. Table 43, p. 229.

[1]Violent crimes are offenses of murder, forcible rape, robbery, and aggravated assault.

[2]Property crimes are offenses of burglary, larceny-theft, motor vehicle theft, and arson.

[3]Non-Index Crimes include all other forms of crime and status offenses listed in the FBI Uniform Crime Reports (see Table 3-1).

Minority groups that are designated by **ethnicity** are *differentiated from the dominant group on the basis of cultural rather than physical differences* (Schaefer, 1979:9). Many millions of people, representing every other nation on earth, have immigrated into the United States. Over time, as they learned and accepted the language, norms, and beliefs of the dominant culture, most of these new citizens and their descendants were assimilated and "Americanized." However, some groups have retained a residual of pride in their "old country" heritage, reflected in ethnic values, traditions, and practices that have been perpetuated to distinguish particular subcultures within the United States.

As in their studies of racial backgrounds, criminologists have found that official statistics on juvenile delinquency also vary with ethnicity. Of special importance in this regard is the large ethnic minority classified by government agencies as Hispanic or Chicano, which includes anyone of Spanish, Mexican, Puerto Rican, Cuban, or other Latin American background in the United States (Frey, 1997:48). The Hispanic segment of the population totaled 22 million in the 1990 census and is growing five times faster than the non-Hispanic population. About 35 percent of the Hispanic population in the United States is under 18 years of age, compared with 25 percent of the population of non-Hispanic origin. (del Pinal and De Navas, 1990:1).

The FBI Uniform Crime Reports have indicated that Hispanic young people also account for a disproportionately larger share of juvenile arrests (*FBI Uniform Crime Reports, 1989, 1990*). The reader is strongly cautioned to avoid racial and ethnic stereotypes of criminal involvement based on statistical summaries; as Chapter 4 demonstrates, there is no valid biological explanation for high rates of juvenile delinquency for any group. The most plausible explanations point to social forces that negatively impact upon many members of these minority groups which tend to generate delinquent behaviors. (You will find additional discussions of youth from racial and ethnic minority groups involved in delinquency in Chapters 4 and 12).

Place of Residence and Arrest Statistics

For as long as arrest statistics have been compiled in the United States, numbers of arrests have been highest in the large cities, moderate in suburban communities, and lowest in rural areas. This numerical pattern partially reflects the fact that a larger part of the population has lived in urban areas for well over a century. However, the likelihood of an individual being arrested also has consistently varied with place of residence. FBI arrest data confirms that the larger the city, town or community, the higher the arrest rate. For example, in 1995, cities with over 250,000 residents had an arrest rate of 7.78 per 100,000 inhabitants, while smaller cities with populations from 25,000 to 49,999 recorded a lower rate of 5.35. The point is further underscored by the arrest rate of 4.25 for suburban county agencies.

While the number of offenses cleared by arrest still reflect a heavily urban concentration, the gap in arrest rates between cities, suburban communities, and rural areas has been narrowing. Numerous studies have suggested that this changing geographical pattern of arrests reflects the centrifugal expansion of urban population and concomitant social problems into the smaller communities ringing the central cities (Bardo and Hartman, 1982; Harries, 1974; Hurley, 1994; Weeks, 1996). The tendency toward the equalization of arrest rates between large cities and the suburbs also may indicate a greater sensitivity of law enforcement agencies and the public to the incidence of crime and delinquency in middle class, suburban districts. Table 3-4 summarizes the 1998 arrest statistics for persons under 18 years of age according to urban, suburban, and rural areas.

Urban and suburban youngsters are very similar in the kinds of crimes for which they are arrested, with each group closely paralleling on Index offenses. In contrast, rural youths are more likely to be involved in less serious crimes and status offenses than their urban and suburban counterparts. Several sociological theories of urban delinquency will be presented in Chapters 6 and 12.

TABLE 3-4 1998 Arrests of Persons Under Age 18 by Urban, Suburban, and Rural Place of Residence

Population Group	Crime Index Total	Violent Crime[1]	Property Crime[2]
CITY ARRESTS UNDER AGE 18	1,547,057	415,893	1,131,164
Percent Under Age 18[3]	19.4	12.3	21.9
SUBURBAN COUNTIES[4]: ARRESTS UNDER AGE 18	278,580	80,415	198,165
Percent Under Age 18[3]	17.8	11.8	20.2
RURAL COUNTIES: ARRESTS UNDER AGE 18	111,286	32,650	78,636
Percent Under Age 18[3]	15.5	9.4	18.0

Source: Derived from Federal Bureau of Investigation. 1999. *Crime in the United States, 1998: Uniform Crime Reports.* Washington, DC: U.S. Government Printing Office. Table 28, pp. 207–208.

[1]Violent crimes are offenses of murder, forcible rape, robbery, and aggravated assault.

[2]Property crimes are offenses of burglary, larceny-theft, motor vehicle theft, and arson.

[3]Percentage under age 18 of total offenses in that category for all ages.

[4]Excludes central cities and suburban city law enforcement agencies within metropolitan areas.

Juvenile Court Statistics

The National Juvenile Court Statistical Reporting Program was initiated in 1929 by the Children's Bureau, a division of the United States Department of Labor which began issuing annual reports on cases of children processed through a sample of juvenile courts. These reports included juveniles who had violated a state law or municipal ordinance, as well as children who were dependent or neglected and who required special proceedings to determine custody or adoption, permission for medical treatment, and other miscellaneous conditions. In short, the Juvenile Court Statistics Reporting Program was intended to furnish an index of the general nature and extent of the kinds of problems brought before the juvenile courts. For our purposes we will consider just those juvenile court proceedings focusing on delinquent behavior. In 1975, the Juvenile Court Statistical Reporting System was transferred to the National Center for Juvenile Justice and Delinquency Prevention in the United States Department of Justice. The practice of publishing annual summary reports has continued.

Unfortunately, from its inception, the Juvenile Court Statistical Reporting Program has had a two- to four-year time lag between the collection of data and the actual publication and presentation to the public of annual reports. For example, in preparing this text, the authors have used the most currently available juvenile court statistics which were collected for 1996 and published in 1999! Obviously, the snail's pace compilation and publication of such vital data are of considerable consternation to analysts and authors.

Methodology

Cases of young people accused of law-violating behavior can be referred to juvenile court intake by law enforcement agencies, social agencies, schools, parents, probation officers, and victims. However, law enforcement officers are the primary source of referral with three out of every four delinquency cases referred from that source.

Juvenile courts operate a two-track system for processing delinquency cases. Which track is selected for a given case depends upon the seriousness of the offense, number of previous contacts the youth has had with the police, the quality of evidence, the subjective opinion of screening personnel, and other variables. In general, the choice is between informal or formal disposition.

In an informally handled (or nonpetitioned) case, court intake personnel make a decision to divert the matter away from the court system, thus operationalizing an informal, less punitive approach. In most nonpetitioned cases, the youth is released, often with a warning. He or she may be referred to another agency for counseling, voluntary community service, or a restitution program to compensate victims.

More serious delinquency cases are assigned to the formal track that begins with the filing of a petition, affidavit, or other legal instrument used to initiate court action. These petitioned cases are scheduled on the official juvenile court calendar for adjudication by the judge. In a formal hearing, if a judgment of guilty is reached, the court is asked to assume jurisdiction over the youth. Final court disposition may involve a fine, restitution, probation, institutionalization, or some combination of these sanctions.

Traditionally, national estimates of juvenile court activity have been based on data encompassing both petitioned (formal) and nonpetitioned (informal) cases. In recent years, however, the responsibility for juvenile court intake screening has become more and more diversified. In some jurisdictions, city and county government agencies other than the juvenile courts provide screening and diversion services that formerly were a more exclusive function of the juvenile courts. Consequently, the multiple definitions and conceptualizations of delinquency at the screening level—impacting especially on those cases selected for nonpetitioned, informal treatment—seriously eroded confidence in estimates of the number and characteristics of juvenile offenders processed through the juvenile justice system. Moreover, questions were raised regarding the legitimacy of including nonpetitioned cases diverted away from the juvenile courts—often by other agencies—in annual summaries of juvenile court activities. Consequently, beginning in 1985, national summaries and projections of juvenile court activities have been based only on petitioned or formally adjudicated cases of delinquency and status offenses (Snyder et al., 1989).

Juvenile Court Statistics, 1996, provides a detailed portrait of these cases, including the offenses involved, sources of referral, demographic characteristics of offenders, detention practices and case dispositions. This picture is based on analyses of 1,757,600 individual case records from nearly 1,800 courts. Thus, national estimates were generated using data from courts with jurisdiction over 67 percent of the nation's youth population at risk in 1996 (Snyder and Sickmund, 1999).

Although annual compilations of juvenile court data were originally intended to measure the workloads of the nation's juvenile courts, the expanded and refined methodology and nationwide network of participating juvenile courts also has provided another overview of the magnitude and more serious dimensions of juvenile crime in the United States.

Findings

In 1996, courts with juvenile jurisdiction disposed 1,757,600 cases of juvenile delinquency (see Table 3-5). Delinquency cases encompassed juveniles charged with the eight Uniform Crime Index offenses against persons and property, drug law violations, and public order offenses, such as disorderly conduct and public drunkenness. In addition, 162,000 juvenile status offenders were processed through juvenile courts in 1996. These status offenses included running away, truancy, ungovernable behavior, and liquor law violations. Altogether, 1,919,600 delinquency and status offense cases were handled through United States juvenile courts in 1996.

Table 3-5 indicates that between 1994 and 1996, the number of delinquency cases processed by juvenile courts increased by 13 percent. The largest growth was experienced in drug law violation cases, where the caseloads increased by 46 percent. The number of cases within each of the other three general offense categories also increased. Between 1994 and 1996 the number of person offense cases formally processed by the courts increased by more than 13 percent, while the number of property and public order cases increased by approximately 9 percent and 10 percent, respectively. Overall, Table 3-5 reveals that while the number of cases in most categories handled by juvenile courts continued to increase in 1996, they were less than the extraordinary increases between 1990 and 1994.

It is also interesting to note in Table 3-5 that there were also significant increases in the number of cases processed through juvenile courts during this recent seven-year period for most status offense categories.

TABLE 3-5 **Longitudinal Comparisons of Delinquency and Status Offense Cases Handled by U.S. Juvenile Courts: 1990, 1994, and 1996**

Offense	Number of Cases			Percent Change	
	1990	**1994**	**1996**	**1990–94**	**1994–96**
Delinquency	1,299,200	1,555,200	1,757,600	+20%	+13%
Person[1]	243,500	336,100	381,500	+38%	+13%
Property[2]	751,500	803,400	874,400	+7%	+9%
Drugs	71,100	120,200	176,300	+69%	+46%
Public Order	233,200	295,600	325,400	+27%	+10%
Status Offense	92,700	126,900	162,000	+37%	+28%
Runaway	15,100	21,500	25,800	+42%	+20%
Truancy	26,900	36,400	39,300	+35%	+8%
Ungovernable	12,600	15,700	20,100	+25%	+28%
Liquor	29,200	33,600	44,800	+15%	+33%
Other[3]	9,000	19,800	32,000	+121%	+62%

Source: Data derived from Snyder, H. N., and Sickmund, M. 1999. *Juvenile Offenders and Victims: 1999 National Report.* Pittsburgh, PA: Office of Juvenile Justice and Delinquency Prevention, U.S. Department of Justice. pp. 157 and 166.

[1]Offenses against persons (or violent crimes) are court cases of murder, forcible rape, robbery, and aggravated assault.

[2]Property crimes are offense cases of burglary, larceny-theft, motor vehicle theft, and arson.

[3]The category of "other status offenses" includes cases such as curfew violations, smoking tobacco, and violations of a valid court order.

In 1996, the large majority of young people involved with juvenile courts were male. Figure 3-1 indicates that males accounted for 77 percent of delinquency cases. When the volume of delinquency offenses was controlled for type of crime it was found that an almost identical percentage of males was responsible for crimes against persons, property crimes, and public order offenses. The number of delinquency cases involving females increased 76 percent between 1987 and 1996, while cases involving males increased 42 percent.

Status offense cases processed by juvenile courts in 1996 fell into a very different pattern of male/female participation. Females were adjudicated for 41 percent of all status offense cases. When status offense cases were categorized by specific types it was found that females accounted for approximately 45 percent of cases involving truancy and ungovernable behavior petitioned to juvenile courts in 1996. Sixty percent of runaway cases involved females.

Figure 3-2 graphically compares the white and nonwhite levels of involvement in delinquency cases processed by juvenile courts in 1996. During that year, white youths were the subjects of adjudication in 66 percent of all delinquency cases. When the racial background of delinquency case offenders was tabulated for specific crime categories, it was found that white youths were petitioned to juvenile court for 59 to 70 percent of crimes against persons, property crimes, drug violations, and public order offenses.

The preponderance of white over nonwhite involvement in juvenile court proceedings was even more pronounced in the adjudication of status offenders. According to *Juvenile*

FIGURE 3-1   Sex Characteristics of Delinquency Cases by Offense, Petitioned to U.S. Juvenile Courts

Delinquency	77%	23%
Person	75%	25%
Property	77%	23%
Drugs	86%	14%
Public Order	77%	23%
	Male	Female

Source: Data derived from Snyder, H. N., and Sickmund, M. *Juvenile Offenders and Victims: 1999 National Report.* Office of Juvenile Justice and Delinquency Prevention, U.S. Department of Justice (September 1999), p. 148.

Court Statistics, 1996, white youngsters accounted for 70 to 75 percent of all runaway, truancy, and ungovernable behavior cases processed through the courts.

Although whites represent nearly two-thirds of all cases disposed of by juvenile courts in the United States, the number of nonwhites brought before juvenile courts is much larger

FIGURE 3-2   Race Characteristics of Delinquency Cases by Offense, Petitioned to U.S. Juvenile Courts

Delinquency	66%	34%
Person	59%	41%
Property	70%	30%
Drugs	65%	35%
Public Order	64%	36%
	White[1]	Nonwhite

[1]In 1996, whites made up 82 percent of the nation's youth population at risk. In both the population and court data, nearly all youths of Hispanic ethnicity were included in the white racial category.

Source: Snyder, H. N., and Sickmund, M. 1999. *Juvenile Offenders and Victims: 1999 National Reports.* Pittsburgh, PA: Office of Juvenile Justice and Delinquency Prevention, U.S. Department of Justice. p. 150.

than their share of the national population. Smith et al. (1980), however, presented evidence that racial minorities in juvenile courts are more likely to have had prior referrals and to be committed to correctional institutions, and less likely to receive lenient treatment such as probation by juvenile courts than are whites for the same offenses.

Occasionally a delinquency case is transferred to criminal court if the offense is especially serious and the offender is deemed to have adult responsibility. The number of such delinquency cases transferred to criminal court jurisdiction were 49 percent more in 1997 than in 1987. This growth reflects the increase in petitioned cases coming to juvenile courts, though cases transferred to criminal courts represented just 1 percent of all petitioned delinquency cases in 1997 (Puzzanchera, 2000).

The findings reported here regarding the number and categorization of delinquency and status offenders processed through U.S. juvenile courts are in general harmony with findings based on arrest statistics in the FBI *Uniform Crime Reports.*

The Composite Delinquent Profile: Typical or Stereotypical?

By combining findings and conclusions based on the two national official sources of juvenile delinquency data, it is possible to construct a composite picture of the "typical" delinquent. According to annual arrest statistics compiled by the FBI and the records of delinquency and status offense cases petitioned to juvenile courts, this composite juvenile delinquent is disproportionately male, between 15 and 18 years of age, a member of a racial or ethnic minority, and has a prior record of both status and criminal offenses. In addition, Cantwell (1983), Goettling (1989), and numerous others have reported that juvenile offenders reflect a higher incidence of unstable home life because of parental separation, divorce, desertion, or death. They are also often characterized by chronic poverty, little motivation or success in school, and few occupational opportunities. The probability is also statistically high that officially defined juvenile delinquents reside in urban, lower class, slum neighborhoods. A strong linkage also appears between the violent behavior of some juveniles and their having been exposed to extreme abuse and violence within their own families (Cantwell, 1983:37).

Unfortunately, such composite summaries—based on the simple statistical majority and averages of arrested and/or adjudicated youths—portray an oversimplified and distorted image of juvenile delinquents and the delinquency problem. The next section of this chapter demonstrates that the generalizations that comprise the "composite" or "typical" delinquent are based on data that have several serious deficiencies. A vast number of delinquents do not fit the statistical model. In addition, in recent years several studies have sparked a vigorous debate regarding the so-called "correlates of delinquency." While gender, social class, race/ethnicity, and the quality of family life remain statistically significant in describing a large number of juvenile delinquents, some investigators consider these characteristics as somewhat illusory as causal variables (Elliott and Huizinga, 1983; Hindelang et al., 1979; Tittle et al., 1978). Finally, such broad-stroked portrayals of the "typical" juvenile delinquent may be more stereotypical than typical. It has been repeatedly suggested that youth possessing certain easily identifiable traits and backgrounds may be socially prejudged and thereby encouraged to follow a course leading to delinquent behavior (Matza, 1964). All of these variables will be extensively discussed in subsequent chapters.

Limitations of Official Delinquency Data

Arrest Statistics

A decided advantage of the annual FBI crime reports is that juvenile arrest data are now available for almost all cities, and the *Uniform Crime Reports* cover about 96 percent of the nation's population. However, there are several intrinsic and probably insoluble problems associated with the use of data based on arrests. First, the number of arrests is a questionable index of crime and delinquency because law enforcement motives, techniques, and success vary widely from time to time and from place to place. For example, a low arrest rate may indicate little criminal or delinquent activity in a particular community. A low arrest rate also can mean that the police force is inactive or ineffective in that area. Conversely, a high arrest rate may mean that there is a high level of criminal and delinquent activity in a particular city. A high arrest rate can also mean that the police are making arrests on slight pretext or pursuing a highly publicized "war on crime and delinquency" for political purposes. In some places campaigns emanating from city halls to "make our streets safe" are not uncommon during election years. Police activity then may be intensified as large numbers of vagrants, prostitutes, gamblers, delinquents, and other "undesirables" are caught in the police dragnet. Much less publicized is the rapid release of most "suspects" and the inflation of local arrest statistics.

Similarly, researchers argue that conclusions based upon official statistics should be tempered by the observation that law enforcement may be more rigorous in lower-class neighborhoods inhabited largely by racial and ethnic minorities (Siegel, 1995:71). Smith and Visher (1981) examined variations in police arrest practices. They found that the decision to take a suspect into custody is influenced by such extralegal factors as the dispositional preferences of victims, the race and demeanor of the suspect, and the presence of bystanders. "Specifically, members of socially disadvantaged groups such as blacks and Hispanic youths are more likely to be taken into custody independent of the seriousness of their behavior" (Smith and Visher, 1981:167). The point here is that while the FBI has attempted to standardize definitions of various crimes for law enforcement personnel and agencies participating in the Uniform Crime Reporting Program, no way has yet been devised to standardize the subjective decision-making processes involved in making arrests which can statistically inflate or deflate the participation of some groups in crime and delinquency (Yablonsky and Haskell, 1988).

A second fundamental problem with the *UCR* arrest statistics is that they tell us nothing about juvenile crime that is undetected, unsolved, or unreported. According to popular belief, the police, astute television detectives, and federal marshals "always get their man." On the contrary, there is overwhelming evidence that numbers of arrests and court referrals reveal only the visible tip of the crime/delinquency iceberg.

Many violent crimes often go unreported. According to the Department of Justice (1983), many victims fail to report assaults and thefts because they feel that these are "private matters" or that the police can or will do nothing about them. Probably most of the status offenses and less serious instances of juvenile delinquency never become a matter of public record or concern. Many thousands of juveniles are confronted daily by parents, teachers, neighbors, and law enforcement officers who administer informal warnings, censures, punishments, or other controls over nonconforming youthful behavior. Such informal procedures are especially characteristic of small towns and rural areas, as illustrated by the youthful Halloween disturbance described at the end of Chapter 2 (Perk, 1985).

Juvenile Court Statistics

One of the most serious and chronic problems encountered with annual compilations of juvenile court data is the lack of representation from several states. For example, in 1994, nearly half of the states (23) either failed to submit reports, or irregularities and errors in recording the characteristics and dispositions of cases processed through their juvenile courts made their data partially unacceptable. Thus, while the procedures used to generate national estimates of court activity control for the size of a community, the volume of cases referred to reporting courts, the age, race, and offense characteristics of those cases and other factors, no procedure can completely overcome the fundamental threats to validity caused by the absence of a random sample in which every case has an equal chance of being included in the data (Butts, et al., 1996). In 1996, juvenile court statistics covering just 67 percent of the nation's youth population at risk—were included in estimates of juvenile court activity for that year (Snyder and Sickmund, 1999). The fact remains that nearly 33 percent of the nation's juvenile population at risk of becoming delinquent was not included.

A second factor affecting the validity and reliability of juvenile court statistics is the apparently insurmountable problem of variance in definitions and coding categories for criminal offenses among the data suppliers. This inconsistency in reporting procedures generates a difficult heterogeneity and overlapping in the national data.

A third dilemma confounding the use of juvenile court statistics centers directly on the estimating procedures used by the National Center for Juvenile Justice in projecting from the sample of reporting courts the total court activity and populations served in given areas. Periodic changes in boundary lines, population size, and composition of many juvenile court jurisdictions make longitudinal comparisons of court activity tentative and often conjectural.

Over half a century of recording and reporting of juvenile court case dispositions passed before steps were taken to correct or reduce the effects of those basic methodological flaws. Consequently, a number of years of consistent data gathering and analysis will be needed before The National Juvenile Court Reporting System Program can achieve a high degree of longitudinal and comparative credibility, beyond recent years. Thus, while official surveys of juvenile court proceedings are helpful in measuring court caseloads at a given time, the incomplete and estimated nature of the data invalidate their use for making comparisons between years and between some states and communities.

The fourth limitation of juvenile court statistics is that every new referral of a juvenile to a court is regarded as a case. Therefore a youth referred to a court three times during the course of a year is counted as three cases. While this procedure is appropriate for measuring caseloads, it would contribute to inflation of the data if it were used to measure the number of juvenile delinquents in a given area. On the other hand, many youths are petitioned to a juvenile court as a single case—but having committed multiple offenses. The inclusion of such cases tends to deflate the reported number of juvenile offenses in each court jurisdiction.

Unofficial Sources of Delinquency Information

Self-Report Studies

Some of the limitations of the FBI *Uniform Crime Reports* and the *Juvenile Court Statistics* as indices of the scope and nature of the national delinquency problem are overcome by

Each year, approximately one-and-three-fourths million cases of delinquency are processed through U.S. juvenile courts. Data from such cases are compiled and published annually.

self-report studies. A large number of researchers, rather than relying on official reports of arrests and court dispositions, have drawn samples of various populations and have directly inquired through survey questionnaires about their respondents' previous delinquent behavior. This approach, aimed at adolescents and young adults not identified by law enforcement agencies as juvenile offenders, is designed to reveal and measure undetected and unreported instances of juvenile delinquency.

The most comprehensive and useful study of this type to date is the National Longitudinal Survey of Youth 1997 (NLSY97).

The first wave of NLSY97 interviewed a nationally representative sample of nearly 9,000 youth who were between the ages of 12 and 16 at the end of 1996. The interviews were conducted in 1997 and early 1998. The survey asked youth to report whether they had engaged in a variety of delinquent or other behaviors that may lead to future delinquency. These youths will be interviewed annually to track changes in delinquent and other deviant behaviors (Puzzanchera, 2000:1).

BOX 3-1   Concept Application

The following experience was related in a paper anonymously and voluntarily submitted to one of the authors by a female student enrolled in a Juvenile Delinquency course.

"Undetected and Unreported Delinquency: The Missing Statistics"

I was a juvenile delinquent. Juvenile delinquency to me is like a disease. It grows inside of you and becomes an obsession. It takes over everything you do. I can write about my experience now with some objectivity because it is over. But I still feel pangs of guilt and regret for some of the things I have done and tried to do.

It does not seem likely that a delinquent could come from a respectable, conservative, upper middle class family with every kind of advantage available to an adolescent. But it can happen and happen very easily, even to a girl like me from that kind of background.

I was a victim of the busing system in my state. Not that the idea of desegregation and busing is totally bad, but in many cases it can cause more harm than good—especially with younger kids who must be separated from their familiar neighborhoods and other family members that might restrain them from getting in trouble. I was forced to catch a bus at seven o'clock every morning to travel to a high school twelve miles away from my home while my older brothers attended a high school less than a mile away.

My delinquent phase started when I was in the eighth grade. First I was pressured by my peers to try smoking cigarettes. I haven't kicked that habit yet. Next came the pot smoking. "Oh, I'll try it just this once" I could hear myself saying. Some harder drugs came next. Speed, quaaludes, reds, yellow jackets, and black mollies were names I heard and used regularly. Soon I was up to a $50 to $100 weekly drug habit. All this by the time I was a sophomore in high school. And nobody knew, except for my few so-called "connections." Certainly not my parents who thought that I was a perfectly well-adjusted high school student. Both of them worked and they placed top priority on their careers and material success. They assumed that if they supplied a comfortable home, nice clothes, and a healthy allowance, that I had everything I needed—especially since I didn't complain about anything or tell them about my "private" life. Somewhere in the back of my mind, I was confident that I could get out of the new lifestyle I was following before I developed any serious habits.

My grades began to suffer, especially when my friends and I began to ditch school regularly. And I soon learned how to do a reasonable forgery of my mother's name on notes excusing my absences from school for "illness" or other lies. A large group of us regularly took off from school together and hung around in shopping malls, pool halls, and alleys.

The vandalism, things we did for fun, came later. I was never really involved, but always around. But one too many times, I was there and we got caught, just for smashing some windows for kicks. One trip to the "pokey" was enough for me. No report to our parents was made, thank God. I was literally "scared straight."

Of course, there were always unusual happenings at school. For instance, I can remember a shooting in the cafeteria. One guy just pulled a gun on another and shot him in the hand. Many fights occurred. I was even subjected to one once. I was just banged up a bit. And to think it was all over a lousy cigarette. I lost. I didn't have a menthol one. After that, I carried a knife. And, in a desperate moment, I could or might have been forced to use that knife.

Needless to say, there was always the talk of prostitution and promiscuity. Talk of the "tricks" the night before always fascinated and horrified me at the same time. Luckily, I never contacted that realm of delinquency.

Not all of my experiences in high school were bad. Some teachers really cared. I grew out of my juvenile delinquency phase. In a way I'm glad of what I experienced but I wouldn't want anyone else to go through it. I learned some important lessons. I learned the value of constructiveness, and I will do something good in my life. I was a lucky delinquent. I'm no longer involved in drugs of any kind. Now my education is everything. Plus the fact, that I grew up. Now I'm aged nineteen going on thirty-five, a decent, conservative, well-adjusted, upper middle class college student.

*   *   *   *

Continued

BOX 3-1   *Continued*

As a review of this chapter, what characteristics of the young woman in this account are contrary to those derived from official arrest statistics to typify the "average" juvenile delinquent? Do you agree that this self-reported, delinquent experience is evi-

dence that much delinquent behavior goes undetected, unreported, and does not result in arrest? Did you ever participate in any illegal act prior to your eighteenth birthday that, if detected or reported, could have led to your arrest?

Findings from the NLSY97 were astonishing. For example, one in seven 12-year-olds has engaged in assaultive behaviors, and one in four has purposely destroyed property.

Self-report studies clearly show that delinquent behavior is far more common than is indicated by official data (e.g., Jensen and Eve, 1976; Elliott and Huizinga, 1984). Findings from repeated self-report studies led The President's Commission on Law Enforcement and Administration of Justice (1968:55) to conclude that "enormous numbers of young people appear to be involved in delinquent acts." This finding can be generalized to apply to the entire population:

> *Evidence indicates that over 90% of all Americans have committed some crime for which they could be incarcerated. The observation does not deny that crime may be more concentrated in some groups, but only that it is unlikely to be absent in others. (Bohm, 1986:197)*

Self-report surveys can be expensive and time consuming, and the absence of an ongoing national unbiased sample presents a virtually insurmountable methodological problem. In spite of these limitations, such studies clearly support the contention that official statistics fail to completely measure the volume of delinquency and the incidence of many specific offenses.

Table 3-6 summarizes data from two self-report surveys, independently administered by the authors to 591 undergraduate students attending two western state universities in 2000. A large majority of the subjects were white and they were about equally divided between males and females. Because they were not randomly selected, no assumption can be made that these 591 students accurately represent the total population of youth at risk of committing delinquent behavior, or even the overall student population at their schools. Nevertheless, even within these limitations, some remarkable findings emerged (Table 3-6).

While one-third of the 591 subjects at the two universities had shoplifted, and had damaged property and inflicted physical harm to others, and nearly three-fourths had purchased and/or consumed alcoholic beverages, and 12 percent had taken an automobile without the owner's permission—only about 7 percent of the subjects had ever been arrested for any reason while under the age of 18! This figure is fairly close to national arrest statistics. In 1998, there were 1,855,002 arrests of persons under age 18 for all offenses, which includes multiple arrests during the year for the same individuals. Even if we assume that this total number of arrests represents 1,855,002 separate individuals, that number still equals just 2.6 percent of the national population under age 18. Based on additional information derived from self-report studies, we can conclude that juvenile delinquency is much more common and widespread than official statistics would lead us to believe. The similarity of findings

TABLE 3-6   Self-Reported Delinquent Behavior by Students at Two Western U.S. Universities

Type of Offense	University A (N 311)		University B (N 280)	
WHILE UNDER THE AGE OF 18, DID YOU EVER:	YES	NO	YES	NO
1. Get arrested?	6.5%	93.5%	12.3%	87.7%
2. Break into a place?	13.1%	86.9%	11.4%	88.6%
3. Shoplift?	30.0%	70.0%	26.2%	73.8%
4. Steal something worth less than $100? (Do not include shoplifting.)	21.4%	78.6%	25.0%	75.0%
5. Steal something worth more than $100?	9.7%	90.3%	11.7%	88.3%
6. Beat up or hurt someone on purpose?	27.6%	72.4%	25.9%	74.1%
7. Get into fist fights or brawls? (Do not include what you counted in Item 6.)	36.2%	63.8%	42.9%	57.1%
8. Ruin, break, or damage someone else's property on purpose?	41.9%	58.1%	30.9%	69.1%
9. Take a car without the owner's permission?	12.2%	87.8%	11.3%	88.7%
10. Take money or something of value from someone through threats with knife or gun?	00.0%	100.0%	2.2%	97.8%
11. Have sexual intercourse?	73.5%	26.5%	69.3%	30.7%
12. Violate curfew?	82.2%	17.8%	64.9%	35.1%
13. Skip school without parents' knowledge?	63.9%	36.1%	63.4%	36.6%
14. Defy parents? (Do not include skipping school and curfew violations).	55.8%	44.2%	58.7%	41.3%
15. Purchase and/or consume alcoholic beverages or illegal drugs?	75.8%	24.2%	71.5%	28.5%

Source: Bynum, J., and Thompson, W., Unpublished data from self-report surveys conducted at two western U.S. universities, 2000.

from "University A" and "University B" and with those from other self-report studies confirms a reasonable degree of reliability for this measuring technique.

Research conducted by Maynard Erickson and Lamar Empey (1963) demonstrated how data generated from self-report studies can be combined with official statistics on arrests and court referrals to produce a more complete account of juvenile delinquency. They found that court records accurately revealed which juvenile offenders demonstrated persistent patterns of more serious misbehavior, thus facilitating societal identification of juveniles who may have incorporated the delinquent role more decisively into their lifestyles. At the same time, self-report studies help us to comprehend more precisely the magnitude of delinquency among young people in general.

Critics of self-reports have questioned the honesty of respondents who may falsify their answers to make themselves "look good" by denying that they committed delinquent acts when they actually have done so; and of respondents who may exaggerate their true delinquent acts (Jesness, 1987). Such objections to self-reports are largely overcome by the use of anonymous questionnaires, which tend to frustrate subjects who may view the survey situation and their responses as a status-gaining opportunity. Also, it can be assumed that if respondents falsify information, as many are likely to exaggerate their delinquency as are likely to deny it. Hence, these falsifications will offset each other within a large sample.

Travis Hirschi (1969) effectively countered the suspicion about respondents' dishonesty with data derived from police records and his own self-report study of those same youths. He found a strong similarity between the numbers and kinds of self-reported offenses of incarcerated juvenile delinquents and those listed in their official records. While this finding supports arguments for the validity of both measures, Hirschi (1969:64) contended that police records are *less* valid than self-reports as a measure of delinquency:

> *As defined, every delinquent act committed by a person is witnessed by him; he cannot commit delinquent acts without knowing it (otherwise, there is nothing to explain). Obviously, the police do not have such omnipresence.... In short, the records of the police are, on a priori grounds, a weaker measure of the* commission *of delinquent acts than presumably honest self-reports.*

In addition to aiding researchers in ascertaining the actual dimensions of juvenile delinquency, self-report studies also have challenged the widely held view that since African Americans and Hispanics are overrepresented in official statistics, they must have a stronger proclivity toward delinquent behavior. Summarizing a number of self-report studies (Voss, 1963; Winslow, 1967; Chambliss and Nagasawa, 1969; and Donovan, 1977), Arnold and Brungardt (1983:152) concluded that:

> *...analyses consistently indicate that whites' offenses are so similar in number and type to those of the minority groups that the official data appear to be highly distorted.... [The] differences revealed do not approach the magnitude of the differences in official data.*

Thus, while we cannot claim the absence of empirical documentation (national arrest and juvenile court statistics), that underclass and minority youths are more likely to be involved in delinquency than their white, middle-class counterparts, self-report studies have made the argument of the so-called "correlates of delinquency" more problematic and less emphatic.

Michael Hindelang and his associates (1979), in their insightful focus on the traditional correlates of delinquency, may have resolved the issue. They reviewed the research literature and found that studies of delinquency that use official records and those utilizing self-report surveys typically have measured different types of behaviors; official data tend to reflect more serious offenses, while self-report studies tend to measure much more common and less serious types of behavior. In other words, the notion that official and self-report methods produce discrepant results with respect to sex, race, and social class is largely illusory because the two methodologies tap different domains of behavior. They noted:

> *...other evidence from victimization surveys, studies of the reliability and validity of self-reports, and studies of biases in criminal justice processing, suggest that both official data and self-reports provide valid indicators of the demographic characteristics of offenders,* within the domain of behavior effectively tapped by each method. *[italics in original](Hindelang et al., 1979:995)*

Victimization Surveys

Another useful source of juvenile delinquency information is the victimization surveys conducted by the United States Department of Justice and a number of private researchers. These studies focus on victims and their recollections of the crimes, the circumstances, and the offenders. Some of the variables included are the approximate age, sex, race, and other demographic characteristics of assailants and victims, the relationship between victim and offender, the types of crime, and the circumstances surrounding the crime.

The most ambitious victimization surveys have been conducted by the Law Enforcement Assistance Administration of the Department of Justice, beginning in 1972. This agency, together with the Census Bureau, operationalized an ongoing National Crime Survey to measure the victimization of persons ages 12 and over, households, and commercial establishments. Twice each year data are obtained through interviews with a representative national sample of about 49,000 households (containing approximately 100,000 individuals over age 12), from which rates of victimization for persons and households are generated. Currently, the National Crime Victimization Survey focuses on the personal crimes of rape, robbery, assault, and larceny, and the household crimes of burglary, larceny, and motor vehicle theft (*Criminal Victimizations in the United States, 1992,* 1994).

Like self-report studies, victimization surveys have the advantage over arrest and juvenile court statistics in offering an avenue through which to explore and estimate the extent of unreported crimes, especially when victims are allowed to respond anonymously. Law enforcement officers and researchers are convinced that vast numbers of offenses are not brought to the attention of police. For example, forcible rape is grossly underreported. The actual number of forcible rapes is thought to be several times greater than is reflected in official statistics (Barlow, 1987). Many rape victims may understandably shrink from the embarrassment of reporting and detailing the experience to the police and in open court (The President's Commission on Law Enforcement, Task Force Report, 1968). Thus, like self-report studies, victimization surveys are also more likely to uncover information about more serious types of unreported crimes. Table 3-7, listing the reasons victims give for *not* reporting crimes against them to the police, clearly establishes the usefulness of such surveys as an adjunct to arrest statistics in achieving a more complete picture of crime and delinquency.

Although there is some variation from city to city in victimization rates, the surveys of both national and city samples have produced findings in agreement with self-report studies; that is, only about a third of all crimes are reported to the police (Klaus et al., 1983). In 1996, less than a third of crimes overall were reported to law enforcement officials. About half of all violent crimes were reported to the police.

Victimization studies also have supplied important and frightening facts about the victims of crime. Citing Bureau of Justice statistics, *Parade* (1987:15) announced that "it's downright dangerous to be a teenager in this country":

> *...teens are more than twice as likely as adults to be the victims of rape, robbery, assault and crimes of violence. In the violent-crime category, for example, more than 60 of every 1,000 teens were victims,...compared to 27 of every 1,000 adults.*

In a 1997 report to the nation commissioned by President Clinton to assess the overall well-being of America's youth, we find that the number of youth who are victims of violent

TABLE 3-7 Percent Distribution of Reasons for Not Reporting Victimizations to Police, by Type of Crime

	Object Recovered, Offender Unsuccessful	Private or Personal Matter	Reported to Someone Else	Lack of Proof	Police Would Not Want To Be Bothered	Police Inefficient, Ineffective, or Biased	Fear of Reprisal	Too Inconvenient or Time-consuming	Other Reasons and Reasons not Given
All personal crimes (14,756,040)[1]	24.0%	6.4%	16.1%	11.0%	8.0%	3.6%	1.3%	4.1%	25.5%
Crimes of violence (3,813,310)[1]	18.1%	17.6%	13.4%	7.1%	7.4%	5.3%	4.3%	4.5%	22.3%
Rape (97,880)[1]	5.7%	24.7%	16.9%	10.0%	1.6%	1.7%	10.9%	6.4%	22.1%
Robbery (667,550)[1]	19.3%	6.6%	5.3%	14.5%	9.5%	11.1%	5.2%	6.2%	22.3%
Aggravated assault (705,630)[1]	16.1%	18.1%	8.6%	7.5%	6.6%	6.6%	6.9%	4.2%	25.4%
Simple assault (2,342,240)[1]	18.8%	20.3%	17.0%	4.8%	7.2%	3.3%	3.0%	4.0%	21.6%
Crimes of theft (10,942,720)[1]	26.0%	2.4%	17.1%	12.3%	8.2%	3.0%	0.3%	3.9%	26.8%
All household crimes (11,310,570)[1]	30.3%	5.3%	3.9%	12.0%	10.3%	3.2%	0.7%	3.2%	31.1%
Burglary (3,114,100)[1]	25.5%	5.4%	8.4%	11.7%	8.8%	4.5%	0.9%	2.6%	32.2%
Household larceny (7,516,340)[1]	32.4%	5.2%	2.2%	12.0%	10.7%	2.6%	0.6%	3.1%	31.2%
Motor vehicle theft (680,120)[1]	29.3%	6.2%	2.8%	13.7%	11.5%	4.1%	0.0%	6.6%	25.8%

Source: Abridged from U.S. Department of Justice. *Criminal Victimization in the United States, 1991*. Washington, DC: U.S. Government Printing Office, 1992. Table 112, pp. 110–111.

[1]NOTE: Number of reasons shown in parentheses. Some respondents may have cited more than one reason for not reporting victimizations to the police. Some estimates are based on small samples.

BOX 3-2   Controversial Issue

Juvenile Violence: Guns and the U.S. Constitution

Nationwide, there is a growing concern over juvenile delinquency, especially the frightening level of juvenile violence. Teenagers are two and a half times more likely than adults to be involved in violence (Jennings, 1993).

> *Causal factors pertaining to juvenile violence are multifarious. Many social scientists believe that much of the violence reflects a breakdown in families, schools, and other societal institutions. Some studies suggest that 70 percent of juvenile offenders come from single-parent homes* (FBI Crime in the United States: Uniform Crime Reports, 1991, 1992:279). *(See Chapters 7, 9, and 10 for detailed discussion.)*

Another factor commonly associated with violent crime in general is the tremendous proliferation in illegal weapon usage.

> *The United States is the most heavily armed nation on earth. Its 255 million people possess more than 200 million guns—74 million rifles, 66 million handguns, and 62 million shotguns....*
>
> *America is the most violent nation in the world.... In 1990, handguns murdered 10 people in Australia, 22 in Great Britain, 68 in Canada, and 10,567 in the United States* (Landers, 1993:F4).
>
> *American youngsters are 12 times more likely to die by gunfire than their counterparts in the rest of the industrialized world* (Meyer, 1997:9C).

Guns, in the hands of frightened, angry, and immature youths, can seem to offer quick solutions to their problems. Peter Jennings, in his 1993 ABC Special "Kids in the Crossfire" reported that "35 percent of kids can get their hands on a gun" and that "one in five high school students carries a weapon to school." The results are predictable. The number of juvenile homicide offenders tripled between 1984 and 1994 (up to more than 26,000)—the increase is all firearm-related. Nearly half of juvenile offenders' victims are other young people. Between 1984 and 1995, according to the Office of Juvenile Justice and Delinquency Prevention, "7 in 10 juvenile homicide offenders were killed with a firearm" (Snyder et al., 1996:1, 22, and 24). Gun violence claims nearly 5,000 children under age 18 every year (*USA Today*, 2000). According to the Center for Disease Control and Prevention, "More people, 10 through 19 years of age are killed by guns than any other cause."

> *The National Association of Children's Hospitals and Related Institutions examined discharge records from 44 acute care children's hospitals and found...that children wounded by gunfire ran up bills that averaged $14,434 in 1991. That is just about what four-year private colleges charged for tuition, room and board that same year. The association counted only the hospital charges, not doctor bills or the costs of lifetime rehabilitation for the maimed (*Manteca Bulletin, *November 26, 1993. Page A–7).*

It may come as a surprise to the student reading such overwhelming statistics to learn that gun control continues to be a hotly debated topic among the citizenry in general and periodically in the legislatures of state and federal governments. Some senators and members of Congress, supported by the powerful National Rifle Association, have vigorously argued that the issue is much broader than the assumption that "guns cause crime" and over-simplified solution that "fewer guns will reduce violence." The NRA contends that "Guns don't kill people, people kill people."

The leaders and lawyers of this influential special interest group perceive their position as ultimately founded on an irrevocable constitutional right for citizens to bear arms:

> *A well-regulated militia being necessary to the security of a free State, the right of the people to keep and bear arms shall not be infringed* (Constitution of the United States, Amendments, *Article II).*

In summary, proponents of proposed gun control laws urge more rigorous background checks, waiting periods, and age parameters for would-be gun

Continued

BOX 3-2   *Continued*

purchasers (particularly of handguns) as a positive step toward reducing crime rates. On the other hand, opponents to gun control laws see in them a major threat to American freedom. The NRA contends that under such laws, criminals can still easily buy illegal firearms on the black market and "when guns are outlawed, only outlaws will have guns."

*   *   *   *

After reflecting on the statistics regarding youth violence and the controversy over gun control, what is your position on the issue? Can you think of other, related causes and possible solutions?

Sources

Federal Bureau of Investigation. 1992. *Crime in the United States: Uniform crime reports, 1991.* Washington, DC: U.S. Governement Printing Office.
Funk & Wagnall's Standard Reference Encyclopedia, 1991. "Constitution of the United States." Vol. 7. New York: Standard Reference Works.
Jennings, Peter. 1993. Kids in the crossfire. American Broadcasting Company. Program of November 6, 1993.
Landers, Ann. 1993. Column in *Fort Worth Star-Telegram* (Newspaper) on September 19, 1993. Section F, Page 4.
Manteca Bulletin. 1993. "Gun attacks kill 15 american youths each day." November 26, 1993. Page A-7.
Meyer, T. 1997. CDC says gunfire is killing U.S. kids. *Medford Mail Tribune.* February 9, 1997. Page 9C.
Snyder, H. N., Sickmund, M., and Poe-Yamagata, E. 1996. *Juvenile Offenders and Victims: 1996 Update on Violence.* U.S. Department of Justice. Washington, DC: U.S. Government Printing Office.

crime escalated to 118 per 1,000 in 1994 (Knight, 1997). At the same time, teenage victims of personal crimes are least likely to report crimes to the police, compared with other age groups (*Criminal Victimizations in the United States, 1991,* 1992).

The major limitation of the victimization data collected by the National Crime Surveys is that the victims are the only source of information. For maximum validity, their perceptions and conclusions regarding such factors as the race and age of offenders should be made just after the crimes have been committed. It is understandable that judgment could be faulty and distorted by reason of the stress associated with the crime. In addition, victims have personal contact with offenders only in such crimes as rape, robbery, assault, and personal larceny, whereas the majority of crimes against persons and property are outside these categories. Thus, while systematically gathered reports from victims help researchers to determine the magnitude and trends of some crimes by incorporating measurements and projections of the unreported dimension, doubts remain about the complete accuracy and specificity of the victims' reports (McDermott and Hindelang, 1981).

A second criticism of victimization surveys centers on the long list of serious crimes that are excluded. For example, murder, kidnapping, forgery, driving under the influence of drugs, and status offenses are seldom included on victim questionnaires. Edward Wells and Joseph Rankin, in their widely cited study (1995) of the efficacy of crime victims' surveys, acknowledge that the National Crime Victimization Survey is not equally reliable for all types of victims and offenses, and that "young persons are less reliably represented in the NCVS due to such factors as sampling frame of the survey, form of the questionnaire, interview, and wording of questions." (1995:287). In spite of these shortcomings, Wells and

Official crime statistics, reported by law enforcement agencies, represent only the tip of the iceberg—just a portion of our national delinquency problem. Many juvenile offenses are undetected, unreported, or dealt with informally without arrest.

Rankin provide a strong defense of victimization surveys as a useful supplement to compilations of arrests and other official sources of crime data.

The Magnitude and Trends of Juvenile Delinquency

In view of the recognized limitations of the data with which they must work, social scientists, criminologists, law enforcement officers, and others who seek to measure crime and delinquency may be tempted to agree with Disraeli, who exclaimed: "There are three kinds of lies: lies, damned lies, and statistics" (also attributed to Mark Twain) (Wheeler, 1976:7). Nevertheless, the conjunction of official and unofficial data, especially when gathered over a period of years, *does* present a fairly clear pattern of juvenile delinquency.

In total, American young people account for a large and often disproportionate share of our national crime problem.

At the same time, Table 3-8 presents some encouraging data and a dramatic reversal of escalating juvenile arrests. Table 3-8 compares arrest data for youths under age 18 in the eight offense categories comprising the Crime Index during three recent, sequential periods of time: 1991, 1994, and 1998. It is clear that the long trend of rising juvenile crime in the United States has ended. Between 1994 and 1998, arrests of youths for violent offenses and property offenses consistently declined 19 and 17 percent respectively. The most pronounced reductions were in murder (47 percent), robbery (29 percent), and motor vehicle theft (39 percent).

Although criminologists, sociologists, and other authorities in the field have not reached an explanatory consensus for the recent and significant decline in juvenile arrests, several partial and promising interpretations of the data have been suggested. Scholars have variously credited more vigorous law enforcement, proactive and preventive social programs aimed at youths at risk of becoming delinquent, enhanced economic and occupational opportunities, and smaller proportions of the national population in the delinquency-prone adolescent years. Although each of the above arguments is supported by some evidence, a conclusive causal explanation for the decline in juvenile arrests must await additional data and investigation. At this point we can safely say that the improvement can be traced to a variety of causes (Sniffen, 1999; *TELEMASP Bulletin, Vol. 6, No. 1 and 2,* 1999; Witkin, 1998).

However, a word of caution is order. Despite a six-year decline in the number of juvenile arrests (1995–2000), it is premature to declare the resolution of this serious social prob-

TABLE 3-8   **Longitudinal Comparisons and Trends of Arrests of Persons Under Age 18 for Crime Index Offenses**

	Number of Persons Under Age 18 Arrested			
	1989	**1994**	**1998**	**Change (1994–1998)**
Offense Charged				
Murder	1,759	2,379	1,243	−47.8%
Forcible rape	3,443	3,618	3,299	−8.8%
Robbery	19,579	29,498	20,987	−28.9%
Aggravated assault	37,080	52,011	45,202	−13.1%
Burglary	91,957	88,958	74,044	−16.8%
Larceny-theft	275,014	311,690	269,315	−13.6%
Motor vehicle theft	57,250	55,437	33,431	−39.7%
Arson	5,003	7,489	5,714	−23.7%
TOTALS				
Violent crimes[1]	61,861	87,506	70,731	−19.2%
Property crimes[2]	429,224	463,574	382,504	−17.5%
Crime Index Total	491,085	551,080	453,235	−17.8%

Source: Federal Bureau of Investigation, 1999. *Crime in the United States, 1998: Uniform Crime Reports.* Washington, DC: U.S. Government Printing Office. Tables 32 and 34, pp. 214 and 216.

[1]Violent crimes are offenses of murder, forcible rape, robbery, and aggravated assault.
[2]Property crimes are offenses of burglary, larceny-theft, motor vehicle theft, and arson.

lem. With over one and three-fourth million persons under age 18 still arrested each year, and one out of every 16 youths between ages 10 and 17 annually processed through a juvenile court, it is still unequivocally clear that juvenile delinquency remains a challenging phenomenon in the United States.

In addition, short-term, statistical reversals have occurred in the past and often turned out to be temporary anomalies before prevailing demographic, economic, and social factors returned arrest data to the more dominant and longitudinal pattern and direction. Also, the reality of self-report data again confirms that recorded delinquent behavior through arrest and juvenile court statistics represent only a small portion of youthful law-breaking; and that a vast reservoir of "unofficial" delinquency remains (McGehee, 2000).

Nevertheless, the present reduction in juvenile arrests is a very positive and hopeful development that warrants national commitment to continue the trend.

Addendum: A Balanced Perspective on Youth

After struggling through a chapter such as this—under an avalanche of crime data on young people (much of it negative)—a more balanced and complete portrayal of American youth is appropriate. The deviant and his or her behavior are generally more visible and reportable news because the public is titilated and excited by nonconformity. Thus, we need to remind ourselves that even though 1,855,002 youths were arrested in 1998, nearly 27 million other young people between 10 and 17 years of age were *not* arrested that year. The great majority of American youth do not come into serious conflict with the behavioral expectations and law-enforcement agencies of society. In fact, there are many instances every day of young people responding in supportive, responsible, even heroic ways, to the highest and noblest values and standards of civilized society. The two brief stories that follow are examples of this generally underreported phenomena:

TEEN SAVES CHILD FROM CREEK

PORTLAND (AP)—A teenager jumped into a frigid creek and saved a 4-year-old boy who was spotted floating face-down. Chris Cottrill, 17....stripped off his outer clothes, plunged into the creek and pulled the boy onto a concrete bank. Cottrill then performed cardiopulmonary resuscitation on the child until paramedics arrived. "I started yelling at him, 'Come on! Stay with me!" Cottrill [said]. "I hope ...that his parents know that whatever the outcome, I tried to save him" (Ashland Daily Tidings, 2000:B1).

S.F. TEEN RUNS TOWARD RESPONSIBILITY, AIDS COLUMBINE VICTIM

DENVER—While he was watching the Columbine High School tragedy unfold from his San Francisco home..., 15-year-old Rashad Williams decided he had to do something to help.

On Tuesday, he did just that, handing shooting victim Lance Kirklin a check for $18,000.... Kirklin, 16, was among 22 students who were injured in the rampage.

BOX 3-3   Cross-Cultural Focus

Juvenile Delinquency in Russia

Before the 1990–1991 economic and political upheaval in the former Soviet Union, and the new experimentation with democracy, there was little open discussion of crime and delinquency in that communist nation. In response to inquiries from visiting journalists and researchers from abroad, Soviet police and state officials were often defensive and denied that such problems existed in any magnitude in the Soviet Union. Trapped in the uneasy logic of Marxist-Leninist doctrine, these spokesmen had little choice in the matter. According to socialistic ideology—poverty, greed, exploitation, and other social causes of crime are eliminated as society progresses toward a communistic utopia.

It was in this stultifying system that David Shipler found himself in the 1970s. He was the Moscow Bureau Chief for the *New York Times* and, in the best tradition of American news reporters, he was in pursuit of the facts regarding crime and juvenile delinquency in the Soviet Union.

Crime statistics are a state secret, I was informed by the Ministry of Internal Affairs after weeks of unsuccessful attempts to get an interview there. News items on violent crime are kept off television. General-circulation newspapers never report crimes when they occur, only selected cases after they have been solved, when some moral point or sociological analysis can be made.... The instinct is to protect the society's image, and the rationale is to avoid publicity that could make the violence contagious. (Shipler, 1989:230)

Undaunted, Shipler set out to pierce the shroud of official state dogma and discover the scope and details of crime in the Soviet Union. After many months of conversations and interviews with Russians from all walks of life, and after exhaustive research through law libraries and other specialized publications, Shipler developed a frightening picture of crime as a major and growing social problem in that nation. Much of it involved an epidemic of murders, rapes, beatings, muggings, and burglaries committed by teenagers from 14 to 18 years of age. The reliability of Shipler's findings was supported

by an earlier but much briefer account of runaway juvenile crime in Russia by Hedrick Smith (1985):

When I was in Irkutsk, the rector of the university there told me that the most rapidly growing faculty was the law faculty because so many Siberian cities were requesting lawyers. One reason was, it turned out, that police forces wanted law-trained university graduates to help cope with juvenile delinquency. (Smith, 1985:194)

The causes of the spiraling incidence of serious juvenile crime in the Soviet Union since World War II are strikingly similar to those often cited to explain American social problems since the beginning of the twentieth century. Soviet criminologists have pinpointed major demographic and social changes associated with rapid industrialization and urbanization. Millions of vulnerable village folk must adjust to urban life and, as old values and stabilizing relationships become obsolete, divorce rates escalate and family control is weakened. The disorientation and anonymity of the mass society is conducive to nonconformity behavior (Hollander, 1969).

Even high-ranking government officials appeared to be ignorant or unconcerned about the magnitude of juvenile crime in the Soviet Union. Shipler found that even the head of the Central Committee's Department of Education, S. P. Trapeznikov, was unable to get any crime statistics. Prior to the new "openness" introduced by President Gorbachev in 1990, the Soviet Union was organized to discourage negative reporting, even within official ranks. Consequently, there was a national effort to suppress any bad news that might reflect negatively on the state or agencies and officials at lower levels.

Among those who conceal data to avoid bringing criticism on themselves are school teachers and principals. In Irkutsk, after two boys had raped a girl, the high school's principal and teachers tried to hush up the crime, a teachers' journal reported, dismissing it as a "childish prank" and pleading with the victim and her parents to drop charges.... It

Continued

BOX 3-3 *Continued*

turned out that principals avoided reporting all crimes so that their schools would not be listed as performing poorly. Local police commanders also suppressed statistics.... "If I were to send in to the city militia headquarters the genuine figures about crime in my district," the commander of the 130th was quoted as saying, "I would not last a day in my job. That is what they all do; I am not the only one. Juvenile crime is a scourge in Moscow and in other cities as well." (Shipler, 1989:243–244)

In Moscow, a special task force was organized by concerned city officials and citizens to measure the true magnitude of crime and juvenile delinquency within the city, and to probe for possible causes. When the group's work was completed and a report submitted, findings were clearly unwelcome and summarily dismissed. Trapeznikov, head of the Central Committee's Department of Education, called the picture "exaggerated," rejected any relationship between crime and poverty, and branded the report "antisoviet."

As the individual nations that once comprised the Soviet Union move into the twenty-first century and intensify their experiment with capitalism, they are caught in the vortex of rapid and often traumatic social change. Reports continue to proliferate that the political collapse of the Soviet Union has been followed by widespread unemployment and family impairment. For example, Candice Hughes (1993) graphically describes the lifestyle of thousands of children and teenagers who are ignored, neglected, and abused by their parents—and roam the streets of Moscow as juvenile offenders. These Russian youths, lost in a tide of social change, are characterized as cynical, hedonistic, and committed to the pursuit of money through any illegal means that might be available. Russian authorities now openly express their concern and hope that revitalized families, schools, and social welfare agencies can soon effectively address their growing juvenile delinquency problem.

Sources

Hollander, P. 1990. *A converging social problem: Juvenile delinquency in the Soviet Union and the United States.* British Journal of Criminology 9 (April): 148–166.

Hughes, C. 1993. *Boys' life on the streets in Moscow.* Fort Worth Star-Telegram, September 19, 1993: Section AA, p. 1.

Shipler, D. K. 1989. *Russia: Broken idols, solemn dreams* (2nd ed.). New York: Time Books (a division of Random House, Inc.).

Smith, H. 1985. *The Russians* (3rd ed.). New York: Time Books (a division of Random House, Inc.).

He was shot five times at close range, including once in the face, and nearly bled to death.... Kirklin's jaw was shattered and he faces at least four more reconstructive surgeries. His medical bills are expected to top one million dollars and he has no health insurance.

[Rashad Williams,] a freshman at San Francisco's Archbishop Riordan High School, who runs the 400- and 800-meter events for his school's track team, sought sponsors in Kirklin's name and entered the 7½-mile Bay to Breakers Race in May....

Williams raised $14,000 in the race. In the weeks that followed, checks worth an additional $4,000 poured in....

Williams' mother, Sheila Burton-Harris, said she was not surprised. "This is nothing new to us. Rashad will give money to a student who doesn't have lunch money; he'll give $5 to a homeless person just after he's gotten it from me" (San Francisco Examiner, 1999:A9).

Despite alarming crime rates, it is impossible to be pessimistic about America's youth when we still produce young people like Chris Cottrill and Rashad Williams!

SUMMARY

This chapter focused on the challenging task of measuring the magnitude of juvenile delinquency in the United States in response to such questions as:

1. Approximately how many people under age 18 are directly involved in crime each year?
2. What kinds of crime are most common among American young people?
3. How do such variables as gender, race, ethnicity, and place of residence affect the incidence and kinds of juvenile offenses that are committed?
4. What are the trends in juvenile delinquency? Is it increasing or decreasing?

Evolving from these concerns, two continuous national, data-gathering programs were instituted. The Federal Bureau of Investigation collects, summarizes, analyzes, and reports arrest data from a network of city, county, and state law enforcement agencies and compiles this information in its annual Uniform Crime Reports. These FBI reports include the incidence of juvenile arrests for various crimes and tabulate for such variables as age, gender, race, and place of residence. The second official source is the National Center for Juvenile Justice and Delinquency Prevention of the Department of Justice which collects and summarizes data on case dispositions submitted from juvenile courts across the nation. The annual reports on Juvenile Court Statistics also identify and summarize those court dispositions by type of offense and a limited number of demographic variables.

Other sources of systematically collected data on juvenile delinquency include self-report studies and victimization surveys. Self-report studies are usually questionnaires directed at samples of the population under study, in which subjects are asked about their participation in delinquent and/or criminal activities. The advantage of self-report studies is that they identify and

measure some of the vast amount of undetected and unreported criminal and delinquent behavior. Victimization surveys are designed to accomplish the same objective. However, the subjects are asked to indicate crimes perpetrated against them and their property, and, if possible, to describe the offenders by age, sex, and race. The most ambitious victimization survey is conducted on a regular basis and targets a representative sample of housing units in the United States. The U.S. Department of Justice supervises this survey and issues annual reports of findings.

All of these data-gathering programs suffer from serious methodological limitations regarding validity and reliability. For example, arrest statistics are subject to distortion due to variable law enforcement techniques and success in different jurisdictions. Some data are incorrectly tabulated and reported. In addition, arrest data present a picture only of offenders who were apprehended. Juvenile court data have been plagued by nonprobability sampling techniques, reporting irregularities and fluctuating court jurisdictions. Self-report studies and victimization surveys have been criticized for biased samples and inflated or deflated reports that severely limit generalizations to larger populations.

In spite of these shortcomings, the accumulation and combination of all these data on delinquent behavior over a long period of time present a clear and consistent conclusion that American young people generally account for a disproportionately large amount of criminal activity. According to official statistics, underclass, minority group males represent the most typical juvenile delinquents—a finding that has been moderated by unofficial statistics. While most juvenile delinquency is composed of status offenses and property crimes, there are a large number of violent crimes against persons. Overall, between 1995 and 2000, there has been an encouraging downward trend in the number of juvenile arrests in the United States.

Concept Integration

Questions and Topics for Study and Discussion

1. Define each of the first 8 crime categories of the *FBI Uniform Crime Report*. Why are they of major significance? Do you know anyone who has committed any of these major offenses? Do you know a victim of any of these crimes? Was the offense reported and the offender arrested?

2. Explain how information on crime and delinquency is collected for the *FBI Uniform Crime Reports,* the National Juvenile Court Statistical Reports, self-report studies, and victimization surveys. What are the advantages and limitations of each of these data-gathering techniques?

3. List and explain each of the variables that compose the composite profile of the "typical juvenile delinquent." Is this a completely reliable and valid portrayal of juvenile delinquents in the United States? Explain your answer.

4. Discuss the statistical evidence of delinquent behavior among racial minorities. How can we explain the high rates of juvenile delinquency among such minority groups by looking at their social environment and economic background?

5. What are the most recent trends in crime and delinquency as reported in this chapter?

6. Discuss the statistical evidence of delinquent behavior by female juveniles. How can we explain the increasing rates of delinquency by young females in recent years?

References

Adler, F. 1975. *Sisters in crime.* New York: McGraw Hill.

Arnold, W. R., and Brungardt, T. M. 1983. *Juvenile misconduct and delinquency.* Boston: Houghton-Mifflin.

Ashland Daily Tidings. 2000. Teen saves child from creek. (January 11):B1.

Bardo, J. W., and Hartman, J. J. 1982. *Urban sociology.* Itasca, IL: F. E. Peacock Publishers, Inc.

Barlow, H. D. 1987. *Introduction to criminology* (4th ed.). Boston: Little Brown.

Bohm, R. M. 1986. Crime, criminal and crime control policy myths. *Justice Quarterly* 3 (June):193–214.

Butts, J. A. Offenders in juvenile court, 1994. *Juvenile justice bulletin.* U.S. Department of Justice, Office of Juvenile Justice and Delinquency Prevention. National Center for Juvenile Justice. Pittsburgh, PA.

Cantwell, M. 1983. The offender. In *Report to the nation on crime and justice: The data* (M. W. Zawitz, Ed.). Bureau of Juvenile Statistics, U.S. Department of Justice. NJC-87068. (October):29–40.

Chambliss, W. J., and Nagasawa, R. H. 1969. On the validity of official statistics: A comparative study of white, black, and Japanese high school boys. *Journal of Research in Crime and Delinquency* VI (January):71–77.

Chesney-Lind, M., and Sheldon, R. G. 1998. *Girls: Delinquency and juvenile justice* (2nd ed.). Belmont, CA: Wadsworth.

Craig, Y. 1996. Fires set by children up sharply. *Fort Worth Star-Telegram.* March 24:A1, 29.

Criminal Victimizations in the United States, 1991. 1992. Rockville, MD: U.S. Department of Justice, Office of Justice Programs; Bureau of Justice Standards.

Del Pinal, J. H., and De Navas, C. 1990. *The Hispanic population in the United States* (March, 1989). Washington, DC: U.S. Government Printing Office.

Diegmueller, K. 1987. The forgotten juveniles: Crimeless criminals. *Parade* September 3:14–15.

Donovan, J. E. 1977. A typological study of self-reported deviance in a national sample of adolescents. Unpublished Ph.D. dissertation. Boulder: University of Colorado.

Elliott, D. S., and Huizinga, D. 1983. Social class and delinquent behavior in a national youth panel, 1976–1980. *Criminology* 21 (May):149–177.

Elliott, D. S., and Huizinga, D. 1984. The relationship between delinquent behavior and ADA behaviors. Paper presented at the ADAMHA/OJJDP Research Conference on Juvenile Offenders with Serious Alcohol, Drug Abuse, and Mental Health Problems. Bethesda, MD, April 17–18, 1984.

Erickson, M. L., and Empey, L. T. 1963. Court records, undetected delinquency and decision-making. *Journal of Criminal Law, Criminology and Police Science* 54, No. 4 (December):456–469.

Federal Bureau of Investigation. 1976. *Crime in the United States: Uniform crime reports—1975.* Washington, DC: U.S. Government Printing Office.

———. 1990. *Crime in the United States: Uniform crime reports—1989.* Washington, DC: U.S. Government Printing Office.

———. 1999. *Crime in the United States: Uniform crime reports—1998.* Washington, DC: U.S. Government Printing Office.

Figueira-McDonough, J. 1984. *British Journal of Criminology* 24 (October):325–342.

Forsyth, C. J., and Foster, B. D. 1993. Trends in female criminality 1943–1991. *Free Inquiry in Creative Sociology* 21 (November):135–139.

Frey, W. H., with First, C. L. 1997. *Investigating change in American society.* Belmont, CA: Wadsworth Publishing Co.

Goettling, A. 1989. Patterns of homicide among children. *Criminal Justice and Behavior* 16:63–80.

Harries, K. D. 1974. *The geography of crime and justice.* New York: McGraw-Hill Book Co.

Hindelang, M. J., Hirschi, T., and Weis, J. 1979. Correlates of delinquency: The illusion of discrepancy between self-report and official measures. *American Sociological Review* 44 (Dec.):995–1014.

Hirschi, T. 1969. *Causes of delinquency.* Berkeley: University of California Press.

Hurley, D. 1994. They said it couldn't happen here. *Family Circle.* April 26, 1994:75–84.

Jensen, G., and Eve, R. 1976. Sex differences in delinquency: An examination of popular sociological explanation. *Criminology* 13:427–448.

Jesness, C. F. 1987. Early identification of delinquent-prone children: an overview. In *Prevention of delinquent behavior* (J. D. Burchard and S. N. Burchard, Eds.). Newbury Park, CA: Sage.

Karchmer, C. L. 1984. Young arsonists. *Society* 22 (November/December):78–83.

Klaus, P. A., Rand, M. R., and Taylor, B. M. 1983. The victim. In *Report to the nation on crime and justice: The data* (M. W. Zawitz, Ed.). Bureau of Justice Statistics, U.S. Department of Justice. NJC-87068. (October):17–27.

Knight, H. 1997. Report probes well-being of U.S. youth. *San Francisco Chronicle.* July 3, 1997:A13.

Manley, D. 1979. Status offenders—Helping them cope. *The Sunday Oklahoman* June 17, 1979:23.

Matza, D. 1964. *Delinquency and drift.* New York: John Wiley.

McDermott, M. J., and Hindelang, M. J. 1981. *Juvenile criminal behavior in the United States: Its trends and patterns.* National Institute for Juvenile Justice and Delinquency Prevention, LEAA, U.S. Department of Justice. Washington, DC: U.S. Government Printing Office.

Parade. 1987. Tough for teenagers. March 22:15.

Perk, S. K. 1985. Juvenile pranks or criminal behavior. Conference paper: Midsouth Sociological Association.

Poe-Yamagata, E., and Butts, J. A. 1996. *Female offenders in the juvenile justice system.* U.S. Department of Justice, Office of Juvenile Justice and Delinquency Prevention. National Center for Juvenile Justice. Pittsburgh, PA.

Puzzanchera, C. M. 2000. Delinquency cases waived to criminal court, 1988–1997. *OJJDP Fact Sheet (February, 2000 #02).* U.S. Department of Justice. Washington, DC.

Puzzanchera, C. M. 2000. Self-reported delinquency by 12-year-olds, 1997. *OJJDP Fact Sheet (February, 2000 #03).* U.S. Department of Justice. Washington, DC.

San Francisco Examiner. 1999. Teen runs toward responsibility: Aids Columbine victim. (October 29):A9.

Santoli, A. 1986. How should we handle young offenders? *Parade.* (April 20):16–19.

Schaaf, D. 1986. The fire starters. *Friendly Exchange* (August):16–19.

Schaefer, R. T. 1979. *Racial and ethnic groups.* Boston: Little Brown.

Schiraldi, V. 1998. Exaggeration of juvenile crime drives stiffer penalties. *Medford Mail Tribune.* (Jan. 10):3A.

Siegel, L. J. 1995. *Criminology* (5th ed.). St. Paul, MN: West Publishing Co.

Smith, D. A., and Visher, C. A. 1981. Street-level justice: Situational determinants of police arrest decisions. *Social Problems* 29 (December):167–177.

Smith, D. D., Finnegan, T., and Snyder, H. N. 1980. *Delinquency 1977: United States estimates of cases processed by courts with juvenile jurisdiction.* Pittsburgh, PA: National Center for Juvenile Justice.

Snyder, H. N., Finnegan, T. A., Nimick, E. H., Sickmund, M. H., Sullivan, D. P., and Tierney, N. J. 1989. *Juvenile Court Statistics, 1985.* U.S. Department of Justice, Office of Juvenile Justice and Delinquency Prevention, National Center for Juvenile Justice. Pittsburgh, PA. April.

Snyder, H. N., and Sickmund, M. 1999. *Juvenile offenders and victims:* 1999 national report. U.S. Department of Justice, Office of Juvenile Justice and Delinquency Prevention. National Center for Juvenile Justice. Pittsburgh, PA.

Snyder, H. N., Sickmund, M., and Poe-Yamagata, E. 1996. *Juvenile offenders and victims: 1996 update on violence.* U.S. Department of Justice, Office of Juvenile Justice and Delinquency Prevention. National Center for Juvenile Justice. Pittsburgh, PA.

Stahl, A., Sickmund, M., Finnegan, T., Snyder, H., Poole, R., and Tierney, N. 1999. *Juvenile court statistics*

1996. Washington, DC: Office of Juvenile Justice and Delinquency Prevention. Pittsburgh, PA.

TELEMASP Bulletin. 1999. Why the drop in crime? Part IV. Vol. 6, Numbers 1 and 2. April and May of 1999.

The 1967 President's Crime Commission Report: Its Impact 25 Years Later. 1994. (Edited by John Conley). ACJS Monograph Series. Cincinnati: Anderson Press.

The President's Commission on Law Enforcement and Administration of Justice, Task Force Report. 1968. *The challenge of crime in a free society.* New York: Dutton.

Tittle, C., Villemez, W., and Smith, D. 1978. The myth of social class and criminality. *American Sociological Review* 63 (December):643–656.

Toufexis, A. 1989. Our violent kids. *Time Magazine.* June 12, 1989:52–58.

United States Department of Justice. 1974. First Annual Report of the National Institute of Law Enforcement and Criminal Justice. LEAA. Washington, DC: U.S. Government Printing Office.

1974. *Standards and goals for juvenile justice.* Washington, DC: U.S. Government Printing Office.

1983. *Report to the nation on crime and justice: The data* (M. W. Zawitz, Ed.). Bureau of justice Statistics. NJC-87068. (October).

USA Today. 2000. Society in the crosshairs. (March 2): 14A.

Voss, H. L. 1963. Ethnic differentials in delinquency in Honolulu. *Journal of Criminal Law, Criminology, and Police Science* LIV (September):322–327.

Weeks, J. R. 1996. *Population* (6th ed.). Belmont, CA: Wadsworth Publishing Company.

Weller, R. H., and Bouvier, L. F. 1981. *Population, demography and policy.* New York: St. Martin's Press.

Wells, L. E., and Rankin, J. H. 1995. Juvenile victimization: Convergent validation of alternative measurements. *Journal of Research in Crime and Delinquency* 32 (August):287–307.

Wheeler, M. 1976. *Lies, damn lies, and statistics. The manipulation of public opinion in America.* New York: Laurel Edition, Dell.

Winslow, R. W. 1967. Anomie and its alternatives: A self-report study of delinquency. *Sociological Quarterly* VIII (Autumn):468–480.

Witkin, G. 1998. The crime bust. *U.S. News and World Report.* May 25:28–40.

Wooden, W. S. 1985. Arson is epidemic—and spreading like wildfire. *Psychology Today* 19 (January):23–28.

Yablonsky, L., and Haskell, M. R. 1988. *Juvenile delinquency* (4th ed.). New York: Harper and Row.

PART

II

CAUSES OF
JUVENILE DELINQUENCY

Introduction: Theory and the Etiology of Juvenile Delinquency

In Part I, we defined juvenile delinquency as "illegal conduct by a juvenile that reflects a persistent delinquent role and results in society regarding the offender as seriously deviant." Even though a very large proportion of juvenile delinquency is composed of such relatively trivial status offenses as running away from home, chronic school truancy, and curfew violation, a persistent pattern of youthful involvement in many serious crimes against persons and property qualifies juvenile delinquency as a national social problem.

Now, after our discussion in Part I of "what is delinquency?" and "who are the delinquents?" we are ready to investigate the "why" of juvenile misconduct. In other words, how do we explain seriously deviant and antisocial behavior by young people? The study of **etiology**— *the cause(s) of an event, phenomenon, or behavior*—is a common inquiry and exercise in the scientific community and many academic disciplines. For example, the quest to explain biological variations in certain animal species prompted Charles Darwin to develop the theory of evolution. Similarly, Isaac Newton's observations of falling objects led him to conceptualize the law of gravity and other theoretical principles regarding cause and effect in the physical world. The application of the scientific method of investigation and theory building in the social sciences is somewhat more complicated than in the biological and physical sciences because of the incomparable complexity of human subjects and the ethical considerations involved in subjecting them to fully controlled laboratory test conditions. Nevertheless, within these limitations, sociologists and other students of human behavior are on the same etiological quest to explore, identify, understand, and explain the cause(s) of social phenomena. Serious efforts to establish valid and reliable findings and conclusions involve a103

n objective, systematic approach to observation, data collection, and the testing of hypotheses. Finally, if findings and conclusions warrant, the ultimate result of the research enterprise may be the generation of explanatory theories.

In popular usage, the term "theory" means a "hunch" or a calculated guess that explains why some event occurs, or the possible relationship between cause and effect variables. To the lay person, a theory often suggests mere speculation, based on unfounded assumptions and little factual data, concerning an event or a form of behavior. For example, in hypothetically reconstructing events leading up to an automobile accident, an onlooker might speculate: "My theory of what happened is that the driver fell asleep and ran off the road." Or, as it was erroneously "theorized" in 1971, by extending voting rights to 18-year-olds, young Americans between 18 and 21 would generally and enthusiastically take advantage of the opportunity to participate in the political process.

To the scientist or researcher, the term "theory" means much more than an "off-the-cuff" guess or estimate. To these scholars, a **theory** is *a general statement that systematically and objectively relates concepts or variables together to explain events or behavior.* If a theory is valid, it correctly predicts that identical relationships, events, or behaviors will occur in the future if the conditions and circumstances are identical.

A large number of scholars from many disciplines, utilizing many approaches and methodologies, have attempted to develop causal theories explaining why some juveniles become delinquent. There has been considerable variation in the adequacy of these theories as they have been exposed to continual scrutiny and testing. In some cases, theories of delinquency have been modified, expanded, or discarded as inadequate explanations. Other theories have survived relatively intact as useful contributions to delinquency etiology. The five chapters comprising Part II present the more interesting, prominent, and useful theories of deviant behavior in general, and juvenile delinquency in particular.

Chapter 4 begins with an overview of eighteenth-century philosophical speculations regarding the causal origins of criminal behavior. There follows a more detailed discussion of the nineteenth-century biological determinism and the "born criminal" suggested by Cesare Lombroso, the twentieth-century constitutional typology and the "mesomorphic delinquent" described by William Sheldon, and others who argued that criminal and delinquent behavior can be traced to genetic and physiological factors. The chapter concludes with a discussion of more current and methodologically sophisticated efforts to establish causal linkage between biology and juvenile delinquency, as well as some controversial insights offered by sociobiology.

Chapter 5 surveys the early and contemporary concepts and contributions of psychiatrists and psychologists in explaining juvenile delinquency. These psychogenic theories perceive the delinquent's misbehavior as symptomatic of an underlying neurological or learning disability or some form of emotional or personality maladjustment. Psychoanalysis and projective tests—as techniques for probing the unconscious dimension of the human mind—are also explained.

Chapters 6, 7, and 8 provide an extensive treatment of the major sociological theories of juvenile delinquency, including social strain, cultural transmission, social learning, social control, social labeling, and radical theories. These sociological explanations share and amplify in various ways the basic premise of those who pursue sociological investigations and theory construction—that delinquency and most other human behaviors emerge as part and product of those human groups, interactions, and relationships that comprise the individual's social context and environment. Each section of Chapters 6, 7, and 8 concludes with a synopsis of contributions and criticisms of the various sociological theories of juvenile delinquency.

4 BIOLOGICAL EXPLANATIONS OF JUVENILE DELINQUENCY

Reading Objectives

The reading of this chapter will help you achieve the following objectives:

1. Explain the nineteenth century effort of Cesare Lombroso to link biological or physical characteristics with criminal behavior.
2. Compare and contrast the "rational individual responsibility for behavior" of the Classical School of Criminological Thought with the "biological determinism" of the Positive School of Criminology.
3. Become more aware of how society often casually and carelessly applies biological causes to human behavior in everyday life.
4. Describe the twentieth century research of William Sheldon and of Sheldon and Eleanor Glueck who tried to establish a causal relationship between body type and juvenile delinquency.
5. Discuss several recent areas of investigation that focus on gender, age, abnormal chromosomal and electroencephalograph patterns, diet, physical appearance, and other biological variables as possible causal backgrounds for some antisocial behavior.
6. Critique the weaknesses and limitations of theories of deviant and delinquent behavior that are based on biological and physiological variables.
7. Understand how the inclusion of social factors such as the attitudes and reactions of one's social group can reinforce the relationship between biological or physical characteristics and a tendency toward deviant and delinquent behavior.

Introduction

In Part 1, we examined the questions "What is juvenile delinquency?" and "Who are the delinquents?" Our understanding of the issues and answers raised by those initial questions form the foundation for the discussions in Part II of the theoretical causes of juvenile delinquency. In other words, there was a logical need to define the *What* and the *Who* of juvenile delinquency before we consider the *Why*.

Many explanations of misconduct have been suggested. From the dawn of recorded history, philosophers, theologians, political leaders, and social thinkers have conjectured that deviance and antisocial behavior might be traceable to demons, original sin, or people's insatiable and self-serving lust for power, gratification, and material possessions. The development of the "age of science" offered a plethora of additional explanations—all claiming to be based upon scientific reasoning.

The Link between Biology and Behavior: Myths and Folklore

The notion that there is an intrinsic relationship between human physical traits and behavior is also very old. For example, Franz Joseph Gall (1758–1828) speculated that mental faculties and traits of character—such as acquisitiveness, benevolence, destructiveness, spirituality, combativeness, and imitativeness—are manifested in separate portions of the brain. **Phrenology,** as Gall's system was called, noting that individuals vary in these traits of character and personality, further *contended that there is a positive relationship between these specific cerebral functions and the formation or shape of the human skull.* Although phrenology has been repeatedly and convincingly disproved anatomically and physiologically, the belief and fad was popularized by practitioners claiming to ascertain these mental characteristics and behavioral propensities by measuring the shape, irregularities, and protuberances of the skull.

History also is replete with fallacious suggestions from many writers that geographic location is reflected in temperament and behavior. For example, the Greek historian Polybius (200–118 B.C.) wrote, "There is an inevitable tendency for society to yield to climatic influences and these influences cause personality and physical differences in people." The Roman Paulio expanded on this view:

> *Southern European people are keen in intelligence due to the keen air. Northern peoples are sluggish, chilled by the air. People in warm climates have passionate natures; people in cold climates are stolid.*

The Frenchman Jean Bodin (1530–1596) held a related view: "Northern climate causes people's life fluids to make them cruel…but loyal to the government." Mondescuer, in a callous expression of unwitting male chauvinism, wrote:

> *In the South the women mature early due to the climate and marry early to older men. Since women are inferior in wisdom to their more experienced husbands, this affects the woman's social status.*

Unfortunately, ethnic and racial biases and slurs still persist in some places where a disvalued ethnic background is equated with undesirable behavior. For example, there are still those who erroneously generalize that "all Irishmen drink too much"—perhaps traceable to the large quantities of Irish whiskey exported to the United States during the Prohibition Era. Similarly, the Germans have been stereotyped as "militaristic" due to the political circumstances in their nation preceding World Wars I and II. And African Americans have suffered for generations the degrading and simplistic assumption by some unenlightened whites that there is an affinity between being black and "a preference for fried chicken and watermelon."

Such allusions to a mystical linkage between biological inheritance or physical appearance and human behavior often appear as taken-for-granted truisms in the language and culture of a people and, sadly, often affect important relationships and decisions. The life chances of many people, ranging all the way from marriage to employment, can be negatively influenced by such unfair stereotypes and unfounded generalizations as "People with red hair are hot-tempered"; "Fat people are always jolly"; and "Tall men make the best leaders." Only in recent decades has objective and sympathetic attention been given to the universal and longstanding stigma imposed on left-handed people. Michael Barsley (1966) carefully documented the history of prejudice and even persecution experienced by a large and visible minority who favor the use of the left hand and, therefore, were falsely assumed to be sinister, deviant, or criminal in some way.

In the theater and motion picture industry, physical appearance has consistently been related to character and behavior. Actors generally portray transparent characters whose personalities, motives, and actions must be obvious to the audience and easily interpreted. Thus, on the stage or screen, each character is usually unidimensional—presented as either "good" or "bad." It was a common joke for many years that cinema "westerns" always portrayed the hero as physically attractive, well groomed, idealistic, God-fearing, wearing a white hat, and kind to women, children, and horses. On the other hand, the villain was quickly identified as ugly, slovenly, uncouth, ignorant, immoral, cruel, and (of course) wearing a black hat. Only in the movies are the "good guys" and the "bad guys" so easily and dichotomously sorted out. People and situations are much more complex in real life and defy immediate character evaluation. Unfortunately, however, in real life as in the cinema, physical appearance is often the basis for quickly imputing character and judging behavior.

The Classical School of Criminological Thought

The first organized inquiry and hypothesis regarding criminal deviance emerged in the eighteenth century. Charles Montesquieu (1689–1755), Cesare Beccaria (1738–1794), Jeremy Bentham (1748–1832), and other Enlightenment writers propounded a "naturalistic" approach to explaining criminal behavior by contending that the only acceptable explanations for human conduct are to be found in man himself. From that beginning, the **Classical School of Criminological Thought** was developed. The Classical theorists were guided by the assumption that humans are rational, reasoning individuals who weigh and control their actions and destinies. The focus was upon the criminal as totally responsible for personal behavior. Thus, according to Graeme Newman's *The Punishment Response* (1978), appropriate punishment "to suit the crime" would not only encourage the reformation of offenders, but discourage criminality in the general populace. The idea was that a person would conform to the standards and behavioral expectations of society in order to avoid physical pain—like a bull with a ring in his nose. Punishment was thought to be appropriate under most circumstances and for most offenses because it was assumed that crimes were the result of free will based on conscious, reasoned decisions.

While the Classical position did not clearly differentiate between children who violated laws and adult offenders, the later **Neoclassical School** recognized that not all persons are equally rational and personally responsible for their behavior. Consequently, "judges were allowed some discretion in dealing with the young, the mentally disturbed, and those confronted with unusual circumstances that decreased responsibility" (McCaghy and Capron, 1997:9). Nevertheless, the Classical/Neoclassical approach has been severely criticized. Its fatal flaw lay in overlooking how society is a major force in shaping human behavior, including criminality. Even if the highly questionable assumption of equal rationality among humans is valid, social inequality is a pervasive reality. An individual's decision to engage in criminal activity is based on much more than the simple equation and anticipated balance of pleasure minus pain. Levels of poverty, alienation, and social status, and numerous other forces and factors also must be taken into account.

Deterrence Theory

The classical and neoclassical theme that harsh and immediate punishment will discourage many offenders from repeating their misconduct has reemerged as the guiding premise in a number of contemporary suggestions for the treatment and prevention of juvenile delinquency. This approach, known as Deterrence Theory, encompasses a wide variety of "get tough" policies and programs—ranging from the reinstitution of corporal punishment in some schools to calls for more youth to face adult criminal courts and to receive longer jail sentences for their serious delinquencies. The deterrent effect of such uncompromising societal responses is assumed to strike directly at recidivism and chronic offenders and is enthusiastically promoted by Ernest van den Haag (1975), a professor of jurisprudence at Fordham University, and numerous others.

A ghastly extension of "punishment to suit the crime" has been portrayed on public television in Iraq, where convicted thieves have suffered brutal brandings and amputations— without anesthetic. "As a device to intimidate political opposition and reduce crime, the mutilations may be tragically effective" (*Time,* 1995:46).

Deterrence Theory as a prevention and treatment strategy for juvenile delinquents has the same limitations as the original Classical School of Criminological Thought— largely centered on an oversimplified and overgeneralized set of causal assumptions regarding human behavior. Not only do complex background factors vary widely from person to person, but not every individual is rational and thus fully accountable for his or her conduct (See Chapter 15 for additional discussion and applications of Deterrence Theory).

The Positive School of Criminology

The first efforts to apply scientific and systematic research methodology to establish the principle of biological determinism as the fundamental cause of criminal behavior occurred in the late nineteenth century. Implicit in the deterministic model is that a given thing cannot simply appear out of nothing or nowhere; it is determined or caused by some other thing, event, or phenomenon in the environment. Biological and physical scientists, in their study of plants, animals, and objects, already had found the deterministic explanation very useful in reasoning from cause to effect or, inversely, from effect to cause. This approach attracted a number of nineteenth century researchers and theorists, including some early criminologists, who enthusiastically tried to apply various forms of biological determinism to crime and juvenile delinquency. (Albanese, 1993).

Cesare Lombroso (1835–1909), an Italian army physician, who is often referred to as the "Father of Criminology," measured the jawbones, skulls, hands, and other physical traits of a group of prisoners and proposed that criminals are biological reversions to an earlier, more primitive stage of human development (Ferrero, 1911). The ideas of Lombroso and his followers formed the basis of the **Positive School** of criminology and constituted a reaction to the earlier Classical School. Whereas the Classical School theorists had assumed that humans are rational and endowed with free will, and thus able to calculate the advantages and costs associated with any course of action, the positivists denied the existence of free will and argued that each person is born with an innate propensity toward certain forms of behavior. In other words, just as people inherit specific physical traits, reflective of their genetic background, so, too, the positivists contended, some people are motivated by an inborn tendency toward behavior that may be criminal according to the standards of society. Lombroso viewed this antisocial human behavior as an almost genetically programmed response, much as lower animals are driven by instinct. This biological inheritance, Lombroso felt, when joined with conducive social circumstances and opportunities, irresistibly moves some individuals to act as they do.

From his late nineteenth-century study, Lombroso concluded that there is a *born criminal type,* "bestial" in appearance, and characterized by "low cranial capacity; retreating forehead; highly developed frontal sinuses;…early closing of the cranial sutures;…tufted and crispy hair; and large ears…[and] relative insensibility to pain" (Lombroso, 1911:365). In short, Lombroso identified the *born criminal* as one whose body structure and criminal behavior are dual manifestations of an underlying **atavism,** that is, *a biological throwback to a savage, lower phase of human evolution.* Such persons (*homo delinquens*), he reasoned, are biological and social misfits in a society of modern men (*homo sapiens*) whose civilization includes extensive behavioral restrictions.

Lombroso later refined and expanded his original thesis on the born criminal to include other types whose antisocial behavior he traced to biological or physiological traits. For example, the etiology of the *insane criminal,* according to Lombroso, may be linked to diseases or abnormalities of the mind. The *criminaloid* was different from the born criminal only in that his predatory conduct was less savage and more occasional. Lombroso described the *criminal by passion* as characterized by a romantic sensitivity and capacity for altruistic motives in the commission of crime—and thus contrasting sharply with the born criminal.

The premises, methodology, and conclusions of Lombroso and the Positivistic School of Criminology have been subjected to intense scrutiny and criticism by subsequent investigators, who cite the weaknesses of descriptive data, broad generalizations from few cases, and the absence of comparative control groups of nonprisoners (Goring, [1913] 1972). At the same time, more charitable scholars have applauded Lombroso for at least implementing a rudimentary scientific approach to criminology and for ultimately acknowledging the impact of sociological causes of crime interacting with inherited traits and tendencies to produce antisocial behavior (Wolfgang et al., 1972).

Twentieth-Century Constitutional Typologies

Biological explanations of crime and delinquency have continued to fascinate many investigators. For example, William Sheldon and associates (1949) equated personality and character with body type and contended that youths with a certain physical appearance have an inherited and enhanced potential for delinquent behavior. According to Sheldon, three distinct body types can be identified and characterized:

1. **Endomorph.** Physically characterized as having a rotund, soft, fleshy body. The endomorph tends to be easygoing, gregarious, and self-indulgent in temperament.
2. **Ectomorph.** A slender and fragile body, with small features and weak appearance. The ectomorph tends to be a loner, introspective, and emotionally high-strung.
3. **Mesomorph.** The body is generally muscular and firm, with a strong frame and resilient constitution. The mesomorph tends to be energetic, impetuous, and insensitive.

Sheldon compared 200 boys referred by social agencies and courts to a center for problem children in Boston with 4,000 college males and found the center's children to be more mesomorphic. He concluded that although mesomorphy does not predestine youths to delinquent behavior, it is the constitutional background most favorable to delinquency, since the mesomorph has the emotional makeup and physical resources to "translate impulse into action" and to become a predatory person (Cohen, 1966:51).

In 1950, Sheldon and Eleanor Glueck, a husband-wife team of researchers, reached conclusions similar to those presented by William Sheldon. The Gluecks compared 500 white male delinquents with 500 white male nondelinquents and agreed with Sheldon that mesomorphs apparently possess higher delinquency potential than youths having other body types. They stressed that while a mesomorphic body does not make delinquent behavior inevitable, the aggressive, muscular youth seems more likely to relieve his tensions and frustrations in ways that society defines as troublesome and delinquent.

Broad generalizations from the Sheldon and Glueck studies cannot be made, since both suffer from serious methodological problems. These efforts to correlate physical characteristics with a delinquent propensity have been severely criticized by other scholars (e.g., Clinard and Meier, 1998; Cohen, 1966) for lack of objectivity and nonrepresentative samples. For example, black, middle class, female, and more intelligent delinquents are conspicuous by their absence. Furthermore, the studies based their findings on the small proportion of youngsters who had been caught and were under treatment. This is a sampling bias that badly distorts the findings. Those who have been apprehended represent the unsuccessful delinquents. They tell us nothing about the successful ones! Finally, if mesomorphy represents a constitutional predisposition to delinquent behavior, what of the millions of persons who fit this body type but are not delinquent?

While the limitations of the constitutional typologies are extremely formidable, Sheldon and Eleanor Glueck made their argument for the connection between biology and behavior more convincing when they extended a linkage to social variables. Their statement that "A physical characteristic may be socially defined and treated in ways which encourage criminal behavior" is a noteworthy contribution (Hartl et al., 1982:557–558). Observations and perusal of juvenile court procedures and records indeed reveal that those youths who are aggres-

Sheldon's Body Types

| Endomorph | Ectomorph | Mesomorph |

(Illustration by Marilyn R. Thompson)

sive, socially assertive, nonsubmissive to authority, and essentially mesomorphic in physique, are those most likely to be arrested and committed to a correctional institution. This topic is expanded in Chapter 8 in a discussion of how society assigns the "delinquent label."

The Continuing Search for the Biological Connection

Many criminologists, researchers, and theorists are still searching for a direct link between human biology and human behavior. In view of the extensive societal commitment to alleviate the juvenile delinquency problem, such ongoing investigations are worthwhile. Although findings thus far are often discredited or inconclusive, several lines of investigation warrant our attention in the context of this chapter.

BOX 4-1 Concept Application

The following anecdote describes an experience of one of the authors who encountered a young woman who demonstrated how the negative social evaluation of physical characteristics can result in deviant behavior. As you read it, look for the synthesis of biological and social variables that may be causally related to deviance and delinquency.

"An Ugly Girl"

When I was fresh out of graduate school and relatively inexperienced in my new academic role, I found myself thrust into a traumatic conflict situation that I will never forget. In addition to my teaching duties, I was asked to serve on "The Student Counseling Committee." That mild title belies the gut-level, arena-like confrontation I experienced at my first meeting with the committee.

My first sense of impending disaster occurred when I arrived and discovered that the committee functioned with a rotating chairmanship and—like a game of tag or Russian Roulette—I was "it"…

Immediately the door opened and the first student came in for "counsel." To my astonishment, a powerfully built and angry young woman was ushered into the committee room. It became quickly apparent that she had been there before and that she was unimpressed with the committee—especially the green young sociologist at the head of the table. She turned out to be an extremely formidable adversary.

The reason for her periodic visits with the Student Counseling Committee was her continuous and unprovoked verbal assaults upon her teachers and other students. Occasionally, she would punctuate her words with a slap or a kick. She was not only unpleasant and uncooperative, but loud and rude in all of her social contacts. She was a bully. As a consequence, she was feared, hated, and socially isolated. Other students rejected her; teachers were driven to exasperation, but agreed that she was a superior student. Her trademark was a sharp tongue with which she mercilessly belittled the physical shortcomings of others. Even during our interview, she scornfully referred to the baldness, fatness, crooked teeth, and other imperfections of the committee members. To every overture we made, she replied in the same insolent and insulting manner.

…I quickly leafed through her dossier on the table in front of me and discovered that she had scored exceptionally high on an intelligence test. She was not stupid; quite the contrary. "But why is she acting this way?" I kept asking myself. "If we can explain her strange behavior, perhaps we can help her…"

It was a grim and tension filled situation as the young woman berated the school, teachers, students, the committee, and me. Finally, as I sought to blunt her attack and grope for some insight, I asked pointedly, "Young lady…what is wrong with you?" She recoiled momentarily before lashing out again. But her reaction led me to believe that she did have some conscious inkling of why she behaved as she did. A bit later, when she paused for breath in her tirade, I demanded of her: "Tell me what is wrong with you." She looked around the room and shuddered. And we were dumbfounded as she covered her face with her hands and cried out one of the most pitiful stories I have ever heard. "I'm so ugly!" she began.

The basis for her incorrigible and deviant behavior (often officially classified as "juvenile delinquency") had been laid in her early childhood. Her parents had openly compared her with more winsome sisters, and with grotesque humor referred to her as "the ugly duckling in the family." She felt rejected because of prominent facial features and a boyish, muscular build. Her dilemma deepened when she became the target of cruel nicknames and taunts in elementary school. Not only did she accept the negative and painful appraisal as valid, but acted as she surmised an "ugly person ought to act." As she talked, I was reminded of the classic commentary of W. I. Thomas on the social psychology of human behavior: "A thing is real as it is real in its consequences." Ultimately, that socially injured and stigmatized young woman transformed her hurt into hatred. She felt that her survival was at stake so she went on the offensive and struck back at society.

While her case was extreme, a negative evaluation of personal physical appearance is a common problem among adolescents. Many young people, already under the strains associated with moving into adulthood, become dismayed when they compare themselves with the illusory physical ideals of peer and reference groups. Failing to meet group stan-

Continued

BOX 4-1   *Continued*

dards for physical appearance can result in great personal stress and damaged self-esteem (Wright, 1989). Stolz and Stolz (1944) extensively interviewed ninety-three teen-age boys and eighty-three teen-age girls regarding their physical characteristics and their relative attitudes about their appearance. Nearly all of them were worried about something. Boys were distressed by lack of size, particularly height, eyeglasses, fatness, poor physique, lack of muscular strength, unusual facial features, and skin blemishes. Girls were concerned about tallness, fatness, facial features, late development, skin blem-

ishes, thinness, large limbs, and eyeglasses. There is considerable evidence that this adolescent anxiety over undesirable appearance can be translated into antisocial behavior. (Agnew, 1984).

*   *   *   *

Based upon the information available in the short story about the "ugly" girl, what evidence can you find to support the view that biological factors, when joined with social definitions, can cause or reinforce antisocial behavior, from the viewpoints of the Positivists, William Sheldon, and Freda Adler?

Source

Adapted from Jack E. Bynum. 1987. *So you think you are ugly? Applied Sociology.* Pp. 17–19. Acton, MA: Copley Publishing Group.

Recommended Reading

Jackson, L. A., and Fitzgerald, H. E. 1988. "What is beautiful is good": The importance of physical attractiveness in infancy and childhood. *Child International,* published by Eltan Limited; London, England. Pp. 26–40.

Gender

In Chapter 3, statistical evidence was presented showing that males commit much more crime and delinquency than females. Each year, more males than females have been arrested for violent crimes and property crimes in the eight Index offense categories. This gender variation in crime rates is consistent in virtually all societies.

It has been popularly believed that part of the difference in crime rates between males and females in our country may be attributed to biological differences (such as hormones that predispose men to aggressive behavior). However, much of the difference is due to the contrasting gender roles that men and women are socialized to play. Traditionally, most boys and young men have been socially encouraged to be aggressive and competitive. Such attributes were generally considered useful in achieving occupational success and upward social mobility. On the other hand, girls and young women were expected to achieve only the family-oriented and home-based objectives of marriage and motherhood. These nurturing female roles were associated with a dependent, pliant, and nonaggressive disposition (Chance, 1988).

There is accumulating evidence that much of the difference in delinquency rates between the sexes is a product of variations in parental restrictiveness, values, socialization, and cultural opportunities and expectations experienced by young males and females (Hagan, J. A. et al., 1985).

Girls and boys do not inhabit the same worlds, and they do not have the same choices. This is not to say that girls do not share some circumstances and qualities with boys (notably class and race), but even the manner in which these affect the daily lives of young people is heavily mediated by gender (Chesney-Lind and Shelden, 1998:241–242).

Nevertheless, the statistical picture of male/female offenses has begun to change in recent years. Slowly at first, and then at an accelerated pace, role restrictions have been lifted for many women and more options have become available. At the same time, female participation in crime and delinquency has increased. Between 1981 and 1997, the arrest rates for female juveniles increased twice as much as arrest rates for juvenile males. More specifically, female arrest rates for weapons law violations nearly tripled during that same time period, while the male rate nearly doubled. In 1997, females between ages 16 and 17 accounted for 21 percent of all juvenile arrests for aggravated assault (Snyder and Sickmund, 1999:115 and 136). According to Freda Adler (1975:1) "The phenomenon of female criminality is but one wave in this rising tide of female assertiveness…"

Traditional gender roles demonstrate a possible link between biology and social expectations. Males have been encouraged to be more aggressive and competitive, while females have been expected to remain in the background in supportive and nurturing roles. Some theories have related this "macho" posturing to certain kinds of male delinquency.

Statistics compiled in the United States, Italy, France, Germany, and Russia have recorded a marked rise in violent crimes committed by women in recent decades. For example, of 52 alleged terrorists captured in Germany, 22 were women; since 1970 murders by women have increased 87 percent and cases of assault and battery by 45 percent (Brothers, 1985). Several experts have related this increase in aggressive criminal behavior to the recent emancipation of many women from their traditional passive and subordinate roles in male-dominated societies. Leon Salzman (1980), Clinical Professor of Psychiatry at the Albert Einstein College of Medicine, reported that there was no biological reason for females to be less aggressive, except that being aggressive had no meaning in a woman's life until she had the same possibilities as a man.

Race and Ethnicity

The national statistics on juvenile arrests are compared and contrasted in the previous chapter for white, black, American Aborigine (Indians and Eskimos), Asian or Pacific Islander, and Hispanic subgroups. It is clear that there are statistically significant variations in arrest rates in the United States when comparing racial and ethnic groups. Parallel findings from other sources concur that the rates of delinquency for Chinese-Americans, Japanese-Americans, and Jews, for example, are lower than the rates for the rest of the population. On the other hand, the arrest rates for African Americans and Hispanics are higher than those of other groups (*FBI Uniform Crime Reports, 1996* and *1999*). However, these findings are moderated by self-report studies (see Chapter 3) which suggest that the discrepancy between white and black involvement in juvenile crime is not as pronounced as indicated by arrest statistics. (Hindelang, Hirschi, and Weis, 1979, 1981). Some of the racial differences manifest in official arrest data may be traced to differential treatment accorded the races by law enforcement and the juvenile justice system.

Data from several sources (Final Report, 1986; Huff, 1986; Klein, 1969; Miller, 1975; Short and Strodtbeck, 1965; Thrasher, 1927) have identified the racial and ethnic composition of urban youth gangs. They found that the racial and ethnic composition of gangs reflects that of the population in their urban environment; gang members are more often recruited from minority groups with less power and prestige; and most gangs are racially/ethnically homogeneous and exclusive:

> ...*the various cities differ in the racial makeup of their gangs. For example, in Philadelphia and Detroit, the overwhelming number of gang members are black. In New York and Los Angeles, Hispanic gangs predominate. San Francisco's small gang population is mostly Asian....* (Siegel and Senna, 1997:340).

Great caution must be exercised lest the reader assume that the aforementioned data prove that there is an inherent connection between racial or ethnic background and delinquent behavior. In addition to the social bias often reflected in arrest statistics, when a long-range analysis of criminal and delinquent rates and patterns in urban areas is utilized, the high incidence of such antisocial behavior appears related more to the poor socioeconomic circumstances of minority groups than to the biology of race or ethnicity. Clifford Shaw and Henry McKay (1969) followed a number of different ethnic groups such as the Irish, Polish, and Italians over time as they improved their general occupational, educational, and income levels, and moved from the grim, inner-city tenements and slums into better neighborhoods. In all instances, the crime and delinquency rates for each group fell as higher social status was achieved. The current occupants of inner-city, underclass areas are mostly black and Hispanic minorities, and these groups manifest the typical high crime and delinquency rates of previous area residents. It is expected that as the present minority group residents improve their socioeconomic situations and move to better neighborhoods, they too will experience reduced rates of crime and delinquency.

The present deteriorated social circumstances of many African Americans in contrast to other ethnic or racial groups cannot be ignored as viable contributing factors to their involvement in crime and delinquency.

> *The black poverty rate is triple that of whites, and the unemployment rate is double. Black infant mortality not only is double that of whites, but may be rising for the first time in a decade. We have reached the point where more than half of the black children born in this country are born out of wedlock—most to teenage parents.... The officially acknowledged high school dropout rate in many metropolitan areas is more than 30 percent (Howard and Hammond, 1991:142).*

Age

In Chapter 1, we discussed the legal importance and usefulness of chronological age in defining the boundary line between juvenile delinquency and adult crime, as well as the level of an offender's accountability. In future chapters, the human life course will be presented as a framework for insights regarding societal treatment of individuals based on their various and changing ages. However, in the context of this chapter, we want to look at how a person's age—as a biological factor and phenomenon—may be causally related to his/her delinquent behavior.

There is convincing documentation that the age of youthful offenders is generally associated with the beginning, intensity, and end of their criminal careers. Statistical analysts of criminal patterns and trends have long recognized that such conduct is more common among adolescents and young adults than in other age groupings. According to the U.S. Department of Justice,

> *That young people commit crime at a high rate is no revelation. Age is so fundamental to crime rates that its relationship to offending is usually designated the "age-crime curve." This curve, which for individuals typically peaks in the late teen years, highlights the tendency for crime to be committed during an offender's younger years and to decline as age advances (Blumstein, 1995:3).*

In view of the data on age patterns of youthful offenders, several promising biological hypotheses have been advanced as possible explanations for teenage involvement in crime. For example, Editha Nottelmann of the National Institute of Mental Health has reported on research linking misbehavior during puberty to hormonal changes. She and her colleagues at the NIMH and the National Institute of Child Health and Human Development measured the blood levels of seven hormones in 56 boys and 52 girls between the ages of 9 and 14. At the same time other researchers assessed the youngsters' social adjustment and behavior. They found that boys with a profile of lower testosterone and higher androstenedione and girls with lower dehydroepiandrosterone sulfate levels were more likely to exhibit delinquent behaviors. Major fluctuations and imbalances in these key hormones can occur at the onset of puberty (*Emporia Gazette,*1985).

Delbert Elliott and Rhonda Dibert, in a related line of inquiry, have formulated extensive conceptual models linking the onset of adolescent sexual behavior with several demographic variables (e.g., race, social class, and family structure) as a concomitance and developmental progression to minor and major delinquencies. Again, the empirical study of Elliott and Dibert strongly implies a biological connection between age and deviant behavior. (Elliott and Dibert, 1991).

D. Wayne Osgood et al. (1988) go even further in their research report, "The Generality of Deviance in Late Adolescence and Early Adulthood." These investigators used self-report data from young people to support the previously established finding that a wide range of deviant behaviors are positively correlated with one another during the same life stage for many young people.

> *There are two plausible general explanations for such correlations.... The first is that engaging in one form of deviant behavior leads to engaging in others as well ...particularly that drug use leads to crime. The second explanation is that different deviant behaviors are related because they have shared influences. For example, the factors that lead people to become sexually active at an early age might be the same as (or at least overlap) those that lead them to use marijuana (Osgood et al., 1988:81).*

Osgood and his colleagues go on to suggest that their data and the congruence of similar background factors behind numerous deviant behaviors might lead to the identification of a general syndrome of deviance and, by extension, a general explanatory theory of juvenile delinquency and other forms of nonconformity by young people.

Maturation Theory

Just as new prospects for theoretical development may be emerging regarding chronological age as an important biological determinant in the genesis of delinquency, similar attention is being focused on the age of offenders and the termination of their delinquent careers. While juvenile delinquency is an advance predictor for many youths who later become adult criminals, it is also true that most delinquent youngsters change for the good. It is a matter of general consensus among sociologists and criminologists (supported by considerable data) that young people typically seem to mature and "grow out" of their deviant behavior—usually without the assistance or sanctions of law enforcement or other control agencies of society.

> *One of the longest standing and most agreed upon facts about criminals is that the older they become the less likely they will be to continue their criminal involvements.... Virtually all criminologists, whatever their theoretical persuasion,*

appear to operate with a common image of the age distribution (Hirschi and Got-
tfredson, 1983). The influence of age and cessation of crime has generally been
referred to as the "maturation effect" (Blumstein et al., 1986; Hirschi and Gottfred-
son, 1983). Walter Reckless summed up this phenomenon by concluding that "crime
is like a fast rising storm which peaks during adolescence and young adulthood,
blows strongly for awhile and eventually subsides in middle age" (Sandhu, 1974)
(Entire quotation from Jackson, 1993:7).

Robert Sampson and John Laub, in their study, *Crime in the Making* (1993), found that
delinquents who reform do so because they get attached to a structured social institution.
Strong ties to a job or a spouse can reduce one's criminal behavior to about zero.

Certainly, the maturation effect, or Maturation Theory as it has been called in recent
years, warrants further study as a biological and/or social threshold between delinquent behavior and conformity. There is considerable speculation among theorists on exactly why
and how most offenders later come to terms with society and conform as they mature and
grow older. In this respect, the theory may have important implications for the social control
of serious deviance as discussed in Chapters 15 and 17.

Genetic Crime Causation: The XYY Hypothesis

Before we discuss chromosomal abnormalities as a possible biological cause of crime and delinquency, a brief review of basic genetics will prove useful. Each human cell has 46 chromosomes. Upon conception, each parent donates 23 gene-carrying chromosomes concerned with
the transmission and development of hereditary characteristics. These chromosomes combine
into 46 chromosomes in the offspring. Among the 46 chromosomes is a set which determines
sex. The female has two X chromosomes, referred to as XX. The male has one X and one Y
chromosome, referred to as XY. The X chromosome, because it is inherited from the mother,
is believed by some to convey gentle and passive traits; the Y chromosome, inherited from the
father, is thought to carry tough and aggressive traits. Normal males, then, described as 46XY,
are those in whom gentle and tough characteristics supposedly balance each other.

Occasionally, a male will have an extra Y chromosome, indicated by the symbol
47XYY. Although males with this chromosomal abnormality comprise only about one-seventh
of one percent of the male population, the existence of an extra Y chromosome has led to
the XYY hypothesis: "Men cursed with this rare cellular structure are predisposed to violent, antisocial acts" (Rosenberg et al., 1982:6).

The major characteristics of these people are that they are a little mentally re-
tarded, have too much acne on their faces, stand taller than the average normal
male, and—most importantly—have a strong tendency to be unusually aggressive.
Thus it has been theorized that the extra Y chromosome can drive the XYY male
into committing a dangerous, violent crime such as murder (Thio, 1998:73).

The XYY hypothesis has fueled a rash of speculation and some research efforts to collect
supporting data. Richard Fox (1971) studied inmates of prisons and mental institutions and
found that as many as three percent displayed the 47XYY characteristics, compared to an estimated frequency for the abnormality of 0.13 percent among the population at large. In addi-

tion, several highly publicized, violent crimes between 1942 and 1968 were found to have been committed by individuals with an XYY constitution. Richard Speck, who in 1967 murdered eight nurses in Chicago, was alleged to have the 47XYY trait. The quality of such information is overstated and highly questionable as a basis for establishing a valid connection between human genetic background and antisocial behavior. Not to be overlooked is the fact that the vast majority of murderers apparently do not have an XYY chromosome pattern. Moreover, the sample of prisoners who have been tested is biased, since many criminals are not confined in institutions and therefore not subject to chromosomal analysis. Nor is the true prevalence of XYY in the general population known. Put differently, no one can tell how many XYY men are noncriminals and serve as model members of their communities.

Social scientists hasten to point out that the suspected connection between biology and behavior is more complex than it appears. Even though an extra Y chromosome may have the potential to lead its carrier to violent behavior, sociocultural factors supply the triggering mechanism and largely determine whether the potentiality will become an actuality. As one geneticist admits:

> *A social mechanism is entirely possible. Large, possibly slightly retarded, males may be ridiculed...and may respond aggressively. In any case, it would appear that of the total amount of violence in our society only a very small part is contributed by XYY individuals (McClearn, 1969:1003).*

Despite the absence of convincing empirical evidence supporting a possible connection between chromosomal abnormality and criminal behavior, several premature and radical proposals have been made to incorporate the idea into correctional practices, even as a predictive tool for identifying potential delinquents. For example:

> *[The most] frightening...is a suggestion made in 1971 by Arnold Hutschnecker, one of President Nixon's personal medical advisors. Hutschnecker, a physician, proposed a massive program of chromosomal screening for every six-year-old in the country. He suggested that "hard core" six-year-olds showing evidence of criminal potential be sent to "therapeutic" camps where they could learn to be "good social animals." This particular plan was sent to Elliot Richardson, Secretary of Health, Education and Welfare, for consideration. Richardson turned down the plan "because it was not feasible to implement on a national scale, at that time." (Hunt, 1973; Moran, 1978:347; cited in Thornton and Voigt, 1992:120–121).*

Concerned over popularized speculation and gross generalization that "crime is in the genes" (Wilson and Herrnstein, 1985), more cautious criminologists (Gibbons, 1990:199) continue to question research methodology and suggest that we may be seeing bad research rather than bad genes (Walters and White, 1989).

Diet and Deviant Behavior

One of the more plausible and promising areas of contemporary research into possible organic causes for misbehavior is the apparent association between dietary deficiencies and biochemical irregularities which cause some youngsters to become hyperactive, unruly, and

BOX 4-2   Cross-Cultural Focus

The Study of Twins and Adopted Children in Scandinavia

For over 50 years, the study of twins has suggested a tantalizing avenue of inquiry for researchers pursuing the illusive relationship between human biology and antisocial behavior. Twins offer unique opportunities to identify, separate, compare, and contrast the effects of heredity and environment.

Genetically and in physical appearance, twins are classified into two categories. Fraternal twins are no more similar than single-birth siblings. On the other hand, identical twins result from the double fertilization of a single egg. They have exactly the same genetic blueprint and look much alike.

Criminologists who have done research on twins have been motivated by the general assumption that if delinquent behavior is an inherited propensity, twins should be similar in such conduct since they share a common genetic makeup. It soon became apparent, however, that this approach contained a serious methodological flaw. Odd Steffen Dalgard and Einar Kringlen (1976), in their "Norwegian Twin Study of Criminality," argued convincingly that because of their uniformities, twins are treated as twins by society. Twins almost always are reared together in the same family, they share the same social experience at school, and they elicit the same societal responses from their community. Consequently, critics have contended, the similar behavior of twins—delinquent or otherwise—may result from their social environment as well as from genetic inheritance.

In order to resolve this dilemma and more rigorously separate and control social influences in testing the hypothesis that serious deviant behavior has a genetic basis, researchers turned to the study of adopted children. The most extensive and promising investigations of this type have been conducted by Sarnoff Mednick and his associates in Denmark where detailed, longitudinal data on the criminal involvement of adoptees, and their biological and adoptive parents, were made available to the researchers.

In 1971, the Mednick group analyzed the records of criminal behavior for 1,146 male adoptees and their biological and adoptive fathers. These researchers also began a similar but larger study in the 1980s of over 14,000 male and female adoptees.

This latter study also included the records of criminality of biological and adoptive mothers and fathers. The methodology was strengthened in both studies as adoptees were matched carefully for age, gender, place of residence, and occupational status of fathers with nonadoptee control groups of equal size. The many interesting findings and conclusions that emerged from the Danish studies of Sarnoff and his colleagues included the following:

1. They found that 31 percent of the biological fathers of convicted male delinquents had criminal records compared to just 13 percent of the adoptive fathers of the same youth group (Hutchings and Mednick, 1977).

Social scientists in their studies of twins are trying to unravel the complex interplay between nature and nurture—biology and environment—as these two powerful forces may be related to the delinquent behavior of some children later in life.

2. The biological mothers of convicted female adoptees were significantly more likely to have more criminal convictions to their credit than the adoptive mothers of the same cohort of young female adoptees (Mednick et al., 1986).

Continued

BOX 4-2　*Continued*

The Mednick group concluded from their extensive adoption studies that there is an important and persistent relationship between criminal parents and the criminal behavior of their biological offspring. The fact that the children in their samples had been separated from their natural parents and raised by adoptive parents underscores the possibility of a genetic connection (Mednick and Gabriella, 1984).[1]

Social scientists have continued to criticize adoption research on methodological grounds. As yet, they argue, the complex and confounding effects of nature and nurture are not disentangled and adequately controlled. For example, there was wide variance in age at adoption of subjects. Ideally, all adopted subjects should have been removed as very-young infants from their biological parents and other elements of their original social environments. Even more disturbing to validity is the fact that the Danish adoption agencies went to considerable pains to match biological and adoptive parents on socioeconomic status and other important social variables— thus effectively duplicating and perhaps reinforcing the original social milieu of many subjects.

Sources

Dalgard, O. S., and Kringlen, E. 1976. A Norwegian twin study of criminality. *British Journal of Criminology* 16, 213–232.

Hutchings, B., and Mednick, S. A. 1977. Criminality in adoptees and their adoptive and biological parents: A pilot study. In S. A. Mednick and K. A. Christiansen (Eds.). *Biological bases of criminal behavior.* New York: Gardner Press.

Mednick, S. A., and Gabriella, W. F. 1984. Genetic influences in criminal convictions: Evidence from an adoption cohort. *Science* 224, 25 (May):891–894. (Copyright 1984 by the American Association for Advancement of Science.)

Mednick, S. A., Moffitt, T., Gabrielli, W., and Hutchings, B. 1986. Genetic factors in criminal behavior: A review. In D. Olweus, J. Block, and M. Radke-Yarrow (Eds.). *Development of antisocial and preschool behavior.* Orlando, FL: Academic Press.

Rosen, C. M. 1987. The eerie world of reunited twins. *Discover* 8, 9 (September):36–46.

[1] A large and ongoing study involving several hundred sets of twins and a limited number of triplets (reared together and separately) was launched in 1979 by Thomas Bouchard, Jr. at the University of Minnesota, Minneapolis. While not directly focusing on delinquent and criminal behavior, Bouchard and his associates' effort to disentangle the effects of heredity and environment include evaluating their subjects for such traits as impulsiveness, aggressiveness, stress reaction, and alienation (Rosen 1987). Ultimately, such information could prove to be extremely useful to students of deviant and antisocial behavior.

delinquent. Students of nutrition as it relates to human behavior are amassing considerable and convincing evidence that children who develop poor nutritional habits can grow into disturbed adolescents and violent adults (Rimland and Larson, 1981). "Because their bodies are smaller,...and because their minds and bodies are still developing, children are especially vulnerable to the dietary risks we all experience" (Reed et al., 1983:118).

The popular overconsumption of junk foods and refined carbohydrates by youths in the United States is increasingly suspected by researchers as a culprit in stimulating some aggressive and antisocial behavior. Not only can such foods quickly raise blood sugar levels, but they may temporarily impair the brain's ability to perceive, process information, and regulate behavior. Lonsdale and Shamberger (1980) examined a group of children whose marginal malnutrition was traced to a junk food diet high in sugar. The devastating effects included reduced self-control and troublesome behavior. Lonsdale and Shamberger (1980: 210) concluded:

Scientifically, we have reason to believe that this approach to diet is changing the balance of neurological transmission which is the hallmark of the function of the brain and the central nervous system. It means that the quality and quantity of nu-trition can change your behavior.

Criminologists Alexander Schauss and Clifford Simonsen, along with University of Puget Sound chemistry professor Jeffrey Bland, conducted an analysis of the diets of chronic juvenile offenders (Schauss et al., 1979). They found that on average the juveniles ingested 32 percent more sugar than a control group of children who were behaviorally disordered but had no criminal record (Reed et al., 1983). A remarkable experiment was conducted by Stephen Schoenthaler and Walter Doraz (1983) in which refined sugar was drastically reduced in the diets of 276 incarcerated youths. Honey and molasses were substituted for sugar, fruit juices took the place of beverages with high sugar content, and so forth. In a short while the dietary modifications apparently resulted in behavior modification among the subjects. Schoenthaler and Doraz (1983) reported that physical assaults, fighting, thefts, and various other forms of disobedience were reduced by nearly 45 percent.

A study conducted by scientists at the Massachusetts Institute of Technology (Matthews, 1983) has raised some doubts about the premise that the consumption of high sugar products by children is the sole or determining culprit in producing unacceptable behavior. These researchers think that it is the colossal amount of caffeine children ingest in soft drinks and iced tea that causes hyperactivity. Caffeine also interferes with the way the brain processes stimuli. Another contradictory opinion has emerged from controlled experiments conducted by Richard Milich and William Pelham (1986) on the effects of sugar ingested by school children. They found little support for the suggested relationship between diet and antisocial conduct.

Nevertheless, studies continue to accumulate in the quest for a subtle but direct link between diet and deviant behavior. Food additives and preservatives—previously considered generally safe for human consumption—are now suspected of causing numerous allergic reactions including hyperactivity, learning disability, and aberrant behavior. For example, Schauss and his associates (1979) discovered that hundreds of chronic juvenile offenders drank on average 12 to 15 eight-ounce glasses of milk per day! The researchers theorized that preservatives in the milk caused the impaired behavior. While commercial food producers are likely to be dismayed and to challenge such findings, such promising research inquiries regarding causal linkages between diet and criminal or delinquent behavior should be encouraged.

Brain Malfunctions

Since 1959, the administration of the electroencephalograph (EEG) test to criminal and delinquent offenders has aroused considerable interest. The theory holds that the brains of some deviants emit electric waves of abnormal frequency. While some fragmentary findings support this contention in a very general and tenuous way, much more refined and systematic research needs to be done in this area:

> *In 143 cases…a high percentage of EEG changes was found among abnormal personalities…It was emphasized that the EEG may only answer the question as to the existence of a brain lesion which in turn is frequently causally associated with behavioral disturbances (Schulz and Mainusch, 1971).*

Similarly, many studies searching for connections between hyperactivity, brain damage, and delinquent behavior have produced inconsistent and controversial findings. For example, Lee Robins (1978) and James Satterfield (1978) found unusually high incidences of hyperactivity among the delinquent children in their studies. This hyperactivity, or *hyperkinesis,* is characterized not only by frenetic activity, but often by learning disabilities, extreme aggressiveness, and the inability or refusal to clearly distinguish between right and wrong. The conclusion that this deviant behavior has a biological connection is based on the hypothesis that some of these hyperkinetic children may be suffering minimal brain damage due to birth injury and/or heredity. Other researchers (Broder et al., 1978; Conrad, 1975) vigorously disagreed. The latter group not only challenged the basic premise of "minimal brain damage" as a valid diagnosis, but found no evidence supporting such a biological connection with deviant or delinquent behavior.

Another avenue of inquiry has focused on the association between learning disability and youth crime. A 1975 survey of all youngsters admitted to correctional institutions in Colorado found that an astonishing 90 percent had some form of learning disability (Poremba, 1975). The learning disability known as dyslexia has come under special scrutiny. **Dyslexia** is *a brain malfunction whereby visual signs are scrambled.* For example, the dyslexic child might see the letters and words on this page in reverse order or perhaps upside down. Consequently, average skills in reading, spelling, and arithmetic are impossible to attain if the malady remains undiagnosed. Until recent years, little was known about this type of cognitive abnormality, and teachers often misinterpreted the learning difficulties of apparently healthy children as laziness. Sometimes dyslexic children are assumed to be retarded; as their frustration and alienation deepens, they often become emotionally maladjusted, hostile, and delinquent. Ultimately, this learning disability can lead to their being expelled from school or dropping out entirely and never reaching full intellectual potential (Eitzen, 1986:398; Murray, 1976). A growing public awareness of dyslexia and its implications about learning and disciplinary problems for afflicted children has led to the creation of special diagnostic and educational programs in most states.

A more current and promising research approach in this area has sought to synchronize events from both nature and nurture that may be causally related to violent and delinquent behavior in some youths. In the 1990s, several investigators found statistical support for the thesis that children who have experienced traumatic birth complications plus early rejection by their mothers are likely candidates for violent criminality later in life.

> *In 1993, Stephen Buka and Felton Earls of the Harvard School of Public Health reviewed the body of research in the scholarly journal* Health Affairs. *The best predictors of violent behavior included prenatal and perinatal complications. Considerable evidence links these complications with brain dysfunction, including impaired intelligence and attention deficit disorder, which have been linked with antisocial and delinquent behavior later on....*

Many of the same factors were outlined in a 1993 National Research Council report, *Understanding and Preventing Violence.* According to that report, adult violent offenders displayed certain personality features as children, including hyperactivity, risk-taking, acting impulsively, poor attention span, low IQ, and low empathy. They also tended to be abused or neglected and lacked parental nurturing.

The report also lists neurobiological factors linked to poor school performance and poor relationships with other children, which are then linked with later aggressive behavior. Key among these are childhood head injuries, inadequate prenatal care, and ingestion of lead paint (Friend, 1994: 5D).

Among other areas of investigation into brain disorders as they relate to juvenile and adult criminality include a focus on brain tumors (Kletschka, 1966), epilepsy which may be related to diminished self-control (Pollock, et al., 1983), and a growing interest in the effects of environmental pollution on the brain and concomitant high delinquency and crime rates in urban areas (Londer, 1987).

> *Evidence that chemicals in the air we breathe affect our brains is growing. Scientists suspect that the airborne toxins turn some people to violence. In Los Angeles, for example, and other cities, hot weather can worsen the effects of pollution. That's when some people, goaded by bad air, come out swinging (Londer, 1987:6).*

It is expected that the hypothesized ecological connections with brain malfunctions and delinquency will continue to be challenging research topics.

Sociobiological Explanations

One of the most imaginative and controversial directions for scholarly inquiry on the biological basis for deviant behavior lies in the relatively new field of sociobiology, which combines elements of several biological subareas in explaining social behaviors among animals and humans. A major proponent is Edward O. Wilson (1975), a Harvard University zoologist specializing in the study of insect life. Wilson (1978:16) defines **sociobiology** as follows:

> *The systematic study of the biological basis of all forms of social behavior, in all kinds of organisms, including man...[is a] hybrid discipline that incorporates knowledge from ethology (the naturalistic study of whole patterns of behavior), ecology (the study of the relationships of organisms to their environment), and genetics in order to derive general principles concerning the biological properties of entire societies.*

Sociobiologists maintain that social behavior is a product of evolutionary history and genetics. Just as Charles Darwin traced the evolution of physical traits, sociobiologists attempt to do the same for social behaviors. It is generally accepted that some of the social behavior of monkeys and apes was adapted in the long course of evolution into their biological endowment. That is, behavior that promotes survival is passed on to the offspring of such species through inherited genes. This involves temperament and personality traits as well as physical characteristics. Thus, for male animals, physical traits that assist in the hunt, such as quickness and motor skills, are supplemented by an aggressive disposition. For females, the biological ability to become pregnant is supported by nesting and nurturing instincts. Sociobiologists claim that these and many other predispositions toward personal and species survival are genetically programmed into the organism.

Despite the fact that no one has yet isolated any of those genes in humans, some sociobiologists have enthusiastically made wholesale transfer of the conclusions regarding the assumed life-and-death genetic struggle of lower animals to human beings. For example, they explain kinship ties, social bonding, and the incest taboo as reflecting unconscious inborn needs to protect and perpetuate one's own genetic endowment. Similarly, according to some sociobiologists, several million years of human biological-genetic evolution have made us aggressive, acquisitive, and apparently amoral at times, since these characteristics and behaviors can enhance gene survival. Thus, through sociobiological reasoning, another deterministic explanation has been made for what ordinarily appears as deviant, criminal, and delinquent behavior.

The position that perceives human behavior as genetically programmed has elicited vigorous opposition from those espousing the view that human conduct is, in general, culturally relative. Austin Turk (1969: 10–11) spoke for many social scientists by arguing that validation of biological-predisposition hypotheses would require us to agree that there are persons born to commit certain acts that will invariably be criminal—anywhere and everywhere. On the contrary, Turk contends:

> *There is apparently no pattern of human behavior which has not been at least tolerated in some normative structure. While there do seem to be universal categories of norms (e.g., norms limiting the use of violence) no specific explicit or implicit rule has ever been shown to be present in all human societies... From the absence of universal norms it follows that research on the etiology of any specific form of "criminal" behavior must inevitably be culture-specific and time-bound, because the phenomenon under study will change from culture to culture...*

In addition to the criticism that sociobiology does not take culture into account, and that culture is dominant over most genetic, inherited, behavioral tendencies, other opponents contend that the application of animal instincts to human beings is nothing more than a grossly imperfect transfer by analogy. Thus, sociobiologists assume: they are animals and we are animals; all species are the result of a long evolutionary process; therefore the same inherited survival needs and instincts that characterize other primates also may be invoked to explain human behavior. Critics of sociobiology argue that these assumptions are simplistic in light of the sophistication and complexity of the human organism and human societies. Finally, critics point out that the essential principles and hypotheses of sociobiology are scientifically untestable and therefore remain nothing more than interesting speculations.

SUMMARY AND CONCLUSION

We began this chapter by exploring some of the myths and folklore that attempted to directly link biology to behavior. We pointed out how many of these attempts led to racial and ethnic slurs and created some unfair stereotypes.

The eighteenth century gave rise to the Classical School of Criminological Thought, which assumed that crime/delinquency was the result of the exercise of free will and logical, rational thought. The Neoclassical School

BOX 4-3   Controversial Issue

Heredity Versus Environment in Deviant and Delinquent Behavior

Numerous efforts are being made to utilize sociobiology in the study of deviant behavior. For example, Sarnoff A. Mednick (1977), in harmony with the sociobiological perspective, argued that law-abiding behavior must be learned; that it is not inherent in people to conform to the normative behavioral expectations that prevail in their social group. Mednick theorized that people learn to conform because they are afraid to deviate. He acknowledged that this learning process is an intrinsic part of the culture content of a people. Furthermore, he indicated that the vast majority of cases of deviant and criminal behavior can be traced to socioeconomic and situational factors that temporarily neutralize the socially learned avoidance of punishment. Nevertheless, there remains a very small number of deviant individuals whose antisocial behavior falls into a consistent pattern and for which there is no apparent social cause. Mednick's research concentrated on that minority of offenders and suggested that their habitual misconduct is caused by an autonomic nervous system that is biologically unique to them. Their autonomic nervous system recovers very quickly from threats and fear of social punishment for misdeeds, thus reinforcing their ability to inhibit previously learned conformity responses:

> As Mednick points out, his is a learning theory. It is a social learning theory to the extent that people's behavior is influenced by previous reactions of others. It is a biological theory to the extent that biological factors (in this case, the ANS) regulate the efficiency of the learning process. (McCaghy and Capron, 1997:43)

Thus far, the main thrust of sociobiology has been centered on animal behavior. However, as new findings accumulate and subsequently are extended to explain human behavior, we may expect renewed controversy and debate between extremists in both the biological and social science camps. As one scholar put it:

> Unfortunately, most of the debate concerning genetic aspects of human behavior has been highly emotional and, hence, extremist in each direction. On the one hand, many social scientists advocate that human beings are born as tabula rasa, blank slates with infinite potential to become anything at all, depending only on experience. On the other end of the spectrum is extreme genetic determinism, in which free will and the capacity for self-betterment are denied, and we are literally prisoners of our heredity. As usual in such outlandish debates, the truth doubtless lies somewhere in between. (Dobzhansky, 1976: 169) [italics in original]

Other leading scholars in sociobiology have taken a moderating and compromising position. Barash (1982:146) cautiously declared that sociobiologists are justified in assuming an influence of genetics in human behavior although not necessarily a controlling influence. On the other hand, most social scientists feel that any conclusions regarding the validity of sociobiology are premature and must await the empirical testing and theoretical scrutiny to which all established theories have been subjected.

Sources

Barash, D. P. 1982. *Sociobiology and behavior* (2nd ed.). New York: Elsevier.

Dobzhansky, T. 1976. The myths of genetic predestination and of tabula rasa. *Perspectives in Biology and Medicine* 19:156–170.

McCaghy, Charles H., and Capron, Timothy A. 1997. *Deviant behavior: Crime, conflict, and interest groups.* (4th ed.). Boston: Allyn and Bacon.

Mednick, Sarnoff A. 1977. A biosocial theory of the learning of law-abiding behavior. In S. A. Mednick and K. O. Christioasen (Eds.). *Biosocial bases of criminal behavior.* New York: Garden Press.

modified the assumptions of the classical theorists by allowing for extenuating circumstances, and recognized that not all people are equally rational. This allowed for some discretion and differential treatment for young offenders, or adults who were adjudged mentally incompetent.

In the late nineteenth century, the Positive School of Criminology developed, and through the leadership of men like Cesare Lombroso attempted to scientifically link biological and physiological characteristics to criminal behavior. This biological determinism laid the foundation for twentieth century research which sought to attribute character, personality, and delinquency potential to the shape of one's body. As the search for a biological connection to delinquency has continued, research has been conducted on many biological variables such as sex, race, age, ethnicity, genetics, diet, and brain malfunctions (Fishbein, 1990).

In an attempt to link biological determinism with the contributing influence of social and cultural factors, sociobiological explanations for delinquency emerged. Sociobiologists insist that social behavior is a product of evolutionary history and genetics. Hence, delinquent behavior is viewed as being genetically programmed into certain individuals.

Social scientists have acknowledged that genetics, biology, and physiology may all play an important role in understanding juvenile delinquency. However, they insist that it is the manner in which these traits are manifested and dealt with in a social and cultural context that explains deviant behavior.

It is apparent that the Gluecks' insightful conclusion—that physical characteristics may be socially defined and treated in ways that encourage criminal or delinquent behavior—sheds light on the probable relationship between biology and sociology (Horton, et al., 1997:82). C. R. Jeffery (1979) suggested that the interaction between biological traits and social factors represents a powerful force in producing deviant or delinquent behavior.

Donald Shoemaker (2000:22) utilized the diagram shown in Figure 4-1 to illustrate and argue that there is more than one plausible connection between the biological makeup of a youth and the youth's delinquent behavior. For example, the long arrow represents the direct relationship between biological factors or medical conditions such as a brain tumor or a dietary problem that can lead to juvenile misconduct. This direct causation approach bypasses social and cultural factors that may combine with biological and/or physiological traits to produce delinquent behavior. The latter possibility is depicted by the shorter arrows in Figure 4-1 that link unfavorable biological factors with negative circumstances in the social environment such as an unhappy home life, inadequate parental nurturing and role models, poor academic performance in school, and/or the presence of delinquent peers in the neighborhood. Together, these biological and social factors interact to produce or generate antisocial behavior in the youth.

Concept Integration

Questions and Topics for Study and Discussion

1. Reexamine the research of Lombroso, Sheldon, and the Gluecks. Identify and critique their methodology, findings, and conclusions.

2. What are the main assumptions of the Classical School of Criminological Thought and the Positive School of Criminology? What are the differences

FIGURE 4-1   Relationship Between Biological and Social Factors in Producing Deviant and Delinquent Behavior

Source: Adapted from Shoemaker, D. *Theories of Delinquency*. New York: Oxford Press, 2000:22. Reprinted by permission.

between these two early approaches to explain criminal behavior?

3. Discuss and explain the hypothesized links between the following variables:
   (a) The XYY chromosome and criminal behavior.
   (b) Abnormal EEG patterns and deviant or criminal behavior.
   (c) Diet, biochemical irregularities, and misbehavior.

4. Crime statistics show that males commit more violent crimes than females. Based on your reading of this chapter, why might this be so? Is this pattern changing? If so, why?

5. Carefully define and explain "sociobiology." How does this field of study attempt to bridge the social and biological sciences? What contribution may sociobiology make toward an understanding of human behavior?

6. Why are rates of crime and delinquency highest in the inner city? How did Shaw and McKay explain the relationship between race/ethnicity, socioeconomic status, place of residence, and rates of crime and delinquency?

7. What did the Gluecks mean by their statement: "A physical characteristic may be socially defined and treated in ways which encourage criminal behavior?" Give several examples.

8. Define the following terms and concepts: biological determinism, atavism, constitutional typology, phrenology, endomorph, ectomorph, mesomorph, electroencephalograph, tabula rasa, chromosomal abnormality, dyslexia, Deterrence Theory, and maturation effect.

References

Adler, F. 1975. *Sisters in crime.* New York: McGraw-Hill Book Co.

Agnew, R. 1984. Appearance and delinquency. *Criminology* 22, 2 (August):421–440.

Albanese, J. S. 1993. *Dealing with delinquency: The future of juvenile justice* (2nd ed.). Chicago: Nelson-Hall Publishers.

Barsley, M. 1966. *Some of my best friends are left-handed people.* Hollywood, CA: Wilshire Book Company.

Blumstein, A. 1995. Violence by young people: Why the deadly nexus? *National Institute of Justice Journal.* Washington, DC: U.S. Department of Justice, Office of Justice Programs, National Institute of Justice. August, 1995:2–9.

Blumstein, A., Cohen, J., Roth, J., and Visher, C. 1986. *Criminal careers and "career criminals".* Washington, D.C.: National Academy Press.

Broder, P. K., Peters, G. W., and Zimmerman, J. 1978. The relationship between self-reported juvenile delinquency and learning disabilities: A preliminary look at the data. Omaha, NE: Creighton University Institute for Business, Law, and Social Research.

Brothers, J. 1985. Women and violent crime. Fort Worth, TX: *Star Telegram.* June 15, 1985:D-3.

Chance, P. 1988. Biology, destiny, and all that. *Across the Board.* July/August 1988, pp. 19–23.

Chesney-Lind, M., and Shelden, R.G. 1998. *Girls: Delinquency and juvenile justice* (2nd ed.). Belmont, CA: Wadsworth Publishing Company.

Clinard, M. B., and Meier, R. F. 1998. *Sociology of deviant behavior* (10th ed.). Ft. Worth: Holt, Rinehart and Winston.

Cohen, A. K. 1966. *Deviance and control.* Englewood Cliffs, NJ: Prentice-Hall.

Conrad, P. 1975. The discovery of hyperkinesis: Notes on the medicalization of deviant behavior. *Social Problems* XXIII, 2 (April:12–22).

Eitzen, D. S., and Zinn, M. B. 1997. *Social problems* (7th ed.). Boston: Allyn and Bacon.

Elliot, D. S., and Dibert, R. L. 1991. Delinquency and sexual behavior: Concomitance and developmental progression. National Youth Survey. Institute of Behavioral Sciences, University of Colorado. Boulder, CO. Nov. 18, 1991.

Emporia Gazette (Newspaper). 1985. Misbehavior during puberty linked to hormonal changes. Emporia, KA. May 28, 1985.

Erikson, E. 1956. The problem of identity. *Journal of the American Psychiatric Association* 4, 1 (January): 56–121.

Federal Bureau of Investigation. 1996. *Crime in the United States: Uniform Crime Reports—1995.*

Washington, DC: U.S. Government Printing Office.

Ferrero, G. L. 1911. *Criminal man according to the classification of Cesare Lombroso.* New York: Putnam.

Final report, state task force on youth gang violence. 1986. Sacramento, CA: California Council on Criminal Justice.

Fishbein, D. H. 1990. Biological perspectives in criminology. *Criminology* 28, 1:27–72.

Fox, R. G. 1971. The XYY offender: A modern myth? *Journal of Criminal Law, Criminology and Police Science* 62, 1:63.

Friend, T. 1994. Violence-prone men may be both born and made. *USA TODAY,* December 14, 1994:5D.

Gibbons, D. 1990. From the editor's desk: A call for some "outrageous" proposals for crime control in the 1990s. *Crime and Delinquency.* 36, 2 (April): 197–203.

Glueck, S., and Glueck, E. 1950. *Unraveling juvenile delinquency.* Cambridge: Harvard University Press.

Goring, C. [1913] 1972. *The English convict: A statistical study.* Montclair, NJ: Patterson Smith.

Hagan, J. A., Gillis, R., and Simpson, J. 1985. The class structure of gender and delinquency: Toward a power-control theory of common delinquent behavior. *American Journal of Sociology.* 90:1151–78.

Hartl, E. M., Monelly, E. P., and Elderkin, R. D. 1982. *Physique and delinquent behavior.* New York: Academic Press.

Hindelang, M. J., Hirschi, T., and Weis, J. G. 1979. Correlates of delinquency: The illusion of discrepancy between self-report and official measures. *American Sociological Review* 44 (December): 995–1014. 1981. *Measuring Delinquency.* Beverly Hills, CA: Sage.

Hirschi, T., and Gottfredson, M. 1983. Age and the explanation of crime. *American Journal of Sociology* 89:552–584.

Horton, P. B., Leslie, G. R., Larson, R. F., and Horton, R. L. 1997. *The sociology of social problems* (12th ed.). Saddle River, NJ: Prentice Hall.

Howard, J., and Hammond, R. 1991. The hidden obstacles to black success: Rumors of inferiority. In *Annual editions: Human development, 1991/1992.* (Larry Fenson and Judith Fenson, Editors). Guilford, CT:142–146.

Huff, C. R. 1988. Youth gangs and public policy in Ohio: Findings and recommendations, unpublished report at the Ohio Conference on Youth Gangs and the Urban Underclass. Columbus, OH: May 25, 1988.

Hunt, J. 1973. Rapists have big ears: Genetic screening in Massachusetts. *The Real Paper,* July 4, 1973:4.

Jackson, L. L. 1993. *Success under probation and parole supervision: A maturation and gender comparison.* Unpublished Master's Thesis. Stillwater, OK: Oklahoma State University. May, 1993.

Jeffery, C. R. 1979. *Biology and crime.* Beverly Hills, CA: Sage.

Klein, M. 1969. Violence in American juvenile gangs. In D. Mulvihill, M. Tumin, with L. Curtis (Eds.). *Crimes of violence.* National Commission on the Causes and Prevention of Violence, Vol. 13. Washington, DC: U.S. Government Printing Office, p. 1429.

Kletschka, H. D. 1966. Violent behavior associated with brain tumors. *Minnesota Medicine* 49:1835–1855.

Londer, R. 1987 Can bad air make bad things happen? *Parade Magazine.* August 9, 1987. Pp. 6–7.

Lombroso, C. 1911. *Crime, its causes and remedies* (trans. H. P. Horton). Boston: Little, Brown.

Lonsdale, D., and Shamberger, R. J. 1980. Red cell transketolase as an indicator of nutritional deficiency. *American Journal of Clinical Nutrition* 33 (February):205–211.

Matthews, F. 1983. Diet to help you beat the blues. *National Examiner.* July 26, 1983. P. 31.

McCaghy, C. H., and Capron, T. A. 1997. *Deviant behavior: Crime, conflict, and interest groups* (4th ed.). Boston: Allyn and Bacon.

McClearn, G. E. 1969. Biological bases of social behavior with specific reference to violent behavior. In D. Mulvihill, M. Tumin, with L. Curtis (Eds.) *Crimes of violence.* Staff Report to the National Commission on Causes and Prevention of Violence, Vol. 13. Washington, DC: U.S. Government Printing Office, p. 1003.

Milich, R., and Pelham, W. 1986. Effects of sugar ingestion on the classroom and playground behavior of attention deficit disordered boys. *Journal of Counseling and Clinical Psychology* 54:714–718.

Miller, W. 1975. *Violence by youth gangs and youth groups as a crime problem in major American cities.* Washington, DC: U.S. Government Printing Office.

Moran, R. 1978. Biomedical research and the politics of crime control: A historical perspective. *Contemporary Crises* 2:335–357.

Murray, C. A. 1976. *The link between learning disabilities and juvenile delinquency.* Washington, DC: U.S. Department of justice.

Newman, G. 1978. *The punishment response.* Philadelphia: JB Lippincott.

Osgood, D. W., Johnston, L. D., O'Malley, P. M., and Bachman, J. G. 1988. The generality of deviance in late adolescence and early adulthood. *American Sociological Review* 53 (February):81–93.

Pollock, V., Mednick, S. A., and Gabrielli, Jr., W. F. 1983. Crime causation: Biological theories. In *Encyclopedia of Crime and Justice,* Vol. 1 (Sanford H. Kadish, ed.). New York: Free Press.

Poremba, C. D. 1975. Learning disabilities, youth and delinquency: Programs for intervention. In H. R. Myklebust (Ed.) *Progress in learning disabilities,* Vol. 3. New York: Grune and Stratton, pp. 123–149.

Reed, B., Knickelbine, S., and Knickelbine, M. 1983. *Food, teens, and behavior.* Manitowoc, WI: Natural Press.

Rimland, B., and Larson, G. E. 1981. Nutritional and ecological approaches to the reduction of criminality, delinquency, and violence. In *Journal of Applied Nutrition,* 33, 2. (In R. A. Weisheit and G. Culbertson (Eds.). *Juvenile delinquency: A justice perspective* (2nd ed.). 1990. Prospect Heights, IL: Waveland Press, Inc., pp. 55–68.

Robins, L. N. 1978. Aetiological implications in studies of childhood histories relating to antisocial personality. In R. D. Hare, and D. Schalling (Eds.) *Psychopathic behavior; Approaches to research.* New York: John Wiley, pp. 252–272.

Rosenberg, M. M., Stebbins, R. A., and Turowetz, A. (Eds.) 1982. *The sociology of deviance.* New York: St. Martin's Press.

Salzman, L. 1980. *Treatment of the obsessive personality.* New York: Jason Aronson, Inc.

Sampson, R., and Laub, J. 1993. *Crime in the making.* Cambridge: Harvard University Press.

Sandhu, H. S. 1974. *Modern corrections: The offenders, therapies and treatments.* Springfield: Charles C. Thomas, Publisher.

Satterfield, J. H. 1978. The hyperactive child syndrome: A precursor of adult psychopathy? In R. D. Hare, and D. Schalling (Eds.) *Psychopathic behavior: Approaches to research.* New York: John Wiley, pp. 329–346.

Schauss, A., Simonsen, C., and Bland, J. 1979. Critical analysis of the diets of chronic juvenile offenders, Part 1. *Journal of Orthomolecular Psychiatry,* 8, 3:149–157.

Schlapp, M. G., and Smith, E. H. 1928. *The new criminology.* New York: Boni and Liveright.

Schoenthaler, S., and Doraz, W. 1983. Type of offenses which can be reduced in an institutional setting using nutritional intervention. *International Journal of Biosocial Research* 4:74–84. And item, Diet and crime. In *International Journal of Biosocial Research* 4:29–39.

Schulz, H., and Mainusch, G. 1971. Contribution of clinical electroencephalography to forensic expert opinion. Summarized in *Abstracts on Criminology and Penology.* W. K. Nagel (Ed.) 11, 478:138–139. The Hague: A. E. Klewer, Deventer.

Shaw, C. R., and McKay, H. D. 1969. *Juvenile delinquency in urban areas.* Chicago: University of Chicago Press.

Sheldon, W., Hartl, E. M., and McDermott, F. 1949. *Varieties of delinquent youth.* New York: Harper & Row.

Shoemaker, D. J. 2000 (4th ed.). *Theories of delinquency: An examination of explanations of delinquent behavior.* New York: Oxford University Press.

Short, J. F., and Strodtbeck, F. 1965. *Group process and gang delinquency.* Chicago: University of Chicago Press.

Siegel, L. J., and Senna, J. J. 1997. *Juvenile delinquency: Theory, practice, and law.* (6th ed.) St. Paul, MN: West.

Snyder, H. N., and Sickmund, M. 1999. *Juvenile offenders and victims: 1999 national report.* U.S. Department of Justice, Office of Juvenile Justice and Delinquency Prevention. Pittsburgh: National Center for Juvenile Justice.

Spergel, I. 1964. *Racketville, slumtown, haulberg: An exploratory study of delinquent subcultures.* Chicago: University of Chicago Press.

Stolz, H. R., and Stolz, L. M. 1944. Adolescent problems related to somatic variations. Chapter V. *National Society for the Study of Education.* Adolescence, 43rd Yearbook.

Thio, A. 1998. *Deviant behavior* (5th ed.) New York: Addison-Wesley.

Thornton, W. E., Jr., and Voigt, L. 1992. *Delinquency and justice* (3rd ed.). New York: McGraw-Hill, Inc.

Thrasher, F. 1927. *The gang.* Chicago: University of Chicago Press.

TIME. 1995. February 6, 1995:46.

Turk, A. T. 1969. *Criminality and legal order.* Chicago: Rand-McNally.

van den Haag, E. 1975. *Punishing criminals: Concerning a very old and painful question.* New York: Basic Books.

Walters, G. D., and White, T. W. 1989. Heredity and crime: bad genes or bad research? *Criminology* 27 (August):455–479.

Wilson, E. O. 1975. *Sociobiology: The new synthesis.* Cambridge: Harvard University Press. 1978. *On human nature.* Cambridge: Harvard University Press.

Wilson, J. Q., and Herrnstein, R. J. 1985. *Crime and human nature.* New York: Simon & Schuster.

Wolfgang, M. E., Figlio, R. M., and Sellin, T. 1972. *Delinquency in a birth cohort.* Chicago: University of Chicago Press.

Wright, M. R. 1989. Body image satisfaction and adolescent girls and boys: A longitudinal study. *Journal of Youth and Adolescence* 18, 1:71–83.

5 PSYCHOGENIC EXPLANATIONS OF JUVENILE DELINQUENCY

Reading Objectives

The reading of this chapter will help you achieve the following objectives:

1. Explain the psychological concepts of the unconscious and personality as motivating sources of human behavior, including juvenile delinquency.
2. Describe some of the techniques and tools used by psychiatrists and psychologists, such as psychoanalysis and projective tests, to trace symptomatic conduct disorders to deeply hidden mental stress and conflict.
3. Outline and discuss some of the specific theories developed by psychiatrists and psychologists to explain the causes of juvenile delinquency.
4. Perceive psychologically based juvenile delinquency as organized into a typology of various causes and kinds of misbehavior.
5. Be aware of some major limitations and weaknesses of the psychogenic approaches to identifying and explaining the causes of juvenile delinquency.

Introduction

March 30, 1981, was a cool and rainy day in Washington, D.C. Ronald Reagan, the fortieth President of the United States, was concluding a speech to a labor union convention at the Washington Hilton Hotel. Outside, on the sidewalk near a doorway, a small crowd of people huddled under umbrellas and waited for a glimpse of the President as he exited from the hotel. As the President's entourage came into view, a murmur of friendly greeting came from the crowd, and President Reagan turned to wave and smile before entering the limousine that would carry him back to the White House.

Suddenly, a young man stepped forward on the sidewalk and simultaneously pulled a small automatic pistol from his pocket. Before anyone could react, he assumed a shooter's crouch and rapidly fired at the President. One bullet entered the brain of White House Press

John Hinkley, Jr., the young man charged with the attempted murder of President Ronald Reagan, was finally institutionalized at St. Elizabeth's Mental Hospital in Washington, D.C. Prior to the attack, an armed and ominous Hinkley made this self-portrait with a Polaroid camera.

Secretary, James S. Brady. A Secret Service agent and a Washington policeman were also gunned down and lay sprawled on the sidewalk. Another bullet entered President Reagan's chest, broke a rib, punctured a lung, and lodged near his heart.

In that one frightening and chaotic moment, John W. Hinckley, Jr. became more than just the youngest would-be assassin of a United States President. In Hinckley's long trial that followed his assassination attempt, there was a renewed and intense focus on insanity as an explanation for criminal behavior and as a valid legal defense (Camper et al., 1982). No effort was made to deny that Hinckley had attacked the President's party with murderous intent. After all, news reporters had captured the entire episode on videotape, from the firing of the gun by the expressionless John Hinckley, Jr., to the moment when he was disarmed, subdued, and arrested at the scene. The facts that he had purchased the gun and ammunition with assassination in mind, that he had previously stalked President Carter, that his March 30 attack on President Reagan had been carefully planned, and that he was caught with "the smoking gun in his hand" were readily acknowledged, but received much less attention than Hinckley's mental processes and state of mind leading up to the assassination attempt.

Legal scholars agree that criminal conduct is not enough to elicit sanctions from society. It must be demonstrated to the satisfaction of the court that a criminal offender has **mens rea**—*a guilty mind or evil intent,* in order to be punished. In other words, it must be conclusively established that the offender consciously intended to break the law (Halleck, 1966; Willing, 2000).

Thus, Hinckley's trial was a contest between the professional opinions of psychiatrists, those called as expert witnesses by federal prosecutors, and those who testified for the defense. The prosecution sought to establish that Hinckley was legally sane and therefore fully responsible for his criminal conduct. On the other hand, attorneys for the defense sought to convince the jurors that Hinckley's mental illness was so severe that he lacked substantial capacity to appreciate "the wrongfulness of his acts and could no longer control his own conduct" (*San Francisco Chronicle,* 1981:24). When the long trial ended, John W. Hinckley, Jr. was declared to have "diminished mental capacity" at the time of the assassination attempt. He was sent to St. Elizabeth's Mental Hospital in Washington, D.C. where he received psychiatric evaluation and treatment.

The legal and moral controversy regarding mental illness as it affects human behavior and individual responsibility for one's behavior is not new, nor have we heard the last of it. And this issue has important implications for our study and understanding of the psychogenic explanations of juvenile delinquency (Hinckley and Hinckley, 1985; Simon and Aaronson, 1988).

The Psychogenic Approach

In the nineteenth century, scholars began to accumulate new and important knowledge about human anatomy, physiology, neurology, chemistry, and general medicine. From that, there were many far-reaching implications and applications for the scientific study of human behavior, including some of the early and unsubstantiated biological theories of crime and delinquency discussed in the preceding chapter. More noteworthy, the discovery of an organic basis for many physical illnesses led to the further discovery of an organic basis for some mental illnesses (Reid, 1996). This latter finding lent impetus to the development of psychiatry and psychology as academic disciplines and serious areas of research and knowledge.

Psychiatry is *a medical specialty concerned with the diagnosis, treatment, and prevention of disordered or abnormal behavior.* After completion of their initial medical school education, some physicians take further specialized training in psychiatry in order to become professional psychiatrists. Because psychiatry is a subarea of medicine, psychiatrists tend to view and conceptualize aberrant behavior as caused by some form of mental illness or abnormality. An easy application of this medical model to deviant behavior of juveniles was widely popularized in the late nineteenth century when The Child Savers, an influential group of social reformers, began to use such terms as "disease," "illness," and "contagion" to describe adolescent crime. They promoted the ideas that criminals were the natural product of biological heritage and corrupt urban environments. The Child Savers, together with some prominent penologists of that time, "presupposed that crime was a symptom of 'pathology' and that criminals should be treated like irresponsible, sick patients" (Platt, 1977:45).

Psychology is *a behavioral science that investigates and associates mental processes with behavior.* Psychologists try to understand why people act the way they do by exploring how they grow up, how they react to and cope with stress and change, how their personalities develop, and how they become disturbed or get into trouble:

> *Unlike psychiatry, which is a medical specialty devoted to the understanding and cure of mental disease, psychology has a broader task, ranging from the laboratory study of simple behavior in animals...to the complicated behavior of human beings in social groups (Rehm, 1983:593).*

Although psychiatry and psychology are independent fields of study, they have much in common. Both focus primarily on individuals and perceive human behavior as originating in the mind. Extreme deviance or delinquency is generally seen by psychiatrists and psychologists as overt symptoms or behavioral expressions arising from underlying personality or emotional maladjustments and as alternatives to mental illness (Halleck, 1971).

In addition, psychiatrists and clinical psychologists "devote much of their effort to helping disturbed, troubled, and mentally ill people" (Rehm, 1983:593) and share many similar diagnostic and treatment techniques. In view of the extensive common ground shared by professionals in these two disciplines, psychiatric and psychological contributions will be discussed together as the *psychogenic approach* to human behavior in general and juvenile delinquency in particular.

The Discovery of the Unconscious

The pioneering work of Sigmund Freud (1856–1939) laid the foundation for the twentieth-century psychogenic approach to understanding and explaining human behavior. Freud was originally trained in medicine and neurology but his interest in the aberrant behavior associated with mental illness led him to conclude that biological, physiological, and genetic attributes cannot completely or adequately account for human behavior. He demonstrated that much human conduct is not consciously motivated. Instead, Freud identified a deep, unconscious dimension of the human mind as the motivating source of many acts (Freud, 1961). The **unconscious** may be defined as *a subterranean mental reservoir of unfulfilled needs, desires, and feelings accumulated throughout life and not ordinarily available to conscious thought.* These unconscious drives may manifest their presence through dreams, mistakes, and symptoms (Ellenberger, 1970).

According to Freud, humans suffer mental conflict because of desires and needs that are repressed into the unconscious mind, often during childhood development of personality, identity, and acceptable social roles. Thus, while an individual's behavior may appear to observers as illogical and even abnormal, the troublesome conduct is actually a purposive expression of specific needs that are submerged in the subconscious mind of the subject.

The Formation of Personality

The concept of personality has been another intriguing focus for the study and explanation of human behavior by those employing the psychogenic approach. **Personality** refers to *the unique organization of relatively stable psychological traits possessed by an individual, as revealed by one's interaction with people, events, situations, and other components of the environment.* For example, "enthusiastic," "energetic," "fun-loving," and "idealistic" are some descriptive personality traits that seem to characterize many young people. But if a youth is cheerful and upbeat one day and sad or depressed the next day, we would have some difficulty in ascertaining a dominant personality pattern. A psychologically healthy person maintains a certain consistency and identifiability of personality most of the time that is apparent in the day-to-day presentation of self.

Freud and his colleagues contended that the normal adult personality has three fully developed components: the *id,* the *ego,* and the *superego.* Each of these three dimensions of the human personality performs critical, complex, and interrelated psychic and social functions for the individual.

At birth, the infant's personality is largely unidimensional, dominated by the **id**—*a set of primitive, self-centered impulses and instincts.* The sensuous and hedonistic id seeks immediate gratification and has no sense of time or reality. The spontaneous id functions to enhance the survivability of the infant organism. During the first few years of life the individual develops an ego and a superego. We may conceive of the **superego** as *an antithetical or opposite force that restrains the impulsive id.* The superego is developed in the individual through socialization, and represents socially conditioned and culturally learned moral values and a sense of right and wrong. It includes the formation of conscience and an ego ideal. Whereas the id clamors for self-satisfaction, "The ego ideal represents what we should do and the conscience gives us guilt feelings when we do 'wrong'" (Yablonsky and Haskell, 1988:355).

The **ego,** in Freud's model, is *that part of the personality or self that arbitrates between the demands of the id and the socially sensitive and idealistic superego.* The more pragmatic ego is designed to unify extreme personality positions into balanced, behavioral responses to stimuli. If successful, it directs behavior toward satisfaction of urges consistent with a knowledge of social and physical reality. By living in harmony with the reality of the social situation through the ego, the individual may postpone immediate gratification but does not abandon those personal desires.

Freudian Theory as an Explanation of Crime and Delinquency

Freud's theoretical contributions regarding the mental or psychic origins and motivations for human behavior have been adopted, adapted, expanded, and applied by numerous other psychiatrists and psychologists to the inner conflicts, personality maladjustments, emotional problems, and feelings of insecurity, inadequacy, and inferiority among their patients. In addition, Freud's insights have guided countless psychogenic efforts to identify and explain the mental cause or causes of such conduct disorders as sexual deviations, alcoholism, drug addiction, crime, and juvenile delinquency.

As a common example, Freud and many neo-Freudians have argued that crime is an outgrowth of the repressed, unconscious, emotional traumas of childhood (Sykes, 1980:8;

Samenow, 1984). According to this view, most crime is a result of an imbalance in the offender's ego between uncontrolled drives (the id) and society's expectations about behavior (the superego). Often, the problem is ascribed to an overly strict superego in which the offender, as a child, was socialized with a supercharged, unconscious sense of guilt. In such cases, as drives are repressed, pressures build up until the drives become manifest in abnormal and dangerous ways. Freud (1961) contended that children and adults often misbehave in order to be punished, which then temporarily relieves their guilt. On the other hand, much deviant and delinquent behavior has been credited to a deficient or underdeveloped superego, which fails to intervene or restrain the antisocial impulses of the id. These individuals were also inadequately conditioned to internalize "the socially adequate responses which society requires them to integrate into some form of 'conscience'" (Eysenck, 1979:13).

In both examples just cited, the psychiatrist or clinical psychologist would likely look to the subject's early childhood relationship with parents for explanatory causes of the disordered behavior. It is suggested that the socialization imposed by overly strict or overly permissive parents can create in their offspring a mental condition in which the ego is insufficient to perform its assigned task of mediating between the id and the superego.

Psychoanalysis

In addition to substantiating the existence of the unconscious and introducing the concepts of the id, ego, and superego in personality formation, Freud and his followers also developed various techniques for probing and examining the unconscious forces and motives that energize human behavior:

> *The most ambitious and intensive form of psychotherapy is represented by Freudian psychoanalysis…The intention is to afford the individual insight into the unconscious motivation of his behavior and to allow the development of a "healthy" personality structure. Frequently, the aim is not the removal of the symptom, rather it is to solve the unconscious problems which have led, according to psychoanalytic theory, to the development of a particular symptom. The major technique is that of free association, in which the individual is asked to say everything which comes into his mind without any effort to select or repress. This material, together with the individual's reports on his dreams, is then explored and interpreted by the analyst (Feldman, 1978:234).*

Free association, or *saying whatever comes to mind,* is still the basic tool of psychoanalysis. But psychiatrists and psychologists have continued to develop instruments designed to elicit the unconscious, subjective responses of their patients. Prominent among them is a wide variety of projective tests.

Projective Tests

Projective tests are founded on the principle that a patient undergoing psychoanalysis will reveal deep characteristics and unconscious feelings such as hatred, fear, frustration, and aggression, when expressions and responses are most unrestricted and unstructured. For instance, if the subject is asked to say something or respond to some external stimuli for which there are no previously well-learned conventional responses, it is assumed that hidden, sublimated emotions, motives, drives, and personality traits are likely to guide responses. Consequently, projective tests such as the Rorschach are specially designed to elicit these unconscious projections.

The Rorschach Ink-blot Test

The Rorschach Test was created by Hermann Rorschach in 1921 and utilizes a series of ink-blots as undefined visual stimuli. Each ink-blot in the series is produced by placing drops of ink on a sheet of paper, which is then folded and opened to form an unfamiliar, random pattern (Figure 5-1).

It is assumed by the psychoanalyst administering the Rorschach Ink-blot Test that if an individual is asked to identify what is perceived in the vague and unstructured ink-blots, definitions and responses *must* come from the subjective, subconscious self and are *not* determined by any familiar, prelearned, objective definition of the stimuli. It is further assumed that the responses reflect important (though hidden) emotions, drives, and motives that originated early in the subject's life and experiences. The patient's responses to the series of ink blots are carefully examined and catalogued for evidence of consistent patterns and themes, and then interpreted by the psychoanalyst as an explanation of the subject's disorders.

Projective Tests and Homicidal Children

Enthusiastic advocates of projective tests have suggested a wide range of diagnostic applications, including the identification and explanation of paranoia, schizophrenia, phobic re-

FIGURE 5-1   An Ink-Blot Pattern Similar to Those in the Rorschach Ink Blot Test

actions, and other neurotic and psychotic conditions. One of the most controversial applications has been proposed by some zealous psychiatrists who believe that projective tests could help to identify, in advance, those children most likely to commit murder. The idea is based on the assumption that youths with delinquent propensities go through an early *predelinquent stage* before the delinquent personality and identity are fully developed (Hakeem, 1957–58). The position is taken that children afflicted with this condition of latent delinquency will become delinquent unless there is remedial intervention. For example, Dr. Edward Glover, a renowned British psychiatrist and psychoanalyst, submitted a memorandum to the Royal Commission on Capital Punishment, on behalf of the Institute for the Scientific Treatment of Delinquency, which contended that children liable to commit murder could be detected in early childhood, even in infancy, with projective tests such as the Rorschach. He called for psychoanalytical prediction of future homicidal children in order to prepare programs of prevention. Here is a small portion of the amazing dialogue between the Chairman of the Commission and Dr. Glover:

> *[Dr. Glover]: …I have no hesitation in saying that the crux of the whole approach to the problem of murder and the problem of prevention or punishment lies in an adequate psychiatric attack at the right point. The right point is theoretically at any age, from birth upwards, but in practice between the ages of 2 1/2 and 8. There should be an adequate service of child guidance, including the use of batteries of tests; and we feel fairly convinced that although you would not recognize all the potential murderers,…you would strike seriously to the root of the problem of murder and its prevention…*
>
> *[The Chairman]: Can you at that stage identify those who have these potentialities in them?*
>
> *[Dr. Glover]: That can be done quite rapidly. There are so-called projective techniques of examination which are valuable, because they eliminate subjective bias on the part of the examiner and of the case examined. They have now arrived at a state of, not perfection, but adequacy, so that it is possible to take a child who is to all appearances merely an inhibited child, without any history of bad behavior, and discover that he is potentially violent…(Minutes of Evidence Taken from the Royal Commission on Capital Punishment, 1949:501; Reported in Hakeem, 1957:58).*

Critics of projective tests, including many psychologists and psychiatrists, point out that these instruments are limited in their usefulness because their reliability and validity are still uncertain (Kuhlen, 1952; Vold and Bernard, 1986). While they may be helpful in minimizing the subjective intrusion of the psychotherapist during the actual testing situation, there are inadequate safeguards against the subjective biases of the person who later synthesizes and interprets the subject's responses.

The most severe criticism of projective tests is aimed at their use in identifying and diagnosing innocent persons as potential criminals—*before* they are guilty of serious offenses. Sociologists see this psychoanalytical approach as grossly unfair to the subjects, leading to unavoidable social stigma as they are evaluated by professionals using such character-tainting labels as "predelinquent" or "potential murderer" (see the discussion on labeling theory in Chapter 8). In addition, the United States criminal justice system prohibits arresting, punishing, and/or rehabilitating people *before* they have committed a criminal offense. However, additional delinquency prediction instruments were developed in the 1940s and 1950s (The Minnesota Multiphasic Personality Inventory and the Glueck Social Prediction Table). These popularized techniques, plus the projective tests, helped to maintain the predelinquent model and the notion that very young children should be the diagnostic focus for latent criminality (Lubove, 1965; Mennel, 1973). For example, former Jackson County (Oregon) Circuit judge L. L. Sawyer confidently stated:

> *You can recognize future criminals back in the second grade.... And because that's where it starts, the early grades of elementary school are the best battleground for attacking crime (Mitchell, 1972:2).*

Finally, the tide began to turn in the 1970s as the accuracy of these predictive instruments was seriously challenged by new research (Hamparian et al., 1978).

> *Review of the results of these two efforts, when combined with the results of more recent research, reveals that prediction of delinquency is a stubbornly elusive task. In particular,* most methods of predicting delinquency are inaccurate approximately two-thirds of the time *(Lundman, 1993:37–38.).*

The difficulty of predicting adolescent violent behavior based on a scrutiny of childhood characteristics and background was also underscored by a multi-method, longitudinal study of Oregon youth. An in-depth comparison was made between a group of violent adolescent arrestees and a group of non-violent arrestees. The findings generally supported the contention of the researchers that violent offenders show the same background as frequent but nonviolent offenders (Capaldi and Patterson, 1996:206).

Delinquent Acts as Symptoms

A basic tenet of the psychogenic approach to explaining and treating juvenile delinquency is that delinquent acts are symptoms—an obvious and natural application of the psychiatrist's medical training and jargon to the study of human behavior. Delinquency is not traditionally viewed by the psychiatrist and the clinical psychologist as behavior that is primarily learned from associates, or that springs from frustrating social circumstances, or that is the outcome of some social process such as labeling (as do sociologists). Rather, they view delinquent conduct as a manifested symptom of **psychopathology:** *some internal neurological disorder or deeply hidden personality disturbance.* Psychiatrists typically consider the delinquent act or symptom as "the sick or hurt child's cry for help." These clinicians generally would agree that such children do not consciously seek psychiatric treatment when they are disturbed enough to need it. The psychoanalytic literature contends that overt delinquency is an indirect appeal for help in resolving some internal conflict (Shoemaker, 2000).

Several psychogenic theorists and practitioners have looked with suspicion upon a number of other common childhood activities besides outright delinquent behavior which, if carried to excess, may be viewed as symptoms of some underlying emotional disturbance or personality maladjustment. William Healy and Augusta Bronner (1957), Raymond Kuhlen (1952), and others have variously associated bed-wetting, nail-biting, interest or activity in sports, nervousness, and movie attendance with personality deviations and possible delinquency. This medical model approach is discussed further in Chapter 14, and prevention and treatment strategies based upon these alleged predelinquency symptoms are discussed in Chapter 16. Critics of these suggestions contend that the preoccupation with so-called behavioral symptoms as indicators of predelinquency cannot only blur the boundaries for socially tolerable behavior, but can also place virtually everyone under suspicious scrutiny. Furthermore, the psychoanalyst's reliance upon such symptoms is really evidence that the patient's inner mental life is not subject to direct observation and it is difficult to offer objective proof or empirical evidence supporting psychogenic assessments (Johnson, 1974).

Conduct Disorders

The insistence that delinquent behavior is basically an external symptom of a psychopathological disturbance is a major point of psychological theory and debate with many social scientists. This psychogenic theme is clearly demonstrated in the *Diagnostic and Statistical Manual of Mental Disorders* of the American Psychiatric Association (1987). For example, in the APA Manual the term *conduct disorder* is used to describe the behavior of adolescents who manifest a repetitive pattern of actions that violate the rights of others and major conduct norms. Youths with conduct disorders usually exhibit their unsettling and often threatening behavior in a social setting and may include bullying and cheating in games and school work.

> *Although the adolescent may project an image of toughness, self-esteem is usually low. Angry outbursts, low frustration tolerance, irritability, and reckless behavior are frequent characteristics. School achievement in reading and language skills is below the expected ability and age level (White, 1989:314).*

Specific criteria suggested by the American Psychiatric Association (1987) for the use of clinicians in the diagnosis of conduct disorders include at least three of the following during a period of six months:

1. Frequent lying.
2. Running away from home overnight twice, or one runaway without returning.
3. Frequent truancy from school or for older adolescents absence from work.
4. Stealing without confrontation with the victim on more than one occasion (for example, shoplifting).
5. Vandalism and destruction of property.
6. Breaking and entering into houses, cars or buildings without permission from property owners.
7. Deliberate fire-setting activity (arson).
8. Cruelty to animals.
9. Frequent initiation of physical fights.

10. The use of weapons in physical fights on one or more occasions.
11. Stealing with physical confrontation of victims in muggings, purse snatchings, extortions, and armed robberies.
12. Forcing another person into sexual activity, such as rape or prostitution.
13. Physical violence and cruelty toward people. Even homicidal assault can occur in the later stages of conduct disturbance.

The consistent application of the medical model by the American Psychiatric Association is reflected in the usage of such terms as "conduct disorder," "diagnosis," and "the later stages." The recommended diagnostic formula of "at least three of the following during a period of six months" presents an overwhelming temptation to social scientists who ask: "Why a minimum of three offenses before the adolescent is diagnosed as having a conduct disorder?" Surely one rape or two armed robberies within any period of time ought to qualify anyone for a "diagnosis of conduct disorder"!

Other Psychogenic Explanations of Juvenile Delinquency

Though Freudian and neo-Freudian theories probably have been the most influential, several other prominent psychogenic explanations of crime and delinquency merit discussion. It will become clear to the reader that there is considerable overlap among some of these theoretical constructs, and their difference is often a matter of emphasis. Moreover, underlying all of the psychogenic and biological approaches to etiology is a fundamental belief that criminals and delinquents are aberrant individuals, possessing some quirk of mind or body that is not manifest in the rest of the population.

Early Theories of Feeblemindedness

A bridge between the biological explanations discussed in the last chapter and the psychogenic theories accounting for crime and delinquency may be seen in the studies of feeblemindedness during the early decades of the twentieth century. Just as Lombroso (1911), Sheldon (1949), and other biological determinists argued that some individuals are constrained to antisocial behavior by a genetic or physiological predisposition, Goddard (1920), Healy and Bronner (1926), and other psychologists contended that mental deficiency is a primary cause of crime and delinquency. This interest was further stimulated by the popular studies of the Juke and Kallikak families that purported to trace inherited feeblemindedness and criminal tendencies through several generations (Dugdale, 1910; Estrabrook, 1916; Goddard, 1927). These assumptions have been subsequently discounted.

Such conclusions rested heavily upon the early application of measures of intelligence to institutionalized juvenile offenders. These were developed for the measurement of an individual's Intelligence Quotient (IQ), which is the ratio of a person's Mental Age (MA) to Chronological Age (CA). Thus, an IQ score of 100 means that one's MA and CA coincide at the national average. The higher the IQ, the brighter the individual; the lower the IQ, the more pronounced the retardation is assumed to be.

BOX 5-1 Controversial Issue

The Debate Over Television Violence, Childhood Personality Development, and Criminal Behavior

The authors are indebted to Professor Joe L. Wheeler who has chronicled since 1959 the research and reports on the effects of television on the minds and behavior of children and youth. The following excerpt is from Wheeler's authoritative book, *Remote Controlled* (1993, Review and Herald Publishing Association).

In April [1992], there appeared in the Washington Post a landmark article on television titled "Primal Screen" by Don Oldenburg. He pointed out that...the youth arrest rate for murder, manslaughter, forcible rape, robbery, and aggravated assault increased by 16 percent between 1989 and 1990....

Oldenburg then moved on to a just-released major study ("Big World, Small Screen"), conducted by the American Psychological Association, and 5 years in the making. The findings confirmed earlier suppositions: the child who watches 2 to 4 hours of TV a day will have witnessed 8,000 murders and 100,000 other acts of violence before leaving elementary school.

Oldenburg also discussed in depth the findings of Dr. Leonard Eron of the University of Illinois. Dr. Eron's study is considered major because it spans over three decades and chronicles the lives of the same people. In it, for the first time there was conclusive proof of the staying power of TV imagery:....

The more hours of television the children watched when they were 8 years old...the more serious were the crimes they were convicted of by the time they were age 30, and the more aggressive they were under the influence of alcohol, and the more severely they punished their own children.

According to this 30-year study, the most risky age for TV violence is during the first 10 years of a child's life. "Until children reach the double digits," says Eron, "they find it very difficult to differentiate between what's real and what's not real on TV" ("Primal Screen," Washington Post, April 7, 1992).

In the June 10 issue of Journal of the American Medical Association, *the proverbial smoking gun was finally found so that it could be introduced in the case against TV as conclusive evidence....According to Dr. Centerwall of the University of Washington, television is directly responsible for 10,000 homicides, 70,000 rapes, and 700,000 injurious assaults every year—roughly about half of all serious crimes. According to Dr. Centerwall's long postulated theory: 10 to 15 years after a society embraces television, expect a dramatic increase in murders and other serious crimes. That's just enough time, he notes, for the first generation weaned on television to reach adulthood and move into their most crime-prone years. He first noted it in the case of the U.S. and Canada, but thought maybe the fulfillment of his postulate might have been a fluke. However, television did not become prevalent in South Africa—because of strong government controls—until 1974. So it was that, as the years passed, he watched South Africa with baited breath. But sure enough, about 10 to 15 years later, South Africa's murder rate soared 56 percent! (counting only crimes committed by Whites against Whites)....*

Centerwall concluded with some advice to the nation's doctors: "Children's exposure to television and television violence should become part of the public health agenda, along with safety seats, bicycle helmets, immunization, and good nutrition. One-time campaigns are of little value. It needs to become part of the standard package."

In August of 1992, a landmark event occurred: TV Guide *itself, a magazine which is normally viewed as an apologist for the entire television industry, shocked media scholars by their cover story: "Is TV Violence Battering Our Kids?"—one of the harder hitting such articles during the last couple of years. Featured were a number of big names in the American arena.*

Continued

BOX 5-1   *Continued*

Neil Hickey observed that "More tele-vised violence than at any time in the me-dium's history is flowing into American homes. It is coming from many more sources than ever before—from video, pay-per-view, and cable, as well as from the broadcast net-work and stations. The overwhelming weight of scientific opinion now holds that televised violence is indeed responsible for a percent-age of the real violence in our society. What is new is that psychologists, child experts, and the medical community are just now be-ginning to treat televised violence as a seri-ous public health issue—like smoking and drunk driving—about which the public needs to be educated for its own safety and well-being." (Wheeler, 1993:98–101).

Additional support for these concerns over violence in televised programs has come from a three-year study conducted by a team of researchers at four uni-versities. The research was financed by the cable television industry. A 1998 report on the project sta-tistically verified that the number of violent pro-grams appearing in prime time has increased significantly in recent years. Moreover, Barbara Wilson, a senior researcher on the study and a com-munications professor at the University of Califor-nia at Santa Barbara pointed out that nearly 75 percent of violent scenes on television contained no remorse, criticism, or penalty for the violence which sends "the message that violence is condoned" (*San Francisco Chronicle,* 1998:A-3).

In response to these compelling research find-ings and a growing public outcry against graphic media portrayals of violence, the television enter-tainment industry has vigorously defended its pro-gramming policies. For example, the argument—"Which came first: the chicken or the egg?"—has been applied to the debate. Some program producers have declared that U.S. culture is historically violent and our television is simply reflecting what already exists in society; and to do anything less would be dishonest or inadequate reporting.

Industry rebuttals to warnings and threats of government regulation of television suggest a bitter and complex constitutional fight. They contend that television, like the print media, have certain inalien-able rights embedded in the First Amendment to the U.S. Constitution which guarantees that Congress will not interfere with the freedoms of religion, speech, and publishing the news. With this in mind, television apologists counter, government regulation would amount to censorship. In their view, self-po-licing by the television industry is the only viable option.

*   *   *   *

What psychogenic concepts and theoretical ex-planations of juvenile behavior are illustrated in the Wheeler report? What positions do you, your par-ents, your classmates, and the course instructor take on the issue of the possible relationship between television violence, childhood personality develop-ment, and delinquent behavior?

Many psychologists, with the popularized IQ tests, helped to replace the previously dominant idea that delinquents are somehow biologically defective with the newer notion that they are mentally defective. From this perspective, juvenile delinquents are viewed as retarded or lacking the mental capacity to know the difference between right and wrong; or cannot foresee serious consequences of misbehavior for themselves and for others; or can-not avoid being induced into crime by others.

In more recent decades, psychologists, educators, and other scholars have expanded their knowledge of how people learn, of how sociocultural variables and learning opportunities af-fect the accumulation of information by different individuals and groups, and of how test con-struction and administration procedures can affect responses to so-called Intelligence Tests. In addition, the ability of IQ tests to indicate or predict delinquent behavior has been widely chal-lenged. IQ measurements of incarcerated or institutionalized offenders is a biased representa-

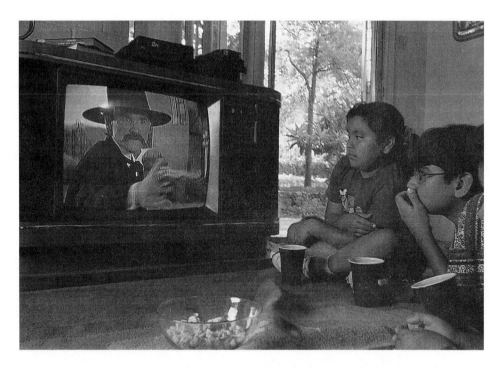

There is an ongoing public debate between many specialists in child development and spokespersons for the television entertainment industry regarding the impact of mass media portrayals of violence on impressionable children.

tion of the criminal and delinquent population since the subjects are those who were caught and convicted. Such scores tell us nothing about those who are successful in their deviance and avoid detection or apprehension. The preponderance of current, empirical evidence also fails to support the proposition that delinquents are inherently less intelligent than the general population (Samenow, 1984:19). Instead, it would be more accurate to say that low IQ scores often are related to poor educational opportunities, and the likelihood of being officially identified as a delinquent is much greater in the most deprived socioeconomic groups whose educational opportunities are drastically circumscribed (Menard and Morse, 1984).

A contrary view was espoused by Travis Hirschi and Michael Hindelang (1977) and by Rolf Loeber and Thomas Dishion (1983) who reviewed research and literature on low IQ scores and delinquent behavior. These investigators pointed to low IQ scores as a key foundational variable for many youths that, when combined with negative circumstances in the home, neighborhood, and other elements of the social environment, can generate an indirect connection between mental incompetency, low self-esteem, and delinquency.

Neurological Abnormalities

It was a rather natural development for psychiatric research and theory as a medical specialty to advance the premise that some individual offenders may be suffering from a brain abnormality or some form of neurological damage. This psychogenic approach has variously linked criminal and delinquent behavior with congenital brain defects, a mental impairment induced by a tumor, or the residual neurological effects of an earlier injury.

Numerous cases have been documented in which atypical, deviant, and antisocial behavior can result from pressures, lesions, and other injuries to those vital areas of the cerebrospinal system that are closely associated with intellect, emotion, inhibition, and self-control. Not infrequently, the "problem child" with a conduct disorder is finally found to have suffered from a severe trauma to the brain at an earlier stage of development (Roth, 1968). Douglas (1960) found significant correlation between premature birth (associated with a greater incidence of minor brain damage than normal birth) and "bad behavior" of school children as rated by their teachers.

Richard Speck, who was convicted in 1967 of the slaying of eight student nurses in Chicago, is cited as a classic example of how neurological impairment from blows on the head may be a contributing factor in criminal behavior:

> *Before Speck's trial began, psychiatrist Ziporyn spent over 100 hours interviewing him. In a book written afterward he quoted Speck at length: "When I was playing in a sandbox I hit myself on the head with a claw hammer. Accidentally, I knocked myself out. Then, a few years later—I must have been about 10—I was playing with some kids. They chased me and I climbed a tree. I...lost my hold. I fell on my head. My sister found me. She thought I was dead." Speck's tale of head injuries continued: "About five years after that, I did it again...I was running down a street and ran my head into a steel awning rod. I was knocked out again." In Ziporyn's opinion "Speck was a killer because his brain was damaged." And he reached the conclusion that the "lethal outburst was inevitable" (Adams, 1976:49).*

A contemporary research application of this hypothesis was conducted by Antonio Damasio at the University of Iowa College of Medicine and appeared in the journal *Nature Neuroscience* (Damasio, 1999). Damasio and his colleagues identified two rare cases in which brain injuries during infancy prevented people from learning normal rules of social and moral behavior. As adults they showed no guilt or remorse for bad conduct because, it was assumed, their previous brain injuries prevented their normal socialization. In light of a sample of just two cases, this study must be considered exploratory rather than conclusive. Much additional work needs to be done on the possible linkage between neurological damage and subsequent antisocial behavior.

In their ongoing search for empirical evidence linking mental processes and malfunctions with antisocial behavior, psychiatrists and neurologists have turned to highly sophisticated medical technology to measure and interpret brain activity. One method of studying nervous system functioning is to record the electrical activity of the brain. The summated electrical activity of the neurons in the brain is so great that it can be recorded through electrodes attached to the outer surface of the head. Such recordings are known as electroencephalograms (EEGs). One finding from this technique is that different patterns of electrical activity in the brain accompany different levels of alertness. For example, one kind of brain wave is recorded when a person is asleep and another pattern is recorded when the person is excited. Some researchers believe EEG data suggest that the brains of many criminals and delinquents do not function normally. They point out that antisocial behavior may develop following the appearance of brain tumors, head injuries, or the onset of diseases like encephalitis and epilepsy; and that the incidence of abnormal EEG waves is greater among persons who chronically violate important social norms than among conformists (White, 1981). Thus far, however, the findings based on the use of electroencephalographic examinations are contradictory (Shah and Roth, 1974).

Considerably more research comparing larger groups of representative juvenile offenders with nonoffenders needs to be conducted in this important area before there can be general acceptance that neurological abnormalities offer a credible explanation of juvenile delinquency. Although there are some instances in which *violent* offenders suffer from some mental anomaly (Pincus, 1979), research has yet to demonstrate consistent correlations between neurological disorders and delinquency. Nor is there convincing evidence of a general association between mental retardation, epilepsy, or the constitutional aspects of personality with juvenile delinquency (Krisberg and Austin, 1978). A more balanced viewpoint accepts the fact that brain abnormalities are found in many cases of violent misbehavior, although this is rarely the single causal factor. Rather, neurological defect, damage, or malfunction, when joined with negative factors in the home and other segments of the social environment, contribute to the development of delinquent propensities in some individuals (Narramore, 1966).

The Flawed Personality

The theories and research findings of psychiatrists and psychologists have greatly increased our understanding of why people behave as they do. The development and dynamics of human personality have been their most fruitful areas of inquiry, as extensions or alternatives to Freud's early and basic conceptualizations.

In the common language of the layperson, the word "personality" usually refers to a person's social skills. We often use the term as a synonym for "charm," "pleasant disposition," or "verbal agility." The term also may refer to the most striking impression that an individual makes on other persons. Thus, we may say, "She has a shy personality" or "He has an aggressive personality" (Mischel, 1982:264). However, as pointed out earlier in this chapter, the professional psychologist uses the term **personality** more precisely in referring to *relatively stable psychological traits possessed by an individual.* In other words, each person maintains a certain consistency of character, an identifiability that endures through time, by which that person can be recognized.

The basic unit of personality organization and psychogenic analysis is the personality trait. A **personality trait** is *a distinguishing feature, quality, or disposition of mind or character.* Personality traits are virtually countless, and include such emotions and associated behaviors as anxiety, fear, anger, religiosity, cheerfulness, and so forth. Each individual's personality probably contains most personality traits to a greater or lesser degree. And each personality trait is regarded as a dimension that ranges from high to low:

> For example, anxiety is a trait that varies from the greatest anxiety to the least anxiety. Most people have some degree of anxiety along the scale between the two extremes. Psychologists have studied such personality dimensions as aggressiveness,

dependency, and extroversion/introversion. People differ greatly in the degree to which they show such traits (Mischel, 1982:264).

Personality theorists maintain that an individual's relatively stable behavioral patterns reflect specific personality traits of measurable strength. Moreover, the particular combination and magnitude of personality traits within a given individual represent the perceptions, concepts, and tendencies that motivate actions in certain situations. Thus, the composition and functioning of human personality has been a rich field of exploration for those scholars seeking psychogenic explanations for deviant behavior, crime, and juvenile delinquency.

The Psychopath/Sociopath

Some of the important work in this area has focused on the identification, description, and causal explanation of the psychopathic personality. The **psychopath** *has a "flawed personality" in the sense that he or she has failed to internalize some of the major values and norms of society.* As a result of this incomplete or unsuccessful socialization, the superego part of the personality that monitors the individual's deportment as "conscience" is partially defective and impotent. The psychopath lacks self-control or internal restraints in the face of temptation and shows little genuine guilt or remorse for crimes committed (Rabin, 1961; McCall, 1999). The term "sociopath" is replacing the older term "psychopath" and thus implicitly recognizes that social forces are also involved in the development of the condition.

We may compare this unsuccessful socialization and the development of the "flawed personality" metaphorically with an unsuccessful smallpox vaccination. By law, virtually every child in the United States is required to receive a smallpox vaccination prior to commencing the first grade of school. Thanks to the medical technology that gave us the smallpox vaccine and the state laws requiring its general use, we have eradicated this dread epidemic disease. Most of us carry a small scar as evidence that we were successfully inoculated with smallpox vaccine and rendered immune to the disease. Occasionally, a child does not develop the usual, localized, and temporary reaction to the smallpox vaccine and we say that "the inoculation did not take."

Somewhat similarly, the transmission and learning of the basic values, norms, laws, beliefs, and attitudes of a shared culture are considered vital to societal survival. The transmission of culture content from older generations to succeeding generations is accomplished through the process of *socialization.* Through socialization—the shared experience and exposure to our cultural knowledge—each of us learns and internalizes a repertoire of generally accepted social norms, roles, and behavioral expectations. Most of us rather consistently demonstrate in our personalities and characters the learned cultural conformity of our society.

Just as with the smallpox vaccination, however, occasionally someone does not experience successful socialization. Perhaps the socialization process was inconsistent or the culture content unclear and therefore the internalization of normative behavioral expectations "did not take." In such cases, the person may manifest extreme nonconformity and even antisocial, criminal deviance. That individual's personality and behavior tend to reflect a lack of concern or an inability to clearly distinguish the difference between right and wrong. Hervey Cleckley (1976), in his book, *The Mask of Sanity,* pointed out that whereas most people suffer from anguish and guilt for wrongdoing, true sociopaths (or psychopaths) are loose and easy. They have little sense of regret and cannot seem to learn from experience. Often they have superficial charm and above-average intelligence. But they keep doing wrong. Starting out perhaps as truants and juvenile vandals, they may proceed along criminal paths through theft, robbery, rape, or murder to become the classic recidivists who are released only to be reinstitutionalized. This emphasis on failed childhood socialization leading to aggressive and predatory adolescence often characterizes the contributions of developmental psychologists (Bandura and Walters, 1959).

Distinctive Patterns of Criminal Thinking

In addition to investigating psychoses and antisocial personality disorders, psychologists continue to search for traits that can be studied as potential sources of crime and delinquency. One approach is to give batteries of tests such as the Minnesota Multiphasic Personality Inventory (MMPI) to both criminals and noncriminals. These tests contain questions about the beliefs, values, attitudes, feelings, and habits of the subjects. The purpose is to distinguish between criminal and noncriminal personality traits and profiles. As yet, no distinguishing and consistent criminal personality type has been isolated (Johnson et al., 1979:34–35).

A variation of the search by personality inventory for the etiology of antisocial behavior is based on a central premise common to most psychogenic explanations of behavior: we are seeing a person's reaction to a situation or issue as defined and interpreted by the individual, perhaps subconsciously. Therefore, observers must refrain from the rigid imposition of societal standards of good or bad, or a definition of the situation external to the individual under examination. Psychiatrists and psychologists believe that the individual's subjective and personal needs must be the focus for study and understanding. With this assumption in mind, Samuel Yochelson and Stanton Samenow (1976) and others have sought to identify the specific motives and thinking patterns of criminals.

Yokelson and Samenow strongly suggest that some criminals show distinctive character traits early in life that become more conspicuous with age. The "criminal child" (and later the adult criminal), they say, is hyperactive, egocentric, a chronic liar, and able to counter fears of punishment and pangs of conscience with a unique "shutoff mechanism." Most surprising of all, habitual offenders—those who have murdered, raped, and stolen, who have committed thousands of crimes from their youth—thought they were good people undeserving of punishment (Hernon, 1980).

This controversial approach is sometimes implemented through extensive interviews in an effort to determine exactly what the offender was thinking prior to and during the time when the crime was committed. It has been well documented, however, that when adult and juvenile "offenders discuss what they were thinking while committing a crime, they often seek to slant what they reveal so it is socially acceptable" (Zastro 1992:46). Psychologist Samenow (1984:17) in *Inside the Criminal Mind,* underscored this problem in acquiring reliable information from offenders:

> *When they are interviewed after being apprehended, criminals invariably relate a tale of horrors about their early lives. They seize upon any hardships in their lives, real or made up, to justify their acts against society. By portraying themselves as victims, they seek sympathy and hope to absolve themselves of culpability.*

Adolescent Identity Crisis

The next psychogenic explanation of juvenile delinquency to be reviewed here focuses on the role confusion and behavioral experimentation common among many American youths as they make the social adjustments associated with their awkward transition from childhood to adulthood. The concept of an "adolescent identity crisis" not only builds on the earlier theoretical constructs of the subconscious and personality development, but incorporates a strong sociological element with its emphasis on adolescent role modeling as a response to external social forces (this aspect is further explored in Chapter 11, The Youth Subculture). Part of the popularity for this theory must be credited to Erik Erikson (1956; 1968), who presented a convincing picture of delinquent behavior as a reflection of the inadequacy felt by many young people as they seek to establish new self-identities and social acceptance to go along with their newly acquired biological maturity.

According to Erikson (1968:50), a psychologically healthy adult has successfully integrated the self and social aspects of identity. Such an individual has achieved an **ego-identity**— *a persistent "sameness and continuity" within oneself that coincides with a consistently shared fundamental character and meaning with others.* Ego-identity is acquired during the formative adolescent years as youths mature and experiment with various poses and roles until they "find themselves" and their new roles and statuses in society.

Erikson contended that it is normal for "gaps" to exist in the personalities of young people that can lead to an identity crisis for some. Until these gaps are "filled in" by experience, the youth's personality pattern and behavior may be unpredictable at times, reflecting a state of **ego-diffusion,** which is the opposite of ego-identity. This *personality presentation of diffusion or inconsistency in ethics, roles, loyalties, and behavior,* is characteristic of many adolescents and often worries and irritates adults who may have forgotten their own adolescent waverings.

Sometimes the significant adults in the youth's life (parents, teachers, and others) may misinterpret the young person's desire and need to experiment with trial roles and to disengage from total adult authority in a quest for self-identity and adulthood. When the adults who previously successfully controlled the youth's behavior are confronted with what they perceive as a vacillating, rebellious teenager, they may overreact with stern, corrective measures designed to reform and restructure the young person's life. Unfortunately, these authoritarian adults do not realize that the adolescent's "bad" behavior is often just a tentative and temporary experiment at role-playing while seeking to solidify autonomy and self-identity. Misinterpretation and overreaction to minor adolescent nonconformity by the important adults in the life of the youth may, according to Erikson, actually precipitate a serious alienation of the youth and reinforce the tendency to choose a genuinely negative and antisocial role.

In addition to the effect of negative feedback from parents and others who express dismay over youthful posturing with nonconforming roles, the ultimate choice of a delinquent role can be exacerbated by the availability of genuine antisocial role models in the youth's environment. Dorothy Rogers (1977), in *The Psychology of Adolescence,* pointed out that as youngsters experiment with different roles they often fantasize an ego-ideal. The **ego-ideal** is *a personality, character, or image to which the youth may aspire.* While youths are testing their independence from traditional authority figures, they may admire and seek to emulate persons whose behavior is the antithesis of parental expectations:

> *...flamboyant crooks, lurid heroes and heroines lend glamour to erotic or vicious behaviors and afford a measure of catharsis for tendencies ordinarily repressed. Such figures...represent the romantic longings of almost everybody's adolescence.*

Adolescents often experience unfulfilled aspirations, identity crises, and loneliness that may lead to some forms of juvenile delinquency.

Even gangsters may serve as worthy ego-ideals. During the prohibition era, a certain notorious gangster was a hero-in-absentia for a good many adolescent boys. Their hero was portrayed as having certain desirable traits—courage, loyalty, and kindness to the poor—which his teenage followers tried to emulate (Rogers, 1977:196).

Insufficient Moral Development

According to Kenneth Keniston (1970), the early Freudian concept of superego development provides an important foundation for more contemporary studies of moral development and delinquent youth.

The first major contribution in this area was made by Jean Piaget (1948), who focused on mental cognition—how people think and understand. Piaget proposed that children develop their cognitive awareness and reasoning in four identifiable stages as they grow older and have a wider experience with their society and the world. Each successsive stage of biological and mental maturation involves an increased ability to deal with reality. The newborn human infant, according to Piaget's experiments, relies totally on sensory contact in dealing with its environment. By about age two, the child is mastering a growing vocabulary and can mentally distinguish between physical or objective reality and things that cannot be sensed directly. In a few years, usually about age eight or nine, the individual has the intellectual skill to perceive numerous causal connections in his or her surroundings; that is, "to understand how and why things happen, which yields far greater ability to manipulate their environment" (Macionis, 1999:126–128). Finally, in Piaget's model, the maturing adolescent is capable of more complex and abstract thought. For example, the youth no longer sees that one must obey rules just because they are expressed and enforced by parents, teachers, or the police. At this stage of mental and moral development, the youth has personally internalized and subscribed to a set of moral values and precepts.

In 1975, Lawrence Kohlberg, building on Piaget's work, presented an elaborate theory of moral development that has suggested psychogenic implications and explanations for crime and delinquency. Kohlberg declared that mental comprehension of right and wrong and corresponding behavior develop in childhood through three distinguishable, sequential, and evolving levels or stages (Kohlberg, 1981).

LEVEL ONE: *Preconventional Level of Moral Development.* This elementary phase of mental and moral reasoning characterizes childhood between the ages of four and ten. The child is generally responsive to the rules of right and wrong as defined by his or her parents, teachers, and other personal authority figures. The child's moral judgments and subsequent conduct are based on self-interest, and acts are interpreted as good or bad in terms of physical gratification or punishment.

LEVEL TWO: *Conventional Level of Moral Development.* This intermediate stage of mental and moral reasoning prevails among adolescents (and most adults, according to Kohlberg). At this level, the individual is less egocentric and more sociocentric as his/her world and orientation expands. The youth typically subordinates the will and conforms behavior in harmony with the expectations of society. Through internalization of social norms, the individual now shares the common desire to support and protect the existing social structure. This perspective can function to guide mental and moral decisions.

LEVEL THREE: *Postconventional Level of Moral Development.* In this final and advanced stage of moral reasoning, the individual's judgment and ethical decisions have matured and transcended the personal and social demands that determined past behavior. At this highest level, one's approach to moral decisions of right and wrong are autonomously based on universal principles of justice that one has cognitively discovered and adopted along with a world view of humanity and of right and wrong (Muuss, 1975).

The mental and moral development ideas of Piaget and Kohlberg have been the basis of considerable speculation and some research in the ongoing quest to find out why some young people turn to delinquency and some do not. For example, Scott Henggeler (1989) reported that the majority of juvenile delinquents in research samples were clustered at the lowest level of Kohlberg's moral development scale in which behavior is largely motivated by self-gratification and a pragmatic avoidance of deviance for fear of punishment. On the other hand, nondelinquent youth were more likely to rank at higher levels of moral reasoning, characterized by idealism, generosity, empathy for others, and a universal concern for justice. The tentative conclusion is that juvenile delinquents may be more prone than nondelinquents to commit illegal and antisocial acts because they have insufficient moral development.

In 1983, Kohlberg and his associates extended the moral development model again by suggesting that increased maturity provides "an insulating effect against delinquency" (Jennings, Kilkenny, and Kohlberg, 1983:311), thus theoretically accounting for the fact that most delinquents eventually grow out of their delinquency.

The moral development theories of Piaget and Kohlberg have been challenged on several grounds. First of all, many key terms and concepts lack definitional consensus. For example, *morality* and *rules* cannot be separate from their cultural or subcultural context, which can supply different meanings for different groups. Second, Piaget and Kohlberg may have made some questionable assumptions concerning the mental processes of *thinking* and *learning.* Not only are these processes impossible to observe and difficult to test, but other researchers indicate that there is no certainty that the transition from one cognitive level to another is as patterned or well-correlated with chronological age as suggested by Piaget and Kohlberg. Moreover, the relationship between thinking and behavior is not as clearcut and consistent as suggested by the moral development theorists. Finally, Kohlberg's methodology has been faulted for two intrinsic biases:

> *First, his emphasis on college learning as a prerequisite for critical thinking as well as moral maturity has been called elitist. Second, his levels of moral maturity have been described as sexist [since his subjects were mostly young boys] (Thornton and Voight, 1992:52).*

Nevertheless, supporters view the concept of insufficient moral development as a promising theoretical direction for future research and new insights regarding the causes of juvenile delinquency.

A Psychological Typology of Delinquency

A **typology** is *a classification system that organizes a diversity of information or objects into predetermined and orderly categories.* For example, in Chapter 3, we referred to two general kinds of crime: violent crime and property crime. That is a simple but useful typology. The FBI *Uniform Crime Reports* is an annual summary and very extensive typology of all the various types of criminal offenses committed in the United States during a given year.

Psychiatrists and psychologists have been extremely productive in generating typologies of mental illness, personality types, and aberrant behavior. A large number of these psychogenic typologies have classified juvenile delinquency according to patterns of behavior, symptoms, personality disorders, and causes. (For examples, see Abrahamsen, 1960; Eysenck and Eysenck, 1968; Hewitt and Jenkins, 1947; Lamson, 1986.)

A very comprehensive classification scheme of delinquency was contributed by Theodore Ferdinand (1966), who synthesized many previous and often incomplete psychogenic typologies. Ferdinand's typology, phrased in terms of psychoanalytical theory, contains three general kinds of delinquent behavior under which are subsumed nine specific delinquent types (Table 5-1). It suffers the shortcomings of most typologies in that it oversimplifies the division of complex material into broad and somewhat artificial, overlapping categories. Nevertheless, Ferdinand's system offers a useful framework for a wide-ranging discussion of a number of specific forms of delinquent behavior that may be traced to psychological causes.

TABLE 5-1   **Ferdinand's Typology of Delinquency**

I. **Impulsive Delinquency**

1. The Unsocialized Aggressive Child
2. The Self-Centered Indulged Delinquent
3. The Psychopath (or Sociopath)
4. The Sexual Pervert

II. **Neurotic Delinquency**

1. The Inadequate Delinquent
2. The Crystallized Delinquent

III. **Symptomatic Delinquency**

1. The Kleptomaniac
2. The Pyromaniac
3. The Sexual Delinquent

Source: Ferdinand, T. N., *Typologies of Delinquency,* New York: Random House, 1966: 179–197. Reprinted by permission.

I. Impulsive Delinquency

This kind of misbehavior is acted out spontaneously, vigorously, and with little sense of guilt. The personalities of these individuals are basically antisocial—against or in opposition to society. According to Ferdinand (1966:177), "such adolescents become delinquent because their own imminent impulses throw them into direct conflict with the mores of their society." Binder (1987) supplies a detailed picture of this kind of psychogenic delinquent who

> *can neither endure frustration nor postpone gratification. A poorly formed and inef-*
> *fective superego, stemming from inadequate handling in infancy, cannot overcome*
> *the pleasure-seeking forces of the moment, and the result is truancy, sexual of-*
> *fenses, theft, and other delinquent acts (1987:20).*

Ferdinand identifies four subtypes within this general category: the Unsocialized Aggressive Child, the Self-Centered Indulged Delinquent, the Psychopath, and the Sexual Pervert.

1. The Unsocialized Aggressive Child
This type is characterized and dominated by feelings of frustration, hostility, and explosive aggression toward anyone unfortunate enough to encounter the child's rage. It is suggested that the genesis of this lack of self-control and sympathy may be traced to the family of origin wherein the mother subjected the child to unrelenting rejection (Hewitt and Jenkins, 1947).

2. The Self-Centered Indulged Delinquent
The mood swings and alternating behavior of this youth resemble the "split personality" of the Dr. Jekyll/Mr. Hyde syndrome. This delinquent is able to make an easy and rapid tran-

sition from a friendly personable attitude to one of unreasonable dangerous fury. The source of the antisocial personality structure and behavior of the self-centered, indulgent delinquent also lies in the family of origin in which the mother is the main power figure and is overly attentive to the children (especially the male children) while the father plays only a marginal and insignificant role.

3. The Psychopath

The psychopath, or sociopath as this type is more commonly referred to today, seeks immediate gratification of personal desires regardless of the consequences for others:

> *The classic description of the psychopath states that he appears emotionally warm and charming but that he is incapable of close interpersonal relationships. If he becomes involved in crime, it is probably as an individual, not as part of the gang (McKeachie and Doyle, 1966:515).*

While the exact cause(s) of psychopathic development is/are widely debated among psychiatrists and psychologists, some researchers point to organic brain disorders, such as tumors and head injuries (White, 1981). Others emphasize the lack of primary relationships with adults during infancy that can result later in a youth incapable of experiencing caring emotions for other people (Fenichel, 1945). In either case, the net result is an unsocialized individual who lacks the normal personality development that ordinarily restrains one from impulsive, aggressive, irresponsible, and amoral manipulation and exploitation of others.

4. The Sexual Pervert

By this now outmoded term, Ferdinand referred to the juvenile who manifests deviant feelings and behaviors toward members of the same sex. Homosexuality may be either a permanent or a temporary practice. In an adult, homosexual tendencies are usually more persistent and fully developed; in a juvenile they are more likely to be impulsive, experimental, and transitory but are still considered as delinquent.

Although homosexual behavior is generally considered by the public as deviant from traditional societal expectations, law enforcement and public sanctions have become more inconsistent in recent times, possibly due to a slowly growing tolerance for those with alternative sexual orientations.

II. Neurotic Delinquency

With this term, Ferdinand was referring to psychoneuroses, which are disorders that are functional in origin, that is, there is no observable damage to nervous tissue or to any organic structure. The neurotic delinquent's personality is often stressful and confused, causing the youth to make faulty responses to ordinarily clear social norms and situations. Consequently, the juvenile's misbehavior is usually "an attempt to correct an imbalance or distortion in the inner dynamics of his personality" (Ferdinand, 1966:187–188). Ferdinand illustrated this general classification of psychogenic delinquency with two subtypes: The Inadequate Delinquent and The Crystallized Delinquent.

1. The Inadequate Delinquent

Ferdinand's primary example of the neurotic delinquent is a youth whose personality is inadequate, that is, the youth is unable to cope with the increasingly complex and demanding social environment concomitant with approaching adulthood. To this delinquent, the role expectations and growing responsibilities are often overwhelming. "Eventually," Ferdinand (1966:189) said, "his ego, in effect, goes on strike" and he becomes vacillating, indecisive, and inadequate.

Erik Erikson (1956) contributed very useful insights regarding adolescent personality development as the psychogenic cause for the "inadequate delinquent." He viewed the emergence of delinquent behavior in such youths as related to their problems in establishing a personally and socially satisfying identity.

2. The Crystallized Delinquent

Ferdinand utilized the metaphor of the colorless, transparent quartz crystal to describe a kind of delinquent whose misbehavior clearly and transparently functions as a convenient means of relief from a pervasive and disruptive sense of inner guilt and interpersonal tensions. The basis for this psychological explanation of juvenile delinquency can be traced to Sigmund Freud (1961), who observed how surprising it was to find that an increase in the unconscious sense of guilt could turn people into criminals. Freud reached this conclusion after examining many adults, ordinarily law-abiding, who admitted to crimes when they were children. "His psychoanalysis of these patients indicated that they had committed the crimes precisely because they were forbidden and because doing them led to a sense of mental relief" (Adams, 1976:51).

III. Symptomatic Delinquency

According to Freudian psychoanalytical theory, everyone is confronted with innate psychological demands to satisfy basic sexual and aggressive needs. Some persons, when denied legitimate gratification of these basic needs in conscious behavior, will repress them into the unconscious where—like the pent-up energy and pressure of a dormant volcano—these unfulfilled needs may burst forth as symptomatic, illegitimate, delinquent behavior. Thus, symptomatic delinquents seem compelled to violate the laws of society by the pressures of unfulfilled needs suppressed in their unconscious minds. Ferdinand cited the kleptomaniac, the pyromaniac, and the sexual delinquent as examples and subtypes of the Symptomatic Delinquent.

1. The Kleptomaniac

Early psychoanalytical theorists often traced an ungovernable desire to steal to sexual frustration, with the act of theft and the item stolen symbolically representing unconscious sexual needs and maladjustments. Other studies refined and expanded this thesis. For example, Grosser (1952) suggested a link between the sex of the juvenile offender and the kinds of things that are stolen. Among the youth he studied, Grosser found that boys were somewhat diversified in their choices of items to steal, apparently motivated more by the lure of illicit gain or the adventure entailed in the situation. Girls, on the other hand, appeared to be more selective, preferring to steal cosmetics, jewelry, or clothing. From this finding, Grosser hypothesized that the stolen items symbolically reflect the sexual orientation and/or objectives of the offenders. In other words, boys may hope to gain a measure of masculine status through money or through daring to risk getting caught; and girls may aspire to gain in feminine status through grooming, beauty, and clothing. Several other researchers have challenged Grosser's thesis, contending that shoplifting and other forms of theft are motivated by many complex variables, such as the socioeconomic status of the offender and the opportunity for theft, which seriously confound any correlation between theft and the offender's sexual orientation.

2. The Pyromaniac

The second example of Ferdinand's Symptomatic Delinquent has an obsessive fascination with firesetting and is an extremely serious threat to life and property. Psychogenic explanations of this form of deviance have varied through the years. Early theorists, following Freud, also associated arson with sexual drives and viewed it as a symbol of unfulfilled needs. They suggested that the excitement of the fire and subsequent efforts to extinguish it metaphorically and subconsciously functioned as a form of sexual release.

"Today, most psychologists and psychiatrists intentionally avoid use of the word pyromaniac—an archaic term employed more as a catch-all category for those who set fires for no apparent reason other than to obtain sensual gratification" (Karchmer, 1984:79). More recent theorists have viewed the compulsive, habitual arsonist from a wider perspective.

> *These juveniles set fires for a variety of reasons. Some are simply the kids whose cries for help went unanswered and whose firesetting behavior became a conditioned response to deal with stress. For others, firesetting is an act of vandalism, a cover for other crimes or a way of creating excitement. These kids are likely to torch objects and structures that appear safe to burn, such as an abandoned building...(Wooden, 1985:24).*

3. The Sexual Delinquent

A sexual deviation is generally perceived as an act that is contrary to the dominant sexual mores of the society in which it occurs. If the deviation is also seen as offensive or threatening to the society, it may be treated as illegal or criminal. In this final subtype of symptomatic delinquency, Ferdinand grouped together fetishism, exhibitionism, and voyeurism.

Fetishism is *the sensual gratification derived from touching a typically nonerotic part of the body of a person or a piece of clothing belonging to someone.* **Exhibitionism** is *the deliberate exposure of one's own genitalia,* thus affirming potency or sexuality through the shock registered by the viewer. **Voyeurism** is *the secretive watching of persons who are in private or intimate situations,* thus manifesting the subconscious needs and maladjustments of the spectator.

Compared to other forms of juvenile misbehavior, these psychologically based aberrations seem to have low incidence. Ferdinand (1966:197) agreed with Fenichel (1945) that such sexual deviations, usually found in males, "can be traced back to childhood fears of castration." Some more contemporary studies contend that Fenichel's explanation is incomplete and cannot be generalized to all who demonstrate these unacceptable behaviors; for example, it does not take into account certain key social factors, such as the absence of sex education or legitimate opportunities for sexual gratification.

Criticisms and Limitations of the Psychogenic Approach

Psychiatric and psychological theories of criminal and delinquent behavior have been help-ful to our understanding and treatment of many conduct disorders and many individual de-linquents. However, as with other causal explanations, they are not without their theoretical and methodological weaknesses.

Critique of Theoretical Assumptions and Concepts

Marshall Clinard and Robert Meier (1992:51) criticized psychogenic explanations of devi-ant behavior stating that they "…blur the line between 'sickness' and simple deviation from norms." In other words, the medical analogy comparing delinquent acts with physical ail-ments lacks generality and is unconvincing, since only a small proportion of juvenile mis-conduct can be traced to an organic cause, of either the mind or the body. The metaphor of the delinquent act as a symptom of underlying emotional maladjustment is seldom grounded in reality and, in fact, glosses over individual responsibility for behavior. In ad-dition, Clinard and Meier (1998:69) disagreed with the assumption that "…adult behavior and personality are almost wholly determined by childhood experiences, most of them in the family, whereas evidence suggests that behavior varies according to social situations and social roles and that personality continues to develop throughout life."

Sue Titus Reid contended that the psychogenic terms are vague, so vague that they may be described as the unknown. No operational definitions for such concepts as *id, ego, su-perego,* or *unconscious* are given (Reid, 1991). Finally, there is no consensus or agreement among psychiatrists and psychologists concerning the objective criteria to be employed in assessing degrees of mental well-being or mental aberration.

Critique of Research Methodology

The methodological problems associated with most studies applying the psychogenic ap-proach to the analysis of criminal and delinquent behavior are well summarized by Reid (1996). The research has been based on samples that are too small, that have usually been selected from among psychiatric patients and often from among institutionalized subjects, and the use of control groups has not been adequate. The focus on the individual seldom generates group patterns of behavior and prevents generalization. And, as discussed earlier in this chapter, projective techniques are open to the subjective interpretation of the analyst. J. E. Farley (1987:152–153) succinctly summarized these methodological problems:

> *Although there is limited evidence that psychological disorders may cause some crime, there is little empirical support for the argument that they cause much crime. So far as studies of the topic have been able to tell, the mix of psychological types among criminals does not differ greatly from that among the general popu-lation. Lunde (1970), for example, argued that the incidence of psychosis is no higher among murderers than among the general public.*

BOX 5-2 Concept Application

The Psychological and Social Impacts on Victims of Crime and Delinquency

Criminology and sociology, as scientific fields of study, have existed for about a century. During most of this time, their main focus has been on the offender and criminal behavior. However, in recent decades, attention and interest have developed about the *victim* as an integral part of the crime situation. Scholars from these disciplines now see crime and delinquency more as an interactive process, and research often encompasses the victim, his or her role, the criminal-victim relationship, and the immediate and subsequent impact of the offender's illegal conduct on the victim (Viano, 1976; Elias, 1986).

It is now well recognized that the trauma inflicted by criminal predation often transcends the immediate and physical experience of the victim. The identification and resolution of latent and longitudinal anxiety, guilt, depression, and other personality disruptions resulting from confrontation with criminal behavior draw heavily upon the expertise of psychologists and psychiatrists (Dadrian, 1976:40–41). For example, juvenile sex offenders as well as their victims are likely to be in need of psychotherapeutic counseling.

> ...thousands of children and teenagers...are committing crimes of sexual abuse, usually against other children. Perhaps most disturbing to professionals is the age of these offenders.
>
> They enter treatment programs at 15, 13, 10, and even 8 years of age.... The Pittsburgh-based National Center for Juvenile Justice reports that, from 1976–1986, the national arrest rate for 13- and 14-year-olds accused of rape doubled.... For the lesser category of sex offenses such as exhibitionism, grabbing, fondling, and other similar attacks, the arrest rate for 13- and 14-year-olds increased by 80 percent over the past decade....
>
> "I've been working with these kids for 15 years now," said Judith Becker, a psychiatrist at Columbia University's New York State Psychiatric Center. "The age of the perpetrators has been decreasing. When I first got involved, the average age of the victims was 12. Now it's 8."
> (The Orange County Register, *1989:A7*)

Rape and child abuse are not finished acts after they have occurred, but are likely to be part of an ongoing process, in which participants may continue to suffer negative personal and social repercussions. These *post-traumatic stress disorders* are associated by psychologists and psychiatrists with a long and varied list of symptomology, including low self-esteem, running away, loneliness, and suicidal feelings (Janus et al., 1987:52). In addition, the generational repetition of many forms of deviance is of great concern to scholars who have repeatedly found that adults often perpetrate the same illegal acts with which they themselves were victimized as children. Charles Manson, who masterminded the brutal Tate/LaBianca murders, has been identified as an extreme case of psychic trauma suffered as a child, reflecting in later crime:

> It was at Plainfield Indiana Boys School that Charles Manson was first homosexually attacked and raped. Thereafter he too engaged in homosexuality.
>
> From Manson's records at the National Training School for Boys, Washington, D.C., a profile emerged.... His first caseworker found him a "sixteen year old boy who has had an unfavorable family life, if it can be called a family life at all" and "aggressively antisocial." Three months later: "It appears that this boy is a very emotionally upset youth who is definitely in need of some psychiatric orientation."
>
> ...because of his diminutive stature, his illegitimacy, and the lack of parental love, he is constantly striving for status with the other boys.... (Wooden, 1976:50–51)

In recent years, victimization studies have been an important methodological and analytical tool in the hands of social and behavioral scientists in understanding the magnitude and causes of adult and juvenile crime, and in developing appropriate treatment strategies.

Continued

BOX 5-2   *Continued*

Sources

Dadrian, Vahakn N. 1976. "An attempt at defining victimology." Pp. 40–42. In Emilio C. Viano (ed.) *Victims and society.*
    Washington, DC: Visage Press, Inc.
Elias, Robert. 1986. *The politics of victimization: Victims, victimology, and human rights.* New York: Oxford.
Janus, Mark-David, Arlene McCormack, Ann Wolbert Burgess, and Carol Hartman. 1987. *Adolescent runaways:*
    Causes and consequences.
Juvenile sex offenders, victims are increasing, abuse counselors say. 1989. *The Orange County Register* (California),
    May 30, 1989.
Viano, Emilio C. 1976. *Victims and society.* Washington, DC: Visage Press, Inc.
Wooden, Kenneth. 1976. *Weeping in the playtime of others.* New York: McGraw-Hill Book Company.

Critique of Psychogenic Applications to Crime and Delinquency

The notion that there is a personality trait or type that is peculiar to criminals and/or delinquents has come under close scrutiny. Gordon Waldo and Simon Dinitz (1967), for instance, reviewed all 94 psychological explanations published between 1950 and 1967. They found little evidence that personality traits could predict delinquent involvement.

> *Tannenbaum (1977) reviewed personality studies from 1966 to 1975. He found that "personality tests, per se, are no better predictors of criminal personalities than were those of ten years ago..." (Albanese, 1993:48).*

Theorists who contend that some psychological factor makes delinquents different from nondelinquents have difficulty in explaining the preponderance of conforming behavior in those who possess the suspected psychological trait. At the same time, self-report studies consistently show that most people have committed delinquent acts sometime during their lives (Klein, 1987). With these data-supported findings before us, it seems futile to try to find an explanation of widespread behavior based on an alleged psychological abnormality, for, by definition, *abnormal* means *unusual,* or *out of the ordinary.*

Gwynn Nettler (1984:28) reported how efforts to expand the legal defense of insanity to include all those personality and emotional weaknesses and defects that afflict human beings have encountered skepticism and disagreement from the legal and psychological professions:

> *While 77 percent of the psychiatrists expressed confidence in their expert testimony in criminal trials, only 44.5 percent of the lawyers expressed confidence in psychiatric expertise...As might be expected, the two professions disagreed also on the relationship between serious criminal activity and mental illness...[While]* half *of the psychiatrists believed that "anyone who commits a serious crime is mentally ill" or "most people who commit serious crimes are mentally ill," only a* third *of the lawyers agreed (Nettler, 1984:28).*

There is also a growing public complaint that psychogenic (and biological) explanations of crime and delinquency are being used by many offenders to reject personal responsibility for their antisocial behavior. It has become common, these critics argue, for theories tracing misbehavior to some irresistible force or factor in the culprit's psyche or genetic blueprint to serve as a viable courtroom defense and justification for horrific crimes. Examples in recent years include the following:

- The campus strangler of a female student whose attorney suggested that his client was just acting out his unconscious anger and unfulfilled needs.
- The Los Angeles mob that brutally attacked and critically injured a passing truck driver claimed they were caught up in the contagious excitement and spontaneity of the moment.
- The infamous "Twinkie Defense" that contended that the murderer of the San Francisco mayor and city supervisor was less culpable due to a dietary biochemical imbalance.
- The gang leader whose violent and criminal lifestyle was credited to low self-esteem.

To sociologists, the critical dilemma of the psychogenic approach is that it attempts to explain juvenile delinquency and many other forms of deviant behavior on the basis of individual characteristics, but the explanations it offers about how individuals developed those characteristics are often social. Thus, they take an unnecessarily circuitous and often erroneous route to the more viable causal variables. For example, psychoanalytic theory emphasizes inherent drives and emotional stress, but social interaction with parents and others during childhood and adolescence is what can produce an imbalance between those drives and learned social expectations about behavior. "Hence, the ultimate cause of the problem is to be found in the social experiences that led to the development of the personality pattern" (Farley, 1987:153). Though psychogenic explanations may help in the treatment of individual cases, increasingly, criminologists have turned to societal forces for explanations of behavior.

SUMMARY

This chapter began by defining and explaining the psychogenic approach to crime and delinquency. The fields of psychiatry and psychology were defined, pointing out their similarities, areas of overlap, and significant differences.

Sigmund Freud's concepts regarding the "unconscious" and personality formation were then reviewed. Freudian theory was applied to crime and delinquency, primarily attempting to explain these forms of deviant behavior as resulting from problems in personality development. We briefly summarized how psychoanalysis has been used in the treatment of criminals and delinquents.

Freudian theory and psychoanalysis led to the development of a variety of projective tests designed to identify maladjusted individuals, including those likely to commit delinquent and criminal offenses. This medical model approach to delinquency contends that delinquency is a symptom of deeply embedded psychological problems. It is further suggested that if identified early enough, and corrected, future delinquency and criminality can be avoided.

Other psychogenic explanations included feeble-mindedness, neurological abnormalities, flawed personalities (such as the psychopath or sociopath), and the adolescent identity crisis. In an attempt to categorize and explain a wide variety of delinquent behaviors, psychologists and psychiatrists constructed extensive typologies. For example, Theodore Ferdinand attempted to classify virtually all cases of juvenile delinquency by assigning them to three broad categories: impulsive, neurotic, and symptomatic.

There are a number of theoretical and methodological weaknesses in the psychogenic approach to juvenile delinquency. Suffering from questionable theoretical assumptions, and small and nonrepresentative samples, the psychogenic approach has failed to provide empirically tested and supported causal explanations for delinquent behavior. While it does provide some useful insights, only a few delinquents seem to suffer from organic brain disorders, or seriously maladjusted personalities. The majority of juvenile delinquents are physically and psychologically similar to the nondelinquent population.

From a sociological perspective, the psychogenic theories fail to view delinquency in its broader social context, and to acknowledge the impact of the many social and cultural factors that influence and shape human behavior. In Chapter 6, and throughout the remainder of this book, we turn to these social and cultural variables in order to more fully understand juvenile delinquency.

Concept Integration

Questions and Topics for Study and Discussion

1. Briefly define the psychogenic approach to explaining and interpreting human behavior and list its shortcomings and limitations.

2. What did Judge Sawyer mean when he said: "You can recognize future criminals back in the second grade"? Do you agree with him? Why or why not?

3. Based upon your reading of this chapter, briefly outline the contributions of Sigmund Freud, Hermann Rorschach, Erik Erikson, and Lawrence Kohlberg. Compare and contrast the ideas of Freud and Erikson regarding the development of human personality as they may relate to juvenile delinquency.

4. What do psychiatrists mean when they say "The delinquent act is the hurt child's cry for help"? Do you agree with them? Why or why not?

5. Outline the specific psychogenic explanations of juvenile delinquency discussed in this chapter.

Which one makes the most sense to you? Which one seems least logical to you?

6. What is a psychopath (or sociopath)? Have you known or read of anyone who seemed to manifest this particular kind of personality? Could there be other explanations for his or her behavior besides personality maladjustment?

7. What is a typology and how is such a system useful in analyzing and understanding psychologically based juvenile delinquency? Try to think of examples from your reading or your experience for each of the kinds of delinquent behavior and delinquents in Ferdinand's typology.

8. List and explain the arguments on both sides of the debate over television violence, childhood personality development, and criminal behavior.

References

Abrahamsen, D. 1960. *Psychology of crime.* New York: Columbia University Press.

Adams, V. 1976. *Human behavior: Crime.* New York: Time-Life Books.

Albanese, J. S. 1993. *Dealing with delinquency: The future of juvenile justice* (2nd ed.). Chicago: Nelson-Hall Publishers.

American Psychiatric Association. 1987. *Diagnostic and statistical manual of mental disorders* (3rd ed., rev.).

Bandura, A., and Walters, R. A. 1959. *Adolescent aggression.* New York: The Ronald Press.

Binder, A. 1987. An historical and theoretical introduction. In *Handbook of juvenile delinquency* (H. C. Quay, Ed.). New York: Wiley.

Camper, D., Kasindorf, M., Clausen, P., Monroe, S., Shapiro, D., and Taylor, J. 1982. The insanity plea on trial. *Newsweek* (May 24, 1982:56–61). Produced by ARIC Press.

Capaldi, D. M., and Patterson, G. R. 1996. Can violent offenders be distinguished from frequent offenders: Prediction from childhood to adolescence. *Journal of research in crime and delinquency* 33 (May, 1996):206–231.

Cleckley, H. M. 1976. *The mask of sanity* (5th ed.). St. Louis: C. V. Mosby Co.

Clinard, M. B., and Meier, R. F. 1992. *Sociology of deviant behavior* (8th ed.). Fort Worth: Harcourt Brace Jovanovich.

Clinard, M. B., and Meier, R. F. 1998. *Sociology of deviant behavior* (10th ed.). Fort Worth: Harcourt Brace Jovanovich.

Comstock, G. A., and Rubinstein, E. A. (Eds.) 1972. Television and Social Behavior. Reports and Papers, Volume III: *Television and adolescent aggressiveness.* A Technical Report to the Surgeon General's Scientific Advisory Committee on Television and Social Behavior. Washington, DC: U.S. Government Printing Office.

Damasio, A. 1999. Brain injury and antisocial behavior. *Nature Neuroscience.* November, 1999.

Douglas, J. W. B. 1960. Premature children at primary schools. *British Medical Journal* 1 (1960):1008.

Dugdale, R. 1910. *The Jukes.* New York: Putnam.

Ellenberger, H. 1970. *Discovery of the unconscious: The history and evolution of dynamic psychiatry.* New York: Basic Books.

Erikson, E. 1956. The problem of identity. *Journal of the American Psychiatric Association* 4:56–121.
1968. *Identity: Youth and crisis.* New York: Norton.

Estrabrook, A. 1916. *The Jukes in 1915.* Washington, DC: The Carnegie Institute of Washington.

Eysenck, H. J. 1979. *Crime and personality.* (2nd ed.). London: Routledge and Kegan Paul.

Eysenck, H. J., and Eysenck, S. B. F. 1968. A factoral study of psychoticism as a dimension of personality. *Multivariate Behavioral Research* (special issue) 15 (1968).

Farley, J. E. 1987. *American social problems: An institutional analysis.* Englewood Cliffs, NJ: Prentice-Hall.

Feldman, M. P. 1978. *Criminal behavior: A psychological analysis.* New York: John Wiley.

Fenichel, O. 1945. *The psychoanalytic theory of neurosis.* New York: Norton.

Ferdinand, T. N. 1966. *Typologies of delinquency: A critical analysis.* New York: Random House.

Freud, S. 1961. The ego and the id. *The complete psychological works of Sigmund Freud.* Vol. 19: 12–68. London: Hogarth.
1963. *An outline of psychoanalysis* (Trans. James Strachey). New York: Norton.

Goddard, H. 1920. *Efficiency and levels of intelligence.* Princeton, NJ: Princeton University Press.
1927. *The Kallikak family: A study in the heredity of feeble-mindedness.* New York: Macmillan.

Grosser, G. 1952. *Juvenile delinquency and contemporary American sex roles.* Ph.D. Dissertation. Cambridge: Harvard University.

Hakeem, M. 1957–1958. A critique of the psychiatric approach to the prevention of juvenile delinquency. *Social Problems* 5:194–206.

Halleck, S. 1966. Current psychiatric roles in the legal process. *Wisconsin Law Review* Spring: 379–401.
1971. *Psychiatry and the dilemmas of crime.* Berkeley: University of California Press.

Hamparian, D. M., Schuster, R., Dinitz, S., and Conrad, J. P. 1978. *The violent few: A study of dangerous juvenile offenders.* Lexington, MA: Lexington Books. Pp. 54–55 and 133–135.

Healy, W., and Bronner, A. J. 1926. *Delinquents and criminals—Their making and unmaking.* New York: Macmillan.
1957. *New light on delinquency and its treatment.* New Haven, CT: Yale University Press.

Henggeler, S. 1989. *Delinquency in adolescence.* Newbury Park, CA: Sage. p. 26.

Hernon, P. 1980. Two researchers startled by findings on criminals. Newhouse News Service. *World Tribune* (February 3, 1980). P. 18-A.

Hewitt, L. E., and Jenkins, R. L. 1947. *Fundamental patterns of maladjustment.* Springfield, IL: State Printer.

Hinckley, Sr., J. W., and Hinckley, A. A. 1985. *Breaking Points.* Chosen Books, Inc.

Hirschi, T. and Hindelang, M. J. 1977. Intelligence and delinquency: A revisionist review. *American Sociological Review* 42:571–586.

Jennings, W., Kilkenny, R., and Kohlberg, L. 1983. Moral development theory and practice for youthful and adult offenders. In *Personality, theory, moral development, and criminal behavior* (W. Laufer and J. Day, Eds.). Lexington, MA: D.C. Heath.

Johnson, E. 1974. *Corrections and society* (3rd ed.). Homewood, IL: Dorsey Press.

Johnson, G., Bird, T., and Little, J. W. 1979. *Delinquency prevention: Theories and strategies.* Washington, DC: U.S. Department of Justice, LEAA.

Karchmer, C. L. 1984. Young arsonists. *Society* (Nov.–Dec.):78–83.

Keniston, K. 1970. Student activism, moral development, and morality. *American Journal of Orthopsychiatry,* 40 (4):577–592.

Klein, M. 1987. Watch out for that last variable. In *The causes of crime: New biological approaches.* (S. A. Mednick, T. E. Moffitt, and S. A. Stack, Eds.). Cambridge: Cambridge University Press.

Kohlberg, L. 1981. *The psychology of moral development: The nature and validity of moral stages.* New York: Harper & Row.

Krisberg, B., and Austin, J. 1978. *The children of Ishmael.* Palo Alto, CA: Mayfield Publishing Co.

Kuhlen, R. G. 1952. *The psychology of adolescent development.* New York: Harper and Brothers.

Lamson, A. *Psychology of juvenile crime.* 1986. New York: Human Sciences Press, Inc.

Loeber, R. and Dishion, T. 1983. Early predictors of male delinquency: A review. *Psychological Bulletin* 94:68–99.

Lombroso, C. 1911. *Crime, its causes and remedies* (Trans. H. P. Horton). Boston: Little Brown.

Lubove, R. 1965. *The professional altruist.* Cambridge: Harvard University Press.

Lunde, D. T. 1970. *Murder and madness.* San Francisco: San Francisco Book Co.

Lundman, R. J. 1993. *Prevention and control of juvenile delinquency.* (2nd ed.). New York: Oxford University Press.

McCall, W. 1999. Born to be bad? Why kids commit crimes. *Ashland Daily Tidings,* Ashland, OR May 28:1.

McKeachie, W. J., and Doyle, C. L. 1966. *Psychology.* Reading, MA: Addison-Wesley.

Macionis, J. J. 1999. *Sociology.* (7th ed.). Englewood Cliffs, NJ: Prentice-Hall.

Menard, S., and Morse, B. J. 1984. A structuralist critique of the IQ-delinquency hypothesis: Theory and evidence. *American Journal of Sociology* 89 (May):1347–1378.

Mennel, R. M. 1973. *Thorns and thistles.* Hanover, NH: University Press of New England.

Mischel, W. 1982. Personality. *The World Book Encyclopedia,* Vol. 15. Chicago: World Book, Inc., 264–270.

Mitchell, L. 1972. Criminal beginnings in elementary schools. *Ashland Daily Tidings:* Ashland, OR, November 6:2.

Muuss, R. E. 1975. *Theories of adolescence.* New York: Random House.

Narramore, C. M. 1966. *Encyclopedia of psychological problems.* Grand Rapids, MI: Zondervan Publishing House.

Nettler, G. 1984. *Explaining crime* (3rd. ed.). New York: McGraw-Hill Book Co.

Piaget, J. 1948. *The moral judgment of the child.* Glencoe, IL: Free Press.

Pincus, J. H. 1979. Mental problems found in delinquents. *Tulsa World,* April 30:10.

Platt, A. M. 1977. *The child savers: The invention of delinquency.* (2nd ed.). Chicago: University of Chicago Press.

Rabin, A. I. 1961. Psychopathic personalities. In *Legal and criminal psychology* (H. Toch, Ed.). Hinsdale, IL: Holt, Rinehart and Winston.

Rehm, L. 1983. Psychology. *Academic American Encyclopedia,* Vol. 15. Danbury, CT: Grolier, Inc., pp. 593–598.

Reid, S. T. 1996. *Crime and criminology* (8th ed.). Hightstown, NJ: McGraw-Hill.

Rogers, D. 1977. *The psychology of adolescence* (3rd ed.). Englewood Cliffs, NJ: Prentice-Hall.

Roth, M. 1968. Cerebral disease and mental disorders of old age as causes of antisocial behavior. In *The mentally abnormal offender* (Rueck and Porter, Eds.). Boston: Little Brown, pp. 35–38.

Samenow, S. E. 1984. *Inside the criminal mind.* New York: Times Books.

San Francisco Chronicle. 1981. A report that Hinckley is sane. *San Francisco Chronicle,* July 23:24.

San Fancisco Chronicle. 1998. No regret, no remorse. *San Francisco Chronicle,* April 17:A-3.

Shah, S. A., and Roth, L. H. 1974. Biological and psychophysiological factors in criminality. In *Handbook of criminology* (D. Glaser, Ed.). Chicago: Rand McNally, p. 120.

Sheldon, W. 1949. *Varieties of delinquent youth.* New York: Harper and Brothers.

Shoemaker, D. J. 2000 (4th ed.). *Theories of delinquency: An examination of explanations of delinquent behavior.* New York: Oxford University Press.

Simon, R. J., and Aaronson, D. E. 1988. *The insanity defense on trial.* New York: Praeger.

Sykes, G. 1980. *The future of crime.* Washington, DC: Alcohol, Drug Abuse, and Mental Health Administration, National Institute of Mental Health.

Tannenbaum, D. J. 1977. Personality and criminality: A summary and implications of the literature. *Journal of Criminal Justice* 5:225–235.

Thornton, W. E., and Voight, L. 1992. *Delinquency and Justice* (3rd ed.). New York: McGraw-Hill, Inc.

Vold, G., and Bernard, T. J. 1986. *Theoretical criminology* (3rd ed.). New York: Oxford University Press.

Waldo, G., and Dinitz, S. 1967. Personality attributes of the criminal: An analysis of research studies: 1950–1965. *Journal of Research in Crime and Delinquency* 4:185–201.

Weinberg, S. K. 1952. *Society and personality disorders.* Englewood Cliffs, NJ: Prentice-Hall.

White, J. L. 1989. *The troubled adolescent.* New York: Pergamon Press.

White, R. W. 1981. *The abnormal personality* (5th ed.). New York: The Ronald Press.

Willing, R. 2000. When children kill, who takes the blame? *USA Today.* March 3:3A.

Wooden, W. S. 1985. Arson is epidemic—and spreading like wildfire. *Psychology Today.* January, 1985: 23–28.

Yablonsky, L., and Haskell, M. R. 1988. *Juvenile delinquency* (4th ed.). New York: Harper & Row, Publishers.

Yochelson, S., and Samenow, S. E. 1977. *The criminal personality.* Vol. I (1976) and Vol. II (1977). New York: Jason Aronson Co.

Zastrow, C. 1992. *Social problems: Issues and solutions.* (3rd ed.). Chicago: Nelson-Hall.

6 SOCIOLOGICAL EXPLANATIONS OF JUVENILE DELINQUENCY

Social Strain and Cultural Transmission Theories

Reading Objectives

The reading of this chapter will help you achieve the following objectives:

1. Define and explain the sociological perspective in explaining human behavior in general and juvenile delinquency in particular.
2. Understand the principles and purposes of theory building as this intellectual exercise applies to the explanation of delinquent behavior.
3. Define and explain specific sociological concepts and theories of deviant and delinquent conduct, including Strain or Anomie Theory and Cultural Transmission Theory.
4. Apply these sociological theories of human behavior to explaining juvenile delinquency.
5. Summarize the contributions and limitations of the various sociological theories of deviance and delinquency discussed in this chapter.

Introduction

Sociology is a comparatively young academic discipline, yet its influence upon modern criminology and contributions to theoretical explanations of deviant behavior have been more extensive and enduring than the preceding theories of biological determinism and psychological maladjustment. Despite some meaningful contributions to our understanding, the biological and psychological explanations tend to neglect a most prominent aspect of deviance, that is, like any other human activity, deviant behavior is inherently social in nature. For an individual to be deviant or delinquent, he or she must be involved with other people.

Sociologists, in explaining and interpreting human behavior, consistently have maintained that human behavior is intrinsically social and that "social facts should be explained by other social facts and not by psychological, biological, or any non-social facts" (Durkheim 1950:18–22). More specifically, sociological explanations stress that juvenile delinquency emerges from the complex network of social groups, institutions, and human interrelationships that exist in a society. Therefore, in order to better understand juvenile delinquency, we must examine it within the social context in which it occurs. While sociologists are not unanimous in pinpointing the exact causes of juvenile delinquency (or any other kind of nonconformity or deviance), the ubiquitous and inseparable social nature of human behavior is the common thread throughout all sociological attempts to explain delinquency.

Before we present the major sociological theories of juvenile delinquency in Chapters 6, 7, and 8, it is important to briefly define theory and explain its purpose.

Theory

The study of **etiology**—*the cause(s) of an event, phenomenon, or behavior*—is a common inquiry and exercise in the scientific community and many academic disciplines. Ideally, systematic and controlled observations, data collection, and the testing of hypotheses will result in valid and reliable findings that then can be stated in a theoretical explanation of what has occurred (Lastrucci, 1967). In other words, a **theory** is *a general statement that accurately relates cause and effect variables together so as to explain events or behavior.* Thus, sociologists, in their pursuit of theoretical explanations of delinquency, have linked youthful misconduct to the home, family, neighborhood, school, peer group, and a host of other variables found in the juvenile's social milieu.

Sociologists agree that causation is present if three conditions are met (Cole, 1980). First, causation can occur only if the independent variable exists *before* the dependent variable. That is to say, the "cause" must precede the "effect." For example, it has been theorized that young people exposed to dominant adult criminal elements in their neighborhoods have increased opportunity to learn and participate in delinquent behavior. In other words, the presence and availability of adult criminals as role models is the causal independent variable, and exists before the emergence of delinquent behavior, the affected or dependent variable, in this line of reasoning.

Second, if causation exists, then change in the independent variable also affects the dependent variable, but in a different way. Thus, if a youngster is removed from the old neighborhood and surrounded by a preponderance of neighborhood models and influences favorable to law-abiding behavior, the youth would be less likely to commit delinquent acts.

Finally, causation cannot be established until researchers have ruled out the influence of other possible independent variables. The way to do this is to analyze the effect(s) of each possible independent variable, while keeping constant all other possible independent variables. Referring back to the previous example, perhaps the degree of stability and cohesiveness of the child's family and home environment is the true independent variable that determines whether the youth will actually participate in delinquent activities, and not the older established criminal elements that exist in the neighborhood. It is conceivable that a strong and secure family and home life may insulate many children from becoming juvenile

delinquents, regardless of their neighborhood environment, whereas children from fragmented and dysfunctional families are those most likely to gravitate toward the available
criminal models in their area.

It is much more difficult to identify and control for possible antecedent or intervening
variables that can confound conclusions regarding causality in social science research than
in the laboratory conditions of the chemist or physicist. It follows, then, that sociological
theories explaining the cause(s) of juvenile delinquency (or other social phenomena) are
more tentative and subject to continual scrutiny, verification, and possible modification. As
Schur (1973:170–171) noted:

> *In their interminable search for "causes," sociologists have produced no definitive
> "solution" to delinquency problems. They have, however, alerted us to many mis-
> conceptions and blind alleys, and begun to show us the direction that policy might
> sensibly take.*

In order to conceptually understand the various sociological explanations of juvenile
delinquency, we have divided them into six major categories—organized and presented in
three chapters:

1. Social Strain theories.
2. Cultural Transmission theories.
3. Social Learning theories.
4. Social Control theories.
5. Labeling theories.
6. Radical and Conflict theories.

While categorical typologies are useful structures and formats for organizing and pre-
senting a mass of data or information, it must be acknowledged that the theoretical categories
that supply the framework for Chapters 6, 7, and 8 are neither exhaustive nor mutually exclusive. Thus, they share the common weaknesses of virtually all typologies in the social and
behavioral sciences. In attempting to group together major theoretical explanations of juvenile delinquency that share a major conceptual basis it becomes clear to the astute reader that
the real world of cause and effect of human behavior cannot be so easily packaged in discrete
categories. As demonstrated in all such endeavors, the etiological theories often merge, overlap, and build on each other. Moreover, these sociological theories are presented in only approximate order of chronological development. In fact, the theories often were formulated
simultaneously as the research and intellectual products of contemporary scholars.

The first two types of sociological explanations—Social Strain Theories and Cultural
Transmission Theories—will be presented in this chapter. The other four kinds of sociological theories are discussed in Chapters 7 and 8.

Social Strain Theories

The theoretical explanations of deviance and delinquency that are grouped together in this
category share the underlying assumption that nonconforming behavior arises out of social
circumstances in which individuals or groups experience normative confusion or disruption.

Confronted with a new, traumatic, or frustrating social situation, some people respond in a deviant and perhaps criminal manner.

Durkheim's Concept of Anomie

Emile Durkheim, in his landmark study of suicide ([1897] 1951), developed the concept of **anomie** to characterize *the condition of a society or group with a high degree of confusion and contradiction in its basic social norms.* Durkheim traced the unusually high suicide rates during periods of serious economic depression, severe political crises and upheavals, rapid societal change, and other unstable social conditions, to the absence or sharply reduced efficacy of normative regulation during such times. Under such conditions, Durkheim hypothesized, the usual rules that restrain us from committing socially unacceptable acts can become weakened or suspended for some members of society. In this state of anomie, sometimes referred to as "normlessness," it is difficult for some individuals to know exactly what is expected of them. In extreme cases, such persons may be "free" to take their own lives. Durkheim contended that unusually high suicide rates could be predicted from a careful study of prevailing social conditions.

Merton's Theory of Anomie

Suicide is just one form of deviant behavior. In 1938, Robert K. Merton modified and expanded Durkheim's concept of anomie into a general theory that would help explain many different kinds of deviant behavior (Merton, 1957). As a result of this conceptual connection with Durkheim's early work, Merton's more fully developed **Strain Theory** of deviant behavior is often referred to as **Anomie Theory.** There are very few sociological theories that are broad enough in basic concepts and assumptions to encompass a wide spectrum of deviant behaviors with any degree of specificity. A general theory is like an umbrella. Just as several different individuals may find shelter under a shared umbrella, so Merton's general theory of anomie offers an organized framework of logical explanations that can be applied to several kinds of deviant behavior including juvenile delinquency.

Merton perceived anomie as a state of dissatisfaction arising from a sense of discrepancy between the aspirations of an individual and the means that the person has available to realize these ambitions. In his essay on anomie as related to deviant behavior, Merton observed that Americans are exposed to powerful socialization processes that stress the success ethic. Consequently, nearly everyone has internalized the culturally approved goal of "getting ahead," that is, making money, accumulating material possessions, and achieving high social status based on money and occupation. At the same time, our society gives a clear message regarding the culturally approved means to achieve these lofty objectives. We are encouraged to strive for them as society says we should: attend school, work hard, save money, lead lives of virtue, thrift, patience, and deferred gratification, and ultimately we hope to realize our dreams of material success. However, Merton maintained that some people, particularly among the disadvantaged lower classes,[1] unhappily realize that they will not be able to achieve those idealized goals through the legitimate means that society

---

[1]*Underclass* is the more acceptable term today. However, in order to maintain consistency in usage and avoid confusion, we will use the term *lower class* when discussing or referring to older, classic studies.

endorses. They may lack the academic background to attend college, and the only jobs available to them may be unskilled, low-paying "dead-end jobs" that lead to neither promotion nor financial security. Yet, the desire to fulfill the internalized objectives persists. This juxtaposition of idealized, socially approved goals, and the reality of reduced life chances and opportunities for achievement in the socially approved ways, places many individuals in a state of helpless and hopeless frustration or anomie. Denied legitimate opportunities, the rules of the game may come to have diminished importance. What really matters to such anomic individuals is not how one "plays the game" but whether one "wins." Under such circumstances, some persons will turn to illegitimate means to attain the culturally approved goals. However, Merton contended, not everyone who experiences the anomic frustration over blocked goals will resort to criminal behavior. Other avenues of adaptation are also open. Merton's Typology of Modes of Adaptive Behavior is an innovative contribution and is the heart of his general theory of deviance.

In his Typology of Modes of Adaptive Behavior, Merton schematically identified five logically possible behavioral patterns for individuals as they respond to the culturally approved goals and institutionalized means for achieving those idealized objectives that predominate in American society (Figure 6-1). Merton stressed that these are role adaptations and not personality types. People may readily shift from one of these roles to another.

The first adaptation is *Conformity,* which encompasses most members of our society. These are individuals who accept both the culturally approved success goals and the institutionalized work ethic for achievement. Thus, their behavior generally conforms to societal expectations.

The other four possible adaptations in behavior represent deviant responses to one's recognition of the conflict between cultural goals and institutionalized means in the context of his or her related state of anomie. Adaptation Number II is *Innovation* and characterizes those individuals who subscribe to the typical cultural goals of monetary and material success but realize that they lack the socially approved and legitimate means to achieve those goals. They become dissatisfied, frustrated, and anomic, and resort to innovative, norm-violating

FIGURE 6-1 Merton's Typology of Modes of Individual Adaptive Behavior

	Individual Adaptations	Culturally Approved Goals	Institutionalized Means of Achievement
I.	Conformity	(+)	(+)
II.	Innovation	(+)	(−)
III.	Ritualism	(−)	(+)
IV.	Retreatism	(−)	(−)
V.	Rebellion	(−,+)	(−,+)

Source: Merton, R. K. Social structure and anomie. *American Sociological Review* 3 (1938):676.

NOTE: (+) signifies "acceptance" by the individual.
(−) signifies "rejection" by the individual.
(−,+) signifies "rejection of existing goals and means and the substitution of new goals and means" by the individual.

behavior to achieve the coveted cultural goals. This adaptation to blocked goals is often a criminal or delinquent response (Bernard, 1990).

Behavioral Adaptation Number III is *Ritualism* and involves a rigid adherence to the culturally approved methods for getting ahead and making progress. However, like a caged squirrel on a treadmill, the individual's overconformity isn't really going to "pay off." In time, perhaps the person will realize that the attained level of achievement will not equal the level of aspiration or effort. This person also experiences a feeling of despair and anomie, and may ultimately modify or abandon the idealized cultural goals, but persists at a ritualized, unfulfilling line of work.

Adaptation Number IV is *Retreatism*. Here the individual, in anomic frustration, abandons both cultural goals *and* the institutionalized means for attaining them. In a sense, the person gives up in the struggle to reach the seemingly unreachable goals via unrewarding methods, and retreats from a social system and a culture that imposes such unreasonable "ends" and "means." This adaptation is reflected in the retreatist behavior of some runaways, drug users, and alcoholics who turn their backs and seek to escape from the struggle for material success and other socially approved values.

The fifth behavioral adaptation is *Rebellion*. In this case, the individual malcontent, angry over the anomic situation experienced, rejects both the culturally approved goals and the institutionalized means of achievement. In their place are substituted new goals and new means of achievement. The individual interprets the disjunction between prevailing cultural objectives and the approved means for their accomplishment as patently unfair, and the call for a new social order is a typical response of the social reformer or revolutionary.

Cohen's "Delinquent Boys"

Albert Cohen (1955) elaborated upon Merton's anomie explanation of deviant behavior with his theory that a large amount of delinquent behavior results from blocked goals and "status frustration." According to Cohen, lower class boys want to achieve success and higher social status, just like middle and upper class boys. Yet, due to their unpromising social circumstances, they find that they are blocked from achieving status (especially in school). Essentially, Cohen reported, lower class boys who aspire to increased social status in a dominant, middle class value system can respond in one of three ways:

1. The "college-boy" response.
2. The "corner-boy" response.
3. The "delinquent-boy" response.

The "college-boy" response roughly corresponds to Merton's Conformity mode of adaptation. In this case, the lower class youth accepts the challenge of the middle class value system and, through higher education and deferred gratification (foregoing small immediate rewards for larger long-term rewards), attempts to achieve social status by conforming to middle class expectations. This response is chosen by comparatively few lower class boys, according to Cohen, because their limited financial resources make chances for college graduation and occupational success extremely low.

Probably the most common response in Cohen's scheme is the "corner-boy" response, which involves the youth's withdrawal into a subculture of working class boys who share a mutual set of values by which status can be gained within the group without having to conform and compete with middle class society. This is analogous to Merton's Retreatism mode of adaptation to anomic conditions. While this group is not specifically delinquent in its purpose, the boys who choose this response are likely to become involved in delinquent activities (especially status offenses such as truancy, smoking, and alcohol consumption).

The final response in Cohen's typology is the "delinquent-boy." Boys in this group—manifestly similar to the youths who make Merton's Innovation and Rebellion adaptations—become frustrated with their inability to gain status through conventional means. Consequently, they develop what Cohen referred to as a delinquent subculture, whose values and behavior are antithetical to those espoused by the middle class. Paradoxically, in acting out their subcultural values, these boys find themselves in harmony with the expectations of their group, but are perceived as nonconforming delinquents by the larger society.

The similarities between the theories of Merton and Cohen are striking. However, some major differences do exist. Merton's approach tended to focus on individual responses to social situations, whereas Cohen's approach was much more oriented toward group responses. Also, Merton viewed criminal deviance as practical and utilitarian in nature, whereas Cohen (1955:25) saw delinquency as more "nonutilitarian, malicious, and negativistic."

Cloward and Ohlin's "Delinquency and Opportunity"

Richard Cloward and Lloyd Ohlin (1960) further added to the social strain approach to explaining delinquent behavior with their concept of "illegitimate opportunity." Like Cohen, they also accepted Merton's view that lower class juveniles generally internalize the standard success goals. They also agreed with Merton and Cohen that the blockage of these goals can lead to status frustration for some youths and place them in a position of untenable strain. This situation can then result in a sense of alienation and anomie in which those affected may turn to delinquent, illegitimate means to achieve an increment in status. It is at this point that Cloward and Ohlin moved their theoretical formulation beyond those suggested by both Merton and Cohen.

Cloward and Ohlin contended that while lower class juveniles have differential opportunities for achieving success through *legitimate* means, they also have differential opportunities for achieving it through *illegitimate* means. They pointed out that there are some areas in which illegitimate opportunities for youth to acquire success and status are not readily available. In such surroundings, some juveniles may be totally frustrated with their locked-in lowly status and lack of opportunity to achieve the idealized success goals. Lacking even deviant or delinquent opportunities, their frustration is unrequited and their aspirations remain unfulfilled. In situations where there *are* illegitimate opportunities, Cloward and Ohlin saw response to anomic frustration as being group-oriented. However, the type of delinquent response depends upon the *kind* of illegitimate opportunity available to the youths. Thus, in contrast to Cohen who saw blocked goals leading to a rather standard delinquent gang response, Cloward and Ohlin delineated three possible delinquent subcultural responses. In other words, while anomic status frustration over blocked goals could well be a common denominator in groups of lower class boys scattered throughout a city,

Cloward and Ohlin contended that some youth, in "retreating" from their own sense of frustration over failure to achieve socially approved status and success, may turn to a gang-related, drug subculture.

the particular form of collective, delinquent response any given group might make would depend on the kind of delinquent opportunity available to the group.

Cloward and Ohlin presented three types of juvenile gangs, each characterized by different kinds of delinquent activities:

1. The "crime-oriented gang."
2. The "conflict-oriented gang."
3. The "retreatist-oriented gang."

The kinds of gangs and delinquent responses that are generated depend, according to Cloward and Ohlin, upon the differential opportunities available in their environments.

The first response of underclass youths to their collective sense of unjust deprivation and alienation described by Cloward and Ohlin involves such criminal activities as theft, fraud, and extortion. The criminal orientation of this group of young people is elicited and orchestrated by adult criminal elements that operate in the neighborhood or district in which this group of disenchanted and anomic youths reside. In the perceived absence of a legitimate opportunity structure, they become vulnerable to the influence of adult criminals whose activities and prosperity have relatively high visibility in the area. The adult criminals are in a position to serve as viable role models and mentors for youths feeling the disappointment and frustration of blocked avenues to success. According to Cloward and Ohlin, the criminal alternative and the opportunity for enhanced social status lead these boys into instrumental delinquency, in which they serve as "apprentice criminals" under the direction and control of adult professionals.

The second anomic response of the youths described by Cloward and Ohlin is the formation of a conflict-oriented gang. Again, the emergence of this particular pattern of gang delinquency is contingent upon the kind of opportunity available to the gang members. Cloward and Ohlin suggested that youthful gangs that turn to fighting and violence as important means of securing status live in areas where both conventional and criminal opportunities are either absent or very weak. In other words, the conflict-oriented activities of these street gangs develop under conditions of relative detachment from all institutionalized systems of opportunity and social control, either legitimate or illegitimate. These are neighborhoods where opportunities for upward social mobility are essentially nonexistent, conventional law enforcement agencies are weak, and where opportunities to participate with adult criminals in their illegal but successful operations are also absent. In such areas frustrated and discontented youths often must generate their own status hierarchy in physical combat with one another and with society.

Cloward and Ohlin termed the third kind of collective, delinquent response as the retreatist-oriented gang. While this response is a *group* reaction to social strain engendered by blocked success opportunities, it is similar to Merton's fourth Mode of Individual Adaptation, in which the actor disengages and retreats from the larger society. Cloward and Ohlin depicted the members of the retreatist gang as overwhelmed with feelings of failure, despair, and normlessness. These youths withdraw into the restricted world of their group and center their attention and activity upon the consumption of drugs in quest of physical or emotional "highs." In this way, they not only demonstrate their contempt for the normative standards of conforming society, but mask their sense of failure. As with the other two types of delinquent gang responses, the development of the retreatist group and its characteristic behavior depends upon the presence of certain opportunity structures in the members' environment. There must be easy access to sources of drugs and the lore of drug use in the area where the potential gang members live. The genesis of a drug subculture in lower class neighborhoods is often aided by "rapid geographical mobility, inadequate social controls, and other manifestations of social disorganization" (Cloward and Ohlin, 1960:178).

One of the most innovative ideas put forward by Cloward and Ohlin centers on how youths are recruited or motivated to abandon the quest for material success and social status and adopt a retreatist orientation. Just as it requires some opportunity and aptitude to achieve societal goals in the culturally approved ways, so too, one must also have a measure of opportunity and certain physical or organizational abilities in order to acquire success through crime or delinquency. Therefore, Cloward and Ohlin suggest, youths failing in both legitimate and illegitimate approaches to material success and social status are *double failures*. These "double failures" are most likely to demonstrate their anomic frustration in a retreatest gang response.

Contributions of Social Strain Theories

In summary of the social strain theories put forward by Merton, Cohen, and by Cloward and Ohlin, deviance and delinquency are viewed as primarily a result of the social structure in which they occur. Juveniles who grow up in communities where access to culturally approved objectives by conventional means is denied, and where a large degree of social disorganization is present, are likely to find themselves in situations where the social norms governing behavior are not clearly defined. It follows, according to social strain theories, that these youngsters may discover that delinquent activities supply opportunities to achieve social identity and social status.

For many years, Social Strain Theory, with its fundamental postulates of anomie and social disorganization, dominated sociological explanations of deviant and delinquent behavior. It is an inherently sociological approach; and, because official arrest statistics seem to support the idea that juvenile delinquency is primarily a lower class phenomenon, strain theory has offered a great deal of explanatory power. More recently, a number of researchers have rallied in support of Merton's Social Strain Theory as basically correct in a broad sense, if not in all particulars (Bernard, 1990; Menard, 1995).

The strain theories of delinquency have contributed to an understanding of the relationship between the status frustration experienced by lower class youths and poor performance in school. For example, Polk and Schafer (1972) indicated that poor school performance and the feelings of frustration due to blocked educational opportunities of economically disadvantaged youths have been linked to juvenile delinquency (this phenomenon and its relationship to delinquency is further explored in Chapter 10).

Although Merton made no direct application of his anomie theory to juvenile delinquency, it is widely regarded as one of the most influential and useful formulations in describing and explaining the process behind many forms of deviant and delinquent behavior. A number of other social scientists were quick to recognize the potential of Merton's general theory of deviance in explaining why at least some juveniles become delinquent (Farnsworth and Leiber, 1989).

Perhaps the greatest contribution of the strain theories has been in its application to gang delinquency (discussed in detail in Chapter 12). Cohen, Cloward and Ohlin, and others effectively applied the basic assumptions of anomie and the strain theories to help explain the formation and activities of juvenile gangs. Irving Spergel (1964), for example, studied lower class gangs, and while his typology of gangs differed from the one constructed by Cloward and Ohlin, he documented that juvenile gangs indeed tend to specialize in certain types of delinquent activities.

While debate continues over whether lower class youths actually internalize middle class aspirations and goals as assumed by the proponents of strain theory, and while most juvenile delinquency does not involve juvenile gangs, the strain theories emphasized the importance of socioeconomic status, neighborhood environment, and adaptation to the social structure as being important variables in the understanding of delinquency. These contributions have provided insight into some types of juvenile delinquency, especially those related to the activities of lower class gangs.

Criticisms and Limitations of Social Strain Theories

A number of weaknesses in the explanatory arguments of strain theory have been advanced. For example, the anomie theory of deviance, while useful in explaining some kinds of lower class nonconformity, makes some questionable assumptions about the situation of lower class people. It assumes, first, that people from the lower social classes develop about the same level of aspiration for themselves as do people from the more favored classes. Studies of lower class subjects show that this is not always the case, that lower class people tend to develop a fairly realistic assessment of their lowered life chances and adjust their expectations accordingly (e.g., Han, 1969).

Another apparent assumption of the anomie theory that may be faulty is the generalization that structural frustration causes delinquency (Agnew, 1984). Sanders (1976:31) challenged this assumption by asking:

> …why is it that only a relatively few members of the lower socioeconomic strata commit delinquent acts frequently? Why are boys ten times more likely to engage in delinquent acts than girls in the same social position?

Travis Hirschi (1969) pointed out that most delinquent boys eventually become law-abiding adults, which is a potential source of embarrassment to the strain theorists. Indeed, most delinquents do come to terms with society as they mature. They do *not* graduate into a life of adult crime. Typically, as they mature, they abandon juvenile crime and misbehavior. But their eventual reform cannot be explained by changes in the lower class conditions that purportedly forced them into their initial deviance.

In *Delinquent Boys* (1955), Cohen's main focus was on the nonutilitarian behavior of lower class juveniles. It was at this point that Sykes and Matza (1957) cast doubt upon Cohen's theory by contending that the delinquent gangs they studied stole in order to get money for entertainment—which merely demonstrated that they were impractical adolescents, rather than "nonutilitarian."

Cohen's point that lower class youths make a delinquent response as a frustrated attack upon middle class standards also has been targeted for criticism. Kitsuse and Dietrick (1959) argued that the initial motives of youths for joining gangs and participating in delinquent activities are many and varied, ranging from self-preservation in the neighborhood to the desire for friends.

Cloward and Ohlin's theory of Differential Opportunity also has been subjected to sharp criticism. The main complaint has been that the theory's emphasis on a set of delinquent subcultural reactions to perceived lack of economic opportunity ignores other major factors in delinquency causation. For example, Bordua (1962) charged that Cloward and Ohlin had a tendency to ignore the life histories of their delinquent subjects. The delinquents of Thrasher, Cohen, Miller, and other theorists were presented as having family, school, and other background experiences that affected their subsequent delinquent behavior. "On the other hand, Cloward and Ohlin's delinquents seem suddenly to appear on the scene sometime in adolescence, to look at the world, and to discover: 'There's no opportunity in my structure!'" (Bordua, 1962:255).

Cohen (1966) pointed out that Cloward and Ohlin suggested a false dichotomy between "legitimate opportunities" and "illegitimate opportunities." He argued:

> …the same things are typically, and perhaps always, both. [For] example, identical firearms can be used to kill deer in season; or deer, policemen, and estranged spouses out of season. It is one of the most fundamental and pervasive dilemmas of social life that all legitimate power, whether over things or people, can be used to implement or to violate social norms (Cohen, 1966:110).

Cloward and Ohlin's contention that youthful gangs specialized in criminality, fighting, or drug use also has been challenged. Numerous studies consistently have shown delinquent gangs to be engaged in a wide variety of illegal activities (Short et al., 1963; Kulik et al., 1968).

Another common complaint regarding the Theory of Differential Opportunity centers on the rather rigid typological structure (a criticism also shared by Merton's Anomie Theory and most other behavioral typologies). Lemert (1967), Short (1963), and Bordua (1962) all contended that the assignment of groups to one or another category is too mechanistic, that is, much gang delinquency in working class areas is more spontaneous and unstructured than Cloward and Ohlin would have us believe.

A persistent criticism of Strain Theory in general is that Merton, Cohen, and Cloward and Ohlin—while suggesting helpful explanations of underclass delinquency—fail to offer any direct insights regarding delinquency in the middle and upper classes. This may be a moot point since most strain theorists never claimed etiological generality beyond the lower class.

Perhaps a more telling deficiency in Strain Theory is the shortage of viable applications to female delinquency of any class. Ruth Triplett and Roger Jarjoura (1997) point out that "although gender and social class are two of the best known correlates of crime and delinquency, criminologists have shown surprisingly little interest in exploring how these variables intersect in the etiology of deviant behavior" (p. 287). Their research findings add significant details to the idea of blocked goals leading to individual strain and possibly illegal conduct—for females as well as males. More specifically, Triplett and Jarjoura "suggest that gender and class are both important factors shaping educational expectations and through them, the likelihood of delinquency involvement" (1997:287). John Hoffman and Susan Su (1997), in their "Strain Theory Assessment of Sex Differences," found that stressful life events have similar impact on delinquency and drug use among both females and males.

Cultural Transmission Theories

Another line of theory building was established in 1938 with a focus on the contradictory and often competitive cultural content of different social groups. The underlying assumption was that the heterogeneity of the population associated with twentieth-century industrialization and urbanization resulted in an inharmonious mixture of ethnic, religious, political, and social class subcultures, each with its own distinctive beliefs, traditions, values, norms, and behavioral expectations. Moreover, it was assumed to be self-evident that the proximity of these diverse segments of the urban population would lead to unavoidable culture conflict as each group judged its own standards as correct and normal and those of other groups as deviant and delinquent.

Sellin's Theory of Culture Conflict

Thorsten Sellin, a criminologist, laid important groundwork for this theoretical approach to explaining criminal and delinquent behavior with the publication of *Culture Conflict and Crime* (1938). Sellin, in explaining fluctuating crime rates in different parts of urban society, noted that values, customs, and standards of conduct were not uniform throughout the population. On the contrary, many districts and neighborhoods of our large cities seem to

BOX 6-1   Controversial Issue

Social Structure as a Proposed Cause of Urban Crime and Delinquency

Roland Chilton's 1991 longitudinal analysis of urban crime and arrest rates forms the basis of his thought-provoking challenge to several theories of crime and delinquency:

[The] estimated non-white incarceration counts…have increased more rapidly than the white incarceration counts.… Black Americans already constitute about 48 percent of the jail population and 46 percent of the prison population. They are greatly over-represented in relation to their numbers in the U.S., where they make up about 12 percent of the population.…

To make sense of the arrest and incarceration patterns, I think we will need to abandon suggestions that physiologically or psychologically aberrant individuals have increased in some random or haphazard way. We will also have to abandon suggestions that it is the misconduct of police, prosecutors and judges that is producing this dismaying trend. I believe we will have to look at widespread practices and procedures occurring in the larger society. In short, I think we will need what is at heart a structural explanation to understand the patterns shown above.…

One of the most plausible explanations for these differences was suggested by Robert Sampson (1987), building on the work of William J. Wilson (1980).… who emphasized the importance of institutions—entrenched ways of doing things—over an emphasis on individual stress and strain. Sampson focused on changes in both family and economic arrangements. He suggests that the economic position of many adult black men increases rates of crime and delinquency through its impact on family life.… If long-term marital commitment and family life suffer because of lack of steady, good paying jobs, the result may be criminal conduct by the next generation—not necessarily by those who are currently unemployed.…

In suggesting that the major cause of the observed increase in black crime is structural, I am suggesting that a number of large changes in urban America have produced social and economic conditions that have reduced the possibilities for much of the crime-limiting socialization of children that occurred in the past, and that still occurs in most suburban and small town areas.…

It is ironic that, as the rights of black Americans in relation to other citizens have increased, and after official legal segregation has been virtually eliminated, there should be increased economic and social segregation in U.S. cities. However, this is clearly what happened as all-black areas of most cities grew in size and as the white populations of most cities either withdrew to other all-white areas or moved to the suburbs.…

The situation was made worse by the reduction of employment possibilities for central city residents with the movement or closing of many urban industrial plants. In my view, it was these changes that produced the profound changes in family arrangements we have seen among large segments of the black population.

The consequences of these losses of employment opportunities was not simply psychological strain for the adults involved. These changes also created situations where there was less time and money for the care and training of children. I am suggesting that this isolation or exclusion from stable employment created more unstable and disadvantaged families.…

It is the combined impact of increasingly segregated cities, increasingly impoverished cities, and dramatic changes in employment opportunities and family life that has produced the increases in robbery and other predatory crime in most American cities (Chilton, 1991:2–3, 7–9).

Continued

BOX 6-1 *Continued*

Charles Murray (1992) has offered a satirical and stinging rebuttal to the structural etiology of crime espoused by Chilton and others:

> *Beginning in the early 60's…American social policy toward poor and disadvantaged youths underwent a transformation.… Poverty, it was concluded, is caused by structural features of capitalism. If a student misbehaves in school or a young man snatches a purse or a young woman has a baby without a husband, these are expressions of or a response to social conditions beyond their control. Value judgments themselves are inappropriate. Having a baby without a husband is a choice, not a sin or*

> *even necessarily a mistake. It is society that must change, not individuals; the rich must see the errors of their ways, not the poor the errors of theirs. To hold people accountable for their behavior is unjust—blaming the victim. Root cause must be corrected (Quoted in Bennett, 1994:67).*

* * * *

Chilton and Murray each have their allies as they take opposite positions in an ongoing public debate in assigning causal responsibility to individuals or society for crime and delinquency. In view of the many related factors and theories discussed in Part II of this text, where do you stand on the issue?

Sources

Bennett, William, J. 1994. *The index of leading cultural indicators.* New York: Simon & Schuster.
Chilton, Roland, 1991. Urban crime trends and criminological theory. *Criminal Justice Research Bulletin* 6 (3). Criminal Justice Center, Sam Houston State University. Huntsville, TX.
Murray, Charles. 1992. The legacy of the 60's. *Commentary,* July, 1992.
Sampson, Robert J. 1987. Urban black violence: The effect of male nobleness and family disruption. *American Journal of Sociology,* 93:348–382.
Wilson, William J. 1980. *The declining significance of race: Black and changing American institutions* (2nd ed.). Chicago: University of Chicago Press.

represent the ethnic culture of foreign countries more than the general culture of the United States. Additionally, the various social classes also occupy their own subcultural "islands" where their own distinctive beliefs, norms, and behaviors prevail.

If these different groups were not in direct geographical and social contact with each other and with the larger society, their behavior would not be subject to comparison and evaluation so closely. However, because such diverse groups coexist in proximity to one another, chronic and abrasive culture conflict often ensues. Thus, Sellin concluded, culture conflict creates a great potential for misunderstanding and antagonism, especially among the subordinate, lower class groups regarding what is conforming and what is deviant behavior. Even the definitions of crime and delinquency can become culturally relative and subject to interpretation within the cultural context of particular groups and neighborhoods in which assimilation into the dominant society is incomplete (Cole, 1993).

Burgess' Concentric Zone Theory

Considerable evidence of the distinctive spatial patterns and concentrations of minority groups, social classes, and specialized land uses was amassed during the 1920s and 1930s by sociologists Robert Park, Ernest Burgess, R. D. McKenzie, and others in the forefront of human ecology, a newly emerging sociological subarea. For example, Burgess (1925), using Chicago as his model, demonstrated the variation in naturally formed urban areas, each occupied by a particular part of the population and reserved for a particular land use, such as commercial, lower class housing, middle class housing, and so forth. Burgess hypothesized that these population groupings and specialized land uses develop as a series of concentric zones spreading out from the dominant and dynamic city center and that this pattern characterized the industrial city of his time (Figure 6-2).

Burgess pinpointed Zone II as an urban environment especially conducive to a wide variety of individual maladjustments and social problems, including crime and delin-

FIGURE 6-2   Burgess' Concentric Zone Pattern of Urban Development

Source: Burgess, E. W. "The Growth of the City: An Introduction to a Research Project." In Park, Burgess, and McKenzie (Eds.), *The City.* University of Chicago Press (1925), pp. 47–62. Reprinted by permission.

quency. Zone II, The Zone of Transition, was so designated because it was the area most subject to rapid change. Population was ever-shifting as waves of new and generally impoverished immigrants settled first in the crowded tenements to begin their American experience. Many of the neighborhoods in Zone II reflected the cultural and ethnic identity of groups of inhabitants from Ireland, Poland, Italy, and other foreign countries (Figure 6-3).

Zone II also was called The Zone of Transition because it lay between the more prosperous and expanding commercial center of the city and the more established residential areas of blue-collar workers in Zone III. Thus, encroachments, invasions, and successions of new

FIGURE 6-3   Burgess' Concentric Zone Pattern of Urban Development

Source: Burgess, E. W. "The Growth of the City: An Introduction to a Research Project." In Park, Burgess, and McKenzie (Eds.), *The City.* University of Chicago Press (1925), pp. 47–62. Reprinted by permission.

groups of people and new land uses, and other forms of social change, were most obvious and traumatic in Zone II. To people living in such an area, nothing seems to be permanent, as society is in a continual cycle of settlement and resettlement, of disorganization and reorganization.

A number of researchers investigated these urban dynamics of social disorganization, industrialization, population movements, and changes in neighborhoods to determine their influence on crime and delinquency. For example, W. I. Thomas and Florian Znaniecki, in their study *The Polish Peasant* (1927) examined social disorganization in a Polish neighborhood of Chicago. They noted the failure of existing social rules and norms to control behavior, and they documented their observations that the home, neighborhood, church, and friendship groups lost some of their influence to control behavior in an environment of rapid social change.

Shaw and McKay's "High Delinquency Areas"

Clifford Shaw and Henry McKay (1942), influenced by the early ecological studies coming from the University of Chicago, charted the spatial distribution of crime and delinquency on maps of Chicago and other cities. They discovered that crime and delinquency and other social pathologies had definite patterns and areas of concentration in the urban community. They listed their findings as follows:

1. Juvenile delinquents are not distributed uniformly over the city of Chicago but tend to be concentrated in areas adjacent to the central business district and to heavy industrial areas.
2. There are wide variations in the rates of delinquents between areas in Chicago....
3. The rates of delinquents tend to vary inversely with distance from the center of the city (Shaw and McKay, 1931:383–385; also see Cox and Conrad, 1996).

The areas identified by Shaw and McKay with a high incidence of juvenile delinquency were called High Delinquency Areas. Their data pointed to the same central districts of the city identified by Burgess as the Zone of Transition whose substandard, slum housing was occupied by poor underclass residents, often immigrants and ethnic minorities, with problems of adjustment similar to those uncovered in the classic study by Thomas and Znaniecki (1927).

Shaw and McKay concluded that delinquency rates reflected the kinds of neighborhoods in which children were raised. They contended that deteriorated poverty-ridden areas of cities tend to produce social disorganization which, in turn, produces delinquency. In their view, high delinquency areas are characterized by local values and norms that are sometimes contrary to the values, norms and best interests of the larger society. A local subculture develops that successfully transmits these antisocial values and norms to younger generations growing up in the area. (Also see Lundman, 1993:59–62).

Miller's Focus on Lower Class Culture

Walter Miller (1958) offered a different explanation of adolescent misbehavior as a product of its cultural context. Miller's theory disagreed with the reactive subculture theories of Cohen and of Cloward and Ohlin which portrayed groups of lower class delinquents responding in anomic frustration to their blocked access to idealized, middle class, success goals.

The lower class, inner-city, slum environment—often characterized by poverty and disorganization—has been linked with juvenile delinquency by many social theorists and reformers.

Rather, Miller proposed that lower class culture contains an effective body of values, norms, and behavioral expectations in its own right. Moreover, children and youths from lower class families and neighborhoods internalize their culture content just as thoroughly as young people from the middle class learn their culture. It follows, Miller argued, that much of what Cohen, Cloward and Ohlin, and others interpreted as a lower class, delinquent reaction to the unfair imposition of middle class values was actually a reasonable reflection of their own lower class values.

Miller's theory rightly belongs in this section of Cultural Transmission Theories because the origin and motivation for the aggressive and often antisocial conduct is successful lower class socialization. According to Miller, the youth's delinquency results not from a lack of commitment to middle class cultural values, but from a commitment to lower class cultural values. Thus, lower class conformity does not harmonize with the behavioral expectations of the dominant middle class.

In circumventing the "delinquent subculture" as etiologically related to the objectionable conduct, Miller went directly to the lower class in general and identified six "focal concerns" or "values" that have high priority for young males:

1. **Trouble.** Chronic anxiety over possible confrontation with law enforcement personnel and the consequences of illegal behavior. Staying out of "trouble" is a major, practical concern of many lower class people.

2. **Toughness.** The exhibition of physical prowess; fearlessness; masculinity. Miller saw this kind of posturing as extremely important to lower class boys who come from female-based households (dominant mothers and absent fathers) and who are trying to establish a male identity. Thus, they equate femininity with weakness.
3. **Smartness.** Display of verbal agility; quick-wittedness; ability to outsmart.
4. **Excitement.** Thrill-seeking; taking a chance; fighting over women.
5. **Fate.** A tendency to trust in luck; to assume that what will be, will be.
6. **Autonomy.** The need to feel independent and free from external authority. Here again, the youth can publicly manifest his bravado by declaring: "I can take care of myself!"

Miller believed that such class-specific focal concerns or values develop because the social classes are continually being separated and segregated from each other spatially, economically, and socially. Hence, youths are likely to develop values and behaviors distinctive of their own class. The internalization of lower class values combined with a need to demonstrate their "manhood" can, according to Miller, cause some young males to defy authority and participate in fighting and other activities that, in turn, could be interpreted by middle class people as a predisposition to juvenile delinquency.

Contributions of Cultural Transmission Theories

The four theoretical formulations presented in this section offer significant contributions in data, concepts, and fresh insights that help explain juvenile delinquency. Each one is like a different lens on a microscope that reveals new and fascinating details regarding the content of culture and subculture as it relates to delinquent behavior.

Sellin's Culture Conflict Theory recognized early the pluralistic nature of society in the United States. Rather than viewing society as a homogeneous entity wherein unchallenged, universal norms prevail, Sellin emphasized the vast diversity of groups and subcultures within the larger society. Many of these ethnic and social class subcultures come into contact with one another in the urban environment—a contact made unpleasant and abrasive by conflicting codes of conduct. Crime and delinquency as a precipitate of culture conflict between dominant and subordinate social groups is convincingly detailed.

Burgess (1925) paid careful attention to ecological space relationships as human groups interact in a crowded, heterogeneous, urban environment. He pointed to the ethnic enclaves in Chicago and other large cities that generate and reinforce subcultures with territoriality, social identity, and solidarity. The more entrenched and resistant the subculture is to assimilation, the greater the likelihood of normative conflict, especially for younger generations in subordinate subcultures. This was the idea behind the concept of "the marginal man" suggested by Burgess' colleague, Robert Park (1928) who, followed by Everett Stonequist (1937), traced the alienation and delinquency of many children of immigrants to their marginal social status and identity as they are caught between two conflicting cultural systems. These second-generation residents of the ethnic area were exposed to the norms, traditions, and language of the "old country" in their homes and neighborhood and, at the same time, experienced the socialization of their American school and peer group. Thus, they became "marginal"—without complete commitment or assimilation into either of the conflicting cultures.

Shaw and McKay (1942) incorporated an ecological dimension from Burgess into their criminological scrutiny of Chicago. They identified distinctive spatial patterns of crime and delinquency that corresponded with specific ethnic and social class areas, particularly in the inner city. Perhaps Shaw and McKay's greatest contribution was the discovery that High Delinquency Areas of Chicago usually retained that statistical reputation in spite of major changes in the ethnic composition of the population in the areas. Repeated collection, examination, and comparison of population and crime data for those troubled areas revealed that they were inhabited by successive waves of poor immigrants from various European countries. Over time, older immigrant groups improved their economic standing with better jobs, experienced a measure of assimilation, and moved further out from the central city into more stable and affluent residential areas. Their places in the old, least desirable neighborhoods were taken by the most recently arrived immigrant groups. As each ethnic group escaped from inner-city blight and poverty, it manifested lower rates of juvenile delinquency, while rates remained extraordinarily high in the old areas adjacent to centers of commerce and heavy industry, irrespective of the ethnicity or national origin of the new residents. From this, Shaw and McKay (1969) concluded that the delinquency-producing factors are inherent in the socioeconomic conditions of the community, not in the racial or ethnic composition of the population.

Miller (1958) embarked in a different direction in making his contribution to Cultural Transmission Theory. His focus on lower class culture identified a set of basic values that can activate lower class, adolescent behavior that, in turn, may be perceived as overly aggressive and delinquent by middle class people. Miller did not justify lower class gang delinquency; rather, his analysis adds significantly to our understanding of why lower class youngsters become delinquent. While such behavior may reflect a culturally relevant quest for manhood, it is still often dangerous and undesirable. David Brownfield's research (1990) found empirical support for Miller's contention that such highly esteemed attributes as toughness and autonomy are particularly strong predictors of delinquent behavior.

Criticisms and Limitations of Cultural Transmission Theories

The studies of Burgess (1925), Thomas and Znaniecki (1927), Shaw and McKay (1942)—as well as the work of Cloward and Ohlin (1960) discussed under Strain Theories—all strongly suggest that social disorganization often characterizes individuals and groups living in high delinquency areas. This assumption has been seriously questioned. A number of more recent studies have concluded that lower class neighborhoods are not without social organization. Rather, their social organization is different from that found in middle class areas.

Shaw and McKay implied that social disorganization was most prevalent in areas whose local institutions were unable to control the behavior of local residents. Certainly, many of the families, schools, churches, and formal law enforcement agencies appear weakened and impotent in high delinquency areas. The strength of local organizations is to a large extent a function of local participation, and participation in such organizations is most likely among people who have positive feelings about their neighborhoods (Bursik, 1984:403). On the other hand, in areas of oppressive poverty, status deprivation, and urban blight that withers hope, local residents may give up on traditional institutions and develop a form of social organization more realistic to their prospects and satisfying to their needs. Certainly, William Whyte's *Street Corner Society* (1981) and other similar studies indicate that there is a high degree of social organization in slum neighborhoods. While the nature of that social organization is different from larger, middle class society, it is no less meaningful and viable to participants. Jane Jacobs, in *The Death and Life of Great American Cities* (1961:53, 57), insightfully described the more casual and less structured social organization of inner-city neighborhoods:

> *Reformers have long observed city people loitering on busy corners, hanging around in candy stores and bars and drinking soda pop on stoops, and have passed a judgment, the gist of which is: "This is deplorable. If these people had decent homes and a more private...outdoor place, they wouldn't be on the street!"*
>
> *This judgment represents a profound misunderstanding of cities. It makes no more sense than to drop in at a testimonial banquet in a hotel and conclude that if these people had wives who could cook, they would give their parties at home.*
>
> *The point of both the testimonial banquet and the social life of city sidewalks is precisely that they are public...*
>
> *Formal types of local city organizations are frequently assumed by planners and even by some social workers to grow in direct, common sense fashion out of announcements of meetings, the presence of meeting-rooms, and the existence of problems of obvious public concern. Perhaps they grow so in suburbs and towns. They do not grow so in cities. Formal public organizations in cities require an informal public life underlying them, mediating between them and the privacy of the people of the city.*

Delinquency area studies also have been criticized by other researchers on the ground that official statistics of arrests and court appearances, used to measure the amount of delinquency for such areas, probably are biased because of more rigorous law enforcement, compared to more affluent, middle and upper class suburbs (see Chapter 3).

Another complaint regarding the logic of the High Delinquency Area thesis is that such urban areas may be *collectors* of deviants rather than the *generators* of deviant behavior. In other words, the socioeconomic conditions and social disorganization of the local community may not be the primary causal variables of crime and delinquency in the area. This argument holds that the real antecedent variable is the pre-existing condition or propensity to illegal behavior in some persons prior to their movement into the high delinquency neighborhood. For example, the district of cheap bars and saloons commonly referred to as "skid-row" does not produce alcoholics. Rather, many people who already have a serious drinking problem gravitate to skidrow because they can merge without difficulty into an area subculture and lifestyle similar to their own. Similarly, "the red light district" does not produce prostitutes. Many prostitutes will move there to find a supportive subculture and other people who share their values and behavioral expectations. The same reasoning can be applied to some of the criminal and delinquent elements that inhabit high delinquency areas. It is conceivable that they brought with them certain character flaws or social circumstances in their families that were already conducive to juvenile delinquency as they settled in the area.

Walter Miller's "Lower-class Culture as a Generating Milieu of Gang Delinquency" (1958) has been limited by a lack of generality. More specifically, the "focal concerns" and "female-based households" described by Miller do not equally characterize the lower class residents of Black, Hispanic, Irish, and Italian enclaves in our cities.

Miller's thesis and other theoretical explanations of lower class delinquency share an inability to generalize to just *one* lower class racial or ethnic group. Some Strain and Cultural Transmission theorists have portrayed an oversimplified, homogeneous picture of lower class values and behavior that fails to adequately take into account the diversification of culture and dynamics of social class mobility *within* certain groups. For example, since the 1960s, there has been a bifurcation of lower class black America splitting into an underclass that seems likely never to escape and an upwardly mobile middle class (Lemann, 1986). Thus, two contrasting versions of black life have emerged.

On the one hand, poverty is even more deeply entrenched for many blacks and is characterized by extraordinarily high and rising rates of unemployment, school dropouts, welfare dependence, single mothers, crime and delinquency. This *underclass* (a nomenclature also shared by portions of the white and Hispanic populations) has been defined by Michael Morris (1989:125) as:

> ...*a segment of the poor who are not only economically deprived, but who manifest a distinctive set of values, attitudes, beliefs, norms, and behaviors....*

Miller's observations have been applauded for identifying some focal concerns of the underclass. On the other hand, they are hardly an adequate depiction of those members of the black lower class who are demonstrating higher achievement and lower delinquency rates; who are now moving out of the ghettos and into the middle class.

> *The clearest line between the two groups is family structure. Black husband-wife families continue to close the gap with whites; their income is now 78 percent as high (Lemann, 1986:33).*

In view of the more pronounced heterogeneity of the lower class, Miller's 1958 formulation may have lost some contemporary relevance for just the lower class.

Concept Integration

Questions and Topics for Study and Discussion

1. Explain the sociological perspective regarding human behavior and social phenomena. How does it differ from the biological determinism and psychogenic explanations presented in previous chapters?

2. What is a theory as the term is used by the social scientist and the researcher?

3. List the major assumption(s) underlying the Social Strain Theories of delinquency etiology. Identify

and discuss several prominent sociologists and their respective concepts and contributions to the social strain approach. What are some of the weaknesses and limitations of social strain explanations?

4. List the major assumption(s) underlying Cultural Transmission Theories of delinquency etiology. Identify and discuss several prominent sociologists and their respective concepts and contributions to

BOX 6-2   Concept Application: "Searching for Causal Explanations of Contemporary School Shootings"

Several decades ago, Walter Miller (1958) identified "trouble, toughness, smartness, excitement, fate, and autonomy" as highly regarded, lower class, cultural values. Miller suggested that the acting out of these "focal concerns" represents the achievement of manhood and respect to many lower class males (Anderson, 1998). On the other hand, these attitudinal and behavioral traits may be interpreted as "delinquent" by police officers and other members of more favored classes.

Recently, in the wake of numerous violent attacks by young males in U.S. schools, Miller's theoretical concepts may have a fresh and broader application. A common theme and clue has emerged in many of these shocking reports: a number of these angry young gunmen were obsessed with a reckless, fatalistic desire to publicly display toughness and autonomy, and to get even for some real or imagined insult. In many cases, their violent bid for recognition and reputation was triggered by an accumulation of what they considered disrespectful and degrading taunts. Here are a few examples:

LITTLETON, COLORADO: *They were so different from their peers, who ridiculed them for wearing black trench coats even in the summer.... Students are beginning to describe how a long-simmering rivalry between the sullen members of their clique and the school's athletes escalated and ultimately exploded in...[the] week's deadly violence that left more than a dozen dead and 22 wounded at Columbine High School* (Johnson and Copeland, 1999, 1A0).

A suicide note, purportedly written by one of the attackers, was defiant and ominous: *"Your children who have ridiculed me, who have chosen not to accept me, who have treated me like I am not worth their time are dead. THEY ARE (expletive) DEAD.... I may have taken their lives and my own—but LET THIS MASSACRE BE ON YOUR SHOULDERS UNTIL THE DAY YOU DIE.... You may think the horror ends with the bullet in my head, but you wouldn't be so lucky"* (Ashland Daily Tidings, 1999:A1).

SPRINGFIELD, OREGON: *At Thurston High School Kipland Phillip Kinkel, a skinny, freckle-faced 15-year-old...walked into the cafeteria, pulled a 22-caliber rifle out from under a khaki trench coat and calmly fired more than 50 rounds among the 400 teenagers in the cafeteria. Two boys died and 23 other youngsters were injured....*

The Springfield carnage represented the sixth time in the past eight months that one of America's public schools has been the scene of a fatal shooting.

Many of the reputed perpetrators apparently felt like outsiders. They were...kids who were out of the mainstream—unhappy, searching for their place, and suffering ridicule (Witkin, et al., 1998:16, 17).

There is growing evidence that the phenomena of explosive high school violence is occurring in other parts of the world.

UPPER NAZARETH, ISRAEL: *Educators say they are alarmed by youngsters drawing knives instead of settling disputes verbally, or at worst, with their fists....*

The first killing took place...during a break at the Yigal Alon High School. A group of boys were standing in the yard, and one asked another for a lick of his ice cream. A ninth-grader, Yevgeny Yakobovich...quipped that the boy with the ice cream wouldn't share because "he is fat and a miser."

The boy who was teased decided to take revenge and rallied four friends. The five went home after school to pick up knives, a baseball bat and a pair of brass knuckles, then headed to the park where Yevgeny liked to play.

They stabbed, beat, and kicked Yevgeny until he slumped on the ground.... Police said the suspects returned to their homes and went to sleep, as though nothing had happened ("Teen Violence Leaves Israel Looking for Answers" in *The Dallas Morning News*, 1999:8A).

Several of the theoretical explanations of youthful crime presented in Chapters 4, 5, 6, 7, and 8 of this

Continued

BOX 6-2   *Continued*

book—including Walter Miller's focus on cultural values—offer helpful insights concerning these current reports of high school violence.

Perhaps the most exciting implication of this new application of Miller's concepts is the expansion of so-called "lower class values" to encompass some hostile, antisocial posturing and behavior of middle class youth. Such an application garners a larger measure of generality for Miller's causal explana-tion. Peter Jennings (1999) underscored this point by pointing to the cultural context of violence: "Boys don't cry; but they are encouraged to be tough, manly, and to fight back" (Jennings, 1999, ABC, "Boys at Risk").

A more detailed discussion of current school violence, together with suggestions for prevention and control, can be found in Chapter 10, "Schools and Delinquency."

Sources

Anderson, E. 1998. *The code of the streets.* New York: W. W. Norton.
Jennings, P. "Boys at Risk." *American Broadcasting Company,* November 15, 1999.
Johnson, K., and Copeland, L. "Long-simmering feud may have triggered massacre." *USA Today,* April 22, 1999:A1.
"Suicide note contains more death threats." *Ashland Daily Tidings* (Oregon). April 24, 1999:A1.
"Teen violence leaves Israel looking for answers." *The Dallas Morning News* (Texas). June 12, 1999:8A.
Witkin, G., Tharp, M., Schrof, J. M., Toch, T., and Scattarella, C. "Again." *U.S. News & World Report,* June 1, 1998:16–18.

the cultural transmission approach. What are some of the weaknesses and limitations of Cultural Transmission Theories?

5. Compare and contrast the problems of first- and second-generation immigrants in the United States and in northern Europe. How do these problems help explain juvenile delinquency in these groups?

6. What are the similarities and differences between Merton's Theory of Anomie, Cloward and Ohlin's Theory of Differential Opportunity, and Miller's concept of Lower Class Culture as a Generating Milieu of Gang Delinquency?

References

Agnew, R. 1984. Goal achievement and delinquency. *Sociology and Social Research,* 68 (July):435–451.

Bernard, T. J. 1990. Angry aggression among the truly disadvantaged. *Criminology* 28 (February):73–96.

Bordua, D. J. 1962. Some comments on theories of group delinquency. *Sociological Inquiry* 32 (Spring): 245–260.

Burgess, E. W. 1925. The growth of the city. In R. E. Park, E. W. Burgess, and R. D. McKenzie (Eds.). *The city.* Chicago: University of Chicago Press, pp. 47–62.

Bursik, R. J. 1984. Urban dynamics and ecological studies of delinquency. *Social Forces* 63 (December):393–413.

Cloward, R. A., and Ohlin, L. E. 1960. *Delinquency and opportunity.* New York: Free Press.

Cohen, A. K. 1955. *Delinquent boys: The culture of the gang.* New York: Free Press. 1966. *Deviance and control.* Englewood Cliffs, NJ: Prentice-Hall.

Cole, A. 1993. Diversity revisited. *Modern Maturity.* (August–September):10, 12.

Cole, S. 1980. *The sociological method: an introduction to the science of sociology* (3rd ed.). Chicago: Rand McNally.

Cox, S. M., and Conrad, J. J. 1996. *Juvenile Justice* (4th ed.). Dubuque, IA.: Wm. C. Brown Publishers.

Durkheim, E. [1895] 1950. *The rules of sociological method.* Glencoe, IL: Free Press. [1897] 1951. *Suicide: A study in sociology.* (Trans. J. A. Spaulding, and G. Simpson): New York: Free Press.

Farnsworth, M., and Leiber, M. J. 1989. Strain theory revisited: Economic goals, educational means, and delinquency. *American Sociological Review* 54 (April):263–274.

Han, W. S. 1969. Two conflicting themes: Common values versus class differential values. *American Sociological Review* 34 (October):679–690.

Hirschi, T. 1969. *Causes of delinquency.* Berkeley: University of California Press.

Hoffman, J. P., and Su, S. S. 1997. The conditional effects of stress on delinquency and drug use: A strain theory assessment of sex differences. *Journal of Research in Crime and Delinquency* 34 (February):46–78.

Jacobs, J. 1961. *The death and life of great American cities.* New York: Vintage Books.

Kitsuse, J., and Dietrick, D. 1959. Delinquent boys: A critique. *American Sociological Review* 24 (April): 208–215.

Kulik, J. A., Stein, K. B., and Sarbin, T. R. 1968. Dimensions and patterns of adolescent antisocial behavior. *Journal of Consulting and Clinical Psychology* 32 (August):375–382.

Lastrucci, C. L. 1967. *The scientific approach.* Cambridge, MA: Schenkman.

Lemann, N. 1986. The origins of the underclass. *The Atlantic Monthly* (June):31–68.

Lemert, E. 1951. *Social pathology.* New York: McGraw-Hill.

Lundman, R. J. 1993. *Prevention and control of juvenile delinquency* (2nd ed.). New York: Oxford University Press.

Menard, S. 1995. A developmental test of Mertonian anomie theory. *Journal of Research in Crime and Delinquency* 32 (May):136–174.

Merton, R. 1938. Social structure and anomie. *American Sociological Review* 3 (October):672–682.
1957. *Social theory and social structure* (2nd ed.). New York: Free Press.

Miller, W. B. 1958. Lower class culture as a generating milieu of gang delinquency. *Journal of Social Issues* 14 (Summer):5–19.

Morris, M. 1989. From the culture of poverty to the underclass: An analysis of a shift in public language. *The American Sociologist* 20 (Summer):123–133.

Park, R. E. 1928. Human migration and the marginal man. *American Journal of Sociology* 33 (May):893.

Park, R. E., Burgess, E., and McKenzie, R.D. 1924. *The City.* Chicago: University of Chicago Press.

Polk, K., and Schafer, W. B. (Eds.). 1972. *School and delinquency.* Englewood Cliffs, NJ: Prentice-Hall.

Sanders, W. B. 1976. *Juvenile delinquency.* New York: Praeger.

Schur, E. 1973. *Radical non-intervention: Rethinking the delinquency problem.* Englewood Cliffs, NJ: Prentice-Hall.

Sellin, T. 1938. *Culture conflict and crime.* New York: Social Science Research Council.

Shaw, C. R., and McKay, H. D. 1931. *Social factors in juvenile delinquency: Report on the causes of crime,* Vol. II. Washington, DC: National Commission on Law Observance and Enforcement.
1942. *Juvenile delinquency and urban areas.* Chicago: University of Chicago Press.
1969. *Juvenile delinquency and urban areas* (revised ed.). Chicago: University of Chicago Press.

Short, J. F., Jr., Tennyson, R. A., and Howard, K. I. 1963. Behavior dimensions of gang delinquency. *American Sociological Review* 28 (June):411–428.

Spergel, I. 1964. *Racketville, slumtown, and haulberg.* Chicago: University of Chicago Press.

Stonequist, E. H. 1937. *The marginal man.* New York: Charles Scribner's Sons.

Sykes, G. M., and Matza, D. 1957. Techniques of neutralization: A theory of delinquency. *American Sociological Review* 22 (December):664–670.

Thomas, W. I., and Znaniecki, F. 1927. *The Polish peasant in Europe and America.* New York: Knopf.

Triplett, R., and Jarjoura, G. R. 1997. Specifying the gender-class relationship: Exploring the effects of educational expectations. *Sociological Perspectives* 40 (2):287–316.

Whyte, W. F. 1981. *Street corner society* (3rd ed.). Chicago: University of Chicago Press.

SOCIOLOGICAL EXPLANATIONS OF JUVENILE DELINQUENCY

Social Learning and Social Control Theories

Reading Objectives

The reading of this chapter will help you achieve the following objectives:

1. Understand more fully the advantages and shortcomings of typologies of sociological theories accounting for juvenile delinquency.
2. Define and explain specific sociological concepts and theories of deviant and delinquent conduct, including Social Learning Theory and Social Control Theory.
3. Apply these sociological theories of human behavior to explaining juvenile delinquency.
4. Summarize the contributions and limitations of the various sociological theories of deviance and delinquency discussed in this chapter.

Introduction

Chapter 7 continues the discussion of the six major categories of sociological theories that have been advanced to explain juvenile delinquency. Chapter 6 encompassed Social Strain and Cultural Transmission theories. This chapter covers Social Learning and Social Control theories. As stated in Chapter 6, there is unavoidable overlap in all of these sociological theories—both historically and etiologically. In many instances, the earliest theorists to pursue a particular approach were contemporaries who often built on, expanded, or reapplied each other's work. In addition, their common quest for causal explanations of juvenile delinquency often entailed the same variables, and usually focused on youthful misconduct in the United States.

Moreover, the sociological theories expounded in Chapters 6, 7, and 8 do not readily lend themselves to microscopic and macroscopic division and classification.

> *Microscopic sociology refers to the study of the smallest social units, that is, individuals and their thoughts and actions. Macroscopic sociology focuses on larger social units such as groups, organizations, cultures, and societies....For convenience, we can divide the range of social phenomena into the microscopic and macroscopic realms, but we should recognize that many social phenomena fall in the middle of the continuum and are difficult to categorize as strictly microscopic or macroscopic (Kammeyer et al., 1997:7).*

This principle aptly describes sociological theories of juvenile delinquency which, more often than not, are mixtures of microscopic and macroscopic sociology. For example, Robert Merton's contribution to Social Strain Theory (discussed in Chapter 6) focuses on *individual* adaptation to anomic frustration over the disjunction of institutionalized success goals and culturally approved means of achievement prevalent in the *larger* society. Somewhat similarly, as you will see in the next chapter, Labeling Theory involves the personal, deviant reflection in an individual's behavior of a negative appraisal of his or her character by the normative standards, mass media, or other social forces in *society.*

In seeking logical organization of a myriad of sociological theories, it is also tempting to separate them into broad social structure and social process categories. *Social structure* refers to the way that society is put together; its institutional arrangements and functions; the hierarchy of social classes and how they relate to one another. And, indeed, some crime and delinquency can be traced to weaknesses and conflicts in social structure. *Social process* refers to the dynamic interaction between and among individuals and groups as they relate to peers, family, school, and other social institutions and agencies. Without question, some juvenile misconduct has evolved from the negative and unproductive personal relations of some youths with processes and institutions of society. However, the etiological or causal roots of juvenile delinquency cannot be placed wholly and neatly in social structure and social process categories. For example, in this chapter we will see that Sutherland's Theory of Differential Association involves not only the social learning of criminal values and techniques in intimate groups, but also the availability of such alternative socialization in underclass neighborhoods of economically disadvantaged residents. Likewise, as is detailed in the next chapter, radical theorists such as Karl Marx and his followers perceived criminal deviance as a logical and legitimate reaction of outraged workers against the manipulation and economic system of the dominant ruling class. Clearly, Radical Theory contains elements of both social structure and social process.

In the absence of stronger organizing criteria, we have chosen to systematize our presentation of sociological theories of delinquency with a typology containing six categories of overarching substantive similarities. In other words, we have examined the sociological theories for similarities in sociological content, explanatory approach, and focus in delinquency etiology. The theories were then grouped together in a typology of six classifications of sociological explanations of delinquency causation:

1. Social Strain theories.
2. Cultural Transmission theories.

3. Social Learning theories.
4. Social Control theories.
5. Labeling theories.
6. Radical theories.

The first two kinds of sociological theory were discussed in Chapter 6. The next two types of causal explanation—Social Learning and Social Control theories—are presented in this chapter. The last two types of sociological explanations of juvenile delinquency—Labeling and Radical theories—will be analyzed in Chapter 8. However, as we cautioned in Chapter 6, while typologies of sociological theory are extremely useful tools for organizing, teaching, and learning a large mass of material, the absence of discrete categories and the unavoidable conceptual overlap must always be kept in mind. Again, our discussion of each category of sociological theory examines the work of several major and representative contributors to that explanatory approach.

Social Learning Theories

The social learning approach to explaining crime and delinquency is dominated by the assumption that virtually all human behavior is socially learned. Consequently, deviance, like conformity, must be learned through the complex process of socialization. **Socialization** refers to *"the process whereby individuals learn and internalize the attitudes, values, and behaviors appropriate to persons functioning as social beings and responsive, participating members of society"* (Encyclopedia of Sociology, 1974:272). In other words, socialization is learning to participate in group life through the acquisition of culture. Social learning theorists view juvenile delinquency as another pattern of learned behavior that some juveniles are taught through social interaction with the family, peer group, and other major agents of socialization.

Sutherland and Cressey's Theory of Differential Association

One of the most popular and durable of the social learning theories is the Theory of Differential Association developed by Edwin Sutherland and Donald Cressey (1943). They stated that most criminal behavior is learned through contact with criminal elements and patterns which are present, acceptable, and rewarded in one's physical and social environment. Sutherland and Cressey argued that this is why juvenile delinquency rates vary among social groups and neighborhoods. In more stable and prosperous neighborhoods, the socialization of the young is largely dominated by values that stress conformity to middle class standards and respect for law enforcement agencies. On the other hand, in a High Delinquency Area, delinquent behavior may be an integral part of the area culture. In the presence of a "criminalistic tradition," youths have the opportunity to associate with those who can teach them alternative and illegal behaviors. Thus, Sutherland and Cressey called their explanation of juvenile delinquency the Theory of Differential Association. They summarized their theory with a set of nine propositions:

1. Criminal behavior is learned.
2. Criminal behavior is learned in interaction with other persons in a process of communication.

3. The principal part of the learning of criminal behavior occurs within intimate personal groups.

4. When criminal behavior is learned, the learning includes (a) techniques of committing the crime, which are sometimes complicated, sometimes very simple; and (b) the specific direction of motives, drives, rationalizations, and attitudes.

5. The specific direction of motives and drives is learned from definitions of the legal codes as favorable or unfavorable.

6. A person becomes delinquent because of an excess of definitions favorable to violation of law over definitions unfavorable to violation of law.

7. Differential associations may vary in frequency, duration, priority, and intensity.

8. The process of learning criminal behavior by association with criminals and criminal patterns involves all the mechanisms that are involved in any other learning.

9. While criminal behavior is an expression of general needs and values, it is not explained by those general needs and values, since noncriminal behavior is an expression of the same needs and values. (Sutherland and Cressey, 1978:80–83)

The sixth proposition is at the heart of differential association theory: "A person becomes delinquent because of an excess of definitions favorable to violation of law over definitions unfavorable to violation of law." The picture is one of the youth subjected to a variety of influences; some endorse the rejection of the law and suggest deviant behavior; others uphold the normative standards of society and recommend conformity. By analogy, the youth is activated like a balance scale, as the two antagonistic forces of socialization strive for supremacy. On one side are placed the "definitions favorable to violation of law"—perhaps the negative influence of a street gang; on the other side are placed those "definitions unfavorable to violation of law"—perhaps the positive influence of parents. According to the reasoning of Sutherland and Cressey, if the definitions favorable to law violation outweigh the definitions unfavorable to law violation, the balance scale is tipped and the youth slips into juvenile delinquency. However, the struggle for supremacy in directing the individual's behavior between the two accumulating and antithetical definitions is subject to several subtle and complex nuances. As Sutherland and Cressey stated in their seventh proposition: "Differential associations may vary in frequency, duration, priority, and intensity." Thus, the actual point of commitment to either a conforming or a deviant career will vary widely among individuals.

Glaser's Concept of Differential Identification

Daniel Glaser (1956) supplemented Sutherland and Cressey's Theory of Differential Association by adding the concept of Differential Identification. Viewing Sutherland and Cressey's theory as too mechanistic, Glaser emphasized the individual's ability to make choices and take on social roles. Glaser contended that it is not merely association with criminals or delinquents that is important, but the extent to which the individual *identifies* with those who are involved in criminal and delinquent patterns of conduct:

> *During any period, prior identification and present circumstances dictate the selection of the persons with whom we identify ourselves. Prior identifications which have been pleasing tend to persist (Glaser, 1956:441).*

Social learning theories suggest that, when delinquent behavior such as fighting, is positively reinforced by peers, juveniles are likely to continue or repeat the deviant behavior.

According to Glaser, criminal or delinquent role models can be real or imaginary, nearby or far away—thus allowing for human ability to identify with certain individuals (and learn from their behavior) without direct association. For example, the mass media, notably television and motion pictures, have come under continuous scrutiny and sharp attack as a powerful socializing agent that can influence some children to seek to replicate the violence they have seen on the screen. As far back as 1971 the Surgeon General's Advisory Committee concluded that children whose parental attitudes on violence, prior socialization, and emotional makeup predispose them to imitate or to be incited by violent content on television were most likely to try to transfer the fictionalized aggression into real life (US Department of Health, Education and Welfare, 1971:10). In this context, and from the perspective of Glaser's differential identification, the fantasized heroics and aggression of Rambo or The Terminator can become viable role models for some youngsters. (See Chapter 5, Box 1 for a current analysis of television's influence on children.)

Akers' Theory of Differential Reinforcement

Ronald Akers is one of the principal theorists behind the view that deviant (and delinquent) behavior is learned and acted out in response to rewards and reinforcements that are available in the individual's environment. Burgess and Akers (1966) reported that Sutherland and Cressey failed to specify the learning process in their Theory of Differential Association and therefore sought to improve differential association theory by incorporating some basic concepts from B. F. Skinner's (1938) operant conditioning. In their synthesis of sociology and psychology, Burgess and Akers said that people are motivated to behave in certain ways if they have been rewarded for doing so. Likewise, they are discouraged from repeating behavior for which they have been punished or denied positive reinforcement. Akers collaborated with others in refining the Theory of Differential Reinforcement into a series of propositions that detail the process of learning and performing deviant behavior through interaction with individuals and groups who have the power to bestow gratification, social status, and other commensurable rewards (Akers et al., 1979; Lanza-Kaduce et al., 1982). Moreover, Akers recognized the impact of public acclaim and reward of selected individuals for certain kinds of behavior. These individuals may then serve as role models for many others who, in experiencing vicarious reinforcement, are also encouraged to imitate the rewarded behavior (Akers, 1985).

Contributions of Social Learning Theories

The social learning approach to explaining delinquency has enjoyed considerable support from many sociologists. Its emphasis on the socialization process as well as the influence of peer and reference groups clearly identifies the sources of delinquent behavior as social in nature. Numerous studies have supported the basic concepts of the social learning approach, especially as proposed by Sutherland and Cressey's Theory of Differential Association (e.g., Short, 1957; Reiss and Rhodes, 1964; Thompson et al., 1983). Going beyond scientific studies, the basic postulates of the social learning theories also appeal to many "common sense" assumptions about human behavior. The old axioms that "one rotten apple can spoil the barrel" and "birds of a feather flock together" implies that individuals' behavior is greatly influenced by those with whom they associate and identify.

The social learning theories as propounded by Sutherland, Glaser, and Akers have had wide application to juvenile delinquency. An especially helpful aspect is the understanding of the sociological and psychological dynamics of drug and alcohol use and addiction.

> *Sutherland's development of the principle of differential association to account for the "specific direction of motives and drives" has been particularly pertinent to the study of drug and alcohol use among adolescents. Primary group associations and favorable attitudinal definitions have emerged as the key causal factors* (Orcutt, 1983:221).

Research conducted by Richard Johnson, et al., (1987) confirmed the supposition that the best predictor of the extent of a youth's involvement in delinquent behavior is the number of his or her delinquent associates. Their findings also support the view that differential association with situational pressure to join others is most relevant to adolescent drug use.

The introduction to illegal drugs and persistence in their use is clearly a part of an individual's social experience. The further linkage with delinquency was argued by W. D. Watts and Lloyd Wright (1990), whose statistical correlations revealed that self-reported alcohol, tobacco, marijuana, and other illegal drug use were all significantly related to both minor and major delinquency for groups of Mexican-American, black, and white males.

In a study on marijuana use, James Orcutt (1987:354) further supported differential association theory and concluded that the theory can be readily empirically tested, and "...perhaps no other theory of deviance can generate such exact conditional predictions about the initiation of any deviant act."

A more recent study by Karen Heimer (1997), using sophisticated methodology and analysis of data from a national sample of males, found very strong support for learning theories of delinquency. Her "results show that violent delinquency is a product of learning definitions favorable to violence, which itself is determined directly and indirectly by association with aggressive peers..." (Heimer, 1997:799).

Schicor (1983) also applauded the generality of theories that employ socialization as an explanatory factor in human behavior. He contended that socialization is an acceptable and meaningful approach to an understanding of delinquency whether one is looking at societies dominated by capitalistic or by socialistic political ideology.

Criticisms and Limitations of Social Learning Theories

Despite much support, the social learning approach to explaining illegal behavior by juveniles is not without weaknesses. Several of the criticisms are shared by other theoretical contributions discussed in this chapter, such as the questions raised by Jack Gibbs (1966) and others that the relationship between delinquency and association with other delinquents may in fact be just the opposite of Sutherland and Cressey's view. It may well be that as delinquents are rejected by the conforming segments of society they are forced to seek association with each other. From this perspective, high delinquency areas and delinquent groups *do not generate* delinquency, but merely *collect* and concentrate it. Thus, the social learning theories of Sutherland, Glaser, and Akers may not explain the original causes of crime, but simply describe a process whereby criminality is transmitted and perpetuated in some delinquents.

Critics also have questioned the generality of social learning theories (a charge that can be leveled at almost any sociological theory, since exceptions to explanatory schemes are legion!). In this instance, it has been argued that social learning theories do not cover crimes of impulse or passion, or delinquencies springing from emotional maladjustment.

Another flaw in social learning theories and other explanations involving delinquency areas is that even in areas with the highest crime and delinquency rates, there are many nondelinquents. It has been suggested that some children are insulated from primary contact and intimate association with neighborhood delinquents by their own unaggressive dispositions and/or careful parental supervision. In addition, many other juveniles are only episodically or superficially involved in delinquent activities. In any case, the fact remains that deteriorated, poverty-stricken areas containing lower class minorities and criminal elements do not produce delinquency in *all* young people residing there.

David Matza (1964) offered another interesting alternative to Sutherland and Cressey's theory of differential association and other causal explanations of this kind. Contrary to those theorists, Matza contended that deviants do not consistently give moral support to one

BOX 7-1   Concept Application: "Going into the Automobile Business"

Each year, nearly half of all motor vehicle thefts in the United States are committed by persons under the age of 18. In 1991, there were 70,659 arrests of people under age 18 for stealing automobiles (*FBI Uniform Crime Reports—1991,* 1992:223). Charles McCaghy and his associates (1977), in their comprehensive study of "Auto Theft: Offender and Offense Characteristics," found that while some middle class youths are motivated to steal cars for fun and joyriding, urban lower class black youths are responsible for most auto thefts, for economic profit. These youths often steal cars so they can be stripped and the parts sold, or so the intact vehicles can be sold on the "black market." T. W. Burke, in his "Armed Carjacking: A Violent Problem in Need of a Solution" (1993), reported on the escalating danger to motorists from this type of criminal behavior. Burke estimated that 60 percent of all armed carjackers are under 21 years of age with the most common offender being a young male in his late teens or early 20s. Although President Bush, in response to public alarm, signed an "Anti-Car Theft Act" in 1992 making armed carjacking a federal offense, the incidence of such violence continues to be very high. In 1993, the assault and murder of several vulnerable tourists during carjackings prompted the German government to advise German citizens traveling abroad to avoid Florida.

The following anecdote was related to one of the authors by a student enrolled in one of his off-campus courses.

"Going into the 'Automobile Business'"

If I had not known otherwise, Mike could easily have been mistaken for one of the typical male college students who regularly sit in my classes at the state university. He was 23 years old; naturally gregarious with a disarming grin; wanted to get more education and ultimately a good job; and he liked football, girls, and automobiles—*especially automobiles.*

But we were not on the university campus, nor was Mike a typical 23-year-old student. I was teaching a university extension course at a federal reformatory and Mike was serving a 10-year sentence for "Grand Theft: Auto." He was assigned to assist me with the logistics of the classroom such as inmate attendance at my lectures, seating arrangements, distribution of books, paper, examinations, and other supplies, and so forth. Consequently, we had numerous opportunities to talk, both formally and informally, and an unusual degree of trust and rapport was established.

I soon learned that although Mike was a high school dropout, he was bright and articulate. Moreover, he was streetwise and very cynical. During the last 11 years he had "graduated" from adolescent play group to youth gang to professional auto theft ring; from school yard to city streets to prison yard. He asserted proudly: "I can get into nearly any car without breaking a window and I can start over half of them without a key." At first, such declarations sounded like just so much bravado and bragging, but later when I had the opportunity to review Mike's official records, it became abundantly clear that he was a very professional automobile thief. His file record dated back to age 12 and was filled with documentation of confrontations with police and juvenile courts, and a multitude of suspected, alleged, and proven crimes against society.

Based on our series of discussions, I was able to reconstruct the course of events that finally brought Mike to the federal reformatory. He had grown up in the underclass slum neighborhoods of St. Louis and Chicago. The family was poor, characterized by his father's unemployment, with five people living in three small rooms and sharing a toilet and tub with two other families. They wore second-hand clothing that didn't fit; and they were often cold, hungry, frustrated, and angry. Mike played in the streets of his neighborhood with boys of similar backgrounds.

Mike reported that high school was a particularly trying ordeal for youths from the poorer neighborhoods:

> *There were dudes there who had plenty of money, who wore nice clothes, and even drove cars to school. My ol' man didn't even own a car. We walked everywhere, or rode the bus if we had the fare. The teachers always gave us that bull about getting an education, working hard, and being successful. Man, it was un-*

Continued

BOX 7-1   *Continued*

real! I got out of there as soon as I could. Be-
sides, I was flunking anyway.

On the streets of the city, Mike found other boys
with similar experiences who shared his feelings of
rejection, alienation, and hopelessness. Then, one
day, he recalled:

> *We spotted a parked, unlocked car with the*
> *keys just hanging there. It was like an invita-*
> *tion! We looked and laughed and someone*
> *dared me to get in. Well, I wouldn't have done*
> *it, but the guys were all watching me. So, I got*
> *in, and so did they. I was just fourteen, but I*
> *could drive it. We decided to borrow it for*
> *awhile, circle around the high school, and try*
> *to pick up some girls. However, something*
> *went wrong. The car swerved over a curb and*
> *got banged up a lot. Somebody saw us, and the*
> *cops picked me up. Later, a judge put a judg-*
> *ment against my father to pay for the damage.*
> *And he pulled out of the family after that.*

There were other joyriding experiences for
Mike and his friends. It was never hard to find a car
in which some negligent driver had left the ignition
key and the boys could not resist the temptation to
"cruise the streets" and enhance an otherwise boring
day or night.

At about age sixteen, Mike began associating
with a street gang in his neighborhood. He described
how the gang was inclined to "steal anything that
wasn't nailed down." Sometimes they stole food
from grocery stores "because they were hungry, or
just for the hell of it." One would distract the clerk,
while another filled his pockets and sneaked out the
door. This same technique was used in clothing and
hardware stores for merchandise they could sell or
trade on the streets. Mike specialized in automobile
parts—hubcaps, tires, and radios. A couple of older
gang members showed Mike how to "hotwire" an
automobile and thus start it by bypassing the ignition
switch. The boys also discussed which types of cars
were easiest to steal, and the older boys told Mike
that the "high dollar" cars were best to steal, because
"they were easy to wire, and the owners always had
enough insurance" to cover their losses.

Mike complained bitterly about social conditions in his old urban neighborhood. There were no
job opportunities and "the poor got no help and no
respect," he said:

> *Even though I had a few dollars and better*
> *clothes, even my own family and the neigh-*
> *bors called me a "no good hood." So, finally, I*
> *decided to have the game as well as the name,*
> *and got more involved in illegal activities.*
> *And, at least I had the guys in the gang who*
> *appreciated me.*

As Mike grew older, however, many of those he
knew best in the gang started dropping out. Some
got married, several took jobs, some went to jail, and
one or two even went back to school. Mike took a
different course:

> *As for me, I had made friends with some older*
> *men in the area who were into the rackets, you*
> *know, some were "hustling prostitutes," oth-*
> *ers were pushing drugs, or into gambling. But*
> *the ones that really appealed to me were in the*
> *"used car business." They made lots of money*
> *and drove big cars. I hung around their "ga-*
> *rage" and got acquainted.*

As Mike described it to me, the "garage" was a
basement with painted-over windows and a large automobile door that opened off a back alley. It was
"open" only from midnight until dawn. When Mike
was about 20, he was invited to "go into the automobile business" with the men at the garage. It was a
professional auto theft ring comprised of eight men
with a highly specialized division of labor: two of
them were the "pickups" who cruised side streets
and unattended parking lots near theaters and bars.
They would locate automobiles they wanted, prefer-
ably large and expensive. With special tools and sets
of keys they were usually able to open and drive off
the automobile with minimal difficulty. Mike became one of these "pickup men."

Three other men were garage "mechanics."
Their job was to change odometer readings, license
plates, and even engine and body manufacturers'
identification numbers. They could repaint an automobile and have it out of the door in 24 hours. Another

Continued

BOX 7-1   *Continued*

man had the task of producing or procuring false registration documents. The other two men had the responsibility of transporting and selling the stolen and altered automobiles, often many hundreds of miles away in other states.

The scheme was successful for a long time until, as Mike summarized his career in the "automobile business," "one guy got caught, and in order to get a lighter sentence for himself, he led the cops to the garage, and we were all picked up."

*   *   *   *

As you reflect on this case study, consider the various sociological explanations of deviant and delinquent behavior presented in chapters 6 and 7. How do they fit as causal explanations for Mike's juvenile delinquency and ultimate criminal career? Which theories seem most applicable to Mike's case?

Sources

Burke, T. W. (1993). Armed carjacking: A violent problem in need of a solution. *Police Chief* 60 (January):18–24.

Federal Bureau of Investigation. *Crime in the United States: Uniform crime reports—1991.* Washington, DC: U.S. Government Printing Office. 1992.

McCaghy, C. H., Giordano, P. C., and Henson, T. K. Auto theft: Offender and offense characteristics. *Criminology* 15 (3) 1977:367–385.

another by approving deviant acts. He pointed out that most delinquents share with nondelinquents the view that their antisocial behavior and that of their peers is wrong. Thus, the idea that the purposeful teaching and learning of delinquent values and techniques occur as more experienced delinquents intimately communicate with youthful novices is misleading. Even among adult criminals, there is a measure of respect for and acknowledgment of the legitimacy of major social norms. We seldom hear of criminals, incarcerated or otherwise, endorsing and encouraging kidnapping, assassination, child molestation, and other serious offenses. In fact, many times, persons imprisoned for a particularly shocking or heinous crime must be isolated from other inmates for their own protection.

In spite of efforts to revise, clarify, and expand Sutherland and Cressey's original Theory of Differential Association by Glaser (Differential Identification), Akers (Differential Reinforcement), and others (DeFleur and Quinney, 1966), the most valid criticism remains. A large number of researchers have expressed difficulty in operationalizing the variables involved in order to empirically test social learning theory (Gottfredson and Hirschi, 1990; Short, 1960; Stickland, 1982; Warr, 1993). For example, the reasoning behind the concept of a "criminalistic tradition" is somewhat circular; that is, *criminalistic tradition* is viewed as creating high rates of crime and delinquency, yet the only way we can identify it is by identifying an area as having high rates of crime and delinquency. Crime and delinquency rates are measurable; criminalistic tradition is not (Reiss and Rhodes, 1964).

Social Control Theories

Whereas the three sociological approaches already discussed (as well as the biological and psychological explanations of previous chapters) have attempted to answer the question "What causes delinquency?" the social control approach also asks "What causes con-

Many thousands of stolen, vandalized, and abandoned automobiles litter our city streets every year. Nearly 39,000 youths under age 18 are arrested for motor vehicle theft each year.

formity?" Albert Cohen (1966:1) succinctly stated the inseparable nature of deviance and conformity:

> *Why do so many people insist on behaving in certain ways despite rules to the contrary? Or, to turn the question around: Why, despite the manifest convenience and utility of violating rules, do so many people insist on complying with them so much of the time? Our view is that these are two ways of putting the same question, because in order to explain why men behave, we would have to know those circumstances that make the difference between complying with rules and not complying, and in order to explain why men do not behave, we would have to know the same.*

While the search for answers to these two questions may lead down similar paths (looking at environment, family, peers, social class, and the socialization process), the assumptions behind the theoretical approaches are vastly different. In the previously explored theories is the central idea that deviants are somehow inherently different from conformists. This leads to the assumption that juveniles can be divided neatly into two distinct categories: delinquents and nondelinquents. This division seemingly is supported by official data showing that of those young people arrested and processed through the courts for delinquent behavior, a disproportionate number of them are from lower class minority groups (Erickson and

Empey, 1963). The delinquent/nondelinquent notion is again reinforced when we recall that much of the theory that we have studied thus far in explaining the presence and persistence of juvenile delinquency rests heavily on those statistical findings. Thus, while offering many valuable insights into anomie, culture conflict, subculture response, and the social learning of delinquent behavior, those theories consistently suggest that delinquency is largely a lower class phenomenon, and is clustered together with other social problems such as poverty, unstable family life, and central-city slum neighborhoods.

With increasing frequency, social scientists and criminologists are declaring that the delinquent/nondelinquent dichotomy is an oversimplification of juvenile behavior regarding social norms. It has become apparent that young people cannot be easily classified into those two opposite types. As Cloward and Ohlin (1963) stated:

> *Deviance and conformity generally result from the same kinds of social conditions. People are prone to assume that those things which we define as evil and those which we define as good have their origins in separate and distinct features of society. Evil flows from poisoned wells; good flows from pure and crystal fountains. The same sources cannot feed both. Our view of this phenomenon is different (Cloward and Ohlin, 1963:37–38).*

This broader perspective on the origins of juvenile delinquency also is supported by unofficial data. Self-report and victimization studies show that a great deal of juvenile delinquency is undetected, unreported, or informally handled. In fact, there is considerable evidence that the majority of youths commit the same illegal acts for which only a small minority are officially categorized as delinquent.

The Social Control theories discussed in this section include a focus on conformity as an approach to identifying and explaining the causes of deviance and juvenile delinquency. The social control approach does not view deviance as abnormal. All of us, from this perspective, contain the inherent potential to commit deviant acts. The reason, then, that people do not commit deviant acts is seen as a result of effective restraint or social control.

Reckless' Containment Theory

Walter Reckless (1961) considered conforming and nonconforming behavior as two alternative responses to the control system that regulates human conduct. The control system was perceived by Reckless as a double line of defense that protects society against serious deviance. One protective barrier is socialized into each member of society and is comprised of such personal attributes as *self-control, self-concept, and internalization of social norms.* This defense barrier is called **Inner Containment** and represents *the ability of the person to resist temptations to deviate and to maintain normative loyalty.* The strength of inner containment varies from individual to individual.

The social group or society to which one belongs also supplies the other line of defense. But this barrier to serious deviance is external to the individual and is called Outer Containment. **Outer Containment** is *the formidable array of legal demands and prohibitions that keep most people within the behavioral bounds of their society.* The ability of the formal laws that comprise outer containment to control behavior also can vary from person to person.

Together, this double defense line is called **Containment Theory** and, when functioning adequately, is designed to control the individual and protect society from deviant or antisocial behavior. Applying this theory to delinquency, Reckless contended that the barriers of inner and outer containment are subjected to the onslaughts of powerful "push factors" within the individual and "pull factors" within the individual's social environment. **Push factors** are *such variables as mental conflict, anxiety, alienation, and frustration.* **Pull factors** are *such variables as membership in a street gang or participation in a criminal subculture.* If there is some weakness in this carefully balanced control system, conformity will give way to deviance, and even delinquent behavior.

Sykes and Matza's Techniques of Neutralization

Gresham Sykes and David Matza (1957) argued that much delinquency occurs because many young persons, under simultaneous pressure from the larger society to conform and from a peer group or subculture with conflicting values and norms urging them to deviate, extend a set of psychological defense mechanisms to justify delinquent behavior. Thus, they are able to rationalize their actions with a set of sliding, situational ethics. Sykes and Matza appropriately called their construction of the delinquency process **Techniques of Neutralization.**

According to Sykes and Matza (1957) juvenile delinquents are not members of a deviant subculture which adheres to a totally different set of norms. Nor are they victims of anomie or norm confusion as a result of social disorganization. On the contrary, most juveniles who commit delinquent acts know what the norms are, and, for the most part, have respect for those norms. Sykes and Matza contended that most delinquents experience a sense of shame or guilt for their actions. Why then do some juveniles refrain from delinquency or commit only a few sporadic acts, while others repeatedly violate the laws? The answer, Sykes and Matza indicated, rests with juveniles' ability to rationalize their actions in such a way as to neutralize their negative impact (from the point of view of the delinquent offender). As they stated:

> *It is our argument that much delinquency is based on what is essentially unrecognized extension of defenses of crime, in the form of justifications for deviance that are seen as valid by the delinquent but not by the legal system of society at large (Sykes and Matza, 1957:667).*

Specifically, Sykes and Matza cited five major techniques of neutralization:

1. Denial of Responsibility. The delinquent contends that delinquent acts are due to forces beyond one's control (e.g., environment, family situation, poverty). This leads to what Sykes and Matza described as a "billiard ball" conception of self in which some juveniles see themselves as "acted upon" rather than "acting."

2. Denial of Injury. The delinquent insists that although a law was violated, nobody was actually hurt. Acts of vandalism and theft become interpreted as mere pranks. Victims are often insured, and thus compensated for their losses. Since much juvenile misconduct is defined by adults as harmless or normal, the youth can appeal for social support for this neutralization technique.

Teenagers enjoy hanging out together. David Matza, in his *Delinquency and Drift,* argues that some juveniles experience an occasional "episodic release" from usual ethical restraints that allows them to act out nonconforming and mischievous roles.

3. Denial of the Victim. Even if the delinquent must accept responsibility and admit that someone was hurt (as in cases of willful assault), often the delinquent reinterprets the wrongful act as some form of rightful retaliation. The victim may be depicted as one deserving of injury. The urban "sport" of "fag bashing" (assault on homosexuals) by juvenile gangs is often justified by participants on the basis that the victim was a "pervert" and therefore deserved punishment.

4. Condemnation of the Condemners. The delinquent may shift the attention away from personal actions to the motives or behaviors of those who show disapproval. This "turning of the tables" is used to put the accuser on the defensive, and demonstrates the tactical stance that "the best defense is a good offense." For example, parents scolding a child for curfew violation may be reminded that they too on occasion come home late without notifying the family. Many parents are faced with this neutralization technique in regard to youthful behaviors such as drinking or smoking, in which the parents themselves may engage.

5. Appeal to Higher Loyalties. The delinquent argues that the social expectations and demands of smaller groups (friends, gangs, siblings, etc.) must take precedence over the social expectations of the larger society. Conformity to peer pressure or doing something "for the good of the group" can neutralize the negative aspects of the act committed.

Sykes and Matza, in their initial exposition of Techniques of Neutralization in 1957, did not fully develop the linkage between background factors and the repertoire of justifications so readily available to delinquents when confronted with their misdeeds. Consequently, the listed Techniques of Neutralization appeared to many readers as transparent excuses for criminal responsibility. In a subsequent paper, Matza and Sykes (1961) expanded and reinforced their argument by maintaining that juveniles also subscribe to a "subterranean" adult value system,

> ...*which tacitly encourages the pursuit of thrills and irresponsibility among juveniles. This underground system of values...also contributes to adolescent justifications for delinquency by allowing one to charge that "Everyone is doing it, so why can't I?" (Shoemaker, 2000:151).*

Matza's major work, *Delinquency and Drift,* was first published in 1964 and contains his fully developed version of Control Theory. He expanded on the neutralization concept and expressed the view that since most juvenile delinquents conform most of the time, they evidently are able to alternate loyalty between different sets of norms—between conformity and nonconformity. In other words, juvenile delinquents experience a kind of "episodic release" from normal moral restraints that permits them to intermittently act out the deviant role. Matza presented a picture of the delinquent as occasionally free to "drift" with ease between conformity and nonconformity.

From this perspective, delinquents are not propelled into their deviance by irresistible biological forces, psychological maladjustments, or even social circumstances, but instead rather casually "drift" into it through an ongoing mental process of temporary negation of conventional normative expectations. Virtually every juvenile commits delinquent acts, just as every juvenile commits acts of conformity. According to Matza, the juveniles most likely to violate major norms repeatedly are those who most successfully rationalize their delinquent acts through the techniques of neutralization. Thus, conventional social restraints and mechanisms of social control are temporarily and effectively overcome by many juveniles.

Hirschi's Social Bond Theory

One of the most tested theories of adolescent crime was presented by Travis Hirschi in his book *Causes of Delinquency* (1969). Unlike most earlier theorists, Hirschi (1969:34) did not set out to explain why some juveniles violate the law, but sought to explain why some do not. Hirschi attacked Strain theorists for depicting the delinquent as typically a lower class gang member, forced into delinquency by the frustrating realization of underachievement of common societal goals. Likewise, Hirschi rebuked the Cultural Transmission theorists for their standard picture of the "innocent foreigner" who, in a failed attempt to understand and obey what are perceived as the irrelevant rules of the larger society, turns to deviant but more satisfying norms of a subgroup.

The main building block of Hirschi's theoretical construction is the social bond that attaches a person to the basic values and expected behaviors of society. In general, the social bond is established early in childhood through a natural attachment to parents, peers, teachers, and others who manifest and model the expected conformity and respected sanctions.

Quite simply, according to Hirschi, if the social bond is firmly intact for an individual, there will be no pattern of delinquent behavior. Conversely, if the social bond is weakened or absent, juvenile delinquency can be expected.

More specifically, Hirschi enumerated and detailed four elements of the social bond that tie the individual to conventional society and thus prevent juvenile delinquency.

1. Attachment. This emotional dimension of the social bond explains conformity as emanating from sensitive regard and respect for one's fellow human beings. It signifies how much one really cares about other people.

2. Commitment. This component of the social bond encompasses the individual's pursuit of idealized and conventional objectives, such as the development of an occupational career and the establishment of a reputation for virtue. The ideological commitment to such enterprises functions as a buffer against nonconformity.

3. Involvement. The individual's preoccupation and heavy investment of time and effort in conventional pursuits serve to ensure conformity by reducing the availability for deviant activities.

4. Belief. This element of the social bond entails one's perception of the moral worth of societal norms. If the laws are perceived as right and proper, they probably will be respected; if the individual entertains doubts about the viability or validity of social norms, it is altogether likely that he or she will violate them.

Hirschi asserted that there is wide variation among people on the degree of their attachment, commitment, involvement, and belief in conventional behavior and thus variability in their individual ability to resist deviant and delinquent conduct. He said that delinquents tend to have relatively weak social bonds and consequently feel little remorse for violating generally accepted social standards.

Contributions of Social Control Theories

The Social Control Approach is more eclectic than some of the other approaches to explaining delinquency. For example, Reckless' Containment Theory embodies some of the ideas of the Social Learning Approach in that inner containment most logically would be developed through the process of socialization in interaction with positive influences in one's social environment, as described by Sutherland and Cressey (1943). Sandhu (1977:58), in an enthusiastic endorsement of Containment Theory, also referred to its eclectic quality:

> *A most useful theory, the one that explains the largest amount of criminal and delinquent behavior, is the containment theory of Reckless. It not only combines both the sociological and psychological theories, but also fills in the gap between the two. It satisfactorily answers the persistent question: Who succumbs and who remains immune to crime when exposed to a crime-provoking situation? It takes into account both the macro and micro levels of explanation.*

Reckless and various associates conducted several intensive longitudinal studies of boys in a high delinquency area who did not become delinquent (Dinitz et al., 1962; Reckless et

BOX 7-2   Controversial Issue

Religiosity and Juvenile Delinquency

The idea that "Religious beliefs and practices can inhibit criminal deviance," or—stated conversely—"The lack of religious involvement can enhance the likelihood of criminal behavior," represent persistent, intriguing, and controversial hypotheses.

The long debate over the possible impact of religiosity on criminal and delinquent conduct has usually ebbed and flowed within the context of Social Control Theory. On one side of the issue some criminologists and sociologists have contended that there is little empirical support for the suggested inverse relationship between religiosity and criminal deviance; that findings are contradictory and spurious—strongly influenced by peer groups, types of crime, and other intervening variables (Merton, 1957; Schur, 1969; Sutherland and Cressey, 1978). "A few early scholars even maintained that, rather than innoculating adherents against waywardness, religion actually promotes crime" (Bonger, 1916; Lombroso, 1918; and Gannon, 1967—all cited in Evans, Cullen, Burton, Denaway, Payne, and Kethineni, 1996:44).

On the opposite side of the issue, a number of contemporary criminologists and sociologists have vigorously contended that there is growing evidence that the absence of religion in the lives of criminal and delinquent offenders contributed—at least in part—to their antisocial behavior (e.g., Burkett and White, 1974; Jensen, 1981; and Ellis, 1987). Emile Durkheim (1951), one of the most respected sociological theorists, supported this position when he posited "that religion is a crucial integrative mechanism for maintaining social order and fostering common beliefs and values" (Benda, 1997:163).

In agreement with this latter contention that religious socialization and commitment of young people can reinforce social bonding to community standards and stem the tide of juvenile delinquency, a myriad of new social control policies and programs have been suggested. These new initiatives range from alliances between police and street preachers in approaching youth gangs (Woodward, 1998), to resurrecting the concepts of sin, shame, and repentance in juvenile courtroom proceedings (Alter and Wingert, 1995), to posting the Ten Commandments in schools (*Medford Tribune,* 1999:A1). All of these hopeful efforts are based on the supposition that a quick infusion of personal morality, responsibility, and respect for the life and property of others can be successfully integrated into human character, personality, and behavior.

At present, it is too early to evaluate the efficacy of these initiatives, but many thoughtful scholars are urging more extensive and refined research testing of the original and controversial hypotheses that sparked this debate.

*   *   *   *

As you think about the absence of religiosity as a possible contributing factor in producing delinquent behavior, can you identify any variables that might be used to measure the level of a person's religiosity?

Sources

Alter, J., and Wingert, P. The return of shame. *Newsweek.* February 6, 1995:21–23.

Benda, B. B. 1997. An examination of a reciprocal relationship between religiosity and different forms of delinquency within a theoretical model. *Journal of Research in Crime.* 34 (May):163–186. Sage Publications, Inc.

Burkett, S. R., and White, W. 1974. Hellfire and Delinquency: Another look. *Journal for the Scientific Study of Religion* 13:455–462.

Durkheim, E. 1951. *Suicide: A study in sociology* (Originally published in 1897). New York: The Free Press.

Ellis, L. 1987. Religiosity and criminality from the perspective of arousal theory. *Journal of Research in Crime and Delinquency* 24 (3), August, 1987:215–232.

Evans, T. D., Cullen, F. T., Burton, V. S., Dunaway, R. G., Payne, G. L., and Kethineni, S. R. 1996. Religion, social bonds, and delinquency. *Deviant Behavior: An Interdisciplinary Journal* 17:43–70.

Jensen, G. F. 1981. *Sociology of Delinquency: Current Issues.* London: Sage.

Medford Tribune (Oregon Newspaper). 1999. Congressional vote allows posting of Ten Commandments in schools. June 6, 1999:A1.

Continued

BOX 7-2 *Continued*

Merton, R. K. 1957. *Social Theory and Social Structure* (2nd ed.). New York: Free Press.
Schur, E. M. 1969. *Our Criminal Society.* Englewood Cliffs, NJ: Prentice-Hall.
Sutherland, E. H., and Cressey, D. R. 1978. *Criminology* (10th ed.). Philadelphia: JB Lippincott.
Woodward, K. L. 1998. The new holy war. *Newsweek.* June 1:26–28.

al., 1956; Scarpitti et al., 1960). They sought to establish a relationship between the level of a child's self-concept and the development of successful inner control in resisting the temptation to become delinquent.

Reckless and Dinitz asked school teachers of 12-year-old white boys to nominate "good" and "bad" boys. In subsequent interviews with these boys, the researchers found that the "good boys" also perceived themselves as good boys, planned to complete high school, and looked upon their friends and families in a favorable light. In contrast, the "bad boys" already had developed an unfavorable self-image. They did not plan to graduate from high school. Moreover, they did not like their families and assumed that they and their friends would get into trouble.

Four years later, in a follow-up study of the same subjects, it was found that their previous self-concept assessments were significant predictors of future behavior and events:

> *...nearly all of the good boys were still in school and had had little or no trouble with the law. On the other hand, 39 percent of the bad boys had been in a juvenile court an average of three times (Sandhu, 1977:49).*

Regarding these findings, Dinitz et al. (1962:517) observed:

> *We believe we have some tangible evidence that a good self-concept, undoubtedly a product of favorable socialization, veers slum boys away from delinquency, while a poor self-concept, a product of unfavorable socialization, gives the slum boy no resistance to deviancy, delinquent companions, or delinquent sub-culture.*

A study by Thompson and Dodder (1986) reported successful operationalization of the inner and outer containment variables in a manner conducive to empirical investigation. Factor analysis of data collected from a varied sample of 677 subjects from public high schools and juvenile correctional institutions generally supported Reckless' theory. Control of delinquency potential was related to favorable self-image, goal orientation, frustration tolerance, retention of norms, internalization of norms, availability of meaningful roles, and reinforcement. A major finding was that Containment Theory provided valuable explanatory insights regarding delinquency across three of four race and sex categories (for white males, white females, and black males).

Sykes and Matza's *Techniques of Neutralization* (1957) and Matza's expanded construction in *Delinquency and Drift* (1964) have received mixed reviews and partial support from other theorists and researchers in the field. Nevertheless, Matza's assumption that juvenile delinquents casually and intermittently fluctuate their loyalty and behavior between conformity and deviance seems reasonable and convincing (Goodman, 1962). In a study of institutionalized females, Regoli and Poole (1979) found support for the argument that delinquents drift into and out of delinquent behavior. Their findings offered evidence that the internalization of values proscribing delinquent involvement had taken place but that some individuals were episodically released from moral constraint so they could engage in delinquency. They also found support for Matza's and Sykes' "subterranean values" idea that delinquent conduct reflects hidden and more permissive adult values (Regoli and Poole, 1979:53). Earlier research (Short and Strodtbeck, 1965; Krisberg, 1974) also found general acceptance of middle class, conventional values among juvenile gang members, which is consistent with Sykes and Matza.

Control or Containment Theories, more than the other explanations of delinquency presented earlier in this chapter, have provided points of departure for empirical testing. Hirschi (1969) offered a rigorous definition of delinquency suitable to quantitative research and then proceeded to conduct research to test his social bond theory. His research methodology was systematic and thorough as he surveyed a broad sample of youths from a California city and, with reference to rates and kinds of delinquency, examined the basic bonding elements that tie individuals to society. The empirical evidence was consistent with Hirschi's theory as he demonstrated how variation in the strength of these ties is associated with the commission of delinquent acts. More specifically, Hirschi found that juvenile delinquents were not as attached to parents, peers, and teachers as were nondelinquents. Delinquents were less involved in conventional behavior and were less conforming than nonoffenders. One of the most important conclusions emerging from Hirschi's study was that his social bond theory cuts across social classes. Hirschi found that the lower class child is no more likely to commit delinquent acts than the middle class child. Furthermore, Hirschi contended that a broken home and a working mother have very little significance for delinquency (Hirschi, 1969).

A number of subsequent researchers have generated support for Hirschi's theory. For example, Michael Hindelang (1973) enhanced the predictability of Hirschi's theory by partially replicating the finding that variations in the strength of social bonding are linked to the likelihood of delinquent behavior. A revised model of Hirschi's social bond theory was operationalized in a research project conducted by Michael Wiatrowski et al. (1981), and indicated that large correlations do exist between Hirschi's four bond elements and participation in delinquent conduct. Rick Linden (1978) questioned the view that separate theories are required to explain the delinquency of lower and middle class boys, and turned to Hirschi's theory which does not postulate class differences. He tested Hirschi's theory with data derived from a large sample of white boys attending public junior and senior high schools in Contra Costa County (California). The data combined information from school records, police records, and from a questionnaire administered to the subjects. Linden found that the nature and amount of self-reported delinquency did not vary greatly by social class, nor did the amount of official delinquency. He concluded that Hirschi's theory "explained both the self-reported and official delinquency of boys from different classes equally well suggesting that a general theory of delinquency involvement is possible" (Linden, 1978:428). LeGrande Gardner and Donald Shoemaker (1989) examined and compared Hirschi's social control theory as it applied to urban and rural youth. They found that weak or incomplete social bonding, as conceptualized by Hirschi, is significantly associated with delinquency and generally in the predicted direction for both subgroups.

More recently, Marianne Junger and Inike Marshall (1997) used Social Control Theory to model the self-reported delinquency in a sample of 788 Surinamese, Moroccan, Turkish, and Dutch boys (all living in the Netherlands). The multivariate analyses found that the key propositions of the social bond (as stated by Hirschi) are interrelated in the same way among all four ethnic groups. "The variables most consistently related to delinquency among the four subsamples are beliefs in conventional values, virtual (family) supervision, (school) conflict, and participation in unconventional leisure activities" (Junger and Marshall, 1997:79).

Criticisms and Limitations of Social Control Theories

The social control theorists' explanations of juvenile delinquency have drawn fire from proponents of other approaches. Cohen and Short (1958) indirectly struck at the heart of Reckless's Containment Theory by rejecting the notion that delinquency is an inherent potentiality in all human beings. In other words, the idea suggests greater biological determinism and more freedom from deviant influences in the environment than is sociologically tenable for some. Matza, who prefaced his own version of control theory in *Delinquency and Drift* (1964) with a critique of hard biological, psychological, and sociological determinism, also rejected uncontrolled human nature as the sole source of delinquent behavior. Matza sought to resolve the motivational dilemma of Social Control Theory by perceiving the offending behavior not as a simple response to human nature, but as a response to the temptation of certain circumstances facing the adolescent. Matza utilized the concept of "will" which may be activated by the individual's realization that the deed can be accomplished without apprehension, or by the need to demonstrate daringness to others. Thus, temporarily free from conventional restraints and willfully motivated, the youth can "drift" into delinquency. Nevertheless, Matza's theory also has not been spared criticism. With his combination of will and drift, Matza may have constructed a contradiction in terms and a semantic quagmire that confounds more than clarifies. With the exercise of will, the casual drift into delinquency seems overstated. If "drift" accurately describes the process, the concept of "will" is much too strong in conjunction. It is difficult to have it both ways.

Hirschi (1969:230) has been a forthright critic of his own social bond theory:

> *The theory underestimated the importance of delinquent friends; it overestimated the significance of involvement in conventional activities. Both of these miscalculations appear to stem from the same source, the assumption of "natural motivation" to delinquency. If such natural motivation could legitimately be assumed, delinquent friends would be unnecessary, and involvement in conventional activities would curtail the commission of delinquent acts.*
>
> *In other words, failure to incorporate some notions of what delinquency does for the adolescent probably accounts for the failure of the theory in these areas.*

Marvin Krohn and James Massey (1980) examined the overall and relative effects of the elements of Hirschi's Social Bond Theory on four separate measures of deviance using data from a sample of 3,065 adolescents. While the magnitude and direction of the observed relationships moderately supported the theory, Krohn and Massey found that the elements

BOX 7-3 Cross-Cultural Focus

Criminality Among the Children of Immigrants in Western Europe

The population dynamics and composition of the United States have always included a strong immigrant factor as successive waves of new residents have arrived from other parts of the world. Their chronic marginality, strain, conflict, and other problems are a recurring and productive theme for students of juvenile delinquency in this country. In general, second generation immigrants—the adolescent children of the original newcomers—often were credited with more than their proportionate share of juvenile crime (Sellin, 1938; Sheu, 1986).

Traditionally, immigration into the industrially developed nations of western and northern Europe was considered a temporary labor arrangement with most incoming residents from southern and eastern Europe commonly idealizing an ultimate return to their homelands. However, soon after World War II, many of these "foreign" enclaves of alien groups took on a more permanent character. By 1970, they had put down roots and produced children—the so-called "second-generation immigrants." In recent years, criminologists in the host countries of West Germany, France, Great Britain, the Netherlands, Sweden, and Switzerland have focused their growing research interest in the criminality of immigrants on those second-generation children of parents who came from a variety of eastern European, Mediterranean, African, and Asian nations. Martin Killias (1989) performed a valuable service to scholars by collecting and reviewing these scattered empirical studies and identifying similarities, differences, and patterns in findings and conclusions.

Killias structured his comparative analysis around three fundamental questions: 1) Do second-generation immigrants suffer from differential treatment at the hands of police and court personnel? 2) Do youths from immigrant families engage in crime more frequently than native-born youths with deeper historic roots in the nation? 3) What are the most viable explanations for higher crime rates among second-generation immigrants?

Regarding the issue of possible police and court discrimination directed against ethnic and racial minorities that could artificially inflate their de-

linquency statistics, studies from Great Britain and Holland only were available to Killias. While these data were inconclusive, he found little support for the thesis of unfair police and adjudication practices against the children of immigrants.

In answering the second question concerning the incidence of delinquent behavior by second-generation immigrants in northern and western Europe, Killias found a close correspondence with the earlier prototype of such phenomena in the United States. History does indeed repeat itself—at least in the statistical picture emerging from studies in France, Britain, West Germany, Sweden, and Switzerland. Not only has juvenile crime increased significantly in these countries since World War II, but Killias verified that the children of immigrants contributed much more crime than their proportionate share of the population.

British as well as German studies also suggest that there may be considerable variation among immigrant youths according to the origin of their parents, although the German subsamples are too small to allow any firm conclusions in this regard....But Asians are regularly cited for their low official crimes rates, in Britain...as well as elsewhere. (Killias, 1989:18)

The third question raised by Killias—"How do we account for the higher crime rates among second-generation immigrants?"—also suggested a return to the American experience for an explanation. After rejecting Sellin's 1938, culture-conflict perspective and Ross's 1937 view that the offender's economic deprivation explained juvenile delinquency by second-generation immigrants in northern and western Europe, Killias turned to the "values and attitudes among immigrants and their position within the host country's social structure" (p. 20). Based on research conducted in Switzerland, Killias concluded that an application of Strain Theory offered the most promising explanation. Investigators found that the original, parent-generation immigrants reduced their levels of

Continued

BOX 7-3 *Continued*

aspiration and frustration by continuing to utilize the standard of living in their home country as a point of reference in evaluating their current situation. On the other hand, their children—the second-generation im-

migrants—were much more likely to refer to living conditions in their country of residence when assessing their achievements. It follows that their level of discontent and crime rate increased accordingly.

Sources

Killias, M. 1989. "Criminology among second-generation immigrants in Western Europe: A review of the evidence." *Criminal Justice Review,* Vol. 14, No. 1, Spring, 1989:13–26.
Sellin, T. 1938. *Culture conflict and crime.* New York: Social Science Research Council.
Sheu, C. J. 1986. *Delinquency and identity: Juvenile delinquency in an American Chinatown.* Albany, NY: Harrow and Heston.

of the bond were more predictive of the less serious forms of deviance than they were of the more serious forms. Their findings also suggested that commitment to academic pursuits and commitment to extracurricular activities had different effects on deviant behavior for males than for females. Overall, the variables used by Hirschi to measure attachment were slightly stronger in predicting male delinquency than they were for female delinquency. In conclusion, Krohn and Massey acknowledged sufficient support for the theory's major hypotheses but called for further research and evaluation.

Concept Integration

Questions and Topics for Study and Discussion

1. What are the advantages and shortcomings of typologies? Outline several typologies with which you are familiar, including the typology of sociological theories of juvenile delinquency that was used to organize Chapters 6 and 7.

2. What is the difference between microscopic sociology and macroscopic sociology? How do these concepts apply to sociological theories of juvenile delinquency?

3. Define the concepts of social structure and social process. What sociological theories presented in Chapters 6 and 7 can be characterized by these two terms? Why?

4. List the major assumption(s) underlying the Social Control Theories of delinquency etiology. Identify and discuss several prominent sociologists and their respective concepts and contributions to the social control approach. What are some of the weaknesses and limitations of the social control explanations?

5. List the major assumption(s) underlying Social Learning Theories of delinquency etiology. Identify and discuss several prominent sociologists and their concepts and contributions to the social learning approach. What are some of the weaknesses and limitations of the social learning approach?

References

Akers, R. L. 1985. *Deviant behavior: A social learning approach* (3rd ed.). Belmont, CA: Wadsworth.

Akers, R. L., Krohn, M. D., Lanza-Kaduce, L., and Radosevich, M. J. 1979. Social learning and deviant behavior: A specific test of a general theory. *American Sociological Review* 44 (August):635–655.

Brownfield, D. 1990. Adolescent male status and delinquent behavior. *Sociological Spectrum* 10 (April–June):227–248.

Burgess, E. W., and Akers, R. L. 1966. A differential association reinforcement theory of criminal behavior. *Social Problems* 14 (Fall):128–147.

Cloward, R. A., and Ohlin, L. E. 1963. *Delinquency and opportunity*. New York: Free Press.

Cohen, A. K. 1966. *Deviance and control*. Englewood Cliffs, NJ: Prentice-Hall.

Cohen, A. K., and Short, J. F., Jr. 1958. Research in delinquent subcultures. *Journal of Social Issues* 14 (3):20–36.

DeFleur, M., D'Antonio, W., and DeFleur, L. 1971. *Sociology: Man in society*. Glenview, IL: Scott, Foresman and Company.

Dinitz, S., Scarpitti, F. R., and Reckless, W. C. 1962. Delinquent vulnerability: Across group and longitudinal analysis. *American Sociological Review* 27 (August):515–517.

Encyclopedia of Sociology. 1974. *Encyclopedia of Sociology*. Guilford, CT: Dushkin.

Erikson, M. L., and Empey, L. T. 1963. Court records, undetected delinquency and decision-making. *Journal of Criminal Law, Criminology and Police Sciences* 64 (4):456–469.

Flowers, R. B. 1990. *The adolescent criminal: An examination of today's juvenile offender*. Jefferson, NC: McFarland & Company.

Gardner, L., and Shoemaker, D. J. 1989. Social bonding and delinquency: A comparative analysis. *The Sociological Quarterly* (30) (3):481–500.

Gibbs, J. P. 1966. Conceptions of deviant behavior: The old and the new. *Pacific Sociological Review* 9 (Spring):9–14.

Glaser, D. 1956. Criminality theories and behavioral images. *American Journal of Sociology* 61 (March):433–444.

Goodman, P. 1962. *Growing up absurd*. New York: Random House (Vintage).

Gottfredson, M. R., and Hirschi, T. 1990. *A general theory of crime*. Stanford, CA: Stanford University Press.

Heimer, K. 1997. Socioeconomic status, subcultural definitions, and violent delinquency. *Social Forces* 75 (March):799-833.

Hindelang, M. J. 1973. Causes of delinquency: A partial replication and extension. *Social Problems* 20 (Spring):471–487.

Hirschi, T. 1969. *Causes of delinquency*. Berkeley: University of California Press.

Johnson, R. E., Marcis, A. C., and Bahr, S. J. 1987. The role of peers in the complex etiology of adolescent drug use. *Criminology* 25 (November):323–340.

Junger, M., and Marshall, I. H. 1997. The interethnic generalizability of social control theory: An empirical test. *Journal of Research in Crime and Delinquency* 34 (February):79–112.

Kammeyer, K. C. W., Ritzer, G., and Yetman, N. R. 1997. *Sociology* (7th ed.). Boston: Allyn and Bacon.

Krohn, M. D., and Massey, J. L. 1980. Social control and delinquent behavior: An examination of the elements of social bond. *The Sociological Quarterly* 21 (Autumn):529–543.

Lanza-Kaduce, L., Akers, R. L., Krohn, M. D., and Radosevich, M. J. 1982. Conceptualization and analytical models in testing social learning theory. *American Sociological Review* 47 (February): 169–173.

Linden, R. 1978. Myths of middle class delinquency: A test of the generalizability of social control theory. *Youth and Society* 9 (June):404–432.

Matza, D. 1964. *Delinquency and drift*. New York: John Wiley.

Orcutt, J. D. 1983. *Analyzing deviance*. Homewood, IL: Dorsey Press.

———. 1987. Differential association and marijuana use: A closer look at Sutherland (with a little help from Becker). *Criminology* 25 (2):341–358.

Reckless, W. 1961. A new theory of delinquency and crime. *Federal Probation* 25 (December):42–46.

Reckless, W., Dinitz, S., and Murray, E. 1956. Self concept as an insulator against delinquency. *American Sociological Review* 21 (December):744–746.

Regoli, R. M., and Poole, E. D. 1979. Assessing drift among institutionalized delinquents. *Journal of the American Criminal Justice Association* 42 (Winter/Spring):47–55.

Reiss, A. J., Jr., and Rhodes, A. L. 1964. An empirical test of differential association theory. *Journal of Research in Crime and Delinquency* 1 (January): 5–18.

Sandhu, H. 1977. *Juvenile delinquency: Causes, control, and prevention*. New York: McGraw-Hill.

Scarpitti, F., Murray, E., Dinitz, S., and Reckless, W. C. 1960. The "good" boy in a high delinquency area:

Four years later. *American Sociological Review* 25 (August):555–558.

Schicor, D. 1983. Socialization: The political aspects of a delinquency explanation. *Sociological Spectrum* 3 (January–March):85–100.

Shoemaker, D. J. 2000. *Theories of delinquency.* (4th ed.) New York: Oxford University Press.

Short, J. F., Jr. 1957. Differential association and delinquency. *Social Problems* 4 (January):233–239. 1960. Differential association as a hypothesis: Problems of empirical testing. *Social Problems* 8 (Summer):14–25.

Short, J. F., Jr., and Strodtbeck, F. L. 1965. *Group process and gang delinquency.* Chicago: University of Chicago Press.

Skinner, B. F. 1938. *The behavior of organisms.* New York: Appleton-Century-Crofts.

Strickland, D. E. 1982. Social learning and deviant behavior: A comment and critique. *American Sociological Review* 47 (February):162–167.

Sutherland, E. H., and Cressey, D. R. 1943. *Principles of Criminology.* Philadelphia: JB Lippincott. 1978. *Criminology* (10th ed.). Philadelphia: JB Lippincott.

Sykes, G. M., and Matza, D. 1957. Techniques of neutralization: A theory of delinquency. *American Sociological Review* 22 (December):664–670.

Thompson, W. E., and Dodder, R. A. 1986. Containment theory and juvenile delinquency: A reevaluation through factor analysis. *Adolescence* 21 (Summer):365–376.

Thompson, W. E., Mitchell, J., and Dodder, R. A. 1983. An empirical test of Hirschi's control theory of delinquency. *Deviant Behavior* 5:11–22.

United States Department of Health, Education and Welfare. 1971. Washington, DC: National Institute of Mental Health.

Warr, M. 1993. Age, Peers, and delinquency. *Criminology* 31 (February):17–25.

Watts, W. D., and Wright, L. S. 1990. The relationship of alcohol, tobacco, marijuana, and other illegal drug use to delinquency among Mexican-American, black, and white adolescent males. *Adolescence* 97 (Spring):171–181.

Wiatrowski, M. D., Griswold, D. B., and Roberts, M. K. 1981. Social control theory and delinquency. *American Sociological Review* 46 (October):525–541.

8

SOCIOLOGICAL EXPLANATIONS OF JUVENILE DELINQUENCY

Labeling and Radical Theories

Reading Objectives

The reading of this chapter will help you achieve the following objectives:

1. Define and explain specific sociological concepts and theories of deviant and delinquent conduct, including Labeling Theory and Radical Theory.
2. Apply these sociological theories of human behavior to explaining juvenile delinquency.
3. Summarize the contributions and limitations of the various sociological theories of deviance and delinquency discussed in this chapter.
4. Explore the idea that delinquent activity is motivated in many youths by the "fun and entertainment factor."
5. Recognize the importance and need for a general, all-encompassing theory of juvenile delinquency and the difficulty and complexity in achieving such an objective.

Introduction

Part II of this book focuses on the biological, psychological, and sociological explanations of juvenile delinquency. Much of our discussion is on the continual testing and refining of these causal theories by researchers in the field. It is extremely important to prove and confirm the validity of proposed theories of cause if we ever hope to control this serious social problem. Later in the text, you will see how some of these theoretical constructs and concepts have become the foundations of prevention and treatment programs for antisocial deviance and juvenile delinquency.

In previous chapters, we identified six major groupings of sociological theories of delinquency. In Chapter 6 we covered Social Strain and Cultural Transmission theories. The subjects of Chapter 7 were Social Learning and Social Control theories. Now, in Chapter 8, the last sociological explanations of juvenile delinquency will be presented—Labeling and Radical theories.

Labeling Theories

One of the most popular sociological explanations of juvenile delinquency and other forms of deviance is based on how society perceives, judges, and reacts to the behavior in question. It is appropriate to preface our explanation of Interactionist Theory—or Labeling Theory, as this formulation is commonly known—by briefly reviewing **social status** and **social roles,** and how we acquire these dimensions of personal identity (see Chapter 1 for a more thorough treatment).

Social status is *an individual's prestige position in relation to others in his or her social group or society.* Social status also can refer to the prestige position of a group in relation to other groups. The level of social status or prestige held by a person is determined by the social group as every member is ranked from high to low. Some status or prestige is automatically **ascribed** to a person as a consequence of biological characteristics such as sex or age. Individuals also may receive some unearned and vicarious status based upon the wealth and power of their parents. Some social status can be changed or **achieved** through personal effort, especially in an open class society that encourages its members to strive for upward social mobility. Considerable social status may be derived from one's level of education and occupation.

The level of social status assigned to an individual also may be modified by taking on new roles. Thus, not only is the prestige position held by a person founded on inheritance and personal achievement, but also on the social role(s) occupied. A **social role** is *the set of behavioral expectations that accompanies a particular status.* As people grow older and have new experiences, society often changes their social statuses, and assigns new roles to them. For example, your life course will probably encompass the successive roles of child, sibling, adolescent, college student, spouse, parent, grandparent, and retiree, to name just a few. With each role assignment (and the related status position), society hands the individual a rather carefully structured "script" containing behavioral expectations to be fulfilled.

When each of us, as individual members of society, is made aware of the role assignment and the behavioral expectations associated with that role, we usually comply. To conform to the social expectations of our group or society is much easier than to digress from them. Societal judgments regarding a role assignment and the behavioral expectations regarded as appropriate for that role are very powerful forces and influences impacting upon the individual. Thus it becomes normative and virtually mandatory for the individual to comply with the role "label" that has been applied to him or her by manifesting the expected behavior.

The fundamental sociological principles of social status, social roles, and social expectations comprise the foundation for the Labeling Theory of deviant and delinquent behavior. For even a deviant role can be assigned by society to some persons who, in the judgment of society, seem to warrant such a negative label. Labeling Theory concentrates less on the de-

*"Dear, now would be a good time to tell him
that this type of behavior may eventually lead
to a clash with the criminal justice system and
subsequent criminal labeling."*

viant acts themselves and instead focuses on the actor and the audience and their perceptions of each other (Gibbs, 1966). Howard Becker (1963:9) defined and described labeling
as an interactive process:

> *Social groups create deviance by making the rules whose infraction constitutes de-
> viance. The deviant is one to whom that label has successfully been applied. De-
> viant behavior is behavior that people so label.*

For example, if a person becomes known in society (community, school, neighborhood, etc.)
as an alcoholic, prostitute, juvenile delinquent, or by any other negative label or reputation,
the social status or prestige position of that individual is ranked accordingly. Moreover, with
the label goes a new role and set of social expectations. The person is expected to behave in
harmony with the social role assignment. In other words, labeling is a public declaration of
one's social identity; of what society perceives and expects the individual to be. Thus, in one
sense, societal labeling is being publicly "branded." It is extremely difficult to escape the label—whether rightly or wrongly applied—because it leads to a redefinition of the relationship
and expectations between the person labeled and the other members of society. Labeling Theory strongly suggests that the causal explanation for much juvenile delinquency, as well as a
large share of the responsibility, can be traced to society itself.

Early Contributions to Labeling Theory

The labeling approach has its theoretical roots in some of the early ideas of social psychologists such as Charles Horton Cooley and W. I. Thomas. Cooley ([1902] 1964), in his classic concept of the **Looking-Glass Self,** observed that *an individual's self-evaluation and*

self-identity are basically a reflection of one's perception of other people's reactions to his or her conduct. Broadly applied to adolescent behavior, juveniles use those with whom they interact like a mirror that reflects back an image (a social identity), which is then internalized as part of the youths' self-concepts. If juveniles perceive that others view them as delinquent, they are very likely to accept that label.

W. I. Thomas (1931) contributed the concept of **Definition of the Situation** which essentially means that *when people define a situation as real, it becomes real in its consequences.* This thought-provoking concept further illuminated the process whereby certain acts are socially defined as deviant or delinquent and the juvenile who commits an act so defined becomes labeled as "delinquent." This is similar to Robert Merton's idea of the **Self-fulfilling Prophecy** as a catalyst for eliciting future behavior of the prescribed kind. According to Merton (1968), when the members of a social group define a person or event in a certain way, they may in fact shape future circumstances and activities so that the anticipated and projected behavior comes to pass.

Tannenbaum's Concept of "Tagging"

In 1938, with the publication of *Crime and Community* by Frank Tannenbaum, an innovative application of the labeling perspective was made to criminology. Tannenbaum emphasized the treatment of the offender that makes a hardened criminal out of the accidental or occasional one. Thus, the greater evil lies in the societal treatment, not in the original act. Tannenbaum (1938:17–19) called this demonization process *tagging* and pointed out:

> *There is a gradual shift from the definition of the specific acts as evil to a definition of the individual as evil, so that all his acts come to be looked upon with suspicion. In the process of identification his companions, hangouts, play, speech, income, all his conduct, the personality itself, become subject to scrutiny and question. From the community's point of view, the individual who used to do bad and mischievous things has now become a bad and unredeemable human being…The young delinquent becomes bad because he is defined as bad and because he is not believed if he is good…The process of making the criminal, therefore, is a process of tagging, defining, segregating, describing, emphasizing, making conscious and self-conscious; it becomes a way of stimulating, suggesting, emphasizing, and evoking the very traits that are complained of…*

The process of tagging led to Tannenbaum's (1938:8, 20) somber conclusion: "The adult criminal is usually the delinquent child grown up…The person becomes the thing he is described as being."

Lemert's Primary and Secondary Deviance

As we have unfolded the development of each theoretical explanation of deviance and delinquency, we have tried to demonstrate how successive theorists have added to the accumulating store of insights, concepts, and knowledge until the full theoretical formulation eventually takes shape and comes into view. Nowhere is this process of theory building more obvious than in the emergence of the labeling perspective of deviance and delinquency. While the modern labeling approach is often attributed to the work of Edwin Lemert (1951), it is obvious that he stood on the shoulders of numerous earlier theorists, as he synthesized and refined their work as foundation stones for his own contributions.

Lemert's expansion of Labeling Theory was in his concern for the consequences of an individual's being labeled on future behavior. Remember, Cooley indicated that an individual's evaluation of self is basically a reflection of other people's reactions. It follows that if the labeled person believes in the societal label, then the process of labeling can be a critical determinant of the subsequent deviant or conforming career of the individual.

In discussing the dynamics involved in becoming a juvenile delinquent, Tannenbaum implied that there is a progression between two types of criminal or delinquent acts. One is the *first* act, which the child considers as innocent but which adults define as delinquent. The second is the *final* behavior, which both the child and adults define as delinquent. Lemert went further than Tannenbaum, and made explicit the distinction between these two behavioral steps in deviance. He called the first one **primary deviation** and the second, **secondary deviation. Primary deviation** occurs when *an individual may commit a deviant act (or several deviant acts), but does not internalize the deviant self-concept and continues to occupy the role of conformist.* **Secondary deviation** occurs when *an individual's self-concept is altered and the deviant role is personally assumed.*

The labeling approach to explaining juvenile delinquency has the potential of going beyond the questions of how society defines, labels, and punishes the deviant, "or how group members alter their social expectations and behavior" in relation to the person. The theory poses the surprising question of how the revised self-concept of the socially labeled and stigmatized individual can possibly lead to the "emergence of stable patterns of deviance" (DeFleur et al. 1971:385).

Becker's Developmental Career Model

Howard Becker is one of the leading practitioners of the labeling perspective. In his book, *The Outsiders* (1963), he propounded the view that deviance, like beauty, exists in the eye of the beholder. No act is intrinsically deviant, but must be defined as such. He emphasized that societal perception of an act as deviant can automatically impute a generalized deviant role to the individual. Everett Hughes (1945:357) described this process as taking on a **master status**—*a status which "…tends to overpower, in most crucial situations, any other characteristics which might run counter to it."* As Becker (1963:34) said:

> *Treating a person as though he were generally rather than specifically deviant produces a self-fulfilling prophecy. It sets in motion several mechanisms which conspire to shape the person in the image people have of him.*

Perhaps Becker's major contribution to Labeling Theory was his introduction of the notion of a developmental process that precedes the attainment of a deviant or delinquent identity and career. We are indebted to Becker's (1963) study of marijuana users which prompted him to outline an unfolding sequence of steps that could lead an individual to unreserved commitment and participation in a deviant career.

Becker argued that the identity and state of being a "confirmed marijuana user" develops over time. It has history and longitudinal development. For example, Becker (1963:23) found that the developmental process for becoming a confirmed and consistent user of marijuana included the following sequence of related steps or stages: (1) the person must have access to the drug; (2) he or she must experiment with it; and (3) the individual must continue its use. Each of these steps toward the final condition involves subtle changes in the individual's attitudes and perspective, as well as behavior. Becker (1963:23) noted:

> *Each step requires explanation... We need, for example, one kind of explanation of how a person comes to be in a situation where marijuana is readily available...,and another kind of explanation of why, given the fact of its availability, he is willing to experiment with it in the first place. And we need still another explanation of why, having experimented with it, he continues to use it... That is, no one could become a confirmed marijuana user without going through each step.*

"The circumstances that determine movement along a particular path include properties of both the person and of the situation." The personal component involves the individual's susceptibility and vulnerability to the drug; the situational component in the developmental process consists largely of feedback from other actors, who witness it, and how they respond to the individual's use of marijuana (Cohen, 1966:104). According to Becker and other labeling theorists, it is within the social situation and context that the user of marijuana can encounter sanctions and a labeling experience that can stimulate further progress and development of a deviant career.

The developmental model or developmental process suggests considerable explanatory power for many other forms of deviant and delinquent behavior besides the use of marijuana. In addition, Becker's formulation also helps to moderate the rigid delinquent/nondelinquent dichotomy by perceiving delinquent behavior at various stages of development, intensity, and commitment.

Contributions of Labeling Theory

A significant contribution of the labeling approach to explaining the causes of juvenile delinquency is its analytical division of nonconforming behavior into primary and secondary deviance. Of equal importance is the focus on the societal perception and reaction to the initial deviant act and the subsequent revision in self-concept that enables the actor to continue into a more stable pattern of deviant behavior. Thus, as Matza (1969:891 164, 196) pointed out:

> *...we see how the effort of society to remedy or control deviance ironically becomes a factor in producing deviance. This paradoxical development runs against common-sense which usually sees social control efforts as an effective response rather than a cause of deviant behavior.*

Wide application of the labeling perspective has been made in critiques of law enforcement procedures and the juvenile justice system. Piliavin and Briar (1964:214) contended that many dispositions made by police officers in cases of suspected juvenile offenders are

Some social and personal labeling is effectively symbolized and communicated in clothing styles and predictive of the wearer's values and behavior. For example, high school and college students may derive identity and solidarity by wearing their school colors and names—much like a label. On the negative side, gang members also gain satisfaction, status, and identity by labeling themselves and wearing their ominous gang colors and names (see Chapter 12).

based on intuitive character assessments which, in turn, are founded on the youth's group affiliations, age, sex, race, grooming, dress, and demeanor:

> *...the official delinquent, as distinguished from the juvenile who simply commits a delinquent act, is the product of a social judgment, in this case a judgment made by the police. He is a delinquent because somebody in authority has defined him as one, often on the basis of the public face he has presented to officials rather than of the kind of offense he has committed.*

The labeling process that occurs during police/juvenile encounters on the streets is further discussed in Chapter 13.

Similarly, Cicourel (1968) used a labeling approach to show differential treatment between lower and middle class families in the administration of justice. He indicated that ad hoc interpretations and imputations of character, family life, and future possibilities—often retained in official and unofficial files by schools, police departments, and courts—not only negatively and unfairly label some youths, but literally predestine them for future litigation.

Regarding juvenile delinquency, Edwin Schur emerged as one of the more outspoken proponents of the labeling perspective. In his book *Radical Non-intervention* (1973) he asserted that we must rethink the delinquency problem. The label of delinquency has been so overused and so widely applied that it covers everything from talking back to parents and truancy, to forcible rape and first degree murder. As Schur pointed out, both the terms "juvenile" and "delinquent" are ascribed statuses. That is to say, they are labels assigned to some youths by the society in which they live. Schur insisted that so-called delinquents are neither internally nor externally different from nondelinquents except for the fact that they have been officially processed by the justice system and so labeled.

A less radical labeling viewpoint of criminal and juvenile justice procedures has been set forth by Hugh Barlow (1987). He asserted that criminologists and legal authorities have long attempted to distinguish between those acts of **mala in se**—*considered inherently evil* (such as murder and rape) and **mala prohibita**—*those considered evil only because they are prohibited* (such as gambling and alcohol consumption by minors). The labeling approach provides valuable insights into the latter category, as a vast number of the acts committed by juveniles that come to be labeled as delinquent clearly fall under it. The wide variety of acts which become treated as status offenses for juveniles are not considered evil in and of themselves, but merely have been labeled as inappropriate behavior for juveniles.

Additional support for the labeling argument has been derived from the 1993 research of David Ward and Charles Tittle. Despite some methodological problems in gathering data, their findings suggest that "sanctioning and labeling of norm violators significantly affects the likelihood that an offender will develop a deviant identity and that such identities significantly affect the likelihood of recidivism" (1993:60). However, Ward and Tittle hasten to caution that the traditional labeling process is just one of several ways that recurring deviance may be produced. Moreover, labeling may be more relevant in explaining minor acts of deviance and delinquency than for major offenses.

Criticisms and Limitations of Labeling Theory

The reviews of Labeling Theory are mixed and contradictory. The weaknesses cited by critics are diametric opposites to the strengths referred to by proponents. For example, much has been made of Labeling Theory's focus on societal reaction as a key factor in producing deviance (e.g., Becker, 1963; Erikson, 1964). In response, Gibbs (1966) suggested that the approach is defective in that it tends to deny the existence of deviance as any reality apart from the process of social adjudication of deviance. Gibbs indicated that this approach cannot tell us why one person rather than another commits deviant acts. He argued that the usefulness of the approach is in its understanding of the societal response to deviance, while leaving the original or primary deviance unexplained. However, labeling theorists like John Kitsuse (1972) have countered that Labeling Theory was never intended as an explanation of primary deviation from societal norms.

David Bordua (1967:48) challenged the depiction of societal reaction as a force totally external to the passive (and often innocent) actor, moving the actor to a secondary and more stable pattern of deviance. He pointed out that juvenile delinquents often have coveted, encouraged, and cultivated such labels as "tough" or "bad" for themselves as a matter of pride. Gang members often have flaunted their presence and staged a confrontation with the police because their subsequent arrests are often sources of "rep" among their peers (Werthman and Piliavin, 1967). On the other hand, punishment, societal labeling, and stigmatization for wrong-doing can be effective in deterring offenders from pursuing a course of continual law violation. It is *not* axiomatic that those guilty of primary deviance and subjected to the labeling process will ultimately move on to secondary deviance (Akers, 1985).

As a counterbalance to Barry Glassner's (1982:75) contention that "during the past few decades, more sociological research has derived from the labeling perspective than from any other model of deviance," a number of sociologists complain that "labeling theory lacks empirical verification and that therefore its pronouncements should be considered with caution" (Bordua, 1969:121). Moreover, L. N. Robins (1975) argued that it is unlikely that the proponents of the perspective will subject Labeling Theory to empirical study since they are the sociologists most suspicious of "hard" data. He contended:

> *In short, labelling [sic] theorists believe that deviance in a society is largely the product of attempts to measure or record it, Like Archimedes, who realized he would have to stand outside the earth if he were to move it, the sociologist accepting labelling [sic] theory has nowhere to stand from which he or she can observe the "natural" rates against which the size of the distortion in official rates and rates based on interviews can be measured, to estimate the impact of labelling [sic] (Robins, 1975:21).*

Labeling Theory has been used to indict the juvenile justice system, charging that police, courts, and other agencies tend to negatively evaluate and label some suspected delinquents, thus increasing their likelihood of further involvement in secondary deviance. This contention was strongly disputed by Foster et al., (1972), who found that labeling by the juvenile justice system during an early stage of processing did not produce changes in self-concept or increased delinquency by their subjects. Similarly, Terence Thornberry (1979) found that the handling of delinquent youths in a stern manner generally did not result in greater criminality, as Labeling Theory suggests. Along the same line, Bordua (1967:154) and Gibbs (1966:50) charged that labeling theory does not take into account the positive aspects of societal reaction to deviant or delinquent behavior. Many children and youths are diverted from further misbehavior and delinquency by the serious and even threatening response of parents, teachers, and police officers to an initial offense. Even an uncomplimentary label and dire predictions about where a delinquent course can lead has deterrent value for many juveniles.

More recent research on the logic and explanatory power of Labeling Theory continues to generate mixed and contradictory findings. For example, Lawrence Sherman found inconsistent support for the hypothesis that "the process of repeatedly being arrested and labeled affects individuals' self-image and later behavior such that they come to accept this definition of themselves" (Sherman and Berk, 1984; Sherman and Douglas, 1992).

> *Sherman's work showed…not everyone who is labeled comes to see him or herself in that way and increase his or her deviant behavior. This probably reflects the fact that each of us has many components to our self-identities (Stockard, 1997:138–139).*

BOX 8-1 Concept Application

Juvenile Delinquency as Creative Short-Term Hedonism: "Crime is Fun!"

The well-established sociological theories presented in Chapters 6, 7, and 8 variously assert that juveniles are constrained to engage in delinquent behavior by frustrating social circumstances, involvement with delinquent peers, the impact of class conflicts and cultural prescriptions, ineffectual social bonding and control, and negative societal labeling. All of these etiological efforts are more or less sociologically deterministic, leaning heavily on social forces external to the individual.

In recent years our attention has been attracted by a surprising new emphasis in explaining juvenile misconduct. Although investigators have long observed the game element and the pleasure experienced by many youngsters participating in illegal activities (Shaw and McKay, 1931), the possible importance of this hedonistic dimension as an explanatory variable is a more contemporary suggestion. For example, Richards et al. (1979) found that their middle class subjects readily identified delinquency as "play" and "fun." Jack Katz, in his *Seductions of Crime: Moral and Sensual Attractions of Doing Evil* (1988), contended that criminal behavior cannot be fully understood or explained without grasping how it is experienced or what it means to the actor.

If we grasp the subjective interpretation of the experience, Katz argues, we will find that crime has a sensual, magical, creative appeal that is lacking in most conventional, law-abiding acts. The "central problem" for the criminologist, Katz argues, "is to understand the emergence of distinctive sensual dynamics" (p. 4). Doing evil, he writes, is motivated by a quest for moral transcendence, righteousness in the face of challenge, boredom, humiliation, or chaos. Deviance has authenticity, Katz believes, an attractiveness that uplifts, excites, and purifies. To understand crime as a strictly rational pursuit, as the desperate need to wallow in self-flagellation, as the manifestation of a mental disorder, or the enactment of straightforward

cultural or subcultural dictates, is to miss the point spectacularly. Deviance is the existential pursuit of passion, a "lucid" enterprise, with clear-cut winners and losers, a fevered, out-of-one's-head experience, a world of beauty all its own, accessible only to the righteous, the daring, the members of a kind of soulful elite. (Goode, 1990:7)

This possible extension of delinquency theory is refreshingly simple and straightforward, and therefore potentially embarrassing to some theorists who may wonder how they could have overlooked the obvious allurement and sensuality of deviant behavior. Without question, while delinquency is often illogical and dangerous, it is also exciting and stimulating to a great many youngsters. One of the authors made this serendipitous discovery when interviewing several youthful gang members in California cities. In response to inquiries regarding the motivation for their criminal conduct, all the usual social causes were cited—ranging from broken homes to slum neighborhoods to the lack of educational and occupational opportunities. In addition, some of the more candid and articulate informants added something more. They excitedly alluded to the unparalleled adrenalin rush and emotional high associated with the risk entailed in their illegal adventures. As I pursued my inquiry of "Why do you break the law?" one youth metaphorically adapted the mountain climber's traditional response to the challenge: "Because it is there. The law is just waiting there to be broken; so I break it!" (Bynum, 1993).

Many sociologists will deny that Katz's reasoning is a unique contribution to causal explanations of deviance and delinquency. Rather, they contend that the hedonistic aspects of misbehavior are already incorporated in existing Social Learning and Cultural Transmission Theories. Further, these critics challenge the "crime is fun" explanation as an empirically unsubstantiated and premature conclusion.

Continued

BOX 8-1 *Continued*

Short-term hedonism may be the explanation for the spontaneous destruction by attendants at the Woodstock '99 festival in Rome, New York.

Sources

Bynum, J. E. "The California street gangs: Motivations and methods." Unpublished research report. October 1, 1996.

Goode, E. "Symposium: Phenomenology and structure in the study of crime and deviance." *Contemporary Sociology* 19, 1:5–12. 1990.

Katz, J. *Seductions of crime: Moral and sensual attractions of doing evil.* New York: Basic Books. 1988.

Richards, P., Berk, R. A., and Forster, B. *Crime as play: Delinquency in middle-class suburbs.* Cambridge, MA: Ballinger. 1979.

Shaw, C. R., and McKay, H. D. *Social factors in juvenile delinquency: Report on the causes of crime,* Vol. II, Washington, DC: National Commission on Law Observance and Enforcement. 1931.

Radical Theories

Radical Theory is an organized body of evidence and argument that dramatically departs from more established and accepted criminological theories. Such revisionist approaches have a recurring history in sociology and often are precipitated by major social problems and a growing conviction among some innovative thinkers and theorists that the existing and widely applauded explanations of what is happening and why are incomplete or inaccurate. For example, during the 1960s and early 1970s the widespread civil rights struggle, the Vietnam

War, and other social upheavals became the catalysts that sensitized many people to the gross suffering and glaring inequities among human beings and led to the questioning of dominant economic, social, and criminological theories. A number of articulate sociologists and criminologists expressed their discontent with the theoretical status quo by calling for fundamental revision of explanations of deviant and criminal conduct (e.g., Chambliss, 1974; Quinney, 1974; and Turk, 1969). This radical new criminology focused on the generation of laws and legal institutions by affluent and politically influential groups that not only perpetuate their elitist power and position but also unfairly discriminate against the underclass with a criminal label. The radical theorists complained that traditional criminology emphasized the categories set up by the criminal law and "the kinds of common crimes believed to be associated with the poor and powerless" (Michalowski, 1985:314, 315).

Consistent with the labeling perspective, radical theorists view adult crime and juvenile delinquency as labels that often are selectively applied to specified individuals and groups whose behavior is particularly disturbing to those who are in a position to attach such labels and implement social sanctions. However, labeling theorists usually focus on the microsociological context of interaction and postulate that the deviant label and role can be imputed in communities of any size and for a multitude of reasons. On the other hand, radical theorists take a macrosociological approach by contending that the criminal or delinquent label arises from conflicts between different social classes as their vested interests and values clash, and as law enforcement is differentially applied to these social classes.

The Marxian Heritage

The philosophical and ideational roots of radical theories of deviant and delinquent behavior can be traced back to the writings and conflict perspective of Karl Marx ([1867] 1967). Marx saw capitalism as an evil economic system that intensified and perpetuated the separation and ranking of social classes. He contended that by virtue of their ownership and control of the means of production, the bourgeoisie (capitalist class) were able to maintain their power, materialistic and hedonistic lifestyle, and domination over the disadvantaged proletariat (working class).

In his writings, Marx pointed to a growing awareness and alienation among workers of the world as they toiled to maintain productivity and profit for their capitalist overlords. Karl Marx and Friedrich Engels ([1848] 1979) developed a conflict interpretation of human society, behavior, and social phenomena in which they called for the revolutionary overthrow of capitalistic political, economic, and social structures and the radical reorganization of society. They pointed to an inevitable war of the classes in which the downtrodden and pauperized proletariat would revolt and ultimately establish a classless society in which people could not be exploited to satisfy the greed of a small, wealthy, and powerful upper class.

Although Marx did not focus his Conflict Theory explicitly on explaining crime or delinquency, many subsequent scholars expanded and applied his basic thesis to those phenomena. Radical Theories of delinquency are built upon the conflict perspective and generally agree with Marx that the unequal distribution of wealth and power is the major causal explanation behind norm-violating behavior. The theoretical contributions of Richard Quinney, David Greenberg, and Herman and Julia Schwendinger are such extensions of the Marxian argument and examples of radical theory of crime and delinquency.

Quinney's Social Reality of Crime and Delinquency

Richard Quinney emerged in the 1970s as one of the most prominent spokespersons for radical criminology in the United States. According to Quinney (1975), crime and delinquency can be best understood in relation to how a society creates its criminal laws, defines crime and delinquency, and what practices it implements to control its citizens. Quinney distinguished between what he called the "official reality of crime" which purports that law violation threatens social order and public safety, and the "social reality of crime" which reflects the less visible definition that any act which threatens those in power is legally prohibited and considered criminal or delinquent.

Quinney's (1975:37–41) radical theory of criminal behavior contains definite undertones of Marxian class conflict and was summarized in six propositions:

1. The Official Definition of Crime: Crime as a legal definition of human conduct is created by agents of the dominant class in a politically organized society.

2. Formulating Definitions of Crime: Definitions of crime are composed of behaviors that conflict with the interests of the dominant class.

3. Applying Definitions of Crime: Definitions of crime are applied by the class that has the power to shape the enforcement and administration of criminal law.

4. How Behavior Patterns Develop in Relation to Definitions of Crime: Behavior patterns are structured in relation to definitions of crime, and within this context people engage in actions that have relative probabilities of being defined as criminal.

5. Constructing an Ideology of Crime: An ideology of crime is constructed and diffused by the dominant class to secure its hegemony.

6. Constructing the Social Reality of Crime: The social reality of crime is constructed by the formulation and application of definitions of crime, the development of behavior patterns in relation to these definitions, and the construction of an ideology of crime.

It is abundantly clear from the context of Quinney's *Social Reality of Crime* (1970) that his use of the term "crime" encompasses juvenile delinquency as well as illegal conduct by adults. It follows that the six propositions comprising the nucleus of Quinney's radical theory represent an explanation for the definition and creation of crime and delinquency, as well as the societal responses. Quinney views criminal and delinquent behavior as largely a result of the repressive efforts of the dominant class to control subordinate classes.

In his book, *Class, State, and Crime,* Quinney (1980) outlined two broad categories of criminal activity. The first is what he called *crimes of economic domination and repression.* These crimes include the unlawful acts committed by members of the ruling class in order to maintain their social supremacy. Part of these activities, according to Quinney, involve the constant efforts of government and law enforcement officials to criminalize those behaviors of the working class which appear to threaten the existing social order. In order to control the masses, Quinney argued that the lower class must be coerced or duped into believing that the laws that repress them actually protect them.

The second type of criminality Quinney called *crimes of accommodation and resistance.* These are the crimes committed by members of the working class in an effort to survive the oppression of the ruling class. Expanding on Marxian theory, Quinney postulated that in a

Radical theorists such as Richard Quinney and David Greenberg, building on Marx's conceptualization of lower class frustration and alienation, contend that much juvenile delinquency reflects a popular label imposed on the poor and powerless.

capitalist society the poor and the powerless are forced into crime for survival. Predatory and parasitic property crimes such as vandalism, theft, burglary, and robbery are explained as resulting from the impoverished situation of the underemployed, the unemployed, and the unemployable (Bartol and Bartol, 1989:275).

Quinney's radical theory can be applied to juvenile delinquency in two important ways. First, it implies that activities and conduct by youths which are perceived by adults as threats to the authority and privileged status enjoyed by adults are those most likely to be defined and punished as delinquency. Second, it indicates that underclass and minority youths are far more likely to be involved in activities that are seen as threatening the existing social order, and hence, far more likely than their white middle and upper class counterparts to be punished by legal authorities.

Greenberg's Focus on Adolescent Frustration

David Greenberg (1977) made a direct application of conflict and radical theory to juvenile delinquency by linking it to the high level of frustration experienced by many adolescents in a capitalist society. As Robert Merton (1957) pointed out in his Theory of Anomie (Chapter 6), in a country like the United States there is tremendous pressure on everyone to achieve certain culturally approved objectives. There is a general consensus that these objectives are money, material possessions, and other symbols of economic success. Greenberg forcefully added that the precise nature of these success goals depends upon one's place in a rigidly structured and age-graded life course. Adolescents, for example, are subjected to virtually uncompromising peer pressure to conform to certain prescribed codes of appearance and behavior. At the same time, pressures from older generations and the larger society in the form of laws requiring school attendance and minimum-age work regulations effectively restrict the opportunities of teenagers in the job market and lock them into their unfulfilling age-status roles. Based upon this situation, Greenberg identified several sources of potential frustration among adolescents in a capitalistic society that can motivate many to delinquent conduct.

Most prominent among adolescent frustrations can be the lack of money by the poor to participate socially, or at least symbolically, with more affluent teenage members of the youth subculture. The absence of funds for popular clothing, cosmetics, recorded music, and automobiles may lead to shoplifting, burglary, automobile theft, or perhaps to dealing illegal drugs in order to attain these items. These pressures may be negligible for those youths fortunate enough to have parents who are sympathetic and economically able to fulfill the needs and desires characteristic of their children's age and status position in society. On the other hand, Greenberg argued, less affluent minority and lower class youths may feel compelled by their economically disadvantaged situation to engage in juvenile delinquency.

A second source of adolescent frustration cited by Greenberg as related to a proclivity to engage in criminal conduct is failure to achieve respect in school. A weak academic performance or aptitude coupled with stigma imposed by teachers and classmates may be interpreted by a youngster as valid appraisals of his or her worth as a person and ultimate chances for success. Such a demoralized youth, according to Greenberg, is a prime prospect for antisocial and delinquent behavior. Such negative school experiences are more commonly found among members of the underclass.

A third source of economically determined juvenile misconduct suggested by Greenberg is inability of huge numbers of lower class youths and adults to find gainful employment. Greenberg suggested that unemployed and underemployed males are especially vulnerable to anxiety regarding their "manhood" and are likely to feel a critical inadequacy in fulfilling social expectations associated with the adult male role. This frustration may lead to an overemphasis on toughness, and lead to aggressive acts, including fighting, assault, rape, and even homicide.

Schwendingers' Instrumental Theory

Radical theories in the Marxist conflict tradition consistently contend that a person's status position in the social class structure is the key factor in explaining that individual's illegal behavior. Capitalism, according to Marx and those who espouse this theoretical approach, generates competitiveness, acquisitiveness, and the exploitation of others, and consequently reinforces the division and mutual antipathy of the "have" and "have not" social classes. Each member of society is assigned membership somewhere in the stratified ranks of social classes based upon his or her success in controlling and/or accumulating the profits and products of economic endeavors. Thus, radical theorists argue, the stage is set for all kinds of illegal behavior resulting from the alienation of many lower class individuals and groups. Official arrest and court statistics seem to confirm that crime and delinquency are largely lower class phenomena. On the other hand, radical theorists suggest that the capitalistic system, which encourages a certain amount of surplus labor and unemployment, together with the legal system and law enforcement, is organized to ensure such an outcome.

Herman and Julia Schwendinger (1985) expanded and extended these basic premises from the Marxist conflict perspective in developing their own innovative Radical Theory. While affirming that delinquency still can be explained by a youth's social class status, the Schwendingers added that significant amounts of "criminality can be found among youth in all stations of life" (1985:3). As was noted in Chapter 3, self-report studies support this contention, by indicating that middle class youths are about equally involved in delinquent conduct as members of the lower class.

To this, the Schwendingers added their main theoretical insight: the parents' social class is not the most important variable in determining the delinquency potential for adolescents. Rather, the youths' relative status position among other teenagers is the best predictor of delinquency. Herman and Julia Schwendinger identified several relatively exclusive, stratified status formations—or distinctive social networks formed by the youths themselves—which roughly correspond with some of the more traditional social classes. These stradom formations of youth tend to be based upon common values, interests, and activities, and separate members of one social network from other youth groupings. The Schwendingers outlined the following prominent social networks among American youth:

1. *Socialites,* which may be referred to as "elites," "frats," "soshes," or "preppies," which are generally comprised of upper middle class, college-bound youths.
2. *Greasers,* also called "hoods," "homeboys," "thugs," or "hodads." This group is largely comprised of lower class and minority youths.
3. *Intellectuals,* who are often called "brains," "bookworms," or "nerds."

Not all youths neatly fit into one or another of these categories. There can be considerable overlap of individuals who comfortably interact with more than one group. There likely will be some individuals who do not readily identify with any of these social strata or networks in a given school or community. There is also considerable crossover based on a blurring of socioeconomic background. For example, athletes may be identified as "jocks" and those interested in skateboards may be known as "skaters" regardless of the socioeconomic status of their families. Nevertheless, in spite of such irregularities, the Schwendingers posited that virtually all youths will find some specific clique with which they can identify.

The theoretical formulation developed by Herman and Julia Schwendinger to explain juvenile delinquency is called **Instrumental Theory.** This theory describes the misbehavior as motivated by calculated and selfish designs upon the victims—not dissimilar from the rationalizations of the "greedy bourgeoisie" so vividly described by Karl Marx. The delinquent has a utilitarian attitude regarding the illegal act as well as of the victim as a "legitimate" object of exploitation ("What's in it for me?") (Carey and McAnany, 1984:138).

Moreover, the Schwendingers' Instrumental Theory conceptualized delinquency as importantly linked to a youth's social network, contending that members of some stratum formations are much more likely to become delinquent than others; and that the delinquent conduct manifested by members of one stratum or social network may vary significantly from the kind of delinquency most common in other groups. For example, youths with economically deprived backgrounds are not only more likely to become involved with the network identified as "greasers," but are apt to participate in theft, burglaries, and perhaps violence (especially if they join a gang). On the other hand, middle class youths who are identified as "socialites," while perhaps equally delinquent, are more likely to engage in truancy, vandalism, shoplifting, and less violent forms of law violation. Thus, in another sense, membership in a particular stratum or subgroup has an "instrumental" function—serving as a vehicle for a social identity and enhancing opportunity and motivation for various specialized activities—even juvenile delinquency. Youths identified as "intellectuals," regardless of their parents' social class, are much less likely to become involved in serious illegal behavior.

Contributions of Radical Theories

In our study of the various theoretical perspectives and approaches that explain human behavior, we must be cautious that some viewpoints are not summarily rejected simply because personal biases and preferences interfere with objective considerations. Radical criminology is in danger of such a fate because it is philosophically linked with **Marxist Conflict Theory** and boldly calls for revolutionary revision of the political and economic institutions that are assumed to define crime and delinquency in support of upper class domination of the underclass. The United States has a long history of costly political and military confrontation with socialism, communism, and other dimensions of Marxist activism and it may be difficult for some to conceive of any positive contributions from radical theories to our understanding of juvenile delinquency. However, Radical Theory offers several helpful insights regarding the causes of delinquency.

A major contribution of radical theories is that they call attention to the lack of power and resultant alienation experienced by young people living in any society dominated by adults. Juvenile statutes, for the most part, reinforce expectations for children and youths to conform to norms which reflect adult values about appropriate behaviors. When those norms are violated, youths are confronted by a juvenile justice system which is similarly dominated by adults. Many young people feel powerless in this adult world. In Marxian terms, these juveniles experience a growing alienation, class consciousness, and class cohesion, much like any other powerless group of people.

Radical theories also underscore the prejudice and discrimination experienced by youths who are members of racial and ethnic minorities. Radical theorists forcefully argue that minority youths are subjected to differential and unequal treatment at the hands of school officials, law enforcement officers, and juvenile court judges. An awareness of their social handicaps, in a perceived conflict with a hostile society, enhances the attractiveness of illegal means to attain economic success to some underclass and minority youths. The economic determinism behind some juvenile crime was graphically illustrated to one of the authors during recent field research on urban street gangs. During the course of the investigation, there was an opportunity to briefly interview several youths after their conviction for possession and selling of crack cocaine. Although they were high-school dropouts, they were very "street smart" and mercenary about their profession as drug dealers. In response to a naive inquiry regarding why they didn't pursue their formal education and seek an honest job, one 17-year-old youth answered with a question: "How much money did you make last year?" Momentarily thinking that his response was tangential and unrelated, the researcher asked: "What does my income have to do with the illegal activities for which you have been convicted?" "Well," he countered, "I made nearly $100,000 last year, doing my thing; and no income taxes. How much did you clear?!" It seems that some of our most popular and traditional theories of juvenile delinquency have underemphasized the importance of class conflict and economic determinism which are central tenets of Radical Theory.

An example of the relatively new interest in and influence of the radical approach to explaining crime and delinquency can be seen in the heated debates it has sparked among criminologists and sociologists. Its support by some scholars is evidenced by the formation of a learned society known as the Union of Radical Criminologists. This group holds meetings, circulates newsletters among its members, and focuses on research which utilizes the conflict perspective and radical theory applied to the study of crime and juvenile delinquency.

Another contribution of the radical theories is that they force more conventional criminologists and sociologists to consider alternative theoretical explanations for deviance, crime, and delinquency. Crime and delinquency (in the minds of radical theorists) often are contrived nomenclatures imputed to underclass offenders who are actually the victims of the system rulers. By shifting the focus away from individual delinquents and on to the macroscopic social, economic, and political forces which create and enforce the laws defining delinquency, these theories encourage society to examine and question the juvenile justice system. Even if these theories do not provide a comprehensive explanation for delinquent behavior, such an examination and critical analysis of the juvenile justice system can be very beneficial.

Criticisms and Limitations of Radical Theories

As with other theoretical schools of thought that have been put forward to account for juvenile delinquency, Radical Theories not only have offered significant insights but have been subjected to critical evaluation. James Short (1990:135), for example, observed that capitalism and socialism have much in common and their dichotomous division into "good" and "evil" systems is not as simple as radical theorists suggest:

> *All advanced industrial and postindustrial societies "reproduce surplus labor" and capitalist and socialist nations alike apparently undergo similar changes in crime patterns in various stages of development. Profitability and competition in international markets motivate capitalist, socialist, and mixed economies;...Thus,*

while many of the facts upon which Marxist and other "radical" theories are based are generally accepted, much debate centers on specific interpretations. Although the levels and types of unemployment and the levels of alienation of labor vary a great deal among nation-states, they are more or less constant features of capitalist, socialist, and mixed economies in today's economically interdependent world.

Lamar Empey and Mark Stafford (1991:499) noted the failure of Radical Theory to empirically test its propositions as an important limitation of its explanatory power:

It has failed to explain why age and sex continue to be better predictors of crime than social class. And it has failed to indicate why, contrary to all of the lessons of history, sociology, and anthropology, delinquency can be expected to disappear in a truly socialist society—why such a society could be expected to avoid the disorienting, often crime-producing conditions that all advanced societies—capitalist and noncapitalist—are now experiencing. In terms of traditional scientific standards, at least, the theory has been deficient.

Other analysts have also pointed out that the theoretical causes of delinquency are not solely rooted in socioeconomic class conflict. Rather, there is considerable, legitimate overlap with Radical Theory of key variables from other theoretical orientations. The concept of "lower class alientation," for example, must be shared with Social Strain and Cultural Transmission theories.

David Schicor (1983) contends that "socialization"—so useful in social learning theories—is a meaningful approach to understanding juvenile delinquency, whether looking at capitalist or socialist societies. Although Marxian and radical theorists must rely heavily on socialization as a causal factor in accounting for cultural materialism and lower class inability to fulfill such expectations, they have tended to discount the importance of this basic concept. The reason, according to Schicor, is the overpoliticization of delinquency research by some Marxian and radical theorists. The idea of socialization (the internalization of societal norms and values by members of society) "is conservative in the sense that it is meant to support and maintain the status quo and is not intended to support or further social change" (1983:95).

Finally, while it has been oft repeated and appeals to logical supposition, a direct link between economic conditions and crime has never been systematically established. Marxian theory contends that the lower classes feel exploited and alienated and consequently strike out at those who are repressing them. The greater involvement of lower class individuals in highly visible street crimes such as homicide, assault, robbery, burglary, larceny-theft, and automobile theft seems to support this assumption. What is puzzling, however, is why the great majority of victims of these crimes also are members of the lower class.

Richard Quinney (1975) attempted to address this question by suggesting that the reason violent and property crimes committed by the poor against the poor are so heavily policed and punished is because they threaten the general social order, and the ruling class fears that victimization will spread beyond the lower class and into their ranks. Still, radical theories and the class-conflict perspective do not adequately explain why members of the lower class would vent their frustrations and aggression against poor people of similar economic circumstances.

An Overview of the Sociological Explanations

Chapters 6, 7, and 8 have provided an outline and analysis of the major theoretical constructs that comprise the sociological view of juvenile delinquency. The six categories we have created are not absolute, discrete, exhaustive, or mutually exclusive. Instead, we have grouped together various sociological theories which generally share common assumptions and concepts. Rather than attempting to adhere to any single theoretical approach, such as Social Strain, Cultural Transmission, Social Learning, Social Control, Labeling, or the Radical perspective, we have introduced each one as offering reasonable causal explanations for juvenile delinquency, together with appropriate summations of contributions and weaknesses.

We also have avoided the temptation to attempt the development of a single general theory to explain all delinquents and all the acts defined as juvenile delinquency. Even without total synthesis, the various approaches and the specific theories and concepts presented here can, in combination, shed a great deal of light on the social problem we call juvenile delinquency. Going beyond the limitations of the biological and psychological approaches, the sociological explanations show delinquent behavior to be a very complex social phenomenon. Delinquency is a social act, from the very inception of the norms which govern juveniles, to the social institutions which affect juveniles, the environment in which the juveniles live, the socialization to which they are subjected, and the process whereby their actions are judged by others as conforming or deviant. Juvenile delinquency does not exist in a social vacuum. Each of the six sociological approaches to the problem contributes a measure of understanding to some of the dynamic social factors involved in delinquency etiology.

Concept Integration

Questions and Topics for Study and Discussion

1. What are the advantages and shortcomings of typologies? Outline several typologies with which you are familiar, including the typology of sociological theories of juvenile delinquency that was used to organize Chapters 6, 7, and 8.
2. What is the difference between microscopic sociology and macroscopic sociology? How do these concepts apply to sociological theories of juvenile delinquency?
3. Define the concepts of social structure and social process. What sociological theories presented in Chapters 6, 7, and 8 can be characterized by these two terms? Why?
4. List the major assumption(s) underlying Social Labeling Theories of delinquency etiology. Iden-

tify and discuss several prominent sociologists and their concepts and contributions to the social labeling approach. What are some of the weaknesses and limitations of the social labeling approach?
5. List the major assumption(s) underlying the Radical Theories of delinquency etiology. Identify and discuss several prominent sociologists and their respective concepts and contributions to the radical theory approach. What are some of the weaknesses and limitations of the radical explanations of juvenile delinquency?
6. In your judgment, which of the various sociological theories in Chapters 6, 7, and 8 explaining the cause(s) of delinquency makes the most sense? Why? Which one makes the least sense? Why?

BOX 8-2 Controversial Issue

The Continuing Quest for a General Theory of Juvenile Delinquency

The integration and unification of theoretical concepts and contributions from a broad spectrum of approaches into one overarching explanation of juvenile delinquency has been a tantalizing and controversial objective for many sociologists. The formulation of a general theory of etiology that encompasses multiple racial, ethnic, environmental, gender, and social class variables in accounting for delinquency is no small task. Thus far, it has been an impossible task. Nevertheless, a number of serious efforts have been made by sociologists to develop the ultimate and definitive theory explaining why some children become juvenile delinquents while others do not. Some have suggested expanded versions of their favorite theories as fulfilling this objective. Still others have sought to blend portions of some theories into overall eclectic approaches with varying scope and success. A few examples will illustrate the many scores of efforts along this line.

Stephen Cernkovich (1978) challenged the bifurcation of causal explanations of juvenile delinquency based on "supposed class-linked differences." Cernkovich's approach emphasized the similarities in "conventional value orientations of delinquent adolescents across socioeconomic strata.... [and their adherence to common] subterranean value orientations" (1978:443).

Delbert Elliott and his associates (1983) partially integrated traditional Strain, Social Control, and Social Learning Theories into a synthesized perspective to account for delinquency and drug use. They postulated that "involvement with and commitment to delinquent peers is the most proximate cause of delinquency and drug use and mediates the influence of weak bonding to parents, school, and conventional norms" (1985:85).

Jeffrey Segrave and Douglas Hastad (1985) used self-report data from a sample of high school students to develop three path analysis models showing that variables derived from Strain, Cultural Transmission, and Social Control theories explain significant, though small proportions of the variance in male and female delinquency.

Another useful approach towards the integration of major sociological theories of delinquency

was initiated by Hennessey Hayes (1997) who analyzed a sample of data derived from a National Youth Survey. Hayes incorporated elements of Labeling, Differential Association, Social Learning, and Social Control theories into a model designed to help explain both initial and continued delinquency. Hayes reasoned that

> ... *social controls, such as those provided by the family, significantly affect the development of delinquent peer associations and the associating with delinquent peers increases the likelihood of primary delinquency.... Thus, newcomers may be socialized within delinquent peer groups and may learn new delinquent norms and values, which serve to heighten the likelihood of engaging in delinquent behavior.... More frequent involvement in delinquency then may increase the likelihood of being observed by members of conventional groups and finally may elicit an informal reaction (informal parental labels).*
>
> *The effects of parental labels in this study were most dramatic in the maintenance of delinquent peer relationships, which further increased the likelihood of secondary delinquency (Hayes, 1997:177-179).*

In all cases, a commonly acceptable "grand theory" of juvenile delinquency has eluded formulation. There are still numerous unanswered questions regarding the validity and reliability of these theoretical suggestions. So far, methodologically sound, empirical testing has been only partial, or in some cases, totally lacking. Consequently, predictability and generality remain tentative at best for such theoretical offerings (Osgood et al., 1988).

Considerable interest in formulating a general theory of social deviance which encompasses juvenile delinquency was generated by a panel of scholars who gathered in Albany, New York in 1987. The participants included Ronald Akers, Jack Gibbs, Travis Hirschi, James Short, Terrence Thornberry, and a number of other distinguished sociological

Continued

BOX 8-2   *Continued*

theorists. The objective of the Albany Conference was to bring together leading scholars in the field of deviance to address some of the more important issues surrounding the integration of competing theories. For example, Short (1990:7; 1998:28) suggested that the considerable overlap among academic disciplines in their shared interest in delinquency and delinquents could offer a rationale and fertile common ground for the integration of theoretical explanations.

Several promising interdisciplinary approaches to the etiology of deviant and delinquent behavior have been made within the last decade. Especially noteworthy is the resurgence of interest in the role of heredity in determining criminality. Hans Eysenck's intriguing thesis incorporates psychological and sociological elements in his conclusions regarding "genetic determinism" in the study of personality differences and similarities between twins and adopted children. In asserting that genetic factors may be partially responsible for antisocial conduct,

Eysenck's theory could best be termed as a "biologically-rooted conditioning theory" (Eysenck, 1980). He maintains that individuals refrain from law breaking to the extent that they are adequately socially conditioned and acquire an internalized conscience....Thus, the undersocialization of the conscience is the key to antisocial and criminal behavior (Kraska, 1989:2).

Alan Booth and D. Wayne Osgood (1993) turned their attention to the influence of varying levels of the male hormone, testosterone, in contributing to antisocial behavior in a large sample of men. They found "a significant and moderately strong relationship between testosterone and adult deviance, and this relationship...is largely mediated by the influence of testosterone on social integration and on prior involvement in juvenile delinquency" (1993: 93). In other words, testosterone is one of a complex constellation of biological and social factors that are causally involved in subsequent deviant behavior.

One of the most recent and ambitious effort toward an integrated and general theory of crime and delinquency has moved from the planning stage to implementation. A nationwide and methodologically sophisticated investigation will focus on these research questions:

Why do some children and adults who share similar characteristics and experience similar life circumstances become criminals while others do not? How are drugs and crime intertwined in the development of criminal careers? At what age and developmental stage do we have the best opportunity to intervene with programs to decrease the number of individuals who progress to more serious antisocial behavior and criminology? (Massive Study, 1990:2).

The longitudinal series of studies began in 1993 and focuses on seven cohorts of individuals from birth to age 18. The initial group includes 1,000 boys and 1,000 girls from urban neighborhoods. Funded thus far by the National Institute of Justice and the MacArthur Foundation, the ten-year project may ultimately cost $80 million dollars (Geyelin, 1992:B6).

The research agenda for the program integrates biological, behavioral, and sociological perspectives and contributions in tracking the individual and social factors impacting on the development of pro and antisocial behavior. The project director is Felton Earls, Professor of Human Behavior and Development at the Harvard School of Public Health. Co-director is Albert Reiss, Professor of Sociology at Yale University.

Scholars and theorists from many academic disciplines, as well as law enforcement agencies and personnel, all eagerly look forward to the findings and conclusions from this massive study. If enough interest continues to be generated towards the integration of divergent theoretical explanations of social deviance, some day a more eclectic theory of juvenile delinquency causation may become a reality. Meanwhile, it remains our task to glean from existing theories the most appropriate concepts, variables, and explanations which provide some measure of understanding of juvenile delinquency.

Continued

BOX 8-2   *Continued*

Sources

Booth, A., and Osgood, D. W. 1993. The influence of testosterone on deviance in adulthood; Assessing and explaining the relationship. *Criminology* 31 (February):93–102.

Cernkovich, S. 1978. Value orientation and delinquency involvement. *Criminology* 15 (February):443–458.

Elliot, D. S., Huizinga, D., and Ageton, S. 1985. *Explaining delinquency and drug use.* Beverly Hills: Sage.

Eysenck, H. J. 1980. The biosocial model of man and the unification of psychology. In A. J. Chapman and D. M. Jones (eds.). *Models of man.* Leicester: British Psychological Society.

Geyelin, M. Study to focus on what leads youths to crime. *The Wall Street Journal.* June 5, 1992. pp. B1 and B6.

Hayes, H. D. 1997. Using integrated theory to explain the movement into juvenile delinquency. *Deviant Behavior: An Interdisciplinary Journal* 18:161–184.

Kraska, P. B. 1989. The sophistication of Hans Jurgen Eysenck: An analysis and critique of contemporary biological criminology. *Criminal Justice Research Bulletin* 4:1–6.

Massive study will trace developmental factors that cause or prevent criminality. 1990. *National Institute of Justice Reports* 220 (May/June):2–3.

Osgood, D. W., Johnston, L. D., O'Malley, P. M., and Bachman, J. G. 1988. The generality of deviance in late adolescence and early adulthood. *American Sociological Review* 53 (February):81–93.

Segrave, J. O., and Hastad, D. N. 1985. Evaluating three models of delinquency causation for males and females: Strain theory, subculture theory, and control theory. *Sociological Focus* 18 (January):1–17.

Short, J. F., Jr. 1990. Exploring integration of the theoretical levels of explanation: Notes on juvenile delinquency. In *Theoretical Integration in the Study of Deviance and Crime: Problems and Prospects.* Albany, NY: Unpublished proceedings of the Albany Conference, May 7–8, 1987. *Delinquency and society.* Englewood Cliffs, NJ: Prentice-Hall.

Short, J. F., Jr. 1998. The level of explanation problem revisited—the American Society of Criminology (1997 Presidential Address). *Criminology* 36 (February):3–36.

References

Akers, R. L. 1985. *Deviant behavior: A social learning approach* (3rd ed.). Belmont, CA: Wadsworth.

Bartol, C. R., and Bartol, A. M. 1989. *Juvenile delinquency: A systems approach.* Englewood Cliffs, NJ: Prentice-Hall.

Barlow, H. 1987. *Introduction to criminology* (4th ed.). Boston: Little Brown.

Becker, H. 1963. *Outsiders: Studies in the sociology of deviance.* New York: Free Press.

Bordua, D. J. 1967. Recent trends: Deviant behavior and social control. *Annals of the Academy of Political and Social Science* 369 (January):149–163. 1969. On deviance. *Annals of the Academy of Political and Social Science* 312:121–123.

Carey, J. T., and McAnany, P. D. 1984. *Introduction to juvenile delinquency: Youth and the law.* Englewood Cliffs, NJ: Prentice-Hall.

Chambliss, W. 1974. The state, the law, and the definition of behavior as criminal or delinquent. In Daniel Glaser (Ed.). *Handbook of criminology.* Chicago: Rand McNally.

Cloward, R. A., and Ohlin, L. E. 1963. *Delinquency and opportunity.* New York: Free Press.

Cohen, A. K. 1966. *Deviance and control.* Englewood Cliffs, NJ: Prentice-Hall.

Cooley, C. H. [1902] 1964. *Human nature and the social order.* New York: Schocken Books.

DeFleur, M., D'Antonio, W., and DeFleur, L. 1971. *Sociology: Man in Society.* Glenview, IL: Scott, Foresman and Company.

Empey, L. T., and Stafford, M. C. 1991. *American delinquency: Its meaning and construction* (3rd ed.). Belmont, CA: Wadsworth.

Erikson, K. 1964. Notes on the sociology of deviance. In H. Becker (Ed.). *The other side.* New York: Free Press, pp. 9–22.

Foster, J., Dinitz, S., and Reckless, W. 1972. Perceptions of stigma following public intervention for delinquent behavior. *Social Problems* 20:202–209.

Gibbs, J. P. 1966. Conceptions of deviant behavior: The old and the new. *Pacific Sociological Review* 9 (Spring):9–14.

Glassner, B. 1982. Labeling theory. In M. M. Rosenberg, R. A. Stebbins, and A. Turowetz (Eds.). *The sociology of deviance.* New York: St. Martin's Press, pp. 71–89.

Greenberg, D. F. 1977. Delinquency and the age structure of society. *Contemporary Crises* 1 (April): 189–224.

Hayes, H. D. 1997. Using integrated theory to explain the movement into juvenile delinquency. *Deviant Behavior: An Interdisciplinary Journal* 18: 161–184.

Hughes, E. C. 1945. Dilemmas and contradictions of status. *American Journal of Sociology* 50 (March):353–359.

Kitsuse, J. I. 1972. Deviance, deviant behavior, and deviants: Some conceptual problems. In Williams J. Filstead (ed.), *An introduction to deviance: Readings in the process of making deviants.* Chicago: Markham, pp. 233–243.

Lemert, E. 1951. *Social pathology.* New York: McGraw-Hill.

Marx, K. [1867] 1967. *Capital: A critical analysis of capitalist production,* vol. 1. New York: International Publishers.

Marx, K., and Engels, F. [1848] 1979. *The communist manifesto.* New York: International Publishers.

Matza, D. 1964. *Delinquency and drift.* New York: John Wiley.
1969. *Becoming deviant.* Englewood Cliffs, NJ: Prentice-Hall.

Merton, R. 1957. *Social theory and social structure* (2nd ed.). New York: Free Press.
1968. *Social theory and social structure* (enlarged ed.). New York: Free Press.

Michalowski, R. J. 1985. *Order, law, and crime.* New York: Random House.

Osgood, D. W., Johnston, L. D., O'Malley, P. M., and Bachman, J. G. 1988. The generality of deviance in late adolescence and early adulthood. *American Sociological Review* 53 (February):81–93.

Piliavin, I., and Briar, S. 1964. Police encounters with juveniles. *American Journal of Sociology* 70 (September):206–214.

Quinney, R. 1970. *The social reality of crime.* Boston: Little, Brown and Co.
1974. *Critique of legal order: Crime control in capitalist society.* Boston: Little, Brown and Company.
1975. *Criminology: An analysis and critique of crime in America.*
1980. *Class, state, and crime* (2nd ed.). New York: Longman.

Robins, L. N. 1975. Alcoholism and labelling theory. In W. R. Gove (Ed.). *The labelling of deviance.* Beverly Hills: Sage, pp. 21–33.

Schicor, D. 1983. Socialization: The political aspects of a delinquency explanation. *Socialization Spectrum* 3 (January–March):85–100.

Schur, E. 1973. *Radical non-intervention: Rethinking the delinquency problem.* Englewood Cliffs, NJ: Prentice-Hall.

Schwendinger, H., and Schwendinger, J. J. 1985. *Adolescent subcultures.* New York: Praeger.

Sherman, L. W., and Berk, R. A. 1984. The specific deterrent effects of arrest for domestic assault. *American Sociological Review* 49:261–272.

Sherman, L. W., and Smith, D. A., with Schmidt, J. D. and Rogan, D. P. 1992. Crime, punishment, and stake in conformity: Legal and informal control of domestic violence. *American Sociological Review* 57:680–690.

Short, J. F., Jr. 1990. Exploring integration of the theoretical levels of explanation: Notes on juvenile delinquency. *Delinquency and Society.* Englewood Cliffs, NJ: Prentice-Hall.

Short, J. F., Jr., and Strodtbeck, F. L. 1965. *Group process and gang delinquency.* Chicago: Univ. of Chicago Press.

Stockard, J. 1997. *Sociology: discovering society.* Belmont, CA: Wadsworth.

Tannenbaum, F. 1938. Point of view. *Crime and Community.* Boston: Ginn and Co., pp. 8–22.

Thomas, W. I. 1931. *The unadjusted girl* (Revised edition). Boston: Little, Brown and Co.

Thornberry, T. P. 1979. Sentencing disparities in the juvenile justice system. *The Journal of Criminal Law and Criminology* 70 (Summer).

Turk, A. T. 1969. *Criminality and the legal order.* Chicago: Rand McNally.

Ward, D. A., and Tittle, C. R. 1993. Deterrence or labeling: The effects of informal sanctions. *Deviant Behavior: An Interdisciplinary Journal* 14: 43–64.

Werthman, C., and Piliavin, I. 1967. Gang members and the police. In D. J. Bordua (Ed.). *The police.* New York: John Wiley.

PART III

JUVENILE DELINQUENCY IN A SOCIAL CONTEXT

Introduction: Collective Behavior and Social Groupings

Part I of this book explained the sociological perspective and emphasized the inherently social nature of juvenile delinquency. In Part II we presented the major theoretical explanations for delinquency. Now, in Part III, we look at juvenile delinquency within the social context of collective behavior. **Collective behavior** refers to *behavior motivated and influenced by an individual's membership in or identification with a social group.* There are a variety of different types of social groups which impact upon human behavior. Three of the most important and readily identifiable are primary groups, secondary groups, and reference groups. The **primary group** is *a relatively small intimate group characterized by face-to-face interaction.* **Secondary groups,** on the other hand, tend to be *somewhat larger groups characterized by more formal interaction which are usually organized for a specific purpose.* A **reference group** is *a group with which an individual has a strong sense of identification regardless of his/her actual membership in the group.* The four chapters in Part III look at examples of these types of groups and explore their relationship to juvenile delinquency.

Chapter 9 looks at the family—a primary group which is typically the first social group that teaches an individual basic attitudes, values, beliefs, and appropriate behaviors. This chapter traces the historical development and changing role of the traditional American family. We emphasize the family's role in influencing juveniles' behavior and summarize the importance of social variables such as social class, family size, birth order, and the nature of family interaction in terms of their relationship to juvenile delinquency. The effect on children of mothers working outside the home is explored, and various techniques of parental discipline are reviewed in regard to their theoretical link to delinquency. Research on the assumed link between broken homes and delinquency is summarized and discussed, and the chapter ends with an overview of the family's role in delinquency prevention.

In Chapter 10, we look at the secondary group of the schools, develop the concept of the school as a social arena, and emphasize its role as a major agent of socialization transmitting the dominant attitudes, values, and beliefs of society to American youths. We explore how the school acts as a "screening device" in distributing academic credentials, and how, in some situations, it becomes a "combat zone" for those who socially interact there. We look at the relationship between schooling and delinquency, and conclude the chapter by exploring ways in which schools might become more actively involved in delinquency prevention.

Chapter 11 explores the phenomenon of the youth subculture, which serves as an important reference group for adolescents, its widespread influence on American teenagers, and its possible link to juvenile delinquency. The important sociological concepts of **culture, subculture,** and **counterculture** are defined, and the origin, development, and perpetuation of a youth subculture is placed within a sociological context. Distinctive elements of the youth subculture such as values, dress, grooming, fads, and language are described along with their possible relationship to juvenile delinquency. The influence of mass media on American youth is discussed and serious social problems linked with the youth subculture— running away, prostitution, teenage drug usage, and permissive sexual practices leading to increased numbers of teenage pregnancies—are explored.

Chapter 12 deals with one of the most misunderstood dimensions of juvenile delinquency—the gang. The youth gang is one of the more difficult types of social groups to categorize. As we discuss in Chapter 12, some contend it is a primary group, others view it as a loosely constructed secondary group, and still others see it as more closely resembling a reference group for some inner-city youths. As we point out in the chapter on gangs, this has led some researchers to categorize it as a fourth type of social grouping, the **near group** resting on a continuum between the extremes of an unorganized mob at one end and the primary group at the other, and *characterized by diverse membership, loose organization, ambiguous leadership, and impermanence.* While most delinquency does *not* involve juvenile gangs, juvenile delinquency is much more likely to take place within a group context than to be the act of an isolated individual youth. In this chapter we look at the phenomenon of "predatory youth" and the subtle social processes which occur when the play groups of some children evolve into full-fledged juvenile gangs. The organization of gangs is viewed from a sociological perspective, and motivations for joining a gang are explored. The participation of females in gang delinquency is summarized, and some of the major sociological theories which focus on explaining the formation of juvenile gangs are reviewed.

As you read Part III, keep in mind the discussion of the basic social nature of juvenile delinquency presented in Part I, as well as the many theoretical explanations for the causes of delinquency presented in Part II. Apply them to the material presented in these four chapters. You should note that while none of the theories presented in Part II can fully explain *all* of the types of delinquency discussed in Chapters 9, 10, 11, and 12, they can provide valuable insights regarding the roles played by the family, the schools, the youth subculture, and the juvenile gang in relationship to juvenile delinquency.

9 THE FAMILY AND JUVENILE DELINQUENCY

Reading Objectives

The reading of this chapter will help you achieve the following objectives:

1. Understand the changing role of the family in U.S. society.
2. Identify how the family acts as a primary agent of socialization for youth in our society.
3. Explain how family variables such as social class, family size, the nature of family interaction, and parental discipline relate to juvenile delinquency.
4. Summarize the research relating broken homes to delinquency.
5. Understand the impact of parental discipline upon youths and how various techniques of discipline may relate to delinquency.
6. Explore how the family may serve as an insulator against juvenile delinquency.

Introduction

Part III of this book explores juvenile delinquency in a social context and how membership in social groups and collective behavior impact upon human behavior. This chapter discusses one of the most important social groups in which juveniles participate—the family. For most juveniles, the first social group to which they belong is their **family of origin.** The **family of origin** *is the family in which the child grows up,* and today, in western nations like the United States, it *usually consists of only the parents and children.* This concept of family need not be limited to biological relatives, and would include adoptive parents and their children. In other words, we are referring to the first family setting to which the child is exposed, and which serves as the primary socializing agent for the youth. This family also may be referred to as the **family of orientation.**

The Changing Role of the Family

The shift in American society from being predominantly rural prior to the Industrial Revolution to predominantly urban after the turn of the century had tremendous impact upon the family institution. As Marcia and Thomas Lasswell (1982:10) pointed out, "Although the dramatic move away from the farm was not the result of changing ideas about love, marriage, and the family, it certainly had a profound effect on all of these."

Agrarian America often is depicted as being characterized by the **extended family** *in which several generations (which may include parents and their children, grandparents and other close relatives) lived under one roof, shared and cooperated in the economic, social, and psychological support of the family.* There is some question whether the extended family was actually the predominant type of family or not. Research indicates a lack of evidence that early families in the United States typically followed the extended family pattern. According to Rudy Seward (1978:44), "The extended family was the exception rather than the rule." Whether it was extended or not, there is virtually unanimous agreement that the family was much larger in agrarian America. Children typically grew up in the same household as their parents. Families were usually large, hence, family rules had to be negotiated among several people. If the family was an extended one, the oldest male assumed the role of head of the household, and was viewed as the ultimate source of power and discipline.

Often steeped in misinformed nostalgia, this earlier version of family life was not idyllic, as is sometimes portrayed in novels and movies, or in the minds of those who lament the decline of the family as they envision it. Life was tough in preindustrial America and families faced a variety of problems on a daily basis, not the least of which was their very survival. However, there were aspects of family life in preindustrial America that limited the likelihood that youths would get into trouble with law enforcement officials. While children were growing up, they rarely found themselves lacking supervision from adults or older siblings. There almost always was a parent, grandparent, or some other adult around to set limits on a child's behavior, or to mete out punishment should these limits be exceeded. Another important factor was the cultural attitudes toward childhood and adulthood during that time. In agrarian America the role expectations for children and adults were fairly explicit. Children were assigned chores and expected to help around the house and farm (or store if they happened to live in town), but were exempted from responsibilities associated with adulthood. When children reached an age when they were physically and mentally capable of assuming the work responsibilities of adults (usually somewhere after the onset of puberty), they began to be treated as adults by family, friends, and the community. This clear transition from child to adult resulted in changing role expectations for youths who began to make plans for marrying and starting families of their own. The marriage ceremony symbolically marked the *rite of passage* into adulthood. The concept of adolescence had not been developed (Rogers, 1985); hence, much of the marginality experienced by juveniles today did not exist.

That is not to say that young people did not violate norms in preindustrial U.S. society. They certainly did. However, most norm violations were handled by the family through parental discipline. If fairly minor violations occurred outside the home, they were usually handled informally, as local constables typically knew everybody in the community and either disciplined the youngsters themselves, or reported the behavior to their parents. When serious violations occurred, one of two things was likely to happen: either the child's parents were held legally accountable for their child's actions; or the child was held responsible and treated as an adult (Reid, 1996).

Increasing Importance of the Nuclear Family and the Creation of "Adolescence"

The shift from an agricultural to an industrial society, and the concomitant transition from rural to urban residence for the majority of our citizens, had lasting impact upon family size and structure. Urban life put new demands on the family, many of which were not compatible with the traditionally larger or extended family pattern. For example, families went from being units of production to units of consumption. Families also needed to be located near industry, and if necessary be mobile enough to move should the father's place of employment change. A result was that families became smaller. As Dorothy Rogers (1985:228) noted:

> *At one time adults considered adolescents as an economic asset, useful in performing numerous household chores or in earning their keep. However, household appliances, urbanization, and labor laws have taken away most of the tasks that children used to perform, and some parents find children an economic burden.*

As economic and social constraints acted upon the family, the large nuclear or extended family pattern gave way to the smaller **nuclear family** as the norm. The **nuclear family** was *limited to the husband and wife and their children, and was characterized by smaller size, greater independence for its members, and more geographical and social mobility.* Along with this transition to smaller nuclear families the characteristics previously mentioned in regard to extended and larger nuclear families were dramatically altered. The number of adults and older siblings available in the nuclear family to supervise the behavior of children was diminished. As the small nuclear family emerged, typically one parent (the father) went off to work, leaving only one adult (the mother) to supervise the children.

Further complicating the situation was the emergence of the concept of **adolescence**— *a socially created life stage between childhood and adulthood.* No longer were role expectations clearly delineated for adults and children. The enactment of child labor laws prohibited children from working in the factories, and with the emergence of the concept of adolescence, routine chores and responsibilities were no longer assigned to physically capable youth. Instead, for a period of one's life (roughly from about 10 to 16 years of age) youths found themselves in a social paradox where they were neither allowed the tolerance of behavior granted children, nor afforded the rights and responsibilities associated with adulthood. "Appropriate" behavior for teenagers became somewhat ambiguous, leading to the marginality of the juvenile status. Adolescence came into its own during the periods of the Great Depression and World War II, as older youths left school for part-time and full-time jobs to help support their families. The marginality of adolescence was increased because despite the fact that these youths were assuming adult roles, they were not afforded the rights, privileges, responsibilities, and status of adulthood (Klein, 1990). As the normative expectations for youth became less clearcut, the void gave rise to what many refer to as the youth subculture as adolescents struggled for a sense of identity and a set of attitudes, values, and beliefs to which they could adhere.

Contemporary society presents the family with an everchanging set of circumstances, causing the family to be redefined, restructured, and realigned in a variety of ways. Researchers disagree as to what relationship these changes may have to juvenile delinquency, but studies consistently show that the family is among the most influential factors in delinquency (U.S. Dept. of Justice 1999a,b). Divorce, changing sex roles, working mothers, increased leisure time, economic pressures, and the increasing expectation for upward social mobility have all exerted numerous pressures on the family and the individuals within it.

Of the aforementioned changes, the effects of mothers working outside the home and divorce have been the most researched regarding their possible connections to juvenile delinquency. These two variables have received so much attention from researchers that they will be discussed later in separate sections of the chapter.

The Family as an Agent of Socialization

Socialization refers to the *process whereby individuals learn and internalize the appropriate attitudes, values, beliefs, and behaviors of a particular culture.* This complex social learning process has appropriately been referred to as "people-making" by family therapist Virginia Satir (1972).

Socialization is a lifelong process. Virtually everybody with whom an individual comes in contact can influence the socialization process, but for the most part, sociologists contend that the major agents of socialization consist of the family, school, church, peer group, and mass media. Debate arises over which of these agents of socialization exerts the most influence; however, in almost all cases, the family is the first agent of socialization with which a child comes in contact. As Robert Bell (1983:437) pointed out, "In most cases the important agency for transmitting the culture is the immediate family... it gets [children] first, keeps [them] longest and is [their] major source of cultural imperatives." Larry Bumpass (1984:621–622) concluded it is "the 'family of orientation' that serves as the reference point for the transmission of social values." Thus, the family has the first opportunity to socialize the individual to the particular set of ideas, values, beliefs, and behaviors that family members deem appropriate.

Further, while the family cannot totally control outside influences upon its members, it can have significant impact in shaping the extent to which the child will be exposed to the other major agents of socialization. Whether a child attends church, and if so, what kind, is usually determined by parents early in the child's life. Likewise, the decision to own a television and how much and what type of viewing will be allowed is at least initially a prerogative of the family. The child's first peer group is usually not chosen freely, but is often determined by the parents' choice of friends. Quite often, the first play group of most children consists of the children of their parents' adult friends and neighbors. Once children venture outside the home their initial peer group is largely determined by the geographic boundaries of the immediate neighborhood. Thus, parents' choice of residence (or socioeconomic circumstances which dictate place of residence) largely determine the initial peer group for most children (Colvin and Pauly, 1983). Neighborhood characteristics can also greatly influence a youth's likelihood of becoming involved in delinquent activities (Elliot et al., 1996). While school attendance is required by law, the choice of private versus public, church-related versus secular, or in which school district a child lives is largely determined by the parents.

One of the most important ways in which a family socializes its young members is through the process of *role modeling*. Social learning theorists contend that an important part of the process of learning social role expectations occurs through the observation and subsequent identification with and imitation of those who already fill those roles (e.g., Bandura and Walters, 1963). Consequently, a significant part of the socialization of children consists of them observing their parents and older siblings in everyday social interaction. While parents verbally instruct their children in regard to the "do's" and "don'ts" of social behavior, the children also learn simply by watching their parents and older siblings. A substantial amount of the delinquency literature indicates that juveniles whose parents and/or older siblings violated the law, committed violence, or committed other forms of deviance are more likely to become involved in illegal and deviant behavior (e.g., Hogan and Kitagawa, 1985; Barnes et al., 1986; Lauritsen, 1993; Heimer, 1997). While the biological theorists might cite these studies as verification that criminality is inherited, from a sociological perspective the studies emphasize the importance of social environment, social learning, socialization, and role modeling.

There is considerable evidence that juveniles learn their attitudes toward the law, law enforcement officials, and law violation from those with whom they associate (e.g., Sutherland and Cressey, 1978). The social group from which children are likely to learn their first attitudes toward the law is the family. Thus, the early childhood socialization process cannot be overestimated in its importance in developing the foundation of attitudes, values, and behaviors likely to lead to conforming or law violating behavior in adolescence and young adulthood. Evidently, the family influence and its importance in early socialization are significant in virtually all societies (Schicor, 1983).

Working Mothers and Juvenile Delinquency

The phenomenon of large numbers of married women working outside the home is a fairly recent one, which has undoubtedly impacted upon the U.S. family, but researchers cannot seem to agree on what the specific nature of that impact has been upon the children in the family. When "Rosie the Riveter" stepped into the factory to take the place of her husband, who had marched off to war, the event was viewed as temporary. The results, on the other hand, were long lasting. Women proved that they were capable of working in factories alongside men, or in place of them. During that time, however, they also were expected to return home to perform all of their "wifely" and "motherly" duties, such as cleaning, cooking, and childrearing, which were not expected of their male counterparts. To a large extent, this expectation remains today. If women with young children are employed outside the home, their family responsibilities are often considered paramount and the job, while important, comes second (Hochschild, 1997).

Over the decades since World War II, women increasingly assumed their place in the employment market and have gone to work outside the home in record numbers. Many researchers on the family view this phenomenon as being one of the greatest changes that has occurred in the traditional view of marriage. In 1900 only one out of five women was employed outside the home, and most of them were single; however, by 1970, more than half (54%) of all women between the ages of 45 and 54 were in the labor force, and the number of working married women with children under the age of 6 more than doubled between 1960 and 1975 (Bell, 1983:265–267). Claire Brindis (1986:6) reported that over 50 percent of all mothers were in the labor force, including women with children under the age of 6 who were the most likely to be considered full-time homemakers.

Today, over 65 million American women and over 70 percent of mothers work outside of the home. One of the major problems faced by working mothers is finding adequate child care for their children. The number of working women with children is large, and there is not enough organized child care to help them. Bell (1983:267) estimated that "organized daycare centers, cooperative programs, nurseries, and preschools together take care of no more than 10 percent of the children of working mothers." The changing structure and size of the U.S. family means that in most cases there are no other adult family members available to care for the children in the home. Some mothers make arrangements with nonworking mothers to watch their preschoolers or to watch their school-aged children for a brief period of time before or after school. However, in many cases, the children must fend for themselves. The phrase **latchkey children** is used to describe the numerous *school-aged children who return home after school to an empty house.* The U.S. Bureau of the Census estimates that there are more than 1.6 million grade-school aged children left unsupervised after school (AP, Washington, 1994). Susan Byrne (1977) contended that the latchkey children are much more likely to get into trouble than children who return home to a parent.

Opinions differ as to whether latchkey children represent a form of neglect that leads to delinquency, or if they mature more quickly and learn a sense of responsibility that makes them less likely to become delinquent.

BOX 9-1   Controversial Issue

"Latchkey Children: Independence or Neglect?"

Brandon and Mica step off the school bus at approximately 4:00 p.m. every day. They wave goodbye to their bus driver and all their friends on the bus. Then they walk the two blocks to their home. When they reach their house, Brandon, who is the older of the two at age 12, reaches into his shoe to retrieve his housekey, unlocks the door for his 8-year-old sister, and they go inside. After relocking the door, Brandon and Mica proceed through their daily ritual. Brandon pours each of them a glass of milk while Mica unwraps the cookies, brownies, donuts, or similar snack that was left for them on the kitchen counter earlier that morning. They retire to the family room where Mica watches her favorite cartoon show and Brandon begins working on his homework.

Brandon and Mica are not orphans; nor are they victims of a broken home, severe neglect, or any other form of child abuse. Rather, they are part of the legions of "latchkey" children who return home from school each day to an empty house to await the arrival of their parents, both of whom work outside the home. In their case, they are not home alone for an extended period of time. Their mother teaches at the high school, and arrives home around 4:30 p.m. each day, approximately 30 minutes after the two children. If their mother must attend a meeting, run an errand, or is otherwise delayed, the two children are sometimes in the home alone until approximately 5:30 p.m. when their father, who teaches at the local university, usually arrives.

Brandon and Mica have been carefully schooled in their role of latchkey children. Their mother and father have established some basic house rules regarding their activities while in the home alone. They are not allowed to play outside or have house guests, are strictly forbidden from cooking, and do not answer the door under any circumstances. If the phone rings, they take a message, informing the caller that their mother is "in the shower" and cannot come to the phone at the moment. Their mother's and father's work phone numbers are posted near each of the telephones right below the emergency 911 number, and right above the phone number of their next-door neighbor, who is usually at home in the afternoon.

Brandon and Mica's parents are concerned about their children's welfare, and greatly fear the possibilities of harm coming to their children while home alone. Their mother's greatest fear is that of fire, and despite the presence of smoke alarms in every room, the practiced fire drills, and other precautions taken, she worries that if a fire should break out, the children would panic. Their father's major concern is related more to the possibility of personal harm which might come to the children from walking in on an intruder, or from someone noticing that the children walk home alone from the bus stop every day at the same time.

On the positive side, Brandon and Mica's parents have noticed a growing sense of independence and responsibility on the part of the two children over the past 2 years in which they have been coming home to an empty house. Brandon is remarkably mature for his age, and takes the responsibilities associated with his role as the older sibling quite seriously. He is very confident of his ability to take care of himself and his younger sister for the brief period that they are alone each afternoon. He has begged his parents not to hire a babysitter, although his parents continue their search for somebody to stay with the children during that period of time. Mica also has shown increased confidence in her own abilities, and no longer relies on her mother or father to perform minor tasks for her when she is physically capable of doing them for herself. Mica's mother remarked that when she was home waiting for the children when they came home from school, "they couldn't even get themselves a glass of water—or at least, they wouldn't; now they take the initiative to help themselves when they can."

Brandon and Mica are far from unique. They happen to be from a middle class background with well-educated parents, both of whom are pursuing professional careers. Many other children are in the same situation. Others come from lower class backgrounds where their parents are employed in unskilled or semiskilled occupations. There are as many possible scenarios as there are social situations for families, but one common element seems to permeate today's American family: more and more

Continued

BOX 9-1   *Continued*

of them rely upon two paychecks. Either by choice or by necessity, many American families are characterized by the dual-income phenomenon and, consequently, the number of children who must spend a portion of the day in the home alone without adult supervision is growing.

* * * *

Some researchers lament the phenomenon of "latch-key children" as being a form of child neglect, and predict that children left alone in the home even for a brief period of time are more likely to become juvenile delinquents. On the other hand, some research

has indicated that the children of working mothers tend to be well adjusted and no more likely to become delinquent than children whose mothers stay at home. What do you think? Should children be left alone in the home without adult supervision? If so, at what age should parents allow their children to be in the home unsupervised? In your opinion, are "latch-key children" more or less likely to become involved in delinquency? How do you feel about the case of Brandon and Mica? Are they being neglected, or are they becoming independent and learning to assume responsibility?

Despite the rhetoric associated with the detrimental effects on children of working mothers, there has been little research actually linking higher rates of delinquency to the children of mothers working outside the home. In fact, Sheldon and Eleanor Glueck (1950), Travis Hirschi (1969), Mary Reige (1972), and Elizabeth Harvey (Recer, 1999) all found insignificant differences in rates of delinquency when comparing children of working mothers to those whose mothers did not work outside the home. Another study indicated that working mothers often make a point of spending more time with their children when they are home in order to compensate for the time away from them (Hill and Stafford, 1979). And, in a nationwide poll, 41 percent of mothers employed outside the home indicated that they believe they spend more time with their children than their mothers did with them (CNN, 1993). Moreover, studies show that day care has far less effects on infants and children than their experiences in the home (NY Times News Service, 1996; Washington Post, 1997).

There also is the notion that the *quantity* of time spent between parents and children may be less important than the *quality* of the time spent. Parents who consciously make up for lost time with children because of work may attempt to enhance the quality of interaction during what limited time they do have with their children. Bell (1983:272–273) indicated that as a result of time constraints on working women:

> *...a great deal of stress may be placed on the quality of time spent with children rather than the quantity. Many working mothers devote their undivided individual attention to their children in the relatively short time they have with them.*

As suggested by Hirschi (1983), this may be more effective in reducing the likelihood of delinquency than merely the mother's presence in the home. A 5-year study conducted by John Guidubaldi and his associates indicated that children of working mothers tended to do better in school, were absent fewer days, and had better communication skills than children whose mothers did not work outside the home (AP Washington, 1986:15). Their study indicated that mothers who stayed home expressed more confidence that they were good parents than did working mothers, but because mothers who worked outside the home were more worried about their parenting they seemed "to make an effort to spend 'quality time' with their offspring" (AP Washington, 1986:15).

There is also some evidence of detrimental effects when the mother works outside the home. Adam Booth and his associates (1984) found that any change in a wife's employment status can contribute to marital instability. They found that a wife's employment weakens marital stability, especially if she works more than 40 hours per week. Their research primarily examined the impact that working outside the home by the wife had on the husband-wife relationship, however, and did not examine its effects on the children in the family. The Lasswells (1982:361) reported that "having both parents employed outside the home is usually stressful to children only if the parents are suffering from stress about it." Contemporary research on the children of working mothers dispels most of the presumptions about its possible link to juvenile delinquency (Woodruff, 1994).

Other Family Variables and Juvenile Delinquency

The importance of the family in socializing its young members is without question. What is much less clear is which variables within the family context are related to the problem of juvenile delinquency. While the possibilities are almost infinite, at least four variables have emerged in delinquency research which provide the basis for various theories of delinquency causation: social class, family size (and birth order), the nature of family interaction, and parental discipline.

Social Class

The first social status of a child is that of the family. Whether a child is born into an impoverished family, a blue-collar working class family, a middle class professional family, or a wealthy family is totally beyond the child's control, yet has profound impact upon his or her life. This *ascribed status* affects choice of neighborhood, attitudes and values, parental discipline, education, career choices, and even life expectancy (Hollingshead, 1961; Silverman and Dinitz, 1974; Colvin and Pauly, 1983; Hogan and Kitagawa, 1985).

Lower class juveniles are more likely to be arrested than middle or upper class youths; hence, they comprise more than their proportionate amount of the official data on delinquency. Several sociological theories of delinquency causation attempt to explain why lower class youths might be more prone to commit delinquency than their middle and upper class counterparts. Self-report studies, however, indicate that delinquency exists among all social classes, but that lower class youths are more likely to be officially processed. Lower class youths are more likely to come into contact with the police (Piliavin and Briar, 1964). They are also more likely to be arrested and petitioned to juvenile court (Goldman, 1963; Smith and Visher, 1981; Fagan et al., 1987; Lundman, 1996); if petitioned, they are more likely to be adjudicated delinquent (Axelrod, 1952; Arnold, 1971; Fagan et al., 1987); and, if adjudicated delinquent, more likely to receive a severe disposition by the court (Axelrod, 1952; Arnold, 1971; Thornberry, 1973; Fagan et al., 1987). Whether the lower class commit more delinquency, or are merely more likely to be caught and processed, the family's social class emerges as an important variable. Likewise, whether upper class youths actually commit less delinquency (Empey and Erickson, 1966), or are just less likely to be apprehended and adjudicated, the importance of their social status cannot be denied.

The family's social class also affects the socialization experienced within the family. Walter Miller (1958) argued that lower class values were distinctively different from those of the middle and upper class. He viewed the focal concerns of the lower class as involving *trouble, toughness, smartness, excitement, fate,* and *autonomy,* all of which he contended led to gang delinquency. While Miller's assertions are highly questionable in that these same focal concerns may be emphasized by juveniles in general, regardless of social class, few would argue that social class does not impact upon one's set of values. Bell (1983:448) summarized some of the values he believes vary by social class:

> *There are social class differences in values that are passed on to the children. The middle class are more apt to stress values dealing with self-direction, such as freedom, individualism, initiative, and creativity. Working class parents are more apt to stress values of conformity to external standards such as orderliness, neatness, and obedience.*

Other researchers have linked social class to different types of parental discipline and other aspects of family interaction and have indicated that other family factors such as relative deprivation, family size, amount of supervision, and styles of discipline may mediate some of the effects of social class (Strong and Devault, 1986; Tittle and Meier, 1990; Larzelere and Patterson, 1990; White and Kaufman, 1997). From a sociological perspective, socioeconomic status is an important determinant of social behavior.

Family Size and Birth Order

Psychologists and sociologists long have emphasized the importance of parents in personality development, but research indicates that the number of siblings and the child's place in the birth order are also importantly related to delinquency (e.g., Pfouts, 1980; Steelman and Mercy, 1980; Kidwell, 1981; Hirschi 1969, 1983; Glueck and Glueck, 1968; Nye, 1958, 1974; McCord et al., 1959). Hirschi (1969) indicated that large families tend to lack financial resources, discipline, and adequate socialization. Walter Toman (1970:45) also saw family size as an important variable indicating, "After all, as families get larger, children turn to each other for what they cannot get from parents." Michael Rutter (1980) attempted to more directly relate family size to problems which might lead to delinquency. He indicated:

> *First, large family size is quite strongly associated with overcrowding and socio-economic disadvantage. Secondly, there is probably less intensive interaction and less communication between the parents and the children in large families if only because parental time has to be distributed more widely. Thirdly, parental discipline and supervision may be more difficult when there are a lot of children to look after. Fourthly, some of the children may have been unwanted. Fifthly, in some cases the lack of family limitations may reflect general parental qualities of inadequate foresight and planning (Rutter, 1980:155).*

Numerous arguments could be raised regarding Rutter's assertions. For example, although rural families tend to be larger than urban, place of residence is evidently an intervening variable. Urban delinquency rates tend to be much higher than rural. To date, family size consistently emerges as an important variable in delinquency studies and seems most consistent with Social Learning Theory (see Chapter 7) in that exposure to sibling delinquency is almost always positively related to delinquent conduct (Brownfield and Sorenson, 1994). However, family size appears to be a relevant variable for further research as to its possible relationship to juvenile delinquency.

The Gluecks (1968), Nye (1974), and McCord et al. (1959) saw birth ordinal position as an important variable associated with the likelihood of delinquency. Their research suggested that the first child tends to relate well to adults and experiences the undivided attention of parents for a period of time. First-born children apparently accept their parents' ways of doing things much more readily than do later-born children. Bell (1983:456) even contended that "…parents attach greater importance to first-born than to later-born children." Loretta Blerer (1980) also concluded that first-born children were less likely to become involved in delinquency because they tend to relate well to adults and internalize rules and regulations established by parents. The first-born also may act as a "third parent" to younger siblings, thus identifying more strongly with adult roles than subsequent children. The later child, however, tends to be intensely competitive and feel a strong "need not to conform" in order to contrast with the "conservative older sibling" (Blerer, 1980:52).

The youngest child also seems somewhat more insulated against delinquency. The youngest child benefits from the experience parents have gained in childrearing while also gaining from the experience of having older siblings as role models. Bell (1983:456) pointed out that the older sibling "who is further along in the socialization process but still relatively close in age actions to the younger sibling, may be a more effective agent of socialization than the much older adult parents." The "baby" of the family typically receives a great deal of attention from parents and older brothers and sisters, which may make the youngest child less likely to become involved in delinquency.

Middle children sometimes may get "lost" in the childrearing process. They are not usually given the responsibility and meaningful roles assigned to the oldest child, but also are not granted the tolerance and freedom from responsibilities afforded the baby of the family. Hirschi (1969, 1983), Nye (1958, 1974), and McCord et al. (1959) all found middle children to be more likely to be delinquent. It may be that middle children feel relatively deprived of parental attention as compared to the oldest and youngest children, and perceive getting in trouble as one method of gaining attention from adults.

Family size and position in the birth order impact upon the socialization process and are relevant variables to be considered in the study of delinquency. In the ongoing argument of heredity versus environment, it is often ignored that different children in the same family experience different *social* environments. When answering questions about why children of the same parents (and hence, same environment) have such different personalities, Blerer (1980:52) stated, "The fact is that it is *not* the same environment: each child, depending upon his [or her] birth order position is born into an environment that is entirely different from that into which any of his [or her] siblings is born." Lasswell and Lasswell (1982:323) confirmed "that the addition of each child changes the family structure…not only does each sibling change the parents' relationship…but also the children's relationships." The extent to which family size and birth order are related to delinquency poses interesting prospects for future sociological research.

Family Interaction

The dynamics of family interaction include infinite possibilities, and undoubtedly vary between and within families, depending upon which family members are involved and what circumstances surround the given situation. However, there are certain identifiable types and patterns of family interaction between parents and children which appear on a fairly consistent basis throughout much of the research on the family and delinquency. Parental rejection, for example, has been shown to be an important factor leading to delinquency (Simons, et al., 1989), whereas strong attachment to, and involvement with family have been consistently linked to non-delinquency (U.S. Dept of Justice, 1999a).

Family violence has been shown to be even more consistently related to problematic youth. Murray Straus and his associates (1980) indicated that violence ranging from spanking and shoving to shooting and stabbing has become a common element of social dynamics in an increasing number of American families. It has been estimated that annually over 50 million Americans are victims of physical violence at the hands of family members (US News and World Report, 1979:60–61). The California Commission on Crime Control and Violence Prevention indicated that millions of American children are violently abused, molested, or seriously neglected by their parents each year (Strong and DeVault, 1986:459). Family violence does not only involve parents abusing children; it is estimated that "138,000 children use a gun or knife on a sibling each year" (Lasswell and Lasswell, 1982:382).

Numerous studies have linked violence within the family (especially abuse by one or both parents) to juvenile misbehavior and delinquency (e.g., Gil, 1970; Steinmentz and Straus, 1973; Gelles and Straus, 1979; Straus et al., 1980; Kratcoski, 1982). The violence-begets-violence theme suggests that children who are socialized in a family environment in which violence is the norm are much more likely to commit violent behavior and to perceive violence as a viable solution to problems (Straus et al., 1980; Hamner and Turner, 1985). Some researchers contend, however, that the link between child maltreatment and delinquency may be somewhat exaggerated (Zingraff, et al., 1993).

Besides the issue of physical violence, the overall relationship between parents and children appears relevant to understanding delinquency and its relationship to home environment. Numerous studies indicate that parental conflict and other aspects of family stress are linked to adolescent behavior—especially delinquency (e.g., Ambert, 1999; Acock and Demo, 1999; Plunkett and Henry, 1999). David Abrahamsen (1960:43) pointed out that "homes racked with a great deal of tension…may produce a great deal of hostility and arguing which threatens family cohesiveness and could lead to delinquency." McCord et al. (1959:83) contended, "Quarrelsome, neglecting families actually had a higher crime rate than homes in which permanent separation disrupted the family" and suggested that homes characterized by neglect and conflict were more likely to produce delinquents than those broken by divorce. August Aichorn (1969:164) indicated that in homes where youths are confronted with constant bickering and quarreling, they often leave the home and take "refuge in the streets." As we shall see in Chapter 11 when juveniles take to the streets, their likelihood of involvement in delinquency and with the police is great. Stephen Cernkovich and Peggy Giordano (1987) concluded that patterns of interaction within the family are more important in explaining delinquency than structural factors such as family size and broken or intact home. Social control theorists contend that attachment to parents is a significant element of the "social bond" and extremely important in insulating a child against delinquency. Hirschi (1969:88) indicated that children who had developed a strong social bond with their parents were more likely to feel the "psychological presence" of their family when out in the social world. He viewed "affectional identification, love, and respect" as important delinquency inhibitors (Hirschi, 1969:91). Later research confirmed that the social bond with parents was an important variable in family interaction for reducing the likelihood of delinquency (e.g., Jensen, 1972; Gove and Crutchfield, 1982; Rosen, 1985; Cernkovich and Giordano, 1987; U.S. Dept. of Justice, 1999).

Parental Discipline

An acknowledged role expectation in U.S. society is that parents will discipline their children. The nature, type, and extent of the discipline varies a great deal, as do attitudes about what constitutes appropriate disciplinary measures.

In colonial America, children generally were viewed as the property of their parents (especially the father), and virtually any disciplinary method deemed appropriate by the parent was permitted. Corporal punishment was used fairly regularly, as the "spare the rod and spoil the child" school of childrearing tended to dominate. In fact, some colonies actually had what were called "stubborn child laws," which allowed parents to kill their children for serious or continuous misconduct (Straus et al., 1980). The severity of discipline legally sanctioned in colonial America is documented in a law from one of the colonies which read:

> *If any child or children above 16 years old of competent understanding, shall curse or smite their natural father or mother, he or they shall be put to death unless it can be sufficiently testified that the parents have been very unchristianly negligent of the education of such child...if any man have a rebellious or stubborne [sic] son of sufficient years and understanding, that is to say, 16 years of age or upwards, which shall not obey the voice of his father or the voice of his mother, yet when they have chastened him will not harken unto them...such son shall be put to death, or otherwise severely punished (Calhoun, 1960:42).*

While such extreme measures were very rare, general attitudes regarding the disciplining of children supported the unquestioned authority of the parent. As time passed, attitudes toward children changed, and laws were passed to protect children. Corporal punishment was still used, but laws prohibited excessive physical abuse. Today, attitudes toward parental discipline are varied, but every state has laws designed to protect children from parental abuse. Discipline in the U.S. family ranges from corporal punishment to no punishment at all, with virtually everything in between. In general, parental attitudes have become more tolerant with less severe methods of punishment being used. Strong and DeVault (1986:375–377) summarized contemporary childrearing strategies into the following categories:

1. Authoritarian. Typically require absolute obedience; parents maintaining control seems most important; "Because I said so" is typical response to child's questioning of authority. More typical of lower class and working class families.

2. Permissive. Child's freedom of expression and autonomy are valued; parents are sometimes manipulative using such terminology as "do what we want you to do because you want to do it"; typical of middle class families.

3. Authoritative. Relies on positive reinforcement and infrequent punishment; encourages autonomy within reasonable limits; more typical of upper middle and upper class families.

Parental discipline is involved in the concept of delinquency in a variety of ways. If nothing else, in virtually every state parents can petition their own children to juvenile court for refusing to obey them. Usually handled under the umbrella of "incorrigibility," this type of misbehavior is treated as a status offense.

Beyond the possibility of parents bringing the court's attention to their own child's misbehavior, parental discipline influences the development of the juvenile in a multitude of other ways which lead to or prevent delinquency. For example, Robert Larzelere and Gerald Patterson (1990) found that the apparent effects of socioeconomic status on delinquency could be significantly mediated by parental monitoring and consistency of discipline.

When strict discipline takes the form of corporal punishment, however, it may contribute to behavioral problems as opposed to deterring them. A study released by the American Medical Association showed that the more a parent spanks a child, the worse that child acts over time (Schulte, 1997). While parental violence is linked to delinquency, strict discipline by parents is not. The McCords and Zola (1959) found that consistency in discipline was more important in insulating against delinquency than the method used. Tommie Hamner and Pauline Turner (1985) suggested that parents adhere to the following guidelines if punishment is to be successful:

1. *Before punishment is administered, the child should know clearly what the expectations for his [or her] behavior are and what consequences will occur if these expectations are not met.*
2. *Punishment should follow the act immediately.*
3. *Punishment needs to be deserved and understood.*
4. *Punishment needs to be related to the act.*
5. *Punishment should be administered within a context of love and respect (Hamner and Turner, 1985:45).*

Hirschi (1983:15) further emphasized the importance of parental discipline:

The parent who cares for the child will watch his or [her] behavior, see him [her] doing things he [or she] should not do, and correct him [or her]. Presto! A socialized decent human being.

Admittedly, Hirschi may have oversimplified the complex art of disciplining children, but his point may be valid. Paying attention to their children's behavior, and then doing something about misbehavior, represents a basic element of the socialization process and the internalization of norms supporting conforming behavior. He pointed out some potential problems that might enter into the socialization process and thwart the prevention of delinquency:

1. *The parents may not care.*
2. *The parents may care, but may not have the time or energy to monitor the child's behavior.*

While discipline is important, research shows that spanking rarely achieves the desired results and, instead, may encourage children to resort to violence in dealing with others.

3. *The parents may care, may monitor the behavior, but may not see anything wrong with it.*
4. *The parents may care, may monitor the behavior, may view it as wrong, but might not have the inclination nor the means to impose punishment (Hirschi, 1983:15).*

Any of these factors might negatively affect the socialization process and lead to delinquency. The first factor would be a situation wherein the parents deserve "blame" for not properly socializing their child to internalize social norms and refrain from law violation. However, the second example implies that if both parents work, or a child is raised in a one-parent family, the parent may not be able to monitor the child's behavior. Scenario three alludes to a situation wherein the parent knows that the child has violated a norm, but sees nothing wrong with the child doing so. In a pluralistic society, if certain norms have no meaning for parents, they are not likely to enforce them within the family setting. Finally, the last situation addresses the problem faced by many parents in attempting to discipline their children. Sometimes, in an attempt to get along with their children, parents tolerate behavior that they know is wrong simply to avoid confrontation. Or, in other cases the inability to handle the youth or actual fear of the child (if the parent is physically smaller and/or weaker than the child) might prohibit intervention and punishment even though the parent(s) clearly feel(s) the situation warrants it. One study estimated that "8 million children—18 out of every 100, most of them teenagers—assault their parents" (US News and World Report, 1979:60–61). Regardless of the reasons, when parents fail to discipline their children, the burden is likely to shift to other agents of social control such as school, police, and the courts.

Larzelere and Patterson (1990) concluded that spending time with children, good communication, supervision, monitoring behavior and holding youths accountable are the most effective delinquency prevention tools for parents. They also noted that positive reinforcement for desired behavior is a more effective form of discipline than punishment for undesired behavior.

Broken Homes and Delinquency

There has been much debate over the relationship between broken homes and juvenile delinquency. **Broken home** usually *refers to any family situation in which one of the parents is not present on a permanent basis.* **Intact home** *is used to describe a family situation in which both parents are consistently present in the home.*

A common theme in much of the earlier literature on juvenile delinquency was that broken homes contributed to delinquency causation (e.g., Shideler, 1918; Gilling, 1933; Parsons, 1947; Glueck and Glueck, 1950; Monahan, 1957). Since the family usually serves as the primary agent of socialization, a logical assumption was that any disruption in the family institution, especially something as significant as divorce, was likely to have negative impact upon the socialization process. Thus, social learning theories and social control theories tended to link broken homes to delinquency.

The number of marriages in the United States ending in divorce increased dramatically during the twentieth century. The number of divorces per 1,000 population was 1.6 in 1920; 3.5 in 1970; 5.3 in 1979 (National Center for Health Statistics, 1980) and then dropped slightly to 4.6 in 1991 (Hoffman, 1992: 941). Only about 5 percent of all marriages in the 1860s ended in divorce (Preston and McDonald, 1979) while about 50 percent of marriages of the 1970s were estimated to terminate through divorce (Weed, 1980). Andrew Cherlin (1981) pointed out that the divorce rate doubled during the decades of the 1960s and 1970s. As divorce rates have increased, so has speculation about the impact of divorce upon juveniles and its assumed relationship to juvenile delinquency.

Empirical research on the relationship between broken homes and delinquency has provided mixed results and led to a variety of interpretations and conclusions. Ivan Nye (1958) contended that the broken home had a stronger relationship to status offenses (especially truancy and running away) than to serious delinquency. John Johnstone's (1978) and Joseph Rankin's (1983) research, some 20 and 25 years later, essentially came to the same conclusion. Research by Thomas and associates (2000) indicated that single-parent family structures were directly linked to sexual risk taking and indirectly linked to alcohol use and abuse. Nye (1958) concluded that the broken home was related to delinquency among girls more than for boys. Susan Datesman and Frank Scarpitti (1975) also viewed the broken home as having differential impact on boys and girls, with the relationship to delinquency being stronger for girls. Rachelle Canter (1982), on the other hand, contended that boys were as affected as girls by the breakup of their parents.

Talcott Parsons (1947) promoted the idea that divorce was particularly dysfunctional for the development of young males because it created anxiety about their masculine identity. He viewed that anxiety as leading to **compulsive masculinity,** or *an overemphasis on what were considered "manly" characteristics,* which was likely to result in antisocial behavior. Jackson Toby (1966) amplified this theme 20 years later, and contended that compulsive masculinity was likely to develop in families where the father was absent. Compulsive masculinity,

A divorced father picks up his daughter for a weekend visitation. Research is mixed as to whether there is a possible link between families broken by divorce and delinquency.

he claimed, was linked to delinquency, especially violent behavior. Ira Silverman and Simon Dinitz (1974) generally agreed that the absence of a male role model led to exaggerated masculinity and in an attempt to assert their masculinity, many young males commit delinquency. Barbara Cashion (1982) refuted these assumptions, however, indicating that her research findings on female-headed families showed that delinquency was not higher among juveniles in homes where the father was absent when the variable of socioeconomic status was controlled. Among other factors, children from broken homes generally experience a loss of socioeconomic status, which might indirectly contribute to their delinquency (Li and Wojtkiewicz, 1992).

Other research on delinquency has questioned the relationship between broken homes and delinquency, especially the assumption that broken homes *cause* delinquency. Studies suggest that juveniles from broken homes are treated differently by juvenile courts (Smith, 1955; Singer, 1993). Thus, studies linking broken homes to delinquency which used youths who had been adjudicated delinquent, and especially studies which used institutionalized samples, were called into question. Monahan (1957) confirmed that youths from broken homes were much more likely to be referred to juvenile court, while those from intact homes were more likely to be dismissed during intake. Further, he found that juveniles from broken homes were more likely to be institutionalized than placed on probation (Monahan, 1957). A study of Massachusetts youths found that while prior record, nature of offense, and other legal variables were important factors in disposition, many social caseworkers viewed single-parent families as less capable of handling delinquents, and, consequently, were more likely to recommend that they be placed in some type of juvenile facility (Isralowitz, 1981). Youthful offenders from single-parent families are also more likely to be remanded to adult courts and face grand jury indictments than are juveniles from intact homes (Singer, 1993).

In an excellent overview of the research on broken homes and delinquency, Karen Wilkinson (1974) indicated that the variable of broken home has fluctuated in its importance to sociological research on delinquency. She suggested that perhaps the reason that sociologists have emphasized the broken home in delinquency causation more at some times than at others is because the relationship between broken home and delinquency has indeed been different during different periods of time. Wilkinson went on to say that if the concept of broken home is going to be utilized in sociological theory it must be refined. She suggested that it is likely to have a different impact upon a juvenile if the home is broken as a result of the death of one of the parents as opposed to divorce or desertion. Richard Hardy and John Cull (1973) confirmed that the loss of a parent through death was not nearly as likely to lead to delinquency as the loss of a parent through divorce or separation. Wilkinson (1974) pointed out that if the broken home factor in delinquency is going to be meaningful, it must be incorporated into a broader theory of delinquency causation such as Hirschi's (1969) control theory.

The relationship between broken homes and delinquency is, at best, ambiguous. Divorce is a much more common phenomenon in American society today than ever before. Data indicate that approximately 50 percent of all marriages end in divorce and there has been a tremendous increase in the number of children living in single parent families (U.S. Bureau of the Census, 2000). With divorce rates so high, it might even be argued that broken homes have become the norm. If not the norm, at least the negative attitudes and stigma associated with divorce have been reduced greatly and divorce has become much more socially accepted (Thornton, 1985). Whether the increased number of homes split by divorce has caused increased delinquency is debatable. If social agencies such as Big Brothers/Big Sisters and day care centers can help fill the void in a child's life caused by the absence of one of the parents, the juvenile may be no more likely to engage in delinquency than would a child from an intact home. Further, it might even be argued that the juvenile who has experienced a broken home eventually receives more adult supervision and has more adult role models. Statistics indicate that most of those who divorce soon remarry, and it is estimated that 15 million minor children now live in step-families with an increase of nearly a million every year (Lasswell and Lasswell, 1982:430). Children of divorced parents are likely to have two families, not one, and four adults involved in the socialization process as opposed to two.

Some research emphasizes the nature of the relationship between parents and children as being more importantly related to delinquency than whether the home is broken or intact (e.g., Cernkovich and Giordano, 1987). Lawrence Rosen and Kathleen Neilson (1982:134) concluded that "the concept of broken home no matter how it is defined or measured, has little explanatory power in terms of delinquency." A study by Margaret Farnworth (1984) came to essentially the same conclusion. Homes characterized by tension, even in intact families, may produce situations which could lead to delinquency (Abrahamsen, 1960:43). McCord et al. (1959) suggested that homes characterized by neglect and conflict were more likely to produce delinquents than those broken by divorce. Suzanne Steinmentz and Murray Straus (1973) reaffirmed that idea in a study indicating that children who experienced family violence were more likely to commit violence than those who had not. With increasing divorce rates, it is likely that the possible relationship between broken homes and delinquency will continue to capture the interest of researchers.

The Family and Delinquency Prevention

How one perceives the role of the family in delinquency prevention is directly linked to one's view of the role of the family in delinquency causation. The disparate findings of sociological research in this area suggest that a multicausal approach needs to be taken which assesses the variety of ways in which the family impacts upon its individual members.

Many of the problems of juvenile delinquency appear related to the marginal status accorded adolescents in American society. One of the ways in which the family might effectively attempt to prevent delinquency is to create clearly defined and meaningful social roles for its younger members. Societal and parental expectations should be consistent, well defined, and clearly articulated to children. Whether both parents are present in the home or not appears less important than the quality of the relationship established between the child and the parent(s) who is/are present.

Parental supervision and consistency in discipline also appear to be important insulators against delinquency. Much of the controversy over the relationship between broken homes and delinquency causation may be mediated by looking at the extent of parental supervision. Donald Fischer (1983) concluded that high parental supervision is a significant variable in lower delinquency rates even under other adverse social conditions, and other studies have indicated that unsupervised youths are far more likely to get into trouble than those who are well-supervised (Agnew and Palmer, 1989). One parent who is intimately involved in the supervision of the child's behavior may be more effective in preventing delinquency than two parents who show little or no interest in their children's behavior or who are distracted from their parental responsibilities by marital stress. While studies linking broken homes, physical and emotional abuse, and other family problems to delinquency causation create much controversy, there is almost irrefutable evidence that a stable family life characterized by love, concern, consistency in discipline, and adequate parental supervision is related to less likelihood of delinquency. Allen Liska and Mark Reed (1985:558) concluded that parents "are the major institutional sources of delinquency control;" Larzelere and Patterson (1990) and former U.S. Attorney General Janet Reno concurred that direct parental supervision is the best insulation against delinquency (Cass, 1993). Box 9-2 provides a view of the family's role in delinquency prevention.

The family serves as the first social group to which a juvenile belongs. While church, school, mass media, and peers greatly influence the values and behavior of youths, the family usually has the first opportunity in the socialization process. No doubt, the changing role of the family has altered its preeminence in socializing its young members. Many of the

BOX 9-2   Concept Application

The Role of the Family in Preventing Delinquency

Former U.S. Attorney General Janet Reno contended that strong parenting may be the only "cure for crime," and established what she called a "national agenda for children" in an effort to reduce crime and delinquency in the United States (Cass, 1993:A7). Asserting that "We will never have enough dollars to save everybody if we wait until they are 16 or 17," Reno believes that the first three years of a child's life are the most important for instilling values that will help prevent future delinquency and crime (Cass, 1993:A7). Thus, she contends that if the United States is seriously interested in reducing its crime problem, Americans must reform the way they rear their children.

A Texas juvenile judge echoed Reno's sentiments when he commented on the high rate of violence and disregard for life and property exhibited by many of the teenagers he faces in court. "The problem is not so much the kid being an evil kid, but the family environment," he responded to the Director of the Texas Youth Commission and an Assistant District Attorney who had observed that juveniles today "are much more aggressive and dangerous" and have "a greater disregard for the lives and property of other people…" (AP, Austin, 1993:41A). While these practitioners, like Janet Reno, are not social scientists, their assertions echo many of the findings of sociological and criminological research.

So many studies over the past four decades have linked delinquency to family problems in the home that, in 1990, the Office of Juvenile Justice and Delinquency Prevention cited the need of "preserving families to prevent delinquency" as one of its top priorities (U.S. Department of Justice, 1992; National Institute of Justice, 1992). Three community-based programs across the United States were cited as exemplary and proposed as models for other communities and states to replicate. They included: *Targeted Outreach,* a delinquency intervention program designed and operated by the Boys and Girls Clubs of America; *Court Appointed Special Advocates,* a program that ensures that courts are familiar with, and mindful of, the needs of neglected and abused children; and *Permanent Families for Abused and Neglected Children,* a training and technical assistance project of the National Council of Juvenile and Family Court Judges (U.S. Department of Justice, 1992). Parents Anonymous, perhaps the oldest child abuse prevention organization in the United States, is committed to strengthening families and reducing delinquency. They offer mutual support groups, parental leadership training, and a host of other specialized services and information to families. Research shows that involvement with Parents Anonymous leads to better parenting skills, reduction in physical and emotional abuse, improved self-esteem, better social interaction, and reduced delinquency (Rafael and Pion-Berlin, 1999).

These programs, and thousands of others across the country, acknowledge the central role the family can play in delinquency prevention, and how local communities can intervene and help youths whose families are not fulfilling that role. As one Juvenile Court Judge noted:

> If we're going to make any inroads into the criminal justice system, it's going to be with the juveniles. That's exactly why they are having to spend billions of dollars on new prisons now, because they ignored the juveniles.

Most experts agree, whether practitioners or academic researchers, that any significant effort to reduce and prevent juvenile delinquency must start with the family.

Sources

AP, Austin. 1993. "Rate of violence among Texas kids at a high point." *The Dallas Morning News,* August 21:41A.

Cass, Connie. 1993. "Reno pushes strong parenting as cure for crime." *Fort Worth Star Telegram,* September 19:A7.

National Institute of Justice. 1992. "Breaking the cycle: Predicting and Preventing crime." *National Institute of Justice Journal* 225 August:28–29.

Rafael, T., and Pion-Berlin, L. 1999. Parents Anonymous: Strengthening families. *Juvenile Justice Bulletin,* April, 1999. U.S. Dept. of Justice: Office of Juvenile Justice and Delinquency Prevention.

U.S. Department of Justice. 1992. "OJJDP model programs 1990: Preserving families to prevent delinquency." *Juvenile Justice Bulletin* April:1–4.

functions formerly fulfilled by the family have been abdicated to other social groups and agencies. Yet, the family still plays a fundamental role in shaping the attitudes, values, beliefs, and behaviors that may promote or prevent future law violation (AP, Chicago, 1997).

The social bond between juveniles and their families appears to be one of the most effective insulators against delinquency (U.S. Dept. of Justice, 1999a). As U.S. society has become more highly industrialized, urbanized, and bureaucratized, the juvenile's attachment to the family has become somewhat more difficult to maintain. William Arnold and Terrance Brungardt (1983) agreed that commitment to family is a conformity-producing process and represents a basic American value. But, as they pointed out, family commitment also may be somewhat contradictory to another basic value: individual freedom in interpersonal relations. They hypothesize that "forces detracting from commitment to family demands free persons to interact with others who lack commitments to conformity producing values" (Arnold and Brungardt, 1983:128). In today's urban environment, a multitude of sociocultural influences exist which potentially weaken a juvenile's commitment to family. In Chapter 11, The Youth Subculture, we discuss some of the competing values experienced by juveniles in the social and cultural milieu in which they interact.

As was indicated at the beginning of this chapter, the family has undergone and continues to experience dramatic changes. There is no solitary version of *the* family. Rather, the institution of the family is in a continuous process of transition. Bumpass (1984:621) reported:

> *In 1980, only three-fifths of all children lived in the simple family composed of once-married parents, less than half will live out their childhood in this status. In this context, we must rethink our conceptualization of the family in sociological research.*

In order to more thoroughly assess the family's impact upon juvenile delinquency, the changing role of the family will have to be more fully understood within its broadest sociological context.

SUMMARY

The role of the family in the U.S. has changed a great deal over the past 200 years. The extended or large nuclear family that fulfilled the necessary economic and social functions in a predominantly agrarian society gave way to the smaller more mobile nuclear family as the United States became more urbanized and industrialized.

The family serves as one of the most important agents of socialization in our society, and the first to which most people are exposed. A child's initial attitudes, values, and beliefs typically are learned from family members. Additionally, a child's first play group, place of residence, exposure to religion, and a variety of other experiences primarily are determined by the family of orientation.

There has been tremendous interest in and much disagreement about the impact on children of having mothers who work outside the home. Each year, more women with children of preschool and school age join the U.S. work force. A major problem associated with the increased number of working mothers is the lack of adequate child care facilities available in the United States. This situation has given rise to the phenomenon of "latchkey children" who must spend some time in the afternoons left unsupervised until one or both parents return home from work. Much speculation has occurred regarding the potentially increased likelihood of delinquency among these unsupervised youths. When children are left unsupervised for long periods of time, their opportunities for engaging in delinquent behavior are increased. Research indicates, however, that if working parents are aware of the potentially negative impact of both parents working outside the home and spend "quality time" with their children when possible, that adequate socialization can overcome the negative aspects of temporary lack of supervision.

Some important family variables have been shown to be related to delinquency. Social class, family size, birth order, family interaction, and parental discipline all impact upon a juvenile's likelihood of becoming delinquent.

For many years a causal link was believed to exist between broken homes and delinquency. Data indicated that children of single parent homes were apparently more likely to commit delinquent offenses. However,

subsequent research has indicated that the apparent relationship between broken homes and delinquency may be spurious, and better explained by other variables such as lack of supervision and differential treatment by members of the juvenile justice system.

Because of the significant impact the family has upon children, it potentially can play a vital role in delinquency prevention. Adequate socialization and the development of a strong social bond are important dimensions of the family's delinquency prevention role. The family also can reduce the marginality experienced by adolescents by providing meaningful familial roles and responsibilities. In short, the family's impact upon juveniles cannot be overestimated, and consequently, should remain a major research focus for sociological inquiry into the social problem of juvenile delinquency.

Concept Integration

Questions for Study and Discussion

1. In what ways does the type of family a juvenile experiences (extended or nuclear) affect the likelihood of his or her becoming delinquent?

2. How does the socialization process in the family impact upon the likelihood of a youth becoming delinquent?

3. An increasing number of mothers work outside the home today. In your opinion, are the children of working mothers *more* or *less* likely to become delinquent? Why?

4. How do family variables such as social class, family size, birth order, family interaction, and parental discipline relate to juvenile delinquency?

5. Define the following terms: extended family, nuclear family, family of orientation, role modeling, latch-

key children, broken home, and intact home. How does the understanding of these terms and concepts help us in understanding juvenile delinquency?

6. In what ways can the family become more involved in delinquency prevention?

7. Think of your own family situation when you were growing up. What type of family did you live in (extended or nuclear)? In what ways did your family help prevent you from becoming delinquent? What family situations did you experience which potentially could have promoted delinquency on your part? As a parent, how would you go about trying to prevent your children from becoming delinquent?

References

Abrahamsen, D. 1960. *The psychology of crime.* New York: Columbia University Press.

Acock, A. C., and Demo, D. H. 1999. Dimensions of family conflict and their influence on child and adolescent adjustment. *Sociological Inquiry* 69 (Fall):641–658.

Agnew, R., and Peterson, D. M. 1989. Leisure and delinquency. *Social Problems* 36 (October):332–350.

Aichorn, A. 1969. *Delinquency and child guidance.* New York: International Universities Press.

Ambert, A-M. 1999. The effect of male delinquency on mothers and fathers: A heuristic study. *Sociological Inquiry* 69 (Fall):621–640.

AP Chicago. 1997. They're really not ignoring you. *Dallas Morning News.* September 10, 1997:4A.

AP Washington. 1986. Study says children of working mothers do better in school. *Emporia Gazette* August 25, 1986:15.

AP Washington. 1994. Census data detail kids home alone. *Dallas Morning News* May 20, 1994:12A.

Arnold, W. R. 1971. Race and ethnicity relative to other factors in juvenile court dispositions. *American Journal of Sociology* 77 (2):211–227.

Arnold, W. R., and Brungardt, T. M. 1983. *Juvenile misconduct and delinquency.* Boston: Houghton-Mifflin.

Axelrod, S. 1952. Negro and white institutionalized delinquents. *American Journal of Sociology* 57 (May):569–574.

Bandura, A., and Walters, R. 1963. *Social learning and personality development.* New York: Holt, Rinehart, and Winston.

Barnes, G. M., Farrell, M. P., and Cairns, A. 1986. Parental socialization factors and adolescent drinking behaviors. *Journal of Marriage and the Family* 48 (February):27–36.

Bell, R. R. 1983. *Marriage and family interaction* (6th ed.). Homewood, IL: Dorsey Press.

Blerer, L. M. 1980. The meaning of birth order: First born, last born. *Parents* (March):52–55.

Booth, A., Johnson, D. R., and White, L. 1984. Women, outside employment, and marital instability. *American Journal of Sociology* 90 (November): 567–583.

Brindis, C. 1986. The nation's changing demographic profile: Implications for the family life educator. *Family Life Educator* 5 (Fall):4–9.

Brownfield, D., and Sorenson, A. M. 1994. Sibship size and sibling delinquency. *Deviant Behavior* 15 (Jan.–March):45–61.

Bumpass, L. 1984. Some characteristics of children's second families. *American Journal of Sociology* 90 (November):608–623.

Byrne, S. 1977. Nobody home: The erosion of the American family. *Psychology Today* 10 (May): 40–47.

Calhoun, A. W. 1960. *A social history of the American family: Colonial period.* Vol. 1. New York: Barnes and Noble.

Canter, R. J. 1982. Family correlates of male and female delinquency. *Criminology* 20 (August):149–167.

Cashion, B. G. 1982. Female-headed families: Effects on children and clinical implications. *Journal of Marital and Family Therapy* 8 (April):77–85.

Cernkovich, S. A., and Giordano, P. C. 1987. Family relationships and delinquency. *Criminology* 25: 295–321.

Cherlin, A. J. 1981. *Marriage, divorce, and remarriage.* Cambridge, MA: Harvard University Press.

Chollar, S. 1987. Latchkey kids: Who are they? *Psychology Today* 21 (December):12.

CNN. 1993. Headline News, November 30.

Colvin, M., and Pauly, J. 1983. A critique of criminology: Toward an integrated structural-Marxist theory of delinquency prevention. *American Journal of Sociology* 89 (November):513–545.

Datesman, S., and Scarpitti, F. 1975. Female delinquency and broken homes. *Criminology* 13 (May):35–56.

Elliott, D. S., Wilson, W. J., Huizinga, D., Sampson, R. J., Elliott, A., and Rankin, B. 1996. The effects of neighborhood disadvantage on adolescent development. *Journal of Research in Crime and Delinquency* 33 (November):389–426.

Empey, L. T., and Erickson, M. L. 1966. Hidden delinquency and social status. *Social Forces* 44 (June): 546–554.

Fagan, J., Slaughter, E., and Hartstone, E. 1987. Blind justice? The impact of race on the juvenile justice process. *Crime and Delinquency* 33 (April):224–258.

Farnworth, M. 1984. Family structure, family attributes, and delinquency in a sample of low-income, minority males and females. *Journal of Youth and Adolescence* 13 (August):349–364.

Fischer, D. G. 1983. Parental supervision and delinquency. *Perceptual Motor Skills* 56 (April):635–640.

Gelles, R., and Straus, M. 1979. Violence in the American family. *Journal of Social Issues* 35 (Spring):15–19.

Gil, D. 1970. *Violence against children.* Cambridge, MA: Harvard University Press.

Gilling, J. 1933. *Social pathology.* New York: Appleton-Century-Crofts.

Glueck, S., and Glueck, E. 1950. *Unraveling juvenile delinquency.* Cambridge, MA: Harvard University Press.

1968. *Delinquents and nondelinquents in perspective.* Cambridge, MA: Harvard University Press.

Goldman, N. 1963. *The differential selection of juvenile offenders for court appearance.* New York: National Council on Crime and Delinquency.

Gove, W. R., and Crutchfield, R. D. 1982. The family and juvenile delinquency. *The Sociological Quarterly* 23 (Summer):301–319.

Hamner, T. J., and Turner, P. H. 1985. *Parenting in contemporary society.* Englewood Cliffs, NJ: Prentice-Hall.

Hardy, R. E., and Cull, J. G. 1973. *Climbing ghetto walls.* Springfield, IL: Charles C Thomas.

Heimer, K. 1997. Socioeconomic status, subcultural definitions, and violent delinquency. *Social Forces* 75 (March):799–833.

Hill, C. R., and Stafford, F. P. 1979. Parental care of children. *Journal of Human Resources* 15 (Spring): 219–239.

Hirschi, T. 1969. *Causes of delinquency.* Berkeley: University of California Press. 1983. Families and crime. *Current* 254 (July–Aug.):14–19.

Hochschild, A. 1997. *The time bind: When work becomes home and home becomes work.* New York: Holt Metropolitan Books.

Hoffman, M.S. (Ed.). 1992. *The World Almanac and Book of Facts, 1993.* New York: Pharos Books.

Hogan, D. P., and Kitagawa, E. M. 1985. The impact of social status, family structure, and neighborhood on the fertility of black adolescents. *American Journal of Sociology* 90 (January):825–855.

Hollingshead, A. B. 1961. Elmstown's youth: The impact of social classes on adolescents. New York: John Wiley.

Isralowitz, R. E. 1981. Youth service caseworkers: Social and legal factors affecting their recommendations to place youths in secure care facilities. *Children and Youth Services Review* 3 (3):233–246.

Jensen, G. 1972. Parents, peers and delinquent action: A test of differential association perspective. *American Journal of Sociology* 78 (November):562–575.

Johnstone, J. W. C. 1978. Juvenile delinquency and the family: A contextual interpretation. *Youth and Society* 9 (March):299–313.

Kidwell, J. S. 1981. Number of siblings, sibling spacing, sex, and birth order: Their effects on perceived parent-adolescent relationships. *Journal of Marriage and the Family* 43 (May):315–332.

Klein, H. 1990. Adolescence, youth, and young adulthood: Rethinking current conceptualizations of life stage. *Youth & Society* 21 (June):446–471.

Kratcoski, P. C. 1982. Child abuse and violence against the family. *Child Welfare* 61 (Sept.–Oct.): 435–444.

Larzelere, R. E., and Patterson, G. R. 1990. Parental management: Mediator of the effect of socioeconomic status on early delinquency. *Criminology* 28 (May):301–324.

Lasswell, M., and Lasswell, T. E. 1982. *Marriage and the family.* Lexington, MA: DC Heath.

Lauritsen, J. L. 1993. Sibling resemblance in juvenile delinquency: Findings from the National Youth Survey. *Criminology* 31 (August):387–401.

Li, J. H., and Wojtkiewicz, R. A. 1992. A new look at the effects of family structure on status attainment. *Social Science Quarterly* 73 (September):581–595.

Liska, A. E., and Reed, M. D. 1985. Ties to conventional institutions and delinquency: Estimating reciprocal effects. *American Sociological Review* 50 (August):547–560.

Lundman, R. J. 1996. Demeanor and arrest: Additional evidence from previously unpublished data. *Journal of Research in Crime and Delinquency* 33 (August):306–323.

McCord, W., McCord, J., and Zola, I. 1959. *Origins of crime.* New York: Columbia University Press.

Miller, W. B. 1958. Lower class culture as a generating milieu of gang delinquency. *Journal of Social Issues* 14 (3):5–19.

Monahan, T. P. 1957. Family status and the delinquent child: A reappraisal and some new findings. *Social Forces* (March):250–258.

National Center for Health Statistics. 1980. Births, marriages, divorces, and deaths for 1979. Monthly Vital Statistics Report 28, no. 12, Washington, DC: U.S. Department of Health, Education and Welfare.

NEA Today. 1986. Families. *Today's Education,* NEA *Today* 5 (1):30–41.

New York Times News Service. 1996. Day care found not to harm infant's trust. *Dallas Morning News,* April 21:4A.

Nye, F. I. 1958. *Family relationships and delinquent behavior.* New York: John Wiley.
1974. Emerging and declining family roles. *Journal of Marriage and the Family* 36 (May):238–245.

Parsons, T. 1947. Certain primary sources and patterns of aggression in the social structure of the western world. *Psychiatry* 10 (May):167–181.

Pfouts, J. H. 1980. Birth order, age spacing, IQ differences, and family relations. *Journal of Marriage and the Family* 42 (August):517–530.

Piliavin, I., and Briar, S. 1964. Police encounters with juveniles. *American Journal of Sociology* 70 (September):206–214.

Plunkett, S. W., and Henry, C. S. 1999. Adolescent perceptions of interparental conflict, stressors, and coping as predictors of adolescent family life satisfaction. *Sociology Inquiry* 69 (Fall):599–620.

Preston, S. H., and MacDonald, J. 1979. The incidence of divorce within cohorts of American marriages contracted since the Civil War. *Demography* 16:1–25.

Rankin, J. H. 1983. The family context of delinquency. *Social Problems* 30 (April):466–479.

Recer, Paul. 1999. Study: No lasting harm for working mom's kids. *Dallas Morning News,* March 1, 1999:1A.

Reid, S. T. 1996. *Crime and criminology* (8th ed.). Hightstown, NJ: McGraw-Hill.

Reige, M. G. 1972. Parental affection and juvenile delinquency in girls. *British Journal of Criminology* 12 (January):55–73.

Rogers, D. 1985. *Adolescence and youth* (5th ed.). Englewood Cliffs, NJ: Prentice-Hall.

Rosen, L. 1985. Family and delinquency: Structure or function? *Criminology* 23:553–573.

Rosen, L., and Neilson, K. 1982. Broken homes. In L. D. Savitz and N. Johnson (Eds.). *Contemporary criminology.* New York: John Wiley, pp. 126–135.

Rutter, M. 1980. *Changing youth in a changing society: Patterns of adolescent development and disorder.* Cambridge, MA: Harvard University Press.

Satir, V. 1972. *Peoplemaking.* Palo Alto, CA: Science and Behavior Books.

Schicor, D. 1983. Socialization: The political aspects of a delinquency explanation. *Sociological Spectrum* 3 (Jan–Mar):85–100.

Schulte, B. 1997. Spanking kids may make them worse. *Dallas Morning News,* (August 15):1A; 18A.

Seward, R. R. 1978. *The American family: A democratic history.* Beverly Hills, CA: Sage.

Shideler, E. H. 1918. Family disintegration and the delinquent boy in the United States. *Journal of Criminal Law and Criminology* 8 (January): 709–732.

Silverman, E. J., and Dinitz, S. 1974. Compulsive masculinity and delinquency: An empirical investigation, *Criminology* 11 (February):498–515.

Simons, R. L., Robertson, J. F., and Downs, W. R. 1989. The nature of the association between parental rejection and delinquent behavior. *Journal of Youth & Adolescence* 18 (June):297–310.

Singer, S. I. 1993. The automatic waiver of juveniles and substantive justice. *Crime and Delinquency* 39 (April):253–261.

Smith, D. A., and Visher, C. A. 1981. Street-level justice: Situational determinants of police arrest decisions. *Social Problems* 29 (December):167–177.

Smith, P. M. 1955. Broken homes and juvenile delinquency. *Sociology and Social Research* 39 (May–June):307–311.

Statistical Abstract of the United States. 1990. *Statistical Abstract of the United States* 1990. Washington, DC: U.S. Government Printing Office.

Steelman, L. C., and Mercy, J. A. 1980. Unconfounding the confluence model: A test of sibling size and birth order on intelligence. *American Sociological Review* 45 (August):571–582.

Steinmetz, S. K., and Straus, M. A. 1973. The family as cradle of violence. *Society* 10 (Sept.–Oct.):50–56.

Straus, M., Gelles, R., and Steinmetz, S. 1980. *Behind closed doors: Violence in the American family.* New York: Anchor.

Strong, B., and DeVault, C. 1986. *The marriage and family experience* (3rd ed.). St. Paul, MN: West.

Sutherland, E. H., and Cressey, D. R. 1978. *Criminology* (10th ed.). Philadelphia: JB Lippincott.

Thomas, G., Reifman, A., Barnes, G. M., and Farrell, M. P. 2000. Delayed onset of drunkenness as a protective factor for adolescent alcohol misuse and sexual risk taking: A longitudinal study. *Deviant Behavior* 21 (March–April):181–210.

Thornberry, T. P. 1973. Race, socioeconomic status, and sentencing in the juvenile justice system. *Journal of Criminal Law and Criminology* 64 (1):90–98.

Thornton, A. 1985. Changing attitudes toward separation and divorces: Causes and consequences. *American Journal of Sociology* 90 (January): 856–872.

Tittle, C. R., and Meier, R. F. 1990. Specifying the SES/delinquency relationship. *Criminology* 28 (May): 271–300.

Toby, J. 1966. Violence and the masculine ideal: Some qualitative data. *Annals of the American Society of Political and Social Sciences* 364 (March):19–27.

Toman, W. 1970. Birth order rules all. *Psychology Today* (December):45–49, 68–69.

United States Bureau of the Census. 1981. *Current Population Reports,* ser. P-20, No. 373. Washington, DC: U.S. Government Printing Office. 1982. Marital status and living arrangements: March, 1981. *Current Population Reports,* ser. P-20, No. 372. Washington, DC: U.S. Government Printing Office.

United States Bureau of the Census. 2000. *Statistical abstract of the United States* (120th Ed.). Washington, DC: U.S. Government Printing Office.

United States Department of Justice. 1999a. Highlights of findings from the Rochester youth development study. Washington, D.C.: Office of Juvenile Justice and Delinquency Prevention.

United States Department of Justice. 1999b. Highlights of findings from the Pittsburgh youth study. Washington, D.C.: Office of Juvenile Justice and Delinquency Prevention.

U.S. News and World Report. 1979. Battered families: A growing nightmare. *U.S. News and World Report* (January 15):60–61.

Washington Post. 1997. Day care doesn't hurt kid's learning, study says. *Dallas Morning News,* April 4:1A; 19A.

Weed, J. A. 1980. *National estimates of marriage dissolution and survivorship: United States. Vital Health and Statistics,* ser. 3 no. 19. Hyattsville, MD: National Center for Health Statistics.

White, M. J., and Kaufman, G. 1997. Language usage, social capital, and school completion among immigrants and native-born ethnic groups. *Social Science Quarterly* 78 (June):385–398.

Wilkinson, K. 1974. The broken family and juvenile delinquency: Scientific explanation or ideology? *Social Problems* 21 (June):726–739.

Woodruff, V. 1994. Studies say the kids are all right. *Working Woman* (October):12.

Zingraff, M. T., Leiter, J., Myers, K. A., and Johnsen, M. C. 1993. Child maltreatment and youthful problem behavior. *Criminology* 31 (May):173–188.

10 SCHOOLS AND DELINQUENCY

Reading Objectives

The reading of this chapter will help you achieve the following objectives:

1. Describe and explain the role of the school as an agent of socialization in our society.
2. Identify ways that the schools act as a "screening device," helping to channel students into future failure or success.
3. List ways in which the schools have become a "combat zone" or arena of confrontation between many students and their teachers and school administrators.
4. Describe how the bureaucratic structure of our schools has helped create and perpetuate juvenile delinquency.
5. Identify specific ways the schools can become actively involved in delinquency prevention.

Introduction

Education is one of the basic social institutions and is largely responsible for the transmission of culture, including values and norms, to the members of society. Because of this important socialization function, our society requires that every child attend school for a specified period of time. It follows that virtually every American has an early experience in elementary and secondary school. However, the quality and extent of that educational experience varies among our young people.

Most U.S. children make a relatively easy transition as they move from home to school if the significant adults in these social environments share common values and norms. However, a large number of young people arrive at school painfully aware of the differences between their socioeconomic status and that of their classmates and teachers. They soon learn that teachers and administrators have the authority and responsibility to teach and enforce standards of conduct that are difficult for them to understand and accept. Thus, the school may become an arena of conflict and confrontation for many youths as they develop delinquent patterns of behavior.

The School as an Arena

An **arena** is *a public place where individuals or groups are pitted against each other in struggles to determine dominance and often survival.* According to ethologist Robert Ardrey (1966), **arena behavior** is a *struggle for both status and for territory* and is common in most animal species, including humans. Thus, examples of arena behavior include the battles between male elk during the mating season, ancient gladiator contests, many of our athletic events, and such collective violence as fights between rival street gangs and wars between nations. In the context of our study of juvenile delinquency, the public schools often become the arena where delinquent youths first encounter a society that opposes and resists their behavior.

Schools and the Socialization Process

The school is usually the first social institution beyond the family to be entrusted as a major agent of socialization for children. Basically, the school's responsibilities in regard to socialization are twofold: the transmission of cognitive skills, and the transmission of normative culture.

In the contemporary United States, the teaching of basic cognitive skills has become almost exclusively the domain of the schools. While a great deal of controversy may surround *how* the cognitive skills should be taught, there is virtually unanimous agreement that they *should* be taught. The teaching of the 3 Rs (readin', 'ritin', and 'rithmetic) as well as other basic skills is clearly the primary responsibility of the schools.

The role of the school in the transmission of normative culture is not nearly so clearcut, however. The teaching of normative culture involves the transmission of values, norms, attitudes, and beliefs. According to Emile Durkheim ([1906] 1956:71–72):

> [*Education*] *consists of a methodological socialization of the younger generation…* *It is the influence exercised by adult generations on those that are not ready for social life. Its object is to arouse and to develop in the child a certain number of physical, intellectual, and moral states that are demanded of him[/her] by the political society as a whole and for the special milieu for which he[/she] is specifically destined…From the egotistic and asocial being that has just been born, [society] must, as rapidly as possible, add another, capable of leading a moral and social life.*

Two basic questions arise in regard to the school's attempt to promote the internalization of cultural attitudes, values, and beliefs. First, which specific attitudes, values, and beliefs will be taught? Second, how does the school go about teaching them?

The United States is an extremely diverse, culturally pluralistic society composed of many ethnic, religious, economic, and social class subgroups. These various subcultural groups view life from a wide spectrum of value perspectives. Since compulsory attendance laws require that virtually every child attend school for a specified period of time, the widest possible range of cultural values is represented among the student population as they enter school. On the other hand, the school officials who are charged with the socialization task are typically a much less culturally diverse group. For example, teachers tend to come from white, middle class, Protestant backgrounds. Numerous studies have indicated a strong bias favoring the promotion of middle class values in our public schools (e.g., Cicourel, 1968; Jencks et al., 1972; Farkas, et al., 1990). The vastly divergent backgrounds of students in contrast to the predominantly middle class experience of their teachers can lay the groundwork for unfortunate social confrontations and nonproductive learning situations.

In a study of Chicago public schools, Howard Becker (1952) documented teachers' preferences for white middle class children. In a much more shocking exposé, in his book *Death at an Early Age* (1967), Jonathan Kozol described the cynicism, prejudice, and outright racism he saw lower class black students subjected to by white, middle class teachers in the public schools. And 25 years later, in his book *Savage Inequalities,* Kozol (1991) found that the disparities between predominantly black schools and predominantly white school districts had grown greater rather than smaller. Aaron Cicourel (1968) argued that misbehavior, especially delinquent acts, from lower class youths elicited more severe responses from teachers and school administrators than the same behavior from middle and upper class youths. He indicated that school officials tended to view delinquency on the part of students of middle and higher socioeconomic status as out of character and only situational.

Later studies noted similar findings that students from middle class family backgrounds were more likely to have internalized the values of competitiveness, politeness, and deferred gratification which are more likely to lead to success in the public school experience (e.g. Jencks et al., 1971; Braun, 1976). Carl Braun (1976), for example, found that teachers' expectations were importantly influenced by noncognitive variables such as physical attractiveness, socioeconomic status, race, gender, name, and older siblings. His research indicated that teachers expected lower achievement from students who belonged to minority groups, came from economically disadvantaged homes, were physically unattractive, had unusual or unattractive names, or had older brothers or sisters who had been unsuccessful in their school experience. Other research confirmed that teachers' perceptions of students' work habits and conformity to behavioral norms were most directly linked to grades (Farkas, et al., 1990). Undeniably, a student's family background (especially socioeconomic status) has been linked to educational aspirations (Jencks, 1971; Hurn, 1978; Alwin and Thornton, 1984; Astone and McLanahan, 1991), and educational aspirations appear highly related to educational achievement and success in school (Hurn, 1978).

Juvenile Delinquency and the School Experience

Thus far, our discussion has focused on the attempt to socialize students to the dominant value system in the United States and how that relates to a successful school experience. This takes on additional meaning for understanding delinquency when we further view the relationship between the school experience and the process of becoming a juvenile delinquent. Most studies indicate that poor performance in school and negative school experiences are significantly related to juvenile delinquency (e.g., Brownfield, 1990; Arum and Beattie, 1999). That relationship is far more complex than it may appear, however. As pointed out in the Societal Response definition of delinquency, in order for juvenile delinquency to take place, a social audience must react to an actor and an act, and make an evaluation of them in regard to social appropriateness. As further developed by the Labeling Approach, some group must react to the juvenile's behavior and apply the negative label of "delinquent" to it if the juvenile is going to be considered a juvenile delinquent by society. The variable of social power becomes relevant if there is disagreement over the appropriateness of the act. Individuals, groups, and/or social agencies with the power and authority to label juvenile behavior as wrong and place the label "delinquent" on juveniles so that it becomes a part of their identity are critical in creating the "juvenile delinquent." The schools have that power in our society.

Harry Gracey (1977) described how from their first day of school, children are subjected to authoritarian adults who arbitrarily judge students' behavior as "right" or "wrong" and label students as "good" or "bad" based on those judgments. Referring to kindergarten as "academic boot camp," Gracey contended that the primary purpose of kindergarten is not so much the preparation for the academic experience to come in future grades (as contended by most teachers and administrators), as it is to dramatically socialize children into fitting into the bureaucratic structure of the school system. Gracey (1977:217) stated:

> *The unique job of the kindergarten in the education division of labor seems…to be teaching children the student role. The student role is the repertoire of behavior and attitudes regarded by educators as appropriate to children in school.*

Gracey found that learning classroom routines and submitting to rules and authority are the main elements of the student role. To a large extent, successfully fulfilling the student role means "doing what you're told and never mind why" (Gracey, 1977:225). Hence, those students who are most obedient, whose personal values either agree with or have been successfully subjugated to the teacher's, are most likely to be labeled "good students" and have a successful school experience.

In his book *Creating School Failure, Youth Crime and Deviance,* Delos Kelly (1982) further developed this idea and illustrated how the school's initial labeling has lasting impact on the child's entire educational career. Those students who disobey, question authority, refuse to suppress their own values (values gained from early childhood socialization in the family) are more likely to be labeled "bad students" and be unsuccessful in school. Ironically, this early application of the label "delinquent" (or "predelinquent" for younger children) may encompass students at both ends of the intellectual continuum. In other words, students with the least academic potential, along with the most intellectually curious and innovative students, may be the most likely to violate normative expectations of teachers, and end up labeled as "problem students." According to the Labeling Approach, this negative label has impact upon the juvenile's self-concept and very well may influence future behavior which culminates in the **self-fulfilling prophecy.** Students who are labeled early in their educational career as "dumb," "slow," "mean," or "troublemaker" may engage in the types of behavior which are expected to accompany those student roles. Conversely, students labeled as "bright," "gifted," "polite," and "obedient" are likely to conform to the positive expectations entailed in those roles. A possible example of this may be revealed in the findings that participation in school athletics serves as an insulator against delinquency for some students (e.g., Hastad et al., 1984; Segrave and Hastad, 1984).

Of course, not all negative labels are initiated at school. Parents, neighbors, police, and juvenile courts also may judge certain children to be more problematic than others. Consequently, negative labels and poor self-concepts can be brought from outside the school. In fact, Allen Liska and Mark Reed (1985) contended that parents, not the schools, were the major institutional sources of delinquency control. They found that "...for most adolescents in high school, the good opinion of teachers and school administrators may be considerably less important than that of their parents" (Liska and Reed, 1985:558). The extent to which these factors affect the educational process is not clearly understood, but there is some evidence that they may negatively impact upon the school experience. For example, Kelly (1977) showed that juvenile delinquents, or at least those who had been officially identified by the legal system, were at a significant disadvantage in the classroom.

Schools as a "Screening Device"

One of the important functions of the educational institution in our society is to acknowledge academic performance and intellectual development through the awarding of academic credentials. In this sense, the school is designed to serve as a "screening device." Ideally, everybody in our society is supposed to be provided an equal opportunity in terms of access to our educational system. This supposition is, of course, highly questionable, since we know that individuals have been denied equal access to education on the basis of race, ethnic background, and other social variables. Nevertheless, it has become widely proclaimed in our society that the opportunity for education is a right, and not a privilege. Though everybody is supposedly given equal access to the academic credentials offered by our educational system, it never has been expected that everybody would attain them equally. As Peter and Brigitte Berger (1975:188) indicated, "Since the educational system contains an endless series of hurdles, it is important that not all should succeed in it; it is predetermined that some (indeed, many) should fail to reach the top." Those who have the most potential, work the hardest, and learn the most are viewed as having legitimately earned higher academic recognition than the rest. We logically conclude that our high school graduates are smarter and more diligent than those who dropped out, but not as smart and diligent as those who have earned college degrees. Likewise, Bachelor's degrees signify something different from Master's degrees, and Master's degrees something different from Doctoral degrees. The assumption is that virtually everybody aspires to the highest level of academic certification (a highly questionable assumption), but the schools effectively "screen out" those who are not qualified, so that only the most "deserving" attain the highest credentials (an even more questionable assumption). These academic credentials, in turn, are then used in a variety of ways which affect occupation, income, housing, and virtually all components of lifestyle and social status (Collins, 1971).

The basis for this "screening device" may very well be variables other than intelligence, diligence, and academic performance. Edgar Friedenberg (1959) made a strong case that academic credentials do not certify ability, but the acceptance of larger society's dominant values and norms. Friedenberg contended that academic credentials, more than intelligence and academic performance, serve to signify an individual's willingness to endure the rules. In this sense, he argued that schools tend to preserve the status quo by guaranteeing that those

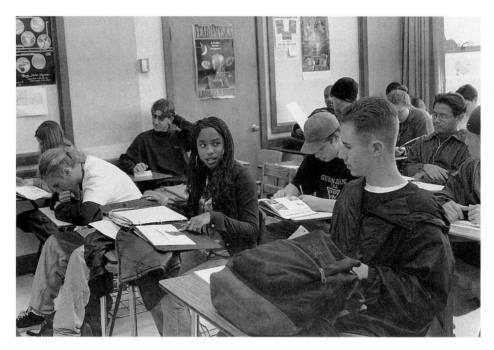

Public schools attract a diverse student body from a wide variety of social backgrounds and value systems. Some research indicates that conformity to dominant norms becomes a major factor in whether students succeed in school or have problems, some of which may lead to juvenile delinquency.

who fail in school also fail in society—a point substantiated by research (e.g., Monk-Turner, 1989). From this perspective, it is no wonder that failure in school and juvenile delinquency are closely related. This phenomenon is not limited to the United States (see Box 10-1).

Mark Colvin and John Pauly (1983) elaborated upon the relationship between family background, school failure, and juvenile delinquency. They pointed out that socioeconomic status of the child's family has been linked to school "tracking," which to a large extent determines a student's immediate peer group. **Tracking** refers to *an educational strategy in which students considered to be roughly equivalent in intelligence, based upon standardized tests, previous academic performance, and other criteria, are placed in the same classroom,* and can have important impact on a child's academic achievement (Gamoran, 1992). Students in a particular "track" often also resemble each other in a variety of ways other than academic abilities. Sometimes, students who have reputations as "behavioral problems" may be placed in the same class, and placed under the supervision of a teacher with the reputation of being a strict disciplinarian. Colvin and Pauly indicated that the initial bond to the school is developed at home by the family, but may be reinforced or weakened by the immediate peer group at school. If placed in a social setting in the school where a

BOX 10-1   Cross-Cultural Focus

Self-Concept and Delinquency Among Chinese School Children

Americans typically perceive Chinese youths as bright, passive, and above all, respectful to their teachers and parents. Rarely do we think of China as having a delinquency problem, and little research appears in U.S. journals on this phenomenon. Young criminal offenders have become a major concern in contemporary China, however. Chinese law provides that youths under the age of sixteen are held criminally liable only if they have committed homicide, robbery, arson, or some other serious offense which greatly threatens social order. Most youthful offenders commit relatively minor infractions and are handled through neighborhood tribunal committees and other local administrative agencies. The handling of juvenile cases and the operation of youth reformatories in China falls under the supervision of the Ministry of Education.

In China, as in the United States, schools not only teach cognitive skills, but also play an important role in the overall socialization process. Students are expected to show great deference and respect to their teachers, and strict conformity to rules is as important

as high academic performance. In this way, Chinese schools act as a screening device, and professors Kwok Leung and Sing Lau (1989) indicated that the relationship between poor school performance and delinquency in China is not appreciably different from that experienced in the United States.

Leung and Lau studied 1,668 seventh- and ninth-grade students in Hong Kong in an effort to determine the relationship between academic performance and self-concept, and the relationship between poor self-concept and delinquency. They summarized that youths who were unsuccessful and frustrated in school often turn to peers for their major source of approval as opposed to parents and teachers. In this peer reference group, they usually seek out and find others who share similar frustrations in school and support delinquent values and behavior. Findings from this study suggest that consistent with studies of U.S. students, peer approval had a stronger influence on self-concept and the promotion of delinquent behavior than the countervailing influence of teachers and parents combined.

Sources

Leung, Kwok, and Sing Lau. "Effects of self-concept and perceived disapproval of delinquent behavior in school children." *Journal of Youth and Adolescence* 18 (August), 1989:345–359.

Worder, Robert L., Sarada, Andrea M., and Dolan, Ronald E. *Criminal justice and public security in China: A country study* (4th Ed.), 1988.

student is surrounded by delinquent peers, "this type of association continues the pattern of reinforcement toward more sustained delinquent behavior" (Colvin and Pauly, 1983:543).

A variety of social cliques tend to form in the school environment. J. Milton Yinger (1982:274) pointed out that the "standard high school subcultures, with their emphasis on sports, fun, and a modicum of learning, are quite different in sociological meaning from groups oriented to truancy, petty theft, masculine hyperaggressiveness, and gang combat." To a large extent, Yinger attributed the youth's fear of failure as part of the motivation to join deviant groups.

High school represents a "defining moment" in most young people's lives (Beattie, 1999:515). School hallways are becoming increasingly an arena of "haves" and "have-nots" and students from less affluent homes and neighborhoods find they are often relegated to lower social standing in school (Johnson, 1998). In large part, a youth's status and social identity are directly connected to school performance. Carl Werthman (1976) compared the identity needs and materials available to adults and to youths. In our society, adult status and identity are typically gained through occupations and affluence. Young males (especially from lower classes), without access to the materials with which to build male identity and social status, will use whatever materials are available in their environment. They may assert their autonomy by fighting with other students or rejecting the rules and authority of the school. The adult authority figures and the normative structure of the school offer a situation of confrontation and risk in which the youth can gain a measure of identity and status from peers. On the other hand, the aggressive, rebellious stance is interpreted by school officials as a predisposition to delinquency and the stage is set for further confrontation and struggle. Research suggests that if these males work while in school, although they may be able to buy some of the material possessions that enhance their status, they may still be more likely to become involved in delinquency (Wright et al., 1997).

Walter Schafer and Kenneth Polk (1976) reported another possible dimension of the school's role in projecting youths into delinquent behavior. They pointed out that educators often perceive a correlation between educational deficiencies and behavior problems and therefore categorically define some youngsters as "stupid" or "bad." As these children become aware of this negative evaluation, their alienation is deepened and they increase their truancy and other forms of delinquency. The possible link between low intelligence and/or learning disabilities and juvenile delinquency is unclear. The hypothesis that "academic competence is linked to delinquency by way of success in and attachment to the school" has been very popular (Hirschi, 1969:115). Travis Hirschi and Michael Hindelang (1977) contended that IQ is an important but frequently ignored variable in juvenile delinquency. Margaret Farnworth and her associates (1985) indeed found that intervention prior to school entry that improves academic potential and future school performance for children categorized as "high risk" for school failure may in fact reduce the likelihood of delinquency. However, they contended that the impact of the preschool intervention was independent of IQ scores.

Much of the apparent link between low IQ, learning disabilities, poor school performance, and juvenile delinquency has been seriously challenged. For instance, Bruce Lane (1980) reviewed the research examining the connection between juvenile delinquency and learning disabilities, and explained that no clear relationship has been established between the two. A study of 12 to 15-year-old boys, separated into groups of learning disabled and nonlearning disabled, indicated no more delinquency on the part of the learning disabled than the others (Broder et al., 1981). Interestingly, however, Paul Broder and his associates (1981) found that the learning disabled group members were more likely to be adjudicated delinquent by juvenile courts. Scott Menard and Barbara Morse (1984) reported similar findings. They argued that the IQ-delinquency hypothesis lacks empirical support and adds nothing to delinquency theory. They indicated that the correlation of IQ with delinquency is not because IQ exerts a causal influence on delinquent behavior, but because, in the schools, it may be selected as the criterion for differential treatment. Another study found that while learning disabled and nonlearning disabled students engage in essentially the same behaviors, learning disabled children are treated differently and are more likely to be considered delinquent (Keilitz et al., 1979).

Dropout and delinquency rates vary greatly across communities, and socioeconomic status, race and ethnicity, and other social and economic variables have been shown to be importantly related to both (Figueira-McDonough, 1993; McNeal, 1997). School dropouts tend to have a hard time finding jobs, and girls who drop out are more likely to become pregnant than those who stay in school (Cantelon and LeBoeuf, 1997). Delbert Elliott (1966) expanded on the problems experienced by some youngsters at school and the alternative responses open to them. Elliott presented some interesting data and hypotheses regarding the variable rates of delinquency for boys from different socioeconomic neighborhoods who dropped out of school. His and later studies (Elliott and Voss, 1974; Jarjoura, 1996), showed that while in school, lower class boys had higher rates of delinquency, but as suggested by strain theories, after lower class boys dropped out of school and took a job, their delinquency rates dropped dramatically. Conversely, middle class boys' delinquency tends to increase when they drop out of school (Jarjoura, 1996). Colvin and Pauly (1983) provided additional insight into why this may occur. While in school, lower class boys experience a great deal of failure. Failure in school may have made these boys "more receptive to the influence of delinquent groups in which they learn specific attitudes, motives, and skills to produce patterned delinquent behavior" (Colvin and Pauly, 1983:524). Out of school, these lower class boys moved into a setting where they could experience some success. Terence Thornberry and his associates (1985) questioned the methodology of these studies, however, and by using longitudinal data from a Philadelphia sample they determined that dropping out of school was positively related to delinquency and later crime over both the short and the long term. Their study indicated more support for the Social Control Theory approach, in that the severing of the social bond with the school apparently resulted in increased delinquency. On the other hand, subsequent studies continue to question the relationship between dropping out of school and later delinquency involvement (Jarjoura, 1993; Figueira-McDonough, 1993; Jarjoura, 1996), and one study even suggests that secondary education related to occupational training lowers the likelihood of delinquency and adult crime (Arum and Beattie, 1999).

J. David Hawkins and Denise Lishner (1987) developed a theoretical model which illustrates how the aforementioned school experiences may be related to juvenile delinquency (see Figure 10-1). The series of arrows in Figure 10-1 show how each of the school-related risk factors is directly and indirectly linked to juvenile delinquency among males. The figure also illustrates both direct and indirect interrelationships among the variables. Finally, the model depicts how these risk factors are also related to dropping out of school. It is important to note that there is no direct relationship indicated between dropping out of school and increased juvenile delinquency among males. Rather, consistent with the research of Elliott (1966) and Elliott and Voss (1974), the model suggests that both delinquency and dropping out are the result of similar negative school experiences. This supports the "...contention that school experiences themselves are factors in delinquent behavior, which, when removed, no longer contribute to [delinquency]" (Hawkins and Lishner, 1987:186). It also supports research findings that dropping out of school may be viewed as the culmination of a long-term process of academic disengagement (Alexander et al., 1997).

One form of delinquency which grows directly from problems in school is that of truancy. In some cities, truancy rates run as high as 30 percent, and there is mounting evidence that juveniles who skip school are more likely to get involved in alcohol, drugs, gangs, and violence (Garry, 1996). Students who are having difficulty in school are most likely to be truant. As Jacob Getzels (1977:74) put it:

What can be more tormenting than to be confronted day after day with a situation in which the language, and value codes seem different in inexplicable ways from those to which you are accustomed—and more a situation in which you cannot

FIGURE 10-1   School-Related Risk Factors for Individual Delinquency Among Males

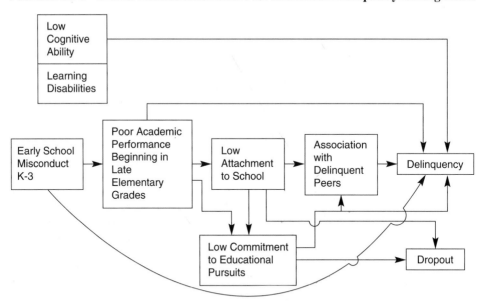

Source: J. David Hawkins and Denise M. Lishner. "Schooling and Delinquency." Pp. 179–221 in Elmer H. Johnson (Ed.), *Handbook on Crime and Delinquency Prevention.* Westport, Connecticut: Greenwood Press (1987), p. 185. Copyright © 1987 by Elmer H. Johnson. Reprinted with permission of Greenwood Publishing Group, Inc.

succeed and from which you are not permitted to escape without threat of severe punishment?

Truancy has become such a problem in some districts that administrators are actually willing to pay students to attend school. For example, at Memorial Junior High in San Diego, the school truancy rate was so high that the school began to pay students 25 cents a day to attend school (Tedrick, 1980:7). The special problem of truancy and what some school districts are doing to deal with it are explored further in Box 10-2.

One of the ways that schools act as a "screening device" is to (perhaps unintentionally) drive away those students who cannot succeed there. As these students grow more frustrated they are much more likely to skip school. Gayle Zieman and Gerald Benson (1980) interviewed junior high school boys who had histories of truancy, and found that they perceived the school as a place of discomfort associated with confrontations and lack of success. Most states have a compulsory attendance law up to a certain age (usually 16) and students below the legal age for dropping out are delinquent by virtue of their truancy.

Beyond the simple act of truancy making the juvenile a delinquent, the juvenile is also likely to get into other kinds of trouble while wandering the streets when school is in session. While this may not be the case when older students drop out to take full-time jobs (Elliott, 1966), it is highly probable that younger students who skip school periodically, to

BOX 10-2 Controversial Issue

"Dealing with the Problem of Truancy"

Most children read of the exploits of Tom Sawyer and Huckleberry Finn with a great deal of excitement, enjoyment, and envy. Those two characters prowled the banks of the Mississippi River, having more fun and excitement in a day than most kids can anticipate in a lifetime. They fished, rafted, chewed tobacco, fought, explored, cussed, and created mischief in a way that Mark Twain portrayed as humorous, enjoyable, and downright lovable. A great many of their exploits occurred while they were in the process of "playing hookey" from school.

Truancy, or "skipping school," is a major problem for families, school districts, and communities across the nation. It is a problem for families, because children are not in school where their parents assume them to be, and they are not receiving the education for which their parents are paying (in the form of taxes, and, in some cases, tuition and other costs). It poses numerous problems for the school. One is that like the parents, school officials do not know where the child is—only where the child is not. Questions of legal responsibility arise if a student is injured while truant. Parents assume the child to be in school, while school officials assume the child stayed home. In such cases, the question of liability is sometimes one that must be determined by the court.

If the student is not hurt, the school still may be. In many states, local school districts are funded on the basis of their ADA (Average Daily Attendance). This means that school funding is based upon some type of formula which pays a specific amount of money per student per day of attendance. Thus, when students are absent, money is lost to the school district. In a large district, truancy can reduce the operating budget by several thousand dollars per year.

Truancy also poses a variety of problems for the community, not the least of which is the crime and mischief youths are likely to engage in while wandering the streets. Vandalism, theft, and other property crimes, along with problems of policing youths who are supposed to be in school, make truancy a nuisance in some communities and a major problem in others. Truancy has been described as a "stepping stone" to other forms of delinquency, and research suggests that students who skip school are often drawn to be-

haviors involving alcohol, drugs, property crimes, gang activities, and violence (Garry, 1996).

As a result of these problems and others, numerous attempts have been made to reduce truancy. Many of these attempts have focused upon more closely policing juveniles in an effort to apprehend truants and return them to school. Ironically, in some school districts, the punishment for truancy is some type of formal suspension from school! Hence, a juvenile who hates school, skips it, and then gets caught, may find that for the next 3 to 5 days it is not necessary to be truant to escape the agony of school. Nevertheless, that is the extent of the efforts of some districts at reducing the problem of truancy.

On the other hand, some districts have been more creative in their efforts to keep students in school. For instance, one school district in Chula Vista, California, adopted a program called "Operation Stay in School" (Superintendent's Communicator, 1982). While it also involves "rounding up" truant students from the streets, it focuses the combined efforts of parents, police, probation officers, and school district staff on preventing truancy. In this program, "spot sweeps" are made of various locations in the area and students who are truant are apprehended and taken to a receiving center to be returned to their parents or guardians. Immediate follow-up action involves counseling whereby everyone is made aware of the legal, social, and personal problems associated with truancy. Results of this program have included improved attendance, reduced vandalism, and a reduction in daytime burglaries. Similarly, in Oklahoma City, a massive effort in which police, school officials, and the community seek to round up truants and place them in an alternative school called THRIVE (Truancy Habits Reduced, Increasing Valuable Education) has been quite successful in reducing truancy and its associated delinquency (Ryan, 1991).

Other districts have been much more innovative and controversial in their battles against truancy. Boston's public schools offer cash to students with perfect or near-perfect attendance and give alarm clocks to students who claim they were absent or tardy because they overslept (AP, Boston, 1998). Memorial Junior High School had the highest truancy

Continued

BOX 10-2 *Continued*

rate in San Diego, California, in 1979, and consequently, lost approximately $132,000 in state attendance funds (Tedrick, 1980). In an effort to reduce the truancy problem, the school began the "cash-for-class" program. For each day of school attendance, the student receives a card stamped "25 cents." Perfect attendance is worth $5 per month. Many argue that students should not be paid, but according to the principal, students aren't really being paid to go to school, but are being rewarded for their attendance. The "pay can be spent only for school-related items such as paper, notebooks, library fines, concerts, and gym clothes and for wholesome foods such as apples and milk" (Tedrick, 1980:7).

The Spring Valley Schools in California developed a lottery of sorts in an effort to reduce their truancy rates (*CNN News,* September 22, 1986). The school decided to give away 73 $1,000 U.S. Savings Bonds at the end of the academic year. All seventh and eighth graders with two or fewer absences were eligible to enter the contest.

A more controversial solution to the truancy problem might be to eliminate compulsory attendance laws, or at least reduce the age limit for mandatory attendance. When juveniles in their midteens feel totally alienated from school, it is unlikely that any creative endeavor to thwart truancy will lure

them into regular school attendance. While Gary, Indiana, did not totally eliminate its compulsory attendance law, it developed an experimental program to alleviate truancy among some of its most chronic habitual truants. These students attended a special school that met for only half a day. Reading and writing were emphasized, but so were free time, drawing, and other activities. Lessons were designed to ensure that students experienced some type of success each day. Interestingly, although attendance was not compulsory, truancy was no longer a problem (Robison, 1960:482–483).

In a society that highly values education, the elimination of compulsory attendance laws sparks heated debate. It should be remembered, however, that compulsory attendance and compulsory education are not synonymous. Those who favor abolition of compulsory attendance laws often cite the old adage: "You can lead a horse to water, but you can't make it drink." Some students simply do not want to be in school and they turn their dislike of school and teachers into disruption, intimidation, harassment, and even violence—creating an environment of fear and frustration (Lawrence, 1998). It is doubtful that much is accomplished educationally when teenagers are forced to attend school against their will.

Sources

AP, Boston, 1999. Schools offerintg cash, clocks to beef up attendance. *The News Telegram,* September 2:5.
CNN News. 1986. Schools attempt to cut truancy, September 22.
Garry, E. M. 1996. Truancy: First step to a lifetime of problems. *Juvenile Justice Bulletin.* Washington, DC: U.S. Dept. of Justice, Office of Juvenile Justice and Delinquency Prevention.
Lawrence, R. 1998. School crime and juvenile justice. New York: Oxford University Press.
Robison, S. M. 1960. *Juvenile delinquency: Its nature and control.* New York: Holt, Rinehart and Winston.
Ryan, M. 1991. They don't skip school anymore. *Parade Magazine* (Sept. 8):8.
Superintendent's Communicator. 1982. Operation stay in school, *Superintendent's Communicator 3* (Sept. 30):2.
Tedrick, D. 1980. School will pay students to cut rate of truancy. AP, San Diego, Emporia Gazette November 1:7.

frequent pool halls, video arcades, shopping malls, or simply roam the streets, are very likely to get involved in other forms of delinquency beyond their truancy. In some cities, police routinely make daytime sweeps of shopping malls searching for truant youths (NBC Nightly News, 1997). By virtue of being on the streets or in malls during school hours, the juvenile is highly visible to police and may be routinely picked up, questioned, and possibly searched. In these cases, the general behavior of the youth which earned a reputation or label of being "smart aleck," "out of control," and "bad" at school is also likely to compound potential problems with the police. As several studies point out, the overall demeanor of juveniles as perceived by the police becomes one of the most significant variables in determining how the police handle the case (Piliavin and Briar, 1964; Lundman, 1996).

Schools as "Combat Zones"

Failing grades, truancy, and dropping out are only some of the responses available to students who do not succeed in the school system. Another way they can respond to the value conflict, frustration, and damage to self-concept that they experience is to fight back. As William Glasser (1978) pointed out, students who cannot cope with an unsuccessful school experience feel they have essentially two options: drop out, or go to school and cause trouble. Compulsory attendance laws can limit those options to the latter, turning some schools into what amount to "combat zones."

One of the prominent psychological explanations of human violence which was developed in the 1930s is the Frustration-Aggression Hypothesis. According to John Dollard and his colleagues (1939), frustration arises when an individual is unable to reach some desired goal. This frustration is then vented in the form of aggressive behavior. While there is much disagreement over the causal link between frustration and aggression today (especially over the early assumption that frustration *must* lead to aggression), it is generally agreed that frustration certainly *can* lead to aggression. Likewise, Merton's Anomie Theory contends that juveniles who cannot pursue culturally prescribed goals through socially approved means become frustrated and often pursue a deviant adaptation strategy to the situation. Given this, it is not totally unexpected that when students find themselves at odds with the school system, are negatively labeled, and cannot achieve success through the approved standards, they will become frustrated. That frustration may be relieved by dropping out (if they are allowed to), or it may be vented through wreaking havoc on the school, teachers, and other students.

Vandalism and Destruction

Juveniles sometimes strike back at the schools with vandalism and destruction. William Sanders (1976:101) reported that schools are the most common target of **malevolent vandalism**—*"activity in which property is destroyed out of malevolent motives on the part of the perpetrators."* The school becomes the target of vandalism because of the juveniles' contempt for the institution. Paul Chance (1984) indicated that vandalism is primarily a result of not liking school and feeling disliked by teachers and administrators. Estimates of the total annual cost of school vandalism in the United States ranged between $100 million to $600 million over 20 years ago (cited in Neill, 1978:305). Today, no comprehensive figures on school vandalism are even kept, but it is safe to assume that the figure is much higher. Vandalism is a property offense and generally not considered to be a violent act. But in this situation we are not referring to the petty types of vandalism which routinely occur at most schools, such as seniors spray painting the year of their graduating class on the sign in front of the building. Although even those types of acts can be costly, they are primarily engaged in for fun and mischief. Rather, we are referring to massive attacks on school property.

James Truckenmiller (1982) identified students' perceived lack of access to educational success as one of the variables most predictive of vandalism. School districts are acutely aware of the problems associated with school vandalism, and many have taken steps to create programs in an effort to reduce it. G. Ray Mayer et al. (1983) reported the results of a 3-year study of 20 schools from 12 school districts which showed that educators could take positive steps to reduce vandalism and other forms of inappropriate student behavior. Patricia Stagliano and Irwin Hyman (1983) found that implementing student conduct codes, student-teacher-community task forces, community training, and legislation requiring the monitoring of school vandalism had all met with at least some success.

Violence and Personal Attacks

Vandalism is not the only form that violence takes in the schools. Sometimes the frustration and anger felt toward the educational system are more openly directed against the teachers and administrators who represent it. Ron Halvorsen and Donald Hawley (1973:56) described the "combat conditions" of teaching in some of the poorer sections of Brooklyn:

> *The school tool shed had a telephone in it, and if things got too difficult an instructor could make a run for it, lock himself in, and then telephone for help. In one classroom the students suspended the teacher out of a fifth-floor window, threatening him, "Teach, if you assign any homework today, we're going to drop you."*

A study of 253 classroom teachers in the Los Angeles public school system in the 1970s indicated that 28 percent of those teachers actually had suffered physical assault (Bloch, 1978). It went on to describe how the reactions to long-term stress among these 253 teachers were extremely similar to combat neurosis. And, in 1991, assaults on teachers had become so common in the state of Florida that three state legislators introduced a bill to allow teachers to zap unruly students with electric "stun guns" (AP Tallahassee, 1991).

A Senate subcommittee report on juvenile delinquency concluded that school violence in the form of vandalism and attacks on people was definitely on the increase (Bayh, 1975). A similar subcommittee report found that the types of crimes found in the public schools encompassed virtually every type of crime found on the streets, including fatal beatings, stabbings, and even rapes of both students and teachers (U.S. Senate Subcommittee on Delinquency, 1977:7–10). The same report found that an alarming number of students were arming themselves with knives and guns for personal protection.

A National Institute of Education report in 1978 indicated that over a quarter of a million secondary school students were physically attacked by other students each month, and blamed some truancy problems on students' fear for their personal safety (Okaty, 1991). A subsequent study by the U.S. Department of Education estimated that 3 million violent crimes and thefts occur per year in U.S. public schools—an average of 16,000 crimes per day (Johnson, 1993). And, an APA Commission report estimated that kids carry an estimated 270,000 guns to school every day (Fields, 1993). Fear of violent attacks is increased when fatal shootings or stabbings over something as trivial as a cigarette lighter are reported (AP, Webbers Falls, OK, 1997).

School violence peaked in the United States during the 1992–93 academic year, but a series of tragic shootings in American schools during the late 1990s focused worldwide attention on schools as "combat zones." A 16-year-old boy rumored to be part of a Satanic cult shot nine of his high school classmates fatally wounding two in Pearl, Mississippi in October of 1997, and only two months later three students were killed and five others wounded in a shooting at Heath High School in West Paducah, Kentucky. Americans were still reeling from the shock of these two school shootings when in March of 1998, two boys, aged 11 and 13 killed four girls and a teacher and wounded 10 other students during a false fire alarm at a middle school in Jonesboro, Arkansas. A month later, a science teacher was shot to death and two students were wounded at an eighth-grade dance in Edinboro, Pennsylvania. The following month, May of 1998, saw two fatal shootings within two days as an 18-year-old honors student killed a classmate in a high school parking lot in Fayetteville, Tennessee, and a 17-year-old boy in Springfield, Oregon opened fire at a high school, killing two and wounding 20 others, after having murdered his parents in their home. On April

Students and teachers flee Columbine High School under police supervision during the 1999 shooting rampage that left 14 students (including the two shooters) and one teacher dead and 23 wounded.

20, 1999, two students entered Columbine High School in Littleton, Colorado, clad in black trench coats and armed with several high-powered weapons and bombs. Before the rampage ended, 12 students and a teacher had been shot to death, 23 students had been wounded, and the two boys had turned the guns on themselves and committed suicide. Police estimated that if the killers had successfully discharged the bombs as planned, hundreds of students and teachers would have been killed or seriously wounded.

These events, like others that preceded them and still others that followed, including a shocking incident in which a first grade girl was shot and murdered in a Michigan elementary school by a six-year-old classmate, reminded Americans that children are not safe from violence even when at school. They also signaled a change in the nature of school violence. Prior to these mass shootings, violence in schools tended to be more one-on-one and motivated by some particular incident between the two students involved. These violent incidents involved large numbers of victims and were much more random in nature. Thus, although the number of specific violent incidents in schools actually decreased during the years 1993 to 2000, the numbers of students killed or injured in such incidents and the sensational nature of the violence in many of these episodes dramatically increased.

Data on school crime are a bit difficult to collect and assess because schools' disclosure of crime information varies greatly from one school district to another. Although colleges and universities are now required to compile campus crime statistics and release them to the public, no similar requirements exists for U.S. elementary and secondary schools. In 1993, President Clinton proposed that a campus-by-campus computerized crime report should be compiled by all schools, kindergarten through 12th grade, so that parents would be aware of potential threats to their children's safety while at school, and after the tragic shooting at West Paducah High School in 1997, President Clinton directed the U.S. Department of Education and Justice to prepare an annual report on school safety.

Even grade schoolers are susceptible to the violence of other students, and often live in fear of the school bullies who torment and sometimes assault them (Herndon, 1993; Annual Report on School Safety, 1998). Studies estimate that one in seven school-aged children is either a bully or a victim, and that this problem directly affects almost five million elementary and junior high school students in this country (Roberts, 1988:52). Referring to this phenomenon as peer terrorism, school authorities from across the United States met at Harvard University in 1987 for a "Schoolyard Bully Practicum" (Bergmann, 1987:A-8). The event, sponsored by the National School Safety Center, emphasized the need for awareness of the widespread problem of violent assaults on the school playgrounds. One school official indicated that these are not just "kids being kids," but are violent attacks against young people (Bergmann, 1987:A-8). Consequently, many students who are the victims of such violence approach their school day with fear and trepidation.

Joan McDermott (1983) examined research on crime and the fear of crime and victimization in the school and community. She suggested that crime and the fear of crime should be viewed in a community context since schools which experienced high rates of crime tended to be located in high-crime neighborhoods. A longitudinal study of 532 young black males and their parents in Philadelphia seems to substantiate McDermott's assumption. In that study, it was found that both the juveniles and their parents had extremely high rates of fear about the boys being victims of crime in the school environment (Savitz et al., 1978). Over one-half of the boys indicated that they had been the victims of robbery, assault, or extortion. Even those who had not been victimized personally expressed a great deal of fear. These youths indicated that they greatly feared being mugged, robbed, and even murdered in school rooms, school hallways, school yards, streets, playgrounds, recreation centers, movie theaters, dance halls, and on public transportation. The study found that parental and juvenile fear of school-based crime was alleviated by truancy, joining gangs for protection, and even relocation to safer schools in safer neighborhoods (Savitz et al., 1978).

Whether high crime neighborhoods lead to crime in the schools, or crime in the schools leads to high crime neighborhoods, has developed as an interesting sociological question. One study found that geographic proximity to a high school increased the likelihood of crime in neighborhoods in San Diego (Roncek and LoBosco, 1983). In fact, that study indicated that residential areas adjacent to public high schools experienced more crime than areas that were more than a block away from those same schools. Dennis Roncek and Donald Faggiani (1985) replicated that study in the city of Cleveland, and discovered similar findings. These studies suggest that crime and violence in the schools, like any other social problem, must be viewed within their broader sociological context, as opposed to being viewed as isolated acts. Crime does not occur in schools in isolation from crime in the rest of society (Lawrence, 1998).

Overgeneralizations are dangerous, and it would be a gross exaggeration to conclude that very many of today's youths are violent sociopaths ransacking the schools and terrorizing administrators, teachers, and fellow students. Nevertheless, the increasing rates of truancy, vandalism, and student violence indicate a significant problem for our schools in regard to juvenile delinquency.

School Safety and "Zero Tolerance"

In many communities, parents are not sitting idly by while their children are being robbed, bullied, and assaulted at school. For example, at Arlington High School in Indianapolis, things became so bad that some concerned fathers formed a group known as "Security Dads" who with the cooperation of school officials took it upon themselves to spend several hours per day patrolling the halls and campus in order to provide a safer environment for their children to attend school (Whittemore, 1992). The Indianapolis story is but one example of how parents can make a difference, and experts almost unanimously agree that parents can make schools safer by simply spending more time there with their children (Greer, 1993).

School officials are very aware of the necessity to provide a safe and secure environment for students, faculty, and all those who enter the school domain. In some schools this has prompted the stationing of full-time uniformed police officers or security guards within the schools. Other schools require all students, school personnel, and visitors to pass through metal detectors upon entrance to school buildings, while still others conduct random checks for weapons, drugs, or other forms of contraband and potentially dangerous items. Additionally, a number of schools prohibit the use of backpacks or book bags that might be used to conceal a weapon or some other dangerous or controlled substance. In an effort to reduce crimes and violence in schools, many school districts participate in a federally funded "Zero Tolerance" program whose aim is to establish schools as "gun-free" and "drug-free" zones. Although it may be defined somewhat differently by various school districts **zero tolerance** generally refers to *school policies that prohibit the possession, use, sale, or supply of any type of weapon, alcohol, or illegal drug on school premises or at any school-related functions.*

These programs, for the most part, have enjoyed fairly widespread public support, but they have not been without their problems and critics. Some argue that the presence of uniformed and armed guards in school buildings convey precisely the wrong image for students, and may inadvertently create a more hostile and potentially violent atmosphere. Others argue that students' constitutional rights are violated when they are required to pass through metal detectors or are subjected to random stops and searches for weapons or drugs without probable cause. And, in some high-profile cases, the zero-tolerance policies of some schools have received widespread media attention for their bureaucratic absurdity as children have been suspended over the possession of nail clippers, mouthwash, or over-the-counter pain relievers (Thompson and Hickey, 1999). Nevertheless, school administrators often find themselves in a very difficult situation when faced with the need to provide an open, inviting, and pleasant learning environment while at the same time trying to ensure that schools are safe and secure.

School as Bureaucracy

Beyond the outright hostility some students express toward the school as a result of their failure, or their inability to relate to the dominant values being expressed there, is the more subtle problem experienced by students in regard to dealing with the bureaucratic structure of the school. Max Weber ([1922]1968) indicated that **bureaucracy** as an *ideal type* is typified by: *a clearcut division of labor; a hierarchy of authority; an elaborate system of rules and regulations; people treated as "cases," not as "individuals"; and a clearcut career pattern for those working within the bureaucracy.* Clearly, the public schools meet the criteria for bureaucracy.

The bureaucratic elements which may create the most significant problems for students are those regarding the elaborate system of rules and regulations and the fact that people often are treated as cases rather than individuals. Certainly, no school could operate without a set of rules and regulations. However, in some situations, the schools, at least as perceived by many of the students, have adopted so many rules and regulations that it becomes virtually impossible to abide by all of them. Further, it seems that in some cases, the rules take precedence over the people who must enforce and abide by them. Rules for the sake of rules are likely to be broken for the sake of breaking them.

Ralph Hummel (1977) discussed the lack of purpose and frustration people experience in a bureaucratic structure. Students who feel they are being treated like numbers, rather than people, are likely to develop a sense of alienation in the school environment. The assembly line model of education which has dominated our educational philosophy since the industrial revolution has led to viewing schools as analogous to factories. Thus, incoming students are seen as raw materials to be shaped, molded, and transformed into finished products (i.e., productive citizens) by those trained and skilled to do so (the teachers). Students' views of teachers and teachers' views of students are affected by the roles they are forced to fulfill within the bureaucratic structure. Students often are amazed to discover that their teachers have a life outside the bureaucratic structure of the school.

The depersonalization, and, in some cases, the dehumanization of the educational process in contemporary U.S. society have taken their toll on young people. Standardized testing, tracking, technological teaching devices, and a variety of other developments in education undoubtedly have made positive contributions to the educational endeavor. However, on the negative side, it must be noted that these developments also have led to increased bureaucratization of the schools. The students, forced to survive in this bureaucratic structure, may find themselves unable or unwilling to cope with it, and hence become involved in a variety of nonconforming activities leading to delinquency.

Schools and Delinquency Prevention

Because of the school's significant role in the socialization of U.S. youth, a large part of the responsibility for preventing delinquency seems to fall upon the school system. Unfortunately, to a large extent, educators and administrators have interpreted this responsibility as meaning they should be on the lookout for those youths most likely to cause trouble, commit delinquent acts, and become adult criminals. This emphasis on individual pathology as an explanation for deviance has been nonproductive and extremely unsuccessful, and the use of standardized tests for predicting potential problem students has come under increased fire. Despite the widespread use of standardized personality inventories, aptitude tests, achievement tests, and tracking, the problem of delinquency has increased rather than diminished.

As pointed out in the earlier discussion on the labeling processes in the schools, these developments in education have, if anything, compounded the problems of delinquency rather than alleviated them. As more potential delinquents are identified, labeled, and acted upon, it is likely that more actual delinquents are produced.

Perhaps one of the most enlightened discussions of this problem and suggestions for modification is provided by Delos Kelly (1982:122):

> *If change is to come about, then I believe that it must begin with the educational system. Not only is this one of our basic social institutions but most children spend at least ten years or more within the system; they also spend many hours each day in school. The same does not exist with many families or the community.*

He goes on to point out that the problems of stereotyping, labeling, degrading, tracking, and programming failure into certain students must be stopped. Kelly (1982: 123-124) calls for an all-out resocialization of parents, teachers, educators, and students in regard to the success-fail philosophy of the schools.

The teacher plays a tremendously significant role in any strategy of changing the orientation of schools in such a way as to eliminate some of the problems of delinquency. Eliminating failure and making students feel accepted and cared for are viable approaches to solving many of the discipline problems in the public schools, and teachers play the most vital role in implementing any school-based strategy for delinquency prevention (Glasser, 1978; Kimbrough, 1986). According to Carl Werthman (1976), when faced with situations in the classroom which threaten serious disruption, the teacher can respond in one of three ways. The teacher can simply overlook any activities other than learning which take place in the classroom, and essentially attempt to teach those who are apparently willing to learn. Rarely do serious problems erupt, because the teacher fails to acknowledge the activities of those who are trying to disrupt the educational process. A second strategy is for the teacher actually to briefly participate in the disruption. Minor disruptions, such as jumping to the window to see a passing firetruck or discussing last night's homecoming game, do not have to be elevated into teacher-student confrontations if the teacher is flexible enough to allow the students these minor distractions for a brief period and then direct them back to the desired classroom activity. The third optional response is for the teacher to react to and confront any activities which do not directly relate to the learning planned for the class. This confrontational approach indicates that the teacher sees extraneous activities not only as disruptive, but as direct challenges to adult authority in the classroom. When the teacher responds in this fashion, an adversarial situation is created in which, if the teacher is to maintain control of the classroom, he/she must win each and every encounter. While some situations may not allow for the first two options (such as fights and other situations which threaten others), the tendency for a teacher to consistently choose the third response is likely to be viewed by the students as overreaction, and may in fact lead to problems in the classroom rather than reduce them. Thus, the personal reactions of teachers to potentially disruptive situations in the classroom cannot be overestimated as potential ways of reducing delinquency in the schools.

Kenneth Polk (1984) also viewed the educational institution as one of the most important elements in delinquency prevention and control. He contended that the number of marginal youths is growing, not only because less successful students continue to have an unpleasant school experience, but also because their future occupational aspirations are severely limited. He proposed that to counter the alienation experienced by these youths, they must be engaged in useful work and be more thoroughly integrated into the school community. William Pink (1984) concurred, viewing effective schools as the most cost-efficient delinquency prevention program. He contended that the current educational system perpetuates a two-trajectory system where the low-trajectory youths (less successful students) are not only ill prepared academically, but also meet with failure in the out-of-school world, creating social situations which generate delinquency and other forms of deviance.

J. David Hawkins and Joseph Weis (1980) also acknowledged the school's importance in delinquency prevention, and viewed the school's role as going beyond academic and intellectual development. They suggested that the school must provide more alternative educational options, such as enhanced skill training. This suggestion was supported by a study which showed that students who received meaningful occupational education in high school were less likely to be incarcerated later as adults (Arum and Beattie, 1999). Hawkins and Weis also suggested that the school take a more active role in the social development process, including education in civil and criminal law. Emphasizing the social context in which the schools operate, they argued for more student input into the educational process and urged schools to draw upon student leaders to exert peer influence in delinquency prevention. They pointed out that the student leaders should not be merely the academic leaders, but also the informal leaders of various social groups and cliques.

Barry Krisberg and James Austin (1978) further emphasized the social nature of the educational process and outlined some ways in which schools could meaningfully change in an effort to reduce delinquency. They suggested that schools might enter into agreements with local communities to enhance their partnership role with the entire community. Their suggestions included utilizing local artisans, craftspersons, and other professionals in the community as guest lecturers. They also suggested revising the curriculum to include local internship programs and viewing the local community as a learning resource. Local museums, libraries, universities, scientific establishments, businesses, and industries all should be viewed as places of learning and instruction. Enhanced school–community relations would better integrate school and community in the educational process and reduce the view that schools are socially set apart from the rest of the world. Further, a number of studies suggest that schools must become more involved in *all* aspects of a student's life, including family, interaction with other private and social institutions, and other interests outside of school (e.g., Fagan and Pabon, 1990). As a result, many school districts are developing comprehensive delinquency prevention plans in cooperation with parents, the police, local businesses, and other available local, state, and federal agencies.

SUMMARY

The educational system did not create youthful misbehavior and juvenile delinquency. The main sources of delinquency reside in the features of broad society; however, schools can either aggravate or reduce the problem according to the way they dispense rewards and punishments to students, provide access to opportunities for success, and react to the problems of students. In this chapter, we illustrated some of the ways in which the schools as public arenas are interwoven into the phenomenon of juvenile delinquency. The schools usually represent the first social institution (outside the family) with which the child must contend.

The major role of the school is that of socialization. For the schools, this process involves not only teaching the necessary cognitive skills expected of all citizens, but also the teaching of what are considered to be appropriate attitudes, values, beliefs, and behaviors. The child's ability to conform to normative expectations of teachers and administrators and adapt to the student role is critical in helping to determine success within that institution.

Success within the educational system is importantly linked to success in the larger society. Those who fail, create problems, cause trouble, and cannot achieve success in school are those who are most likely to be labeled "delinquent," and also to subsequently fail in life.

The success/fail orientation of the educational system often acts as a "screening device" which may alienate the unsuccessful students to the point of truancy or dropping out. Those alienated students who choose to remain in school may do so at great costs to the schools, administrators, teachers, and other students, who become the victims of their violence and vandalism.

While schools cannot be blamed for causing juvenile delinquency, they may be able to play an important role in reducing and/or preventing it. Schools are an integral part of society and the single social institution in which juveniles spend the largest portion of their time. From a sociological perspective, if members of society want to make a serious effort to reduce many of the problems associated with juvenile delinquency, the schools must play a major role.

Concept Integration

Questions and Topics for Study and Discussion

1. Explain how the school acts as a major agent of socialization in our society. Should the school attempt to socialize students in regard to normative aspects as well as cognitive aspects of culture? If so, how can it best do that? If not, why not?

2. Academic credentials have become extremely important in our society. Discuss some ways in which schools determine what level of credentials a student should receive. Should a student's willingness to conform to school rules be a factor in determining academic success? Why? Why not?

3. What is meant by referring to the school as a "combat zone"? What might be done to alleviate some of the conflict in the schools?

4. Schools have become increasingly bureaucratized in recent years. What positive outcomes has bureaucratization had on the schools? What has been the negative impact?

5. What can school teachers and administrators do to help reduce and prevent delinquency in the schools?

6. Discussion topic: Should states require compulsory school attendance? If so, why? If not, why not?

References

Alexander, K. L., Entwisle, D. R., and Horsey, C. S. 1997. From first grade forward: Early foundations of high school dropout. *Sociology of Education* 70 (April):87–107.

Alwin, D. F., and Thornton, A. 1984. Family origins and the schooling process: Early versus late influence of parental characteristics. *American Sociological Review* 49 (December):784-802.

Annual Report on School Safety. 1998. Washington, DC: U.S. Department of Education, U.S. Department of Justice.

AP Tallahassee, FL. 1991. Bill allows Florida teachers to stun their unruly students. *Sunday Oklahoman,* January 20:A11.

AP Webbers Falls, OK. 1997. Oklahoma officials investigate slaying of teen over lighter. *Dallas Morning News,* February, 21:17A.

Ardrey, R. 1966. *The territorial imperative.* New York: Atheneum.

Arum, R., and Beattie, I. R. 1999. High school experience and the risk of adult incarceration. *Criminology* 37 (August):515-530.

Astone, N. M., and McLanahan, S. S. 1991. Family structure, parental practices and high school completion. *American Sociological Review* 56 (June): 309–320.

Bayh, B. 1975. Our nation's schools—A report card: "A" in school violence and vandalism. *Preliminary Report of the Subcommittee to Investigate Juvenile Delinquency.* Washington, DC: U.S. Government Printing Office.

Becker, H. 1952. The career of the Chicago public school teacher. *American Journal of Sociology* 57 (March):470-477.

Berger, P., and Berger, B. 1975. *Sociology: A biographical approach* (2nd ed.). New York: Basic Books.

Bergmann, R. 1987. Purdy: Few bullies in Manteca. *The Manteca Bulletin,* June 9:A-8.

Bloch, A. M. 1978. Combat neurosis in inner-city schools. *American Journal of Psychiatry* 135 (October):1189–1192.

Braun, C. 1976. Teacher expectations: Sociopsychological dynamics. *Review of Educational Research* 46 (Spring):185–213.

Broder, P. K., Dunivant, N., Smith, E. C., and Sutton, L. P. 1981. Further observations on the link between learning disabilities and juvenile delinquency. *Journal of Educational Psychology* 73 (December):838–850.

Brownfield, D. 1990. Adolescent male status and delinquent behavior. *Sociological Spectrum* 10 (April–June):227–248.

Callahan, R. E. 1962. *Education and the cult of efficiency.* Chicago: University of Chicago Press.

Cantelon, S., and LeBoeuf, D. 1997. Keeping young people in school: Community programs that work. *Juvenile Justice Bulletin* (June). Washington, DC: U.S. Department of Justice, Office of Juvenile Justice and Delinquency Prevention.

Chance, P. 1984. Save our schools: Love a vandal. *Psychology Today* 18 (May):17–18.

Cicourel, A. V. 1968. *The social organization of juvenile justice.* New York: John Wiley.

Collins, R. 1971. Functional and conflict theories of educational stratification. *American Sociological Review* 36 (December):1002–1019.

Colvin, M., and Pauly, J. 1983. A critique of criminology: Toward an integrated structural-Marxist theory of delinquency production. *American Journal of Sociology* 89 (November):513–545.

Dollard, J., Miller, N., Doob, L., Mowizer, O. H., and Sears, R. R. 1939. *Frustration and aggression.* New Haven: Yale University Press.

Durkheim, E. [1906] 1956. *Sociology and education.* (Trans. S. D. Fox) New York: Free Press.

Elliott, D. S. 1966. Delinquency, school attendance and dropout. *Social Problems* 13 (Winter):307–314.

Elliott, D. S., and Voss, H. 1974. *Delinquency and dropout.* Lexington, MA: Lexington Press.

Fagan, J., and Pabon, E. 1990. Contributions of delinquency and substance use to school dropout among inner-city youths. *Youth and Society* 21 (March):306–354.

Farkas, G., Sheehan, D., Grobe, R. P., and Shuan, Y. 1990. Cultural resources and school success: Gender, ethnicity, and poverty groups within an urban school district. *American Sociological Review* 55 (February):127–142.

Farnworth, M., Schweinhart, L., and Berrueta-Clement, J. R. 1985. Preschool intervention, school success and delinquency in a high-risk sample of youth. *American Educational Research Journal* 22 (Fall):445–464.

Fields, S. 1993. Time to end teens' new, vicious edge. *Insight,* September 13:28–30.

Figueira-McDonough, J. 1993. Residence, dropping out, and delinquency rates. *Deviant Behavior* 14 (April–June):109–132.

Friedenberg, E. Z. 1959. *The vanishing adolescent.* New York: Dell.

———. 1971. The high school as a focus of student unrest. *Annals of American Academy of Political and Social Science* 395 (May):117–126.

Gamoran, A. 1992. The variable effects of high school tracking. *American Sociological Review* 57 (December): 812–828.

Garry, E. M. 1996. Truancy: First step to a lifetime of problems. *Juvenile Justice Bulletin* (October). Washington, DC: U.S. Dept. of Justice, Office of Juvenile Justice and Delinquency Prevention.

Getzels, J. W. 1977. Why some children do poorly in school. In H. Ehlers (Ed.). *Crucial issues in education* (6th ed.). New York: Holt, Rinehart and Winston, pp. 73–76.

Glasser, W. 1978. Disorder in our schools: Causes and remedies. *Phi Delta Kappan* 59 (January):331–333.

Gracey, H. L. 1977. Learning the student role: Kindergarten as academic boot camp. In D. H. Wrong and

H. L. Gracey (Eds.). *Readings in introductory sociology* (3rd ed.) New York: Macmillan, pp. 215–226.

Greer, C. 1993. How safe is your child's school? *Parade Magazine,* November 7:8.

Halvorsen, R., and Hawley, D. 1973. *From gangs to God.* Washington, DC: Review and Herald Publishing Association.

Hastad, D. N., Segrave, J. O., Pangrazi, R., and Peterson, G. 1984. Youth sport participation and deviant behavior. *Sociology of Sport Journal* 1 (December):366–373.

Hawkins, J. D., and Weis, J. G. 1980. The social developmental model: An integrated approach to delinquency prevention. Seattle: University of Washington Center for Law and Justice.

Hawkins, J. D., and Lishner, D. M. 1987. Schooling and delinquency. In Elmer H. Johnson (Ed.). *Handbook on crime and delinquency prevention.* Westport, CT: Greenwood Press, pp. 179–221.

Herndon, L. 1993. Bullies can make a kid's life miserable—but don't despair. *The Oregonian* (August 26):A1.

Hirschi, T. 1969. *Causes of delinquency.* Berkeley: University of California Press.

Hirschi, T., and Hindelang, M. J. 1977. Intelligence and delinquency: A revisionist review. *American Sociological Review* 42 (August):571–587.

Hummel, R. P. 1977. *The bureaucratic experience.* New York: St. Martin's Press.

Hurn, C. J. 1978. The limits and possibilities of schooling. Boston: Allyn and Bacon.

Jarjoura, G. R. 1993. Does dropping out of school enhance delinquent involvement? Results from a large-scale national probability sample. *Criminology* 31 (May):149-160.

1996. The Conditional Effect of social class on the dropout-delinquency relationship. *Journal of Research in Crime and Delinquency* 33 (May): 232–255.

Jencks, C., Smith, M., Acland, H., Bane, M. J., Cohen, D., Gintis, H., Heyns, B., and Michelson, S. 1972. *Inequality: A reassessment of the effect of family and schooling in America.* New York: Basic Books.

Johnson, D. 1998. School hallways increasingly divided into haves- haves-nots. *Dallas Morning News,* October 18:14A.

Johnson, M. G. 1993. Schools' disclosure of crime information varies. *Ft. Worth Star Telegram* (September 12):A1.

Keilitz, I., Zaremba, A., and Broder, P. K. 1979. The link between learning disabilities and juvenile delinquency: Some issues and answers. *Learning Disability Quarterly* 2 (Spring):2–11.

Kelly, D. H. 1977. Labeling and the consequences of wearing a delinquent label in a school setting. *Education* 97 (Summer):371–380.

1982. *Creating school failure, youth crime, and deviance.* Los Angeles: Trident Shop.

Killackey, J. 1990. Standardized test use comes under criticism. *The Sunday Oklahoman,* April 15:1-A.

Kimbrough, J. 1986. School-based strategies for delinquency prevention. Pp. 193–206 in P. W. Greenwood (Ed.) *Intervention Strategies for chronic juvenile offenders.* New York: Greenwood Press.

Kozol, J. 1967. *Death at an early age.* New York: Bantam Books.

1991. *Savage Inequalities: Children in America's schools.* New York: Crown.

Krisberg, B., and Austin, J. 1978. *The children of Ishmael: Critical perspectives on juvenile justice.* Palo Alto, CA: Mayfield.

Lane, B. A. 1980. The relationship of learning disabilities to juvenile delinquency: Current status. *Journal of Learning Disabilities* 13 (October):425–434.

Lawrence, R. 1998. *School Crime and Juvenile Justice.* New York: Oxford University Press.

Liska, A. E., and Reed, M. D. 1985. Ties to conventional institutions and delinquency: Estimating reciprocal effects. *American Sociological Review* 50 (August):547–560.

Lundman, R. J. 1996. Demeanor and arrest: Additional evidence from previously unpublished data. *Journal of Research in Crime & Delinquency* 33 (August):306–323.

Mayer, G. R., Butterworth, T., Nafpaktitis, M., and Sulzer-Azaroff, B. 1983. Preventing school vandalism and improving discipline: A three year study. *Journal of Applied Behavior Analysis* 16 (Winter):355–369.

McDermott, J. 1983. Crime in the school and in the community: Offenders, victims, and fearful youths. *Crime and Delinquency* 29 (April):270–282.

McNeal, R. B. 1997. High school dropouts: A closer examination of school effects. *Social Science Quarterly* 78 (March):209–222.

McPartland, J. M., and McDill, E. L. (Eds.). 1977. *Violence in schools: Perspectives, programs and positions.* Lexington, MA: DC Heath.

Menard, S., and Morse, B. J. 1984. A structuralist critique of the IQ-delinquency hypothesis: Theory and evidence. *American Journal of Sociology* 89 (May):1347–1378.

Monk-Turner, E. 1989. Effects of high school delinquency on educational attainment and adult occupational status. *Sociological Perspective* 32 (Fall):413–418.

NBC Nightly News. 1997. Police make daytime sweeps of urban shopping malls, May 17.

Neill, S. B. 1978. Violence and vandalism: Dimensions and correctives. *Phi Delta Kappan* 59 (January): 302–307.

Okaty, G. J. 1991. Kids at school/Kids at risk. *Police Chief* 58 (May):39–41.

Piliavin, I., and Briar, S. 1964. Police encounters with juveniles. *American Journal of Sociology* 70 (September):206–214.

Pink, W. T. 1984. Schools, youth and justice. *Crime and Delinquency* 30 (July):439–461.

Polk, K. 1975. Schools and the delinquency experience. *Criminal Justice and Behavior* 2 (December): 315–338.

———. 1984. The new marginal youth. *Crime and Delinquency* 30 (July):462–480.

Polk, K., and Schafer, W. E. (Eds.). 1972. *Schools and delinquency.* Englewood Cliffs, NJ: Prentice-Hall.

Roberts, J. 1988. School yard menace. *Psychology Today* 22 (February):52–56.

Roncek, D. W., and LoBosco, A. 1983. The effect of high schools on crime in their neighborhood. *Social Science Quarterly* 64 (September):598–613.

Roncek, D. W., and Faggiani, D. 1985. High schools and crime: A replication. *Sociological Quarterly* 26 (Winter):491–505.

Rubel, R. J. 1977. *Unruly school: Disorders, disruptions, and crimes.* Lexington, MA: DC Heath.

———. 1979. *Crime and disruption in schools: A selected bibliography.* Washington, DC: National Institute of Law Enforcement and Criminal Justice, U.S. Department of Justice (January).

Sanders, W. B. 1976. *Juvenile delinquency.* New York: Holt, Rinehart and Winston.

Savitz, L. D., Lallix, M., and Rosen, L. 1978. Fear of school-based crimes and rational responses. From *Theoretical perspectives on poverty and school crimes,* Vol. 2. New York: National Council on Crime and Delinquency.

Schafer, W. E., and Polk, K. 1976. Delinquency and the schools. In *Task force report: Juvenile delinquency and youth crime.* The President's Commission on Law Enforcement and the Administration of Justice. Washington, DC: U.S. Government Printing Office, pp. 228–234.

Segrave, J. O., and Hastad, D. N. 1984. Interscholastic athletic participation and delinquent behavior: An empirical assessment of relevant variables. *Sociology of Sport Journal* 1 (June):117–137.

Stagliano, P. A., and Hyman, I. A. 1983. State department of education activities to reduce school violence and vandalism. *Phi Delta Kappan* 65 (September):67–68.

Thompson, W. E., and Hickey, J. V. 1999. Society in Focus: An Introduction to Sociology (3rd ed.). New York: Longman.

Thornberry, T. P., Moore, M., and Christenson, R. L. 1985. The effects of dropping out of high school on subsequent criminal behavior. *Criminology* 23 (1):3–18.

Truckenmiller, J. L. 1982. Predicting vandalism in a general youth sample via the HEW youth development model's community program impact scales, age, and sex. Unpublished paper presented at the 90th Annual Convention of the American Psychological Association, Washington, DC, August 23–27, 1982.

U.S. Department of Health, Education and Welfare. 1978. *Violent schools-safe schools: The safe school study report to the Congress.* Vols. I, II, and III. Washington, DC: U.S. Government Printing Office.

U.S. Senate Subcommittee on Delinquency. 1977. *Challenge for the third century: Education in a violent environment.* Washington, DC: U.S. Government Printing Office.

Weber, M. [1922] 1968. Bureaucracy. In G. Roth, and C. Wittich (Eds.). *Economy and society: An outline of interpretive sociology* (3 Vols.) (Trans. E. Fischoff et al.). New York: Bedminster Press, pp. 956–1005.

Werthman, C. 1976. The function of social definitions in the development of the gang boy's career. In R. Giallombardo (Ed.). *Juvenile delinquency* (3rd ed.). New York: John Wiley, pp. 327–347.

Whittemore, H. 1992. Dads who shaped up a school. *Parade Magazine* (September 27):20–22.

Wright, J. P., Cullen, F. T., and Williams, N. 1997. Working while in school and delinquent involvement: Implications for social policy. *Crime & Delinquency* 43 (April):203–221.

Yinger, J. 1982. *Countercultures: The promise and the peril of a world turned upside down.* New York: Free Press.

Zieman, G. L., and Benson, G. P. 1980. School perceptions of truant adolescent boys. *Behavioral Disorders, Programs, Trends and Concerns of Children with Behavioral Problems* 5 (August):212–222.

11 THE YOUTH SUBCULTURE

Reading Objectives

The reading of this chapter will help you achieve the following objectives:

1. Define subculture and explain what is meant by the concept of youth subculture.
2. Explain those aspects of American society which may lead to the creation and perpetuation of a youth subculture.
3. Identify specific attitudes, values, beliefs, behaviors, and norms characterizing the youth subculture.
4. Understand how participation in a youth subculture may result in committing delinquent acts such as running away, prostitution, status offenses, and various other forms of "middle-class" delinquency.
5. Identify elements of the youth subculture which may constitute countercultures (e.g., teenage Satanism and hate groups which may be involved in serious forms of delinquency and violent crimes).
6. Explore ways in which the youth subculture might be utilized to help control and prevent juvenile delinquency.

Introduction

It seems that every generation of adults worries about the future of society being turned over to its children. History is replete with the theme of elders believing that the younger generation has abandoned the most important attitudes, values, and beliefs of their parents, and that each succeeding group of youngsters almost ensures that society's ruin is imminent. Likewise, as children begin to grow into young adults they marvel at the "old fogeyness" of their parents, teachers, and other older members of society. They often wonder how adults survived so long while being so ignorant, out-of-touch, and old-fashioned. These disparate views have led to the sense of a generation gap between adults and juveniles that has spawned both social speculation and scientific research into the phenomenon often referred to as the **youth subculture.**

In Chapter 9, we looked at the family as the most important primary group to which people belong. We discussed the prominent role that the family plays in socializing its members to internalize the culture of society. We indicated, however, that as children grow up, they also become exposed to a variety of other socializing agents including church, school, peers, and mass media. Chapter 10 focused on the powerful influence of the school and how it may both contribute to, or help prevent, juvenile delinquency. In this chapter, we explore the ways in which the youth's movement outside the family and the school into a larger social world may lead to the development of a sense of social ties to other youths embarking upon the same process. This sense of identity along with a variety of other social factors contribute to the formation of a youth subculture, some elements of which may contribute to the youth's likelihood of committing acts regarded as deviant by adults.

Culture, Subcultures, and Countercultures

Culture is *the entire body of shared and learned beliefs, values, attitudes, traditions, normative expectations, and other forms of knowledge that is passed on from one generation to the next within a society.* Within the dominant culture of larger society, there exists a variety of **subcultures,** *which share most of the attitudes, values, and beliefs of the overall culture; however, they also adhere to certain attitudes, values, beliefs, and norms unique to them, somewhat setting them apart from larger society.* Hans Sebald (1968:205) referred to **culture** as *"a blueprint for behavior of a total society"* and **subculture** as *"the blueprint for behavior of a smaller group within the society."* He illustrated the concept by saying, "there are subcultures for narcotic addicts, longshoremen, inmates in prison, Texas oil men, those in the world of fashion, jazz musicians—and adolescents" (Sebald, 1968:205).

As long as the smaller group accepts and conforms to most of the norms of larger society while maintaining its uniqueness, it is usually considered to be a subculture. However, *when the subculture differs to the point that it rejects the overall attitudes, values, beliefs, and norms of larger society, and offers a substitute normative system,* it becomes a **counterculture.**

A great deal of debate has been waged as to whether U.S. youths constitute a subculture. A number of social and behavioral scientists contend that there *is* a youth subculture and that in order to understand most juvenile behavior (including delinquency) it is necessary to put it in its subcultural context (e.g., Coleman, 1960; Smith, 1962; Schwendinger and Schwendinger, 1985). Some even contend that the youth subculture is in direct conflict with the larger culture created and maintained by adults, and hence, constitutes a youth counterculture (Roszak, 1969; Yinger, 1982). Chapter 12 explains the concepts of deviant and delinquent subcultures and focuses upon gang membership as one form of a counterculture that pits juveniles against the mainstream of adult society. In the remainder of this chapter, we discuss the concept of a youth subculture in the United States in its broadest sense and explore its possible relationship to certain types of juvenile delinquency.

The Creation of a Youth Subculture

Throughout this book, we have emphasized the marginal status accorded U.S. youths. Ralph England (1967) contended that the beginnings of the youth subculture can be traced to the rapid urbanization and industrialization which occurred during the nineteenth century. He indicated that the status of youth became marginal—neither adult nor child. He saw the twentieth century as reinforcing the development of the youth subculture in a variety of ways. After World War II, the United States experienced the creation of a distinct youth culture separated from adults and children. He viewed this youth subculture as based on the values of hedonism and materialism, and supported by enough money to express those values socially. When those values lead to behavior disapproved by adults, delinquency can be the result (England, 1967).

David Gottlieb et al. (1966) agreed that industrialization and the marginal status of youths led to the formation of a youth subculture. They contended that "there is general agreement among many students of adolescent behavior that the emergence of distinct youth cultures is related to the emergence of industrialization" (Gottlieb et al., 1966:ix). According to Gottlieb and his associates, in a modern industrial society there is a prolonged period of adolescence which lacks a clearly defined rite of passage into adulthood. This helps to create an adolescent subculture with distinctive attitudes, values, and behaviors. This notion is supported by research on the rise of a Japanese youth subculture (Kersten, 1993).

Ernest Smith (1962) also linked the marginal status of adolescence to the formation of a youth subculture. He indicated that "the absence of transitional rituals and the prolongation of dependence of American youth lead to parent-youth conflict" (Smith 1962:21). Robert Bell (1983) indicated that there probably always has been some type of conflict between the young and their parents in U.S. society. However, the concept of adolescence and the marginal status of juveniles was not traditional in American society. Rather, as America experienced the shifts from rural to urban and agrarian to industrial, the role expectations for youths became much less clear. According to Dorothy Rogers (1985:8):

> ...*various factors have conspired collectively to designate adolescence as a discrete age stage. First, children inevitably became more separated from adults as society moved from a rural to an urban environment. Second, as cultures became more complex, the stages became increasingly refined, with a definite step-like transition from infancy to adulthood. While some societies ritualize the shift from youth to maturity, those lacking such rites have instead a* youth culture, *or institutionalized adolescence.*

A youth subculture is not unique to U.S. society (as Box 11-1 indicates), but certain characteristics of our culture seem to be particularly linked to the formation and perpetuation of such a subculture. James VanderZanden (1986:38) indicated that western societies have "postponed the entrance of their adolescents into adulthood...[and]...have spawned conditions favorable to the development of unique cultural patterns among their youth." James Coleman (1960:337) suggested this same analysis in his description of the formation of youth subcultures:

> *Industrial society has spawned a peculiar phenomenon, most evident in America but emerging also in other Western societies: adolescent subcultures, with values and activities quite distinct from those of the adult society—subcultures whose members have most of their important associations within and few with adult society.*

BOX 11-1 Cross-Cultural Focus

A Canadian Youth Subculture

In a participant observational field study, Stephen Baron explored the street life of an adolescent subculture on the Canadian west coast. These youths, usually referred to as "punks" by themselves and others, were characterized by their outrageous and distinctive hairstyles and dress, panhandling, allegiance to "punk rock," "heavy metal," or "death rock" music, and a penchant for violence.

The punks chose the streets as their main turf because they provided the youths a sense of autonomy and a source for "action." Panhandling was the primary source of income for members of the subculture, and they often had "contests" to see who could beg the most money in a specified amount of time. In addition to begging, they also engaged in the theft of cigarettes, cassette tapes, liquor, and other items for a quick resale on the streets. Many engaged in the selling of fake drugs or taking money for drugs they were supposed to deliver later, but never did. They often stole food items from local merchants for consumption, and when they needed money quickly, the males "rolled" (mugged) unsuspecting passersby.

While these activities were engaged in for day-to-day survival, they also provided a major source of entertainment for the street youths. A major activity of the punks was simply "hanging out," and when boredom overtook them, they often turned to mischief and violence for fun. Motorists, especially other youths, routinely shouted insults as they drove by and the punks often responded by shouting obscenities or hurling rocks at the cars. Occasionally a window would be broken, or a car would stop, and a fight ensued. Participation in violence, even if the punk was severely beaten, enhanced status within the group.

The punks had almost daily encounters with the police. While most of these interactions were punctuated with mutual hostility, many officers became acquainted with various members of the subculture and often called them by name, asked how they were doing, and admonished them to stay out of trouble, or to take care of themselves. Others hassled the youths frequently, asking for identification or searching them. The punks seemed particularly amused by plainclothes officers who attempted to purchase drugs from them, and had great fun in teasing and taunting the undercover officers.

The Canadian punk youth subculture illustrates the marginality and alienation from the larger culture experienced by many youths. Baron noted that the subculture's resistance to society must be taken seriously as its members were willing to ignore public harassment, fight other groups, and suffer both social and legal consequences in order to symbolically display their contempt for dominant social standards and to express their sense of identity with their distinctive youth subculture.

Source

Baron, Stephen W. "Resistance and its consequences. The street culture of punks." *Youth and Society* 21 (December) 1989:207–237.

Role of the Youth Subculture

It should be pointed out that social and behavioral scientists who support the idea that a distinctive youth subculture exists in the United States are *not* suggesting that U.S. youth in general constitute a delinquent subculture. Rather, they argue that youths, especially teenagers, experience social conditions that may alienate many of them from their parents' generation and many of their parents' traditional social values. This feeling of alienation can

The dress, hairstyles, and demeanor of these youths bind them together in a distinctive youth subculture that may even lead some adults to label them as a potentially dangerous counterculture.

be manifested in a variety of ways, most of which would not be considered delinquent. We will look at some of the specific elements of the youth subculture which might contribute to some forms of delinquency. At this point, we turn our attention to the social situation of American youths and why they tend to experience alienation from the adult world, and why that sense of alienation leads to the formation of a strong sense of identity and cohesion with other youths.

Erich Goode (1994:258) described a subculture as a group whose members:

1. *interact with one another more frequently and more intimately than they do with members of other social categories;*
2. *[have a] way of life, and…beliefs, [that] are somewhat different from members of other social categories; and*
3. *think of themselves as belonging to a specific group, and they are so defined by those who do not share this trait.*

American youths fit this description of subculture fairly well. It should be pointed out, however, that a subculture is not a primary group. Unlike the family, the youth subculture is not characterized by intimate face-to-face interaction. Although many ethnic, religious, social class, and other subcultures often are reinforced by spatial proximity and direct interaction, the existence of a widespread youth subculture indicates that value sharing does not necessarily require direct contact or primary social interaction. Unlike some of the smaller street gangs and other juvenile groups (clubs, fraternities, sororities, etc.) which depend upon the interpersonal contact among members for transmission of values, norms, and social support, a subculture may be widely distributed geographically and without interpersonal contact. However, if a subculture is to perpetuate itself, there must be mechanisms for transmitting its values among members and from one generation to another. Our massive and technologically sophisticated communications network contributes the necessary cohesiveness among youths by affording instant awareness of news and issues relevant to young people, innovations in dress and language, and the rapid sharing of values and norms across the country.

One of the most thorough sociological analyses of the youth subculture in the United States is that of Hans Sebald (1968, 1984). He pointed out that there is not a uniform adolescent subculture, but a very diverse one. He established that important differences exist in youth peer cultures based upon socioeconomic status, age, race, ethnicity, and rural or urban residence (Sebald, 1968:201–202). Despite these differences, however, he contended that there is a sense of unity among virtually all teenagers. "They know they belong together and observe norms and values not necessarily consistent with the adult world's folkways and mores" (Sebald, 1968:203).

Why do subcultures form? What purposes does a youth subculture serve for adolescents? Sebald identified eight commonly agreed upon functions provided by subcultures in general, and showed how these functions are specifically fulfilled by the youth subculture. According to Sebald (1968:206; 1984:207–208), subcultures provide:

1. **Common Values and Norms.** *Typically, youth subcultural values are different from those of children and those of adults.*
2. **A Unique "Lingo."** *Youths speak an argot that is often only partially understood and approved by adults.*
3. **Distinct Forms of Mass Media.** *For example, certain movies, magazines, television programs, and music appeal primarily to the youth subculture.*
4. **Common Styles and Fads.** *This is especially evident in styles of dress, grooming, and make-up.*
5. **A Sense of Belonging.** *Thinking of and referring to one's peer group in terms of "we" instead of "they."*
6. **Unique or Distinctive Status Criteria.** *Adolescents tend to choose different standards for selecting leaders or earning prestige.*
7. **Social Support.** *Teenagers provide one another with a sense of understanding and support for behavior that may violate adult norms.*
8. **Gratification of Specific Needs.** *There are some basic needs of teenagers which larger society prohibits (e.g., sexual activity) and which are provided for in the youth subculture.*

Identifying with a youth subculture alleviates some of the frustrations experienced by juveniles as a result of their marginal status in society. It also provides group support for norms and values that run counter to those of their parents, teachers, and other adults. Membership in the youth subculture also provides a sense of identity and belonging for juveniles.

Although today's teenagers may have less in common with each other than some past generations, they still are very strongly peer-driven and the need to belong is considered crucial (Begley, 2000). The sense that other people are in the same situation as they and understand their problems serves as an important symbolic expression of a sense of belonging for American teenagers. Researchers who most strongly contend that there is a youth subculture tend to focus on three assumptions:

1. *Adolescents suffer a certain amount of turmoil and stress due to their uncertain position in the social structure.*
2. *A teenage subculture develops as a social reaction to this uncertainty and it has a widespread and powerful pattern among American adolescents.*
3. *The adolescent subculture provides a sense of security during the period of adolescent discontinuity (Sebald, 1968:198–200).*

Consequently, the formation of a youth subculture serves as an important frame of reference for teenagers to enhance personal and social identity and give meaning to their lives. Again, the marginal status of juveniles in U.S. society plays an important role in assigning importance to the youth subculture. Very few meaningful social roles are provided for adolescents in the adult world. Smith (1962:26) pointed out, "Contemporary American society provides no clearly defined status-roles for youth, except perhaps the dependent-subordinate ones of children and students." The roles of child and student often alienate youths as they begin to view themselves as young adults. Herman and Julia Schwendinger (1985:34–35) pointed to the marginality of adolescents in the family and school as leading to the formation of youth subcultures.

Distinctive Elements of the Youth Subculture

The persistent conflict between adult and juvenile values appears to contribute to the ongoing phenomenon of the youth subculture. Theodore Roszak (1969:1) proclaimed, "The struggle of the generations is one of the obvious constants of human affairs." This struggle apparently takes place in a variety of arenas. Part IV of this book looks at public arenas in which the confrontation between adults and youths is manifested (the streets and courts). Here, we identify some of the elements of the youth subculture which distinguish it from the larger society and set the stage for potential confrontation with adults. Juveniles differentiate themselves from adults in a multitude of ways, but that differentiation is probably most clearcut in regard to values.

Youth Values

Values *are beliefs and ideas that are held in high esteem by a particular group.* There is great diversity within the juvenile subculture reflective of the pluralism found in the larger society. Variables such as race, age, sex, socioeconomic status, and even geographical location impact upon youth values as they do upon those of adults (Sebald, 1968; Schwendinger and Schwendinger, 1985). There are, however, some rather consistent areas in which

BOX 11-2   Concept Application

The American Youth Subculture: Youth Values in the 21st Century

Is it possible to generalize and accurately describe the values of approximately 23 million American youths ranging in age from 13 to 20? Probably not. But popular polls and some scientific research indicate that the so-called American youth subculture may be stronger and more readily identifiable and influential than ever. Moreover, largely due to mass media, American youth values are exerting powerful influence on adolescents and young adults around the globe. As one sociologist put it, "…the number of adolescents compared to other societal age groups has come roaring back…[and] the importance of teenagers for our collective future cannot be denied…" (Peterson, 1999:426).

Sociologists long have asserted that values are linked to behavior, and consequently, that internalizing certain values may either lead to, or help insulate youths from committing juvenile delinquency (Shoemaker, 2000). Consequently, a brief look at dominant values of contemporary American youths provides valuable insight into the youth subculture of the 21st century and the role it may play in contributing to or helping to prevent juvenile delinquency.

Similar to generations of the past, today's youths are extremely peer-oriented; having friends is not only essential, but also an important part of a teenager's identity. They form cliques, or as they prefer to call them *tribes,* and often identify with each other through distinctive dress, hair fashions, body piercings, or tattoos. On the downside, many of today's youths are highly materialistic, cynical, and somewhat desensitized to hearing harsh language and seeing violence. One youth confessed, "Lying and cheating are standard behavior," and another asserted "There's a lot of anger in my generation—you can hear it in the music" (Begley, 2000:55). Material possessions are highly prized, especially personal beepers and cellular phones, and it appears that common status offenses such as drinking, smoking, curfew violations, as well as petty property offenses such as shoplifting are easily rationalized, and consequently, loom ever larger in America's future.

All is not gloomy on the values front of the American youth subculture, however. Today's teenagers are among the most educationally, occupationally, and professionally oriented of any over the past several decades. And studies show that they are less likely to drive drunk, have unprotected sex, or get into fistfights than youths of the early 1990s. Many of today's youths are passionate about religion and other spiritual matters, and a substantial number of them enjoy spending time with their parents and other adults.

As in past generations, contemporary American youths share numerous values as well as attitudes, norms, and behaviors, which set them apart from adults and help to comprise an identifiable youth subculture. And, as in the past, this youth subculture may simultaneously contribute to, and in some cases help prevent, juvenile delinquency.

Sources

Begley, Sharon. 2000. "A world of their own." *Newsweek,* May 8:53–56.

Kalb, Claudia. 2000. "Unhealthy choices." *Newsweek,* May 8:66–68.

Leland, John. 2000. "Searching for a holy spirit." *Newsweek,* May 8:61–63.

Newsweek. 2000. "Through their own eyes." *Newsweek,* May 8:64–65.

Peterson, Gary W. 1999. "The renewed importance of studying parent-adolescent relations: An introduction. *Sociological Inquiry* 69 (Summer):426–430.

Shoemaker, Donald J. 2000. Theories of Delinquency (4th Ed.). New York: Oxford University Press.

Thomas, George, Alan Reifman, Grace M. Barnes, and Michael P. Farrell. 2000. "Delayed onset of drunkenness as a protective factor for adolescent alcohol misuse and sexual risk taking: A longitudinal study." *Deviant Behavior* 21 (March–April):181–210.

adults and juveniles tend to differ in their value judgments. Two of the most notable are in regard to attitudes toward sex and drugs.

A large amount of research has been conducted on teenagers' attitudes and behaviors related to premarital sex and the use of drugs. Since both of those activities are illegal for juveniles, they are explored in some detail in the next section of this chapter which directly relates the juvenile subculture to the problem of juvenile delinquency. In this section we confine our treatment of youth values to a brief discussion of some of the values of young people which differ from those of adults and which may contribute to the cleavage between the generations.

The contention that youths adhere to a particular set of social values that are different from those of most adults is not to imply that there are no similarities in the value systems of youths and their parents. After all, children are first socialized within the context of their family and learn their first values from their parents and older siblings. Consequently, most youths, especially those with middle class parents, are socialized to the dominant values of society. Cultural pluralism notwithstanding, most teenagers understand the norms of larger society and feel a sense of guilt when they violate them (Sykes and Matza, 1957). How, then, do the values of the youth subculture come into conflict with those of their parents and other adults? It has been suggested that the differentiation of youth values is largely symbolic, and resides not so much in conflicting ideology, as in conflicting lifestyle.

You may remember that in an earlier chapter we discussed sociological theories which contended that a great deal of delinquency can be attributed to the existence of delinquent subcultures (e.g., Miller, 1958; Cohen, 1955). These theorists contended that delinquent subcultures tend to be comprised of lower class youths who take dominant middle class norms and turn them "upside down" (Cohen, 1955). While there is debate over the general explanatory power of these subcultural theories, they may provide insight into the basic value system of U.S. teenagers. Gary Schwartz and Don Merten (1967) suggested that the major subcultural elements of adolescent social life are in the symbolic aspects of their values, beliefs, and standards. "The distinctiveness of the youth subculture is not necessarily that their norms and values are fundamentally at odds with the adult world, but that their evaluative system which provides cultural meaning for their life is vastly different" (Schwartz and Merten, 1967:453).

In other words, many of the distinctive values of the youth subculture are not all that different from the values they were taught by their parents. Rather, the difference resides in the ways that teenagers express those values in their behavior. For instance, Talcott Parsons (1942) used the automobile as an example in which youths take basic social values and reinterpret them in a way that is socially meaningful to them, but leads to behavior that is at odds with the norms prescribed by adults. By the 1930s, the automobile had become a basic part of U.S. culture. Virtually every family owned one and adults highly valued the automobile for its utilitarian purpose—transportation. American youths also highly valued the automobile, but for very different purposes. The automobile, approved and sanctioned by adults for transportation, was used by juveniles for entertainment, drag racing, and other activities frowned upon by adults (Parsons, 1942). By the 1960s, the automobile had taken on even more importance for teenagers, becoming, perhaps, the most important symbol of the youth subculture providing prestige, a place for dating and sexual activities, and a hobby for many teenage boys (Sebald, 1968:257–258).

There are several other basic social values that parents tend to teach their children that the youth subculture expresses in ways that may lead to conflicts with parents, teachers, law enforcement officials, and other adults. For example, *independence* is a basic value in American society. Liberty, freedom, and independence are concepts taught to children from birth. However, when teenagers begin to assert their own independence, they often meet with disapproval from adults. Adults usually conceive of independence, freedom, and liberty in a more nationalistic and abstract sense. When juveniles speak of independence, freedom, and liberty, they typically mean freedom from parents, school, and other adult authority figures and rules. Hence, it is not the value which conflicts with adult society, but the behaviors chosen for expressing it which lead to youths being viewed as deviant.

Another basic middle class American value is *conformity.* While parents encourage individuality, they insist that it be tempered with the ability to get along with others, to be part of an accepted group, and to conform to normative expectations. Evidence suggests that juveniles value conformity as much as their parents, and perhaps even more. Again, the problem does not lie in internalizing the value, but in exhibiting it in behavior. In fact, the youth subculture is probably a result of the strong desire on the part of young people to conform with one another.

A multitude of studies indicate that one of the strongest motivations for behavior among juveniles is their desire to gain and maintain acceptance with their peers (e.g., Smith, 1962; Sebald, 1968; Clasen and Brown, 1985; Schwendinger and Schwendinger, 1985). Gerald Pearson (1958:88) stated, "A fundamental evidence of the existence of youth culture is the compulsive conformity required of its members." Smith (1962:9) explored the phenomenon of the **clique,** *a small primary group within the youth subculture,* and indicated that the clique "sets norms that are often the highest authority for its members and may take precedence over both family and other adult norms." Schwendinger and Schwendinger (1985:106–107) described various youth cliques such as "greasers," "jocks," "surfers," "squares," "intellectuals," and "nerds," and pointed out that whatever the particular clique membership, all were characterized by extreme peer pressure to conform to a particular set of attitudes, values, beliefs, and behaviors.

It is apparent that the peer pressure to conform provides a strong sense of *esprit de corps* and social identity for juveniles. Thomas Cosner and Gerald Larson (1980) contended that the youth subculture is a reaction to the increased demands of the larger society for juveniles to conform while mediating much of the tension and rebellion experienced as a result of their status. This need to conform to and identify with the youth subculture hinges on adherence to its values. Bennett Berger (1963) contended that the youth subculture is not merely a function of one's chronological age. Rather, it is a distinctive set of attitudes, values, beliefs, and behaviors which focus on hedonism, irresponsibility, and expressiveness. Support for the notion that the youth subculture is not totally based on age may be seen in a quote from 1960s "Yippie" leader Jerry Rubin, who, in his forties, declared, "We ain't never, never gonna grow up…we're gonna be adolescents forever!" (Time, 1986:24). The hedonism and irresponsibility on the part of middle class youths in the United States has received widespread attention in the sociological literature on the youth subculture. Lamar Empey (1982:202) summarized some of the research on youth subcultures by pointing out that while there are questions as to the "uniqueness of adolescent subculture, most theorists suggest that it helps to produce an adolescent world of hedonism and irresponsibility, and the more adolescents are involved in it, the more likely they are to be delinquent."

In summary of youth subculture values, Sebald (1968) proposed that American young people are socialized to some basic cultural values which contradict each other. He described some of the "dichotomous values with which juveniles must come to grips" as including: *competition* versus *cooperation; work* versus *leisure; piety* versus *freethinking; individualism* versus *conformity;* and *sexuality* versus *chastity* (Sebald, 1968:145–150). It may well be that identity with a youth subculture provides a temporary social frame of reference for teenagers within which to handle these value discrepancies. Hence, a feeling of group support allows juveniles to validate their behaviors based upon their interpretation of appropriate values and behaviors.

Dress, Grooming, and Fads

Some of the ways in which teenagers express their identity within a youth subculture can be found in their norms regarding dress, grooming, and widespread acceptance of various fads. VanderZanden (1986:38) indicated that the "unique cultural patterns among youth... find expression in fads having to do with musical recordings, entertainment idols, and dance steps, personal adornment and hair styles...." The distinctive and often faddish dress of teenagers clearly operates to set them apart from their adult counterparts. It simultaneously unifies members of the youth subculture while distinguishing them from the larger culture (Richards, 1988; Coker, 1993). Dress, grooming, and personal appearance become the most important vehicles by which juveniles can symbolize their status. Bell (1983) indicated that distinct styles and tastes, especially in regard to personal appearance, develop within the youth subculture. He indicated, "The youth subculture has become highly subject to the dynamics of fashion...[and] the youth culture has produced its own version of the game of keeping up with the Joneses" (Bell, 1983:477).

England (1967) indicated that after World War II, a large market of goods emerged aimed primarily at the youth culture in the United States. Adherence to the normative expectations of youths regarding dress and other material possessions (cars, athletic equipment, stereos, cosmetics, etc.) demands access to a certain amount of money. Sebald (1968:112) indicated that in the mid-1960s, teenagers spent over 1.5 billion dollars annually on entertainment; 700 million dollars annually on records; 450 million on cosmetics and toiletries; and 3.6 million on women's clothing. The cost of albums, stereo equipment, cosmetics, and clothing has increased significantly. Nancy Needham (1986:16) estimated that Americans under the age of 18 spent more than 70 billion dollars annually on everything from breakfast cereal to name brand clothing. The importance to conform to peer expectations regarding these items has not diminished. Consequently, many parents have been confronted by a teenager demanding the purchase of a particular brand of athletic shoe, or some similar item, when a much less expensive brand would have been equally functional. Teenagers are constantly bewildered by their parents' failure to understand that one shoe style is "in" and another is definitely "out." This failure to recognize such a widely known and accepted "fact" only serves to underscore the so-called generation gap.

Juvenile hairstyles also accentuate the existence of a youth subculture and broaden the gap between parents and teenagers in regard to acceptable taste. James McAlexander and

John Schonten (1989) contended that hair more than any single body feature is a central part of a person's identity. Further, they suggested that in a society lacking puberty rites, such as the United States, hairstyles may serve as a symbol of transition from childhood to adolescence, and from adolescence to young adulthood. It seems almost axiomatic that when adults are wearing their hair short, teens will be wearing theirs long, and vice-versa. In the mid-1960s the Beatles launched a revolution in hairstyles for teenage boys. Crewcuts rapidly disappeared, and the "Beatle cut" swept across the United States much to the chagrin of parents, teachers, and other adults. Many schools passed dress and hair codes (it was at about the same time that the miniskirt became the style for teenaged girls) and the battle of generational values once again surfaced. Eventually, adults became more tolerant of the longer hair; ultimately, not only were teen rock stars wearing their hair longer, but so were middle-aged crooners, country and western singers, and talk show hosts. When lawyers, doctors, teachers, and "good ol' dad" followed suit, it was inevitable that the teenagers of America would make the move back to shorter hair. By 1990 "flat tops," "buzzes," "spikes," and other shorter (but deviant) hairstyles dominated the youth culture. One juvenile judge in Houston, Texas believes that hair style is such an important part of a juvenile's identity that he offers to cut delinquents' sentences if they will agree to cut their hair in a more "mainstream" style (AP, Houston, 1993).

Tattoos have become another widespread symbol of the youth subculture (Begley, 2000). Once thought primarily to be the trademarks of sailors, prostitutes, motorcycle gangs, and other social outcasts, tattoos have become a symbolic mainstay of today's youth subculture and tattoo parlors can now be found on small-town squares and in middle-class urban shopping malls. It is estimated that somewhere between 12 million to 20 million Americans have tattoos and tattoos are for Generation X what identity bracelets were for their parents' generation. Interestingly, as youths who were tattooed in their late teens and early twenties marry and start their careers, many of them regret their "badges of rebellion," and seek to have the tattoos removed—a process that is both more painful and more expensive than getting the tattoo in the first place (Marin, et al., 1995).

While various styles of dress, grooming, and cosmetics vary somewhat by race, social class, ethnicity, and other social and demographic factors, juveniles seem to have much more in common with each other than they do with their parents or other adults (Smith, 1962; Sebald, 1968; Wein, 1970; Bell, 1983). As mentioned earlier, the youth subculture is not a small primary group within which all members interact directly with one another. Consequently, the youth subculture becomes very dependent upon the mass media to carry the message of current trends in style to teenagers across the country. This necessitates a communication network primarily aimed at adolescents to express and reinforce their particular values and norms. Those youths who feel the most committed to the youth subculture are most likely to express conformity to its norms.

Mass Media

A perusal of any magazine rack indicates that this mass medium acknowledges the existence of a large youth subculture and makes every effort to cater to its tastes and styles. After World War II, a large number of magazines, books, records, movies, and television shows were aimed at the special interests of the huge youth market (England, 1967; Klein, 1990).

Much to the chagrin of many parents and school officials, tattoos have become an important symbol of the youth subculture.

Today, magazines such as *Teen, Teen Beat, Spin,* and *Rolling Stone* are clearly aimed at youthful consumers and seem almost to simultaneously dictate and reflect teenagers' preference in music. Likewise, *16, Seventeen, Glamour, Teen,* and other magazines cater to a juvenile audience, setting the pace for teen dress and hair styles. *Mad* magazine still satirizes adult life and appeals directly to the sense of humor of junior high and high school students. All of those magazines, and a variety of others, influence and reinforce values of U.S. youth.

Television producers, writers, directors, and commercial advertisers also have recognized the large teen market and have routinely catered to its particular tastes and values. Numerous television programs are aimed directly at teenagers, using popular teenaged stars and models. Market researchers indicate that teenagers spend $56 billion annually, so advertisers aggressively stalk the youth market through all possible avenues (Schwartz, 1990). Frances Lawrence et al. (1986:434) found that adolescents on average watched 147 minutes of television daily—approximately 17¼ hours every week. Lawrence discovered that many of the attitudes, values, and beliefs of adolescents, especially regarding standards of dress and personal conduct, were formed by television. By the mid-1980s, cable television offered 24 hours every day of "rock videos" and music programming aimed specifically at the American youth market, and as we entered the 21st century, these programs were among the most popular with youths in the United States and around the world.

Since the late 1950s, rock music has become one of the most important symbols uniting the youth subculture in America (Kaiser, 1988). It has served as one of the most distinctive ways that youths express their values and rebellion against adult traditions and norms. Adults have always expressed concern over the lyrics and rhythms of popular teen music, and the rap music of the late 1980s and 1990s created such a furor that steps were taken to ban it in several states, and at least label it as offensive in others (Lynxwiler and Gay, 2000) (see Box 11-2).

Writers, producers, and directors of movies also have acknowledged the existence of a youth subculture and have attempted to capitalize on movies geared toward its values. Richard Corliss (1986) described some of the trends in youth-oriented movies over the past few decades. During the 1950s, the movies starring James Dean and Marlon Brando exemplified the rebellion of youth; the 1960s were dominated by Beach Party movies, and later by social protest films; the 1970s gave rise to teen "sexploitation" films such as the Porky series; and the 1980s witnessed what Corliss described as a revamp of the Andy Hardy movies—films characterized by kids struggling with values, drugs, sex, parents, and school (Corliss, 1986). Corliss (1986) discussed the youthful stars such as Molly Ringwald, Anthony Michael Hall, Emilio Esteves, Judd Nelson, Andrew McCarthy, and Ally Sheedy, who affectionately became known as the "Brat Pack" by their young fans. The theme of youths struggling against parental authority also dominated many of the movies of the 1990s, and young stars like Drew Barrymore with on-screen and real-life struggles with drugs, sex, and other teenage and young adult problems emerged as youthful role models. Jennifer Love Hewitt, Scott Wolfe, Sarah Michelle Geller, and a host of other young actors in their teens and twenties helped the youth subculture usher in the 21st century.

Language

One of the most important ways that any subculture can symbolically distinguish itself from the larger culture is by adopting a unique language or jargon. American Old Order Amish speak German, Orthodox Jews speak Yiddish, and various ethnic groups adhere to the language of their homeland in urban subcultural enclaves like Chinatown and Little Italy.

Language also appears to be a vehicle by which teenagers differentiate themselves from adults. According to some researchers, the most important symbolic element of the youth subculture is its distinctive language (Schwartz and Merten, 1967). Smith (1962), Sebald (1968), Rogers (1985), and VanderZanden (1986,1990), to name a few, all pointed to the distinctive jargon of youths as being one of the significant aspects of the youth subculture. Smith (1962:14) saw language as a means for teenagers to "exclude outsiders" and "intensify group identity." Yinger (1982:152–171) pointed out ways in which juveniles reverse language by using words to mean their exact opposite, such as using the word "bad" as a compliment to actually mean "good." For example, when one teenaged male tells another that his car is "really bad," he is paying him a high compliment.

One of the most thorough treatments of the distinctive language of the youth subculture can be found in Sebald's (1968) sociological analysis of adolescence. He contended that teens have created a unique **argot** (*specialized slang, or jargon*) to promote group cohesiveness and

BOX 11-3 Controversial Issue

Censoring Rock Music

Few things more clearly demonstrate the gap between generations than their preferences in music. In the 1940s many concerned parents forbade their daughters to listen to "crooners" such as Perry Como and Frank Sinatra for fear that they would become so caught up in the romantic trance induced by the music that boys would take advantage of them. The 1950s launched rock 'n' roll and the driving beat and suggestive movements of the performers convinced many parents that the music would drive their teenagers into a sexual frenzy. Elvis Presley's first performance, especially his hip movements, on the Ed Sullivan Show was considered so suggestive that cameramen were instructed to show him only from the waist up. The 1960s spawned songs of protest against the Vietnam War and for civil rights, while the 1970s gave rise to "acid rock" and songs espousing free love and experimentation with drugs. The 1980s saw "heavy metal" reach its peak, and many adults were certain that it was connected with illicit drugs, satanic worship, adolescent suicide, and other evils. Popular bands and recording artists did little to dissuade parental fears as they used satanic symbols on their album covers, wore exotic makeup, performed with snakes and other animals, and covered their bodies with offensive tattoos. Each new trend in music popular with teenagers seemed more threatening than those preceding it, and in each decade, adults concerned about the negative impact of popular music on youths instigated movements to burn records, ban radio broadcasts, and censor certain musical artists and their performances.

The dawn of the 1990s saw a renewed and more intense effort at censorship spawned largely by the popularity of "rap" music. Referred to simply as "filth" or "audio pornography" by some, and by others as "attitude" filled with misogyny, anger, and hatred from the ghetto, rap music touched off a tidal wave of censorship efforts across the country. The governor of Florida banned performances by 2 Live Crew, one of the most popular and controversial rap bands, and several states followed suit by attempting to ban the sale of their album "Nasty as They Wanna Be."

Other rap and heavy metal groups also have generated much concern. Perhaps generating the most controversy has been "hip-hop" and the so-called "gangsta rap." Ice-T's controversial song "Cop Killer" brought waves of protest from police organizations and the songs of N.W.A. (Niggaz With Attitude) and other rappers have infuriated the public with their violent, sexist, and racist lyrics, and several radio stations have refused to play their records. The pressing question is whether there is a relationship between violent rap songs and violence in the streets. One youngster convicted of murdering a police officer unsuccessfully used the defense that he was listening to the song "Cop Killer" and therefore should not be held accountable for the shooting. And critics of rap music point to the fact that life is imitating art far too often as a number of popular gangsta rappers have been indicted for violent crimes. Many of the rappers, however, insist that they are simply depicting life on the streets as they know it, and that by shocking the white community with their songs, they may bring about desirable social change (Leland, 1993). Whatever its social impact, this form of urban music simultaneously frightens and attracts the American public and accounts for the sale of approximately 70 million albums per year (Vognar, 1998).

An Oklahoma legislator introduced a bill to put "warning labels" on objectionable records (Hinton, 1990), and an Arizona state senator introduced a "No ID, no LP" bill which would prohibit sales of recordings containing lyrics describing or advocating drug use, satanism, murder, or violence to anyone under the age of 18 (Burgess, 1990). At least twelve other states debated similar legislation. Many of the legislators who favor labeling and censorship bills consider themselves fairly "hip" and admit that they resented earlier attempts to censor the popular rock-and-roll music that they enjoyed as teenagers. Viewing the new heavy metal and rap music as much more dangerous and threatening, however, they believe that their efforts are different.

Research conducted by Amy Binder (1993), however, suggests that attempts to censor heavy metal and rap music may reflect different motives. She analyzed the rhetoric in media accounts from 1985 to 1990 regarding the potential societal dangers of the

Continued

BOX 11-3 *Continued*

two genres of music, and found that although both focused on sex and defiance of authority, the racial compositions of the artists and audiences of the two brands of music primarily shape the way they are perceived. Binder (1993) argued that images and stereotypes of white youths greatly influenced the perceived dangers portrayed by the media as being associated with heavy metal music, whereas dangers associated with rap music were exaggerated by white's fears of stereotypical portrayals of poor, angry, black youths.

Columnist Lewis Grizzard (1990:J-6) put these censorship efforts in perspective, pointing out that "nothing sells like controversy," and urged adults to take a different tack in fighting the offensive music–ignore it. He indicated that much of the music's attraction to teenagers was a result of the horror it generated for adults–their parents. Take away the controversy, he concluded, and the thrill will be gone and "…your children will go back to dyeing their hair orange or whatever else they can think of to drive you crazy."

Sources

Adler, Jerry, and Jennifer Foote. 1990. "The rap attitude," *Newsweek,* March 19:56–59.
Binder, Amy. 1993. "Constructing racial rhetoric: Media depictions of harm in heavy metal and rap music. *American Sociological Review* 58 (December):753–767.
Burgess, Mike. 1990. "Arizona: 'No ID, no LP'" *Dallas Morning News,* March 25:43A.
Grizzard, Lewis. 1990. "Parent-teenager dis-chord: fighting dirty," *Dallas Times Herald,* March 25:J-6.
Hinton, Mick. 1990. "Moore legislator seeking warning on records deemed objectionable," *Sunday Oklahoman,* February 24:1-A.
Leland, John. 1993. "Criminal Records: Gangsta Rap and the Culture of Violence," *Newsweek,* November 29:60–64.
Lynxwiler, John, and David Gay. 2000. "Moral boundaries and deviant music: Public attitudes toward heavy metal and rap." *Deviant Behavior* 21 (Jan–Feb):63–85.

provide boundary maintenance. He contended that many of the terms and idioms used in teen argot provide a form of verbal shorthand, summarizing very complex ideas and meanings into only one or two words (Sebald, 1968:249–251).

The Youth Subculture and Juvenile Delinquency

The focus of this chapter up to this point has been to lay a conceptual foundation for understanding a particular basis for potential juvenile delinquency. When people think of delinquents, listen to television news reports, or read newspaper headlines about delinquency, they are most likely to hear or read about rapes, robberies, murders, and other violent offenses committed by youths. Youth crime is a major problem, and much of this textbook has focused on the typical street crime types of delinquency. Yet, the vast majority of youthful offenses are not serious violent crimes. Rather, a much larger proportion of juveniles who get in trouble with the law commit what would be considered misdemeanors if they were adults, or not crimes at all (status offenses). Consequently, exploring the existence of a youth subculture which promotes values, attitudes, beliefs, and norms that often conflict with adult normative expectations may provide valuable insight for understanding status offenses and nonviolent crimes committed by youths.

Research dealing with the existence of a youth subculture consistently has linked it to middle class delinquency, especially status offenses and nonviolent crimes (Shoemaker, 2000; Empey, 1982). It is highly unlikely that theoretical frameworks attempting to explain rape or murder are also going to explain the motivations for truancy, drug use, or premarital sex. The issue of truancy was addressed in Chapter 10; in this chapter we provide a brief sociological analysis of juvenile runaways, prostitution, juvenile drug use, and premarital sexual behavior in relation to the youth subculture.

Juvenile Runaways

A vast literature has accumulated on the runaway phenomenon in the United States, and numerous theories have been postulated on why youths leave home and what can and should be done about it. Much of the research on running away focuses upon home and family problems which place unusual stress upon the juvenile who finally decides to flee the home environment (e.g., Gullotta, 1979; Roberts, 1981; Morgan, 1982; Whitbeck and Simons, 1990), while others have examined the difference between **runaways**—*those who leave their home*—and **throwaways**—*those who are pushed out of their homes* (e.g., Gullotta, 1979; Adams et al., 1985).

Running away from home is a delinquent act. In 1982, 115,214 juveniles were arrested as runaways (FBI *Uniform Crime Reports,* 1983:176) In 1986, the number climbed to 138,586 (FBI *Uniform Crime Reports,* 1987:174); then it dropped slightly to 135,471 in 1991 (FBI *Uniform Crime Reports,*1992:223); but once again increased to 189,696 in 1995 (FBI *Uniform Crime Reports,* 1996:224). Of course, not all runaways are arrested. Johnson and Carter (1980) estimated that in 1975, over 600,000 children ran away from their homes. The FBI. estimated that there were one million juvenile runaways in 1980 (Wells and Sandhu, 1986:147), and O'Brien (1983) put the estimate at one million runaways per year in the U.S., while more current estimates range from one-half million to 1.3 million (Kaufman and Widom, 1999). Running away from home seems to increase during certain social, political, and economic conditions. Mona Wells and Harjit Sandhu (1986) pointed out that throughout U.S. history, periods of war and social upheaval have been accompanied by increased rates of running away. Lipschutz (1977) also documented specific periods in history when there was an increased incidence of running away. In the twentieth century, the periods of the Great Depression (1930s), World War II (1940s), and the "Flower Child Era" (1960s) saw large waves of runaways in this country.

Wells and Sandhu (1986) concluded that the phenomenon of running away from home seems to result from a combination of "push-pull" factors such as problems at home and pressures of school combined with the allure of perceived freedom and independence. A counselor for runaways in Los Angeles summarized:

> *Kids are not really running away…they are running to something they think is there which isn't there. They think it's just a groovy street scene…which of course, isn't true. There's nothing more revolting than the street scene, but they really don't know it. They think it's really an exciting thing. It's complete freedom, but they don't realize it's kind of hard to have freedom if you're out pan-handling for food… (Wein, 1970:201).*

Jennifer James (1982) confirmed that many runaways are lured to the streets by the anticipation of excitement to be found there, but often become disillusioned with the life they find. While running away is a delinquent act in itself, it is only one aspect of the problem which links running away from home to delinquency. As D. Kelly Weisberg (1985) indicated, many juvenile runaways wind up in jail or prison because they get involved in street crimes such as prostitution, drugs, theft, and violence. Drug usage has been found to be much higher among runaways (especially females) than other youths (Windle, 1989).

Many runaways were either abused or neglected by their parents (Kaufman and Widom, 1999). Once they leave home, runaways are extremely vulnerable prey for pederasts, pimps, and others who spot them on the streets, show them some attention and apparent affection, and offer them a warm meal and a place to sleep. They become easy targets for prostitution (Morgan, 1975; Austin, 1985; Hersch, 1988), child pornography (O'Brien, 1983), and other forms of victimization, especially violence and sexual abuse (Whitbeck and Simons, 1990). In *America's Runaways,* Christine Chapman (1976) discussed the problems that runaway youths face on the streets of major cities. These almost invariably include being taken advantage of by more "streetwise" adults (U.S. Dept. of Justice, 1990). Tom Cox, of the Diggers Creative Society in Los Angeles (a group formed to help street youths), noted:

> *A kid of fourteen can't cope with the streets. Even if they wanted to fool with the illegal part of it, they just can't manage it, they just can't make it. They are going to get busted, or they are going to get into some very bad situations where the people who are sheltering them have nothing to lose. In one case, there's a guy who collects fourteen-year-old boys and sends them out to earn money for him (Cited in Wein, 1970:196).*

Juvenile Prostitution

For both male and female juveniles on the streets, especially runaways, prostitution may become one of the few available routes to survival. Weisberg (1985:4) noted:

> *Since runaway episodes begin impulsively, the runaways seldom brought much money with them, and they frequently found themselves without resources for food and shelter. They might find shelter with strangers, but such as might well be conditioned on an exchange of services involving drug dealing or prostitution.*

Frances Newman and Paula Caplan (1981) verified that a significant number of teenage prostitutes were runaways. Similarly, Patricia Hersch (1988:31) pointed out that "wherever we turn, teenagers are being used for sexual recreation by men—lots of men..." In 1995, 1044 people under age 18 were arrested for prostitution (FBI *Uniform Crime Reports,* 1996:224), and certainly that figure represents only the "tip of the iceberg."

When young girls run away from home, they make easy victims for pimps who prey on their vulnerability. Some of the juvenile prostitutes on the streets appear to have voluntarily entered into prostitution. James (1978) found that some female juvenile prostitutes were from affluent backgrounds but were attracted to street prostitution for the thrill and adventure of it. Many runaway youths conclude that prostitution means "easy money," even

Juvenile prostitutes work the streets of most major cities in the United States.

if not desirable. Many of Weisberg's (1985:57) subjects stressed that prostitution meant easy money, "with 'easy' referring to the short duration of the sexual encounter as well as the lack of difficulty in performing such employment." Some of the juvenile prostitutes actually indicated that they like "the absence of fixed working hours, leaving them to 'do their own thing'" (Weisberg, 1985:57).

The so-called voluntary nature of such prostitution may be nothing more than rationalization for the norm-violating behavior in which the youth is participating. For as Shirley O'Brien (1983:69) pointed out, "It is easy for children desperately in need to turn to pornography and prostitution to support themselves." And Weisberg (1985:78-79) concluded that runaways were most likely to fit into the category of "situational" prostitutes (entering into prostitution temporarily due to specific social and economic circumstances) as opposed to "vocational prostitutes" (entering into prostitution as a career). As O'Brien (1983:69) summarized, "Runaways who have been neglected and abused to a point that their home situation was more troublesome than whatever might be 'out there,' rationalize that food and shelter provided in exchange for sexual favors is better than living in an impossible home environment." Unfortunately, youths who were abused and neglected at home are also very likely to be abused and neglected on the streets and they often get arrested for a variety of street-related crimes (Kaufman and Widom, 1999).

Juvenile prostitution (like adult prostitution) is not solely a form of deviance for females. Runaway boys are also quite vulnerable on the streets and often succumb to prostitution because they see it as a viable means of survival. Research by Calhoun and Weaver

(1996), for example, indicates that many male runaways view prostitution as a "rational choice," after weighing the perceived benefits of financial gain, sexual pleasure, and control of work schedule, against the potential liabilities of getting arrested, possibility of violence, sex with undesirable people, and the possibility of not getting paid for their services. Interestingly, few if any of the young male prostitutes mentioned the fear of contracting AIDS as part of their mental equation when assessing the potential benefits and liabilities of street prostitution. Robin Lloyd (1976:211) estimated that there were approximately 300,000 male prostitutes under the age of 16 in the United States. Prostitution becomes an integral part of life on the streets for juvenile males (Weisberg, 1985; Hersch, 1988). Young males who run away from home find life on the streets extremely difficult and may find themselves exploited by adults for purposes of child pornography (O'Brien, 1983) and prostitution (Wein, 1970; James, 1982; Weisberg, 1985). The tenderloin district of San Francisco attracts numerous runaways, and many young males congregate in that area as prostitutes. The area along Market Street from Mason to Tyler streets has become so well known for having male juvenile prostitutes that it is referred to as the "Meat Rack" (Weisberg, 1985:20).

Young male prostitutes, like females, may enter into prostitution for a variety of reasons. James (1982) found that the largest percentage of adolescent male prostitutes entered the trade out of economic necessity. Hersch (1988) estimated that male juvenile prostitutes often made $75 to $100 per night. On the other hand, an earlier study by Albert J. Reiss (1961) revealed that some male juvenile prostitution was primarily a form of "street hustle" highly supported among delinquent peers. Reiss described a situation in which delinquent males would hang around on the streets posing as prostitutes. When approached by older males they would agree to engage in fellatio for a price. The boys viewed the older male's behavior as homosexual, while rationalizing that their own participation in the act was simply a form of sexual release for which they were paid. Sometimes, after the act, they would even beat the older male to signify their own revulsion at homosexuality. This type of behavior was viewed as very "macho" by the delinquent boys, and never viewed as being a homosexual (Reiss, 1961). Similar activities occur in urban areas where "tough" local teenagers cruise the gay areas, participating in "fag bashing" or "rolling queers" for money. Sometimes these juveniles sell sexual favors to the homosexuals before beating them.

Juveniles and Drugs

In September of 1986, President Ronald Reagan, with wife Nancy alongside, appeared on national network television to "declare war" on drug use in the United States. A series of drug-related deaths of famous athletes and other celebrities, together with network news coverage of widespread drug smuggling and dealing in the United States, clearly had stirred public sentiment to be ready to "take up arms" in that war. Later, President Bush vowed to step up the war against drugs and sent American troops into Panama to capture drug kingpin Manuel Noriega. By 1990, drugs were viewed as America's most serious social problem—especially for youths.

Of course, drug use is not new in the United States. James Inciardi (1986) traced opium use back to the eighteenth century. Later, opium, morphine, and even heroin were openly used for their medicinal values (Inciardi, 1986). The Harrison Act of 1914 regulated most addictive narcotics, and, together with the Supreme Court decisions of *Webb* v. *U.S., U.S.*

v. *Behrman,* and *Lindner* v. *U.S.* it became almost impossible for the estimated 200,000 narcotics users to legally obtain their drugs (Inciardi, 1986:15). Illegal drug markets and dealers emerged, and the nation had a drug problem.

For the most part, drug use was perceived as being associated with lower class urban ghettos and adult derelicts. By the 1950s, it became linked with juveniles, but was mostly viewed as an aspect of youthful rebellion, and was thought to be most clearly associated with lower class ghetto youths and juvenile gangs (Inciardi, 1986).

In the 1960s and early 1970s drug use within the youth subculture came to national attention. Harvard professor Timothy Leary openly advocated LSD use, and the so-called hippie movement preached free love and drugs as mind-expanding experiences. Smith (1962), Sebald (1968), Roszak (1969), Wein (1980), and others all linked drugs to the youth subculture as one of the means by which juveniles could express their rebellion against the adult world. Marijuana appeared to be the drug of choice of the youth subculture, and popular motion pictures such as *Easy Rider* depicted youth cult heroes using drugs the way children might nibble on cookies.

The decade of the 1970s saw the drug-related deaths of rock and roll stars Jimi Hendrix and Janis Joplin. Their music was considered fairly wild by most parents and even some teens. Later, during that same decade, however, Elvis Presley, The King of Rock 'n' Roll, died, and a subsequent investigation looked into possible drug involvement. The 1980s saw numerous drug-related deaths of famous celebrities, many of whom had mass appeal among America's teenagers. John Belushi of *Saturday Night Live* and movie fame died of an overdose, as did the Cleveland Browns star Don Rogers. Two very celebrated cases involved the airplane crash of Ricky Nelson (could the son of *Ozzie and Harriet* have been on drugs as news accounts alleged?) and the cocaine overdose of University of Maryland's All-American basketball star Lynn Bias just 2 days after he signed a lucrative contract with the Boston Celtics. Public awareness of a drug problem mushroomed; virtually everybody wondered just how widespread the problem was, especially among the nation's young people. The drug-related death of teen idol, River Phoenix, in 1993 fanned the flames of concern, as did the death of *Saturday Night Live*'s Chris Farley in 1998.

Approximately 150,000 youths under the age of 18 are arrested for illegal drug usage each year (*FBI Uniform Crime Reports,* 1999), but this too is considered to represent only a small fraction of the illegal drug usage among juveniles. For example, Coryl Jones and Catherine Bell-Bolek (1986:5) cited a study indicating that 61 percent of students surveyed reported trying an illegal drug at some time, and 40 percent had used a drug other than marijuana. Evan Thomas (1986:64) cited a similar study indicating that at the time the survey was taken, 25.7 percent of the high school seniors surveyed had used marijuana within the preceding 30 days. Cocaine had been tried by 17 percent of the students surveyed in 1985 as compared to 10 percent in 1976 (Jones and Bell-Bolek, 1986:6). While some studies suggest that overall drug use declined during the 1980s (Greenwood, 1992), usage of lethal drugs such as "crack" and "ice" made inroads into the nation's high schools at an alarming rate (Gelman, 1990). In their analysis of the widespread drug use among juveniles, Jones and Bell-Bolek (1986) contended that it was a social event in most cases. They suggested that drug abuse was "a function of the adolescent's social interaction and experimentation with life-style" (Jones and Bell-Bolek, 1986:7). Similarly, Glassner and Laughlin (1987) pointed out that adolescent drug use almost always occurs in a social context, and while "peer pressure" may be too strong a term, certainly "peer interaction" is one of the most important influences. Other studies also found drug use among juveniles to be social in nature and cited peer influence as the most important factor (Kandel, 1985; Brownfield, 1990; McGee, 1992). Delbert Elliott et al. (1985) further underscored the influence of peers. They integrated Strain, Social Control, and Social Learning theories into a synthesized perspective to account for delinquency and drug use. They postulated that "involvement with and commitment to delinquent peers is the most proximate cause of delinquency and drug use and mediates the influence of weak bonding to parents, school, and conventional norms" (Elliott et al., 1985:85).

Part of the allure of drugs for youths may be tied to their parents' abhorrence of them. Glassner and Loughlin (1987:1) succinctly pointed out that adolescent drug use scares adults. Evan Thomas (1986:65) indicated that "In the age of youth rebellion, the fact that parents were shocked by drugs was all the more reason for children to take them," and studies indicated that certain types of drug use became more widespread and socially accepted among juveniles (Beschner and Friedman, 1986). The existence of a youth subculture in which value is placed on breaking away from parents may be influential in drug acceptance. Jones and Bell-Bolek (1986:7) stated:

> *Even the identification of drug taking as a severe risk provides a fascination for the risktaking adolescent. For some adolescents, risk is not a deterrent, but a challenge.*

On the brighter side, a 1999 study suggests that fewer teens view illegal drug usage as "cool," and one government report showed that teen use of illegal drugs actually decreased from 1998 to 1999 (AP, Washington, 1999; New York Times News Service, 1999).

Juvenile drug use is illegal; hence it constitutes delinquency. Even the use of drugs that are legal for adults, such as alcohol and nicotine (cigarettes) are deemed inappropriate for youths. The 1990s have witnessed renewed interest in smoking and the use of tobacco products among teenagers—with boys tending to use the "smokeless" tobacco and girls smoking cigarettes and even cigars. Alcohol use has become normative among teenagers and by the upper grades in high school almost all have tried it, with many using it regularly (Gelman, 1990). Studies show that smoking, drinking, and some types of illegal drug usage are increasing among the nation's youth—especially among teen-aged girls (AP, Washington, 1998a,b; Griffin, 1999). Moreover, the use of alcohol, tobacco, and marijuana either singly or in some combination are all significantly related to each other and both minor and violent forms of delinquency (Elliott and Morse, 1989; Watts and Wright, 1990; Dembo, et al., 1992). Research shows that the younger an adolescent is at the onset of drug usage, the more likely he or she is to continue to use them—especially if they associate with peers who use drugs (Zhang et al., 1997). A juvenile subculture which encourages and/or promotes violation of parental norms is likely to accentuate drug taking and related forms of delinquency among its members.

Juveniles and Sex

Perhaps no subject sparks more interest among juveniles and provokes more fear among parents than premarital sexual activity. Smith (1962:5) suggested, "Probably the most im-

portant area within which adult norms attempt to dominate youth behavior is that of sex…"
On the other hand, he contended that the youth culture often dominates adolescent behavior
"particularly in relation to sex activities" (Smith, 1962:7). In a treatise on the youth subculture of the 1920s, Paula Fass (1977) discussed sex mores of the period, and indicated that
peer influence and conformity to peer culture were the most important guidelines youths
considered in regard to sexual behavior. In her book *Barriers Between Women,* Caplan
(1981) found that it was in the area of sexuality that mother-daughter relationships were
most conflictual.

   Not only do parents typically socialize their children to view premarital sexual activities as taboo, virtually all sexual activities are illegal for juveniles. Since juvenile statutes
prohibit premarital sexual behavior for both males and females, one of the status offenses
for which juveniles can be adjudicated delinquent is that of promiscuity. Under Arizona
law, for example, if a youth is under the age of 15, anything more amorous than kissing is
a serious violation of the law and social workers, teachers, parents, or any other adults who
are told of petting activities are legally required to report them to the police (Reuters, 1990).
American society exhibits a double standard, however, more vigorously enforcing virtue
among teenaged girls than boys. When four high school cheerleaders in the small town of
Hempstead, Texas were kicked off the cheerleading squad, one of their parents pointed out
that the girls had not gotten pregnant by themselves, yet no boys were being punished in a
similar fashion (AP, Hempstead, TX, 1993). Official data indicate that females are more
likely to be brought to court for committing sex offenses than males (Chesney Lind, 1977)
but either sex can be petitioned to court for being sexually active. Adolescents must somehow balance the biological and physiological changes which are turning them into sexually
potent young men and women against the traditional values of their parents which discourage adolescent sexuality and the laws of the state which make it illegal. Research suggests
that the scales are not very well balanced.

   A 1986 article in *Ladies Home Journal* estimated that 12 million adolescents (40 percent of all teenagers) were sexually active (Sherman, 1986:199), and a *Newsweek* poll in the
year 2000 showed that about 47 percent of teens reported they had engaged in sexual intercourse (Begley, 2000). Researcher Su Yates commented, "For many kids, you're considered
out of it if you're not having sex—it's a rite of passage" (Sherman, 1986:199). Clearly, the
values of many youths toward premarital sexual activity differ from what most parental
norms allow. Wein (1970:11) interviewed street youths in New York City and Los Angeles
and concluded "Most kids seem to find the *idea* of premarital intercourse quite acceptable"
[italics in the original]. Other studies suggest that the youth culture approves of more than
just the idea. Elizabeth Stark (1986:28) found that among 15- to 17-year-olds, "almost half
of the boys and a third of the girls were sexually active." In a study of college students, Carol
Darling and J. Kenneth Davidson (1986) found that 84 percent of the females and 99 percent
of the males had experienced sexual intercourse before marriage. They indicated that there
was a "major increase over the past 15 years in the numbers of adolescent males and females
engaging in heterosexual intercourse" (Darling and Davidson, 1986:403). Stark (1986:28)
stated that "teenagers are becoming sexually active at younger ages." One poll showed that
most teenagers were having sexual intercourse regularly by the eleventh grade (Gelman
1990). One 15-year-old New Yorker candidly explained, "A virgin today is not the same
thing it used to be—A virgin might be someone who has only had oral sex" (Zeman,

1990:27). And, despite finding a slight drop in the sex rate among teenage girls, for the first time in 25 years, a 1995 study showed that half of all girls between 15 and 19 years of age have had sexual intercourse at least once (AP Washington, 1996).

Invariably, sexual activity among juveniles has led to another social problem: teenage pregnancies—resulting in approximately half a million teenage girls giving birth each year (Gelman, 1990). Stark (1986:28) pointed out that "one out of ten teenage girls in the U.S. becomes pregnant every year and almost half of those pregnancies result in births—30,000 of them to girls under the age of 15." A 1995 study showed that 11.2 percent of teenaged girls become pregnant with pregnancy rates highest among blacks (22 percent) and Hispanics (18 percent) (AP Washington, 1996). Research shows that a host of variables including self-esteem, attitudes toward school, educational aspirations, and religiosity, influence premarital sexual activity and how teenage girls resolve the problem of premarital pregnancy (Plotnick, 1992). Eric Sherman (1986:202) pointed to popular "television shows, music videos, and movies with names like *Losing It* and *The Last American Virgin* as leading adolescents "to believe that *everyone* fools around." Yinger (1982,120) pointed out that when youths "misperceive that 'everyone else' is participating in a particular activity, they may be tempted to join the fictitious 'everyone else.'" Joyce Ladner, a professor of sociology at Harvard, indicated that teenage pregnancy "knows no color…it is not a black problem or a white problem," she stated. "It is an American problem" (Sherman, 1986:202).

When teenagers become pregnant, a host of other problems arise such as whether to keep the baby, get married, have an abortion, drop out of school, and how to handle the situation. Sherman (1986:202) indicated that teens account for 30 percent of all abortions in the United States, with about 450,000 abortions each year. Numerous studies have shown that youths are consistently becoming more liberal in their attitudes toward sex (e.g., Sherwin and Corbett, 1985), and more unmarried teens are opting to keep their babies (Stark, 1986). Stark (1986) pointed out that some teens (both male and female) *want* pregnancy, feeling that it asserts their entrance into adulthood. A reflection of the changing attitudes of many teens toward sex and pregnancy in the 1980s can be found in the lyrics of a popular song by rock superstar Madonna in 1986. In a song entitled "Papa Don't Preach," she declared "I'm gonna keep my baby" (written by Brian Elliot © Elliot/Jacobsen Pub. Co.—quoted by permission). So many young mothers are keeping their babies over the past decade that more than 300 schools in 46 states have started parenting and child care classes for teenaged mothers (Kantrowitz, 1990).

Youth Countercultures and Delinquency

Our discussion of delinquency associated with the youth subculture to this point has focused on nonviolent activities such as running away, prostitution, drugs, and premarital sex. As we noted at the beginning of this chapter, however, subcultures sometimes turn in *countercultures*—groups that reject society's values and norms and replace them with others that run counter to those of the larger culture. In Chapter 12 we will take a look at the counterculture of juvenile gangs, but in this chapter we want to look at two aspects of the youth subculture which constitute juvenile countercultures and sometimes promote serious and violent criminal activities: teenage Satanism and youth hate groups.

Teenage Satanic Groups

Sociologist Marcello Truzzi is quoted as saying that teenage sex no longer shocks parents—"the only thing left is the devil" (Lyons, 1988:163). Over the past few decades, teenagers have shown an increased interest in Satanism, and many popular rock and heavy metal groups have capitalized on this interest. With painted faces and eerie costumes these groups play live concerts and record tapes and compact discs that extol the virtues of animal and human sacrifices, sexual orgies, suicide, and even murder. Rumors abound that Satanic cults are responsible for everything from animal mutilations on Halloween night to human kidnapping and mass murders. Almost every popular television talkshow has featured at least one segment on teenage Satanism; and a recent poll indicated that 63 percent of the respondents viewed Satanism as a "serious threat" to our society, while another 23 percent said it was "somewhat serious" (Zellner, 1995).

The extent of teenage Satanism is not known. The Church of Satan claims that annual sales of the Satanic Bible exceed a half-million copies, but some evidence suggests that law enforcement agencies, concerned parents, school officials, and fundamentalist Christians may account for as many sales as believers and practitioners (Zellner, 1995). Also, while teenage Satanists may indeed be involved in some serious criminal activities including kidnapping and murder, research indicates that teenage Satanists are far more likely to be "dabblers"—youngsters "who listen to rock and heavy metal music with occult themes, have an interest in Satanic imagery, and engage in fantasy role-playing games" (Zellner, 1995:87).

Kathleen Lowney (1995) spent five years conducting participant observation and ethnographic interviews with members of an adolescent Satanic counterculture in the south known as "the Coven." Lowney was told about the group by local police and school officials who were upset by the group's demeanor and dress as well as their Friday night Satanic rituals on the outskirts of town where they met under a bridge by "sacred" candlelight and campfire to summon demons to do their bidding. Lowney's analysis of the group indicated that popular folklore and psychiatric explanations for adolescent Satanism are inadequate. Members of the Coven showed no evidence of being mentally ill. And, while they participated in delinquent activities such as under age smoking and drinking, minor vandalism, occasional truancy, and premarital sex—activities also engaged in by non-Satanic youths—they did not commit any serious crimes. Lowney concluded that in a community steeped in conservative Christian values, the Coven provided a symbolic challenge to the dominant culture. Moreover, it provided an important social collectivity in which its members gained a sense of identity and importance, albeit totally unacceptable by community standards where athletes and cheerleaders were held in high status (Lowney, 1995).

Some youth countercultures *are* involved in serious crimes, however. Among them are the hate groups such as Skinheads, neo-Nazis, and others, who commit crimes of violence against homosexuals, members of racial and ethnic minorities, and various other groups who may become the targets of their hatred.

Youth Hate Groups

During the 1980s, the United States experienced an increase in the number of **hate crimes**—*crimes directed at people because of their race, ethnicity, religion, sexual orientation, or* *some other physical or cultural characteristic that sets them apart from the perpetrator.* These crimes often involve groups such as the Skinheads, Neo-Nazis, Ku Klux Klan, and others, and are most often committed by young men under the age of twenty. These groups are usually comprised of disgruntled working-class and middle-class youths and are formed and maintained under a strong ideological commitment to some "cause" such as white supremacy, racial or ethnic purity, anti-Semitism, homophobia, or a return to some so-called idyllic past (Levin and McDevitt, 1993).

While there are a number of hate groups in the United States today, probably the most visible and well-known are the various groups that refer to themselves as "Skinheads." Their distinctive shaven heads, elaborate tattoos, and black Doc Marten boots are copied from their British counterparts who emerged during the early 1950s in England. It is estimated that there are over 5,000 Skinheads in the United States today, and their crimes range from simple assaults and terroristic threats to serious felonies such as aggravated assault, forcible rape, and murder. By 1995, the increase in violent crimes committed by various hate groups had prompted 29 states to enact special hate crime legislation (Marowitz, 1991; Zellner, 1995).

Why do juveniles join hate groups? The answers probably vary by individuals, but sociologically, the most common explanations focus on marginality, alienation, and scapegoating (Zellner, 1995). We have discussed the problem of marginality experienced by adolescents who are no longer considered children, but not yet treated as adults, throughout this book. This marginality may be combined with strong feelings of alienation—a sense of futility and desperation—linked to family problems, school failure, and/or unemployment. Thus, the appeal of a group who can point to the alleged "source" of these problems—members of minorities, or other vulnerable scapegoats—and offer an avenue for venting frustration and retaliating against the so-called culprits (Levin and McDevit, 1993; Zellner, 1995).

The Youth Subculture and Delinquency Prevention

It should be pointed out again that the youth subculture has not thrown out all adult values and the vast majority of crimes and delinquency associated with it are nonviolent. Consequently, the same subculture which may promote some forms of juvenile delinquency also may serve as a potential preventive. For example, Robert Sherwin and Sherry Corbett (1985) found that while college students had indeed become more liberal in sexual attitudes compared to their counterparts of 1963 and 1971, they had not developed an attitude of "anything goes." Rather, while more sexually active, students also held a stronger belief that sexual intimacy should occur in relationships in which there was a feeling of commitment on the part of the couple. John Roche (1986) contended that in some ways, youths were actually becoming more conservative. When he analyzed pre-marital sex on the basis of dating stages, he found that both males and females were much more permissive in their attitudes toward sex than in their actual behavior. One of his findings was that teens tend to think that everybody else is much more sexually active than they are. He indicated that sexual mores tend first to be generated by parents and early religious training; later, they are influenced more by peers and the media (Roche, 1986). He also suggested that a greater social awareness of sexually transmitted diseases such as herpes II (and AIDS) might make many young people "think twice about engaging in premarital sex" (Roche, 1986:107). Unfortunately, while most teenagers are aware of the potential danger of AIDS, many believe that it simply cannot happen to them, and consequently, despite increased knowledge, sexual behavior has not been significantly altered (Roscoe and Kruger, 1990).

We have discussed the influence of mass media on juveniles. While movies, television programs, and other media aimed at youths might promote rebellious or delinquent behavior, they also can be used to present delinquency prevention messages. For example, rock and roll music has both influenced and reflected the values of the youth subculture. By the mid-1980s, while the themes of many popular rock songs encouraged engaging in sex, drug use, and rebellion against parents, some entertainers used that same forum to encourage young girls to "just say no" to sex. Although these songs were urging girls to limit their sexual behavior, they nevertheless reflected the overall tone of the youth subculture, and did not put parents' minds completely at ease.

During the late 1980s, and into the 1990s, organizations such as Students Against Driving Drunk (SADD) were filling the airwaves with messages against drinking and driving. Likewise, young celebrities made public service announcements on television urging teenagers to enter into contracts with their parents in which they agreed not to use alcohol and drugs, and by 1990, television had launched a major public service campaign against drug usage. Perhaps one of the most influential media efforts aimed at the youth subculture focused on encouraging youths not to start smoking. Again, teenaged celebrities warned youths of the dangers of smoking. More importantly, the campaign not only pointed out the dangers associated with smoking, but also emphasized that it simply was not "cool" to smoke. While some people are skeptical of the impact of these public service announcements, research indicates that they are effective in changing juveniles' attitudes and behaviors in a positive fashion (Ingersoll, 1999).

The youth subculture and its heavy emphasis upon conforming to certain distinctive values, attitudes, beliefs, and norms undoubtedly contributes to certain forms of delinquency. This seems to be especially the case for status offenses and other nonviolent law violations. Thus, that same youth subculture may hold tremendous potential for delinquency prevention. Peer pressure to conform to the law can be just as strong and influential as peer pressure to violate it.

Finally, as suggested by maturation theory, much of the delinquency attributable to membership in a youth subculture is the type that is likely to diminish and desist as juveniles mature into adulthood (see Chapter 4). For example, many of the symbols of youthful rebellion—hairstyles, dress, and even tattoos (which are expensive and painful to remove)— are likely to be discarded as teenagers move into their twenties and thirties and assume the responsibilities of work, marriage, and parenthood (Marin et al., 1995).

SUMMARY

We have reviewed a substantial amount of sociological literature documenting the existence of a youth subculture in U.S. society which perpetuates distinctive attitudes, values, beliefs, and norms that may lead some youths to delinquent behavior. The subculture apparently developed during the latter part of the nineteenth century primarily as a result of industrialization, urbanization, and the increasingly marginal status of adolescents.

Youth values reflect early socialization by family, school, and church, but clearly become more influenced by peers and mass media during adolescence. The values are fairly consistent with the values of the adult culture, but are manifested in many distinctive ways. Fashion, grooming, dress, music, fads, and language are a few of the easily observable vehicles by which youths strive to symbolically differentiate themselves from their parents, teachers, and other adults.

While the youth subculture does not necessarily constitute a deviant subculture, some aspects of it can be directly linked to delinquent behavior, especially in the areas of running away, prostitution, drug use and premarital sexual behavior. Research tends to associate the youth subculture with middle class delinquency, primarily involving nonviolent crimes and status offenses. But, as noted in this chapter, sometimes youth countercultures can be involved in serious delinquency and violent crimes.

The existence of a distinctive youth subculture is open to debate, but it seems clear that the marginal status of adolescents and the lack of any clearcut rites of passage into adulthood in U.S. society have created a social situation which tends to bond youths in spirit if not in ideology. As a result, much of the youthful behavior reflects values supported by their peers and not by their parents or other adults. Friedenberg (1963:4, 9) asserted, "the young disturb and anger their elders, and are themselves angered and disturbed…the plight of the adolescent is basically similar to that of the emigrant in that he can neither stay what he was nor become what he started out to be." While questioning the existence of a distinctive youth subculture, William Arnold and Terrance Brungardt (1983) acknowledged that many youths are uncommitted to the normative system of adults.

Howard Becker (1963) surmised that rules about youthful behavior are made without regard to the problems of adolescence; hence, juveniles are "outsiders" who are often labeled deviant as a result of violating rules which have little or no meaning for them. This relative powerlessness in rulemaking may lead to social alienation, which could result in delinquency. The lyrics to a hit song of the mid-1980s seem to summarize the attitudes of many American youths, as the rock group Twisted Sister chanted:

We're not gonna take it,

No, we're not gonna take it,

We're not gonna take it anymore.

Quoted with permission from "We're Not Gonna Take It" sung by Twisted Sister. (From the album "Stay Hungry" produced by Tom Worman. Atlantic Recording Company, New York, 1984.)

While not all youths are rebellious in attitude, they can undoubtedly relate to the sentiment. Wein (1970:223) described an interview with a 16-year-old "chemistry whiz" on his way to a Rotary Club meeting. It may reflect the strong sense of unity among American teens:

Youth: "Being a part of the subculture I'm in, I don't believe what's going on."

Wein: "What subculture?"

Youth: "Oh, teenagers. Our little subculture."

Wein: "Is there anyone your age whom you would exclude from that?"

Youth: "Oh, probably not…you can't help but be in it."

Acknowledging the existence of a youth subculture and its powerful influence upon adolescent behavior is not the same as identifying all U.S. teenagers as belonging to a delinquent subculture. Rather, the much broader context of a youth subculture provides a meaningful sense of social identity for American youths. It also provides a social context in which adolescent nonconformity to both adult and child normative expectations can be viewed as acceptable. We have demonstrated ways in which that acceptance can promote certain types of juvenile delinquency. Given that fact, it is reasonable to assume that the youth subculture also can provide a significant influence for discouraging and preventing juvenile delinquency.

Concept Integration

Questions and Topics for Study and Discussion

1. Define culture, subculture, and counterculture. What is meant by the concept of youth subculture?
2. Is there a youth subculture in the United States? if so, what are some of the distinctive elements of it? If not, why does there seem to be a sense of unity

among juveniles? Are there other explanations? If so, discuss them.

3. In what ways do youth values differ from those to which they were socialized by adults? In what ways are they similar? How do these similarities

and differences create conflict between juveniles and adults?

4. How do the mass media contribute to the formation and perpetuation of a youth subculture? How do they possibly contribute to juvenile delinquency?

5. In what ways does participation in a youth subculture potentially lead to juvenile delinquency? Are there ways in which a youth subculture might be utilized for delinquency prevention? Discuss some of these.

References

Adams, G. R., Gullotta, T., and Clancy, M. A. 1985. Homeless adolescents: A descriptive study of similarities and differences between runaways and throwaways. *Adolescence* 20 (Fall):715–724.

AP Hempstead, TX. 1993. Ouster of 4 pregnant cheerleaders prompts sexism complaints from Hempstead parents. *Dallas Morning News,* October 3:27A.

AP Houston. 1993. Judge offers to snip time for a snip of hair. *Manteca Bulletin,* November 29:A3.

AP Washington. 1996. Sex rate among teenage girls down for 1st time in 25 years, study finds. *Dallas Morning News,* May 7:10A.

AP, Washington, 1998a. Use of drugs among teens increases, survey finds. *Dallas Morning News,* August 22:6A.

AP, Washington, 1998b. Smoking sharply rises among college students, study finds. *Dallas Morning News,* November 18:11A.

AP, Washington, 1999. Fewer teens using illegal drugs, government says. *Dallas Morning News,* August 19:3A.

Arnold, W. R., and Brungardt, T. M. 1983. Juvenile misconduct and delinquency. Boston: Houghton Mifflin.

Austin, L. 1985. Troubled girls prey for runaway network. *Wichita Eagle Beacon,* March, 17:1A, 6A, 7A.

Becker, H. 1963. *Outsiders: Studies in the sociology of deviance.* New York: Free Press.

Bell, R. R. 1966. Parent-child conflict in sexual values. *Journal of Social Issues* 22 (2):34–44.

Berger, B. M. 1963. On the youthfulness of youth cultures. *Social Research* 30 (Autumn):319–342.

Beschner, G., and Friedman, A. S. (Eds.) 1986. *Teen drug use.* Lexington, MA: Lexington Books.

Brownfield, D. 1990. Adolescent male status and delinquent behavior. *Sociological Spectrum* 10 (April–June):227–248.

Calhoun, T. C., and Weaver, G. 1996. Rational decision-making among male street prostitutes. *Deviant Behavior* 17 (April/June):209–227.

Caplan, P. J. 1981. *Barriers between women.* New York: Spectrum.

Chapman, C. 1976. *America's runaways.* New York: William Morrow.

Chesney-Lind, M. 1977. Judicial paternalism and the female status offender. *Crime and Delinquency* 23 (April):121–130.

Clasen, D. R., and Brown, B. B. 1985. The multidimensionality of peer pressure in adolescence. *Journal of Youth and Adolescence* 14 (December): 451–468.

Cohen, A. K. 1955, *Delinquent boys.* New York: Free Press.

Coker, V. L. 1993. Personal dress often a type of identification for adolescents. *Greenville Herald Banner* (December 7):A14.

Coleman, J. S. 1960. The adolescent subculture and academic achievement. *American Journal of Sociology* 65 (January):337–347.

Corliss, R. 1986. Well, hello Molly! *Time* 127 (May 26):66–71.

Cosner, T. L., and Larson, G. L. 1980. Social fabric theory and the youth culture. *Adolescence* 15 (Spring): 99–104.

Darling, C. A., and Davidson, J. K. 1986. Coitally active university students: Sexual behaviors, concerns, and challenges. *Adolescence* 21 (Summer): 403–419.

Dembo, R., Williams, L., Wothke, W., and Schmeidler, J. 1992. Examining a structural model of the relationships among alcohol use, marijuana/hashish use, their effects, and emotional and psychological problems over time in a cohort of high-risk youths. *Deviant Behavior* 13 (April-June):1985–215.

Elliott, D. S., Huizinga, D., and Ageton, S. 1985. *Explaining delinquency and drug use.* Beverly Hills, CA: Sage.

Elliott, D. S., and Morse, B. J. 1989. Delinquency and drug use as risk factors in teenage sexual activity. *Youth and Society* 21 (September):32–60.

Empey, L. T. 1982. *American delinquency: Its meaning and construction* (Rev. ed.). Homewood, IL: Dorsey Press.

England, R. W., Jr. 1967. A theory of middle class juvenile delinquency. In E. W. Vaz (Ed.). *Middle class juvenile delinquency.* New York: Harper and Row, pp. 242–251.

Fass, P. S. 1977. *The damned and the beautiful: American youth in the 1920s.* New York: Oxford University Press.

Federal Bureau of Investigation. 1999. *Uniform crime reports: Crime in the United States, 1998.* Washington, DC: U.S. Government Printing Office.

Friedenberg, E. Z. 1963. *Coming of age in America.* New York: Random House.

Gelman, D. 1990. A much riskier passage. *Newsweek* (Special Edition) (Summer/Fall):10–16.

Glassner, B., and Loughlin, J. 1987. *Drugs in adolescent worlds: Burnouts to straights.* New York: St. Martin's Press.

Goode, E. 1984. *Deviant behavior* (2nd ed.). Englewood Cliffs, NJ: Prentice-Hall.

Gottlieb, D., Reeves, J., and Tenhouten, W. D. 1966. *The emergence of youth societies: A cross-cultural approach.* New York: Free Press.

Greenwood, P. W. 1992. Substance abuse problems among high-risk youth and potential interventions. *Crime and Delinquency* 38 (October):444–458.

Griffin, L. 1999. Growing pains. *Dallas Morning News,* April 18:1A.

Gullotta, T. P. 1979. Leaving home—Family relationships of the runaway child. *Social Casework* 60 (February):111–114.

Hersch, P. 1988. Coming of age on city streets. *Psychology Today* 22 (January):28–37.

Inciardi, J. A. 1986. *The war on drugs: Heroin, cocaine, crime, and public policy.* Palo Alto, CA: Mayfield.

Ingersoll, S. 1999. Investing in youth for a safer future. *OJJDD Fact Sheet* 98 (April):1–2.

James, J. 1978. Entrance into juvenile prostitution: Progress report, June 1978. Washington, DC: National Institute of Mental Health.
———. 1982. Entrance into juvenile prostitution. Washington, DC: National Institute of Mental Health.

Johnson, R., and Carter, M. M. 1980. Flight of the young—Why children run away from their homes. *Adolescence* 15 (Summer):483–489.

Jones, C. L., and Bell-Bolek, C. S. 1986. Kids and drugs: Why, when and what can we do about it? *Children Today* 15 (May-June):5–10.

Kaiser, C. 1988. *1968 in America.* New York: Weidenfeld and Nicolson.

Kandel, D. B. 1985. On processes of peer influence in adolescent drug use: A developmental perspective.

Advances in Alcohol and Substance Abuse 4 (Spring-Summer):139–163.

Kantrowitz, B. 1990. High school homeroom. *Newsweek* (Special Edition) (Summer/Fall):50–54.

Kaufman, J. G., and Widom, C. S. 1999. Childhood victimization, running away, and delinquency. *Journal of research in crime and delinquency* 36 (November):347–370.

Kersten, J. 1993. Street youths, *Bosozaku* and *Yakuza:* Subculture formation and societal reactions in Japan. *Crime and Delinquency* 39 (July):277–295.

Klein, H. 1990. Adolescence, youth, and young adulthood: Rethinking current conceptualizations of life stage. *Youth & Society* 21 (June):446–471.

Lawrence, F. C., Tasker, G. E., Daly, C. T., Orhill, A. L., and Wozniak, P. H. 1986. Adolescents' time spent viewing television. *Adolescence* 21 (Summer): 431–436.

Levin, J., and McDevitt, J. 1993. *Hate crimes: The rising tide of bigotry and bloodshed.* New York: Plenum Press.

Lipschutz, M. R. 1977. Runaways in history. *Crime and Delinquency* 23 (July):321–332.

Lloyd, R. 1976. *For money or love: Boy prostitution in America.* New York: Vanguard.

Lowney, K. 1995. Satanism as oppositional youth subculture. *Journal of Contemporary Ethnography* 23 (January):453–484.

Lyons, A. L. 1988. Satan wants you: The cult of devil worship in America. New York: Mysterious Press.

Marin, R., Hannah, D., Colin, M., Annin, P., and Gegax, T. 1995. Turning in the badges of rebellion. *Newsweek,* February, 6:46.

Marowitz, W. A. 1991. *Bias crime: The law enforcement response.* Chicago: Office of International Criminal Justice.

McAlexander, J. H., and Schonten, J. W. 1989. Hairstyle changes as transition markers. *Sociology & Social Research* 74 (October):58–62.

McGee, Z. T. 1992. Social class differences in parental and peer influence on adolescent drug use. *Deviant Behavior* 13 (Oct-Dec):349–372.

Miller, W. B. 1958. Lower class culture as a generating milieu of gang delinquency. *Journal of Social Issues* 14 (Summer):5–19.

Morgan, T. 1975. Little ladies of the night: Runaways in New York. *New York Times,* November 16:34–38.

Morgan, O. J. 1982. Runaways—Jurisdiction, dynamics, and treatment. *Journal of Marital and Family Therapy* 8 (January):121–127.

Needham, N. R. 1986. Big bucks in little hands. *NEA Today* 5 (November):16–17.

Newman, F., and Caplan, P. J. 1981. Juvenile female prostitution as a gender constant response to early deprivation. *International Journal of Women's Studies* 5 (2):128–137.

New York Times News Service. 1999. Fewer teens find drugs "cool," study says. *Dallas Morning News,* November 22:7A.

O'Brien, S. 1983. *Child pornography.* Dubuque, IA: Kendall-Hunt.

Parsons, T. 1942. Age and sex in the social structure of the United States. *American Sociological Review* 7 (October):604–616.

Pearson, G. H. J. 1958. *Adolescence and the conflict of generations.* New York: W. W. Norton.

Plotnick, R. D. 1992. The effects of attitudes on teenage premarital pregnancy and its resolution. *American Sociological Review* 57 (December):800–811.

Reiss, A. J., Jr. 1961. The social integration of queers and peers. *Social Problems* 9 (Fall):102–120.

Reuters (News Service). 1990. A kiss is just a kiss—but watch out. *Dallas Morning News,* April 22:2-F.

Richards, L. 1988. The appearance of youth subculture: A theoretical perspective on deviance. *Clothing and Textiles Research Journal* 6 (Spring):56–64.

Roberts, A. R. 1981. *Runaways and non-runaways in an American suburb—An exploratory study of adolescent and parent coping.* New York: John Jay Press.

Roche, J. P. 1986. Premarital sex: Attitudes and behavior by dating stage. *Adolescence* 21 (Spring):107–121.

Rogers, D. 1985. *Adolescents and youth* (5th ed.). Englewood Cliffs, NJ: Prentice-Hall.

Roscoe, B., and Kruger, T. L. 1990. AIDS: Late adolescents' knowledge and its influence on sexual behavior. *Adolescence* XXV (Spring):39–48.

Roszak, T. 1969. *The making of a counterculture: Reflections on the technocratic society and its youthful opposition.* Garden City, NY: Anchor Books.

Schwartz, G., and Merten, D. 1967. The language of adolescents: An anthropological approach to the youth culture. *American Journal of Sociology* 72 (March):453–468.

Schwartz, J. 1990. Stalking the youth market. *Newsweek* (Special Edition, Summer/Fall):34–36.

Schwendinger, H., and Schwendinger, J. S. 1985. *Adolescent subcultures and delinquency.* New York: Praeger.

Sebald, H. 1968. *Adolescence: A sociological analysis.* New York: Appleton-Century-Crofts.

Sherman, E. 1986. Teenage sex: A special report. *Ladies Home Journal* 103 (October):138, 199, 202–206.

Sherwin, R., and Corbett, S. 1985. Campus sexual norms and dating relationships: A trend analysis. *Journal of Sex Research* 21 (August):258–274.

Shoemaker, D. J. 2000. *Theories of delinquency: An examination of explanations of delinquent behavior* (4th ed.). New York: Oxford University Press.

Smith E. A. 1962. *American Youth Culture.* Glencoe, IL: Free Press.

Stark, E. 1986. Young, innocent and pregnant. *Psychology Today* 20 (October):28–35.

Statistical Abstract. 1990. *Statistical Abstract of the United States 1988* (110th ed.). Washington, DC: U.S. Bureau of the Census.

Sykes, G. M., and Matza, D. 1957. Techniques of neutralization: A theory of delinquency. *American Sociology Review* 22 (December):664–670.

Thomas, E. 1986. America's crusade: What is behind the latest war on drugs. *Time* 128 (September 15):60–68.

Time. 1986. Growing pains at 40. *Time* 127 (May 19): 22–41.

U.S. Department of Justice. 1990. Runaways in juvenile courts. *Juvenile Justice Bulletin* (November):1–7.

VanderZanden, J. 1986. *Core sociology.* New York: Alfred A. Knopf.
1990. *The social experience: An introduction to sociology* (2nd Ed.). New York: McGraw-Hill.

Vognar, C. 1998. The rhyme and reason behind hip-hop's mainstream success. *Dallas Morning News,* September 6:J1–J5.

Watts, W. D., and Wright, L. S. 1990. The relationship of alcohol, tobacco, marijuana, and other illegal drug use to delinquency among Mexican-American, black, and white adolescent males. *Adolescence* XXV (Spring):171–181.

Wein, B. 1970. *The runaway generation.* New York: David McKay Co.

Weisberg, D. K. 1985. *Children of the night: A study of adolescent prostitution.* Lexington, MA: Lexington Books.

Wells, M., and Sandhu, H. 1986. The juvenile runaway: A historical perspective. *Free Inquiry in Creative Sociology* 14 (November):143–147.

Whitbeck, L. B., and Simons, R. L. 1990. Life on the streets: The victimization of runaway and homeless adolescents. Unpublished paper presented at the Midwest Sociological Society meeting April 11–14, 1990, in Chicago, IL.

Windle, M. 1989. Substance use and abuse among adolescent runaways: A four-year follow-up study. *Journal of Youth & Adolescence* 18 (August):331–344.

Yinger, J. 1960. Contraculture and subculture. *American Sociological Review* 25 (October):625–635.

Zeman, N. 1990. New rules of courtship. *Newsweek* (Special Edition, Summer/Fall):24–27.

Zellner, W. W. 1995. *Countercultures: A sociological analysis.* New York: St. Martin's Press.

Zhang, L., Wieczorek, W. F., and Welte, J. W. 1997. The impact of age of onset of substance use on delinquency. *Journal of Research in Crime and Delinquency.* 34 (May):253–268.

12 JUVENILE GANGS AND DELINQUENT BEHAVIOR

Reading Objectives

The reading of this chapter will help you achieve the following objectives:

1. Extend the sociological perspective to help you understand and explain group dynamics, that is, in what ways gang behavior is social in origin, social in content, and social in consequences.
2. Understand how neighborhood play groups of juveniles can evolve into delinquent youth gangs.
3. Define and understand the concept of "gang."
4. Comprehend the magnitude of the juvenile gang problem, that is, the number of gangs, number of gang members, and gang involvement in delinquent behavior.
5. List the common motives of members for joining gangs and outline the general organization, officers, and roles within fighting gangs.
6. Understand more clearly the connection between the personal and collective social identity of gang members and their use of rituals, symbols, language, and graffiti.
7. Explore the compositional factors of gangs—social class, race, and gender and link these factors to reasons why gangs are formed and the illegal activities of gang members.
8. Trace gang formation and behavior back to the theoretical causes and explanations developed by sociologists.

Introduction

The theoretical explanations of deviance and delinquency discussed in Part II included the important perspective that human behavior is social in origin. In general, our conduct reflects the powerful influences and effects of our families, neighborhoods, communities, subcultures, and other social forces and groups in which we share membership and with whom we interact. More specifically, we looked at the etiological or causal linkages between a broad spectrum of social variables and delinquent behavior.

In earlier chapters of Part III, we focused directly on the family, the school, and the youth subculture as potential, contextual generators of alienated and delinquent youths. In this chapter we turn our attention to juvenile gangs, whose delinquent behavior is not only social in origin but social in content; that is, they act out their misconduct within supportive and cooperative groups.

Predatory Youths: A National Alarm

TEXAS: *Four teenagers were hospitalized Saturday after being shot during a gang fight in Oakcliff Friday night. A group of high school students had rented a ballroom for a party when a second group of uninvited youths entered and began firing automatic pistols and a shotgun into the ceiling. "Then the youths lowered their guns and began firing at teens believed to be in a rival gang," police said* (Dallas Morning News, *1990:34A).*

CALIFORNIA: *A show of disrespect led to the shooting of a 15-year-old Manteca boy in the Taco Bell parking lot late Tuesday night. Police believe the shooting was gang related and don't have any suspects in custody. The victim said that he and two friends were cruising through the parking lot when two young men in a pickup truck "showed them disrespect by staring at them." The teen then reportedly got out of his car and confronted the two men. They exchanged words before a bullet was fired, striking the youth in the shoulder. The two suspects fled westbound and disappeared (Tressel, 1993:A-1).*

OHIO: *The young people charged in a killing rampage that left six dead bragged about the slayings during a holiday dinner, a newspaper reported.*

Melissa Gomez, who had been a member of the loosely formed group, [said]…that her friends held a Christmas dinner at which the talk quickly turned to the slayings.

She said Heather Matthews, 20, told her: "If you're going to run with us, you need to know what's going on and what's already happened."

She said Ms. Matthews showed off a new pair of tennis shoes and said: "Oh, I killed some girl at the phone booth for them."

Matthews and three other members of the group called the Downtown Posse were charged with murder and robbery in the three-day spree. DeMarcus Smith, 17, and Laura Taylor, 16, were charged with aggravated robbery in juvenile court (Daily O'Collegian, *1993:3).*

Although only a small proportion of juvenile crime in the United States is as violent as reported in these news excerpts, or impacts so tragically on individual victims or society, such acts of collective violence are repeated often enough to warrant our serious concern and study.

The Solitary Delinquent

As with many other forms of deviant behavior, some juvenile crime is committed by solitary individuals acting alone, and this phenomenon must be acknowledged. Opportunities arise for youngsters to make delinquent responses that do not require encouragement from peers or other influential persons. For example, occasional opportunities for crimes may appeal to some juveniles because they can be carried out alone and privately, without an accomplice or even a tolerant witness. Such solitary operatives seek to protect and maintain respectable ties and status within the nondeviant society (Goffman, 1963). Solitary delinquents also may be emotionally or socially maladjusted in some way. They avoid companionship and group interaction and express their frustration or anger in a delinquent, loner role:

> *The solitary delinquent may be a social isolate, who is unable to make friends or who prefers to work or play alone. Throughout society there are people who do not make close affiliations with groups. If such a person is motivated toward delinquency, he would tend to carry out his delinquency alone, just as he prefers to study alone, read instead of play with others, or have a hobby that does not require cooperation. It is normal for him to act as an individual and not as a member of a clique or gang (Cavan and Ferdinand, 1981:225).*

Although nearly a third of the boys who come before the juvenile court have, for one reason or another, committed their delinquencies alone (Cavan and Ferdinand, 1981), little research has focused on the solitary delinquent. As a result, causal explanations are largely speculative.

Many sociologists, while acknowledging the statistical reality of solitary individuals, counter that the popularized picture of "the lone gunman," "the secretive alcoholic," "the closet homosexual," or "the solitary delinquent"—acting out deviant behavior with little or no connection with other members of society—is an oversimplification. Theoretically, it is virtually impossible to conceive of any human behavior as occurring in a complete social vacuum, without an interlocking web of human interaction and totally devoid of social causes, social support, and/or social consequences. Applying this sociological principle to deviant or delinquent behavior, no act can be judged as conforming or nonconforming without the societal audience.

Sociologists often conceptualize each individual and his or her behavior as being at the hub or vortex of a social network (Mitchell, 1979). For example, consider the shoplifter. Although there are professional shoplifting gangs that prey upon retail merchants, (see Box 12-1), much shoplifting involves single individuals, operating alone. However, many observers are oblivious to the social linkages between a solitary delinquent shoplifter and numerous other members of society who, while usually not responsible for the illegal behavior, are nevertheless related to it in some way. Figure 12-1 outlines the shoplifter's social network.

The model of the shoplifter's social network (Figure 12-1) contains only some of the linkages and associations between the individual offender and other people. If we look at the apparently solitary actor closely, we can discern an abstract, dynamic, and complex societal web that connects the individual and the behavior in question to a wide array of other persons and groups which in some way support, influence, or are affected by the behavior. These often inescapable connections and relationships may be voluntary or involuntary, formal or informal, primary or secondary, but the impact of deviant or delinquent behavior on other persons sharing a social network can be extremely negative and traumatic.

FIGURE 12-1   The Shoplifter's Social Network

Group Delinquency

In addition to the sociological principle regarding the social causes and consequences of human behavior, there is considerable documentation that most juvenile delinquency is committed by social groupings of varying size, purpose, and organization.

One of the most extensive studies along this line of inquiry was conducted by Maynard Erickson and Gary Jensen (1977) who administered self-report questionnaires to 1,700 high school students from three small towns and three urban schools in Arizona. The subjects were asked how many times during the past year they had committed each of 18 delinquent acts, and in how many of those times they had been in the company of others. The findings suggested that the youths generally engaged in delinquent behavior when they were with their friends. However, the tendency varied with the type of offense. Group violations were more common with drug offenses and least common with status offenses other than drinking alcoholic beverages and smoking tobacco. The study also found that females were even more likely than males to commit delinquent acts in groups.

The findings of Erickson and Jensen generally agreed with those of similar investigations carried out in other countries. For example, Brunner (1974) found that group membership and processes played a central role in three major types of juvenile crime in Germany; that between 80 and 90 percent of illegal behavior by juveniles involved groups of youths, particularly gang crime, violent crime, and drug abuse.

The group context of juvenile misbehavior should come as no surprise when we recall from Chapter 2 that we human beings share with most other species a strong social imperative that constrains us toward social interaction with others of our kind. Thus, most nonconforming, delinquent behavior—like most conforming, law-abiding behavior—has been widely observed and documented in social groupings. LaMar Empey and Mark Stafford (1991:114, 116) concluded that "the gregarious and companionate character of law-violating behavior" is clearly reflected in self-report studies of juvenile delinquency: "…the preponderant majority of all delinquent acts are committed in groups—whether male or female, black or white, middle- or lower-class."

Paradoxically, the initial social stimulant for potentially serious delinquent behavior by some children has been traced to innocent neighborhood play groups.

The Play Group

The natural, spontaneous, and initially innocuous emergence of neighborhood play groups among urban youngsters was well described in Frederick Thrasher's (1927:26) early study of gangs:

> *On a warm summer evening children literally swarm over areaways and sidewalks, vacant lots and rubbish dumps, streets and alleys…This endless activity has a tremendous fascination,… and it would be a marvel indeed if any healthy boy could hold himself aloof from it…*

The play groups engage in all sorts of childhood games including "hide-and-go-seek," "cowboys and Indians," "pick-up softball," and crap-shooting. These are natural groupings of participants who live in the same area and know each other as well as brothers. In time, as the youngsters grow older, more adventuresome, and more mischievous, such childhood games may become less satisfying. Building on the loosely organized alliances and innocent activities of the play group, some youths begin to experiment with more aggressive and predatory group behavior, directed toward youths outside the group and against society in general. Thus, the "game" is extended over time and territory to include higher stakes and involuntary victim-participants.

Fifty years after Thrasher's landmark study, in a *Time* magazine report (1977), a youth who attended a school for problem youngsters said: "Mugging is like playing a game; kids do it for the fun of it."

Clifford Shaw and Henry McKay (1931:251) also reported on the playful, game-like approach of juveniles at the beginning of their delinquent careers:

> *When we were shoplifting we always made a game of it. For example, we might gamble on who could steal the most caps in a day, or who could steal caps from the largest number of stores in a day, or who could steal in the presence of a detective and then get away. We were always daring each other that way and thinking up new schemes. This was the best part of the game…It was the fun I wanted,*

not the hat. I kept this up for months and then began to sell the things to a man on the west side. It was at this time that I began to steal for gain.

Since the family usually provides the first social setting for childhood play activities, siblings sometimes move on to engage in delinquent behavior together. Seattle, Washington even had a one-family gang: seven brothers, aged 11 to 20, were arrested 192 times during a 9-year period, 1968 through 1976. Enough of the boys were always at liberty to keep up the family tradition (*Time,* 1977).

In more recent years, Ikuya Sato (1987) has focused on this propensity among a great many youngsters to "play" as a prelude and accompaniment to delinquent behavior. He conducted an extensive review of major urban ethnographies describing the playful attitude and approach of youth groups seeking entertainment and excitement in the streets. The developing by-product often turned into juvenile crime. Sato suggests that this common, playful pattern and approach to misconduct by mischievous, daring, and thrill-seeking adolescents is an understudied characteristic of gang behavior. This aggressive play group, according to Sato, offers a promising conceptual framework for explanatory theory building and an alternative to the widely held views that juveniles are thrust into delinquency by their unfortunate circumstances or conformity to deviant subcultural values.

The Juvenile Gang

Some studies have concluded that much juvenile delinquency consists of gangs committing crimes as social activities. For instance, Sarnecki (1983) suggested that committing crimes together satisfies juveniles' needs for togetherness and excitement. Notwithstanding, society shows little tolerance for serious misconduct by youth groups, even if interpreted as "social activities" fulfilling juvenile needs for "togetherness" and "excitement." For while gang members may view their predatory behavior as "fun and games," their victims see it as violent and frightening crime. From the viewpoint of the larger society, there is a great difference between the neighborhood play group and the intimidating street gang. Despite the play group basis for the early association among some gang members, once they advance beyond the occasional and spontaneous prank to a conscious and deliberate pattern of illegal conduct, they become a threat to society.

What Is a Gang?

In its broadest sense, the term **gang** means *a group of persons assembled and acting or working together.* In time, common usage applied the term to places and things utilized by some organized groups of workers. For example, sailors have traditionally referred to the movable bridge used in boarding or leaving a ship at a pier as a "gangplank." Similarly, the opening by which a ship is boarded is the "gangway." Additional applications of the term were made to describe "a set of similar instruments arranged so that they function together." For example, a "gang cultivator" or a "gang plow" is built to turn multiple and parallel furrows. Most fishermen are acquainted with the concept of the "gang hook," which is actually a cluster of several fishhooks with their shanks joined together (*Webster's Third New International Dictionary,* 1986:934).

The term "gang" often has been used to signify a group of close associates or friends with no criminal or antisocial connotations. For example, a generation or so ago "the gang" could have signified a collegial and informal male group whose activities centered on social drinking, cardplaying, and sporting events. In the early part of the twentieth century, several popular songs romanticized that notion with such lyrics as: "Those wedding bells are breaking up that old gang of mine" (Miller, 1981; Lotz et al., 1985:131).

In the late nineteenth century, large sections of the American West were terrorized by gangs of adult criminals. The collective cruelty, robbery, and violence of those outlaw bands reinforced the definition of the gang as a group of persons united in unlawful and antisocial activities. While the word "gang" is still occasionally used in law enforcement, the news media, and by the public in reference to organized groups of adult criminals engaged in extortion, racketeering, theft, and prostitution, the most recent and prominent application has been to hostile groups of urban youths who are reputed to terrorize neighborhoods, victimize innocent people, and fight each other over territory and status. This image of urban gangs involved in crime and delinquency was popularized in recent decades by such motion pictures as *West Side Story, The Wild Ones, The Lords of Flatbush, Rumblefish, The Outsiders, Colors,* and *Boys in the Hood.*

Although several decades of serious attention have been given to juvenile gangs by criminologists, sociologists, and law enforcement personnel and agencies, the great variability among these gangs and the many dimensions of their behavior have confounded the development of an all-encompassing answer to the question "What is a gang?" (Curry and Decker, 1998:2). However, Walter Miller (1975:1), after interviewing law enforcement and social service professionals who dealt with youth gangs in six large American cities, brought together some of the major variables into one of the better working definitions of the term *"gang":*

> *A gang is a group of recurrently associating individuals with identifiable leadership and internal organization, identifying with or claiming control over territory in a community, and engaging either individually or collectively in violent or other forms of illegal behavior.*

In later sections of this chapter we address the multiple variations in gang objectives, orientation, and organization, and offer theoretical explanations for their formation and behavior.

James Short (1987:16–17) extrapolated a useful set of definitional criteria from the gangs he studied with Fred Strodtbeck, contending gangs manifest these characteristics:

1. *recurrent congregation outside the home;*
2. *self-defined inclusion/exclusion criteria and continuity of affiliation;*
3. *a territorial basis consisting of customary hanging and ranging areas, including self-defined use-and-occupancy rights;*
4. *a versatile activity repertoire; and*
5. *organizational differentiation, e.g., by authority, roles, prestige, friendship, or special interest cliques.*

Such academic definitions fail to capture precisely what "the gang" means to its members. A 16-year-old gang member in Hartford, Connecticut *was* able to succinctly summarize the camaraderie, esprit de corps, mutualism, and male bonding in his definition: "What is a gang? You look out for me and I look out for you—that's what makes a gang" (Ramos, 1989:7).

History of Youth Gangs

Antisocial and criminal conduct by members of juvenile gangs is not a new phenomenon. Nor does history exempt any western nation from this form of deviant behavior. Cyril Burt (1925) reported that many troublesome and even dangerous delinquent gangs were present in England during the first quarter of this century. The word "Hooligan" came into common English usage in 1898 to describe the rowdy youths who participated in a regular pattern of civil disorder. The term was derived from the Hooligan gang which engaged in pitched battles with other youth gangs in London.

> The "Hooligans" adopted a uniform dress-style. Bell-bottom trousers with a buttoned vent in the leg, colourful neck scarves, a distinctive style of cap, boots said to be "toe-plated with iron and calculated to kill easily", ornamental leather belts with designs worked in metal studs, and a characteristic "donkey fringe" haircut.... (Pearson, 1984:83).

Thrasher (1936:40) noted in 1936 that tens of thousands of poverty-stricken Russian youths were gravitating to gangs for survival:

> Russia's 100,000 neglected children are said to travel in gangs, winning a precarious living by stealing and finding shelter in deserted buildings and in Moscow and other cities in the sewers and catacombs.

James Inciardi (1978:34–36) documented the presence of youth gangs engaged in criminal activity in American cities during the nineteenth century:

> The earliest gangs consisted almost entirely of Irishmen. The Irish, emigrating to this country in vast numbers and lacking funds, education, and skills, were met with contempt by native New Yorkers and were forced into the city's worst slum— the Five Points district...and lacking other means of earning a living, many developed criminal careers.
> ...The Plug Uglies were formed in the mid-1820's and took their name from the giant plug hats which each member filled with rags and straw to protect their heads during gang battles. The Shirt Tails were so called because they wore their shirts on the outside of their trousers,... These gangs of the Five Points, Bowery, and Hell's Kitchen, which often included hundreds of men and boys, consisted of many small gangs grouped together and led by a supreme chieftain who commanded absolute loyalty ...
> The gangs of youthful and young adult criminals who made war on one another and terrorized the streets of New York were also evident in other cities. Philadelphia had its "Buffaloes," "Blood Tubs," "Rugs," and "Copper Heads";

Baltimore had its "Stringers"; and a group known as the "Crawfish Boys"
plagued the streets of Cincinnati.

Battles over "turf" (territory) between rival gangs often raged for days. One gang war in New York City lasted an incredible 30 years—from the 1830s to the 1860s—and the Army was often called out to restore order. Gang members armed themselves with pistols, muskets, knives, bricks, clubs, brass knuckles, and pikes.

Amazingly, even women joined in the fray. The most famous female fighter was
Hellcat Maggie. Her teeth were filed to points and she wore long fake fingernails
made of brass (Street Wars, 1993:7).

Contemporary Youth Gangs in the United States

The first scholarly investigation of youth gangs in the United States was Frederick Thrasher's (1927) work in Chicago. Although Thrasher verified that a great many of the gangs were organized primarily for conventional participation in athletic, dancing, and other socially acceptable activities, many gang members were routinely involved in collective or individual delinquency.

Number of Gangs and Members

Although the United States has a long history of aggressive youth gangs taking to the streets to battle one another, the police, and to prey upon the citizenry, the statistical magnitude of the gang problem was imprecise and often speculative. Nevertheless, during the 1960s, 1970s, and 1980s, several researchers made significant beginnings to measure the number of gangs and members in selected cities (Miller, 1975; Needle and Stapleton, 1983; Spergel and Curry, 1988; Klein, 1995). These scholars concluded that there has been an alarming increase in gang activity, spreading rapidly across the country, and constituting a serious social problem.

In 1995, fortified by a national concern and funding, the Office of Juvenile Justice and Delinquency Prevention of the U.S. Department of Justice, established the National Youth Gang Center. One of the major tasks assigned to the NYGC was to conduct periodic and methodologically sound, national surveys to obtain comprehensive data on American youth gangs. These annual surveys systematically collect information on reported gang composition and activities from a sample of law enforcement agencies in cities, counties, and communities of varying population size, in all parts of the nation. Data on motorcycle gangs, hate or ideology groups, prison gangs, and exclusively adult gangs were excluded from the survey. The rich data base emerging from these ongoing NYGC surveys have validated earlier projections that large numbers of American youth are seriously involved in gangs and gang-related crime.

At present, the 1997 National Youth Gang Survey is the most recently available report in the series. Of the 3,018 urban and suburban police departments and county sheriffs' departments that received the survey questionnaire, 2,766 responded (a 92 percent response rate).

From these data, it was estimated that 4,712 U.S. cities and counties experienced
gang activity in 1997, down slightly from 4,824 in 1996. There were an estimated

30,500 gangs and 816,000 gang members in 1997, compared with an estimated 31,000 gangs and 846,000 gang members in 1996.... Despite the slight decrease in gang activity from 1996 to 1997, most respondents (45 percent) felt that the gang problem in their jurisdictions in 1997 was "staying about the same," 35 percent indicated it was "getting worse," and 20 percent felt it was "getting better" (Moore and Terrett, 1999:1).

Researchers are greatly interested in the movement of gang members from one law enforcement jurisdiction to another, thus revealing how much gang activity can be traced to more permanent local residents, and how much can be credited to transient or new residents to the area. Most respondents (89 percent) estimated that 23 percent of their gang members were migrants—moving to their jurisdictions with families, to find jobs, join friends, and other social reasons.

The nationwide sample of police and sheriffs' departments participating in the 1997 Youth Gang Survey were also asked to indicate the degree to which gang members had engaged in certain offenses in their jurisdictions. For example, these officers revealed—on the average—that gang members were involved in 28 percent of the aggravated assault and larceny/theft, 27 percent of the motor vehicle theft, and 26 percent of the burglary reports in their areas (Moore and Terrett, 1999). Such statistical evidence strongly supports the contention of many theorists that a youth associated with a gang is much more likely to participate in criminal or delinquent behavior than a youth without gang affiliation (See Chapters 6 and 7).

Locale

Youth gangs have been active in all 50 states. The 10 states reporting the most gangs were (in order) California, Texas, Illinois, Colorado, Arizona, Florida, Missouri, Washington, Oregon, and Utah. The 10 states reporting the most gang members were (in order) California, Illinois, Texas, Ohio, Indiana, New Mexico, Arizona, Florida, Nevada, and Minnesota (Moore, 1997).

Robert Park, in the Editor's Preface to Thrasher's study, reminded readers that:

Gangs are not confined to cities, nor to the slums of cities...Every village has at least its boy gang...composed of those same foot-loose, prowling, and predacious adolescents who herd and hang together, after the manner of the undomesticated male everywhere... (Thrasher, 1927:ix).

However, Park's important generalization has been overshadowed by Thrasher's forceful portrayal of the inner city as the normal and natural habitat of the street gang. The contemporary image of the leather-jacketed, streetwise, and dangerous gangs roaming the inner city streets has prevailed, not only because of their high visibility, but also because of recurring news reports of their criminal activities and the public outcry for protection.

Criminologists and social scientists, supported by the official data on crime and delinquency, often have contributed to the stereotype of the youthful street gang as an inner city phenomenon with their conclusion that urban areas of blighted slum neighborhoods are the focal points of numerous social ills, including juvenile delinquency. The research of Shaw and McKay (1969) supported the belief that delinquency is especially associated with the normative confusion and corruption manifested in the high delinquency areas of large U.S. cities. These writers and numerous others argued that criminal and delinquent behavior is concentrated, encouraged, and reinforced by the prevailing customs and norms of such deteriorated areas (see Chapter 6 for a detailed discussion).

In the lower socioeconomic slum districts of the city, gang behavior can take on a spatial, ecological dimension as members relate and interact with each other and their mutual environment. It has been well documented that urban gang members generally demonstrate a territorial imperative in which they consistently identify and defend boundaries around their 'turf'—the geographical area they intend to dominate. The gang territory may be the immediate neighborhood in which members reside or the area around a recreational center, store, school, park, or pool hall. The familiar range and sense of possession lend social and psychological security and much coveted status and identity to gang members. Similar to the citizens of formally organized nations, gang boys will defend their established boundaries against competing gangs from another area, and other outsiders who are perceived as threatening. Ronald Halvorsen, a former gang member, described this territorial behavior and the careful demarcation of boundary lines:

> *If you were to visit the Coney Island beaches, you would find they are divided into sections by rock walls that run out into the water. These sections are called "bays," and each is claimed by a different gang. The Avenue X gang held Bay 13, and the Swords had Bay 17, up to the Steeplechase Pier. We Beachcombers staked out our claim on Bay 11, just down from the big Cyclone roller coaster. We practically camped there during the summer months. At last, I was really living! (Halvorsen and Hawley, 1973:56).*

Contrary to official arrest statistics and the media emphasis on inner city gangs, considerable evidence shows that delinquent gang activity also exists in suburban communities that ring large cities, small towns, and even rural areas (Wooden, 1995; *Dallas Morning News*, 1990; Muehlbauer and Dodder, 1983). John Johnstone (1981) found intense gang activity in several suburban communities near Chicago. These suburban gangs also lived in rundown tenements whose black majority experienced high levels of unemployment and poverty similar to those found in central city ghettos.

Regarding youth gangs in more affluent communities, over 40 years ago Harrison Salisbury (1958) painted a grim picture of marauding bands of middle-class teenagers, living in fashionable suburbs of Boston and New York, and committing gang rapes and malicious vandalism on schools:

> *A typical outbreak occurred at Maplewood, New Jersey, a fine community of middle-class families, proud of a low juvenile delinquency rate. A gang of boys broke into the Maplewood Junior High School and sacked it. They destroyed the principal's office, wrecked classrooms, carried kerosene and alcohol from the art department into the library, toppled books from the shelves, poured inflammables over them and set fire to the place. School authorities estimated the damage at $300,000 (Salisbury, cited in Vaz, 1967:196).*

James Coleman (1970) charted and described the development of a youth gang in a middle class suburb. Boys frequenting an area near the community library formed a friendship group that evolved over time into a delinquent gang. Their delinquent activities included vandalism, the theft of guns and automobiles, and the illegal use of alcohol and drugs.

By 1997, countless smaller towns and communities were having their own experiences with delinquent gangs. According to Dan Korem, an author and expert on gangs in rural and suburban neighborhoods, "…middle-class communities typically under-report gang statistics by up to 75 percent." However, the suprising growth and potential for criminal activities by such groups are serious concerns to local police and sheriffs' departments.

> **DEERY, N.H. (AP):** *Mike pulls up his shirt to proudly show off the homemade tattoo of the word "Impact" on his chest, a sign of his membership in the all-white, all-suburban Impact gang.…*
>
> *But to some residents of this predominantly white, middle-class bedroom community of 31,000, it means fear, crime, and trouble. (Greenville Herald Banner, 1997:B-2).*

The National Youth Gang Center, in its annual surveys and reports, gives us a complete and up-to-date picture of geographical patterns and trends of gang habitation. It has become crystal clear that the incidence of gangs and their crime-related activities are no longer just a big city problem. The 1996 survey found that gangs were operating in approximately 4,800 U.S. cities and towns, and affecting "more jurisdictions than before, including many smaller communities and rural and suburban areas with no previous gang experience" (Snyder and Sickmund, 1999:77–78). Table 12-1 charts the chronological spread of gangs in recent times to law-enforcement jurisdictions of varying population size and density.

The Motives for Gang Membership

Although a large number of gang members collectively commit deviant and delinquent acts, they rarely cite that as a reason for becoming a gang member. Many gang members contend

TABLE 12-1   Contemporary Onsets of Illegal Gang Activities in U.S. Communities: 1989–1993

Type of Jurisdiction	Percent Reporting Active Gangs	Average Year of Gang Problem Onset
Big cities	74%	1989
Suburbs	57%	1990
Small cities	34%	1992
Rural areas	25%	1993

Source: Snyder, H. N., and Sickmund, M., *Juvenile Offenders and Victims: 1999 National Report.* Department of Justice, Office of Juvenile Justice and Delinquency Prevention. Washington, DC: U.S. Government Printing Office. September 1999.

that they joined a gang out of fear of being alone and vulnerable in a tough neighborhood. Others expressed much the same rationale—that the gang offered an opportunity to develop and maintain a peer group, or friendship network. Certainly this is a natural human desire, made particularly urgent for youngsters who see former associates from their play group and school affiliating with the neighborhood gang. Other reasons given by gang members for joining the gang include boredom, defiance of authority figures, loyalty to one's own racial or ethnic group, adventure, money from the drug trade, and poor relationships with parents and teachers. Thus, in a sense, the gang can represent a surrogate or substitute family for some youths who perceive a lack of rapport and positive interaction with their own biological families.

James Coleman's insightful concept of "social capital" is especially relevant in explaining why some youth seem favorably or unfavorably inclined toward gang membership. **Social capital,** according to Coleman (1988), *is a reservoir of resilience in some individuals that enables them to resist the allure of potentially damaging associates and activities.* Coleman outlined how social capital is acquired initially through nurturing, intergenerational relationships within one's family of origin—particularly through the presence of both parents in the home and the amount of quality time they spend with their children. This thesis has similarities to Social Learning Theory (see Chapter 7) in that the child is more likely to extend internalized, conventional, family values into life in the larger society. On the other hand, the lack of social capital is an important deficit for both young men and women in their efforts to successfully overcome pressures on the street toward participation in crime and membership in gangs.

Other gang boys have suggested that gang membership was the only available avenue open to them to achieve some measure of respect and identity. This unfulfilled need can be especially pressing in lower class neighborhoods where residents who lack status and recognition on the basis of occupations, material possessions, and educational achievements can find social support, security, and a sense of power within a gang of similarly situated persons (Bing, 1991). One gang in New York City is composed largely of deaf boys and young men between the ages of 13 and 35 who are drawn together by their common physical disability and perceived rejection by the larger society. They call themselves The Nasty Homicides, and decorate their hangout and leather jackets with the slogan, "Deaf Power"—a statement of unity and a challenge to all others. Like many other gangs, the Nasty Homicides are potentially violent. According to Short and Strodtbeck (1965), members of delinquent gangs tend to be characterized by a general social disability, lacking skill in interpersonal relations, social assurance, knowledge of the job market, and sophistication in their relations with girls. By displays of toughness and by committing crimes, these unskilled, unemployed school dropouts can assert their masculinity and feel successful in the eyes of friends in the gang (Zastrow, 1992). Short (1987:31), in citing earlier research on gangs, observed that "The greater social skills possessed by gang leaders...and their supportive and nurturant style of leadership...confirm the value of group membership to gang members."

Lewis Yablonsky and Martin Haskell (1988) contended that motivation for gang affiliation is also related to the primary purpose of the specific gang in question. Gangs that focus on social activities such as athletic competition with other groups, dancing, and group discussions (or "bull sessions") attract youths who crave camaraderie and fellowship by engaging in generally innocent activities, and seldom resort to serious crime.

BOX 12-1 Concept Application

The Profit Motive: Group Shoplifting and "The Swarm"

In many cases, the youthful rationale for collective delinquency has moved away from the "fun and games" extension of the play group and the "fraternal hell-raising" of the street gang, to a purposeful economic motive. Several social scientists have begun using economic models to explain the mercenary and predacious emphasis of such gangs and other forms of deviance (Clarke and Cornish, 1985).

> *These rational choice theorists argue that, when faced with a choice, individuals calculate the costs and benefits of various options and, on the basis of these calculations, choose the most profitable option. Such economic models usually assign monetary values to the costs and benefits of various options (Best, 1994:226).*

Some youth gangs have become semiprofessional groups of highly specialized "business" associates, fully committed to the pursuit of financial gain through car thefts, the marketing of illegal drugs, and other criminal operations. Shoplifting gangs are good examples. In contrast to the individual shoplifter discussed earlier in this chapter, shoplifting is also often a group endeavor, not only stimulated and encouraged by peer support (Rosenberg and Silverstein, 1969), but conducive to the development of sophisticated criminal skills and strategies.

William Cobb (1982) described a juvenile shoplifting incident that required considerable nerve, planning, and coordination. He described a scenario in which nine male juveniles, several of whom were known to the store security as previous shoplifters, gathered around a table in the clothing department and obscured the view of security personnel while they shoplifted. In an attempt to catch them, all of the store security personnel (seven people) approached the boys to make clear to them that they were being watched. Meanwhile, on another floor of the store, a group of youths helped themselves to merchandise "secure in their belief that their nine confederates

were keeping the store detectives busy" (Cobb, 1982:374).

Another highly organized and proficient juvenile shoplifting gang recently emerged on the East Coast. New Jersey police reported that a charismatic shoplifting mastermind organized about 20 boys into a gang of thieves for weekend excursions to suburban malls in four states. Each child netted up to $800 worth of designer clothes which were exchanged for money and drugs. As arrests were made, authorities found several boys carrying a typewritten manual that explains how to exchange old clothes from their knapsacks for new clothes in store fitting rooms, how to remove alarm devices from merchandise, and how to spot store detectives.

> *"Mostly you have to use common sense and act cool and you really shouldn't have any trouble," the manual says.*
>
> *"If you see someone pick up a phone on your way out of the store and then hear some bells, those bells are for you," it reads. "Don't run or panic. Just calmly walk out of the store."*
>
> *If a shoplifter gets caught, the manual advises, they "will be out in several hours. The juvenile justice system is such that you will not be held for very long" (The Daily O'Collegian, 1987:8).*

Even more brazen, but less secretive in their intent, is the "swarm assault" utilized by at least one Sacramento, California gang in 1993. The "swarm" is comprised of 10 to 30 young males who suddenly invade and overwhelm a lone convenience store clerk in the middle of the night. They are not only attentive to timing and the element of surprise, but neutralize alarms and security cameras, and focus on high-priced items of merchandise. After assaulting the clerk and plundering the store, the gang members quickly withdraw with their loot (KCBS, 1993).

Continued

BOX 12-1 *Continued*

Sources

Best, Joel. 1994. *Organizing deviance* (2nd ed.) Englewood Cliffs, NJ: Prentice-Hall.
Clarke, R. V., and Cornish, D. B. 1985. "Modeling offender's decisions." *Crime and Justice* 6:147–185.
Cobb, W. E. 1982. "Shoplifting." Pp. 369–376. In L. D. Savitz and N. Johnston (Eds.). *Contemporary criminology.* New York: John Wiley.
Daily O'Collegian. April 17, 1987. Stillwater, OK: Oklahoma State University. P. 8.
KCBS Radio News Report. July 20, 1993. Sacramento, California.
Rosenberg, B., and Silverstein, H. 1969. *The varieties of delinquent experience.* Waltham, MA: Blaisdell.

On the other hand, these authors noted, juvenile gangs whose major pursuit is the procurement of money and material possessions through theft and other illegal activities recruit members who are not only interested in such endeavors but have those skills of organization and guile that will be useful to the gang.

Yablonsky and Haskell's final type of gang was the violent-prone gang whose main function and activity centers on the planning and implementation of intragroup confrontation and conflict in defense of territory or status. New members are attracted into alliances and associations with the gang by the prospects of excitement and violence (Yablonsky and Haskell, 1988:260–264).

Initiation Rituals

Most gangs, whose members are informally organized and have only vague objectives, have no initiation ceremonies or rituals. Youths may become members by virtue of their living in proximity to other gang members or their hangout, or casually interacting with gang members in a play group, at school, or on the streets. Thus, the role and status change from nonmember to member is likely to be a taken-for-granted, natural transition. However, researchers have discovered that some of the more aggressive gangs, in keeping with their ominous names and hostile posturing, do have formal and often violent initiation ceremonies for new members. An older study by Herbert Block and Arthur Niederhoffer (1958) cited a wide assortment of rituals and symbols, including leather motorcycle jackets decorated with the gang's name and logo, distinctive and sometimes radical hairstyles, and scarification and tattooing sessions resulting in the permanent display of gang affiliation.

A longstanding practice among many lower class gangs is to initiate new members with an ordeal of hazing, which often takes the form of physical punishment called "cramping" or "the pink belly." The new applicant for membership is held by two of the older boys while the rest of the gang take turns striking him in the stomach. If he "chickens out" of the ordeal, he is rejected for gang membership. A variation is putting the aspiring member inside a circle of gang members and demanding that he fight his way out. Some more predatory gangs require members to mug somebody—"getting paid," they call it (*Tulsa World,* 1990:A9).

The drive-by killing has been used as an initiation rite for the Crips and Bloods of Los Angeles. "From the comfort of a passing car, the itinerant killer simply shoots down a member of a rival gang or an innocent bystander" (Bing, 1989:51). While such initiation rituals

Shoplifting and other forms of theft from commercial establishments have traditionally been carried out by lone individuals or very small groups. Today, shoplifting has become an organized criminal activity of many youth gangs.

appear cruel, bizarre, and senseless to the outside observer, they represent highly coveted badges of honor, courage, and membership to new gang inductees.

NBC *Dateline* (1993) reported that initiation into some San Antonio, Texas girl gangs involves having sexual intercourse with someone infected with HIV (the virus precursor of AIDS). Another female initiation is called "rolling the dice" in which the digits on the dice determine the number of males with whom the new member must have sex. The slang expression used by the gang for this sexual initiation is "engine to caboose" (i.e., "first to last").

Gang Organization

Frederick Thrasher's (1927) observation that "No two gangs are just alike" is still valid. He indicated:

Wide divergency in the character of its personnel combined with differences of physical social environment, or experience and tradition, give to every gang its own peculiar character. It may vary as to membership, type of leaders, mode of organization, interests and activities, and finally as to its status in the community (Thrasher, 1927:45).

While this complex variability among delinquent gangs confounds the formation of discrete, categorical types, there are some overarching patterns of social organization that can be identified.

In smaller, less goal-oriented youth gangs, one or two older, tougher, more articulate boys with forceful personalities may be the informally acknowledged leaders, who set the pace and determine the nature of the groups' activities. On the other hand, larger and more instrumental gangs have a functional organization, generally reflecting the nature of their orientation and activities. For example, the leadership of such well-known fighting gangs as the Egyptian Kings and Dragons, the Mau Maus, and the Jesters includes the president, vice-president, treasurer, a "light-up man" or "armorer" who maintains the gang's arsenal, and the "war counselor" who serves to identify enemy gangs and arranges for "rumbles" or fights.

Formal and informal alliances may be worked out between gangs that find some practical advantage or benefit in such alliances. Malcolm Klein (1964) identified such affiliations among several traditional gangs in Los Angeles. Typically, a "gang cluster" consists of three or four age-graded male subgroups plus a female auxiliary. Each subgroup maintains its own identity yet clearly affiliates with the overall cluster and its "generic name." In this way, several small and relatively weak gangs can muster a more formidable appearance through their alliance network, in confrontations with rival gangs. A few crime-oriented youth gangs have contacts and working agreements with adult criminals in their areas. This can have far-reaching implications. An exploratory study by John Irwin and Donald Cressey (1977) highlighted the situation in Illinois prisons where there is an importation of organization, roles, and norms from the streets of Chicago to the prison through gangs which retain their organization and identity inside and outside prison walls.

Meetings and meeting places may be loosely defined by most smaller gangs and their members as "anytime" or "all the time," "anywhere" or "everywhere," and a centrally located street corner, shopping mall, or convenience store may serve as gang headquarters. At the other extreme, a few large gangs have become virtually institutionalized in some cities. The Vice Lords in Chicago, for example, created an administrative Board of Directors comprised of representatives from subgroups within the "Vice Lord Nation." Regular weekly meetings were instituted, along with membership fees, and membership cards featuring the Vice Lords' logo—a top hat, cane, and white gloves (Keiser, 1969).

The Near Group

Lewis Yablonsky (1959) complained that most efforts to explain gang organization begin with the imprecise assumption that gangs fit the pattern of the traditionally defined sociological group. His research concluded that the delinquent gang is organizationally midway between the stability of the established group and the instability of the mob. Thus, the gang is a kind of social collectivity in its own right, with characteristics especially suited to meet the varied needs of its members.

One way of viewing human collectivities is on a continuum of organization characteristics. At one extreme, we have a highly organized, cohesive, functioning collection of individuals as members of a sociological group. At the other extreme, we have a mob of individuals characterized by anonymity, disturbed leadership, motivated by emotion, and in some cases representing a destructive collectivity within the inclusive social system. (Yablonsky, 1959:109)

Yablonsky maintained that most delinquent gangs are midway on the group-mob continuum and thus are structurally neither groups nor mobs. He described the gang as a "near group" characterized by "diffuse role definitions, limited cohesion, impermanence, minimal consensus of norms, shifting membership, disturbed leadership, and limited definition of membership expectations" (Yablonsky, 1959:109).

Several other researchers have challenged parts of Yablonsky's generalization. Cohen (1958) and other proponents of the gang subculture concept (see Chapter 6) argued that many gang members share a remarkable consensus regarding norms and roles. Klein (1971) contended that the large majority of gang leaders are *not* sociopathic nor do they otherwise suffer serious emotional maladjustment.

John Hagedorn (1988), on the basis of his study of Milwaukee gangs, confirmed Thrasher's observation on the diversity of gang organization and cautioned against the pyramid stereotype of a hard core of sociopathic criminals leading a broad fringe of impressionable kids.

Milwaukee's gangs come in a variety of forms and shapes, but none that looks like a pyramid....

Each age-group has its own "main-group," its leaders, and its "wanna be's."... The makeup of each of these age groups varies between gangs and over time within each gang. A "wanna be" this week may be in the "main group" next week. (Hagedorn, 1988:89, 90)

Gang Graffiti, Slanguage, and Symbols[1]

Like most other enduring subcultures, street gangs are characterized by their own unique and ever-evolving jargon or language. This *slanguage* is reflected in youth gang graffiti which has been called "the newspaper of the streets" for gang members. Its presence is usually one of the first signs of street gang activity in a neighborhood. While graffiti is a chronic and unsightly eyesore to the larger community, it serves several useful purposes to gangs, including identifying territorial boundaries, giving a roster of members, advertising gang exploits, and communicating messages to rival gangs.

An understanding of graffiti is very important to law enforcement officers who have the responsibility to interrogate gang members and protect society from their illegal activities. Accurate interpretations of graffiti can help to identify the gangs operating in certain areas, identify the members through their monikers or nicknames, aid in monitoring gang

---

[1]The material in this section is part of a larger report, "Field Research of Urban Youth Gangs—1988–95," by Jack Bynum. It is based on compilations from *Report on Youth Gang Violence in California,* prepared by the Youth Gang Task Force in 1980; *Street Gangs of Los Angeles County,* prepared by Mike Poirier in 1982; and *Guide for Identifying Youth Gang Graffiti and Tattoos,* prepared by Esteban P. Castaneda in 1986. The authors thank officers of the Stockton California Police Department who made these handouts available.

challenges and rivalries, and assist in developing leads on suspects of gang related crimes. Figure 12-2 is an example of Hispanic gang graffiti and its interpretation.

The distinctive language employed by various gangs is a virtual code that defies translation by nonmembers. For example, the following sentence contains several unusual words and expressions that are familiar to black street gangs:

> *Yo homey, Dizzy D dropped a dime on cuzz and the man popped a cap at cuzz while he laid a drag on a freak sitting on the benzo.*

FIGURE 12-2   An Example of Hispanic Gang Graffiti and Translation

GRAFFITI	TRANSLATION
AQUI	"AQUI"—meaning "Here" or "Look at this"
C IV$_t^s$	"C"—meaning "Corona" (geographic area claimed by the gang) "IV$_t^s$"—meaning "4th Street Gang"
LOS PERSUADERS	"LOS PERSUADERS"—a subgroup of the 4th Street Gang, responsible for the graffiti
Challo George de Lado Richard	Names and monikers of several gang members: Challo, George, de Lado, Richard
CORONA Ls R	"CORONA" repeated; "Ls"—meaning "Locos" or "Crazy Ones"; "R"— meaning "We're the best"
NOMAS	"NOMAS"—meaning "The one and only"
C/S	"C/S"—a symbol meaning "Con Safos," that is, "There is nothing you can do about it; don't touch; anything you do to this, twice to you."

Source: Castaneda, Esteban P., *Guide for identifying youth gang graffiti and tattoos,* Sacramento, CA.: California Youth Authority, March 26, 1986:4.

In order to effectively decipher the communication within and between gangs and their members, police intelligence units in many cities have compiled extensive lexicons or dictionaries of words and phrases commonly used by black, white, and Hispanic gangs. Table 12-2 lists just a few examples from a lengthy police word book of terms and phrases employed by Blood and Crip gangs.

More formally organized youth gangs also often have a complex system of identifying colors, clothing styles, hand signs, and body language. In Chicago, for instance, there are two large families, or clusters, of interrelated and allied gangs: the People and the Folks.

> *The gangs under the People include the Vice Lords, the Black Cobra Stones, and the El Rukns, as well as the Valley Rocks; under the Folks are the Disciples, the Spanish Cobras, and the Latin Jivers.... The People wear the bills of their caps pointed left, and cross their arms with the right arm on top, while the Folks point their caps to the right and cross their arms with the left on top. Every now and then in Chicago a teenager will be gunned down on the street for the crime of having his arms crossed right-on-top in an area that is Folks turf (Lemann, 1986:13).*

Composition of Gang Membership

The composition of a group or population of people refers to those common demographic traits that best describe or typify the group. For example, if we were studying the behavior

TABLE 12-2   Examples of Terms and Phrases Commonly Used by Members of Crip and Blood Gangs and Translations

TERM/PHRASE	TRANSLATION
Bo	Marijuana
Bullet	One year in custody
Busted, Popped a cap	Shot at someone
Cragared down	Low rider type car or full dressed gang banger
Cuzz	Crip
Drop a dime	Snitch on someone
Durag	Handkerchief wrapped around head
Gang banger	Person involved in gang activity
Get down	Fight
Hood or Set	Neighborhood
Homey, Homeboy	Someone from the same gang; friend
Kicking back	Relaxing; killing time
Lady	Girlfriend
Player	Individual interested solely in girls
Red eye	Hard stare
Sherm, wack, liquid, or juice	P.C.P.
Tray eight	.38 caliber handgun
Trick, hook	Phoney sissy
What set you from?	Asking what gang are you a member of

of a group of college students, information about their sex, race, marital status, social class, and other variables probably would be very helpful in understanding their behavior. The same kind of population data is useful in our analysis of gangs and their behavior. Three population characteristics of gang members are discussed here that will contribute to our overall understanding regarding the formation and delinquent behavior of youthful gangs: social class, racial and ethnic composition, and female participation in delinquent gangs.

Social Class

Official crime reports indicate that juvenile delinquency is statistically concentrated in lower socioeconomic urban neighborhoods. While this conclusion may be tempered by a class bias of law enforcement as reflected in arrest statistics, there is considerable evidence from other studies of the strong relationship between lower class unemployment, poverty, and a high incidence of property crime (Gillespie, 1978). Similar to juvenile delinquents in general, gang members are typically characterized as being from poor neighborhoods with substandard housing in which the residents have little hope for educational or occupational achievements.

A broader picture of social class and juvenile gang membership has emerged from several important studies that found definite groupings of young people in more affluent social classes who participate in delinquent activities. For example, Howard and Barbara Myerhoff (1964), in their observations of middle class gangs, found youngsters informally and loosely organized for many socially acceptable activities. However, drag racing, drinking of alcoholic beverages, sexual activity, and other forms of deviant and illegal behavior often emerged. The middle class subjects of the Myerhoffs' study generally lacked the alienated leadership and violent behavior often attributed to lower class gangs. In addition, and again in contrast to the lower class subjects targeted by most research on gangs, the middle class youngsters did not demonstrate well-developed delinquent values, nor did they define themselves as delinquents or troublemakers. Rather, they fully expected to ultimately abandon their temporary deviant behavior and take conventional and law-abiding places in society. These optimistic feelings about the future were shared by the adults in their environment, thus eliciting more tolerance for middle class juveniles than for lower class or underclass youngsters.

The existence of middle class gangs performing very serious acts of delinquency in fashionable suburban communities was also documented in studies by Muehlbauer and Dodder (1983) and by Salisbury (1958) and was discussed earlier in this chapter. A number of such reports have been brought together in a significant work, *Middle-Class Juvenile Delinquency,* edited by Edmund Vaz (1967).

The Straight Edgers. In contrast to the middle class gangs observed by the Myerhoffs, Edmund Vaz, and other scholars cited in this section, a very recent, middle class, ideology-based gang has emerged. Between 1995 and 1998, an ultra-conservative youth group named "The Straight Edgers" reacted violently against drug and alcohol use, and casual sex by many other youth in society. They take their name from a 1981 song, "Straight Edge," by Ian MacKaye of the band Minor Threat:

> *I'm a person just like you,*
> *But I've got better things to do*

Than sit around and smoke dope…
I've got a straight edge.

Extreme, hardcore Straight Edgers use chains, mace, knives, clubs, beatings, brawls, and vandalism to enforce their abstinent lifestyle in schoolyards, punk rock concerts, and shopping mall parking lots. In Salt Lake City, a crowd of Straight Edgers carved a large "X" on the back of a youth caught smoking marijuana. To underscore their self-styled wholesome lifestyle, Straight Edgers have adopted the "X" as their symbol, "X" being what music clubs stamp on the hands of patrons too young for alcohol (Levinson, 1998).

According to Arlene Levinson (1998), "The typical Straight Edger in Utah is white, male, and middle class, ranging in age from the early teens to early 20's" (Levinson, 1998:3A). The more extreme members of the movement are often strict vegetarians—rejecting all animal products, and involved in violent crimes as part of the Animal Liberation Front.

Racial and Ethnic Composition of Gangs

The United States is composed of a variety of different racial and ethnic groups including blacks or African-Americans, Hispanics, Native Americans, Asian Americans, and whites. From the very beginning of the American experience as a developing nation, tens of millions of immigrants have been added to our national population.

Many of these racial and ethnic groups initially settled in their own urban enclaves, where they often preserved distinctive subcultural values, beliefs, and behaviors with which they were familiar, in spite of an intense social pressure to assimilate or Americanize. Many of the racial and ethnic neighborhoods and districts of our cities still retain place names reflecting the traditional background of the residents such as Little Italy, Chinatown, the Ghetto, and so forth. It follows that many of the youthful street gangs that emerged in these particular urban neighborhoods are racially homogeneous as a natural consequence of families of similar racial and ethnic backgrounds living near one another (Ramos, 1989).

Race and ethnicity are, of themselves, powerful forces that can draw people together into cohesive groups. Birds of a feather do indeed flock together! Moreover, if the race or ethnicity of a group is associated in the minds of group members with social, economic, or political injustices they feel they have suffered, additional solidarity and commitment to group objectives can result. With this in mind, Davis (1978) argued that gang ethnicity should always be considered when the modalities and motivations of gangs are examined. Thus, race or ethnicity can serve as a unifying and sacred cause for some gangs—more symbolic and preeminent than their leather jackets and intimidating names (Moore, 1985). Howard Erlanger's study (1979) of the relationships between the subcultural values of the Hispanic American barrios in East Los Angeles, estrangement from the dominant white society, and gang violence offers a classic example of this phenomenon:

> …while subcultural values of the barrio may be different from those of the Anglo society and may exist independently of Anglo society, they do not directly require or condone violence…[However], under situations of estrangement or alienation from the Anglo society brought about by discrimination or negative images of Chicano culture, young Chicanos may become collectively violent as they respond to

the strong Chicano cultural emphasis on values such as courage and dignity for
males. (Erlanger, 1979:235)

Erlanger described the deep resentment Hispanic Americans felt about the educational
situation in East Los Angeles, in which their children were punished for speaking Spanish,
even among themselves in the schoolyard. Hispanic youth interpreted this as rejection by the
Anglo society, and this scenario elicited a readiness to fight among some youthful barrio
gangs. James Vigil, in his 1997 digest *Learning from Gangs: The Mexican-American Experience,* briefly traces the emergence and evolution of Hispanic gangs in southern California and
other parts of the nation. Beginning in the 1940s as a small number of neighborhood-based
youth groups given to periodic outbursts of destructive behavior, these gangs became very
deadly and violent street entities by the 1990s. Vigil estimates, however, that a still-small
number, between 4 and 10 percent, of Mexican American youth belong to gangs (1997).

Chinese-American youth gangs have a long history in major U.S. cities on the West
Coast. Their criminal activities of extortion (selling of "protection"), and the theft of goods
and services from Chinese-American merchants have become virtually institutionalized
due to the pragmatic tolerance of their victims (Chin, Fagan, and Kelley, 1992).

While Hispanics and African-Americans constituted the majority of gang members in
1996 (Bilchik, July 1999:23), gangs continue to develop in every racial category. One of the

Race and ethnicity are powerful cohesive forces and many urban street gangs reflect the
racial, ethnic, and social characteristics of the neighborhoods from which they emerge.

most recent racial gang groupings is the Vietnamese, emerging from the relatively new, closeknit Vietnamese communities of California (Wyrick, 2000; Senate Subcommittee on Juvenile Justice, 1983). These gangs are particularly violent, utilizing robbery, bombing, extortion, and murder as terror tactics. Several loosely organized Asian gangs in Sacramento, California specialize in midnight attacks on the homes of other Asians, assaulting occupants and stealing money. This group of masked young people, after each three or four day rampage, quietly disbands and fades back into the general population (NBC Report, 1994).

Although the majority of gangs of racial and ethnic minority origin are homogeneous in composition, some demonstrate a degree of racial and ethnic integration in their membership, especially in neighborhoods where housing previously has been well integrated (Bilchik, 1999:47). However, Kobrin and Peluso (1968) in their "Criteria of Status among Street Groups" observed strikingly different levels of social status within the gangs for members of various races. The numerically dominant race carefully retained positions of highest prestige and power within the group.

Racial tension among teenagers isn't new, but during the 1990s, police departments began reporting a trend of new white gangs emerging on the basis of a black-white issue. Groups of young, white males have been organizing to counteract what they perceive as the violation of their "turf" by powerful black gangs. Besides neighborhoods, a gang's turf can extend to schools, malls, girls, and economic status. "Often the trouble arises when a white youth associates with or joins a black gang" (*Dallas Morning News,* 1993:A2). Police at a Youth Crime Seminar in Little Rock, Arkansas said the trend is nationwide and includes children of wealthy parents.

Female Participation in Delinquent Gangs

Chapter 3 underscored the statistical evidence that juvenile delinquents are predominantly male. The same generality applies to gang membership. Traditionally, female involvement in gang delinquency has been more passive than active, with girls and young women functioning as support personnel to male members rather than as equal participants. James Short (1968:4) and numerous other writers aptly depicted these females and their secondary roles and statuses as a branch organization or female auxiliary:

> *The gang world is dominated largely by males…But girls are important, too, for many reasons: as sex objects, hustles to be exploited, sources of prestige among the boys with whom they are associated, and in their own right. "Female auxiliary" groups are not uncommon, and when they exist they perform many functions for boys' gangs and enjoy a degree of autonomy among themselves. Their names characteristically suggest their association with boys' gangs, e.g., Vice Queens (associated with the Vice Kings), Egyptian Cobrettes (associated with the Egyptian Cobras), and Lady Racketeers (associated with the Racketeers).*

It has been reported that before and after gang fights, the girlfriends of gang members sometimes concealed the weapons, since the police have been more hesitant to pursue, search, and arrest females not directly involved in the melee. For the same reasons, and in order to avoid the situation of suspicion and the prospects of interrogation, gang boys congregated on a street corner will break up into subunits of two or three, or pair off with their girlfriends, when a squad car appears in the area. "Similarly, unmarried, older boys will occasionally wear wedding rings in order to bolster their moral status in the eyes of the police" (Werthman and Piliavin, 1967:86).

While auxiliary status has been the most common form of gang participation available to females, there is some evidence that a small minority of gangs permit sexually integrated membership (Hardman, 1969). This phenomenon is more likely in middle class, suburban gangs, whose youthful members have not been seriously alienated from middle class norms and values and still aspire to middle class educational and occupational objectives. This does not mean that females may not be members of lower class urban street gangs, however. Anne Campbell (1991) estimated that approximately 10 percent of the growing gang population in New York City are females ranging in age from 14 to 30.

There is considerable debate among scholars and researchers in the field concerning the statistical increase in female delinquency in some offense categories and female participation in gangs. Freda Adler (1975) has pointed to the revitalization of the feminist movement since 1960, and the greater assertiveness, freedom from traditional restraints, and the more equitable status and opportunity now enjoyed by women, as opening the door for more female involvement in criminal activities formerly dominated by males. On the other hand, Rachelle Canter (1982) flatly denies that girls are catching up with boys in juvenile delinquency. Still others, while acknowledging that girls may have increased their involvement more rapidly than boys in damaging property and theft of items worth less than 10 dollars, insist that girls are not catching up with boys in "fist fighting, gang fighting, carrying a weapon, strongarm theft, and major theft" (Steffensmeier and Steffensmeier, 1980).

Interviews with gang boys seem to support that last position. Data on female participation in gang and nongang delinquency, collected from black male delinquents in the Los Angeles County Juvenile Hall, reveal a systematic exclusion of females from the planning and action stages of delinquent activities. The research, reported by Lee Bowker and his associates (1980), indicated that female presence at a delinquent activity site tended to have a suppressive effect on the activity.

More recent reports have again modified previous findings and reversed conclusions regarding female involvement in gang delinquency. While researchers all the way back to Thrasher (1927) have identified isolated instances of all-female gangs, it now appears that a rapidly growing number of well-organized, crime-oriented gangs of this type are creating a major problem for law enforcement. A CBS News Report (1986) estimated that approximately 1,000 girls are involved in over 100 female gangs in Chicago alone. It was emphasized that these are not sister organizations or auxiliaries to male gangs, but independent female gangs. Similar to their male counterparts, these female gangs stake out their own "turf" or territory, adopt distinctive colors and insignia, and have physical confrontations and fights with rival gangs. The CBS Report documented one case in which a nonmember was badly beaten because she wore a yellow article of clothing and yellow happened to be the official color of a nearby female gang. Another juvenile, a 13-year-old girl, was shot in the head and killed by other gang members because they thought she was a police informant.

The authoritative National Youth Gang Survey extrapolated in 1996 that over 93,000 females accounted for 11 percent of active gang members in the U.S. Although numbers were highest in urban areas, the proportion of female gang members was highest in rural counties (Bilchik, July 1999:20,21).

Female gangs—like male gangs—also vary considerably in motivation and kind of criminal involvement. The Sly Vixens and the Tiny Diablas are both centered in the Watts ghetto of Los Angeles County. The Sly Vixens are into heavy drugs and prostitution while the 14- to 19-year-old Tiny Diablas take a weekly collection to buy guns and contend that their gang "gives them a social structure and sense of identity they would not have otherwise" (Donovan, 1990:33).

Contemporary research on why young females affiliate with gangs offers mixed and inconclusive explanations. Anne Campbell's qualitative study of *The Girls in the Gang* (1991) found that membership in three New York City gangs appealed to lonely and alienated girls from transient and physically violent families. However, a quantitative study by Lee Bowker and Malcolm Klein (1983) on "The Etiology of Female Delinquency and Gang Membership" weakened the previously accepted generalization that females commit delinquent acts or join delinquent gangs because they are socially maladjusted, come from broken and unhappy homes, and do not relate well to the opposite sex. A fuller explanation of the emergence and delinquent behavior of the new, all-female gangs awaits further research investigations.

Female members of the Pico Rivera gang. Female gang membership is increasing rapidly in the United States. In just one city, 70 of the 250 active gangs in San Antonio consist of full or partial female membership.

Gang Violence

As mentioned earlier, law enforcement agencies, criminologists, and others who specialize in the study of juvenile crime generally agree that gang membership increases the likelihood of more serious delinquent behavior (Thornberry and Burch, 1997). The reason, according to Klein and Crawford (1968), lies in the cohesiveness generated in the group, as tough talk, "macho" posturing, and alienation are shared and reinforced. It follows that the individual youth who might ordinarily be intimidated by law enforcement officers and reluctant to violate major social norms can become emotionally involved and committed to acts of bravado and delinquency in the context of the gang (Kennedy and Baron, 1993). But, here again, we must take into account the great variation among gangs in purpose, social class, level of perceived estrangement from the dominant society, and subcultural values.

Most gangs do not have crime as their dominant activity; offenses are committed spontaneously; and most members have temporary gang memberships and short criminal careers (Sarnecki, 1982).

Walter Miller (1966) sought to counter the popular media reports that urban gangs are massively, consistently, and continually involved in violent behavior. His research revealed that while theft and vandalism were common among gang members, violence was not a major activity of urban street gangs, nor a central reason for their existence. Only a small minority of gang members participated in violent crime. When violence did occur, it most frequently involved unarmed physical encounters between male antagonists, usually motivated to defend honor or prestige. More often than not, the fight was between two males:

> *Generally, it was not "ganging up" by malicious sadists on the weak, the innocent, the solitary. It did not victimize adult females. With few exceptions, violent crimes fell into the "less serious" category, with the extreme or shocking crimes rare (Miller, 1966:111).*

During the years since Miller's research, the level and scope of gang violence has dramatically increased. In a later study, Miller (1975) reversed his former position with newer data showing that the rate of murder by youth gangs with firearms was higher than ever before.

R. B. Toplin's (1975) gripping *Unchallenged Violence: An American Ordeal* supported the view that contemporary gangs engage in violence of greater severity than did gangs of past years: "During the 1950's, gangs fought with bottles, clubs, chains, knives, and fists. Now they fight with handguns, revolvers, and shotguns" (1975:81). Many combat-oriented gang members in the 1990s were equipped with such advanced automatic weapons as Uzi submachine guns and Chinese copies of the Soviet AK-47 assault rifle, which can be purchased on the streets of our cities.

In recent years, gang violence continued to undergo modifications in strategy and style. In his *Gangbangs and Drive-bys* (1994), William Sanders describes how the drive-by shooting replaced rumbles as the primary form of gang confrontation. Using automobiles and mobile tactics with manufactured, high-quality weapons and the element of surprise, this form of gang violence is far more deadly than the street melees of the past. Gangbangs is a generic term for a variety of other gang violence including assaults, knifings, killings, and beatings.

Drive-by homicides began to decline in Los Angeles in 1993. Coincidentally, that was also the year that an organized crime syndicate nicknamed "The Mexican Mafia" issued an anti-drive-by edict in the belief that the practice threatened its lucrative drug trade by bringing unwanted attention to the neighborhoods. Many gangs further adapted with the "walk-up" or walk-by shooting in which the gunman attacks his targeted victim face-to-face. This was as easy transition, rationalized by the exaggerated and distorted sense of honor held by gang members: "If you are going to be a man and shoot somebody, at least have the guts to look them in the face and shoot them.... It is more honorable to kill at close range" (*The Medford Mail Tribune,* 1996:8B). The decline in drive-bys did not stem the number of gang homicides which reached an all-time high of 807 in Los Angeles County in 1995.

> *Police say a new menace is appearing in the streets, spud guns, homemade weapons that can hurl raw potatoes into the air.*
>
> *"If it hit someone on the head, it would break their skull," said Martinez [California] police officer Mike Marchiano. "If it hit someone over the heart, it would crush the tissue. It would be like taking a sledgehammer to it."*
>
> *To fire a spud gun, a potato is put in a pipe from 28 inches to 5 feet long and a flammable substance on one end is ignited. The force shoots the potato as fast as 1,000 feet per second. "You cannot see the potato flying through the air, it's going so fast," he told the Contra Costa Times* (The Manteca Bulletin, *1993:A-5).*

Box 12-2 describes the use of another unusual weapon—the pit bulldog—by young gangs in some parts of the country.

Violence touches and terminates the lives of a very large portion of American young people, over and above the conspicuous and aggressive street gangs. This alarming point was underscored by Robert Blum (1987), Director of the Adolescent Health Program at the University of Minnesota, and published in the *Journal of the American Medical Association.* Blum's statistical analysis revealed that three of four 15- to 24-year-old Americans who die are victims of violence. Accidents, primarily auto accidents, account for 53.5 percent of the fatalities and remain by far the leading cause of death in that age group. But homicide deaths among young people have climbed 300 percent in three decades to become the number two killer.

Blum credited these grim statistics on homicide and other forms of violence to the increasing "juvenilization of poverty." He projected that within a few years, one of every five adolescents will live at or below the poverty level. Blum agreed with numerous social scientists that impoverished and hopeless youths are subject to more substance abuse, more adolescent pregnancy, higher school dropout rates, more crime, and higher death rates due to violence.

> *From 1980 through 1994 an estimated 326,170 persons were murdered in the U.S. Of these murder victims, 9% or 30,200 were youth under age 18.... The number of juveniles murdered in 1994 was 47% greater than the number in 1980. In 1980 juveniles were murdered at a rate of 5 per day; in 1994 the rate was 7 per day. The majority (53%) of juveniles killed in 1994 were teens ages 15–17 and 30% were younger than age 6 (Snyder et al., 1996:1).*

BOX 12-2 Concept Application

"The Weapon of Choice: The Dogs of War"

During the summer of 1987, and again in 1990 and 1999, outbreaks of apparently unprovoked attacks by pit bull terriers across the United States received widespread coverage from news media. In Tampa, Florida, a 3-year-old girl required plastic surgery after being suddenly mauled by a pit bull in her neighborhood. A 2-year-old boy was killed by a pit bull in Santa Clara County (California). In Zachary, Louisiana, a woman was hospitalized in serious condition, her arm mangled by a pit bull. She had known the dog since it was a pup. And a Modesto, California, police officer shot and killed a pit bull after the dog severely mauled a man and menaced a group of terrified elementary school children (Walker, 1990:A1).

According to Paul Clancy (1987), since 1983 pit bull terriers have been blamed for 21 of 28 dog-attack deaths. During the first half of 1987, pit bulls were responsible for all six recorded deaths by dog attack.

The dissemination of information about the history, traditional use, physical endowments, and personality potential of the breed did little to alleviate public apprehension:

"These dogs can and do make good pets, but they also can be extremely dangerous," says Sheryl Blair of the Tufts Center for Animals. "They fight to the end and beyond." A cross between bulldog and terrier, the pit bull goes back to early 19th century England where it was bred to fight in the ring. (Clancy, 1987:2A)

As the storm of fear and anger toward the pit bull mounted, city council members in scores of communities moved to enact strict new ordinances to control potentially vicious dogs in general, and pit bull terriers in particular. Paradoxically, the negative publicity for the pit bull proved to be attractive to some people who admired the dog's tenacity, courage, and viciousness. In May of 1987, a man in Lawrence, Massachusetts, after being chased by a pit bull, collapsed and died of a heart attack. While the dog was locked up by the Society for the Prevention of Cruelty to Animals,

six telephone calls were received from people who wanted to adopt the dog:

"That's frightening," says shelter director Carter Luke. "There are a lot of people out there who want the biggest gun, the sharpest knife, and baddest dog they can find. They're turned on by it." (Clancy, 1987:1A)

Much to the chagrin of responsible kennel operators and owners, who contend that the pit bull terrier can be a reliable family pet, some unprincipled breeders have chosen to capitalize on the aberrant demand for vicious dogs and have concentrated on those known bloodlines that produce the more aggressive and antisocial types (*Examiner,* 1990:43). In the hands of an owner who derives some sense of gratification, importance, or power from owning such an animal, these particular dogs can be literally transformed into killers. ABC News (1987) has documented the appearance of pit bull dogs in the arsenals of inner-city street gangs. The gang members strut the dogs as status symbols, and also use them to intimidate crime victims as four-legged guns (Douthat, 1994).

"It's the macho thing to do," says Elaine Newton of Philadelphia's SPCA… "The kids are using them as potential weapons. If you can't get a handgun, get a pit bull. It [is] the one thing that makes them feel superior." (Clancy, 1987:1B)

The *Daily Oklahoman* (1987), an Oklahoma City newspaper, detailed the role of the pit bull terrier as a popular "weapon of choice" in many recent battles between rival gangs. Rather than directly attacking one another with knives and guns, opposing gangs set their dogs against each other in staged combats to the death. These pit bulls, bearing such names as Switchblade and Rambo, are well conditioned and ferocious. Just as in the traditional fights between rival gangs, the stakes can be high. Status and territory ("turf") can be won or lost by the gangs and their members, depending upon whose dogs emerge victorious.

Continued

BOX 12-2 *Continued*

Unfortunately, losers may not live to fight again. Reports persist that those vanquished canine warriors that survive the crushing jaws of their opponents are often executed by being strangled by their disappointed owners.

Sources

Clancy, P. "Pit bulls—best friend or time bomb?" *USA Today.* August 10, 1987:1A;2A.
Daily Oklahoman. "Gangs using pit bulls." September, 6, 1987:2.
Douthat, S. "Pit bulls become the dogs of war for drug gangs, fight promoters." *Fort Worth Star-Telegram* (Texas). November 6, 1994:AA4.
Examiner. "Monster dogs." May 6, 1990:43.
Walker, T. "Rampaging dog destroyed by police." *The Modesto Bee* (California). June 5, 1990:Al.

Drug Franchises and Gang Warfare

As discouraging and alarming as these reports of persistent and collective violence by young people may be, they have proved to be but a prologue for the escalating and bloody urban gang wars that erupted in 1987 and continued to the twenty-first century—though at a slightly reduced pace (Bilchik, August, 1999).

Los Angeles (AP)

Gang violence has disrupted the easygoing life of this sunny city, where the gang related killings last year claimed more than four times the 1987 death toll in Northern Ireland's sectarian bloodshed...

Many residents of the nation's second largest city live in fear of gunmen who often are not men at all but rather children with guns....

The gang killers are children of poverty and come from the city's toughest streets in the mostly black neighborhoods south of downtown or the largely Hispanic districts on the city's east side. (*The Sunday Oklahoman,* 1988:A7)

"In 1989, Los Angeles gangs were involved in 570 slayings, 3,819 assaults with deadly weapons, 93 rapes, and 1,851 robberies" (Donovan, 1990:33). During the first five months of 1990, 40 teenage deaths were attributed to gang violence in Boston. It was the worst increase in gang violence ever reported for the city.

This proliferation of street gangs and violence are sometimes driven by the economics of drug trafficking (Fagan, 1989). Urban districts and perhaps entire cities are being literally franchised for the marketing of "crack" cocaine. Thus, the gangs have become the pushers and enforcers for the international drug trade (*Nightline,*1988).

Several California research investigations have reported that the two most prominent Los Angeles gangs were expanding their drug-trafficking operations to other cities. Verification came from the National Drug Intelligence Center in 1996:

Gangs claiming affiliation with the Bloods or Crips were reported in 180 jurisdictions in 42 states.... Chicago-based gangs were reported in 110 jurisdictions in 35 states (Howell, 1998:11).

A nationwide perspective is offered by the 1996 National Youth Gang Survey: "On average, law-enforcement respondents estimated that 43 percent of the drug sales in their jurisdictions involved gang members" (Bilchik, July 1999:38).

> *Each gang has its own jargon and graffiti, spray-painted on walls and fences to mark its "territory." These gang alliances are proclaimed by the colors they wear: Gangs affiliated with the Crips wear blue, and the Bloods prefer red...*
>
> *"Gangs like the Crips are highly mobile, very sophisticated, Just like businessmen. They've acquired a lot of money through selling drugs. I've seen them operate as far north as Anchorage, Alaska, into Las Vegas, the Southwest, and as far east as New Jersey" [says Gerald Ivory, L.A. county probation officer].*
>
> *"Kids (gang members) are...now flying to other cities, seeking fertile ground to sell their drugs. Being a gang member, I've said, is better than being a Harvard MBA. They never operate in the red." (Davis, 1988:A18)*

Gang Rape

Gang rape is another form of violent crime that involves surprisingly large numbers of American youths. Multiple rape or group rape is almost as common as single rape. Menachem Amir's (1971) study of a large number of rape cases revealed that 43 percent were multiple rapes. The most significant fact about multiple rape, as shown by Amir's data, is that its perpetrators were largely adolescents from 10 to 19 years of age.

In 1989, a new term was added to our lexicon of fear and violence when six New York City youths described their predatory rampage through Central Park as "wilding." They were brought to trial in 1990 for brutalizing and raping a young woman jogger and leaving her for dead with a crushed skull (Kaplan, 1990).

Some psychiatrists interpret gang rape as an expression of latent homosexuality, arguing that the co-rapists have an unconscious wish to have sex with each other. Such an interpretation, according to Alex Thio (1998:87) makes as much sense as the suggestion that several men who rob a store together unconsciously want to rob each other. Actually, participation in a gang rape fulfills a social need rather than a sexual desire, particularly for youngsters who feel peer pressure to prove that they are not "chicken" (Groth and Birnbaum, 1979:115).

One of the startling byproducts of such acts of violence is the failure of many bystanders to heed calls for help from the victim. A vivid example was the 1983 gang rape of a young woman in a bar in New Bedford, Massachusetts. She entered the building to make a telephone call and promptly was assaulted by a group of young men:

> *Despite the presence of numerous patrons other than the several rapists, none intervened. Only after the victim ran naked into the street did a passing motorist provide assistance and summon the police (Ritzer, 1986:461).*

Although such widely publicized events are relatively infrequent, and are not limited to occurrence in large cities, they reflect an apparent pattern of apathy among many urban residents.

Dyads and Triads

A **dyad** *is a social group comprised of just two persons;* a **triad** *is a social group of three persons in social interaction.* These sociological descriptors for very small groups are the focal point of a comparatively recent finding that has weakened the common stereotype of large groups or gangs of youths participating together in collective delinquency.

Beginning with the work of Paul Lerman (1967), who used self-report techniques, the fact emerged that the large group context of juvenile delinquency needed revision. Lerman's research dealt with 700 boys, aged 10 through 19, living in New York City. He determined that until the age of 14 or 15, most of the boys committed delinquent acts together with one or two close friends. At ages 16 through 19, more of the youths could be classified as loners, but pair and triad participation in illegal conduct continued to be the most dominant grouping. While the gang fight—in which squads of youths from opposing neighborhoods meet in armed and angry conflict—still occasionally occurs, most delinquent acts usually involve just two or three close friends, operating together in a less sensational manner. As Michael Hindelang (1986) emphasized in his "With a Little Help from Their Friends," our revised concept of collective delinquency more accurately focuses on a small network of two or three trusted pals and peers. They may well be members of a larger gang, whose values, norms, and behavioral expectations are far from altruistic, but most delinquency is acted out in much smaller social units than the gang.

Explanatory Theories of Gang Formation and Behavior: A Summary and Synthesis

Chapters 4, 5, 6, 7, and 8 are totally devoted to causal theories of juvenile delinquency. Chapter 6 also contains a discussion and critique of several sociological theories related to the etiology of juvenile gangs. Now, in the context of this chapter a brief review and summary of the most prominent explanatory theories of gang formation and behavior are appropriate.

The sociological examination and application of the related concepts of culture and subculture formed the foundation for some major theoretical explications of juvenile gang delinquency. As indicated in Chapter 11, **culture** *is the entire body of shared and learned beliefs, values, attitudes, traditions, normative expectations, and other forms of knowledge that is passed on from one generation to the next within a society.* **Subculture** refers to *the beliefs, values, attitudes, norms, behavior patterns, and accumulated knowledge that characterize subgroups and uniquely set them apart in some ways from the larger society.* These subcultures may be based on social class, occupation, religion, racial or ethnic background, ideology, place of residence, or any number of other variables that can characterize specific subgroups.

Once they had carefully defined culture and subculture, it was a short step for sociological theorists to turn their attention to deviant subcultures and criminal and delinquent subcultures as explanatory social contexts for nonconforming or antisocial behavior.

Deviant subculture is *a term applied to any subgroup that deviates markedly from the generally accepted values, norms, and behavioral expectations of the dominant society.* Such nonconformists as "punk rockers," homosexuals, and religious snake handlers may be classified as members of deviant subcultures because they share with others some beliefs, practices, and lifestyles that significantly set them apart. However, they are not ordinarily perceived by the larger society as major threats to the social order.

On the other hand, a **criminal** or **delinquent subculture** *manifests such extreme and negative nonconformity to the normative prescriptions of the larger society that its members are generally viewed as antisocial—against society.* Sutherland (1939), Shaw and McKay (1942), and other early sociologists/criminologists pinpointed the locus of many of these subcultures in high delinquency areas of central cities, where criminal behavior is supported by the cultural values and prevailing practices of those particular districts. Thus, juvenile delinquents often gain identification and encouragement from other delinquents and from criminal elements in their area with whom they associate. In that environment, such behavior is socially learned, expected, and rewarded. Such youngsters, with strong loyalties and emotional attachment to peers, have also learned to distrust established institutions and authorities. They clash with society because the values of their subculture are in conflict with the laws of the land. Once these youths have become involved in lawlessness, their problems snowball, making it more and more difficult for them to stay out of trouble.

After World War II, the most important advances in understanding the causes of delinquency emerged from studies of urban youth gangs. Collectively, these theoretical formulations are sometimes referred to as "Theory of the Reactive Subculture," though actually this is a group of theoretical constructs. They have in common the idea that misconduct is elicited in lower class youths who have internalized the middle class cultural values and objectives of educational, occupational, and materialistic success and are frustrated in their achievement. For example, Albert Cohen (1958) advanced the theory that gangs develop a delinquent subculture, which represents solutions to the problems of some lower class males. A gang gives them a chance to belong, to amount to something, to develop and demonstrate their masculinity, and to fight middle class society. In particular, the delinquent subculture, according to Cohen, is an anomic response toward resolution of the status problems of lower class boys.

The theoretical contribution of Richard Cloward and Lloyd Ohlin (1960), like Cohen's, is also a spinoff from Robert Merton's (1957) general theory of anomie as an explanation for deviant behavior. As was discussed in Chapter 6, Cloward and Ohlin, while agreeing with Merton and Cohen that the disunion between cultural goals and the inadequate means available for their achievement can create strain for lower class youths, argued that they still need to have the opportunity to break away from the dominant, middle class values and turn to illegitimate means to achieve status and self-esteem. In other words, Cloward and Ohlin's "Theory of Delinquency and Opportunity" postulated that every youth who feels deprived and disadvantaged does not turn to the same alternative illegitimate avenues to success. Even delinquent opportunities may not be readily available in the frustrated youth's social environment. Moreover, not only does the quantity of delinquent opportunity vary from area to area and from neighborhood to neighborhood, but there is a quality differential as well. In recognition of that fact, Cloward and Ohlin suggested that there are three kinds of gang subcultures that can develop—the crime-oriented, the conflict-oriented, and the retreatist/drug-oriented. The type that emerges to satisfy the needs for group support and status among lower class youth depends upon the available opportunity in their local communities.

Walter Miller (1958) disagreed with Cohen and with Cloward and Ohlin that the gang is a reactive subculture whose delinquent behavior is a compensation for lower class failure to reach middle class goals. Rather, Miller scrutinized lower class culture for values that could reflect in behavior identified as delinquent by the dominant, middle class society. Miller's study concluded that lower class culture is characterized by six "focal concerns" or values that could easily be interpreted as troublesome opposition to middle class values or a predisposition to delinquency. These lower class cultural values are **trouble, toughness, excitement, fate, smartness,** and **autonomy,** which, according to Miller, represent highly prized masculinity to lower class boys. Paradoxically, the youth's socialized allegiance to those values can produce delinquent behavior.

These sociological theories of gang delinquency offer many valuable insights into social class differences, culture conflict, and subcultural response. They suggest that gang delinquency is largely a lower class phenomenon and is typically clustered together with other social pathologies such as poverty, unstable family life, and inner-city slum neighborhoods. Box 12-3 indicates that urban youth gangs are not unique to the United States.

As detailed in Chapter 6, the subcultural theories of juvenile delinquency are not without their critics. Some have contended that the entire concept of a subculture of juvenile delinquency is meaningless when compared with more powerful and permanent familial, ethnic/racial, and social class value systems impacting upon young people. David Matza (1964) argued that juvenile delinquents, like all young people, spend only a limited amount of time with each other. They still go to their own homes; many attend school; some have jobs. There are prior and offsetting influences in place to counter the shared alienation that is assumed to lead to the procriminal values of the gang. If juvenile delinquents did belong to a viable delinquent subculture, Matza argued, then those who are caught would not be embarrassed or remorseful, as they so often are. Do these youngsters really have a set of values of their own, or do they actually believe in those of their parents, teachers, and other conforming authority figures with whom they are still in contact?

Travis Hirschi (1969) also challenged the delinquent subculture theories by pointing out that while frightening and highly publicized gang crimes do occasionally occur, most delinquency is committed with one or two companions. Hence, the small dyadic or triadic relationship and interaction is an inadequate base for the development of a subculture or a set of delinquent values. Hirschi further concluded that there is no evidence that delinquent companions and gang membership precede delinquency. Rather, an attitude and interest favorably inclined toward nonconformity will lead a youth to experimentation with delinquent behavior and association with like-minded peers.

More recently, other sociologists and criminologists have focused attention on alternative theoretical explanations of gang delinquency. For example, L. Thomas Winfree and his associates (1994) present a data-based argument that a variation of Social Learning Theory offers the most specific explication of the processes whereby one learns deviant behavior. They found that "gang members were distinguishable from nongang youths more in terms of variables derived from social learning than personal-biographical characteristics, including ethnicity, gender, and place of residence" (1994:167). Winfree and his colleagues have suggested a possible alternative to Cultural Transmission Theories of gang delinquency.

Not to be overlooked is the renewed theoretical emphasis of many theorists on the unfortunate socioeconomic structures and circumstances in which millions of lower class

BOX 12-3 Cross-Cultural Focus

Urban Youth Gangs in Russia

The following interviews with Russian police officers, youthful offenders, and other citizens were conducted by CBS news correspondents Harold Dow, Bernard Goldberg, Dan Rather, and Phil Jones. They are excerpts from a CBS documentary entitled "Moscow Vice" that was the televised topic of *48 Hours* on May 31, 1990.

MUSCLING IN

Harold Dow, CBS News: Moscow in the spring. As hard-lined Communism continues to thaw, a new order is emerging here. But for now, no one knows the rules. Private businesses and cooperatives are flourishing, choice targets for the vanguard in Soviet crime. Nick has the power to enforce his own law. He's the leader of a Moscow street gang.... Nicholas, why do you have to stay strong?

Nick: Because if I don't stay strong, I won't be able to survive the competition. I protect businessmen, that's how I live.

Dow: Legitimate businesses are not the only prey of Moscow's racketeers. When state-run liquor stores close, black marketeers take up the slack, selling booze at inflated prices, and paying street gangs for protection.

Nick: I don't have to beat their face in, if someone doesn't want to pay, we just take his vodka and smash the bottles. Nothing criminal in that.

Dow: Nick and his boys are one of many gangs fighting to control turf. Today, they're setting off to meet a rival gang, competition trying to muscle in.

Nick: They wanted to take our daily bread. They came and started to demand money from the people that nourish us. We told them that we would destroy them if they tried to do that again....

WILD ONES

Bernard Goldberg, CBS News: Ever since Gorbachev began lifting the Iron Curtain, all sorts of light has been flooding into the Soviet Union. In Moscow these days, kids can watch music videos,

beamed in by satellite, from what the old men in the Kremlin used to call the decadent West. But there's also a darkness amidst the light, called juvenile crime.... Vera Kripinova and her 14-year-old daughter Elizabeth, [are] among Moscow's elite. They see the changes, and notice the darkness.

Ms. Kripinova: And lots of people steal because they think—they feel it will be worse in the future, so this is the time—the good time, for stealing. It's not only for children. It's a mentality.

Goldberg [to young prisoner]: Why are you here in jail?

Young Man: I have stolen sneakers.

Goldberg: Sneakers! Sneakers? It's one of the new, hot juvenile crimes in the Soviet Union: sneaker snatching. He traveled 900 miles to steal a pair. Now let me make sure I understand this. You got on a train, some place up the Volga River, traveled a day and a half to Moscow to steal somebody's sneakers? Why sneakers?

Young Man: Just fashion.

Elizabeth Kripinova: Just look at our kids—I go to school and I see that they—you know, they don't believe in anything, really.

Ms. Kripinova: Skeptical?

Elizabeth Kripinova: Yeah, they're very skeptical.

Goldberg: [Then there are] the wild ones, Moscow style. Wheelies in the night. Police call them the rockers. They live in the shadows of the new Soviet Union—part of it, but mostly apart from it. [to a group of rockers] Do you have any dreams? What do kids want to be? What do you hope for in this new Soviet Union?

Rocker: That's a very interesting question. The thing is, that I don't think our generation has anything to dream about.

Goldberg: Whom do you look up to? Do you have any heroes?

Rocker: No, we don't have any heroes, no idols.

Continued

BOX 12-3 *Continued*

Goldberg: Have any of you, honest, been either the victims of crime or have actually committed crimes yourself?

Rocker: We've been victims since we were born. The thing is, first you're a victim and then you become a criminal....

SOMETHING OLD...

Dan Rather, CBS News: A precinct in southwest Moscow. This night, like every night, these cops are on drunk patrol. [to officer] Do you get hardened to this?

Police Officer, Moscow: I haven't become indifferent to their suffering. I think about all of the sorrow that they bring their family members. It makes me very sad.

Rather: Eighty percent of the crime here is linked to alcohol abuse. Its effect may even be more devastating on Soviet society than drugs are in the United States....

...SOMETHING NEW

Phil Jones, CBS News: The drug war, Moscow style.... Andree Dahilenko is a 23-year-old American from San Francisco involved in Moscow's drug war.

Mr. Dahilenko: The situation with drugs here is probably similar to the situation with drugs in the United States, let's say in the 50s or 60s. When it wasn't around all that much.... This program was designed to help the kids stay off the street, stay away from drugs. Their life is so miserable, they consider that taking drugs takes away the pain....

Interpreter: Mostly they're using opium, various amphetamines, chemical mixtures, poppy seed.

Jones: Officially, there are 8,000 registered drug addicts in Moscow, but everyone concedes that the number is much too low.

Adapted from "Moscow vice," 48 Hours. With News Correspondents Dan Rather, Bernard Goldberg, Harold Dow, Phil Jones, and Peter Van Sant. CBS Inc., © 1990. All rights reserved. Originally broadcast on May 31, 1990, over the CBS Television Network. Reprinted by permission.

youths seem to be trapped. These scholars credit the grinding poverty, dysfunctional families, negative school experiences, marginal racial and ethnic statuses, and crime-infested urban neighborhoods with transforming hopeless and helpless children into alienated and angry gangs of delinquents (Anderson, 1994). Too often, such youths demonstrate their total disregard for human life and contempt for the norms and justice systems of the larger society:

> **PROVIDENCE, R.I. (AP):** *As stunned courtroom obsesrvers looked on, one of six Latin Kings gang members accused of murder, drug dealing, and extortion, stood up Thursday, unzipped his pants and urinated.*
>
> *Federal marshalls tackled George "King Animal" Perry and removed all the defendants from the courtroom. U.S. District Judge Mary Lisi called a recess and ordered Perry banished to a cell for the rest of the trial (Stockton Record, 1997:A-4).*

Such criticisms as these have partially undermined the popularity of the subcultural theories of gang delinquency. Yet the works of Cohen, Cloward and Ohlin, Miller, and others, while imperfect, are still viewed as having considerable explanatory power regarding lower class juvenile gang delinquency. However, the failure of these subcultural theories to account for middle class group delinquency has led to new research and theoretical explanations within the past 15 years. In seeking the reasons why youths who have zealous role models, thorough socialization, and abundant opportunities—all conducive to achieving middle class values—become nonconforming and delinquent, attention has been focused on the youth culture argument. As we indicated in Chapter 11, youth itself can be perceived as an age-graded subculture, complete with its own shared attitudes, values, language, symbols, tastes in music, and styles of dress, sharpened and focused by marginal social status and separation from meaningful participation in the larger society. Thus, the youth subculture, functioning as a catalyst for the expression of collective alienation, is a dominant explanation of illegal behavior among the affluent and promising children of the middle class. In Chapter 11, we presented an in-depth discussion of the youth subculture as it relates to juvenile delinquency. (For more on the quest for a new, integrated, general theory of deviance and delinquency, see Box 8-2).

Several innovative and promising community programs for dealing with gang-related delinquency are presented in Chapter 16.

Concept Integration

Questions and Topics for Study and Discussion

1. Imagine yourself as a youth living in a neighborhood contested by two rival street gangs. Would you join one of the gangs? Why or why not?

2. Although gangs are often thought of as having little redeeming value or positive function, can you think of any contributions that even a delinquent subculture can make to the social and psychological well-being of its members?

3. Diagram your own cultural and subcultural memberships and involvements. Be sure to include your social class, occupation (or major field of study in college), church affiliation, and racial/ethnic group (if appropriate). Next, discuss how membership in any of these subcultures can influence a person's values, attitudes, perceptions of what is right and wrong, and behavior.

4. Compare and contrast the locale, racial/ethnic composition, and delinquent behavior of lower and middle class youth gangs. How are gangs organized?

5. Based on your reading of this chapter, how do you explain the fact that even though there are serious violations of the law, middle class youths do not generally consider themselves as delinquent or in trouble with society? Why is this view shared by the adults in their environment?

6. Refer back to the Concept Application in this chapter entitled, "The Weapon of Choice." What characteristics, motives, and social/psychological needs of youthful gang members are exemplified in that short report?

7. Define and give examples of the following terms and concepts: Theory of Reactive Subculture, Theory of Differential Opportunity, lower class culture and focal concerns, the play group, gang, near group, graffiti, dyad and triad, female auxiliary, high delinquency area, gang composition, deviant subculture, social capital, delinquent subculture, social network, and gang rape.

References

ABC News. 1987. The pit bull. *ABC News Report,* August 6.

Adler, F. 1975. *Sisters in crime.* New York: McGraw Hill.

Amir, M. 1971. *Patterns in forcible rape.* Chicago: University of Chicago Press.

Anderson, E. 1994. The code of the streets. *The Atlantic Monthly* 273, 5. May, 1994:81–94.

Bernard, J. 1967. Teen-age culture: An overview. In E. W. Vaz (Ed.). *Middle-class juvenile delinquency.* New York: Harper and Row, pp. 23–38.

Bilchik, S. July, 1999. *1996 National Youth Gang Survey.* U.S. Department of Justice, Office of Juvenile Justice and Delinquency Prevention. Washington, DC: U.S. Government Printing Office.

Bilchik, S. August, 1999. *OJJDP Research: Making a Difference for Juveniles.* U.S. Department of Justice, Office of Juvenile Justice and Delinquency Prevention. Washington, DC: U.S. Government Printing Office.

Bing, L. 1989. *Harper's Magazine* (March):51–59.

Bing, L. 1991. *Do or die.* New York: Harper Collins.

Block, H., and Niederhoffer, A. 1958. *The gang. A study in adolescent behavior.* New York: Philosophical Library.

Bowker, L. H., Gross, H. S., and Klein, M. W. 1980. Female participation in delinquent gang activities. *Adolescence* 15, 59 (Fall):509–519.

Bowker, L. H., and Klein, M. W. 1983. The etiology of female juvenile delinquency and gang membership: A test of psychological and social structural explanations. *Adolescence* 18, 72 (Winter):739–751.

Blum, R. 1987. Contemporary threats to adolescent health in the United States. *Journal of the American Medical Association* 257 (June):3390–3395.

Brunner, R. 1974. Focal points of juvenile crime: Typology and conditions. *Juvenile crime and resocialization.* Congress Report, 1974. Stuttgart, W. Germany: New York: Springer Verlag.

Burt, C. 1925. *The young delinquent.* New York: Appleton.

Campbell, A. 1991. *The girls in the gang.* (2nd. ed.). New York: Basil Blackwell.

Canter, R. J. 1982. Sex differentials in self-reported delinquency. *Criminology* 20 (November):373–393.

Cavan, R. S., and Ferdinand, T. N. 1981. *Juvenile delinquency* (4th ed.). New York: Harper & Row.

CBS News Report. 1986. *CBS News Report,* September 11, 1986.

Chin, K. L., Fagan, J., and Kelly, R. J. 1992. Patterns of Chinese gang extortion. *Justice Quarterly* 9, 4 (December):625–646. Academy of Criminal Justice Sciences.

Cloward, R. A., and Ohlin, L. 1960. *Delinquency and opportunity.* New York: Free Press.

Cohen, A. 1958. *Delinquent boys: The culture of the gang.* New York: Free Press.

Coleman, J. S. 1970. *The circle.* Ludlow, MA: Pro Litho.

Coleman, J. S. 1988. Social capital in the creation of human capital. *American Journal of Sociology* 94 Supplement:S95–S120.

Curry, G. D., and Decker, S. H. 1998. *Confronting gangs: Crime and community.* Los Angeles, CA: Roxbury Publishing Company.

Daily O'Collegian. 1993. Oklahoma State University, Stillwater, Oklahoma. January 12, 1993:3.

Daily Tidings, Ashland, OR, June 5, 1985:5.

Dallas Morning News, Dallas, TX. March 18, 1990: 34A.

Dallas Morning News, Dallas, TX. White gangs organizing, officers say. October 10, 1993:2A.

Davis, C. 1988. Probation officer says gangs operate nationwide. *The Sunday Oklahoman.* Section A, page 18-May 1, 1988.

Davis, J. R. 1978. Neighborhood nonsense: The street war. *Terrorists-Youth, biker and prison violence.* San Diego, CA: Grossmont Press.

Donovan, D. 1990. Meet the world's toughest girls! *Weekly World News.* April 17, 1990:33.

Douthat, S. 1994. Pit bulls become the dogs of war for drug gangs, fight promoters. *Fort Worth Star Telegram* (Texas). November 6, 1994:AA4.

Empey, L. T., and Stafford, M. C. 1991. *American delinquency: Its meaning and construction* (3rd ed.). Belmont, CA: Wadsworth.

Erickson, M., and Jensen, G. 1977. Delinquency is still group behavior: Toward revitalizing the group premise in the sociology of deviance, *Journal of Criminal Law and Criminology* 68, 2 (June): 262–263.

Erlanger, H. S. 1979. Estrangement, machismo, and gang violence. *Social Science Quarterly* 60 (September):235–248.

Fagan, J. 1989. The social organization of drug abuse and drug dealing among urban gangs. *Criminology* 27, 4:633–670.

Gillespie, R. 1978. Economic factors in crime and delinquency: A critical review of the empirical evidence. Hearings, Subcommittee on Crime of the Committee of the Judiciary, House of Representatives, 95th Congress, Serial 47. Washington, DC: U.S. Government Printing Office, pp. 601–625.

Goffman, E. 1963. *Stigma: Notes on the management of spoiled identity.* Englewood Cliffs, NJ: Prentice-Hall.

Greenville Herald Banner. 1997. Teen gangs spreading to suburbia. March 26, 1997:B-2.

Groth, A., and Birnbaum, H. J. 1979. Men who rape: *The psychology of the offender.* New York: Plenum.

Hagedorn, J. M. 1988. *People and folks.* Chicago: Lakeview Press.

Halvorsen, R., and Hawley, D. 1973. *From gangs to God.* Washington, DC: Review and Herald Publishing.

Hardman, D. G. 1969. Small town gangs. *Journal of Criminal Law, Criminology and Police Science* 60, 2 (June):173–181.

Hindelang, M. J. 1976. With a little help from their friends. *British Journal of Criminology* 11, 2 (April):109–125.

Hirschi, T. 1969. *Causes of delinquency.* Berkeley, CA: University of California Press.

Howell, J. C. 1998. *Youth Gangs: An Overview.* (Juvenile Justice Bulletin). U.S. Department of Justice, Office of Juvenile Justice and Delinquency Prevention. Washington, DC.

Inciardi, J. 1978. *Reflections on crime: An introduction to criminology and criminal justice.* New York: Holt, Rinehart and Winston.

Irwin, J., and Cressey, D. 1977. Thieves, convicts, and the inmate culture. In R. G. Leger and J. R. Stratton (Eds.), *Sociology of corrections.* New York: John Wiley and Sons.

Johnstone, J. W. C. 1981. Youth gangs and black suburbs. *Pacific Sociological Review* 24 (July): 355–375.

Kaplan, D. A. with Gonzalez, D. L., and Wilson, L. Will the cameras be rolling? *Newsweek.* June 18, 1990:52.

Keiser, R. 1969. *The vice lords.* New York: Holt, Rinehart and Winston.

Kennedy, L. W., and Baron, S. W. 1993. Routine activities and a subculture of violence: A study of violence on the street. *Journal of Research in Crime and Delinquency* 30 (February):88–112.

Klein, M. 1964. Internal structures and age distributions in four delinquent Negro gangs. Paper presented at the annual meeting of the California State Psychological Association, Los Angeles. Youth Studies Center, University of Southern California (mimeo). 1971. *Street gangs and street workers.* Englewood Cliffs, NJ: Prentice-Hall.

Klein, M. W. 1995. *The American Street Gang.* New York: Oxford University Press.

Klein, M., and Crawford, L. 1968. Groups, gangs, and cohesiveness. In J. F. Short (Ed.). *Gang delin-quency and delinquent subcultures.* New York: Harper & Row, pp. 256–272.

Kobrin, J. P., and Peluso, E. 1968. Criteria of status among street gangs. In J. F. Short (Ed.). *Gang delinquency and delinquent subcultures.* New York: Harper & Row, 178–208.

Lemann, N. 1986. The origins of the underclass. *The Atlantic Monthly.* June, 1986:6–27.

Lerman, P. 1967. Gangs, networks, and subcultural delinquency. *American Journal of Sociology* 63:63–71.

Levinson, A. 1998. Clean-living movement turns ugly. *The Mail Tribune* Medford, OR. January 4, 1998:3A.

Lotz, R., Poole, E. D., and Regoli, R. M. 1985. *Juvenile delinquency and juvenile justice.* New York: Random House.

The Manteca Bulletin. 1993. Manteca, California. July 24, 1993:A-5.

Matza, D. 1964. *Delinquency and drift.* New York: John Wiley.

Medford Mail Tribune. 1996. Close-range shootings replace drive-bys in L.A. August 4, 1996:8B.

Merton, R. K. 1957. *Social theory and social structure* (2nd ed.). New York: Free Press.

Miller, W. B. 1958. Lower class culture as a generating milieu of gang delinquency. *Journal of Social Issues* 14 (Summer):5–19.
  1966. Violent crimes in city gangs. *Annals of the Academy of Political and Social Science* 64 (March):97–112.
  1975. *Violence by youth gangs and youth groups as a crime problem in major American cities.* Washington, DC: U.S. Government Printing Office.
  1981. American youth gangs. in A. S. Blumbert (Ed.). *Current perspectives on criminal behavior.* New York: Knopf, pp. 291–320.

Mitchell, J. C. 1979. Networks, algorithms, and analysis. In P. W. Holland and S. Leinhardt (Eds.). *Perspectives on social network research.* New York: Academic Press.

Moore, J. P., and Terrett, C. P. 1999. Highlights of the 1997 national youth gang survey. *OJJDP Fact Sheet.* No. 97. (March, 1999). Washington, DC: Office of Juvenile Justice and Delinquency Prevention, Department of Justice.

Moore, J. W. 1985. Isolation and stigmatization in the development of an underclass—The case of Chicano gangs in East Los Angeles. *Social Problems* 33, 1 (October):1–12.

Muehlbauer, G., and Dodder, L. 1983. *The losers: Gang delinquency in an American suburb.* New York: Praeger.

Myerhoff, H., and Myerhoff, B. 1964. Field observations of middle-class gangs. *Social Forces* 42 (March):328–336.

NBC *Dateline.* 1993. Television report. September 30.

NBC Television News Report. 1994. Sacramento, California. January 15.

Needle, J., and Stapleton, W. V. 1983. *Report of the National Juvenile Justice Assessment Centers, Police Handling of Youth Gangs.* Washington, DC: Office of Juvenile Justice and Delinquency Prevention, U.S. Department of Justice.

Nightline-American Broadcasting Company. 1988. April 15.

Park, R. 1927. Preface to Frederick Thrasher's *The gang.* Chicago: University of Chicago Press.

Pearson, G. 1984. The original Hooligans. A supplement to *History Today.* May, 1984:83.

Ramos, P. 1989. *The Hartford Courant,* June 4, 1989: D1, D4.

Ritzer, G. 1986. *Social problems* (2nd ed.). (Originally published as *Social Problems* by Rodney Stark in 1975). New York: Random House.

Sagarin, E. 1975. *Deviants and deviance: An introduction to the study of disvalued people and behavior.* New York: Praeger.

Salisbury, H. 1958. The suburbs. *The shook-up generation.* New York: Harper & Row.

Sanders, W. B. 1994. *Gang bangers and drive-bys: Grounded culture and juvenile gang violence.* New York: Aldine De Gruyter.

Sarnecki, J. 1982. *Criminality and peer relations: Study of juvenile delinquency in a Swedish community.* Stockholm, Sweden: Brottsforebyggande Radet.
1983. *Criminal juvenile gangs.* Stockholm, Sweden: Brottsforebyggande Radet.

Sato, I. 1987. *Play theory of delinquency: Toward a general theory of "action."* From a draft of concluding chapter of a doctoral dissertation submitted to University of Chicago.

Shaw, C., and McKay, H. 1931. Social factors in juvenile delinquency. In *Report on the Causes of Crime.* National Commission on Law Observance and Enforcement, Report No. 13. Washington, DC: U.S. Government Printing Office.
1942. *Juvenile delinquency in urban areas.* Chicago: University of Chicago Press.

1969. *Juvenile delinquency and urban areas.* (rev. ed.). Chicago: University of Chicago Press.

Short, J. F. (Ed.). 1968. *Gang delinquency and delinquent subculture.* New York: Harper & Row.
1987. Exploring integration of the theoretical levels of explanation: Notes on juvenile delinquency. In *Theoretical integration in the study of deviance and crime: Problems and prospects.* Albany, NY: Unpublished proceedings of the Albany Conference, May 7–8.

Short, J. F., and Strodtbeck, F. L. 1965. *Group process and gang delinquency.* Chicago: University of Chicago Press.

Snyder, H. N., and Sickmund, M. 1999. *Juvenile offenders and victims: 1999 national report.* Department of Justice, Office of Juvenile Justice and Delinquency Prevention. Washington, DC: U.S. Government Printing Office.

Snyder, H. N., Sickmund, M., and Poe-Yamagata, E. 1996. *Juvenile offenders and victims: 1996 update on violence.* Department of Justice, Office of Juvenile Justice and Delinquency Prevention. Rockville, MD: Juvenile Justice Clearinghouse.

Spergel, I. A., and Curry, G. D. 1988. Socialization to gangs: School-community gang prevention and control study. *Research Report.* School of Social Service Administration, University of Chicago.

Steffensmeier, D. J., and Steffensmeier, R. 1980. Trends in female delinquency: An examination of arrest, juvenile court, self-report, and field data. *Criminology* 18, 1 (May):62–85.

Stockton Record (California). 1997. Gang member urinates in court. April 4, 1997:A-4.

Street wars were worse 100 years ago! 1993. *National Inquirer* 68, 7 (September 7, 1993):7.

Subcommittee on Juvenile Justice. 1983. *Gang violence and control.* Hearings before the Subcommittee on juvenile justice of the Committee on the judiciary. United States Senate, Ninety-Eighth Congress, First Session on Gang Violence and Control in the Los Angeles and San Francisco Areas with a View to What Might Be Done by the Federal Government (Westwood, California, February 7, 1983 and San Francisco, CA, February 9, 1983).

Sutherland, E. 1939. *Principles of criminology.* Philadelphia: JB Lippincott.

Thio, A. 1998. *Deviant behavior* (5th ed.). New York: Addison Wesley Longman.

Thornberry, T. P., and Burch, J. H. 1997. *Gang Members and Delinquent Behavior;* Bulletin. U.S. Department of Justice, Office of Juvenile Justice and Delinquency Prevention. Washington, DC: U.S. Government Printing Office.

Thrasher, F. M. 1927. *The gang.* Chicago: University of Chicago Press.

1936. *The gang* (2nd ed.). Chicago: University of Chicago Press.

Time. 1977. The youth crime plague. *Time* 110, 2 (July 11, 1977):18–28.

Toplin, R. B. 1975. *Unchallenged violence: An American ordeal.* Westport, CT: Greenhaven Press.

Tressel, P. 1993. Manteca teen shot following "staring" match at Taco Bell. *Manteca Bulletin* (July 11, 1993):A-1.

Tulsa World. 1990, Mugging to finance night of dancing led to slaying. *Tulsa World* (Sept. 7, 1990):A9.

Vaz, E. W. (Ed.). 1967. *Middle-class juvenile delinquency.* New York: Harper & Row.

Vigil, J. D. 1997. *Learning from gangs: The Mexican-American experience.* (EDO-RC-97-1, February, 1997). Charleston, WV: ERIC/CRESS Clearinghouse on Rural Education and Small Schools.

Webster's third new international dictionary of the English language. (Philip Babcock, Editor-in-Chief). Springfield, MA. Merriam-Webster, Inc., Publishers. 1986.

Werthman, C., and Pilavin, I. 1967. Gang members and the police. In D. J. Bordua (Ed.). *The police.* New York: John Wiley, pp. 56–98.

Winfree, L. T., Jr., Backstrom, T. V., and Mays, G. L. 1994. Social learning theory, self-reported delinquency, and youth gangs: A new twist on a general theory of crime and delinquency. *Youth and Society* 26 (December):147–177.

Wooden, W. S. 1995. *Renegade Kids, Suburban Outlaws.* Belmont, CA: Wadsworth Publishing Co.

Wyrick, P. A. 2000. Vietnamese youth gang involvement. *OJJDP Fact Sheet #1* (February 2000). U.S. Department of Justice. Washington, DC.

Yablonsky, L. 1959. The delinquent gang as a near group. *Social Problems* 7, 2 (Fall):108–117.

Yablonsky, L., and Haskell, M. 1988. *Juvenile delinquency* (4th ed.). New York: Harper & Row.

Zastrow, C. 1992. *Social problems: Issues and solutions.* (3rd. ed.). Chicago: Nelson-Hall.

SOCIAL CONTROL

The Juvenile Justice System

Introduction: Elements of Social Control

In this book we are studying the social problem of juvenile delinquency from a sociological perspective. In this section, we examine the social processes involved in attempting to control juvenile delinquency.

Sociologists seldom assume that any form of crime or juvenile delinquency can be totally eliminated. As indicated in Part I, norm violation occurs in every society, and, in fact, deviance can be both functional and dysfunctional in its consequences. In this section, we focus upon the juvenile justice system and social processes involved in efforts to control juvenile delinquency. **Social control** refers to *the ways in which society members attempt to regulate the actions of others and reduce the negative impact of behavior which violates social norms.*

Chapter 13 focuses upon juveniles' activities in the social arena of the streets and sidewalks and looks at their encounters with the police. Police discretion is discussed as well as the legal and extralegal factors that influence policing juveniles. The issues of due process and delinquency prevention are also addressed.

In Chapter 14 we examine the juvenile court. The historical background which set the stage for development of the juvenile court is described with emphasis upon the Child Savers movement which dominated social philosophy and policy toward juveniles in the late 1800s. Juvenile court procedures are described with a focus on the issue of due process in the juvenile justice system. Some of the major criticisms leveled at the juvenile court are summarized, with suggestions for reforming the juvenile court of the future.

In Chapter 15, we discuss the sociological concept of social control and summarize methods utilized by society in attempting to correct the behavior of juveniles. Our discussion includes elements of **voluntary, informal,** and **formal** measures of social control and how they are applied to the problem of delinquency. We explore juvenile probation, restitution, incarceration, and we look at the controversial issue of capital punishment for juveniles, the ultimate measure of social control that can be exerted by a society. Finally we discuss and evaluate programs that involve deinstitutionalization, community corrections, and diversion.

As you read these chapters, we urge you to keep in mind the sociological framework, concepts, terms, and knowledge which have been developed through your reading of the first three parts of the book.

13 JUVENILES AND THE POLICE

Reading Objectives

The reading of this chapter will help you achieve the following objectives:

1. To view the public streets as a social arena where juveniles come in contact with adults—especially the police—who may define them as delinquent.
2. Understand and analyze juveniles' encounters with the police and the attitudes and variables that affect that interaction.
3. Identify and explain at least two disparate role expectations involved in policing juveniles and the strain this places on police officers and the youths involved.
4. Understand the role of the police as part of the filtering process in the juvenile justice system in regard to the amount of discretion police officers have in handling juveniles and to summarize the legal and extralegal factors that influence this discretion.
5. Define due process and provide an overview of some of the constitutional and legal issues that influence the handling of juveniles by the police.
6. Identify and explore some of the creative and innovative community policing strategies that have been developed to enhance police/juvenile relations and some of the programs used by police departments in an effort to help prevent juvenile delinquency.

Introduction

Chapter 10 began with a definition and discussion of the concept of *arena,* and then discussed the public schools as an arena where juveniles come in contact with others who may disapprove of their behavior and may even perceive them as delinquent. Another important social arena in which juveniles interact is the streets. "Cruising," "dragging the strip," and simply "hanging out" often bring juveniles by the hundreds of thousands out onto America's streets. In an effort to curb delinquency, many cities have implemented teen curfews to try to limit the nighttime activities of youths, but juveniles continue to see the streets as an important part of their social domain (Ruefle and Reynolds, 1995). These activities bring juveniles together not only with other juveniles, but also with a multitude of adults including people on their way to and from work, shoppers, local merchants, homeless "street people," vagrants, prostitutes, pimps, drug dealers, muggers, and, of course, the police. Encounters with any of these adults could result in a youth being identified as a delinquent, but when it comes to officially being labeled as a juvenile delinquent, the most important interaction that takes place in the social arena of the streets is when juveniles encounter the police.

Juvenile Encounters with Police

If juveniles spend much time on the streets, it is inevitable that they will at some time encounter the police. Younger children are often fascinated by police officers and usually wave to them as they drive by in their patrol cars, or stop and talk to them as they walk their beats. Police departments generally attempt to foster this respect and admiration of the police by sending officers to local elementary schools to talk to children, provide safety tips, and otherwise nurture the image of police as public servants, "helpers," and "friends." In some areas, police officers coach little league baseball and soccer teams to develop better relationships with children. In cities with professional sports franchises, police sometimes give youths football or baseball cards featuring the pictures of famous athletes on the front and helpful safety and crime prevention tips on the back (Shown, 1986). These efforts to enhance juvenile-police relations can be effective, and from childhood through the early teen years, youths generally view the police as "good guys" who can be counted on when they are needed (Bouma, 1969).

As they enter their mid-teens, however, juveniles' attitudes toward the police tend to change, and often become more negative. Many juveniles may resent the authority that the officers represent and some may merely be conforming to peer pressure to "not like cops." Research shows, however, that teenagers' attitudes toward the police vary importantly by race, ethnicity, gender, socioeconomic status, number of contacts with law enforcement officials, and exposure to violence and poverty (Portune, 1971; Hoobler, 1973; Giordano, 1976; Winfree and Griffiths, 1977; Greene, 1993). Whites generally have been found to have more favorable attitudes toward police than African Americans and other minorities; girls tend to view the police more favorably than boys; and youths from middle and upper class families typically have a higher opinion of the police than do those from the lower class. Not surprisingly, the more negative contacts youths have had with police, and the more committed juveniles are to violating the law, the less favorable their attitudes are toward law enforcement officers.

Similarly, while police usually like small children and often go to great efforts to befriend them, they tend to be more suspicious of and less friendly to teenagers on the streets. As discussed in Chapter 11, The Youth Subculture, teenagers often rebel against adult authority, and through their dress, hairstyles, language, and overall demeanor, may exhibit behavior that runs counter to a number of adult values and norms. Since police are adults, and more importantly, are charged with enforcing adult values and norms in the form of laws, it is not surprising that many juvenile encounters with the police become confrontational. Consequently, what may begin as routine encounters between juveniles and police on the streets may sometimes turn hostile in a matter of seconds. If a youth is stopped in an automobile and asked to show a driver's license or proof of insurance, if his or her responses or attitude are interpreted by the officer as being disrespectful or suspicious, the encounter may accelerate beyond a routine traffic stop. It could lead to a confrontation that might result in a search of the vehicle, and possibly even in the officer taking the youth to the police station. These extralegal factors that influence encounters between police and teenagers are explored later in this chapter when we discuss police discretion in handling juveniles.

Again, the sociological concept of *arena* is particularly helpful in analyzing juvenile encounters with police as it sheds light on the struggle for dominance and superiority that often takes place on the streets. One gang member summarized the juvenile-police dilemma:

> *They don't want us in the recreation centers, they don't want us on the streets, they don't want us hanging around the soda fountains, Where the hell do they want us? Home watching TV? We're too old for TV and too young for the bars. We get tired of just hanging around and we have to let off steam—even if it means fighting, stealing cars, breaking windows. They think we're all bad, some kind of punks (Tunley, 1962:40).*

A sixteen-year-old girl summarized the confrontational nature of juvenile encounters with police on the streets:

> *Cops don't care.... They loud talk you and harass you. If you're in their custody, they can say and do anything they want to you. Even off-duty, they are still like that. They think they can do anything because they're the law (Bartollas, 2000:396).*

Because of the somewhat negative attitudes held by many police and juveniles toward each other, it is understandable that their encounters are often confrontational in nature and punctuated by bad feelings, mistrust, and even downright hostility and violence. All of these factors make policing juveniles a challenge.

Policing Juveniles

The police are the most socially visible symbol of the juvenile justice system and are on the "front lines" in identifying, controlling, and processing juvenile delinquents. Law enforcement officers often view policing juveniles as a "no-win" situation. Since many of the offenses by juveniles are petty in nature, and in the case of status offenses, are not even against the law if committed by adults, police are often accused of overreacting and harassing youths when they should be protecting society from more serious offenders. On the other hand, if police ignore youthful pranks, status offenses, or the minor vandalism of juveniles, they soon find that the public expects them to intervene, make arrests, and enforce the legal codes no matter how trivial the consequences of their violation.

Virtually everyone agrees that the police should arrest juveniles who commit serious offenses such as burglary, robbery, rape, assault, and murder, but even in these cases, officers often find their actions more highly scrutinized and open to criticism and even formal sanctions than when they arrest adults for the same offenses. For instance if an officer must use force to apprehend a juvenile suspect, he or she may be far more vulnerable to charges of excessive force or brutality than if the perpetrator were over the age of eighteen. Consequently, police officers often feel that they are caught in a "Catch-22" situation when dealing with juveniles, because if they do not take proper precautions and treat the youths as potentially dangerous, they put themselves at serious risk. Yet, if they handle a juvenile in the same way they would an adult, the general public, and even superior officers and police review boards may "second-guess" their actions as being inappropriate because of the offender's age. A police officer expressed this sense of frustration to one of the authors:

I'm just never sure what to do when it's a kid. I mean, hell, a bullet from a gun fired from a 14 year-old is going to kill me just as dead as one fired from somebody who's twenty-four. But I know if I draw my weapon on a kid, have to wrestle one down, or God forbid, have to shoot one, it could mean my career.

Another officer expressed similar concerns and the predicament the police often find themselves in when encountering juveniles on the streets:

Lots of times when we're chasing a car or confront a suspect on the streets, we don't have any idea how old they are.... I mean, I've chased down cars, had the driver flee on foot...chased 'em half a mile while they turned and shot at me... tackled, handcuffed and arrested 'em while they're kickin', scratchin', cussin', and spittin' at me, only to find when I got 'em down to the station that they were only 14 or 15 years old.

Police frustrations in handling juveniles are often compounded by the lenient treatment juvenile offenders sometimes receive from the District Attorney's office or the courts. Studies show that many officers believe that much of their law enforcement efforts against juveniles are useless, because the juvenile justice system merely "slaps the wrists" of offenders, and turns them back on the streets before the paperwork is even completed (e.g., Skolnick, 1966; Walker, 1983; Gaines et al., 1994).

In order to deal with the special problems of policing juveniles, Berkeley, California established a special "youth bureau" in its department in the 1930s, and in the 1950s both a United States and an International Association of Juvenile Officers were established. A study by the U.S. Department of Justice (1993) showed that in 1990, 95 percent of the large police departments in the United States (departments with over 100 sworn officers) had specific written policy directives for the handling of juveniles and 89 percent of large departments had special units for policing juveniles. Sixty percent of large departments had special gang units; 79 percent had units for dealing with child abuse and 74 percent had special units for handling missing children. The study also revealed that approximately three-fourths of all state police departments and even many small municipal police and rural sheriff's departments had special units for handling juveniles (U.S. Department of Justice, 1993).

These **juvenile officers** often *receive special training in child development, adolescent psychology, sociology, and counseling, in order to better equip them to handle the unique problems associated with policing juveniles.* In some cases, becoming a juvenile officer may involve a promotion in rank or an increase in pay, while in others, it may result in ridicule and teasing from their fellow officers who refer to them as "kiddie cops" or the "diaper squad."

Because of special problems faced in policing juveniles, law enforcement officers, whether regular police, or specially trained juvenile officers, sometimes must fulfill different roles and grapple with what style of policing will be most effective in handling youths. In general there are two major schools of thought on the matter: the *law enforcement role* and the *crime prevention role* (Walker, 1983).

Law Enforcement Role

The first police officers in the United States were volunteer citizens who served as town "watchmen," and "kept the peace" through their vigilance and the mutual cooperation of the community. By the early 1900s, however, a new image of the police had emerged that emphasized the "crime fighting" aspect of police work and focused on their role as law enforcement officers (Thurman, et al., 1993). This role contended that police officers should avoid becoming too closely associated with those whom they patrolled (Williams and Murphy, 1990). The **law enforcement role** requires that *police should concentrate on arresting juveniles who violate criminal laws* (Walker, 1983). In the strictest sense of this view, youths are viewed and treated by the police in essentially the same way as are adults. In departments lacking specialized juvenile units, officers are more likely to adopt the law enforcement role in handling youths because virtually all of their training and experience have been geared toward policing adults. Thomson and Fielder (1975) noted that when police departments changed their primary means of patrolling from officers on foot walking a beat to motorized patrol on motorcycles and in squad cars, policing shifted from an informal, social interactive role to a more formalized law enforcement model. This may be particularly true in regard to policing juveniles, as officers today are more likely to encounter youths in the area of the streets outside the context of neighborhood and family. While officers can still use their discretion in handling relatively minor offenses, their primary duty is typically viewed as enforcing the law, arresting criminals (regardless of age), and protecting society.

As described earlier, however, even when the police are acting in their law enforcement role, they sometimes are expected to handle juveniles differently. This produces a certain amount of **role strain** in that *the set of expectations accompanying one role (i.e., law enforcement officer) may be at odds with fulfilling the expectations of another role (i.e., a concerned adult acting on behalf of a child in trouble)*. In some cases, this strain could even become pronounced enough to constitute **role conflict** *where the fulfillment of one role necessitates the violation of another.* Thus, in addition to being a law enforcement officer, when law violations involve a juvenile offender, the police also must attempt to carry out their duties in such a way as to protect the "best interests" of the child. Consequently, another major goal of policing juveniles is crime prevention.

Crime Prevention Role

When Sir Robert Peel formed the London Metropolitan Police Force in 1829, he indicated that the "duty of police is to prevent crime and disorder" (Inkster, 1992:28). Modeled after the British Constables (see Box 13-1), the **crime prevention role** calls for police officers to *act as social workers, and even surrogate parents, to help juveniles to avoid situations which might lead to delinquency* (Walker, 1983). This role places additional demands on police officers beyond simply knowing the law, responding to criminal complaints, and arresting juveniles suspected of having committed delinquent offenses. Thus, the crime prevention role requires expanded training that includes: enhancement of communication skills (especially listening); public speaking ability; problem-solving techniques; understanding of childhood and adolescent development; and conflict resolution and negotiation skills (Meese, 1993).

When acting in the crime prevention role, officers often assume a **loco parentis,** or *parental role* toward juveniles. In this role, the police anticipate that adolescents will "act up" from time to time, and prefer to handle minor indiscretions informally, reserving arrest and court referral only for serious criminal offenses (Gaines et al., 1994).

Many Americans believe that the mere presence and visibility of police officers helps to prevent delinquency. An Associated Press Poll showed that two-thirds of Americans questioned said that posting police officers in schools not only would help curb school violence but also would help reduce other forms of delinquency such as bullying and petty theft. Moreover, they believed that police officers would not only be additional adults in the school that children could turn to if they felt frightened or threatened in any way, but also would serve as positive role models for students (AP, Washington, 1999).

Police Discretion in Handling Juveniles

One of the most salient issues related to policing juveniles is that of **police discretion**—*the wide latitude police officers have in deciding how to handle juvenile offenders.* During the course of everyday policing, officers face numerous situations where they must decide what is the most appropriate response that will most likely achieve the most desirable outcome

Community policing has been an important part of British policing since its inception. Here two members of the London Metropolitan Police stop to chat with an American teenager.

BOX 13-1 Cross-Cultural Focus

Policing Juveniles in Great Britain

The mainstay of British policing is the unarmed constable, or "Bobbie," who patrols the streets on foot in much the same way as his or her predecessors did over a century and a half ago. Nowhere is this type of policing more evident than in London where the Metropolitan Police Service is charged with protecting and serving London's over 8½ million residents and almost that many tourists and visitors every single day. The vast majority of London's police officers walk a "beat" in pairs interacting informally with the public, answering questions, giving directions, and occasionally springing into action to apprehend a criminal.

When British police officers encounter juvenile lawbreakers they emphasize their social service and crime prevention orientation over their law enforcement roles. Most acts committed by youths under the age of fifteen are not punishable by law, so offenders in that age group are usually informally reprimanded or formally "cautioned" by the police and then turned over to their parents. Between the ages of 15 and 18, constables still prefer to handle offenders informally whenever possible, unless the offense is a serious one, or parents refuse to cooperate with the police.

As in the United States, juvenile crime prevention has become a major focus of policing in Great Britain. The Children Act of 1989 authorized local police agencies to work with families, schools, and other social agencies to focus their law enforcement efforts with youths on delinquency prevention. Strategies have been devised to involve young people in a variety of community projects designed to keep them in school and out of trouble with the law. In London, a Youth Partnership Program was developed in which over 40 schools have created Youth Crime Prevention Panels and over 22,000 elementary school children participate in 27 Junior Citizen Schemes and 15 police/community summer projects. A Volunteer Cadet Corps, involving over 300 youngsters aged 16 to 18, has been organized to involve teenagers in local community projects along with London Metropolitan police officers.

New Scotland Yard and other British police agencies are committed to diverting as many young first-time offenders from the criminal justice system as possible in order to avoid the stigma associated with arrest and prosecution. In recent years, however, the British police and judicial system have come under much scrutiny and heavy criticism for being too lenient toward youthful offenders, and British constables have experienced increased public pressure to arrest juvenile delinquents. Over the past decade, Great Britain has experienced an increase in crime rates, and approximately 25 percent of the known offenders are under the age of 17. Concerns over these trends have prompted the public to question some of the informal policing tactics used by the British police in handling juveniles, and constables now issue more formal cautions and place more youths in custody as a result.

Because the United States derives much of its culture and legal tradition from Great Britain, and many top-level law enforcement officials from both countries exchange ideas, information, tactics, and policing methods, it is not surprising that many similarities exist between the two countries regarding the policing of juveniles. Studies show that, as in the United States, British police officers have much discretion in how they handle youthful offenders, and a variety of legal and extralegal factors help determine the outcome of police encounters with juveniles. British police insist that youths be respectful, and the age, sex, race, attitude, and demeanor of the juvenile during the encounter have at least as much effect on police discretion as do the seriousness of the offense and previous police contacts.

Despite increasing pressure from the public to adopt a stricter law enforcement role in handling juvenile offenders, the vast majority of British police officers interviewed by one of the authors indicated that they believe that all but the "most serious" juvenile offenders will eventually "grow out" of delinquency and are best treated informally. Consequently, the British police both officially and unofficially express a solid commitment to the crime prevention role of policing.

Continued

BOX 13-1 *Continued*

Sources

Becker, J. K. 1973. *Police systems of Europe.* Springfield, IL: Charles C. Thomas.
Holdaway, S. (Ed) 1980. *The British police.* Beverly Hills: Sage.
Holdaway, S. 1984. *Inside the British police.* New York: Basil Blackwell.
Sanderson, J. F. 1993. *Youth crime in London: Prevention through partnership.* London: Metropolitan Police Service.
Thompson, W. E. 1992–1999. Unpublished interviews with officers at New Scotland Yard, London Metropolitan Police Service, and Surrey Police Department, England.

for themselves, the police department, and the community they are sworn to serve (Gaines et al., 1994). Police discretion is so important because it is during the initial contacts between juveniles and police that decisions are made that determine whether the encounter will be handled unofficially, or that the juvenile will be detained and officially processed— thus contributing to the official data on juvenile delinquency as we discussed in Chapter 3. In this way, the police contribute to an important **filtering process,** *determining who does or does not become officially recognized as a juvenile delinquent.* Police catch a large number of juveniles in their huge "net," yet many juveniles are both intentionally and inadvertently allowed to slip through "holes" in the "net" as they are "filtered out" of the adjudication process and the juvenile justice system. For example, of the over one million youths processed by the police in 1992, almost one-third of them were released (FBI *Uniform Crime Reports, 1993*). This trend has continued over the years.

Krisberg and Austin (1978:83) noted that police typically have five basic options in deciding what course of action to pursue with juveniles:

1. *Release, accompanied by a warning to the juvenile.*
2. *Release, accompanied by an official report describing the encounter with the juvenile.*
3. *Station adjustment, which may consist of:*
   (a) *release to parent or guardian accompanied by an official reprimand;*
   (b) *release accompanied by referral to a community youth services agency for rehabilitation; or*
   (c) *release accompanied by referral to a public or private social welfare or mental health agency.*
4. *Referral to juvenile court intake unit, without detention.*
5. *Referral to juvenile court intake unit, with detention.*

What determines which of these options will be exercised by police? First, whether all of these alternatives actually are available to the police often depends upon community resources. Some states, counties, and local communities provide a wide variety of diversionary alternatives to police for dealing with juveniles. Others, however, may provide few if any community resources. In times of economic hardship, budget cutting at state, county, and local levels, and other monetary restrictions, police options may be severely limited as social service agencies for youths are often among the first to be targeted for cutbacks or closure. Consequently, in some communities, for all practical purposes, viable police options may be limited to two: either release the juvenile outright, or petition the juvenile to court.

Also, the overall political climate and changes in public policy play an important role in police discretion (Aaronson et al., 1984). For example, public perceptions of youthful "crime waves," and fear of violence coupled with "get tough" policies of national, state, and local officials may preclude many of the alternatives usually left to police discretion. Still, on a daily basis, decisions made by the police at the time of the encounter with juveniles plays the most important role in determining who will be officially processed as a delinquent.

Common sense would seem to dictate, and many people believe, that the nature of the offense committed by a youth largely determine how police decide to handle a case, and indeed that is a factor. However, research shows that a number of other legal and extralegal factors affect police discretion.

Legal Factors

There are a number of legal factors considered by police that help determine how they handle juvenile offenders. Research indicates that the most common legal factors that affect police discretion are: the seriousness of the offense; number and extent of prior police contacts; the amount and nature of evidence linking the juvenile to the offense; and whether a complainant insists that formal action be taken.

Seriousness of the Offense

Juveniles who commit serious criminal offenses that would be classified as felonies or serious misdemeanors if they were committed by adults are much more likely to be arrested, detained, confined, and petitioned to court than those who commit less serious misdemeanors and status offenses (Piliavin and Briar, 1964; Terry, 1967; Black and Reiss, 1970; Krisberg and Austin, 1978; Lundman et al., 1978; Gaines et al., 1994). Not surprisingly, when juveniles are involved in a murder, the police almost always place them under arrest, detain them, and turn the case over to the District Attorney's office. Likewise, forcible rape, aggravated assault, and robbery usually invoke serious formal responses from the police regardless of the age of the offender.

Yet the seriousness of the offense is only one factor that helps shape police discretion in handling juveniles. Alleged felonies comprise only a small fraction of all police-juvenile encounters (most estimates are between 5 to 10 percent), with the vast majority of juvenile offenses being less serious crimes and status offenses. Yet many of these less serious infractions lead to serious consequences. Thus, several other factors influence police discretion in less serious matters.

Prior Police Contacts

Every police department keeps records of prior arrests and in today's computerized world of data collection, prior records can literally be at a police officer's fingertips in a matter of seconds. However, individual officers often carry a small notebook to keep track of contacts with juveniles whether they lead to official arrest or not, and warn youths that if they encounter them again, even for minor infractions, more serious steps will be taken. In some cases, these contacts may have represented nothing more than a police officer stopping a juvenile on the street and asking a few questions, or taking the youth home to his or her parents. Nevertheless, if the officer encounters this juvenile again, because of the previous contact, he or she may be treated much more seriously.

If a juvenile is taken to the police station for more extensive interrogation, an official record, or "rap sheet," is likely to be kept. Thus, even if a youth simply happened to be in the vicinity of a crime, he or she may become "known" to the police, and likely to be treated more harshly in future police encounters. Aaron Cicourel (1968) found that prior contacts with the police often escalated what would have been a routine minor encounter with a juvenile, that normally would have resulted in an unofficial warning, into a formal police action resulting in arrest and petition to court. Likewise, Terry (1967) found that while almost 40 percent of juvenile arrests involve first-time offenders, only about 7 percent of them are referred to juvenile court; conversely, chronic offenders and repeat juvenile offenders well known to the police were much more likely to be arrested and referred to court. Research suggests that seriousness of the offense and prior police contacts are two very important variables that determine police discretion in handling juveniles (Cohen and Kluegel, 1978; Lattimore et al., 1995). Prior contacts with police are so important that many police departments have developed special policing tactics and programs designed to identify and target chronic offenders—a controversial issue discussed later in this chapter and in Box 13-2.

Evidence

Another factor considered by police in determining how to handle a juvenile is how compelling the evidence is linking the youth to the offense. Logically, police are reluctant to take actions against juveniles or adults if there is little or no tangible evidence linking them to an illegal act. In the majority of cases leading to the arrest of a juvenile, a police officer actually witnesses the commission of the delinquent act (Black and Reiss, 1970). Even in those cases, however, police still exercise wide discretion as to how to handle the case. In one study, it was found that only 13 percent of the suspects were arrested even when police saw them commit the offense (Black and Reiss, 1970). On the other hand, when someone else witnessed law violation and called the police, 19 percent of the suspects were arrested. This suggests that the presence of a complainant may also be an important variable related to the action taken by police.

Complainant

The presence of an audience, complainant, or a victim also influences police discretion in handling juveniles. Smith and Visher (1981) found that the police were much more likely to intervene formally and arrest juveniles when there was an audience present—especially if that audience included an adult willing to sign a complaint. Of particular importance to police discretion is the attitude of complainants and victims if they are present. Studies show that when complainants and victims indicate an unwillingness to cooperate with prosecution or recommend that police handle the situation informally, police almost always comply with the request (Black and Reiss, 1970). On the other hand, when a complainant insists that formal action be taken, police are much more likely to arrest the juvenile and take him or her to the station, even if they decide later not to petition the juvenile to court (Hohenstein, 1969; Black and Reiss, 1970).

While the presence or absence of an audience or victim willing to file a complaint represents a legal factor that influences police discretion in handling juveniles, the attitude of the complainant and his or her willingness or unwillingness to cooperate with the police demonstrates that a number of extralegal factors also affect police-juvenile encounters.

Extralegal Factors

In addition to the legal factors that we have discussed, a number of extralegal factors also have been shown to be related to police discretion in handling juveniles. The extralegal factors most commonly cited in research are: age; sex; race and ethnicity; socioeconomic status; willingness of parents to cooperate with the police; appearance, attitude, and demeanor of the youth; and the characteristics of the police officer involved.

Age

Age is a legal factor in determining how police handle juveniles in that each state defines juvenile delinquency by setting minimum and maximum ages of persons that come under the purview of the juvenile courts. As we have mentioned in Chapter 1, in most states the age range is legally set somewhere between the ages of 7 to 18 with some states setting upper limits at 16, 17, or even 21. But age also becomes an extralegal factor in police discretion as to how youths are treated even if they clearly fit the delimitations established by law. Research shows that below the age of 10, few juveniles are detained or referred to court unless they have committed very serious offenses (Goldman, 1963). Moreover, in some states (Texas, for example), even though children are considered capable of *mens rea* at age 7, their cases will not be heard in a juvenile court before they reach the age of 10. Rather, criminal offenses involving youths under the age of 10 are handled by special family courts, and juveniles are much more likely to be determined as "in need of supervision" and made

Police arrest youths suspected of dealing crack cocaine.

wards of the court for their protection than they are to be adjudicated delinquent and remanded to the juvenile justice system.

Data indicate that one reason for the more lenient treatment of younger juveniles is that their offenses tend to be less serious. But research indicates that over the age of ten, juveniles tend to be handled more harshly by the police with each additional year of age, with those at the upper ages of the juvenile range being most likely to be arrested, detained, and petitioned to juvenile court regardless of the nature of the offense (Goldman, 1963; Terry, 1967; McEachern and Bauzer, 1967).

Understandably, age is a factor in police sometimes handling older youths in exactly the same manner as adults. As mentioned previously, in the heat of the action, police sometimes cannot take the time to check identification to determine a suspect's age. Thus, when youths at the upper age limits of juvenile status are apprehended by the police, especially if they are large and mature in appearance, it may not be until they are being processed at the station that it is discovered that they are under the age of adulthood and must be treated as juveniles.

Sex

For many years, it has been assumed that a "chivalry factor" exists in police work whereby females are treated more leniently by the police than are their male counterparts. Indeed, research confirms that sex is an important extralegal variable that influences police discretion, but in contrast to conventional wisdom regarding the favoritism experienced by females, studies suggest that there may be somewhat of a "boomerang effect" regarding police treatment of females. That is to say, that initially girls are considered to be less "suspicious" by the police, and are less likely to be stopped and questioned unless they have been seen committing a delinquent act. In fact, while a group of teenage boys on the street almost always captures an officer's attention and may lead to a police encounter for "routine questioning," a group of teenage girls is far more likely to be considered potential "victims" rather than potential perpetrators of crime. However, when juvenile girls are suspected of delinquency, and especially if they are seen as violating stereotypical or "traditional" gender roles, evidence suggests that they may be treated more harshly by police than males, and may, in fact, be more likely than boys to be taken to the station for official processing and referral to court for relatively minor offenses (Terry, 1967; Armstrong, 1977; Chesney-Lind, 1977, 1988; Chesney-Lind and Shelden, 1992).

Race and Ethnicity

As was discussed in Chapter 3, racial and ethnic minorities are overrepresented in the official data on juvenile delinquency. While some people suggest that the explanation for this phenomenon is that minority youths commit more serious crimes than do whites (Wilbanks, 1987), most studies suggest that there is far more to it than that. Researchers who have participated in "ride along" programs with the police have observed that members of racial and ethnic minorities, especially those who appear to be "tough guys" or to be affiliated with gangs, are far more likely than whites to be stopped, interrogated, handled roughly, and placed under arrest (e.g., Piliavin and Briar, 1964; Black and Reiss, 1970).

Other studies have confirmed that regardless of the seriousness of offense, racial and ethnic minorities, especially African Americans and Hispanics are more likely to be confronted by the police, and to be arrested, detained, and referred to juvenile court (Goldman,

1963; Smith and Visher, 1981; Dannefer and Schutt, 1982; Fagan et al., 1987; Huizinga and Elliott, 1987; Lundman, 1996a).

Robert Sampson (1986) pointed out that the extralegal variables of race and social class may be so important in determining police actions that they contribute to one of the legal factors (prior offenses) that shape police discretion. He noted that because police are more suspicious of minority youths they stop them more often and make a record of the encounter. Thus, when these youths are stopped again, they are already "known" to the police and may be dealt with more harshly the second time because of these "prior contacts" with police.

Ferdinand and Luchterhand (1970) suggested that the differential treatment of minority youths by white police officers may not simply be a matter of racism. They suggested that because the officers and youths come from such disparate social and cultural backgrounds that there is a basic lack of empathy and understanding for minority values and norms. Their research suggests that socioeconomic status may be a more important variable in determining the nature of police-juvenile encounters than is race and ethnicity.

Socioeconomic Status

One of the most important influences on a person's attitudes, values, and behavior in an industrialized capitalistic society is his or her socioeconomic status (SES). Similarly, social class also significantly affects how individuals are viewed and treated by others. Therefore, it is not surprising that SES is an influential factor in police discretion. With few exceptions, the majority of research on youths' SES and their treatment by police indicate that juveniles from lower socioeconomic strata are more likely to come into contact with police than are members of the middle and upper classes. Furthermore, studies suggest that the police are more likely to officially process and refer lower class juveniles to court than they are youths from higher socioeconomic backgrounds (Terry, 1967; Cicourel, 1968; Thornberry, 1973; Sampson, 1986; Lattimore et al., 1995; Lundman, 1996a).

Sampson (1986:884) concluded that, "Apparently, the influence of SES on police contacts with juveniles is contextual in nature, and stems from an ecological bias with regard to police control, as opposed to a single individual-level bias against the poor." In other words, juveniles who live in lower SES neighborhoods which have been identified by police as "high crime areas" are more likely to come into contact with police who patrol these areas more heavily, and hence experience a greater likelihood of being detained, arrested, and petitioned to juvenile court, than youths who live in so-called "low crime areas" that are not patrolled as frequently. Some police officers indicate that they believe that parents do not play as strong a supervisory role among lower class families as they do in the middle and upper social classes, and therefore, the police must make a more overt show of social control in lower SES neighborhoods to prevent and control delinquency (Cicourel, 1968).

Appearance, Attitude, and Demeanor of the Juvenile

The appearance, attitude, and overall demeanor of the juvenile when confronted by the police emerge as very important variables in influencing police discretion (Lundman, 1996a; 1996b). Piliavin and Briar (1964) found that demeanor was the most important factor in determining how police handle apprehended juveniles. Similarly, Morash (1984) found that juveniles who most closely fit the common image of delinquents held by police were most likely to be arrested. Neatly dressed, cooperative, and well-mannered youths are rarely viewed with suspicion, and if they come into contact with police are very likely to be released with an informal warning. On the other hand, if a youth fails the "attitude test," by failing to show the proper deference or by appearing to be antagonistic, he or she is much more likely to be arrested (Cicourel, 1968; Hohenstein, 1969; Winslow, 1973). Smith and Visher (1981:172) concluded that regardless of other legal and extralegal factors, "failure to display deference toward an officer significantly increases the probability of arrest."

Black and Reiss (1970) discovered an interesting finding regarding the demeanor of youths and their likelihood of arrest. Their study confirmed that unusually disrespectful youths were indeed more likely to be arrested than were reasonably respectful youths. They also discovered, however, that juveniles at the other end of the continuum (those who were unusually respectful to the officers) also had a greater likelihood of arrest. Apparently, officers tend to become suspicious of teenagers who "lay it on too thick" and seem "overly respectful" during interaction. Thus, a youth's demeanor apparently plays an important role in the discretionary decisions exercised by officers, and those juveniles who stray too far from officers' expectations in either direction are likely to suffer harsher treatment than those who conform to the "nice kid" stereotype (Piliavin and Briar, 1964; Black and Reiss, 1970; Lundman et al., 1978; Lundman, 1996a; 1996b).

Willingness of Parents to Cooperate

When parents can be easily contacted by the police and show an active interest in their children and an apparent willingness to cooperate with the police, the likelihood is much greater (especially in the case of minor offenses) that a juvenile will be warned and released to parental custody. Goldman (1963) found that approximately 90 percent of the police officers he interviewed felt that if the parents were readily available and willing to cooperate with the police, and if in the officer's view the home situation was considered to be "satisfactory," then the officer's preference was to handle the youth informally unless he or she had committed a very serious offense. Goldman's findings were supported by the 1967 *Task Force Report on Juvenile Delinquency and Youth Crime* which reported that family situation along with the attitude and conduct of a youth's parents were important criteria affecting police decisions on disposition of juvenile cases.

Characteristics of the Police Officer

In addition to all the legal and extralegal factors that influence police discretion in handling juveniles, a variable that sometimes goes overlooked is the impact that personal and social characteristics of police officers may have on shaping their interactions with youths. The same sociological characteristics of youths that influence police discretion (i.e., age, sex, race and ethnicity, and socioeconomic status) may also be important for the police officer involved. For example, while no study has specifically shown that the age of a police officer affects his or her decisions about handling juveniles, research has shown that the length of service and amount of experience officers have may affect their decision-making processes (Sullivan and Siegel, 1972). In general, the longer police officers have been on the force and the more experience they have had in handling juveniles, the more cynical, dissatisfied, and disgusted they become with the juvenile justice system (Gaines et al., 1994). Other studies have suggested that whether the racial, ethnic, and socioeconomic characteristics between the officers and the juvenile offenders were fairly similar or drastically different also affected police discretion. Officers, like other human beings, tend to relate best to other people who have similar social and cultural backgrounds to them (Wilson, 1968; Ferdinand and Luchterhand, 1970).

Finally, it must be acknowledged that just as a juvenile's attitude and demeanor may affect interaction with police, so too might the attitude, demeanor, and personality of the officer affect the interaction with the juvenile. Some police officers assume a parental attitude toward juveniles and may prefer to handle situations informally whenever possible, while others may view their role in terms of strictly law enforcement, and prefer to handle even minor offenses in a formal matter. Moreover, while some police officers have an uncanny ability to *de-escalate* the intensity or potential for violence in a juvenile encounter by remaining calm and having a calming and reassuring effect on the offender, others may *escalate* the situation simply through their voice, mannerisms, and demeanor.

Both legal and extralegal factors influence police discretion in handling both juveniles and adults. With adults, however, police departments generally have more clearcut guidelines regarding what officers should and should not do in certain situations. More importantly, when handling adults, the U.S. Constitution outlines certain elements of **due process,** or *basic legal rights that must be granted to an individual before he or she can be deprived of life, liberty, or property.* Because they were intended to protect adult citizens accused of crimes, unfortunately, the due process procedures are much less clearcut for handling juveniles.

Police and Due Process

As a result of the popularity of movies and television series about the police, virtually everybody is familiar with the landmark U.S. Supreme Court case of *Miranda v. Arizona,* and its mandate for police procedures. In fact, the results of the case have had such profound impact on arrest procedures that it has created a new verb in police language—to **Mirandize** a suspect—which basically means *to advise the suspect of his or her rights.* In the Miranda decision, the court ruled that at the time of arrest, suspects must be informed by the police that:

> *They have the right to remain silent; if they choose to waive that right, anything they say can and will be used against them in a court of law; they have the right to have an attorney present, and if they are unable to afford one, counsel will be appointed for them (Miranda v. Arizona, 384 U.S. 436, 1966).*

The Miranda decision was handed down in an effort to reinforce constitutional rights guaranteed in the 5th (right against self-incrimination), 6th (right to counsel), and the 14th Amendments (right to due process). The U.S. Court of Appeals for the 9th Circuit and the U.S. Supreme Court have ruled that failure to fully "Mirandize" a suspect may constitute a violation of civil rights and that both the department and the arresting officer may be held liable to the suspect for damages (Ronzio, 1993).

These constitutional rights and the Miranda ruling, however, applied to adults, where a clear adversary relationship exists between the state and its citizens who are accused of crimes. What about juveniles? According to the *parens patriae* doctrine upon which juvenile courts, and hence juvenile statutes were created, the state intervenes *on behalf* of juveniles for their protection—not *against* them for punishment. Therefore, it was not made clear by the U.S. Supreme Court whether juveniles should be accorded the same rights to due process by the police and courts as adults.

In its 1964 *In re Gault* decision, the Supreme Court implied that it intended for police officers and the courts to provide some of the same basic due process rights to juveniles that are granted to adults. However, as we will discuss in more detail in Chapter 14, Juvenile Courts, in many instances, the police and the courts deprive juveniles of some of the basic rights guaranteed to adults who are accused of committing crimes.

Krisberg and Austin (1978:80) indicated, "because the rights of due process and restrictions on evidence are not rigidly adhered to in juvenile courts, police can take advantage of the situation and use search, seizure, and interrogation procedures that would clearly be illegal if used with adult offenders." One of the problems with due process for juveniles is that technically, in most states juveniles are *detained* rather than *arrested* by the police. Although the difference is largely a matter of semantics, it allows the police to circumvent court rulings and department policies regarding due process during and after the arrest of suspects.

In an effort to protect the due process rights of juveniles taken into custody by police, the National Advisory Commission on Criminal Justice Standards and Goals (1973:764) recommended:

1. *Police should warn juveniles of their right to counsel and the right to remain silent during questioning.*
2. *Upon apprehension of a minor, police should notify the parents.*
3. *Any statements made to police or court officers not in the presence of parents or counsel should be inadmissible in court.*
4. *Juveniles should not be fingerprinted, photographed, or otherwise put through the usual adult booking process.*
5. *Juvenile records should be maintained physically separate from adult case records.*

These are only guidelines, however, and not mandatory requirements, so local, county, and state police still may exercise a great deal of discretionary power in handling juveniles (Davis, 1971; 1983). Nevertheless, court rulings, these guidelines, and general public sentiment that juvenile law violators should be treated more like adults have led many police departments to develop procedural policies governing interaction with juveniles that afford the youths most, if not all, of the due process rights afforded adults.

A major issue regarding the due process rights of juveniles is under what circumstances a juvenile can waive these rights. Two very important Supreme Court decisions address this issue. In the case of *West v. United States* (1968), the court ruled that a nine-point analysis should be considered to determine if a juvenile's waiver of rights has validity:

1. *The juvenile's age and maturity level.*
2. *The youth's educational level.*
3. *If the juvenile has knowledge of the substance of the charge(s) and understands his/her rights to remain silent and to have an attorney present.*
4. *Whether the accused has been allowed to contact parents, guardian, attorney, or some other interested adult.*
5. *Whether the interrogation occurred before or after being petitioned to juvenile court, or the filing of an indictment.*

6. *The methods police and/or the District Attorney used for interrogation.*
7. *The length and duration of interrogations.*
8. *Whether the accused had ever refused to give voluntary statements on prior occasions.*
9. *Whether the accused had ever repudiated voluntary statements after interrogation.*

In a later case, *Fare v. Michael C.* (1979) the court extended these criteria to include the *"totality of circumstances,"* insisting that before juveniles can legally waive their rights, "all the relevant circumstances" surrounding the case must be taken into account.

Despite these court rulings, however, and a host of police department policies regarding the due process rights of juveniles, the application of these rights varies greatly from state to state. A review of case and state laws regarding due process rights of juveniles indicates that state practices vary widely, and that police discretion is still one of the most important determinants of how juveniles will be initially handled when they come in contact with the juvenile justice system (Caeti, 1993).

Police, Community Policing, and Delinquency Prevention

We have already discussed the "crime prevention" role assumed by many police officers when handling juveniles, but in most large communities, police departments are also becoming actively involved in delinquency prevention programs. Many of these programs are linked to a renewed interest in **community policing** which *emphasizes cooperative efforts between the police and other members of the community.*

The *Teens on Patrol* program (TOP) in Rochester, New York is an example of a successful police/community program aimed at preventing juvenile delinquency. In this program, over one hundred youths are hired during the summer to patrol city swimming pools, parks, and recreational areas, and to report any suspicious or law-violating behavior to the police. These "junior" officers do not make arrests, but they are officially recognized as city employees and carry police radios that put them in direct contact with uniformed officers. Moreover, it is believed that their mere presence and high visibility discourages teenage crime in those areas (Lipson, 1982). In Tulsa, Oklahoma, juveniles who are first-time non-violent offenders are placed in the Youth Intervention Program where they ride along with police officers for an average of 150 hours. The program is considered quite successful as the youths tend to view the officers as positive role models (Woodbury, 1991).

A number of other proactive strategies designed to enhance police/juvenile relations and to deter delinquency have been developed across the country. In Reno, Nevada, for example, a *Community Action Team (CAT)* was organized for linking police officers to the community in dealing with community problems and preventing crime and delinquency. Several programs were developed by CAT. *COPS + KIDS* program sponsors a picnic each year for over 2,500 underprivileged youths and their parents. Also, the Reno police department participates in the Police Athletic League (*PAL*) program where police officers coach youth boxing and wrestling teams, as well as accompany "at-risk" youths on hiking, backpacking, and camping expeditions. The *NAGs* (Neighborhood Advisory Groups) program in Reno is a cooperative arrangement between police and neighborhood groups that discusses allocation of police resources and crime prevention steps for the community while *GREAT* (Gang Resistance Education And Training) attempts to desensationalize gang membership and educate youngsters about the negative aspects of gang violence in order to deter gang recruitment of new members (Weston, 1993).

In the summer of 1992, the Spokane, Washington, Police Department developed an innovative community policing project called *COPY* (Community Opportunities Program for Youth). Primarily aimed at local youths who were at risk of abusing alcohol or illegal drugs and of joining delinquent gangs, the program involved weekly meetings with police officers, juveniles, and parents in nonthreatening surroundings. Officers chatted informally with the youths in the program and emphasized the positive aspects of law-abiding behavior, staying in school, and developing a conventional work ethic. A follow-up study at the end of the summer that utilized observations, focus group interviews, and survey research indicated very positive outcomes for youths, parents, and the officers who participated in the program (Thurman et al., 1993).

Research shows that despite widespread support for the idea of community policing, crime control remains the central focus of most police departments (Zhao and Thurman, 1997).

Not all police efforts at preventing delinquency have been viewed with unanimously positive community support, however. In fact, some police programs aimed at delinquency prevention are quite controversial (see Box 13-2). Police programs that "target" specific teenagers for constant surveillance and single them out for differential law enforcement practices have become quite controversial and raise a number of civil rights issues.

This police officer and a community volunteer work with students as part of an anti-drug educational program.

BOX 13-2 Controversial Issue

Targeting Serious Habitual Offenders: Delinquency Prevention or Police Harassment?

Over the last two decades, research has consistently shown that a disproportionate amount of juvenile delinquency, especially serious property and violent offenses, is committed by a relatively small segment of the juvenile population. In some cases, as few as 5 percent of all juvenile offenders may be responsible for as much as three-fourths of serious juvenile crime. Moreover, in most cases, these juveniles' criminal careers usually begin when they are in their early teens. In response to these findings, various police departments have developed policing strategies aimed at targeting serious repeat offenders in an effort to "stem the tide" of serious juvenile crime.

In 1983, five cities were selected to implement pilot projects specifically aimed at identifying, catching, and processing serious habitual juvenile offenders. The five cities were: Colorado Springs, Colorado; Oxnard, California; Portsmouth, Virginia; Jacksonville, Florida; and San Jose, California. The goal of the programs was *not* to catch and arrest *more* juveniles, but to identify and target the most serious juvenile repeat offenders in each community and to neutralize, or "incapacitate" them, by taking them off the streets (Kline, 1993; Bassett, 1993).

The *SHO/DI* (Serious Habitual Offender/ Directed Intervention) project in Colorado Springs is typical of the programs established in each of the five cities. It required extensive cooperation among the police, the District Attorney's office, probation services, and the schools. Law enforcement officials developed a complete profile of the 25 to 30 most serious repeat offenders in Colorado Springs. These profiles included detailed physical descriptions, summaries of *modus operandi,* case summaries, traffic offenses, police contacts, drug and alcohol involvement, complete delinquency and criminal records, probation information, and summaries of school records. After the most serious habitual offenders are identified, they are placed under intensive surveillance and arrested for even the most minor legal infraction. The District Attorney then prosecutes to the fullest extent possible, and juvenile judges cooperate in either adjudicating the youths as delinquent and recommending incarceration, or in certifying the youths as adults to stand trial in criminal courts.

An evaluation of the SHO/DI program 10 years after its inception concluded that it has been very successful in identifying, targeting, arresting, adjudicating, and incapacitating the most serious repeat offenders in the community (Kline, 1993). Overall delinquency rates have been reduced and the most serious juvenile offenders have not been allowed to "fall through the cracks" of the juvenile justice system.

While police officials and many members of the general public are delighted with SHO/DI and similar programs, the targeted juveniles, their parents and attorneys, and the American Civil Liberties Union raise some serious civil rights issues related to these police tactics. Their concerns are that, in effect, juveniles identified as serious habitual offenders are not only arrested and punished for offenses they have committed, but also are singled out and targeted for "special" policing—what some argue is tantamount to police harassment and invasion of privacy. Moreover, it is contended that when police encounter unsolved crimes with no substantial evidence or probable suspects, they simply reach into their SHO/DI file and pull out a "likely" suspect to go after. Also, attorneys and civil libertarians argue that these "targeted" youths are arrested and given very stiff penalties for very minor offenses that would be ignored by law enforcement officials if committed by other "nontargeted" youths.

*   *   *   *

Should police officers identify and target certain juveniles for differential law enforcement tactics? What are some of the benefits of programs such as SHO/DI? What are some potential problems associated with such a program?

Sources

Basset, A. 1993. Community-oriented gang control. *Police Chief* 60 (February):20–23.
Kline, E. M. 1993. Colorado Springs SHO/DI: Working smarter with juvenile offenders. *Police Chief* 60 (April):32–37.

The San Antonio police have implemented an innovative but somewhat controversial program designed to reduce violent crime by targeting youths known to own or possess firearms. Dubbed WRAT (pronounced "rat"), this program of Weapons Recovery and Tracking appears to be effective in identifying youths who own or possess firearms, and in its first year of operation the program recovered over 250 firearms from youths; and while there is no empirical evidence of direct cause and effect, during that same period, homicides committed by youths dropped by over 40 percent (David, 1997).

Despite some of the controversies, police departments across the country are renewing their efforts to develop community policing and delinquency prevention programs in an effort to work more closely with other community agencies and individuals to stem the tide of rising violence that is plaguing most major cities and a number of suburban and even rural areas. Since the police represent the front lines of delinquency control and prevention, they usually are an essential part of a juvenile's first official encounter with the juvenile justice system. Thus, along with the office of the District Attorney, they help determine whether youths will find themselves in another significant public arena—the juvenile court.

SUMMARY

The streets constitute a social arena where juveniles—especially teenagers—spend a great deal of their time and carry out a wide variety of social activities. During these activities, youths encounter a number of adults who may initiate the process of defining them as delinquent. The front line of the juvenile justice system in the streets is comprised of the police who encounter juveniles in an array of social situations ranging from "routine" traffic stops and informal interactions to life-threatening criminal activities.

Although young children tend to hold positive attitudes toward the police, teenagers and the police often develop more strained attitudes toward one another that may border on a sense of "mutual hostility." Police often feel trapped in a "damned if you do; damned if you don't" situation when policing juveniles, while teenagers often believe that the police enjoy harassing them and their friends and generally overreact to "harmless fun."

When policing juveniles, officers often vacillate between a strict *law enforcement* and a more flexible *crime prevention role.* Either way, the police may employ a great deal of discretion in handling juveniles. This discretion is influenced by both legal and extralegal factors that help determine how police officers handle juvenile offenders.

Police discretion coupled with the disparity among states' statutory provisions and interpretations of case law raise a number of issues regarding the *due process*

rights to which juveniles are entitled. In some jurisdictions, police department policies dictate that juveniles be afforded all of the basic civil rights and due process procedures that are guaranteed to adults. In others, however, the police may employ vastly different policing techniques with youths that violate many of the basic due process procedures used in handling adults.

Most police departments are now developing and using *proactive* strategies of community policing to help prevent and control delinquency rather than merely *reacting* to youth crime. These strategies include a host of creative and innovative programs to involve police officers with children, adolescents, young adults, and other community members with the goal of developing better police/juvenile and police/community relations. While most of these programs are met with widespread acceptance and community support, a few, such as those that target specific juveniles for intensive police surveillance, are quite controversial and raise some legal and constitutional issues.

In final analysis, the police play a significant role in the *filtering process* that determines the youthful behaviors that can and will be tolerated as well as those that will not. They become the pivotal players in determining who will officially enter the juvenile justice system, be petitioned to juvenile court, and officially become identified as juvenile delinquents.

Concept Integration

Questions and Topics for Study and Discussion

1. How can the concept of "social arena" be applied to the streets? What type of confrontations and "struggles for survival" may take place between juveniles and the police as they interact on the streets?

2. Describe the difference in expectations between the *law enforcement* and *crime prevention* roles fulfilled by the police. How might these differential expectations result in *role strain* and even *role conflict* for police officers?

3. List some of the legal factors that affect police discretion. In your view, which of these factors are most important? Should any of these factors not be considered in handling juveniles?

4. List some of the extralegal factors that affect police discretion. Should any or all of these factors influence police decisions in handling juvenile offenders? If so, which ones? If not, is it possible for police officers *not* to be influenced by these social characteristics?

5. Define *due process*. Should the police afford juveniles the same basic rights of due process that are guaranteed to adults? If so, how should police procedures be changed to insure that juveniles are not denied due process? If not, why not?

6. What innovative community policing strategies have been developed in your community or surrounding communities to enhance police/juvenile relations and prevent delinquency? As a class project, develop a program that police could implement to help prevent delinquency in your local area.

References

Aaronson, D., Deines, C. T., and Musheno, M. 1984. *Public policy and police discretion.* New York: Clark Boardman, Ltd.

Armstrong, G. 1977. Females under the law—"Protected" but unequal. *Crime and Delinquency* 23 (April):108–120.

AP, Washington, 1999. Two-thirds of Americans say police would curb violence. *Ashland Daily Tidings,* Aug. 27:1.

Bartollas, C. 2000. *Juvenile delinquency (5th ed.).* New York: Macmillan.

Bassett, A. 1993. Community-Oriented gang control. *Police Chief* 60 (February):20–23.

Black, D. J., and Reiss, A. J., Jr. 1970. Police control of Juveniles. *American Sociological Review* 35 (February):63–77.

Bouma, D. H. 1969. *Kids and cops.* Grand Rapids, MI: William E. Erdman.

Caeti, T. J. 1993. Juvenile right to counsel: A case and statute analysis. Unpublished paper presented at the Southwest Criminal Justice Educators meeting in Dallas, TX, October 8, 1993.

Chesney-Lind, M. 1977. Judicial paternalism and the female status offender: training women to know their place. *Crime and Delinquency* 23:121–130.

———. 1988. Girls in jail. *Crime and Delinquency* 34:150–168.

Chesney-Lind, M., and Shelden, R. G. 1992. *Girls: Delinquency and Juvenile Justice.* Belmont, CA: Brooks/Cole.

Cicourel, A. 1968. *The social organization of juvenile justice.* New York: John Wiley.

Cohen, L., and Klugel, J. 1978. Determinants of juvenile court dispositions: Ascriptive and achieved factors in two metropolitan courts. *American Sociological Review* 43:162–176.

Dannefer, D., and Schutt, R. K. 1982. Race and juvenile justice processing in court and police agencies. *American Journal of Sociology* 87:1113–1132.

David, W. 1997. The San Antonio youth firearms violence initiative. *Telemasp Bulletin* 3 (February): 1–7.

Davis, S. M. 1971. Justice for the juvenile: The decision to arrest and due process. *Duke Law Journal:* 913–920.

———. 1983. *Rights of juveniles: The juvenile justice system* (2nd ed.). New York: Clark Boardman.

Fagan, J., Slaughter, E., and Hartstone, E. 1987. Blind justice? The impact of race on the juvenile justice process. *Crime and Delinquency* 33 (April): 224–258.

Federal Bureau of Investigation. 1993. *Uniform Crime Reports: Crime in the United States—1992.* Washington, DC: U.S. Government Printing Office.

Ferdinand, T. N., and Luchterhand, E. G. 1970. Inner-city youth, the police, the juvenile court, and justice. *Social Problems* 17 (Spring):510–527.

Gaines, L. K., Kappeler, V. E., and Vaughn, J. B. 1994. *Policing in America.* Cincinnati: Anderson.

Giordano, P. C. 1976. The sense of injustice: An analysis of juveniles' reactions to the justice system. *Criminology* 14 (May):105–106.

Goldman, N. (1963). *The differential selection of juvenile offenders for court appearance.* New York: National Research and Information Center, National Council on Crime and Delinquency.

Greene, M. B. 1993. Chronic exposure to violence and poverty: Interventions that work for youth. *Crime and Delinquency* 39 (January):106–124.

Hohenstein, W. F. 1969. Factors influencing the police disposition of juvenile offenders. Pp. 138–149 in T. Sellin and M. E. Wolfgang (Eds.). *Delinquency: Selected studies.* New York: John Wiley.

Hoobler, R. L. 1973. San Diego: Secondary schools' task force. *Police Chief* 40:28–30.

Huizinga, D., and Elliott, D. S. 1987. Juvenile offenders: Prevalence, offender incidence, and arrest rates by race. *Crime and Delinquency* 33 (April):206–223.

Inkster, N. D. 1992. The essence of community policing. *Police Chief* 59 (March):28–31.

Kline, E. M. 1993. Colorado Springs SHO/DI: Working smarter with juvenile offenders. *Police Chief* 60 (April):32–37.

Krisberg, G., and Austin, J. 1978. *The children of Ishmael: Critical perspectives on juvenile justice.* Palo Alto, CA: Mayfield.

Lattimore, P. K., Visher, C. A., and Linster, R. L. 1995. Predicting rearrest for violence among serious youthful offenders. *Journal of Research in Crime and Delinquency* 32 (February):54–83.

Lipson, K. 1982. Cops and TOPS: A Program for police and teens that works. *Police Chief* 49:45–46.

Lundman, R. L., Sykes, R. E., and Clark, J. P. 1978. Police control of juveniles: A replication. *Journal of Research in Crime and Delinquency* 15 (January):74–91.

Lundman, R. J. 1996a. Demeanor and arrest: Additional evidence from previously unpublished data. *Journal of Research in Crime and Delinquency* 33 (August):306–323.

———. 1996b. Extralegal variables and arrest. *Journal of Research in Crime and Delinquency* 33 (August):349–353.

McEachern, A. W., and Bauzer, R. 1967. Factors related to dispositions in juvenile police contacts. Pp. 148–160 in M. W. Kline (Ed.), *Juvenile Gangs in Context: Theory, research and action.* Englewood Cliffs, NJ: Prentice-Hall.

Meese, E. III. 1993. Community policing and the police officer. *Perspectives on Policing.* Boston: National Institute of Justice, U.S. Department of Justice.

Morash, M. 1984. Establishment of a juvenile police record: The influence of individual and peer group characteristics. *Criminology* 22 (February):97–111.

National Advisory Commission. 1973. *Corrections.* Washington, DC: U.S. Government Printing Office.

Piliavin, I., and Briar, S. 1964. Police encounters with juveniles. *American Journal of Sociology* 70 (September):206–214.

Portune, R. 1971. *Changing adolescent attitudes toward police.* Cincinnati: Anderson.

Ramos, P. 1989. When he was shot, I thought it could have been me. *The Hartford Courant,* June 4:D1, D4.

Ronzio, J. A. 1993. Upping the ante on Miranda. *Police Chief* 60 (May):10–13.

Ruefle, W., and Reynolds, K. M. 1995. Curfews and delinquency in major American cities. *Crime & Delinquency* 41 (July):347–363.

Sampson, R. J. 1986. Effects of socioeconomic context on official reaction to juvenile delinquency. *American Sociological Review* 51 (December):876–885.

Shown, C. Z. 1986. Police distributing chief cards again. *Emporia Gazette,* September 4:1.

Skolnick, J. 1966. *Justice without trial.* New York: Wiley.

Smith, D. A., and Visher, C. A. 1981. Street-level justice: Situational determinants of police arrest decisions. *Social Problems* 29 (December):167–177.

Sullivan, D. C., and Siegel, L. J. 1972. How police use information to make a decision: An application of decision games. *Crime and Delinquency* 18:253–262.

Task Force Report. 1967. *Task force report: Juvenile delinquency and youth crime.* Washington, DC: U.S. Government Printing Office.

Terry, R. M. 1967. Discrimination in the handling of juvenile offenders by social control agencies. *Journal of Research in Crime and Delinquency* 4: 218–230.

Thomson, B., and E. R. Fielder, 1975. Gangs: A response to the urban world. Pp. 149–150 in D. S.

Cartwright, B. Thomson, and H. Schwartz (Eds.), *Gang Delinquency.* Monterey, CA: Brooks/Cole.

Thornberry, T. 1973. Race, socioeconomic status, and sentencing in the juvenile justice system. *Journal of Criminal Law and Criminology* 64 (March):90–98.

Thurman, Q. C., Giacomazzi, A., and Bogen, P. 1993. Research note: cops, kids, and community policing—An assessment of a community policing demonstration project. *Crime and Delinquency* 39 (October):554–564.

Tunley, R. 1962. *Kids, crime and chaos: A world report on juvenile delinquency.* New York: Harper Press.

U.S. Department of Justice, 1993. LEMAS Reports—1990. Pp. 33–71 in R. G. Dunham and G. P. Alpert (Eds.), *Critical issues in policing: contemporary readings* (2nd ed.). Prospect Hts, IL: Waveland.

Walker, S. 1983. *The police in America.* New York: McGraw-Hill.

Weston, J. 1993. Community policing: An approach to youth gangs in a medium-sized city. *Police Chief* 60 (August):80–84.

Wilbanks, W. 1987. *The myth of a racist criminal justice system.* Beaumont, CA: Wadsworth.

Williams, H., and Murphy, P. V. 1990. The evolving strategy of police: A minority view. *Perspectives on policing.* Boston: National Institute of Justice, U.S. Department of Justice.

Wilson, J. Q. 1968. *Varieties of police behavior.* Cambridge: Harvard University Press.

Winfree, L. T., and Griffiths, C. T. 1977. Adolescents' attitudes toward the police: A survey of high school students. Pp. 78–99 in T. N. Ferdinand (ed.) *Juvenile delinquency: Little brother grows up.* Beverly Hills: Sage.

Winslow, R. W. 1973. *Juvenile delinquency in a free society* (2nd ed.). Encino, CA: Dickenson.

Woodbury, R. 1991. Putting the brakes on crime. *Time* (September 2):65.

Zhao, J., and Thurman, Q. C. 1997. Community policing: Where are we now? *Crime & Delinquency* 43 (July):345–357.

JUVENILE COURT

Reading Objectives

The reading of this chapter will help you achieve the following objectives:

1. Understand the concept of "due process" as expressed in the United States Constitution and Bill of Rights.
2. Explain the motives and ideology of the Child Savers together with their positive and negative impacts upon the juvenile justice process.
3. Understand the historical development of the juvenile court.
4. Provide an overview of the implications of the Gault Decision and other major decisions by the United States Supreme Court and their impact upon the legal processing of cases involving juveniles.
5. Describe and explain the procedures of the contemporary juvenile court.
6. Identify some of the major criticisms and limitations of the contemporary juvenile court.

Introduction

In Chapter 10, we introduced the concept of **arena** and illustrated how the schools serve as a social arena in which juveniles strive for social acceptance, a sense of social identity, and a measure of success in an adult-dominated society. In Chapter 13, we further explored this struggle for identity and the confrontations encountered by juveniles in the social arena of the streets. The juvenile court also fits our concept of public arena in much the same way as the schools and the streets. Although it conducts private hearings, the juvenile court symbolically represents society's public disapproval of a youth's behavior and the official response to delinquency by the juvenile justice system.

The United States was founded on the principles and ideals of democracy that all people are created equal under the law and entitled to certain inalienable human and civil rights. So dynamic and compelling was this "American Dream" that the nation's founders successfully revolted and separated from England. A later generation suffered a bloody civil war in order to extend these rights to an enslaved minority.

These fundamental rights were codified in the United States Constitution and the Bill of Rights. For example, the Fourth, Fifth, Sixth, Eighth, and Fourteenth Amendments to the

Constitution combine to guarantee **due process of law** *which are procedures designed to safeguard the rights of persons accused of crimes.*

The Fourth Amendment prohibits unwarranted and unreasonable arrest; the Fifth protects against self-incrimination; the Sixth guarantees the right to counsel and a jury trial, as well as the right to be informed of specific charges and the right to confront witnesses; the Eighth Amendment prohibits excessive bail and fines and cruel and unusual punishment; while the Fourteenth ensures that no state will be allowed to deprive any citizen of right to life, liberty, or property without due process of law.

In light of these basic legal rights, it is one of the greatest paradoxes that American children and youths were denied many of their constitutional rights in the juvenile justice system until the late 1960s. In order to fully understand the evolving legal status and adjudication process of young people in this country, we first need to explore the historical background out of which the contemporary juvenile court developed.

Historical Background of the Juvenile Court

Much of U.S. law is founded on British common law which exempted children under the age of 7 from legal responsibility for misconduct because they were considered incapable of **mens rea**—which means *"evil intent" or "guilty mind," and refers to one's ability to understand right from wrong, to understand the consequences of one's actions, and then willfully commit a wrongful act.* At age 7 and older, children were considered capable of *mens rea* and were held responsible for their actions in the same ways as adults.

The *chancery courts* arose in England in the fifteenth century. Part of the reason for their development was to deal with children's problems. The chancery courts required parents to provide support, supervision, and care for their children. The King of England was established as **parens patriae**—*"the father of his country"—which made the King the "ultimate parent" and gave him the right to care for the children of the state if their parents would not or could not do so.* Although the chancery courts were established primarily to deal with problems such as neglect and abuse rather than behavior problems on the part of youths, their existence set an important legal precedent that would have dramatic impact on juvenile courts some four centuries later. The concept of **parens patriae** established the principle that the state could intervene on behalf of a child even if this involved taking the child from the parents.

Much of eighteenth and nineteenth century criminology, both in theory and in practice, was structured on the traditional assumption that punishment is the best and most appropriate deterrent of crime. Thus, in the absence of definitive laws and a specialized court system for the legal processing of children, juvenile offenders often were treated and tried as adult criminals. As recently as the latter part of the nineteenth century, children were tried in criminal courts in both England and the United States; they were detained in the same jails, tried in the same courts, sent to the same correctional facilities, and sometimes even executed (Sanders, 1970). While the nature of the offense and the age of the offender generally determined the kind and degree of punishment to be exacted, there were enough cases of children who were executed by society to underscore the prevailing notion that people would avoid behavior they have identified with evil and pain.

Prior to the establishment of the juvenile court, at least three developments occurred during the nineteenth century which altered the way youthful offenders were treated:

1. *In 1825, in New York City, the* **House of Refuge** *was established. This provided separate correctional facilities for children (usually between the ages of 7 and 14) after they had been convicted in criminal court.*
2. *In 1841, the city of Boston first tried* **probation,** *or supervised release, a method of treating juveniles outside of a correctional institution, but still under the supervision of the criminal court.*
3. *In 1869, the state of Massachusetts officially established probation with supervision for juvenile law violators (Haskell and Yablonsky, 1978:26).*

These developments were linked to the changing attitudes toward childhood and the creation of the concept of adolescence. They represented a desire to hold young law violators accountable for their actions, but also reflected a movement toward handling juvenile offenders differently from adult criminals. Similar trends occurred in other countries (see Box 14-1).

The Child Savers' Movement

Steps to provide specialized correctional treatment to children and youths were initiated by a group of influential social reformers in the late nineteenth century. The Child Savers, as they were called, were convinced that urban slum life exerted a corrupting influence on idle youths. "However," the Child Savers insisted, "because of their tender age, delinquent youth[s] could be reclaimed from a criminal life if proper steps were taken" (Platt, 1969:45). They were instrumental in shifting the focus away from the criminal nature of delinquency to what was generally considered to be a more humanistic approach built around the medical model and the rehabilitative ideal.

The **medical model** used by the Child Savers diagnosed nonconforming behavior with such analogous terms as "disease," "illness," and "contagion." In other words, within the **medical model** *crime was viewed as a kind of social pathology, and young people manifested the antisocial behavioral symptoms of criminality as a result of being exposed to it in their environment.* The older the criminal, the more chronic the "sickness," and chances of recovery were considered to be less than those for a young person.

The **rehabilitative ideal** *emphasized the temporary and reversible nature of adolescent crime, if remedial measures were strenuously applied at an early age.* Support for the Child Savers' ideology was forthcoming from the noted penologist Enoch Wines who wrote in 1880: "These delinquent children are born to it; brought up for it; and they must be saved" (cited in Platt, 1969:45).

The Child Savers had their greatest impact in changing the reformatory system. The **reformatory** was well established throughout the United States during the middle of the nineteenth century as *a special form of institutionalized discipline for teenagers and young adults.* However, the reformatory was recognized as little more than a school for a later career in crime since youngsters were often indiscriminately thrown together with toughened adult criminals and there was little opportunity for education or resocialization that might prepare a young person for a more constructive life (Platt, 1969:46–54).

BOX 14-1 Cross-Cultural Focus

Development of the Juvenile Court in Canada

As in the United States, the development of a separate juvenile justice system in Canada was closely linked with the Child Savers' Movement. In 1857, two legislative acts were passed to provide special trial procedures and separate institutions for Canadian juveniles. One was an act which called for a more speedy trial for youthful offenders in order to avoid the problems they experienced during long terms of imprisonment prior to going to trial. The other piece of legislation established separate prisons for juveniles. Later, in 1874, Ontario passed an act establishing industrial schools as residential institutions intended to rehabilitate young offenders with less severe punishment than inflicted at earlier reformatories.

The Children's Aid Society was formed in Canada in 1891, with an express goal of having a probation officer assigned to each child brought before the court in an effort to protect the child and see that the court acted in his or her best interests. Although the first juvenile court in the world is considered to have been established in Chicago in 1899, records indicate that in 1892 the Toronto police had established a special "children's court" to hear cases involving youthful offenders and in 1893, Canada passed a comprehensive Children's Protection Act which called for special and separate hearings for juveniles.

Nevertheless, it was not until 1908 (nine years after the passage of the juvenile Court Act which established the first juvenile court in the United States) that Canada passed the Juvenile Delinquents Act establishing the first officially recognized juvenile courts in that country. The new juvenile courts were given exclusive jurisdiction over juvenile cases and emphasized treatment and prevention over punishment. Most youths who appeared before the Canadian juvenile courts were placed on supervised probation with the court's main objective being rehabilitation of youthful offenders so that they would not become adult criminals. Thus, there are striking parallels between the development of juvenile courts in Canada and in the United States.

Sources

Kelso, J. J. "Children's court," *Canadian Law Times and Review* 26, 1908:163–166.
Hagan, John, and Leon, Jeffrey, "Rediscovering delinquency: Social history, political ideology and the sociology of law," *American Sociological Review* 42 (August), 1977:587–598.

By the end of the nineteenth century, the Child Savers had exerted enough political pressure to have laws passed that restructured the reformatory system. According to Anthony Platt (1969:54) the reformatory plan developed by the Child Savers included the following principles:

1. *Young offenders must be segregated from the corrupting influences of adult criminals.*
2. *"Delinquents" should be removed from their environment and imprisoned for their own good and protection. Reformatories should be guarded sanctuaries, combining love and guidance with firmness and restraint.*
3. *"Delinquents" should be assigned to reformatories without trial and with minimal legal requirements. Due process is not required because reformatories are intended to reform and not to punish.*

> *4. Sentences should be indeterminate, so that inmates are encouraged to coop-erate in their own reform and recalcitrant "delinquents" are not allowed to resume their criminal careers...*

In summary of the Child Savers' movement, these reformers seem to have equated juvenile independence with delinquency and sought to exercise extensive and rigid control over most youthful activities. Moreover, they shifted the responsibility for addressing social problems from the private to the public arena—a development that made "child saving" society's responsibility and led to the development of juvenile courts (Block and Hale, 1991). While the principles that guided the restructuring of the reformatory system and the development of special courts for handling delinquent youths were motivated by idealistic and humanistic values, their arbitrary implementation denied multitudes of young people their basic constitutional right to due process.

The Juvenile Court

The mounting pressure for a judicial system that incorporated specialized processing of juvenile delinquents culminated in 1899 when the Illinois legislature passed the *Juvenile Court Act,* creating the first statewide court especially for children. Today there is a juvenile court in virtually every American jurisdiction, with about 2,800 courts hearing juvenile cases.[1] **Juvenile courts** are *judicial tribunals that deal in special ways with the cases of young people.* The juvenile court is not a criminal court; it is a statutory court whose powers and limitations are defined by the laws of the state in which it exists.

Most state statutes regarding juvenile courts do not necessarily create a *separate, independent* juvenile court. Consequently, the role of juvenile judge is only a part-time assignment for many judges (Cox and Conrad, 1996). Martin Haskell and Lewis Yablonsky (1978:27) reported that in 40 states juveniles were handled in courts whose primary purpose was some other function (either family or criminal courts). In those states a judge who sits on another court (usually criminal) sets aside a day to hear juvenile cases. On that day, the court becomes a juvenile court and follows the procedures that are prescribed for juvenile courts in that state.

To distinguish the proceedings of the juvenile court from those of the criminal court where adults are brought to trial, a new vocabulary emerged. Rather than a criminal complaint, a juvenile court "petition" is issued ordering the accused offender to appear in court. Similarly, arraignments have come to be called "initial hearings," and convictions have been renamed "findings of involvements." Finally, sentences have been replaced by the more informal and less threatening term "disposition" (Coffey, 1974:37).

The establishment of juvenile courts in 1899 did *not* mean that children were automatically granted the constitutional right to due process. On the contrary, the Child Savers'

---

[1]This figure is based on estimates from several sources. It is extremely difficult to determine precisely how many juvenile courts exist, since juvenile cases are sometimes handled in separate courts; sometimes in municipal, county, or district courts; and sometimes in family and/or divorce courts.

Appearing before a judge in juvenile court is one of the most direct official confrontations with adult society an adolescent may have to face.

well-intentioned but discriminatory philosophy and practices became officially institutionalized in the juvenile court system:

> *The goals were to investigate, diagnose, and prescribe treatment, not to adjudicate guilt or fix blame. The individual's background was more important than the facts of a given incident; specific conduct relevant more as symptomatic of a need for the court to bring its helping powers to bear than as prerequisite to exercise of jurisdiction. Lawyers were unnecessary—adversary tactics were out of place, for the mutual aim of all was not to contest or object but to determine the treatment plan best for the child (Winslow, 1973:134).*

In 1920, the U.S. Children's Bureau recommended the following as essential characteristics of the juvenile court:

1. *separate hearings;*
2. *informal procedures;*
3. *regular probation services;*
4. *separate detention;*
5. *special court and probation records; and*
6. *provision for mental and physical examinations (cited in Belden, 1920:7–10).*

While the Children's Bureau had no authority to make policy or enforce its guidelines, its suggestions for the operation of juvenile courts had tremendous influence on juvenile court proceedings. Juvenile hearings were almost always private, usually involving only the juvenile, his or her parents, the judge, and a social worker. Juries were not used, as the issue of innocence or guilt was much less the focus of the hearing than was the question "Why is this juvenile present in court?" There was the assumption that the youth needed help or he/she would not be there, and the judge's primary responsibility was to decide how best to handle the situation. The proceedings were conducted informally with very little attention to the ritualistic legal traditions that dominated adult criminal court proceedings. The judge generally addressed the juvenile by first name and asked a number of questions of the juvenile and parents; and the strict rules regarding testimony and evidence in criminal cases were not always applied. Thus, the juvenile hearing in the early juvenile court often resembled an informal conference more than a formal trial.

The traditionally informal and nonlegalistic nature of the juvenile court has changed a great deal in recent years. Today, more juveniles and their families secure legal counsel and more attorneys are involved in juvenile court proceedings. Several significant U.S. Supreme Court cases have impacted upon the legal rights extended to juveniles who appear before the juvenile court. One of the results has been that hearings have begun to take on a more formal atmosphere, and judges tend to handle them similarly to criminal proceedings (Coxe, 1967). And, as we shall see in Chapter 15, today, juvenile courts are more likely to remand violent offenders to adult criminal courts than ever before.

The Juvenile Court and Due Process

Juvenile courts were established for the protection of children, and initially ignored the concept of due process. When a youth was petitioned to the juvenile court, the court philosophically and legally was acting on behalf of the child. Therefore, the adversary relationship which exists in criminal courts (state vs. John Doe) was considered to be absent from the juvenile court. For that reason, the rigid ritual, rules of evidence, and other formal procedures of the criminal court were not established as part of the juvenile court. Consequently, the basic constitutional rights (especially those of due process) traditionally were not accorded juveniles in their hearings.

In 1954, in the *Holmes Case,* the U.S. Supreme Court ruled that since juvenile courts were not criminal courts, the constitutional rights guaranteed to persons accused of crimes did not apply to juveniles (*In re Holmes,* 1954). Holmes was an 18-year old boy who was arrested while riding in a stolen car. As a result of his juvenile court disposition, he was sent to a state training school. Holmes' lawyer appealed the case on the basis that Holmes had not been represented by counsel; had not been properly informed of the charges against him; had not been advised of his rights (especially the right not to testify against himself); that much of the testimony against Holmes should have been deemed inadmissible; and that Holmes had not actually committed an illegal act. In response to the appeal, the Supreme Court reaffirmed the position that an adversary relationship does not exist in juvenile court. Chief Justice Horace Stern asserted that the court was not trying to punish a criminal, but rather to salvage a boy who might become one (*In re Holmes,* 1954). In other words, due process was not necessary since the court was attempting to help and reform rather than punish the youth.

Due process, even in a limited form, was not to become a part of juvenile court procedure until 1967, and then it developed through some rather interesting events. In June of 1964, Gerald Gault, along with another boy, was taken into custody in Gila County, Arizona, for allegedly making obscene phone calls to a neighbor woman. Both of Gault's parents were away from home and were not notified of his detention. On the following day, Gault was petitioned to the juvenile court (although his parents did not see the petition). Gault's mother attended the hearing. The judge informally questioned Gault about the phone calls. The disposition of the case resulted in Gault being adjudicated delinquent and committed to the Arizona State Industrial School for the remainder of his minority (6 years). The same charge against an adult would have resulted in a fine of $5 to $50, or imprisonment for not more than 2 months (Neigher, 1967). The case was appealed based on the issues that Gault had not been advised of his rights (especially against self-incrimination); and was not allowed to deny the charges or cross-examine the only witness against him (Neigher, 1967). The final appeal went before the U.S. Supreme Court, and in what is viewed as a landmark decision in juvenile justice, the Supreme Court in 1967, under Chief Justice Earl Warren, handed down the *Gault Decision (In re Gault,* 1967) which resulted in:

1. *Right to notice of charges against the juvenile.*
2. *Right to counsel.*
3. *Right to face and cross-examine witnesses.*
4. *Right to refuse to answer self-incriminating questions.*
5. *Right to a transcript of the proceedings.*
6. *Right to appeal.*

While the Gault decision was a major development in officially providing a measure of due process in juvenile hearings, care must be taken not to overestimate the impact of the case. The decision did *not* provide to juveniles all the constitutional rights afforded adult criminal suspects. A limitation of the decision is that because of the wording, it is not entirely clear whether the rights outlined therein must be accorded the juvenile or whether those rights can be waived by the juvenile's parents. In many cases that might be a moot point, but in cases where the parents originate a petition against their own child, the difference could be extremely important. Regardless, the Gault decision had tremendous impact on the juvenile justice system. More juveniles began seeking counsel, being represented in their hearing, and appealing their cases (Coxe, 1967). Perhaps the most significant impact of the Gault decision is the recognition by the U.S. Supreme Court that even in juvenile cases an adversary relationship exists, and in order to protect the best interests of the juvenile, at least limited due process must prevail.

Several other important U.S. Supreme Court decisions have impacted upon the issue of due process in the juvenile justice system. For instance, in 1966, the famous *Miranda* decision was issued which ruled that when adults are arrested, they must be informed of their right to remain silent, that any statements made by them can be used against them in court, that they have the right to legal counsel, and that if they cannot afford legal counsel, the court will appoint them an attorney (*Miranda* v. *Arizona,* 1966). The Gault decision implied that these rights also must be afforded a juvenile when taken in custody, although it did not expressly state this. In subsequent U.S. Supreme Court decisions, the Court has contended that juveniles are entitled to the rights against self-incrimination outlined in the *Miranda* decision. There is some question, however, whether juveniles can waive those rights without their parents or attorney being present.

Another important U.S. Supreme Court decision was that of *Kent* v. *United States* in 1966. Morris A. Kent was a 14-year-old boy who had been arrested in 1959 for several housebreakings and attempted purse snatchings. Kent appeared before the juvenile court in the District of Columbia, and was placed on probation. Two years later, while investigating a housebreaking, robbery, and rape case, police found fingerprints at the scene which matched those of Morris Kent. Kent (then 16 years old) was taken into custody and interrogated over a period of 2 days, during which he admitted his involvement in the crime under investigation, and offered information about several other similar offenses he had committed. No record exists to establish when Kent's mother was notified that he was in custody, but after 4 days of his detention, she secured an attorney's services. The attorney filed several motions with the juvenile court including one asking for psychiatric and psychological examination of Kent. After approximately 1 week of detention of Kent, the juvenile judge waived jurisdiction (because he was 16, the juvenile court had exclusive jurisdiction in the case) and recommended that he be held over for trial in the District Court of the District of Columbia. No hearing was held in juvenile court, and there was no response to any of the motions filed by Kent's attorney (including a request that the juvenile court not waive its jurisdiction). Further, the juvenile judge issued no statement of reasons for waiving jurisdiction.

A grand jury was convened and indicted Kent on three charges of housebreaking, three counts of robbery, and two counts of rape. Despite protests by Kent's attorney that Kent was mentally incompetent to stand trial, a trial was held. Interestingly, Kent was found not guilty by reason of insanity on the two rape charges, but was found guilty on the charges of housebreaking and robbery. He was sentenced to serve 5 to 15 years on each count, or a total of 30 to 90 years. The case was appealed to the U.S. Court of Appeals on the grounds that Kent was unlawfully detained and interrogated and was deprived of counsel, and his parents were not notified. Kent's attorney contended that young Kent had been deprived of the basic constitutional rights that would have been granted an adult facing the same charges, yet Kent was tried as an adult in criminal court. The Appellate Court upheld the conviction, and the case eventually came before the U.S. Supreme Court. The Supreme Court ruled that in order for a juvenile court to waive its exclusive jurisdiction, a hearing must be held (*Kent* v. *United States,* 1966). In its opinion, the Court stated, "We do not mean by this to indicate that the hearing must conform with all of the requirements of a criminal trial, or even of the usual administrative hearing; but we do hold that the hearing must measure up to essentials of due process and fair treatment" (cited in Cox and Conrad, 1996:274). Justice Fortas expressed some of the problems associated with the juvenile court, lamenting, "There is evidence, in fact, that there may be grounds for concern that the child receives the worst of both worlds: that he gets neither the protections accorded to adults nor the solicitous care and regenerative treatment postulated for children" (Cox and Conrad, 1996:271).

At least four other Supreme Court rulings had significant impact upon due process in juvenile courts: *In re Winship* (1970), *McKiever* v. *Pennsylvania* (1971), *Breed* v. *Jones* (1975), and *Schall* v. *Martin* (1984). Two of these cases extended the rights of due process in juvenile court (*In re Winship,* 1970; *Breed* v. *Jones,* 1975), and two of them denied specific elements of due process for juveniles (*McKiever* v. *Pennsylvania,* 1971; *Schall* v. *Martin,* 1984). *In re Winship* (1970) addressed the question whether "proof beyond a reasonable doubt" is required during the adjudication stage of a juvenile court hearing when the youth is charged with an act that would be a crime if committed by an adult (cited in Cox and Conrad, 1996:Appendix C). The case involved a 12-year-old boy who allegedly broke into a locker and stole $112 from a woman's purse. While the judge was convinced that Winship had committed the act, he acknowledged that there was not proof beyond a reasonable doubt. Winship was adjudicated delinquent and ordered to be placed in a state training school for a period of 18 months subject to yearly extensions until he reached the age of majority (potentially for 6 years). When his case was brought before the U.S. Supreme Court, the Court ruled that proof beyond a reasonable doubt was necessary in a juvenile court hearing where a crime had been committed. The Court concluded, "civil labels and good intentions do not themselves obviate the need for criminal due process safeguards in juvenile courts" (Cox and Conrad, 1996:277). Further due process rights were guaranteed to juveniles when the Supreme Court ruled that juveniles, like adults, were protected against **double jeopardy,** or *being tried twice for the same offense* (*Breed* v. *Jones,* 1975). In that case, the court ruled that a youth cannot be tried in a criminal court for the same offense for which he/she has been tried as a delinquent in juvenile court.

The Supreme Court sent out mixed signals in regard to its commitment to extending the rights of due process to the juvenile court. In the case of *McKiever* v. *Pennsylvania* (1971), the court ruled that juveniles were not guaranteed the right to a trial by jury. Approximately three-fourths of the states follow that ruling and do not provide jury trials for juveniles (Mahoney, 1985:553). Later, in the case of *Schall* v. *Martin* (1984), the Court held that youths could be held without bail if they were being held for their own protection or the protection of society. In these two cases the court reflected a shift back toward the rehabilitative and protective philosophy of the earlier juvenile court. Consequently, there is some ambiguity as to precisely what rights are guaranteed juveniles when they are petitioned to juvenile court. It appears that in some areas, the extent of due process granted juveniles must be determined virtually on a case-by-case basis. However, based upon the legal precedence set in the aforementioned juvenile cases, in most states, juveniles are advised of their legal rights when detained, parents are notified as soon as possible, and juveniles are allowed legal counsel during all phases of the justice process.

Juvenile Court Procedures

While juvenile court policies and procedures vary across and within states, the juvenile court is generally characterized by three main operational procedures: *intake, adjudication,* and *disposition* (U.S. Dept. of Justice, 1992).

Intake

The intake procedure typically begins when the juvenile court receives a **referral** on a particular youth. In most states, **referral** *simply means that the juvenile's name has been given to the court.* Referrals can come from a variety of sources including police, parents, schools, and others. Typically, the largest number of referrals comes from the police (see Table 14-1).

Upon receiving the referral, one of the officers of the court (usually a probation officer) is assigned to investigate the case to determine how the case best can be handled. A decision must be made on whether to hold or release the child while the case is being investigated. The nature of the referral is the main criterion at that point. When possible, juveniles being

TABLE 14-1   Juvenile Court Referrals by Source

Source of Referral	Number of Referrals	Percent
Law enforcement	969,884	83.9
Parents, relatives	39,304	3.4
School	32,368	2.8
Probation officer	27,744	2.4
Social agency	12,716	1.1
Other courts	25,432	2.2
Other	48,552	4.2
Total	1,156,000	100

Source: Adapted from *Juvenile Court Statistics–1989.* Pittsburgh: National Center for Juvenile Justice, U.S. Department of Justice, 1992.

referred for minor offenses are released into the custody of their parents. If the intake officer views it as appropriate, an intake interview with the youth and the youth's parents or legal guardian may be requested (Miller et al., 1985). More serious offenders, or those who for some reason cannot or should not be released to parents, are usually detained. The district attorney has primary responsibility for this decision. Ideally, the probation officer conducts a thorough investigation into the youth's social background by interviewing teachers, neighbors, and others who might provide insight into the situation. The probation officer then may recommend that the case be dismissed entirely, be referred to some other agency, or may move that a petition be filed with the juvenile court for a hearing. A **petition** is *an official statement which contains the important facts of the case* such as the action which prompted the petition, along with relevant information about the juvenile and the youth's parents or guardians (Caldwell, 1961).

During the intake procedure in some states, the judge also has the option of declaring the juvenile to be an "adult" and ordering that the case be referred to an adult criminal court. In recent years, harsher attitudes toward juvenile law violators have resulted in increased numbers of youths being remanded to adult criminal courts. In 1988, over 4,000 youths were sent to state prisons after being prosecuted and convicted as adults (*Christian Science Monitor,* 1988), and in 1997 the U.S. House of Representatives passed a bill that provided financial incentives for states to remand to adult courts juveniles 15 years of age and older who had committed serious felonies (Reibstein, 1997).

There is some argument as to whether a youth is more likely to be certified as an adult based upon the seriousness of the offense and age (Fagan et al., 1987b) or upon extralegal factors such as the race, ethnicity, and family situation of the offender (Osbun and Rode, 1984; Singer, 1993). As pointed out earlier, as a result of *Kent* v. *United States* (1966), a hearing must be held and justification given for waiving jurisdiction by the juvenile court. Some states have revised their juvenile codes to provide for automatic waiver of juvenile court jurisdiction. For example, in some states a juvenile over the age of 16 who commits an act that would be considered a felony if committed by an adult, is automatically certified as an adult, and handled by adult criminal court. In those states, for a juvenile to be handled in juvenile court instead of the adult criminal court, a **reverse certification** hearing must be held to *declare the youth a juvenile.*

The length of time for intake procedures varies. The court attempts to work as expeditiously as possible while taking the necessary time to thoroughly evaluate a youth's background and social circumstances. According to established juvenile justice standards, the intake process should not exceed 30 days (Miller et al., 1985:242).

Adjudication

If a petition is filed and the youth has a hearing, the adjudication process takes place. **Adjudication** refers to *making a judgment or ruling.* This phase of the juvenile court proceeding is analogous to the trial phase of adult judicial proceedings. The judge (usually with assistance from the probation officer and the district attorney) must decide whether to dismiss charges or adjudicate the juvenile as *neglected, dependent,* or *delinquent.* During this stage evidence will be heard, and the judge will attempt to determine if the reason for which the juvenile was petitioned is valid, and if so, what should be done about it. If the child is adjudicated as neglected or dependent, the court identifies the youth as **INS** *(in need of supervision).* Youths sent to the court as a result of having been neglected, abused, wayward, truant, or runaways are most likely to be adjudicated INS.

A **delinquent** adjudication usually means that *the juvenile has committed a wrongful act for which the judge feels the youth must be held accountable.* Juveniles who have committed acts which would be a crime if committed by an adult are most likely to be adjudicated delinquent.

The adjudication hearing for a juvenile accused of committing a criminal act is very likely to take on many of the characteristics of an adult criminal trial. Attorneys are likely to be used, and in a few states, juveniles are even granted the right to a trial by jury (Mahoney, 1985). There are some notable distinctions, however, most prominent of which is that the juvenile hearing remains closed to the public, whereas adult criminal trials are open. There has been increased pressure to open juvenile hearings to public scrutiny, particularly in light of recent events which have resulted in allowing media coverage (including cameras in the courtrooms) of adult trials (Day, 1984). The protective philosophy of the juvenile court has been reemphasized, however, as juvenile courts steadfastly have refused to hold open hearings for fear of public stigmatization of the youths involved. Louis Day (1984) contended that the increased public interest in juvenile delinquency will heighten the demand for public access to juvenile court hearings and records and ultimately will force the Supreme Court to determine two issues: (1) whether juvenile proceedings are criminal cases, subject to the same constitutional requirements as adult cases; and (2) the degree of access the media and public should have to juvenile hearings.

During the adjudication phase, children brought before the court may have their parents, guardian, and/or legal counsel present. As previously mentioned, while initially established as an informal hearing, the adjudication phase has become increasingly formalized and legalistic. More juveniles and their parents are seeking legal advice and securing counsel for juvenile cases. The juvenile's right against self-incrimination is acknowledged, and juveniles are allowed to present a defense to the charges filed against them. As one Supreme Court Justice noted, "This court believes that although the juvenile court was initially created as a social experiment, it has not ceased to be part of the justice system" (Miller et al., 1985:554).

Disposition

Disposition is *the stage of the hearing most analogous to sentencing in a criminal court.* Occurring after adjudication, it is the process by which the judge must decide the best way to handle the juvenile's case. The judge must attempt to do what is best for the child while also protecting the community and preserving the integrity of the law. At least in philosophy, the disposition is supposed to be oriented toward treatment which will benefit the youth, rather than toward punishment.

During disposition, the judge has several alternatives from which to choose. The district attorney plays an important part in making recommendations to the judge, but the judge has extensive discretionary power in determining the disposition of the case. The judge can choose to dismiss the case and release the juvenile to parents or guardians. Estimates vary, but roughly 50 percent of all juvenile cases are simply dismissed. If the juvenile is adjudicated as INS, the judge can declare the youth a "ward of the court" and order placement in foster care. Because of the insufficient number of adequate foster homes, however, this disposition may be ruled less often than others. If the juvenile's problem is thought to be a re-

Studies indicate that juvenile court dispositions are often affected by whether parents appear in court with the juvenile. Also, judges may be more likely to release youths into the custody of their parents if the parents appear to be willing to cooperate fully with the court.

sult of some type of emotional disturbance, the judge probably will order a psychiatric report and the youth may be sent to a residential treatment center.

If the youth is adjudicated delinquent, the judge has three basic alternatives. The one most widely used is to place the juvenile on formal probation. While on probation, the juvenile must adhere to a specific set of guidelines and meet periodically with an assigned probation officer. If probation is deemed inappropriate, the judge can send the juvenile to a minimum security correctional institution. If the offense is of a serious nature, or the juvenile has appeared before the court several times, the judge may decide to send the offender to a maximum security correctional facility for youths. These institutions often are called "state training schools" and to a large extent operate as prisons for offenders under the age of majority.

Several factors influence the outcome of the dispositional phase of juvenile hearings. As already mentioned, one factor is the extent and variety of alternatives available to the judge. As Mahoney (1985:555) pointed out, "a problem related to plea negotiating for juveniles is that in many juvenile courts there is essentially a small range of disposition alternatives."

Variables such as seriousness of the offense, prior record, age, race, and sex of the offender all enter into the discretionary decision of the juvenile court judge (e.g., Arnold, 1971; Chesney-Lind, 1977; Cohen, 1975; Perry, 1985; Fagan et al., 1987 a,b; McGarrell, 1993; Minor et al., 1997; Leiber and Stairs, 1999). Just as the police are influenced by a variety of extralegal factors such as race, age, and sex of the offender in deciding how to handle juveniles on the street, so are the courts. For example, William Arnold (1971), Terry Thornberry (1973), Robert Perry (1985), Jeffrey Fagan et al. (1987a) and Edmund McGarrell (1993) all found that blacks and youths from lower socioeconomic backgrounds typically received harsher dispositions in juvenile court. Similarly, while it has been generally acknowledged that paternalistic attitudes of police and court officials may lead to lower arrest rates and fewer petitions to juvenile court for females, Meda Chesney-Lind (1977) found that once detained and petitioned to court, females are likely to be treated more harshly than their male counterparts regardless of seriousness of the offense.

Other variables related to dispositional decisions include the extent of demonstrated parental interest in the child and the case (O'Quin et al., 1985; Aurand, 1998), known membership in a juvenile gang (Zatz, 1985) and prior dispositions (Thornberry and Christenson, 1984). Interestingly, through a longitudinal study, Thornberry and Christenson (1984) found that the single most important determinant of the type and severity of disposition levied against a particular youth was the type and severity of previous dispositions. They found that rather than dispositions becoming increasingly severe with each repeat offense by an individual, the same disposition was very likely to be imposed over and over again. Joseph Sanborn (1996) concluded that it is almost impossible to determine precisely the impact of any specific factors on dispositional outcomes.

The Role of Attorneys in Juvenile Court

The role of attorneys in juvenile court is not nearly as clearcut as it is in adult criminal court. It has been only since the Gault Decision of 1967 that they have been formally introduced into the juvenile court proceeding; since then, attorneys have played an increasingly important role in the contemporary juvenile court.

The District Attorney

Each state is divided into judicial districts and periodically a public election is held in each district to elect a prosecuting attorney to represent the state in criminal cases within the district. Thus, when the police or a citizen signs a petition alleging misconduct by a child or young person, the office of the district attorney comes in contact with the youngster. Before this petition is filed with the court and a hearing is scheduled, the district attorney may investigate the case and exercise one of three basic options:

1. Refuse to prosecute for lack of evidence and release the child.
2. Defer prosecution and place the child on informal probation. In many such cases the district attorney may make an arrangement with the child's parents not to prosecute if they will keep the child under close supervision.
3. Expedite the filing of the petition and prosecute the child in the juvenile court for the alleged offense.

Former juvenile judge Ted Rubin (1980) concluded that as a result of the Gault Decision (which provides the right to counsel for juveniles), prosecuting attorneys have taken a much more active role in the juvenile court, especially during the intake phase. We can view the district attorney as the law-enforcing officer in the median position between the police officer and the juvenile court judge. Here, the **filtering process** is continued, as many cases are treated informally and not sent on to court. In this way, many young people avoid an official record of delinquency and the state avoids much expensive litigation. If the petition is formally filed with the court, the court procedures described in the previous section officially begin.

The district attorney can be involved in all three stages of the juvenile court proceedings. This officer may make recommendations to the judge regarding whether the case should be handled in juvenile court or transferred to adult criminal court. Along with a court services officer, the district attorney also advises the judge on adjudication and dispositional alternatives.

The Defense Attorney

The role of the defense attorney in juvenile court is both ambiguous and controversial (see Box 14-2). Since due process has been introduced into the juvenile justice system, more juveniles and their parents are seeking legal representation when appearing in juvenile court. The attorney for the juvenile performs many of the same functions as a defense attorney in criminal court. However, because of the less formal atmosphere of the juvenile court, and the more relaxed rules on testimony and evidence, the youth's attorney may not be able to protect the youth in some of the same ways a criminal lawyer can defend an adult in criminal court. While a juvenile may plead the Fifth Amendment (right not to testify against oneself), this behavior may be more likely to antagonize the judge than to help the juvenile's case. Similarly, Anne Mahoney (1985:556) discovered that in states where juveniles were entitled to jury trials, it was quite possible that such a request might actually produce negative results for the youth because the court could penalize those youths who asked for

BOX 14-2 Controversial Issue

The Use of Attorneys in the Juvenile Court

The Gault Decision of 1967 by the U.S. Supreme Court brought some major changes into the juvenile court process. Lauded as a landmark decision, one of its important effects upon juvenile justice was the determination that juveniles and/or their parents have the right to legal counsel when petitioned to the juvenile court. Since that ruling, many juveniles and their parents have opted to have legal counsel present for their hearings before the juvenile court.

While the role of attorneys in adult criminal court is well established, it remains somewhat ambiguous and controversial in juvenile court hearings. The role of the district attorney in the prosecution of juvenile delinquency has become very similar to that in a criminal case. Since the Gault Decision, prosecutors have taken a much more active role in juvenile court procedures. In fact, Rubin (1980) contended that the intake process of the court is dominated by the prosecutor.

The defense attorney, on the other hand, has a much less clearcut role in the juvenile court. The Institute of Judicial Administration and the American Bar Association (IJA/ABA) suggested in their *Juvenile Justice Standards Project* (1977) that there are three roles that the attorney can fulfill in the juvenile court: (1) officer of the court; (2) guardian; (3) advocate. In the first role, the attorney becomes an aide to the juvenile judge in attempting to help the judge determine what is best for the youth, This role seems most appropriate in cases of neglect, abuse, and other situations in which the juvenile appears before the court more as a "victim" than as an "offender." The guardian role involves a situation in which the attorney takes control of all of the juvenile's interests in the hearing, and, to be effective, requires that the juvenile and the juvenile's parents passively follow all advice given by the attorney. This role seems most appropriate when the juvenile is very young, mentally incompetent, or not accompanied by parents or legal guardian when appearing before the court. The advocate role is the traditional role assumed by attorneys when representing a client in adult criminal court. In this role, the attorney attempts to represent the client's best legal interests, and defends the juvenile against the charges outlined in the court petition. It is the third role which is most likely to be adopted by attorneys secured to represent juveniles who have committed offenses that would be a crime if committed by an adult.

The role assumed by the attorney in juvenile court may be controlled to some degree by the type of juvenile court in which he/she appears, and may be greatly limited by the type of juvenile judge presiding over the hearing. In the due process type of court discussed in this chapter, the attorney probably will have every opportunity to assume the advocate role on behalf of the juvenile. On the other hand, in the traditional court, where the judge assumes almost total control of the hearing, and in which the due process rights of the juvenile are severely limited, the attorney may be severely restricted in choice of role in the proceeding.

The impact of increased involvement of attorneys in the juvenile court is unclear. It is generally agreed that their presence in the juvenile court has increased the formality of court proceedings and made judges more aware of the due process rights of the juvenile, However, research on attorneys' influence on the actual adjudication and disposition rulings by juvenile courts indicates that the presence of attorneys has made very little difference (e.g., Sosin and Sarri, 1976). In a collection of research articles, Sarri and Hasenfeld (1976) found that attorneys' impact upon the juvenile court is minimal, and that virtually all others involved in the court procedures exert more influence over the outcome of the hearing (e.g., judge, social workers, court officers, parents, and juvenile).

Perhaps it is the peculiar nature of the juvenile court which limits the impact that attorneys have had on its proceedings. Based upon the philosophies of protection, treatment, and rehabilitation, while simultaneously charged with acting in the best interests of the juvenile and protecting society, the juvenile court has emerged as a truly unique institution in our society.

It has been argued that attorney involvement in juvenile courts has had a more significant impact upon their proceedings than is readily discernible

Continued

BOX 14-2 *Continued*

from the types of research which have been conducted (Naffine and Wundersitz, 1991). In other words, although adjudication rates and types of disposition do not appear to have been significantly affected, perhaps more subtle changes have occurred owing to attorney representation in juvenile court. While the juvenile court hearing is technically informal, and the judge enjoys wide latitude in terms of discretion, no doubt the presence of legal counsel on behalf of a youth indicates a recognition that the juvenile court is still a legal proceeding and that regardless of the subjective nature of adjudication and disposi-

tional decisions, the rights of the juvenile will be preserved to the fullest extent possible. While the juvenile court was established to act in the best interests of the juveniles brought before it, representation by legal counsel may underscore that effort.

* * * *

Based upon your reading of this chapter and this box, what do you think the role of attorneys should be in the juvenile court? Should every juvenile be represented by legal counsel? If so, why? If not, why not? In your opinion, has the impact of attorneys on the juvenile court primarily been positive? or negative?

Sources

Naffine, N., and Wundersitz, J. 1991. Lawyers in the children's court: An Australian perspective. *Crime and Delinquency* 37 (July):374–392.

Rubin, H. T. 1980. The emerging prosecutor dominance of the juvenile court intake process. *Crime & Delinquency* 26 (July):299–318.

Sarri, R., and Hasenfeld, Y. (Eds.). 1976. *Brought to justice?: Juveniles, the courts and the law.* Ann Arbor: University of Michigan, National Assessment of Juvenile Corrections.

Sosin, M., and Sarri, R. 1976. Due process—reality or myth? In R. Sarri and Y. Hasenfeld (Eds.) *Brought to justice?: Juveniles, the courts, and the law.* Ann Arbor: University of Michigan, pp. 176–206.

jury trials. While the criminal judge's decision hinges upon the legal and technical ramifications of the case, it must be remembered that the juvenile court judge's decision rests primarily upon what the judge considers best for the juvenile. Thus, even though an attorney may provide counsel which legally protects the youth, it may in fact not favorably alter the adjudication and disposition decisions.

Criticisms of the Juvenile Court

Since 1899, when the first juvenile court was established, it has undergone a great deal of scrutiny and criticism from different sectors in society. One of the most prevalent criticisms has been that the juvenile courts are "too easy" on juveniles and have a tendency to coddle and protect what are basically just young criminals. As a juvenile officer in the Los Angeles Police Department put it, "…Some of these hoodlums are back on the street before I finish the paper work!" (Carter, 1976:124).

From its inception, the juvenile court has been viewed almost as a parent, charged with protecting those who are sent to it. The juvenile court was founded upon the philosophies of protection and rehabilitation. In a society where people are reading about teenaged rapists, murderers, and muggers, many citizens question the legitimacy of "protecting" juvenile offenders. A rather bizarre case that brought public attention to this issue occurred in 2000 when police charged 39-year-old Michael Skakel with the murder of his neighbor whom he allegedly bludgeoned to death 24 years earlier when he was only 15 years of age. Initial proceedings took place in a juvenile court due to his age at the time of the murder. This placed a number of legal roadblocks in the case before the District Attorney could eventually get the case remanded to adult criminal court (Lavoie, 2000). Many critics of the court are shocked by its lenient dispositions and believe its philosophy should not be applied to youths who commit serious criminal offenses (Krisberg and Austin, 1978). Police often feel helpless in attempting to control the problem, knowing that many of their efforts at law enforcement will be negated by benevolent, well-meaning, or politically sensitive juvenile judges. Victims of juvenile offenders are often reluctant to file complaints or press charges because previous experience has shown that very little will be done to the juveniles; and often they are back on the streets the very same day, seeking revenge. In some states, the most severe penalty for a juvenile is to be adjudicated "delinquent" and institutionalized for a brief period of time. For example, a case in New York which received much media attention focused on a 15-year-old boy who committed a premeditated and particularly vicious murder. He was merely sent to a juvenile institution for 18 months (AP, New York, 1978). On the basis of such cases, some members of society perceive the juvenile court as more helpless and impotent than benevolent and protecting.

Conversely, another criticism of the juvenile court has been that it is "too hard" on juveniles and tends to overreact to relatively minor offenses. Because a major goal of the juvenile court is to prevent juvenile offenders from becoming adult criminals, there may be a tendency on the part of some juvenile judges to treat relatively minor offenses very seriously in an effort to impress upon the juvenile that any further law violation will not be tolerated. As previously discussed in the Gault case, the punishment for an adult who made an obscene phone call would have been a minor fine or brief incarceration. Instead, Gault was ordered institutionalized for a period of six years! This type of disposition seems extreme in proportion to the severity of the alleged offense. Similarly, in some cases, much of what might be viewed as merely "adolescent mischief" is treated as if it were a major crime in order to "teach the youth a lesson." Unfortunately, the lesson taught may not be the one desired. When petty offenses are treated as major ones, at least in the mind of the juvenile, the difference between the two may become blurred. For example, in a state where murder and truancy might both result in 18 months of institutionalization, the vastly significant difference between the two acts becomes symbolically reduced. Several researchers have linked the widespread procedure of indeterminate sentencing (no specified length of sentence) by juvenile courts to terms of incarceration for juveniles often being longer than those for adults who commit the same offense (e.g., Lightholder, 1978; Sleeth, 1978; ACLU, 1978). Consequently, the question of discrimination against juveniles arises as a legal issue to be addressed. Recent trends in juvenile justice indicate that this issue may be dissipated, as juvenile courts appear to be focusing their attention much more on the smaller number of serious juvenile offenders as opposed to the nonserious status offenders who have traditionally monopolized juvenile court dockets (Regnery, 1986). Nevertheless, the punishment ideology appears to dominate today's juvenile court (Bazemore and Umbreit, 1995).

The absence of total due process continues as another point of criticism of the juvenile court. As a result of the Supreme Court decisions discussed earlier in this chapter, and the increased utilization of legal counsel in juvenile hearings, this criticism has been reduced somewhat. Much of the concern now focuses upon preserving the rights of youths charged with status offenses. Since these youths have not violated criminal laws and are more likely to be adjudicated "in need of supervision" as opposed to "delinquent," their hearings are often much more informal. Consequently, the legal rights of these juveniles may not be protected as much as if they had been arrested for a criminal act. For example, Jan Costello and Nancy Worthington (1981) expressed concern that many states were circumventing the Juvenile Justice and Prevention Act which prohibits the incarceration of status offenders.

Perhaps the most persistent criticism leveled at the juvenile court has been that its jurisdiction is too broad. As former judge of the Denver Juvenile Court Ted Rubin (1976:66) expressed:

> *This court is a far more complex instrument than outsiders imagine. It is law, and it is social work; it is control and it is help; it is the good parent, and, also, the stern parent; it is both formal and informal. It is concerned not only with the delinquent, but also with the battered child, the runaway, and many others...The juvenile court has been all things to all people.*

The criticism is that the juvenile court has tried to be too many different things to too many different people. Rubin (1977) said that the juvenile court must establish an identity which clearly outlines its responsibility. In broadening its jurisdiction to attempt to cover virtually any of the problems which involve juveniles, the court may have inadvertently diluted its ability to successfully handle any of them. Barry Feld (1993:403) laments that "the juvenile court has been transformed from an informal, welfare agency into a scaled-down, second-class criminal court...that diverts status offenders, waives serious offenders to adult courts, punishes delinquent offenders, and provides more formal procedures." This "jack-of-all trades, master of none" image has plagued the contemporary juvenile court.

Francis Allen (1976:417) discussed several of the problems involved in juvenile justice, and pointed out that many of the court's "...difficulties arise from an insufficient conception of the court's role and the court's capabilities." Rubin (1979) further discussed some of the problems encountered by the juvenile court in attempting to handle too broad a range of cases. He contended that there is a definite need for a juvenile court, but it should not be expected to handle all types of cases. For example, he suggested that neglected and abused children should probably be handled by divorce and family courts.

The Multifaceted Juvenile Court

One of the difficulties faced by the juvenile court resides in the fact that there really is no such thing as *the* juvenile court. Rather, juvenile courts vary from state to state in their size, nature, jurisdiction, and procedures. In short, there are a variety of juvenile courts. Throughout this chapter we have compared and contrasted the juvenile court to adult criminal court. In the process, we have discovered that while there are increasingly notable similarities between the two, there remain distinctive differences.

It has been suggested that the contemporary juvenile court no longer resembles the earlier chancery court out of which it developed, but is also unlike adult criminal court. In an attempt to analyze the juvenile court as a "people-processing organization," Yeheskel

Hasenfeld and Paul Cheung (1985) pointed to the multidimensional personality of juvenile courts. They indicated that juvenile courts are faced with a "dual and contradictory mandate" of projecting a "social service orientation," while responding to the more legalistic orientation of preserving "law and order" (Hasenfeld and Cheung, 1985:806). In an effort to explain how the court attempts to fulfill this dual mandate, Hasenfeld and Cheung (1985: 819–820) created the following typology of juvenile courts based upon the proportion of cases handled judicially (formally brought before a judge), and the rate of commitment (proportion of juveniles committed to juvenile institutions):

1. ***Interventionist Court:*** *characterized by a* high *proportion of its cases being handled judicially, and by a* high *commitment rate; this is the traditional juvenile court that emerged from the child-saving movement.*
2. ***Paternalistic Court:*** *characterized by a* low *proportion of cases handled judicially and a* high *commitment rate; this is the most commonly found juvenile court which tries to combine social rehabilitation with community protection.*
3. ***Ritualistic Court:*** *characterized by a* high *proportion of its cases being handled judicially and a* low *rate of commitment; this court exercises its formal judicial authority, but feels less pressure to protect the community.*
4. ***Minimalistic Court:*** *characterized by both a* low *proportion of cases handled judicially and a* low *commitment rate; this court represents an attempt to legally reform juvenile courts by elevating their legal status and removing the judge from the political arena.*

This typology addresses the multidimensional nature of juvenile courts and demonstrates that different courts handle cases in different ways.

David Aday (1986) created a simpler typology of juvenile courts based on important variations in court structure and procedure. He identified two different types of juvenile courts: the **traditional court** and the **due process court.** According to Aday (1986:111) the two courts were distinguishable by the following characteristics:

Traditional Court
1. ***Low task differentiation:*** *decisions about cases are made by court staff;* the prosecutor does not participate in decisions to file formal petitions
2. ***Centralized authority:*** *the judge administers probation and other court services;*
3. ***Low discretion for court services staff:*** *probation staff cannot assign juveniles to informal probation;*
4. ***Status offender jurisdiction:*** *the court routinely handles cases alleging status offenses;*
5. ***Low formalization:*** *adjudication and disposition hearings are not bifurcated.*

Due Process Court
1. ***High task differentiation:*** *court services staff participate separately in decisions; the prosecutor participates in decisions to file formal complaints.*

2. **Decentralized authority:** *the judge does not administer probation or other court services; these services are administered within the State Department of Social Services;*

3. **High discretion for court services staff:** *probation staff assign juveniles to informal probation; the court does not handle such cases;*

4. **Status offender jurisdiction:** *the court routinely handles cases alleging status offenses;*

5. **Low formalization:** *there is no requirement to bifurcate adjudication and dispositional hearings.*

In the *traditional court* the role of the judge is to enact the philosophy of *parens patriae;* consequently, the roles of attorneys, staff, parents, and others in the court are minimized. The traditional court attempts to perpetuate a social service orientation. According to Aday (1986:115), "particularistic characteristics of juveniles and/or offenses influence decisions" and "attorney use represents token compliance with due-process requirements and has no effect on decision making." On the other hand, the *due process court* is dominated by legal factors (especially nature of offenses) in its decision making, and attorneys play a prominent role in determining the outcome of cases (Aday, 1986). In the two types of courts studied by Aday, some interesting data emerged regarding rates of detention, probation, and commitment. We have constructed Table 14-2 to illustrate his findings.

As can be seen in Table 14-2, the traditional court was more likely to detain juveniles before their hearing, but once juveniles appeared before the judge, the largest percentage were likely to be placed on formal probation. The due process court detained far fewer juveniles, electing to simply warn and release almost three-fourths (73 percent) of those with whom it came in contact. The traditional court and due process court differed in severity of dispositions, with almost twice the proportion of juveniles appearing before the traditional court being committed to a juvenile institution as compared to those from the due process court.

The Future of the Juvenile Court

Given the historical development of the juvenile court and the many criticisms directed toward it in recent years, the future of the juvenile court is somewhat unclear. Conservatives,

TABLE 14-2   Dispositions in Traditional and Due Process Courts

	Traditional Court	Due Process Court
Detained juveniles	50.0%	16.1%
Unofficially warn and release	24.3%	73.0%
Placed on probation	63.6%	20.2%
Committed	12.1%	6.9%

Source: Created from data in D.P. Aday, Jr. Court structure, defense attorney use, and juvenile court decisions. *Sociological Quarterly* 27 (1), 1986:112.

This 12-year-old youth is being escorted into juvenile court where he is being charged with the fatal shooting death of his 7-year-old cousin.

moderates, liberals, and radicals all have different views on what the future should hold for the juvenile court, but almost all agree that some changes must and will occur. One of the dilemmas faced by the juvenile court is how to combine the rehabilitative philosophy of *parens patriae* upon which it was founded with contemporary retributive trends that insist the court must punish serious juvenile offenders. Many believe that the juvenile court must adopt an alternative model of *restorative justice,* which sanctions serious criminal behavior while also attempting to return the juvenile to society as a productive citizen (Bazemore and Umbreit, 1995). While there is much disagreement over how to reform the juvenile court, there is some consensus that at least five changes are in order:

1. Limit its jurisdiction.
2. Operate under the provisions of due process.
3. Be administered by competent judges.
4. Have adequate court personnel.
5. Have adequate availability of alternatives for disposition.

It is much easier to list these items than it is to actually implement them, but all of these changes are pragmatically feasible. In the last chapter of this book we explore these and other possibilities for reforming the juvenile justice system.

SUMMARY

The juvenile court is a relatively young institution in the United States, officially established in Chicago in 1899. Yet, the historical and legal traditions of the court are much older and can be traced to the chancery courts of fifteenth-century England. During its short history in this country, the juvenile court has greatly extended its jurisdiction and has had dramatic influence on the lives of those with whom it has come in contact.

The establishment of the American juvenile court roughly corresponded to changing attitudes about childhood and represented a major development in separating youthful offenders from hardened criminals. With its protective philosophy, and overall goal of deterring troubled youths from becoming adult criminals, the juvenile court has made numerous contributions in the handling of juveniles. Perhaps one of its most significant contributions has been its symbolic representation of the notion that the state is genuinely concerned about its youths. It has been there to intervene on the behalf of abused, neglected, and misdirected youths.

Despite its laudable philosophy and numerous accomplishments, the juvenile court also has been the target of widespread criticism from a variety of sources. Too lenient, too harsh, too broad in its scope, too narrow in its power, the juvenile court in the view of many has become an ineffective mockery of what it was meant to be. Partly in response to some of these criticisms, and partly as a result of Supreme Court intervention, the juvenile court has undergone numerous changes since it first came into operation. Probably one of the most prominent changes has been in its shift toward a more formal legalistic approach to juvenile criminal offenses. The introduction of elements of due process and increased involvement of attorneys has altered its once informal omnipotent procedures.

In Chapters 15, 16, and 17, we more thoroughly address the inherently social nature of juvenile justice and the issue of modifying the social structure in an effort to mobilize the total community toward delinquency prevention, treatment, and control.

Concept Integration

Questions and Topics for Study and Discussion

1. Explain "due process" and discuss how its introduction into the juvenile court has influenced the philosophy and operation of the court.

2. List some of the positive and negative influences the Child Savers' movement exerted on the juvenile justice process.

3. Describe the historical development of the juvenile court.

4. Describe and explain the procedures of the contemporary juvenile court. In what ways are they different from those of the adult criminal court?

5. Identify some of the limitations and major criticisms of the juvenile court. What changes might be made in the juvenile court to overcome the limitations and address the criticisms?

References

ACLU. 1978. *Children's Rights Report* Vol. 2, No. 9 (May):8–11.

Aday, D. P., Jr. 1986. Court structure, defense attorney use, and juvenile court decisions. *Sociological Quarterly* 27 (1):107–119.

Allen, F. A. 1976. The juvenile court and the limits of juvenile justice. In R. Giallombardo (Ed.). *Juvenile Delinquency* (3rd ed.). New York: John Wiley, pp. 411–419.

Arnold, W. R. 1971. Race and ethnicity relative to other factors in juvenile court dispositions. *American Journal of Sociology* 77 (September):211–227.

AP New York. 1978. Cold blooded killer is given 18-month sentence. *Tulsa Daily World,* June 30, 1978.

Aurand, A. 1998. Troubled teens course through overburdened justice system. *Ashland Daily Tidings,* May 28:3.

Bazemore, G., and Umbreit, M. 1995. Rethinking the sanctioning function in juvenile court: Retributive or restorative response to youth crime. *Crime & Delinquency* 41 (July):296–316.

Belden, E. 1920. *Courts in the US hearing children's cases.* U.S. Bureau Publication No. 65. Washington, DC: U.S. Government Printing Office.

Block, K. J., and Hale, D. C. 1991. Turf wars in progressive era juvenile justice: The relationship of private and public child care agencies. *Crime and Delinquency* 37 (April):225–241.

Caldwell, R. G. 1961. The juvenile court: Its development and some major problems. *Journal of Criminal Law, Criminology and Police Science* 51 (Jan.–Feb.):493–507.

Carter, R. M. 1976. The police view of the justice system. In M. W. Klein (Ed.). *The Juvenile Justice System.* Beverly Hills: Sage, pp. 121–132.

Chesney-Lind, M. 1977. Judicial paternalism and the female status offender. *Crime and Delinquency* 23 (April):121–130.

Christian Science Monitor. 1988. Kid prisons that don't reform: Hope for rehabilitation outside the prison walls. *The Christian Science Monitor* (September 29):B2–B8.

Coffey, A. R. 1974. *Juvenile justice as a system: Law enforcement to rehabilitation.* Englewood Cliffs, NJ: Prentice-Hall.

Cohen, L. E. 1975. *Juvenile dispositions: Social and legal factors related to the processing of Denver delinquency cases.* Washington, DC: LEAA, U.S. Government Printing Office.

Costello, J. C., and Worthington, N. 1981. Incarcerating status offenders: Attempts to circumvent the Juvenile Justice Delinquency Prevention Act. *Harvard Civil Rights—Civil Liberties Law Review* 16 (Summer):41–81.

Cox, S. M., and Conrad, J. J. 1996. *Juvenile justice: A guide to practice and theory* (4th ed.). Dubuque, IA: Brown and Benchmark.

Coxe, S. 1967. Lawyers in juvenile court. *Crime and Delinquency* 13 (October):488–493.

Day, L. A. 1984. Media access to juvenile courts. *Journalism Quarterly* 61 (Winter):751–756, 700.

Fagan, J., Slaughter, E., and Hartstone, E. 1987a. Blind justice? The impact of race on the juvenile justice process. *Crime and Delinquency* 33 (April):224–258.

Fagan, J., Forst, M., and Vivona, T. S. 1987b. Racial determinants of the judicial transfer decision: Prosecuting violent youth in criminal court. *Crime and Delinquency* 33 (April):259–286.

Feld, B. C. 1993. Juvenile (in)justice and the criminal court alternative. *Crime and Delinquency* 39 (October):403–424.

Flanagan, T. J., and McLeod, M. (Eds.). 1983. *Sourcebook of Criminal Justice Statistics–1982.* U.S. Department of Justice, Bureau of Justice Statistics. NCJ-86483. Washington, DC: U.S. Government Printing Office.

Hasenfeld, Y., and Cheung, P. P. L. 1985. The juvenile court as a people-processing organization: A political economy perspective. *American Journal of Sociology* 90 (January):801–824.

Haskell, M. R., and Yablonsky, L. 1978. *Juvenile delinquency* (2nd ed.). Chicago: Rand-McNally.

Institute of Judicial Administration and American Bar Association. 1977. *Juvenile Justice Standards Project: Standards Relating to Counsel for Private Parties.* Cambridge, MA: Ballinger.

Krisberg, B., and Austin, J. 1978. *The children of Ishmael: Critical perspectives on juvenile justice.* Palo Alto, CA: Mayfield.

Lavoie, D. 2000. Treating 39-year-old slaying suspect as juvenile creates legal maze. *Dallas Morning News,* January 21:7A.

Leiber, M. J., and Stairs, J. M. 1999. Race, contexts, and the use of intake diversion. *Journal of Research in Crime and Delinquency* 36 (February):56–86.

Lightholder, S. O. 1978. Stay no longer—California juvenile court sentencing practices. *Pepperdine Law Review* 5 (3):769–794.

Mahoney, A. R. 1985. Jury trial for juveniles: Right or ritual? *Justice Quarterly* 2 (December):553–565.

McGarrell, E. F. 1993. Trends in racial disproportionality in juvenile court processing: 1985–1989. *Crime and Delinquency* 39 (January):29–48.

Miller, F. W., Dawson, R. O., Dix, G. E., and Parnas, R. I. 1985. *The juvenile justice process* (3rd ed.). Mineola, NY: University Casebook Series, Foundation Press.

Minor, K. I., Hartmann, D. J., and Terry, S. 1997. Predictors of juvenile court actions and recidivism. *Crime & Delinquency* 43 (July):328–344.

Myren, R. A. 1988. *Law and justice: An introduction.* Belmont, CA: Wadsworth.

Neigher, A. 1967. The Gault Decision: Due process and the juvenile courts. *Federal Probation* 31 (December):8–18.

O'Quin, K., Vogler, C. C., and Weinberg, T. S. 1985. Parental interest, juvenile misbehavior and disposition recommendations. Paper presented at the 1985 meeting of the Society for the Study of Social Problems.

Osbun, L. A., and Rode, P. A. 1984. Prosecuting juveniles as adults: The quest for "objective" decisions. *Criminology* 22 (May):187–202.

Perry, R. L. 1985. Differential dispositions of black and white juveniles: A critical assessment of methodology. *Western Journal of Black Studies* 9 (Winter):189–197.

Platt, A. 1969. *The Child Savers.* Chicago: University of Chicago Press.

President's Commission on Law Enforcement and Administration of Justice. 1967. *Juvenile Delinquency and Youth Crime.* Washington, DC: U.S. Government Printing Office.

Regnery, A. S. 1986. A federal perspective on juvenile justice reform. *Crime and Delinquency* 32 (January):39–51.

Reibstein, L. 1997. Kids in the dock. *Newsweek,* May 26:70.

Rubin, H. T. 1976. *The courts: Fulcrum of the justice system.* Pacific Palisades: Goodyear.

——— 1977. The juvenile court's search for identity and responsibility. *Crime and Delinquency* 23 (January): 1–13.

——— 1979. Retain the juvenile court? *Crime and Delinquency* (July):281–298.

——— 1980. The emerging prosecutor dominance of the juvenile court intake process. *Crime and Delinquency* 26 (July):299–318.

Sanborn, J. B., Jr. 1996. Factors perceived to affect delinquent dispositions in juvenile court: Putting the sentencing decision into context. *Crime & Delinquency* 42 (January):99–113.

Sanders, W. B. 1970. *Juvenile offenders for a thousand years.* Chapel Hill: University of North Carolina Press.

Singer, S. I. 1993. The automatic waiver of juveniles and substantive justice. *Crime and Delinquency* 39 (April):253–261.

Sleeth, V. 1978. Child is a child, except when he's not—California's new approach to disposition of youthful offenders. *California Western Law Review* 14 (1):124–152.

Thornberry, T. P. 1973. Race, socioeconomic status, and sentencing in the juvenile justice system. *Journal of Criminal Law and Criminology* 64 (March):90–98.

Thornberry, T. P., and Christenson, R. L. 1984. Juvenile justice decision-making as a longitudinal process. *Social Forces* 63 (December):433–444.

U.S. Department of Justice. 1992. *Juvenile Court Statistics 1989.* Pittsburgh: Office of Juvenile Justice and Delinquency Prevention.

Winslow, R. W. 1973. *Juvenile delinquency in a free society* (2nd ed.). Encino, CA: Dickenson.

Zatz, M. S. 1985. Los Cholos: Legal processing of Chicano gang members. *Social Problems* 33 (October):13–30.

*Supreme Court Rulings Cited**

Breed v. *Jones* (1975). 421 US 519, 95 S. Ct. 1779, 44 L. Ed. 2d 346 (1975).

In re Gault (1967). 387 US 1, 87 S. Ct. 142, 18 L. Ed. 2d 527 (1967).

In re Holmes (1954). 379 Pa. 599, 109A 2d 523 (1954).

In re Winship (1970). 397 US 358, 90 S. Ct. 1068, 25 L. Ed. 2d 368 (1970).

Kent v. *United States* (1966). 383 US 541, 86 S. Ct. 1045, 16 L. Ed. 2d 84 (1966).

McKiever v. *Pennsylvania* (1971). 403 US 528, 91 S. Ct. 1976, L. Ed. 2d 647 (1971).

Miranda v. *Arizona* (1966). 384 US 436, 86 S. Ct. 1602, 1620, 16 L. Ed. 2d 694 (1966).

Schall v. *Martin* (1984).———US———104 S. Ct. 2403, 81 L. Ed. 2d 207 (1984).

15 JUVENILE CORRECTIONS

Reading Objectives

The reading of this chapter will help you achieve the following objectives:

1. Understand the sociological concept of social control and explain how it relates to deterrence theory and juvenile delinquency.
2. Distinguish between voluntary, informal, and formal methods of social control.
3. Define the concepts of juvenile probation, restitution, detention, incarceration, and aftercare.
4. Distinguish between different types of juvenile facilities such as detention facilities, training schools, and group homes.
5. Understand the process by and extent to which juveniles are remanded to adult criminal courts and placed in adult jails and prisons.
6. Summarize the use of capital punishment for juveniles who have been convicted of capital offenses in adult criminal courts.
7. Identify some of the more prominent community corrections programs designed to deinstitutionalize youths and divert them from the juvenile justice system.

Introduction

We repeatedly have emphasized the social nature of juvenile delinquency. Just as we looked to human society and culture in defining delinquency, and for providing insight into causal explanations, we now turn to those same sources for controlling juvenile delinquency.

This chapter focuses upon controlling juvenile delinquency, *not* eliminating it. Most social problems are never fully eliminated. Despite multimillion dollar programs and armies of professionals committed to the eradication of problems such as crime, suicide, mental illness, and juvenile delinquency, the problems persist. Ironically, some of our most strenuous efforts to eliminate a social problem may, in fact, only help perpetuate it, and in some cases, create other problems. For example, as we discuss in Chapter 16, some of our efforts to prevent delinquency have led to a preoccupation with identifying and treating "predelinquents." This attempt at identifying delinquents before they have committed delinquent acts involves identifying dubious "symptoms" in early childhood. Unfortunately, as the labeling perspective indicates, identifying and then treating a child as a "predelinquent" may, in fact, later create the very phenomenon that one is trying to prevent.

This should not discourage us from seeking programs aimed at controlling social problems like delinquency, but should serve to caution us against anticipating the discovery of some type of panacea leading to utopian solutions. A pragmatic objective is to develop realistic social mechanisms for reducing and controlling delinquency. By **social control** we mean *those aspects of society and culture which are designed to reduce the incidence of juvenile delinquency and to minimize its negative impact upon the members of society.*

Every society establishes norms to regulate human behavior and provide guidelines for social interaction. Similarly, societies have established numerous ways of dealing with those individuals who violate the norms (folkways, mores, and laws) of their society. These *methods of enforcing norms* are referred to as **sanctions,** and can be either positive or negative. When people conform to normative expectations they receive positive sanctions in the form of respect, honors, awards, and social acceptance. When they violate norms their behavior is negatively sanctioned, or punished, in an attempt to control their behavior. These methods of social control of deviant behavior can be divided into three general categories: voluntary, informal, and formal, and are linked to the idea of deterrence. First, we will briefly look at deterrence theory, and then we will turn to specific areas of social control.

Social Control and Deterrence Theory

At the heart of all social control is a fundamental belief in **Deterrence Theory**—*that deviance will be discouraged (deterred) if social sanctions for nonconformity are perceived to be certain, swift, and severe* (Gibbs, 1975; Schneider, 1990). Like some of its predecessors, deterrence theory assumes that juveniles are rational, logical beings who prefer to be rewarded for their conformity rather than be punished for their deviance. Thus, the theory contends that if youths know that meaningful social sanctions will be forthcoming, they are less likely to commit delinquent acts.

Deterrence comes in two varieties: (1) **Specific deterrence,** *which involves applying a sanction to an individual in hopes that he/she will not repeat the same or a similar act:* and (2) **general deterrence,** *in which a sanction is applied to an individual in such a way that not only is that individual deterred from repeating his or her deviance, but others who learn of the sanction are also discouraged from committing the same or similar acts.* Ideally, the overall goal of society is to sanction juvenile delinquency in such a way as to incorporate elements of both specific and general deterrence. This is difficult, however, as some people may be more affected by one type of deterrence than another, and some youths learn only from personal experience (specific deterrence), while others can learn vicariously from the experiences of others, which is the key to general deterrence (Paternoster and Piquero, 1995). Chapter 16 discusses a variety of treatment and prevention programs aimed at deterring juvenile delinquency. Box 15-1 deals with the controversial caning of an American teenager in Singapore—a punishment used in that culture in an effort to deter vandalism and other property crimes.

Voluntary Social Control

The most fundamental and effective method of social control is **voluntary control,** which most members of society *impose upon themselves.* Voluntary social control is dependent

BOX 15-1 Cross-Cultural Focus

The Caning of an American Youth in Singapore: Justice or Abuse?

Reports of an American teenager spraying paint on some parked cars is not considered shocking in an era when nightly news reports are filled with incidents of armed robbery, aggravated assault, forcible rape, and murders committed by youths under the age of 18. While such acts of vandalism would not be ignored, they quite likely would warrant a small fine, perhaps some financial restitution to the victims, and six months to a year on probation—if they were committed in the United States. Michael Fay, an 18-year-old from Kettering, Ohio, however, did not receive such a light sentence from the courts in Singapore. In a city where chewing gum is a fineable offense, vandalism of automobiles is taken quite seriously, and Michael Fay was sentenced to four months in prison, a $2,220 fine, and six lashes with a rattan cane on his bare buttocks for his participation in the offense.

Fay's sentence sparked an international debate between East and West over human rights issues, and fueled an age-old argument in the United States over whether the American juvenile and criminal justice systems are too lenient, and should more closely model some of their harsher counterparts in other parts of the world. At one point, President Clinton intervened on Fay's behalf, and while unsuccessful in his request that the young man be spared the caning and released to return to the United States, the Singapore government did decide to reduce the flogging from six lashes to four.

Interestingly, many Americans disagreed with the president's appeal for leniency for Michael Fay, and insisted that America's juvenile and criminal justice systems could learn a valuable lesson from Singapore's. Almost 40 percent of Americans in a *Newsweek* poll indicated that they approved of the punishment (Elliott, 1994). They cited Singapore's unusually low crime rates as evidence that their "get tough" approaches to crime and delinquency are more successful than those practiced in the United States. On the other hand, critics of the Singapore criminal justice system argue that Americans would be ill-advised to turn their back on the U.S. Bill of Rights and copy the harsh example of Singapore. Fay's parents contend that Michael's confession was coerced from him, and there are allegations that other American teens involved in the incident were beaten by the police during interrogation while some Singapore youths who may also have been involved were set free.

* * * *

What do you think? Should teenagers or adult criminals be subjected to corporal punishment? Would caning or other types of corporal punishment act as a specific deterrent to delinquency? Would they serve as a general deterrent? Would incorporating corporal punishment into American corrections represent an innovative approach to deterring crime and delinquency, or a giant step backwards?

Sources

Elliott, M. 1994. Crime and punishment, the caning debate: Should the U.S. be more like Singapore? *Newsweek,* April 18:18–22.
National Review. 1994. Singapore blues. *National Review,* May 16:79.
Newsweek. 1994. I tried to ignore the pain, Interview: Michael Fay on his caning in Singapore. *Newsweek,* July 4:36.
Newsweek. 1994. Singapore: After the caning, "Mike's in pain." *Newsweek,* May 16:41.

upon effective socialization of societal members so that they internalize the shared values and norms of their society. A stable and effectively functioning society depends upon most of its members sharing expectations and agreed-upon standards of social conduct. These shared expectations and standards are important aspects of culture and must be transmitted from one generation to the next through the process of socialization. Effective socialization goes beyond individuals obeying rules because they fear the consequences of violating them. Rather, it involves people conforming to social norms because they have been effectively socialized from childhood and have internalized the norms as their own personal behavioral guidelines. The socialization process involves not only teaching social norms to societal members, but causing individuals to believe in the moral and ethical validity of those norms. Thus, the teaching of social **values,** *attitudes about the rightness and wrongness of acts,* is just as important as teaching people the appropriateness of acts, if not more important. For example, most of us have refrained from committing forcible rape, murder, or armed robbery not only because such acts violate formal norms and are defined as criminal, but also because we believe it is wrong to commit such actions against our fellow human beings. We voluntarily obey many of our criminal laws not because we fear the consequences of violating them, but because most of us believe in the validity of such laws and would never consider violating them. On the other hand, in the aftermath of natural disasters such as floods, earthquakes, hurricanes, and tornadoes, we often see how quickly the restraints learned through socialization can be overcome as the police and National Guard must be called upon to keep some people from looting the remains of the damaged property of their fellow citizens.

Some sociological theories of juvenile delinquency claim that inadequate or unsuccessful socialization leads to delinquency. For example, the Social Learning theories contend that delinquency, as well as conformity, must be socially learned through socialization. Hence, the major agents of socialization—family, religion, school, peers, and mass media—all play an important role in helping a juvenile internalize society's norms.

Walter Reckless (1961) emphasized social control as being the primary, distinguishing element between those who commit and those who refrain from committing delinquent acts. The first layer of insulation against delinquency in Reckless' Control Theory is that of **inner containment.** This inner containment is primarily a result of effective socialization. When juveniles internalize society's values and norms as their own, they are much less likely to violate those values and norms. This element of voluntary social control relies upon the individual's set of values to act as a sufficient barrier to committing delinquent acts. What many of us refer to as conscience is in fact the manifestation of voluntary social control.

Another aspect of voluntary social control developed through effective socialization is the process whereby individuals acknowledge their membership in society and simultaneously recognize society as being part of them. Often referred to as a **social bond** (Hirschi, 1969), this acknowledgment promotes the conformity to social norms, and helps prevent involvement in delinquent acts. Because voluntary control is dependent upon the socialization process, the role of the family cannot be overemphasized. Primary responsibility for teaching appropriate values and behaviors rests with the family. The family's choice of neighborhood, schools, and church attendance all impact upon the socialization process. Perhaps most important are the role models provided in a family by parents and older siblings.

In a society where there are infinitely more potential deviants than there are formal agents of social control, the importance of voluntary social control cannot be overestimated. If juveniles are going to conform to society's rules most of the time it is more dependent upon their willingness to do so, than upon the ability of adults to prevent them from committing delinquent acts. Through effective socialization and the juvenile's developing a sense of attachment to society, most juveniles usually refrain from committing serious delinquent acts.

Informal Social Control

When the internalization of social norms is insufficient for an individual to maintain behavioral control, it may be necessary for the social group to implement a second line of defense against deviance. One of the most effective methods members of a society can use to discourage deviance and encourage conformity is to implement various techniques of informal social control. **Informal social control** mechanisms are *applied by other societal members and include such tactics as gossip, ridicule, humor, ostracism, and peer pressure.* Despite their informality, the impact of these methods of social constraints should not be underestimated. They are especially powerful when exercised by groups characterized by close, informal, face-to-face, interdependent relationships. Hence, the family, peer groups, and members of the immediate neighborhood or other primary social groups can act as extremely important agents of social control in discouraging nonconforming behavior.

Ferdinand Toennies ([1887] 1961) developed a theoretical continuum in an attempt to better understand the nature of social interaction and network of social relationships within different types of social structures. At one end of the continuum was the **gemeinschaft** type of community. The **gemeinschaft** community *is characterized by a smaller population, less complex division of labor, and is dominated by primary face-to-face social interaction.* In this type of community informal mechanisms tend to dominate social control strategies because they are so effective in this type of social structure.

While much of contemporary U.S. society has moved away from the gemeinschaft end of the continuum, there are many smaller communities and even sections of larger cities which closely resemble this type of social organization. For example, in rural America, informal social control mechanisms are still more predominantly utilized than formal types of social control. When a juvenile commits a delinquent act such as getting drunk over the weekend and driving a car through somebody's front yard, it is very likely that the entire community will know about it by Monday morning. Rather than placing the juvenile under formal arrest and levying a fine, it is highly likely that the local sheriff will simply pay a visit to the juvenile's parents. The parents may pay for the damage through some type of informal agreement with the injured party and simply promise the sheriff not to let such an incident happen again. Not only will the parents play a key role in attempting to control the juvenile's behavior through some type of disciplinary action, but the entire community probably will become involved in the social control process. Through whispering, finger-pointing, looks of disgust, and various degrees of ostracism, the community can express its lack of tolerance for the delinquent act and issue a warning that similar acts should not be committed in the future. San Antonio, Texas has had some success with a program where students convicted of vandalism are placed on probation and have a sign put in their front yards that reads "Graffiti Offender on Probation Lives Here." The police and court officials contend that the resulting shame and informal sanctions from the neighborhood are more effective than anything the police or courts could do to try to prevent further acts of vandalism (AP, San Antonio, 1999).

The Old Order Amish provide a good example of the powerful influence of socialization and informal social control in delinquency prevention. One of the most powerful sanctions that can be exercised by the Amish is the *Edict of Meidung,* or shunning, which involves ostracism from the community for serious violations of their normative code.

Ostracism, *the experience of being expelled from a social group,* may serve as one of the most powerful and effective informal social control mechanisms available to a community or social group. Human beings are social by nature, and the inability to interact with others can be extremely punitive. Through real or threatened ostracism, a juvenile's peer group can exert extreme pressure upon individual members to conform to the group's expectations for behavior.

On the negative side, if the group is encouraging delinquency, an otherwise conforming youngster may feel compelled to break the law in order to gain acceptance by friends. Social Learning Theories, especially Differential Association, point out the significance of the peer group in influencing a juvenile into delinquent or nondelinquent activities.

On the positive side, if the peer group demands conformity to the law, the juvenile whose own inner containment is not strong enough to prevent delinquency may be sufficiently constrained by the group. This **outer containment,** as Reckless (1961) called it, serves as another layer of insulation against delinquency for those who have not sufficiently internalized the norms. As Ronald Farrell and Victoria Swigert (1982) indicated, rejection from the group may serve as a significant deterrent for the deviant.

Some of the informal strategies for dealing with less serious juvenile offenders have included trying to involve them in what are considered to be positive activities with more desirable peers and role models. Problem juveniles often are encouraged to join baseball and soccer teams, Boy Scouts, YMCA, and a variety of other youth organizations in the hope that by becoming involved in acceptable group behavior, these juveniles will be less inclined to become involved in delinquency. In the past, as juvenile boys in trouble approached the age of 18, they often were encouraged to join the military service. It was thought that the discipline, rigor, and positive aspects of military life would prevent young men from further law-violating behavior.

Formal Social Control

In large, complex, predominantly urban societies with heterogeneous populations such as prevail in much of the United States, social relations are likely to be secondary as opposed to primary in nature. This represents the other end of Toennies' ([1887] 1961) theoretical continuum, the **gesellschaft** society *characterized by a larger population, a complex division of labor, secondary relationships, and formal social control.* In these social circumstances citizens, legislators, police, and court officials are likely to respond more formally to norm violations by juveniles. Laws are formal codified norms, and their violation is likely to bring about a formal response. On the other hand, occasional drinking, fighting, minor vandalism, and various forms of mischief might be tolerated in a small rural community. But the same behavior in larger towns and cities is likely to be perceived as juvenile crime and a threat to the social order. Therefore, delinquency is likely to evoke outcries for public protection and dictate that formal methods of social control be brought into action.

The schools, police, and courts as agents of social control were discussed in previous chapters. In school, juveniles are likely to experience both informal and formal sanctions for their deviant behavior. All the informal social control mechanisms discussed in the previous section can be imposed by other students, teachers, and administrators. However, the school staff and administrators also can implement a variety of more formal social control procedures. Varying degrees of formal punishment, suspension, and expulsion are ways in which school officials can negatively sanction a student's undesirable behavior. In addition, school officials can petition a student to juvenile court, and initiate formal delinquency proceedings against a youth for serious offenses.

Similarly, the police also can utilize both informal and formal techniques of control. When police officers choose the options of issuing warnings, or questioning juveniles and then releasing them, they are exercising informal social control over the youths' behavior. When neighbors see a teenager being delivered home to the parents in a squad car, many of the informal social control mechanisms such as gossip and ridicule are initiated. Because they are employed as formal agents of social control, however, police are most likely to be associated with the formal sanctions at their disposal. As noted in Chapter 13, police can arrest, detain, create an official record, and petition a juvenile to court for law-violating behavior. Thus, the police emerge as one of the most significant elements of formal social control of juvenile delinquency.

The juvenile court was discussed in Chapter 14, and the formal dispositional alternatives available to it were cited. Once a juvenile appears before the juvenile court, even if released outright, a formal control mechanism has been implemented. Despite its attempt to conduct informal hearings, the court represents an official governmental institution and, hence, is by its very nature a formal agent of social control.

Juvenile Probation

One of the most widely used methods of formal social control for juveniles in the United States is probation. Each year some 1.76 million juveniles are processed through juvenile courts and more than half a million cases result in juveniles being placed on probation (Kurlychek, et al., 1999). Juvenile probation officers usually are involved in the juvenile court's intake procedure, and can be very influential in making recommendations to the juvenile judge. Probation also is one of the dispositional alternatives to incarceration for juveniles. **Probation** is *a form of supervised release in which a juvenile adjudicated as delinquent is allowed to remain free from institutionalization, but must adhere to a strict set of guidelines imposed by the court.* Additionally, the youth is required to report to a probation officer on a regular schedule. Probation is thought to have been used first by John Augustus in Boston in 1841 (Culbertson and Ellsworth, 1985). Augustus bailed out offenders and "in addition to providing them with emotional support, he made efforts to find his probationers jobs" (Culbertson and Ellsworth, 1985:127). When a juvenile lacks the necessary degree of voluntary self-control and does not respond to informal societal pressures to conform, probation can be used to implement some formal restraints. Theoretically, probation is assumed to provide outer containment (or external restraint and control) for a juvenile while simultaneously helping to resocialize the youth to a new set of values which it is hoped will provide sufficient inner containment (or self control). Thus, probation rules generally serve not only to prohibit law violations and establish curfews and other restrictions upon behavior, but they also often are likely to include guidelines such as requiring school attendance beyond the compulsory attendance age, church attendance, charity work, and enforced savings (Imlay and Flasheen, 1971).

Ideally, probation combines both the punitive and rehabilitative aspects of juvenile corrections by negatively sanctioning a juvenile's delinquent behavior and reinforcing dominant social norms. Realistically, because of very heavy caseloads, juvenile probation officers often cannot maintain close contacts with their charges. Further, Carl Imlay and Charles Flasheen (1971) pointed out that many of the requirements of probation are petty and violate the basic constitutional rights of juveniles (such as dress and haircut requirements and mandatory church attendance), and may paradoxically produce a general disrespect for the law as opposed to the desired effect. Curfews have become very popular and some communities have instituted them for all youths, not just those on probation. Research indicates mixed results, however, with curfews seemingly reducing the number of minor offenses by youths, but having little or no effect on more serious crimes (McDowell, et al., 2000).

Some states utilize **shock probation,** which *involves a short prison stay designed to shock the youth and to impress upon him or her the seriousness of the problem and potential consequences of further delinquency.* The "shock" of imprisonment is then followed by a specified term of probation (this is also often referred to as **shock incarceration**).

There is mixed opinion regarding the effectiveness of juvenile probation. As William Sanders (1981:258) reported:

Some children are affected by probation in ways that will either help them or harm them. A probation officer who helps a child overcome a problem that led the juve-

nile to delinquency can be said to "cure" the child. If the probation disposition serves to stigmatize a juvenile, it can be said to harm the youth.

Further, if the juvenile placed on probation refrains from committing subsequent delinquency, we have no way of knowing if this success is *because of* or *despite* the probation experience. In fact, Sanders (1981:259) contended "there seems to be little evidence that probation is any more successful in changing delinquents than doing nothing at all."

Restitution and "Restorative Justice"

Most of the public criticism leveled at juvenile probation has centered on the perception that it is too lenient and allows juvenile offenders to escape punishment and accountability for their criminal actions. Gennaro Vito (1985), however, contended that probation, especially if linked with some form of victim restitution, is punitive, and can be an effective way of diverting juveniles from incarceration while holding them accountable for their law-violating behavior. **Restitution** *requires the offender to compensate the victim (either the actual victim or the state) either in monetary payments or in labor for losses related to the offense.* It is used most often in property offenses such as burglary, larceny-theft, and vandalism in which an actual dollar figure can be placed upon the victim's losses. Calvin Remington (1982) positively evaluated the Ventura Restitution Project, which attempts to make juvenile offenders understand the ramifications of their delinquent behavior and make them take responsibility for their actions, as being a viable social control mechanism. Robert Evans and Gary Koederitz (1983) summarized that restitution coupled with probation is a promising, logical, and effective means of achieving the dual goals of deterrence and punishment for law-violating juveniles. A major study sponsored by the National Center for Juvenile Justice showed that recidivism rates for robbery, assault, burglary, and auto theft were lower for juveniles who were ordered to pay restitution to their victims (Butts and Snyder, 1992).

Victim restitution, when coupled with involvement of community correctional programs, represents a new **restorative justice model** of juvenile justice *which focuses on accountability, restitution, and community involvement in the corrections process.* This model combines punitive and treatment approaches and attempts to "restore" justice to those most affected—the offender, the victim(s), and the community (Bazemore and Day, 1996; Vito et al., 1998).

Juvenile Incarceration

A prominent form of formal social control of juvenile delinquents is incarceration in an institution. As a result of increased violence and probation violations, large numbers of youths are incarcerated each year. Due to antiquated methods of data collection, it is very difficult to know precisely how many youths are being held in juvenile institutions at any given time (Lerman, 1991), but admissions to juvenile detention facilities rose to over half a million new admissions in 1990 and then declined during the mid-1990s (BJS, 1997). There are several types of institutions whose primary purpose is the incarceration of juvenile offenders. In order to simplify categorization of these institutions, James Carey and Patrick McAnany (1984:291) divided them into three basic types: detention facilities, training schools, and group homes.

Detention facilities *serve as places to detain, or hold, juveniles who are awaiting a hearing in juvenile court.* Communities provide various types of detention facilities for

Overcrowding is a common problem at many juvenile detention centers. Here, a youth sleeps on the floor between two bunks because of a lack of adequate facilities.

youths. In cities with large numbers of juvenile offenders, there usually are distinct facilities which separate them from adult offenders. "Juvenile halls," as these centers often are called, usually are located near the juvenile court, and might even be operated in conjunction with the court, thereby housing juvenile probation and parole officers and other juvenile court personnel. In smaller communities, where delinquency is less prevalent, juveniles are more likely to be detained in adult jails.

Rosemary Sarri (1974) conducted a thorough study of juvenile detention facilities, and found that they varied greatly from state to state, and from city to city within states. Although in 1980 Congress passed an amendment to the Juvenile Justice and Delinquency Prevention Act of 1974 calling for the removal of all juveniles from adult jails, in some cases, the juvenile detention center is simply a jail cell (Sarri, 1974; Chang, 1979; Schwartz, 1989). It seems logical that juvenile detention generally would be reserved for the more serious offenders, and in many instances that may be the case. However, we should be reminded that the police often make the decision as to whether to detain a youth, and a variety of factors beyond the seriousness of offense are taken into consideration.

Juvenile **training schools** are *long-term facilities for housing juveniles, and serve a function analogous to adult prisons.* Virtually every state has at least one of these facilities (sometimes one for boys and one for girls). They may operate under various names such as "state industrial schools" or "reformatories," but basically share the common characteristic of being a place where the juvenile court can send a youthful offender for an extended period of time. In some states, these facilities are even called "juvenile prisons" which reflects a trend toward including punishment as part of juvenile correction philosophy (Housewright, 2000). As in adult prisons, security is generally a prominent concern, and custody tends to be of primary importance. However, in keeping with the general philosophy of the juvenile court, there is usually an attempt to integrate treatment and rehabilitation into the custody procedures. Charles Tittle (1974) argued that the widespread belief that prisons and other detention facilities fail to rehabilitate is not justified by the empirical evidence, and suggested that there might well be rehabilitative benefits from incarceration.

These long-term incarceration facilities conform to Erving Goffman's (1961:xiii) concept of a **total institution**—*"a place of residence and work where a large number of like-situated individuals, cut off from the wider society for an appreciable period of time, together lead an enclosed, formally administered round of life."* In other words, juveniles eat, sleep, work, go to school, and play within the confines of the institution. Goffman (1961) discussed the social worlds which are constructed in total institutions in which virtually all spheres of one's life take place within the confines of one social setting, and pointed out that there is often a subterranean social world constructed by the inmates which may run counter to the official social structure of the institution.

The corrections literature is replete with studies analyzing the advantages and problems, successes and failures associated with this type of incarceration. Sanders (1981) pointed out that regardless of the treatment or rehabilitation efforts introduced into long-term incarceration facilities for juveniles, the staffs of these types of institutions tend to be increasingly concerned with basic custodial control. Unfortunately, as in adult prisons, intimidation, stabbings, fights, and rapes are part of institutional life in many of these facilities (*Christian Science Monitor,* 1988; Schwartz, 1989).

Michael Sherraden and Susan Downs (1984) conducted an empirical historical study of the institutionalization of juvenile delinquents from 1820 to 1970, and pointed out that institutionalization rates were highest during the second half of the nineteenth century and again during the 1960s. The resurgence in the institutionalization of juveniles refocused public attention on many of the problems associated with incarcerating juveniles.

Zvi Eisikovits and Michael Baizerman (1982) interviewed 43 violent youthful offenders in one Midwestern state who had been incarcerated in either maximum security youth facilities or adult prisons. In assessing how these youngsters "did time," they found that youths in both types of institutions lost sight of getting out, and instead learned to adapt to the institutional life imposed upon them. The youths learned quickly that violence was the norm in the institution, and that treatment language and jargon could be used to manipulate correctional officials into shortening their sentences. In short, the researchers concluded that the young offenders learned to be "con artists" who did not benefit from the institutionalization, but merely adapted to it. Many officials who deal with delinquency contend that the state training schools are a costly failure (costing anywhere from $20,000 to $45,000 per youth per year) where young law violators are warehoused and hardened into a "lifetime of lawlessness and…become permanent and costly liabilities of society" (Ryan, 1980:21).

The third category of juvenile institutions revolves around the **group home** concept. By 1975, it was estimated that there were some 195 public and 851 private facilities of this type in the United States (Carey and McAnany, 1984:293). These facilities can include halfway houses, drug and alcohol rehabilitation homes, and various types of youth shelters. Juveniles can be placed there either by the courts or parents who feel that a change in home environment will be beneficial for the juvenile. **Group homes** *usually resemble a dormitory type of living facility with juveniles being supervised during parts of the day and at* *night, while being allowed limited participation in the larger community either to attend school or work at part-time jobs.* Box 15-2 examines the controversy over institutionalization versus community treatment in group homes.

One of the forerunners of this type of juvenile institution was the so-called Provo Experiment begun in 1956 in Provo, Utah (Empey and Rabow, 1961). This program involved a group home type of setting and allowed a limited number of juveniles to live together under staff supervision while working and attending school in the larger community. The program was considered highly successful and has been copied in other parts of the country. Other community-based treatment programs for juveniles have been developed as an alter-

---

BOX 15-2 Controversial Issue

Institutionalization Versus Community Treatment

In recent decades, fear of crime and harsher attitudes toward youthful law violators have resulted in over 4,000 juveniles being convicted in adult criminal courts and incarcerated in state prisons. Serious and chronic offenders who are not remanded to adult criminal courts are increasingly being placed in juvenile institutions which approximate prison conditions. These facilities are plagued by fights, stabbings, intimidation, rape, gangs, and other forms of violence.

In 1972, in a bold and controversial move, Massachusetts closed all of its state training schools for juveniles and sought alternatives to incarceration for its delinquents. A popular alternative was group homes located in the community. Numerous other states followed the lead of Massachusetts, either closing all of their juvenile institutions, or significantly reducing their populations by choosing community treatment alternatives for delinquent youths. A popular alternative is placement in a group home located in the community. California, for example, has one of the largest networks of group homes in the nation. Whether group homes are more effective in the treatment and prevention of delinquency than the more traditional and punitive method of incarceration is hotly debated.

While the problems of youths in training schools and prisons have been widely discussed, the alternative of community treatment is not without its problems. For one thing, neighborhood residents often oppose group homes on the basis that they create safety risks and decrease property values. Further, when group homes are established, they often suffer from high turnover in staff, and poor monitoring of the homes and the juveniles. Some counties find that they become the dumping grounds for out-of-county delinquents from larger urban areas that do not have adequate facilities to house their own clients.

Juvenile judges, police officers, youth workers, social workers, and politicians often find themselves in a dilemma over how to handle the rising numbers of juvenile offenders. Adult prisons are overcrowded, and even many ardent "get tough" advocates are reluctant to place youths in them. On the other hand, with little community support and few resources for community treatment, the alternatives sometimes are reduced to "lock'em up," or "turn 'em loose"—neither of which provides a satisfactory solution to the problem. Exacerbating the problem is the lack of systematic evaluation of both institutionalization and community treatment programs to determine their effectiveness (*Law Enforcement News,* 1997).

Sources

"Do you get what you pay for?: With CJ efforts, not necessarily." *Law Enforcement News* 23 (May 15) 1997:1; 18.

"Kids' prisons that don't reform," *The Christian Science Monitor,* September 29, 1988:B2–B8.

Schillinger, Kurt, and Sullivan, C. "Treating kids in the community works in theory, but not always in practice." *The Christian Science Monitor,* September 29, 1988:B2–B8.

native to incarceration. They are discussed in the next chapter, which deals with various treatment strategies and prevention efforts for juvenile delinquency.

There also are a number of privately operated juvenile institutions across the United States. Initially, as many state facilities became overcrowded, and state revenues declined, it was believed that private institutions offered superior alternatives to those of the states. David Schicor and Clemens Bartollas (1990) found, however, that many private juvenile facilities suffered from some of the same problems as state-run institutions. Complicating the problems further, they noted, was that the desire to make profits in the private sector sometimes leads to a higher resident-to-staff ratio, and inadequate professional services. Schicor and Bartollas (1990) summarized that there should be a nationwide effort to evaluate private facilities, a thorough examination of their fiscal policies, and a mechanism for supervision and control of private facilities to see that they at least meet minimum state standards.

Juvenile Aftercare

Another method of formal social control is aftercare. Essentially, aftercare for juveniles is the equivalent of parole for adults. In fact, in some states, the term "juvenile parole" is still used. **Aftercare** refers to *release of a juvenile who has been incarcerated in some type of institutional setting under the supervision of an officer of the court for a prescribed period of time.* In most states the officer of the court involved is a juvenile probation/parole officer who also may have been actively involved in the initial intake process for the youth (see Chapter 14). Upon release, the juvenile meets with an aftercare supervisor and agrees to a specific set of restrictions. These conditions may vary according to various classification schemes used to determine the "risk level" of the youth, but regardless of classification, are usually similar to those of probation (Maupin, 1993). They usually include requirements such as school attendance, curfew, notification of whereabouts, and often a list of specific individuals with whom the juvenile is forbidden to associate. Violation of any of the terms may result in the juvenile being returned to some type of custodial facility. Pragmatically, juvenile aftercare and probation are virtually identical, with the distinction being that probation is used *instead of* incarceration, while parole or aftercare is used *after* incarceration. Both are forms of conditional release under the supervision of an officer of the court.

In an effort to make juvenile aftercare more effective, the Office of Juvenile Justice and Delinquency Prevention launched an Intensive Aftercare Program (IAP) based on four factors: (1) Prerelease and preparatory planning during incarceration; (2) Structured transition that requires participation of aftercare staff; (3) long-term reintegrative activities; and (4) working with offenders and targeted support systems (e.g., family, schools, and community agencies) (Altschuler and Armstrong, 1996). Today, there is more interest than ever in effectively reintegrating juvenile offenders back into the community under supervised release and intensive aftercare (Altschuler, et al., 1999).

Unfortunately, one of the problems with this form of social control is that the large numbers of juveniles on probation and parole at any one time create extremely high caseloads for the court officers. Consequently, it is often difficult for probation and aftercare officers to meet regularly with all their charges, and some juveniles may be able to violate some of the conditions for their release without it coming to the attention of their supervisors. As a mechanism of formal social control, when supervised release becomes unsupervised, its effectiveness is significantly reduced.

Remanding Juveniles to Adult Courts

Increased rates of violence committed by young offenders, frustration with the juvenile justice system, and an increasing public sentiment that we must "get tough" on crime and criminals have led to a popular movement to certify juveniles who commit serious violent crimes as adults and to remand them to adult criminal courts for trial. A national survey conducted by the National Center for Juvenile Justice indicated that 16 percent of all state prosecutors' offices had established written guidelines for certifying juveniles as adults, and two-thirds of the offices reported transferring at least one juvenile case to criminal court during the year (DeFrances and Strom, 1997).

In 1997, the U.S. House of Representatives gave its stamp of approval to the process of certifying serious violent juvenile offenders over the age of 15 as adults by offering $1.5 billion in incentive grants to state juvenile justice systems that incorporated such a provision in their juvenile codes (Reibstein, 1997). Under the house bill, adult trials for juveniles as young as 14 would be routine for violent federal crimes. Many states already have statutes that call for automatically certifying violent offenders over a certain age (usually 15 or 16) as adults, and as we mentioned in Chapter 14, in those states a *reverse certification* hearing must be held to retain jurisdiction over the case in juvenile court. In those states where automatic adult certification does not occur, there is some debate over whether juvenile judges should make the decision to certify juveniles as adults and remand them to adult criminal court, or whether that discretion should reside with the district attorney's office, since he or she is an elected official and is charged with prosecuting violent crimes (AP, Phoenix, 1996).

Interestingly, the movement to remand juveniles to adult courts is motivated by the "get tough" approach in the hopes that they will receive longer and harsher sentences, but research reveals that while the sentences may be longer than those that can typically be meted out by juvenile courts, actual time spent in custodial facilities by youths sentenced in adult courts usually does not exceed what they would have received from a juvenile court (Fritsch et al., 1996).

In New York State, Judge Michael Corriero routinely handles about 160 cases per year involving 13-, 14-, and 15-year-olds charged with armed robberies, aggravated assaults, rapes, and murders. Although he can issue up to life sentences for crimes such as murder, Corriero tries to be "firm, but fair," and he sends almost 60 percent of the young offenders who appear before him for counseling. If they stay out of trouble and are not rearrested within a year, he sentences them to five years' probation (Reibstein, 1997).

Although Corriero's approach may not satisfy the "get tough" advocates, it may reflect a sensible approach to the growing problem of violent juvenile crime. While research on the effects of trying juveniles as adults is sparse, a systematic study was conducted on over 2,700 juveniles who were remanded to adult criminal courts in Florida compared with a matched sample of delinquents who were retained in the juvenile courts. This study found that by every measure and definition of recidivism employed, reoffending rates were greater among those who were transferred to adult courts than those who were retained in the juvenile system (Bishop et al., 1996).

If more juveniles are being certified as adults and remanded to stand trial in adult criminal courts, it follows that more young offenders are also being sentenced to adult jails and prisons. This phenomenon is placing even greater burdens on already crowded local jails and state prison systems whose success in handling adult corrections is questionable.

Juveniles in Adult Jails and Prisons

Between 1990 and 1998 the nation's jail population went over half a million (See Table 15-1). During that same period, the number of juveniles held in adult jails increased almost 400 percent from 2,301 to 8,090. Despite the fact that Congress passed a law in 1980 calling for the removal of all juveniles from adult jails, various state statutes and judicial practices allow juveniles to be incarcerated in adult jails. Slightly over 1,500 juveniles who had been adjudicated delinquent were held in adult jails in 1998. That number represented only the tip of the iceberg, however as an additional 6,500 plus juveniles were housed in adult jails in 1998 because they had been certified as adults and were either awaiting criminal trials in adult courts, or had been sentenced there by adult criminal court judges (Gilliard and Beck, 1999).

TABLE 15-1   Average Daily Population and Number of Men, Women, and Juveniles in Local Jails, Midyear 1990–98

	1990	1991	1992	1993	1994	1995	1996	1997	1998
Average daily population[a]	408,075	422,609	441,889	466,155	479,757	509,828	515,432	556,586	593,808
Number of inmates, midyear[b]	405,320	426,479	444,584	459,804	486,474	507,044	518,492	567,079	592,462
Adults	403,019	424,129	441,780	455,500	479,800	499,300	510,400	557,974	584,372
Male	365,821	384,628	401,106	411,500	431,300	448,000	454,700	498,678	520,581
Female	37,198	39,501	40,674	44,100	48,500	51,300	55,700	59,296	63,791
Juveniles[c]	2,301	2,350	2,804	4,300	6,700	7,800	8,100	9,105	8,090
Held as adults[d]	—	—	—	3,300	5,100	5,900	5,700	7,007	6,542
Held as juveniles	2,301	2,350	2,804	1,000	1,600	1,800	2,400	2,098	1,548

Source: Gilliard, D. K. "Prison and Jail Inmates at Mid-year 1998." *Bureau of Justice Statistics Bulletin.* Washington, DC: U.S. Department of Justice, March 1999:6.

Notes: Data are for June 30 in 1992–95 and 1998; for June 29, 1990; and for June 28 in 1991 and 1996.
Detailed data for 1993–96 were estimated and rounded to the nearest 100. Previously published numbers for 1994 and 1995 have been revised to include only inmates held in jail facilities.

—Not available.

[a]The average daily population is the sum of the number of inmates in a jail each day for a year, divided by the total number of days in a year.

[b]Inmate counts for 1990–93 include an unknown number of persons who were under jail supervision but not confined. Detailed counts for 1994–96 were estimated based on the number of inmates held in jail facilities.

[c]Juveniles are persons defined by State statute as being under a certain age, usually 18, and subject initially to juvenile court authority even if tried as adults in criminal court. In 1994 the definition was changed to include all persons under age 18.

[d]Includes juveniles who were tried or awaiting trial as adults.

In addition to the number of juveniles being held in local jails as adults, states are now sending more violent offenders under the age of 18 to minimum, medium, and maximum security adult prisons. Problems associated with placing young offenders in adult jails and prisons have been well documented (e.g., McGee, 1971; Flaherty, 1990; Soler, 1998), and all too frequently incidents of assaults, forcible rapes, and murders occur when juveniles are housed in adult facilities with older inmates. For example, national attention was focused on the problem of jailing juveniles when an Idaho teenager who was put in jail for $60 worth of traffic violations was tortured and murdered in his jail cell by five cellmates (AP, Boise, 1982). This incident is not unique, and as states are increasingly certifying juveniles as adults, district attorneys, judges, and correctional officials must grapple with the reality that sentencing youths to adult prisons can be tantamount to ordering their execution. On the other hand, some states have demonstrated a willingness to order the execution of juveniles for capital offenses.

Capital Punishment for Juveniles

The ultimate form of social control is capital punishment. The execution of criminal offenders is one of the most controversial elements of the American criminal justice system, and that controversy is compounded when it involves the execution of juveniles or of adults who committed their capital offenses while still under the age of majority (see Box 15-3).

The United States has executed a total of 281 juveniles, and contemporary opponents point out that "America may be alone in the world in executing its young" (Seligson, 1986:5). The first sufficiently documented juvenile execution occurred in Roxbury, Massachusetts, in 1642 when 16-year-old Thomas Graunger was executed for committing bestiality (Streib, 1987:55).

In 1972, the U.S. Supreme Court ruled in the case of *Furman* v. *Georgia* that capital punishment was discriminatory and constituted "cruel and unusual punishment," which is prohibited by the Eighth Amendment to the Constitution. The Court ordered its discontinuance and inmates on death row awaiting execution had their sentences commuted to life imprisonment. However, in 1976, the Supreme Court ruled that three states (Florida, Texas, and Georgia) had rewritten their capital punishment statutes in such a way as to conform to the Constitution. Several states wrote new capital punishment statutes in compliance with the Supreme Court's guidelines, and in some states, these new statutes included the right to execute juveniles who committed capital offenses. In fact, among the 36 states which reenacted the death penalty, nine set no minimum age for execution (Arizona, Delaware, Florida, Maryland, Oklahoma, South Carolina, South Dakota, Washington, and Wyoming) (Seligson, 1986:5). Twenty-seven states enacted capital punishment statutes that specified a minimum age at the time the crime was committed, and several of those set the minimum age below the age of majority. Since that time additional states have added execution to their arsenal of punishments and eight states specify no minimum age. Table 15-2 shows states with capital punishment laws and the minimum ages specified for execution.

The constitutionality of executing juveniles has been legally challenged, but the Supreme Court has never clearly resolved the issue. The Supreme Court finally agreed to decide the issue of constitutionality in the 1982 case of *Eddings* v. *Oklahoma.* However, in a

---

BOX 15-3 Controversial Issue

Should Juveniles Be Executed?

The issue of capital punishment has sparked long and hot debate and has been the focus of several U.S. Supreme Court decisions. Debates over execution become even more heated when it involves juveniles. In modern times, the United States stands alone among major industrialized nations in its willingness to execute minors. Amnesty International reports that since 1979, only eight juveniles have been executed worldwide with public sanction–three of them in the United States. The others included one each in Barbados, Bangladesh, and Rwanda, and two in Pakistan.

Advocates of the death penalty for juveniles basically use the same arguments that support capital punishment for adults. These include accountability for one's actions, retribution, and deterrence. Execution is generally reserved for those convicted of premeditated murder, and in the main, those who support capital punishment for juveniles contend that if youths are old enough to kill, they are old enough to be executed.

Opponents argue that executing juveniles is inhumane and barbaric, and contend it makes little sense to enact adult sanctions for crimes committed by adolescents who lack the maturity and judgment (and thus, the full legal responsibility) of adults. These arguments are punctuated by studies which show that youths on death row suffer from various neurological disorders, learning disabilities, psychotic disorders, and subnormal IQs.

One of the most outspoken critics of juvenile executions is Dr. Victor L. Streib, a law professor at Cleveland State University. Streib contends that juveniles lack the adult maturity and sophistication to form criminal intent comparable to that of adults. Further, he notes that retribution and deterrence could be better served by the imposition of long-term incarceration. Adolescents tend to feel immortal and because they do not fully comprehend the permanence of death, show very little fear of it (as witnessed by many life-threatening risk-taking activities actively pursued by youths). On the other hand, lack of freedom generally is regarded as the most severe penalty imaginable by teenagers. Streib also argues that while adult repeat offenders may be beyond rehabilitation, there is evidence that large-scale changes in behavior patterns are possible as people move from adolescence into young adulthood, and later, middle age.

Finally, perhaps the most cogent argument against executing juveniles relates to the message it sends to youths. The crimes for which most juveniles are executed involve the youths struggling with what seems to be an insurmountable or unsolvable problem. In their frustration and confusion, the immediate, albeit illogical, solution seems to be to kill somebody. It is ironic that this scenario seems to fit the reaction of the government to serious juvenile crime. With mounting youth violence, overcrowded jails, reformatories, and prisons, and no immediate solution to serious juvenile crime in sight, the ultimate solution seems to be to kill somebody.

Sources

Streib, Victor L. *Death penalty for juveniles,* Bloomington: Indiana University Press, 1987.

Streib, Victor L. "Imposing the death penalty on children," pp. 145–159 in *Juvenile delinquency: A justice perspective* (2nd ed.). Edited by Ralph A. Weisheit and Robert G. Culbertson, 1990.

Weisman, Mary-Lou. "Should we execute kids who kill?" *Woman's Day,* May 30, 1989:90–91, 123, 130–131.

---

5 to 4 vote, the court once again avoided deciding the constitutionality issue and simply sent the case back for resentencing, urging the lower court to consider age as a mitigating factor (Streib, 1987). As of this writing, the Supreme Court has failed to rule on the constitutionality of the death penalty for juveniles.

TABLE 15-2   Minimum Age Authorized for Capital Punishment

Age 16 or less	Age 17	Age 18	None specified
Alabama (16)	Georgia	California	Arizona
Arkansas (14)[a]	New Hampshire	Colorado	Idaho
Delaware (16)	North Carolina[b]	Connecticut[c]	Louisiana
Florida (16)	Texas	Federal system	Montana
Indiana (16)		Illinois	Pennsylvania
Kentucky (16)		Kansas	South Carolina
Mississippi (16)[d]		Maryland	South Dakota[e]
Missouri (16)		Nebraska	Utah
Nevada (16)		New Jersey	
Oklahoma (16)		New Mexico	
Virginia (14)[f]		New York	
Wyoming (16)		Ohio	
		Oregon	
		Tennessee	
		Washington	

Source: Snell, T. L. 1998. Capital Punishment 1997. *Bureau of Justice Statistics Bulletin* (December) 1998:5. Washington, DC: U.S. Dept. of Justice.

Note: Reporting by States reflects interpretations by State attorney general offices and may differ from previously reported ages.

[a]See Arkansas Code Ann.9-27-318(b)(1)(Repl. 1991).

[b]The age required is 17 unless the murderer was incarcerated for murder when a subsequent murder occurred; then the age may be 14.

[c]See the Conn. Gen. Stat. 53a-46a(g)(1).

[d]The minimum age defined by statute is 13, but the effective age is 16 based on interpretation of a U.S. Supreme Court decision by the State attorney general's office.

[e]Juveniles may be tranferred to adult court. Age can be a mitigating factor.

[f]The minimum age for transfer to adult court is 14 by statute, but the effective age for a capital sentence is 16 based on interpretation of a U.S. Supreme Court decision by the State attorney general's office.

Repeated public opinion polls between 1933 and 1977 indicated that between one-half to three-fourths of Americans surveyed supported capital punishment (Allen and Simonsen, 1981:249). A 1986 Gallup poll indicated that 70 percent favored the death penalty (Seligson, 1986:5). Those public opinion polls did not survey Americans' attitudes toward the execution of juveniles, however. In late 1986, *Parade,* in an article on capital punishment for juveniles, conducted such a poll. It found that nearly 80 percent of the respondents believed that there should be capital punishment in general, but of those who supported capital punishment, 46 percent said they believed there should be a minimum age for the death penalty (*Parade,* 1987:10). Interestingly, however, of those who indicated that a minimum age should be set for execution, only 11 percent said that the minimum age should be 21 and 23 percent said it should be 18. The rest indicated acceptable minimum ages below the age of majority in most states (*Parade,* 1987:10). Almost 55 percent indicated that there should be no minimum age for the death penalty (*Parade,* 1987:10). While this reader poll did not involve carefully and scientifically selected sampling procedures, it nevertheless reflected a sentiment among many Americans that the state should execute juveniles who have committed particularly heinous offenses.

At least two other more scientific polls on the execution of juvenile offenders have been taken. In 1936, 61 percent of the respondents favored the death penalty in general, and 46 percent approved of it for criminals under the age of 21 (Streib, 1987:33). In 1965, public sentiment toward the death penalty had shifted, and only 45 percent favored capital punishment in general with only 23 percent viewing it as acceptable for offenders under 21 years of age (Streib, 1987:33). Later research showed that despite increasingly favorable attitudes toward the death penalty (76 percent in favor), the support dropped dramatically when respondents were given other punishments or rehabilitation programs as alternative choices (Sandys and McGarrell, 1995).

It should be noted that while all of those currently on death row awaiting execution for crimes committed as juveniles were convicted of homicide, capital punishment has not been reserved only for youths who were hardened killers. The most common offense in juvenile capital punishment cases has been homicide, but juveniles also have been executed for the crimes of arson, assault and battery, attempted rape, bestiality, and robbery (Streib, 1987:62). As Streib (1987:71) noted:

> [his data]...refute the commonly held belief that the penalty has always been reserved for our most hardened criminals, the middle-aged three-time losers. While they are often the ones executed, offenders of more tender years, down even to prepubescence, also have been killed lawfully, hanging from our gallows, restrained in our gas chambers, sitting in our electric chairs, and lying on our hospital gurneys.

Indeed, two juveniles as young as 10 years old have been legally executed in the United States (Streib, 1987:57).

The sentencing of a juvenile to die poses a particularly disturbing question to American citizens. Wayne Thompson, one of the juveniles who was awaiting execution on Oklahoma's death row, focused attention upon the marginality of adolescence, and the dilemma faced by the criminal justice system, when he pointed out that at the time of his offense (and conviction and death sentence) he was only 15 years old, considered too young to be able to legally drive an automobile, and "even now, at 19, if I went to buy a beer, they wouldn't sell it to me" (Seligson, 1986:5). In 1989, Thompson's death sentence was overturned on the basis of mitigating circumstances, but once again the U.S. Supreme Court failed to rule on the constitutionality of the death penalty for crimes committed by juveniles.

Despite "get tough" attitudes toward crime and youthful offenders, many states and local communities have devised some innovative correctional programs for wayward juveniles. The aims of many of these programs include deinstitutionalization, community corrections, and diversion from the juvenile justice system.

Deinstitutionalization, Community Corrections, and Diversion

The juvenile court was founded upon the philosophy of protection and rehabilitation, and its foremost goal has been preventing juvenile offenders from becoming adult criminals. Despite widespread criticism, research indicates that there still is much public support for juvenile rehabilitation efforts (Moon, et al., 2000). Consequently, over the years, juvenile corrections has experienced a noticeable trend toward deinstitutionalization, community corrections, and the diversion of youths from the formal juvenile justice system.

Deinstitutionalization simply means *avoiding the placement of juveniles in correctional institutions.* The Juvenile justice and Delinquency Prevention Act of 1974 called for the development of a series of deinstitutionalization programs for status offenders (Rojek, 1982). Many of the community-based prevention programs discussed earlier in this chapter represented efforts to deinstitutionalize delinquents and return them to their communities for their correctional experience. Deinstitutionalization is most likely to be pursued for nonserious juvenile offenders.

Jerome Stumphauzer (1986:5) summarized the need for deinstitutionalization of juveniles by evaluating the imprisonment of youths in the following manner:

> *A worse social learning program could not be designed: remove the youth from the very society to which he must learn to adapt, expose him to hundreds of criminal peer models and to criminal behaviors he hasn't learned (yet), and use punishment as the only learning principle to change behavior!*

As an alternative to institutionalization and traditional institutional methods, Stumphauzer (1986:9–11) suggested using social teaming techniques as follows:

1. Institutional Programming. If institutionalized, use token economies, positive rewards for conforming behavior, humane approaches to negatively sanction nonconforming behavior, and positive role modeling along with positive reinforcement.

2. Behavioral Family Contracting. Teaching and positively reinforcing nondelinquent behavior in the family setting.

3. Social Skills Training. Teaching the skills of problem solving and relating to authority figures.

4. Probation Contracting. Written agreements between juvenile probation officers and juveniles on probation regarding acceptable and unacceptable behaviors and the attendant rewards and punishments for each.

5. School Programming. Using social learning techniques in the school to emphasize rewards for nondelinquent behavior, rather than focusing all attention on punishing rule-violating behavior.

6. Clinical Behavior Therapy. Training youths in techniques of self-control, anger control, and dealing with stress.

7. Employment Skills Training. Providing youths with necessary job skills, and the skills necessary for finding, applying for, and interviewing for employment.

8. Group Treatment Homes. Group homes using "teaching parents" as models, doing chores with emphasis upon positive reinforcement.

9. Community Change and Prevention. Instead of waiting for delinquency to occur and then making arrests, using positive reinforcement and social learning techniques in parks, recreation centers, housing projects, and so on, to acknowledge, reward, and encourage conforming behavior.

William Sheridan (1967) estimated that approximately 30 percent of all inmates in juvenile correctional institutions were there for committing **status offenses**—*acts that would* *not have been illegal if they had been committed by adults* (such as truancy and running away). He contended that placing these offenders in institutions pinned the "delinquent label" upon them and exposed them to the influence of more sophisticated delinquent peers, increasing the likelihood that they would continue their delinquency upon release. Richard Rettig (1980) argued that juvenile detention facilities were overpopulated with youths who did not belong in institutions. He contended that institutionalization has a place in juvenile corrections, and could provide a positive experience, if it is reserved for those youths who really need to be confined (those who pose a serious threat to the community).

Along with the philosophical arguments for deinstitutionalization, one of its strongest justifications has come from the lower costs. The annual cost of housing one juvenile in a public facility ranges from $25,000 to $47,300 (Allen-Hagen, 1991). Paul Lerman (1968) pointed out that both private and public treatment centers experience high rates of failure, and suggested that it might be better to take some of the institutional allowances for food, clothing, supervisory personnel, and other expenses and allocate them to families of delinquents to be used to help the juveniles in their own homes. High costs and high failure rates have led to the closing of juvenile institutions in some states. Massachusetts, for example, closed all of its state training schools in 1972, and it and other states that followed the example have sought a variety of alternatives to incarceration.

Paul George and Patrick Mooney (1986) pointed out that the Miami Boys Club Delinquency Prevention Program serves approximately 120 hard-core male delinquents for approximately one-third the cost of the state training schools. A 1986 study by the California Youth Authority (reported on CNN Headline News, October 6, 1986) indicated that nearly one-half of the youths incarcerated in California's juvenile institutions were there because of property offenses. The average cost of housing a juvenile in California for 1 year was estimated at $25,000. Members of the California Youth Authority indicated that they believed that many youths are institutionalized who should not be, in response to a resurgent "get tough" attitude toward crime. Ira Schwartz (1984) acknowledged that attitude and pointed out that despite some gains toward more humane and less expensive programs, most states still lack sound programs like those suggested in the Juvenile Justice and Delinquency Prevention Act of 1971.

House Arrest

House Arrest, *a program where youths are confined to their homes and closely supervised by their parents with routine unannounced visits or phone calls from a probation officer,* has become a popular alternative. Specific house arrest programs vary, but most require the youths to attend school, observe a strict curfew, notify their parents (and sometimes the probation officer) of their whereabouts at all times, abstain from drugs and alcohol, and avoid places or companions that might encourage them to get into trouble (Ball et al., 1990). Some of these programs require that the youths wear electronic bracelets, necklaces, or anklets that can be monitored 24 hours a day, and sound an alarm if the detainee strays too far from a certain location or fails to report in at a certain time. The Wayne County Juvenile Court in Detroit developed and evaluated three in-home intensive supervision programs as alternatives to juvenile institutional commitment. When evaluated, the in-home programs were as effective as commitment, but cost only about one-third as much. Both self-reported and official recidivism rates indicated virtually no difference two years later for those committed and those going through the in-home programs (Barton and Butts, 1990). Other research also suggests that, although not a panacea, intensive supervision of juveniles (even those who committed felonies) is an effective alternative to incarceration (Wiebush, 1993; Greenwood and Rand, 1993).

Diversion refers to *an attempt to divert, or channel out, youthful offenders from the juvenile justice system.* Like deinstitutionalization, diversion primarily is intended for status and nonserious property offenders. Richard Lundman (1993) argues that diversion should be the standard response for juveniles who have committed status offenses and non-violent crimes. There is some disagreement over the term "diversion." Dean Rojek (1982:316) pointed out that to some it means "simply the process of turning offenders away from the traditional juvenile justice system," while for others, it "connotes not only a turning away but also a referral to a community alternative." As a result, diversion and deinstitutionalization often are interrelated in community efforts to deal with less serious juvenile offenders.

Youth Service Bureaus

The President's Commission on Law Enforcement and Administration of Justice (1967) suggested the creation of Youth Service Bureaus to work with juvenile offenders in local communities. These bureaus primarily were designed to work with nonserious juvenile offenders, but, depending upon the particular community, provide a wide range of service to youthful law violators. The establishment of Youth Service Bureaus launched the move toward diverting youths, especially status offenders and other nonserious delinquents, from the juvenile court (Sherwood, 1972).

With the money and support provided by federal and state governments during the 1960s and 1970s for social programs aimed toward reducing poverty, crime, delinquency, and other social problems, Youth Service Bureaus gained widespread acceptance. Bureaus were established in virtually every community of any size, and programs were developed to aid juveniles in matters related to family, school, and the law. Although the 1980s brought severe cuts to numerous social agencies and programs, Youth Service Bureaus continue to exist in many communities, working closely with law enforcement, juvenile courts, schools, and other social agencies.

One of the criticisms leveled at the Youth Service Bureaus, and at similar diversionary programs, is that while well-intended, they may involve youths in the juvenile justice system who have committed very minor noncriminal offenses, which might be less problematic if ignored. Frederick Howlett (1973) criticized the Youth Service Bureau as being another manifestation of the "child-saving movement." He suggested that rather than involving such minor offenders in the Youth Service Bureau, communities should redefine their concept of deviance, especially in regard to the types of behaviors they will and will not tolerate on the part of juveniles. We explore this issue in much more detail in Chapter 17, Rethinking the Delinquency Problem.

Scared Straight!

Diversion can take many directions. One of the best known diversionary programs is the *Scared Straight!* program begun by inmates serving life sentences at Rahway State Prison in New Jersey. Roughly based on Deterrence Theory, utilizing the concepts behind shock probation and shock incarceration, this program briefly exposes juveniles to some of the harsh realities of life in a maximum security prison. Small groups of juvenile offenders are taken to Rahway to spend a day inside the institution. The youths are shown the brutal side of prison life, highlighted by a session during which inmates serving life sentences for crimes such as murder, rape, multiple assaults, and other violent offenses, shout at and harass the juveniles through racial epithets, threats, and innuendos about homosexual rape. While there is no actual physical contact between inmates and the youths, the threat of physical violence is ever-present. The program gained national attention when actor Peter Falk hosted an award-winning television documentary on the subject. The program boasted impressive statistics regarding its success rate (90 to 95 percent) in deterring participants from involvement in later delinquency.

John Heeren and David Schicor (1984) analyzed the program and suggested that the documentary was perhaps more successful than the actual program. John Finckenauer (1982) concurred, and seriously questioned the alleged success rate of the *Scared Straight!* program. He conducted a study on youths who had completed the program at Rahway and compared them to a control group of teenagers who had committed similar offenses but who did not participate in the program. His findings indicated that the control group actually fared better in the first 6 months following their initial offenses (in terms of not committing subsequent offenses) than did the group who were exposed to *Scared Straight!* Finckenauer (1982:4) concluded that the *Scared Straight!* program, much like other delinquency prevention programs, is illustrative of what he calls the "panacea phenomenon"—the "…continuing search for a cure-all." This attempt to remedy a very complex social problem by means of a simplistic solution is not new, and as Finckenauer (1982:4) summarized, "The highway of delinquency prevention history is paved with punctured panaceas." Lundman (1993) agreed, and he called for the permanent abandonment of all efforts to "scare" juveniles out of delinquency, contending that these programs lead to *more* not *less* delinquency.

Nevertheless, the documentary appealed to public perception that crime was increasing at an alarming rate, but here was an innovative program that was playing a small part in alleviating it. Following the documentary, several states began steps to implement similar programs. While the Rahway program may not have been the "cure-all" hoped for by many, and its success rate was not the 90 to 95 percent claimed, to many people it seemed like a valid attempt to turn delinquent teenagers' lives around; and after all, perhaps doing something—anything—was better than doing nothing.

In 1992, Norwegian prison officials decided to copy the *Scared Straight!* program at Ullersmo with the expressed goal "to scare youngsters off a path of crime" (Finckenauer and Gavin, 1999:147). Two years later, an Oslo television station aired a controversial documentary very similar to the television program that had been so popular in the United States. The Norwegian public responded far differently, however, than had the American viewers. The Norwegian public was outraged by the barbarism of the program and newspapers criticized it with comparisons to medieval torture, the Nazi regime, and even the Gestapo. Meanwhile, Norwegian criminologists pointed out that the program was ethically questionable, violated traditional Norwegian values, and had little or no deterrent effects on the youths submitted to it. An evaluation of the Ullersmo project discovered that although the youths who participated in it indicated that they were scared by the inmates while inside the prison, almost all of them said that it had no impact on their behavior once they left. Perhaps the most discouraging of the evaluators' findings were that several of the girls who participated in the program became infatuated with one or more of the prisoners and some of the boys came away viewing the inmates as heroes or positive role models (Finckenauer and Gavin, 1999). Norwegian officials terminated the project shortly thereafter.

Despite empirical evidence that the *Scared Straight!* program has little or no deterrence effect on American youths who participate in it, it continues to appeal to the American public and the media who seem frustrated that nothing else seems to work, and, as critics note, because it appeals so strongly to the "myth of deterrence by aversion" (Finckenauer and Gavin, 1999:217).

S.H.A.P.E.U.P.

Inmates serving life sentences at the Colorado State Penitentiary learned of the highly publicized and critically acclaimed *Scared Straight!* program developed at Rahway, and decided to create a similar, but distinctively different, program for at-risk juveniles in Colorado. Their program is designed to bring delinquents to a maximum security prison in order to **S**how **H**ow **A** **P**rison **E**xperience **U**ndermines **P**eople (S.H.A.P.E.U.P.). Unlike the *Scared Straight!* program, inmates involved in S.H.A.P.E.U.P. neither use abusive language nor shout threats at the juveniles who participate in the program. Rather than trying to scare the youths, their goal is to educate them to the realities of prison life. Over the course of a day, the juveniles are given a thorough tour of the maximum security facility including the orientation area, isolation cells, death row, and the ominous gas chamber. Inmates serving life terms candidly and calmly discuss a typical day in prison focusing on the boredom, monotony, deprivation, dehumanization, and violence in vivid but nonsensational terms. A deputy warden shows the youths contraband, including the deadly weapons, that have been taken from inmates during routine searches along with photos of young inmates who have been murdered or committed suicide within the prison walls. At the end of the day an inmate serving life encourages the youths to think about what they saw and whether they want such an institutionalized existence to be part of their futures.

A week later the juveniles return to the prison with their parents. Both the youths and their parents tour the prison, and then meet as a group with the inmates discussing life in prison. The youths are asked to recall all of the fun and meaningful things they have done during the past week—where they went, people they saw, school events, parties, etc., and then are reminded that the inmates have spent 24 hours a day each day of that same week in the prison, doing the same things with the same people.

S.H.A.P.E.U.P. seems to have tremendous impact on the youths who participate in it, and unlike *Scared Straight!,* involves the parents in the process. Also, the follow-up visit apparently reinforces the stark realities presented in the initial prison tour. While it is sometimes difficult to track youths who have participated in the program, data indicate that their recidivism rates are much lower than those who have committed similar offenses but not participated in the program. Moreover, inmates who participate in the program seem to benefit from the program as well, turning idle prison time into a meaningful experience for them and the young people they meet.

PLACE

A less dramatic diversion program developed at Syracuse University in 1984 is called PLACE. First-time offenders between the ages of 12 and 15 attend eight 90-minute classroom sessions in which they are involved in role-playing, mock trials, and discussions on the juvenile justice system and causes of delinquency. They talk to recent victims of property offenses. In one of the sessions they are booked, fingerprinted, and placed in a cell. A study conducted on more than 100 youths who had participated in the program during its first 2 years reported that only 11 percent of the participants had been rearrested (Horn, 1986:72).

VisionQuest

VisionQuest is a Tucson-based private program designed to rehabilitate "hard-core juvenile delinquents through positive experiences and physical challenges in the wilderness" (Gavzer, 1986:8). VisionQuest maintains wilderness camps in Arizona, Pennsylvania, and Florida. The program utilizes a practice involving a *rite of passage* similar to that used by the Crow and Cheyenne Indians. Juveniles in the program are expected to complete three "quests" which include working with wild horses and stubborn mules, a 6-month wagon train experience, and an 8-week program of training wild mustangs. The program is structured to teach the juveniles a strong sense of responsibility and a pragmatic understanding of the need to abide by social norms. After completing their quests, the youths experience a ritual ceremony signifying their accomplishments and marking their entrance into adulthood. One researcher who studied the program indicated that the youths were not merely "…playing cowboys and Indians…," but were "…struggling to cope with real and difficult circumstances without the protection or cocoon of traditional institutional programs" (Gavzer, 1986:10). In addition to the wilderness experiences, the program includes daily schoolwork, the earning of a weekly allowance, counseling sessions, and immediate accountability to adult supervisors for behavior. Approximately 15 states send juvenile offenders to VisionQuest at a cost estimated to be approximately half that of traditional institutionalization. The program is considered to be relatively successful. According to one study, of the approximately 3,000 boys and girls who have gone through VisionQuest, only about one-third return to juvenile institutions (Gavzer, 1986:10).

Juvenile Boot Camps

Juvenile boot camps simultaneously reflect the deinstitutionalization and "get tough" movements in juvenile corrections while also implementing elements of shock incarceration and probation. These programs usually involve relatively short stays (usually 30 to 90 days, but sometimes up to 6 months) in a military-style boot camp. Juveniles usually wear uniforms, sleep in tents or barracks, and rise early in the morning to run, do calisthenics, and perform a variety of military drills and hard labor chores. Drill-sergeant-like supervisors bark orders at the young offenders as they try to shock them into realizing the consequences of their delinquency while instilling discipline in them so that they will refrain from repeating their offenses.

While these boot camps capture a great deal of media attention and satisfy the public's need to "get tough" on young offenders, and for the short-term require youths to be accountable for their actions, their long-term effectiveness is doubtful (Mackenzie and Souryal, 1991; Page, 1999). Arizona, one of the first states to implement boot camps, scrapped the program after seven years, deciding that the $1.5 million per year program was a dismal failure. Data indicated that only 22.6 percent of those admitted to Arizona's boot

New "boot camp" arrivals at the Sumter County Correctional Institution in Florida receive "instructions" from the staff.

camps successfully completed the program and that the recidivism rate was no better than for those who had been placed on probation, placed in traditional institutions, or sent to jail. Arizona's Director of the State Department of Corrections concluded that while the boot camps were great for public relations and were politically popular, they were not good public policy. As one critic of the program concluded, "Officials found out that you don't correct problems by…getting in their faces and calling them scum…marching and making [delinquents] eat bad food isn't going to help a kid with a drug problem" (Schwartz, 1996:49A). Interestingly, as Arizona was scrapping its juvenile boot camps, several other states announced plans to copy it.

Other Diversion Programs

A variety of other diversionary programs have been developed and implemented throughout the United States. Washington, DC, for example, established Project Crossroads as a community-based vocational training program designed to divert young offenders from the juvenile justice system by training them for jobs and assisting them with job placement. A similar program was developed in Baltimore, while St. Louis and Sacramento focused their diversion efforts on home detention and family counseling (Roberts, 1989).

Despite differences in specific aspects of diversionary programs, they all share some common goals. Most important for these programs is to divert juveniles from official adjudication procedures in an effort to avoid the stigma associated with being labeled a juvenile delinquent. Moreover, these programs are designed to ease the caseloads of overcrowded juvenile courts and overworked correctional officials so that their efforts can be focused on more serious chronic juvenile offenders.

Evaluation of Deinstitutionalization, Community Corrections, and Diversion

Several studies have been conducted in an attempt to evaluate various deinstitutional, community, and diversionary programs across the country, and have resulted in mixed findings. Mark Pogrebin and his associates (1984) reported moderate success in the Colorado diversionary programs they evaluated, as did Robert Regoli et al. (1985), although they pointed out that using recidivism rates is not always a valid measure of success. William Selke (1982), on the other hand, assessed the Youth Services Bureau in Michigan as being generally unsuccessful, and generally suffering from insufficient staffing.

Elizabeth Wilderman (1984) evaluated Colorado's diversionary program as reducing recidivism somewhat; but on the negative side, pointed out that it negatively labeled some juveniles simply on the basis of participation in it, whose offenses were so minor that they would have been better handled if ignored. This same theme has tended to dominate the critical assessments of many juvenile diversionary programs. For example, Bruce Bullington and his associates (1978) argued that the interest in diversion and community corrections is faddish and that one of the major problems of these programs is that while they were developed to divert juveniles from the juvenile justice system, they involve juveniles in correctional programs who previously would have been ignored by the formal system. Hence, rather than bringing *fewer* youths into the system, diversion actually brings in *more* (Frazier and Lee, 1992). Rojek (1982:321) registered the same criticism when he pointed out:

> *In theory, diversion is perceived to be a process of deflecting offenders away from the traditional juvenile justice system. However, there is strong evidence that this deflection may result in another form of encapsulation.*

Even the argument of reduced costs has come under scrutiny. Rojek (1982:318–320), for example, indicated that while diversion and community corrections were being touted as more humane and cost efficient, their tendency to "widen the net" and identify more juveniles as delinquent represents a substantial investment of resources toward controlling "questionable acts of deviance." Anne Mahoney (1981) also pointed to the "net-widening" aspects of deinstitutionalization, community corrections, and diversion and raised concerns about increased costs to the families of delinquents who were brought into treatment programs. In a position paper, the National Advisory Committee for Juvenile Justice and Delinquency Prevention (1984) expressed similar concern when it noted that the wording of the Juvenile Justice Act of 1974 has caused federal money to be diverted to handling non-criminal acts of delinquency. The committee recommended that a new federal policy be developed focusing on serious juvenile delinquency. Charles Logan and Sharla Rausch (1985) concluded that efforts at diversion and deinstitutionalization are pointless unless they are accompanied by a movement toward decriminalization of status offenses.

Finally, constitutional, legal, and ethical issues have been raised regarding community corrections and diversionary programs. Bullington and associates (1978) argued against the widespread development of diversionary programs because they viewed them as violating the civil liberties that were assured by the Gault decision. They viewed the biggest problem of diversion as involving disposition without adjudication. Bortner et al. (1985) found that there was differential treatment of blacks by the courts, with black females being more likely to be institutionalized for status offenses, while whites were more likely to be diverted and deinstitutionalized. And, Karen Lucken (1997) warned that as private agencies become more involved in community correctional programs that much of the discretion in the handling of juveniles is being turned over to businesspeople seeking to make a profit as opposed to juvenile justice personnel whose primary concern is supposed to be the youth in trouble.

SUMMARY

In this chapter we have pointed out that every society attempts to encourage conformity to its norms and to control deviant behavior. The three general categories of social control involve *voluntary, informal,* and *formal* mechanisms. Voluntary social control relies upon successful socialization and the internalization of social norms and values. An individual's self-concept, personality, and overall socialization experience help determine the extent to which he/she will voluntarily refrain from committing delinquency. The development of a *social bond* or positive attachment to society seems to create a stronger likelihood of conformity among juveniles.

If a juvenile's internal voluntary control is not strong enough to prohibit law violation, a variety of informal social control mechanisms can be implemented by society. Gossip, ridicule, humor, ostracism, and peer pressure all can help control a juvenile's behavior. The nature of the offense as well as the type of society or community in which the juvenile resides help influence the type of informal social control that may be utilized and its probable effectiveness.

The third type of societal defense against delinquency is formal social control. The schools, police, courts, and various social agencies all play an important role in implementing formal social control measures against juveniles. Formal techniques of social control, such as juvenile probation, incarceration in juvenile institutions, and various community programs are utilized in an attempt to prevent and control delinquency. In serious cases, juveniles may be remanded to adult courts and sent to adult jails or prisons. Capital punishment exists as the ultimate form of social control for juveniles who have committed such heinous crimes that society has deemed execution to be the most appropriate social sanction.

All forms of social control are aimed at the goal of *deterrence* in the hopes of reducing juvenile delinquency by applying negative sanctions to youths who violate society's norms. According to *Deterrence Theory,* if these sanctions are certain, swift, severe, and made known to others, they will not only reduce the likelihood that the specific individual who was punished will repeat his or her delinquency, but also will act as a general deterrent, discouraging others from committing delinquency.

Juvenile delinquency, like other forms of social deviance, is not likely to be eliminated. However, members of society must attempt to alleviate the problems associated with it by minimizing its negative consequences.

Concept Integration

Questions and Topics for Study and Discussion

1. Explain what is meant by the term "social control" and how this concept differs from the attempt to eliminate delinquency.
2. Explain what is meant by "voluntary social control." How is voluntary social control achieved? In what ways can voluntary control of delinquency be made more effective?
3. List and describe several techniques of informal social control that can be utilized against delinquency. In what type of community or society is informal social control likely to be most effective?
4. Give several examples of formal social control of juvenile delinquents. How do these methods differ from voluntary and informal techniques of social

control? In your opinion is formal control *more* or *less* effective than voluntary and informal social control? Why?

5. With the return of capital punishment, individuals in many states are housed on death row awaiting execution for crimes they committed while still legally defined as juveniles. In your opinion, should capital punishment be meted out to juvenile offenders? Why? Why not?

6. Identify some of the contemporary programs of deinstitutionalization, community corrections, and diversion. What are the strengths of these approaches to delinquency? What are some of their weaknesses?

References

Allen, H. E., and Simonsen, C. E. 1981. *Corrections in America: An introduction.* New York: Macmillan.

Allen-Hagen, B. 1991. *Public juvenile facilities: Children in custody 1989.* Washington, DC: *OJJDP Update on Statistics,* U.S. Department of Justice.

Altschuler, D. M., and Armstrong, T. L. 1996. Aftercare not afterthought: Testing the IAP Model. *Juvenile Justice* 3 (December):15–28.

Altschuler, D. M., Armstrong, T. L., and MacKenzie, D. L. 1999. Reintegration, supervised release, and intensive aftercare. *Juvenile Justice Bulletin.* Washington, DC: OJJDP, U.S. Department of Justice.

AP, Boise, 1982. Teen tortured, murdered in jail. *Emporia Gazette* June 2:1982.

AP, Phoenix. 1996. Symington seeks changes in juvenile law. *Dallas Morning News,* November 30:29A.

AP, San Antonio, 1999. Yard Signs Shame Vandals Straight. *Dallas Morning News,* September 28:17A.

Ball, R. A., Huff, R., and Lilly, J. R. 1990. House arrest and juvenile justice. Pp. 168–172 in R. A. Weisheit and R. G. Culbertson (Eds.), *Juvenile delinquency: A justice perspective.* Prospect Heights, IL: Waveland Press.

Barton, W. H., and Butts, J. A. 1990. Viable options: Intensive supervision for juvenile delinquents. *Crime & Delinquency* 36 (April):238–256.

Bazemore, G., and Day, S. E. 1996. Restoring the balance: Juvenile and community justice. *Juvenile Justice* 3 (December):3–5.

Bishop, D. M., Frazier, C. E., Lanza-Kaduce, L., and Winner, L. 1996. The transfer of juveniles to criminal court: Does it make a difference? *Crime & Delinquency* 42 (April):171–191.

BJS. 1997. *Fact sheet on children in custody.* Washington DC: Bureau of Justice Statistics, U.S. Dept. of Justice.

Bortner, M. A., Sunderland, M. L., and Winn, R. 1985. Race and the impact of juvenile deinstitutionalization. *Crime & Delinquency* 31 (January):35–46.

Bullington, B., Sprowls, J., Katkin, D., and Phillips, M. 1978. A critique of diversionary juvenile justice. *Crime & Delinquency* 7 (January):59–71.

Butts, J. A., and Snyder, H. N. 1992. Restitution and juvenile recidivism. Washington, DC: *OJJDP Update on Research,* U.S. Department of Justice.

Carey, J. T., and McAnany, P. D. 1984. *Introduction to juvenile delinquency: Youth and the law.* Englewood Cliffs, NJ: Prentice-Hall.

Chang, D. H. 1979. *Introduction to criminal justice: Theory and application.* Dubuque, IA: Kendall-Hunt.

Christian Science Monitor. 1988. Kid prisons that don't reform: Hope for rehabilitation outside prison walls. *The Christian Science Monitor,* September 29:B2–B8.

CNN Headline News. 1986. California youth authority study. *CNN Headline News,* October 6.

Culbertson, R. G., and Ellsworth, T. 1985. Treatment innovations in probation and parole. In L. F. Travis, III (ed.). *Probation, parole, and community corrections: A reader.* Prospect Heights, IL: Waveland Press, pp. 127–147.

DeFrances, C. J., and Strom, K. J. 1997. Juveniles prosecuted in state criminal courts: Selected findings. *Bureau of Justice Statistics Bulletin.* Washington, DC: Office of Juvenile Justice and Delinquency Prevention.

Eisikovits, Z., and Baizerman, M. 1982. "Doin' time": Violent youth in a juvenile facility and in an adult prison. *Journal of Offender Counseling, Services and Rehabilitation* 6 (Spring):5–20.

Empey, L. T., and Rabow, J. 1961. The Provo experiment in delinquency rehabilitation. *American Sociological Review* 26 (October):679–695.

Evans, R. C., and Koederitz, G. D. 1983. The requirement of restitution for juvenile offenders: An alternative disposition. *Journal of Offender Counseling, Services and Rehabilitation* 7 (Spring–Summer):1–20.

Farrell, R. A., and Swigert, V. L. 1982. *Deviance and social control*. Glenview, IL: Scott, Foresman.

Finckenauer, J. O. 1982. *Scared straight! and the panacea phenomenon*. Englewood Cliffs, NJ: Prentice-Hall.

Finckenauer, J. O., and Gavin, P. W. 1999. *Scared Straight: The panacea phenomenon revisited*. Prospect Heights, IL: Waveland Press.

Flaherty, M. G. 1990. An assessment of the national incidence of juvenile suicide in adult jails, lockups, and juvenile detention centers. Pp. 173–182 in R. A. Weisheit and R. G. Culbertson (Eds.). *Juvenile delinquency: A justice perspective*. (2nd ed.). Prospect Heights, IL: Waveland Press.

Frazier, C. E., and Lee, S. R. 1992. Reducing juvenile detention rates or expanding the official control nets: An evaluation of legislative reform effort. *Crime & Delinquency* 38 (April):204–218.

Fritsch, E. J., Caeti, T. J., and Hemmens, C. 1996. Spare the needle but not the punishment: The incarceration of waived youth in Texas prisons. *Crime & Delinquency* 42 (October):593–609.

Furman vs. Georgia 1972. 408 U.S. 238, 371, 1972.

Gavzer, B. 1986. Must kids be bad? *Parade* March 9:8, 10.

George, P., and Mooney, P. 1986. The Miami Boys Club delinquency prevention program. *Educational Leadership* 43 (Dec.–Jan.):76–78.

Gibbs, J. P. 1975. *Crime, punishment, and deterrence*. New York: Elsevier.

Gilliard, D. K., and Beck, A. J. 1999. Prison and jail inmates, Mid-year 1998. *Bureau of Justice Statistics Bulletin* (March). Washington, DC: U.S. Department of Justice.

Goffman, E. 1961. *Asylums*. Garden City, NY: Anchor Books.

Greenwood, P. W., and Rand, S. T. 1993. Evaluation of the Paint Creek Youth Center: A residential program for serious delinquents. *Criminology* 31 (May):263–279.

Hereen, J., and Schicor, D. 1984. Mass media and delinquency prevention: The case of "Scared Straight!" *Deviant Behavior* 5 (1–4):375–386.

Hirschi, T. 1969. *Causes of delinquency*. Berkeley: University of California Press.

Horn, J. C. 1986. A PLACE to go straight. *Psychology Today* 20 (July):72.

Housewright, E. 2000. Hard time for kids. *Dallas Morning News*, January 4:1A, 6A.

Howlett, F. W. 1973. Is the Youth Service Bureau all it's cracked up to be? *Crime & Delinquency* 91 (October):485–492.

Imlay, C. H., and Flasheen, C. R. 1971. See what condition your conditions are in. *Federal Probation* 35 (June):3–11.

Kurlychek, M., Torbet, P., and Bozynski, M. 1999. Focus on Accountability: Best practices for juvenile court and probation. *JAIBG Bulletin* (August):1–11.

Lerman, P. 1968. Evaluative studies of institutions for delinquents: Implications for research and social policy. Social Work 13 (July):55–64.

———1991. Counting youth in trouble in institutions: Bringing the United States up to date. *Crime & Delinquency* 37 (October):465–480.

Logan, C. H., and Rausch, S. P. 1985. Why deinstitutionalizing status offenders is pointless. *Crime & Delinquency* 31 (October):501–517.

Lucken, K. 1997. Privatizing discretion: "Rehabilitation" treatment in community corrections. *Crime & Delinquency* 43 (July):243–259.

Lundman, R. J. 1993. *Prevention and control of juvenile delinquency* (2nd ed). New York: Oxford University Press.

Mackenzie, D. L., and Souryal, C. C. 1991. Boot camp survey. *Corrections Today* (October):90–96.

Mahoney, A. R. 1981. Family participation for juvenile offenders in deinstitutionalization programs. *Journal of Social Issues* 37 (Summer):133–144.

Maupin, J. R. 1993. Risk classification systems and the provision of juvenile aftercare. *Crime & Delinquency* 39 (January):90–105.

McDowell, D., Loftin, C., and Wiersema, B. 2000. The impact of youth curfew laws on juvenile crime rates. *Crime & Delinquency* 46 (January):76–91.

McGee, R. A. 1971. Our sick jails. *Federal Probation* 35 (March):3–8.

Moon, M. M., Sundt, J. L., Cullen, F. T., and Wright, J. P. 2000. Is child saving dead? Public support for juvenile rehabilitation. *Crime & Delinquency* 46 (January):38–60.

National Advisory Committee. 1984. *Serious juvenile crime: A redirected federal effort*. National Advisory Committee for Juvenile Justice and Delinquency Prevention. Washington, DC: U.S. Government Printing Office (March).

Page, C. 1999. Juvenile boot camps don't live up to hype. *Dallas Morning News*, December 11, 33A.

Parade. 1987. Readers respond on capital punishment. *Parade* January 25:10.

Paternoster, R., and Piquero, A. 1995. Reconceptualizing deterrence: An empirical test of personal and vicarious experiences. *Journal of Research in Crime and Delinquency* 32 (August):251–286.

Pogrebin, M. R., Poole, E. D., and Regoli, R. M. 1984. Constructing and implementing a model juvenile diversion program. *Youth and Society* 15 (March): 305–324.

President's Commission on Law Enforcement and Administration of Justice. 1967. *The challenge of crime in a free society.* Washington, DC: U.S. Government Printing Office.

Reckless, W. 1961. A new theory of delinquency and crime. *Federal Probation* 25 (December):42–46.

Regoli, R. M., Wilderman, E., and Pogrebin, M. 1985. Using an alternative evaluation measure for assessing juvenile diversion programs. *Children and Youth Services Review* 7 (1):21–38.

Reibstein, L. 1997. Kids in the dock. *Newsweek,* May 26:70.

Remington, C. 1982. Restitution can work for serious offenders. *Change: A Juvenile Justice Quarterly* 5 (2):9–10.

Rettig, R. P. 1980. Considering the use and usefulness of juvenile detention: Operationalizing social theory. *Adolescence* 15 (Summer):443–459.

Roberts, A. R. 1989. Juvenile justice: *Policies, programs, and services.* Chicago: Dorsey Press.

Rojek, D. G. 1982. Juvenile diversion: A study of community cooptation. In D. G. Rojeck and G. F. Jensen (Eds.). *Readings in Juvenile Delinquency.* Lexington, MA: D.C. Heath, pp. 316–322.

Ryan, B. 1980. Should delinquents be locked up? *Parade* October 12:21, 23.

Sanders, W. B. 1981. *Juvenile delinquency: Causes, patterns, and reactions.* New York: Holt, Rinehart and Winston.

Sandys, M., and McGarrell, E. F. 1995. Attitudes toward capital punishment: Preference for the penalty or mere acceptance? *Journal of Research in Crime and Delinquency* 32 (May):191–213.

Sarri, R. 1974. *Under lock and key: Juveniles in jail and detention.* Ann Arbor: National Assessment of Juvenile Corrections, University of Michigan.

Schicor, D., and Bartollas, C. 1990. Private and public juvenile placements: Is there a difference? *Crime & Delinquency* 36 (April):286–299.

Schneider, A. L. 1990. *Deterrence and juvenile crime.* New York: Springer-Verlag.

Schwartz, D. 1996. Getting the boot: Arizona dropping camps for youth offenders. *Dallas Morning News,* August 11:47A;49A.

Schwartz, I. M. 1984. New moves in juvenile justice: Alternatives to getting tough are more humane and less expensive. *Public Welfare* 42 (Fall):28–31.

———1989. *(In)Justice for juveniles: Rethinking the best interests of the child.* Lexington, MA: Lexington Books.

Selke, W. L. 1982. Diversion and crime prevention: A time-series analysis. *Criminology* 20 (November):395–406.

Seligson, T. 1986. Are they too young to die? *Parade* October 19:4–7.

Sheridan, W. H. 1967. Juveniles who commit noncriminal acts: Why treat in a correctional system? *Federal Probation* 31 (March):26–30.

Sherraden, M. W., and Downs, S. W. 1984. Institutions and juvenile delinquency in historical perspective. *Children and Youth Services Review* 6 (3):155–172.

Sherwood, N. 1972. *The Youth Service Bureau: A key to delinquency prevention.* Paramus, NJ: National Council on Crime and Delinquency.

Soler, M. 1998. Prosecuting children as adults. *Dallas Morning News,* April 15: 1J.

Streib, V. L. 1987. *Death penalty for juveniles.* Bloomington: Indiana State University Press.

Stumphauzer, J. S. 1986. *Helping delinquents change: A treatment manual of social learning approaches.* New York: Haworth Press.

Tittle, C. R. 1974. Prisons and rehabilitation: The inevitability of disaster. *Social Problems* 21 (3):385–395.

Toennies, F. 1887. 1961. Gemeinschaft and gesellschaft. In T. Parsons et al. (3rd ed.). *Theories of Society* (Vol. I). Glencoe, IL: Free Press, pp. 19–201.

Vito, G. F. 1985. Probation as punishment: New directions and suggestions. In L. F. Travis, III (Ed.), *Probation, parole, and community corrections: A reader.* Prospect Heights, IL: Waveland Press, pp. 73–79.

Vito, G. F., Tewksbury, R., and Wilson, D. G. 1998. *The Juvenile Justice System: Concepts and Issues.* Prospect Heights, IL: Waveland Press.

Wiebush, R. G. 1993. Juvenile intensive supervision: The impact on felony offenders diverted from institutional placement. *Crime & Delinquency* 39 (January):68–89.

Wilderman, E. 1984. Juvenile diversion: From politics to policy. *New England Journal of Human Services* 4 (Summer):19–23.

PART

V

STRATEGIES FOR DEALING WITH JUVENILE DELINQUENCY

INTRODUCTION: Approaching Treatment and Prevention in a Social Context

CHAPTER 16 *Treatment and Prevention Strategies*

CHAPTER 17 *Rethinking the Delinquency Problem*

Introduction: Approaching Treatment and Prevention in a Social Context

In this book we are studying the social problem of juvenile delinquency from a sociological perspective. In this concluding section, we examine the social processes involved in attempting to reduce, treat, and prevent juvenile delinquency.

Sociologists seldom assume that any form of crime or juvenile delinquency can be totally eliminated. As indicated in Part I, norm violation occurs in every society, and, in fact, deviance can be both functional and dysfunctional in its consequences. Strategies for treating and preventing delinquency, therefore, must be developed, practiced, and evaluated in a social context.

Chapter 16 deals with specific treatment and prevention strategies for juvenile delinquency. The chapter begins with a discussion of the treatment **ideology**—*a set of ideas or beliefs on which some established practice is based*—and outlines some of the most prevalent treatment strategies used in dealing with juvenile delinquents. The prevention ideology is summarized and some of the more prominent delinquency prevention programs that have been used in this country are discussed.

Chapter 17 concludes the book with suggestions for rethinking the problem of juvenile delinquency. It reiterates the social nature of delinquency, and makes some specific recommendations for meaningful social change in the way that we view juvenile delinquency and its associated problems. Specific suggestions are made for reducing the marginal status of adolescence, decriminalizing status offenses, standardizing juvenile codes, revising the juvenile court, and modifying juvenile corrections. The chapter, and hence, the book conclude with a proposal for **redefining** juvenile delinquency.

We do not consider Part V or Chapter 17 as "the end." Rather, we hope that the information and discussion presented in these last two chapters stimulate your thinking and elicit your participation in the societal quest to better understand and control juvenile delinquency.

16

TREATMENT AND PREVENTION STRATEGIES

Reading Objectives

The reading of this chapter will help you achieve the following objectives:

1. Understand the treatment ideology in juvenile corrections.
2. Understand the prevention ideology in juvenile corrections.
3. Summarize some of the major juvenile treatment programs in the United States.
4. Summarize some of the major delinquency prevention programs in the United States.
5. Develop a sociological perspective on the treatment and prevention of juvenile delinquency.

Introduction

The previous chapter discussed social control as it involves societal intervention into an individual's life in an attempt to regulate social behavior. When a person's behavior is regarded as deviant, and the decision is made to formally or informally intervene, there are three overriding ideological approaches that society may take: *punishment, treatment,* and/ or *prevention.* Chapter 15 primarily focused upon the punishment ideology, illustrating how societal members inflict social reprimands ranging from gossip and ridicule to imprisonment and death upon those who have violated social norms. Chapter 15 ended, however, by discussing the movement toward deinstitutionalization, community corrections, and diversion, in efforts to keep juveniles out of the criminal justice system. Some of these programs attempted various strategies to prevent recurrences of delinquency and bring us to the subject of Chapter 16.

In this chapter, we focus on the treatment and prevention approaches to the social control of delinquency. From the outset, it should be noted that these three ideological approaches are not mutually exclusive. While proponents of one often view themselves as fundamentally at odds with the ideas of the others, there are marked similarities in the three approaches. All of them represent the attempts of society to regulate the behavior of its members. While these ideologies differ in their specific approaches to dealing with the problem of delinquency, more often than not, delinquency programs integrate aspects of all three (punishment, treatment, and prevention) to some extent.

The treatment and prevention ideologies are particularly compatible. While treatment programs are **reactive** in nature in that they are *implemented after a juvenile has been adjudicated delinquent,* they attempt not only to treat the juvenile delinquent, but also to prevent any future involvement in delinquent behavior. Prevention is a **proactive strategy,** based upon the assumption that if the underlying causes of delinquency can be identified and eliminated *before the delinquency occurs,* delinquent behavior can be prevented.

Treatment Ideology and Delinquency Treatment Programs

The **treatment ideology** *follows the rehabilitative philosophy of the juvenile court.* Treatment programs usually are based upon the assumption that delinquent behavior is a manifestation or symptom of some other deeper problem. The treatment ideology tends to apply the medical model approach to delinquency. Delinquency is viewed as analogous to disease, and treatment programs typically take on medical and clinical characteristics. Consequently, *symptoms* of delinquency are observed, in order to make a proper *diagnosis,* so that the appropriate *treatment* strategy can be pursued.

The treatment ideology takes an individualistic approach to delinquency, viewing delinquents as being socially and psychologically maladjusted or disturbed. Treatment programs attempt to readjust or remove what is disturbing the juvenile so that the youth can overcome the source of trouble, and go on to lead a normal life. Psychiatry and psychology often dominate many of the current treatment strategies in juvenile delinquency, and increasingly, the medical model analogy is being taken literally in some of these programs—especially those aimed at alcohol and drug abuse (see Box 16-1).

Treatment programs can be undertaken either in conjunction with or apart from an institutional setting. Thus, just as treatment philosophies are compatible with the prevention ideology, they need not be totally at odds with the concept of punishment. Many juvenile institutions, particularly state training schools and reformatories, often incorporate various treatment strategies into the process of rehabilitation. While utilizing confinement in an institution as a means of social control and punishment, various treatment strategies are often used to attempt to reform the juvenile and prevent any further delinquent or criminal activity. James Robison and Gerald Smith (1971) pointed out that what has often been viewed as the punishment versus treatment ideologies in corrections is not accurate, as these are not opposites. The two approaches are not mutually exclusive but can be used in conjunction with each other. Robison and Smith contended that it was more accurate to view the choice not as being between treatment or punishment, but between one type of treatment/punishment alternative and another.

A variety of strategies and techniques have been used in the treatment of juvenile delinquents. While it would be impossible (and pointless) to discuss them all, we will describe briefly some of the specific and representative types of treatment programs.

Behavior Modification

Behavior modification is based upon principles derived from research in experimental psychology, and is associated with the work of the prominent psychologist, B. F Skinner

BOX 16-1 Controversial Issue

Applying the Medical Model in the Treatment of Delinquency

One of the most alarming trends in juvenile delinquency over the past decade has been the increased use of alcohol and other drugs by teenagers. In the past, these problems were usually addressed by parents, school officials, social workers, youth agencies, and juvenile court officials. More recently, health-care professionals have become the primary providers of treatment and rehabilitation for youths with alcohol and drug abuse problems.

The health-care industry has become particularly skilled at promoting the medical model of alcohol, drug abuse, and related forms of delinquency, such as truancy, running away, and teen suicide. In sophisticated magazine, newspaper, and television advertisements, both private and public health-care facilities promise beleaguered parents that they can cure everything from failing grades to depression, but focus most heavily on their ability to treat and cure teenagers' alcohol and drug addictions.

By the mid-1980s, the treatment of drug abuse and alcoholism among U.S. teens had grown into a multi-million-dollar industry with virtually every major health care facility in the nation offering some type of treatment program aimed directly at teenagers. Most of these programs are expensive, with parents or insurance companies paying between $200 to $600 per day for treatment.

The major controversy over these alcohol and drug-abuse treatment programs centers on whether they work or not. There has been no systematic longitudinal research on the effectiveness of these programs, but preliminary studies suggest that they are no more effective than earlier less expensive methods. One independent study indicates that 80 percent of the adolescents who complete such programs return to drug or alcohol use within a year (Hollandsworth, 1990). And, another showed that while these programs often are successful during the short term, even with adequate aftercare, they do not seem to be effective over the long term (Sealock et al., 1997). Research indicates that many of these programs use simplistic and punitive behavior modification techniques that have been used for decades in juvenile state training schools. As one researcher put it, "Hospitals are rapidly becoming the new jails for middle-class and upper-middle-class kids" (Schwartz, 1989: 143). Critics charge that although drug and alcohol treatment programs occur in hospitals or hospital-like facilities and are supervised by doctors, very little medicine or science is actually involved. Most medical facilities are anxious to jump on the juvenile psychiatric treatment bandwagon, however, because drug and alcohol abuse programs help fill empty hospital beds, and with laws preventing the incarceration of juvenile status offenders, these programs offer alternatives for parents and juvenile court officials who do not know where else to turn.

From a sociological perspective, these programs fail to recognize the inadequacy of the medical model in explaining juvenile delinquency, even in the areas of alcohol and drug abuse, which indeed have physiological and biological consequences. There is general consensus among prominent researchers that drug and alcohol abuse among teenagers is better viewed as a result of problems in interpersonal and social relationships, and hence not likely to be successfully treated in a program based on the medical model.

Most importantly, medical treatments for socially oriented problems should not be used by parents or juvenile authorities merely as substitutes for harsher criminal sanctions.

Sources

Hollandsworth, Skip. "Can kids on drugs be saved?" *Texas Monthly* 18 (June), 1990:107–111, 153–162.

Schwartz, Ira M. "Being abused at better prices." Chapter 7 (pp. 131–148), in *(In) justice for juveniles: Rethinking the best interests of the child.* Lexington, MA: Lexington Books, 1989.

Sealock, M. D., Gottfredson, D. C., and Gallagher, C. A. 1997. *Journal of Research in Crime and Delinquency* 34 (May):210–236.

(1971). As the term implies, **behavior modification** is *a treatment technique which attempts to modify or change an individual's behavior.* Behavior modification operates on the principle that the consequences of an individual's actions play an important part in determining future actions. If an individual receives gratification, or *positive reinforcement,* from a particular act, the same or similar acts are likely to be repeated in the future. On the other hand, if an individual views the consequences of an act as undesirable, or experiences *negative reinforcement* from a particular behavior, that act or similar acts are unlikely to be repeated in the future.

Behavior modification is compatible with the social learning theories of delinquency and has been used in many juvenile correctional facilities. In a facility wherein the daily behavior of juveniles can be readily observed and evaluated, the principles of behavior modification have been used to reward approved actions, while punishing (or at least *not* rewarding) undesirable behavior. Different methods can be and have been used to provide the positive and negative reinforcement viewed as essential to behavior modification.

For example, juvenile institutions often operate on a "level system" or utilize a merit/demerit approach to encourage incarcerated youths to obey rules and demonstrate acceptable behavior. Typically, level classifications are developed with different behavioral expectations required to move from one level to the next. As juveniles earn merits, or otherwise meet the requirements to move up to the next higher level, they are rewarded with more privileges, and higher status within the institution. For example, an institution which establishes five levels may set five curfew or "lights out" times for the various levels. Those who are on the lowest level might have to be in their rooms with lights out by 9:00 p.m., while those on the next highest level would be allowed to stay up until 9:30; whereas those on the highest level might not be required to be in their rooms until 11:00 p.m. Other rewards and privileges, such as time away from the institution to attend a movie, increased visitation privileges, or increased recreation time, can be utilized to motivate the youths to improve their behavior, and perhaps earn their release, or at least make their stay in the facility more palatable. Conversely, failure to meet behavioral expectations would lead to demerits or being moved to a lower level classification, with the loss of certain privileges.

It is difficult to compare and evaluate the effectiveness of behavior modification in the treatment of delinquents, as different techniques of behavior modification are utilized in a wide range of environments. Elery Phillips and his associates (1971) found the token economy system to be effective in dealing with adolescents, and Robert Rutherford (1975) reported case studies in which the use of behavioral agreements between supervising adults and juveniles was effective in modifying behavior in the home, the school, the community, and the institution. Token economies are utilized in many institutional settings, and can effectively reinforce (either positively or negatively) behavior through the use of tokens, coins, chits (institutional coupons), or some other tangible object which has monetary value within the institution. Behavioral contracts can be utilized in virtually any setting in which those in authority clearly delineate the rules and the appropriate behaviors expected from the youths for receiving certain desired rewards (e.g., good grades, merits, money).

Some problems arise in the use of behavior modification with juveniles. One is that in order to be effective, almost constant monitoring and evaluation of behavior are required. If periods of time elapse when the juvenile's behavior goes unnoticed, unrewarded or unpunished, the principles of behavior modification are violated, and its effectiveness diminished. Another problem is that of determining appropriate positive and negative reinforcements for particular youths and specific behaviors. What is viewed as a reward by some may be viewed with ambivalence or even negatively by others. Thus, appropriate punishment for one youth may only encourage the undesired behavior on the part of another.

Another potential problem related to behavior modification resides in the use of punishment as negative reinforcement. While proponents of the treatment technique view it as humane, its implementation could take on cruel and inhumane proportions. For example, various forms of child abuse might be rationalized by the abusive parent as being appropriate punishment for undesirable behavior. Likewise, with available technology in drugs and equipment, the potential rewards and punishments for behavior are almost unlimited.

Finally, one of the problems with behavior modification involves the extent to which the desired behavioral changes continue once the environment is changed and the anticipated positive and negative reinforcements are not immediately forthcoming. The corrections literature is replete with examples of how the "ideal inmate" does not necessarily become the "ideal citizen" after release. It is difficult yet possible to constantly monitor a juvenile's behavior while institutionalized, but it is virtually impossible in the outside larger society. In society, seldom are all behaviors accompanied by a rigid structure that gives immediate rewards and punishments. Complicating the situation further is that in the larger social world, the juvenile has a variety of reference groups from which the potential rewards and punishments can come. As was discussed in Chapters 9 and 11, the family often must compete with the peer group in reinforcing the values and behavior of youths.

Transactional Analysis

Transactional Analysis is based upon the writings of Eric Berne (1961) and *focuses upon the interpretation of interaction between people.* According to Transactional Analysis Theory, as people interact with one another, their **verbal exchanges,** described as *transactions,* reflect different **ego states** identified as either *parent, child,* or *adult.* The parent state arises out of an individual's identification with parents and is manifested in interactions reflecting or modeling the paternal or maternal role, while the child state reflects an individual's clinging to a past state of dependency. The adult state reflects the fully developed independent and mature self.

In his best seller, *Games People Play,* Berne (1964) described how people shift from one ego state to another in the course of social interaction, primarily through conversation, in an attempt to manipulate others and gain the desired outcome from the interaction. The goal of the therapist is to identify which ego state is the source of the problem for the individual and identify ways in which that person may resolve the problem through moving to another ego state.

In another best seller on transactional analysis, *I'm OK, You're OK,* Thomas Harris (1969) described the potential attitudinal outcomes of interaction. In any social encounter, four potential situations or "life positions" exist:

1. ***I'm not OK, you're OK.*** *This life position reflects a situation typical of many children who, after continually being corrected by their parents and other adults, begin to believe that they are inherently wrong.*

2. ***I'm not OK, you're not OK.*** *Reflects a situation in which individuals still feel that their actions and ideas are wrong, but they also reject the ideas and actions of those who attempt to correct them.*
3. ***I'm OK, you're not OK.*** *Reflects a belief in one's self while rejecting the validity of others (a situation which may characterize the attitudes of many delinquents who feel that they have had adult values and norms imposed upon them and have been unjustly punished for their violation).*
4. ***I'm OK, you're OK.*** *Reflects the acceptance of one's own worth and validity while also accepting the validity of others (Harris, 1969:50–51).*

It is the achievement of the fourth life position which is the goal of the therapist for the client. A variety of counseling techniques, conversations, role playing, and other devices are used in an attempt to develop this attitude in the client.

Transactional Analysis gained a great deal of attention in the late 1960s and early 1970s, and as a result of the two previously mentioned best-selling books, became a part of the "pop psychology" which was widespread in the United States during that period. However, in at least one study of a California state training school, Transactional Analysis was judged to be effective in the treatment of juvenile delinquents (Jesness, 1975).

Reality Therapy

Reality Therapy primarily is associated with the work of William Glasser (1965), and is a *treatment strategy which focuses upon the individual understanding the consequences of one's actions and accepting responsibility for them.* Unlike most psychotherapeutic techniques which dwell upon a person's past in order to understand the causes of present behavioral problems, reality therapy focuses entirely upon the present. Glasser contended that concentrating upon individuals' past experiences was useless in effectively resolving present problems, and potentially could provide excuses and rationalizations which would exempt them from taking responsibility for their own actions.

As a technique for dealing with juvenile delinquents, reality therapy is much less concerned with *why* the juvenile committed the delinquent act, as with *what* can be done to ensure that the youth does not commit the same or similar acts in the future. In fact, why the act was committed is treated as irrelevant. Regardless of what problems the youth may have encountered in childhood—broken home, child abuse, inadequate socialization, poor environment, or other negative circumstances—the *reality* of the situation is that the youth has committed an act resulting in trouble with the law, and now must accept responsibility for that action. You may remember from Chapter 7 that Sykes and Matza (1957) contended that delinquent youths usually realize that they have violated society's norms, and experience a sense of guilt over having done so. However, they rationalize their actions through techniques of neutralization, one of which is *denial of responsibility.* Reality therapy directly attacks that neutralization technique, insisting that juveniles acknowledge that they are responsible for their behavior.

Reality therapy has been used widely with juveniles in both institutional and parole or probation settings. Glasser's research indicated that if the therapist develops an intimate relationship with the youth, gains the youth's trust, and genuinely cares about changing the individual's behavior, it can be very successful. Phillip Cole and Joseph Hafsten (1978) found that when reality therapy techniques were used during juvenile probation, they were effective in changing behavior. Interestingly, one of the elements of Cole and Hafsten's probation program included victim restitution. They believed that some form of restitution symbolically represented the juvenile's acknowledgment of responsibility for the offense. The Ventura Restitution Project specifically aims to make juvenile offenders understand the ramifications of their delinquent behavior by making it clear that they have direct responsibility for their actions (Remington, 1982). While it does not involve the intense individual approach that reality therapy demands, the project is based upon the primary assumptions of reality therapy—that individuals must accept responsibility for and the consequences of their actions.

Another program encompassing the reality therapy approach is "TOUGHLOVE." Described as a "self-help program for parents, youths, and communities," TOUGHLOVE literature points out that the program deals in *behavior, not in emotions.* The program is one of crisis intervention to provide support groups for those whose lives are directly affected by the negative effects of delinquency. Avoiding the assignment of blame, the program emphasizes the need for responsible action on the part of all to alleviate the problem.

Group and Individual Counseling

Many group and individual counseling techniques have been followed in treating juvenile delinquents, both inside and outside institutional settings. Transactional Analysis and Reality Therapy are but two examples of these counseling techniques. It would be impossible to delineate all of the counseling strategies that have been employed. Sometimes, even the simple process of intervening and playing the role of mediator to resolve conflicts between two or more youths can effectively avoid confrontations that could possibly escalate into serious problems or even violent crimes (OJJDP, 2000). Psychiatrists, psychologists, social workers, probation and parole officers, and virtually everybody else who has worked with delinquent youths have engaged in some aspect of individual and group counseling in an attempt to resolve the problems associated with delinquency.

An innovative program called "Discovery," developed in Massachusetts, matches juvenile delinquents with college students who serve as counselors, confidants, and positive role models for the youths. The college students, who have completed a set of prescribed courses in criminal justice, receive college credit for their participation. They meet with the delinquents one-on-one in two-hour sessions between four and ten times during a semester. They also hold group meetings with the delinquents and discuss school, hobbies, dating, relationships, crime, jobs, and other matters of mutual interest. A survey of participants showed that out of approximately 200 juveniles and 200 college students who have participated in the program, all of the college students and over 95 percent of the delinquents expressed satisfaction with it (Greenberg, 1990). The juveniles reported that they had been positively influenced by their college role models, and as a result of the program had begun to think more positively about their futures.

The common elements shared by almost all programs which utilize counseling as part of their treatment strategy is that they tend to view delinquency from an individualistic perspective. Even group counseling techniques operate on the premise that the group can help the individual overcome a particular situation, and resolve the problems which caused the delinquent behavior. With few exceptions, counseling techniques, whether conducted individually or in a group context, are dominated by the psychogenic approach to delinquency and tend to ignore the sociological context in which juvenile delinquency occurs.

Prevention Ideology and Delinquency Prevention Programs

The **prevention ideology** is *based upon the assumption that the best way to deal with the problem of juvenile delinquency is to intervene early and prevent it.* Thus, whether the cause of delinquency is viewed as social, psychological, or physiological/biological, the preventive strategy attempts to identify the causal factors, and to intervene and alter those factors before delinquent behavior occurs.

Delinquency prevention strategies have been dominated by the psychiatric perspective. Michael Hakeem (1957–58) pointed out that even some sociologists working in criminology and corrections have tended to adopt the psychiatric approach to delinquency, viewing the problem of delinquent behavior as being rooted in the individual psyche. That is not to say that sociology has not played a role in delinquency prevention. In a later section of this chapter we illustrate how the sociological perspective has been incorporated successfully into some delinquency treatment and prevention programs.

Many delinquency prevention programs, however, have viewed delinquency as abnormal, and, like the treatment strategies just discussed, have tended to perceive delinquency from the medical model analogy. Delinquency primarily was viewed as an individual anomaly, and as such, early diagnosis, identification, and intervention were considered important for effective prevention.

Early Identification

At the heart of the concept of delinquency prevention is the need to identify as early as possible the behaviors of children that are considered to be "warning signs" of impending delinquency. Prevention strategies assume that there are characteristics of "predelinquency" which, if caught soon enough, may be altered in time to prevent actual delinquency. In a pamphlet entitled "What Parents Should Know About Juvenile Delinquency and Juvenile Justice," Waln Brown (1983:12) provided a checklist for parents of what he considered to be a "partial list of delinquent acts and inappropriate childhood behaviors" for which parents should be on the alert, including behaviors ranging from being moody to actual law violations (see Table 16-1).

A longer and even more exhaustive list of "predelinquency" symptoms was developed by a delinquency prevention project sponsored by the U.S. Children's Bureau in St. Paul, Minnesota. That list comprised virtually all sorts of childhood behavior, including bashfulness, crying, daydreaming, nailbiting, silliness, thumbsucking, and bedwetting (cited in Hakeem, 1957–58). Hyperactivity has also been identified as a "predelinquency" symptom, and Dan Hurley (1985) indicated that early detection and intervention could significantly reduce the likelihood of "high-risk" children becoming criminals.

"Pre-Delinquents" and Early Intervention

The search for symptoms of "predelinquency" has underscored the psychiatric assumption that delinquency is a form of individual pathology that, like a disease, must be diagnosed early and treated before it consumes the person beyond hope of "cure." The important second phase in the prevention ideology is to intervene in the individual's life so as to alter a

TABLE 16-1   Partial List of Delinquent Acts and Inappropriate Childhood Behaviors

Alcohol use	Losses or gains of large sums of money
Bad temper	Lying
Cheating	Moody
Complaints by neighbors	Poor school grades
Cruelty to people or animals	Running away from home
Destructive	Regularly misses family meals
Discipline problems in school	Secretive
Discourteous	Sexual misconduct
Disobedient	Smoking
Drug use	Stays out late
Fighting	Stealing
Hanging out at places that have a bad reputation	Swearing
Inconsiderate	Threatens family members
Irresponsible	Truancy
Lack of friends	Verbally abusive
Law violations	

Source: Waln K. Brown, *What Parents Should Know About Juvenile Delinquency and Juvenile Justice,* The William Gladden Foundation, 1983. Reprinted by permission.

purported predisposition toward delinquency. This raises the question as to what type of intervention is most appropriate. No real consensus has arisen about this dilemma. Any and all of the treatment strategies discussed earlier in this chapter have been proposed and tried, along with numerous other methods to prevent the juvenile from continuing on a path toward delinquency.

In at least one type of situation—youthful arson—early identification and intervention apparently have been successful. Clifford Karchmer (1984) found five juvenile firesetter counseling programs, in San Francisco, Dallas, Los Angeles, Mesa (Arizona), and Prince Georges County (Maryland), in which firefighting personnel offered in-house counseling for young arsonists. A critical factor in the success of these programs apparently rests in the ability to diagnose potential juvenile firesetters as early as possible and begin intensive counseling as soon as possible.

Like the treatment strategies discussed earlier in this chapter, the prevention ideology and most prevention programs fail to put delinquency into its social context. Delinquency is viewed as an individual matter, and attempts to prevent it are primarily aimed at intervening into a person's life in order to alter future behavior. While morally uplifting, most of these preventive programs are sociologically bankrupt. As Alexander Liazos (1974) pointed out, virtually all programs based upon these assumptions have failed miserably.

Jackson Toby (1965) discussed the problems of early identification and intensive treatment of delinquency in regard to some of the problems related to accurate prediction, type of treatment, and its efficacy. He analyzed the Cambridge-Somerville Youth Study and the New York City Youth Board Prediction Study. One of the studies (Cambridge-Somerville) employed the *extrapolation technique* of delinquency prediction, in which youths who had exhibited antisocial behavior are identified and treated. The other (New York City Youth Board) followed the *circumstantial vulnerability approach,* which is based more heavily upon sociological research and identifies those youths whose family and neighborhood characteristics have been linked with delinquency. The problem, according to Toby, was that both studies overpredicted delinquency, and he pointed out that the stigmatization of being identified as predelinquent may exceed or at least offset any benefits that might be derived from treatment. He summarized, "Early identification and intensive treatment, though probably not as erroneous as the flat-world theory, is more a slogan or a rallying cry than a realistic assessment of the difficulties that delinquency control programs must overcome" (Toby, 1965:160).

BOX 16-2 Cross-Cultural Focus

Delinquency Prevention in Japan

In response to a major wave of juvenile delinquency following World War II, Japanese officials created two juvenile guidance centers to spearhead their delinquency-prevention efforts. By the mid-1980s, there were 660 juvenile guidance centers with approximately 70,000 citizens working as guidance volunteers in Japan. Most of these guidance centers operate under the auspices of the Child Welfare Law, but nine of them are managed by municipal police departments as part of the juvenile justice system. Located in a wide variety of communities, the primary purpose of these centers is to identify juveniles who commit minor violations and to intervene and supervise them in an effort to prevent them from becoming serious offenders.

Japanese culture places tremendous emphasis on the family, and it still is considered the most important social institution in preventing juvenile delinquency. These centers represent an organized effort for the community to supplement and reinforce family supervision of youngsters through the cooperation of citizen volunteers and the police. Many volunteers organize patrols looking for juveniles involved in smoking, loitering, curfew violations, shoplifting, and other relatively minor offenses. When detected, these youths are identified as "pre-delinquents" and their names are turned over to the police. Rather than being officially processed through the juvenile justice system, however, these youths are assigned to one of the centers for guidance and supervision.

Evaluations of the effectiveness of these guidance centers are mixed. Some argue that many youths caught in the early stages of delinquency may be diverted from lives of serious crime by this early identification and intervention. Others argue that identifying these youths as "pre-delinquents" and reporting their names to the police apply a negative label which may lead to a self-fulfilling prophecy and produce a "net-widening" effect, eventually bringing more youths into the juvenile justice system. In Japan, as in the United States, the impact of delinquency prevention efforts is difficult to assess, and society runs a risk of inadvertently increasing the very activity it is trying to prevent.

Source

Yokoyama, Minoru. "Net-widening of the juvenile justice system in Japan." *Criminal Justice Review* 14 (Spring), 1989:43–53.

Another problem that arises with delinquency prevention is the legal and moral issues that accompany intervention into a person's life *before* the commission of an illegal act. The U.S. judicial system and juvenile corrections are based upon intervening *after* a wrongful act has been committed and state intervention because of presumed future law violation is unconstitutional and illegal.

Sociological Approaches to Delinquency Treatment and Prevention

While most delinquency treatment and prevention programs traditionally have been dominated by the individualistic approach to delinquency, sociologists also have been concerned with delinquents and reducing the likelihood of their further involvement in delinquent behavior. More comprehensive programs are based on juvenile needs assessment that includes but is not limited to psychological problems, physical problems, sexual abuse, violence, family problems and deviance, educational deficits, and problems related to peer associations (Towberman, 1992). There have been numerous sociological contributions to delinquency treatment and prevention, and sociologists continue to search for new and innovative methods toward this end.

Rather than approaching the problem as being one of individual anomaly or pathology, the sociological approach takes into account the influence of society on the individual.

Studies show that involvement in sports or other recreational activities can help prevent juvenile delinquency. Here, older teenaged boys help organize and supervise teams and become role models for younger boys, thus providing positive activities for both age groups.

Consequently, sociologically oriented programs which have attempted to "treat" delinquents and prevent (or at least reduce) further delinquency have approached delinquency as socially created and defined, and influenced by the social and cultural environment. In this section we briefly examine some of the classic programs that have approached the handling of delinquents from a sociological perspective. Then, we briefly describe some of the more recent attempts to apply a sociological perspective to the problem of delinquency treatment and prevention.

The Chicago Area Project

One of the first and most notable attempts to apply sociological principles to the treatment and prevention of juvenile delinquency was the Chicago Area Project. The Project began in the 1930s, and was developed out of the theoretical framework of Shaw and McKay (see Chapter 6) and what later became known as the Chicago School of Thought regarding delinquency.

Shaw and McKay (1942) identified several Chicago neighborhoods in which crime and delinquency were extraordinarily high (as were other forms of social deviance). They contended that any program attempting to reduce delinquency in those areas would have to be developed in the communities themselves, utilizing human and institutional resources from within the neighborhoods, with only minimal guidance (and necessary funding) coming from external agencies (Shaw and McKay, 1942).

It was obvious that informal social control mechanisms were not working in the high delinquency neighborhoods in Chicago. Shaw and McKay believed, however, that some of those areas, such as the Russell Square neighborhood, known as "the Bush," had sufficient territorial and ethnic identity to effectively utilize local social institutions and some of the authority figures in the neighborhood to reduce and help prevent delinquency (Schlossman and Sedlak, 1983).

The Chicago Area Project was distinctively sociological in its approach. Rather than focusing upon individual delinquents, it focused upon the revitalization of meaningful social networks within the community. One of its first accomplishments was to establish organized recreational facilities for youths in the high delinquency areas. While recreation was not viewed as a resolution for delinquency, the formation of athletic teams and leagues required cooperative group efforts among juveniles and adults in the neighborhoods. In the Russell Square area, there were approximately 15 well-established gangs (Schlossman and Sedlak, 1983). Street workers were called upon to make contacts with the gangs, and help structure recreational activities in an effort to reduce involvement in delinquent activities. The workers were successful in organizing intramural basketball and baseball leagues and involving gang members in organized recreation. Soloman Kobrin (1959) assessed the general accomplishment of the Chicago Area Project as a success.

Shaw and McKay presented reports on official delinquency rates 10 years after the implementation of the Chicago Area Project that indicated substantial declines in official delinquency in the neighborhoods participating in the program. However, the success of the Chicago Area Project was not equal in all neighborhoods. As Steven Schlossman and Michael Sedlak (1983) pointed out, the key to success of the project was the involvement of indigenous leaders. Naturally, the same types of leaders and their abilities would not exist in all neighborhoods.

Kobrin's (1959) 25-year assessment of the Chicago Area Project was favorable. While delinquency was not totally eradicated in the targeted neighborhoods of Chicago, it was apparently substantially reduced. Schlossman and Sedlak (1983) also viewed the project as generally successful, especially the work in the Russell Square area. The Project, however, was not without criticism. Some residents of the community questioned whether workers in the project were too tolerant of delinquents. Because the street workers were willing to work with persistently and seriously delinquent youths, some critics charged that they were indirectly encouraging delinquency. Further, some of the private agencies in the area apparently resented the use of indigenous leaders and what they considered the rejection of their expertise (Schlossman and Sedlak, 1983). Nevertheless, the project stimulated the sociological imagination of scholars around the country, and other cities implemented similar programs in their own communities.

The Mid-City Project

The Mid-City Project was developed in Boston in the early 1950s. The project operated between 1954 and 1957 in lower class slum neighborhoods and focused on executing "action programs directed at three of the societal units seen to figure importantly in the genesis and perpetuation of delinquent behavior—the community, the family, and the gang" (Miller, 1962:168).

The Mid-City Project used street workers to establish close ties with juvenile gangs in Boston. They helped the gangs establish organized recreational activities, club meetings, dances, fundraising dinners, and other acceptable social activities. They also helped gang members with problems related to employment, school, and obtaining legal counsel.

Though based upon the same sociological assumptions which underlay the Chicago Area Project, the Mid-City Project differed in some important ways. For one thing, the Chicago Area Project was envisioned and implemented as a long-term program designed to rehabilitate the community from within. The Mid-City Project, on the other hand, was designed as a 3-year program with three distinctive phases, primarily developed and overseen from outside the community. Another important distinction was that the Mid-City Project relied heavily upon psychiatric counseling techniques. Phase Two (Phase One was the Contact and Relationship Establishment phase, and Phase Three was the Termination Phase) involved the use of behavior modification, individual psychotherapy, and regular psychiatric counseling (Miller, 1962). Thus, while sociologically inspired, like many other treatment and prevention strategies, the Mid-City Project was dominated by the psychogenic model.

Sociologist Walter B. Miller evaluated the Mid-City Project. His final assessment of the program was mixed. Miller (1962) viewed much of the work of the street workers with gangs as successful; however, when he posed the important evaluation question, "Was there a significant measurable inhibition of law-violating or morally disapproved behavior as a consequence of Project efforts?" his answer, with minor qualifications, was "No." The project was not deemed a total failure, however, as some improvement was measured in school performance of participants, and the project played an important part in establishing and strengthening social organizations and institutions within the community, whose efforts at delinquency reduction might not be readily measurable over the short term, but might have some long-term impact.

Mobilization for Youth

Mobilization for Youth was begun in the early 1960s on the Lower East Side of Manhattan, and represented an attempt to apply Richard Cloward and Lloyd Ohlin's (1961) Theory of Differential Opportunity structures in urban slum areas (see Chapter 6) to delinquency prevention in the community. The primary focus of the project was to organize the residents of the Lower East Side into social networks which would open channels of access to legitimate opportunities for achieving success in school, business, government, and other social institutions and agencies (Mobilization for Youth, 1961).

Unfortunately, the Mobilization for Youth project met with a great deal of resistance in the community, and fell far short of its ambitious expectations. Nevertheless, the project applied sociological theory directly to a social problem, and even in its failure, gave credence to the sociological perspective that the nature of the problem of delinquency goes beyond the individual juveniles who commit deviant acts, and that consequently, any meaningful program to control or reduce delinquency must also reach beyond those individuals.

Minnesota Youth Advocate Program

The Minnesota Youth Advocate Program was a school-based program begun in 1971 designed to help youths who had been in correctional institutions readjust to school and the community. The program had four specific objectives: increased school persistence, improved school performance, reduced recidivism, and reduced reinstitutionalization (Higgins, 1978). This program represented the sociological perspective in attempting to effectively reintegrate formerly institutionalized youths back into the social institutions and networks of the community. It required readjustment, not only on the part of the juvenile offender, but also on the part of the school, the family, and the community.

Paul Higgins (1978) evaluated the program on its effectiveness in achieving its four specific goals. When he compared participants in the program with a control group of juveniles who had been released from institutions but not exposed to the program, he found no significant differences between the two groups on any of the four objectives.

Neighborhood Youth Corps and Job Training

Neighborhood Youth Corps programs were developed during the 1960s and implemented in major cities throughout the United States. The thrust of the Neighborhood Youth Corps was to provide vocational training and better work opportunities for disadvantaged and delinquent youths. Like the Mobilization for Youth program, the Neighborhood Youth Corps sought to provide delinquent youths access to legitimate avenues of opportunity.

Gerald Robin (1969) studied the programs of the Neighborhood Youth Corps in Cincinnati and Detroit. He compared stratified random samples of participants in the programs with control group subjects who had applied to the program but had not been accepted. In both cities, Robin found that participation in the Neighborhood Youth Corps program was unrelated to delinquency prevention or reduction. He concluded that the assumption that providing better occupational opportunities for youths in order to reduce delinquency has more theoretical than practical value. B. Dalia Johnson and Richard Goldberg's (1982) evaluation of a Massachusetts vocational rehabilitation program came to much the same conclusion.

Over the past two decades, the Neighborhood Youth Corps has given way to a number of neighborhood centers and programs whose aims are to prevent and reduce delinquency. Project CRAFT (Community Restitution and Apprenticeship Focused Training) offers job training, paid apprenticeships, and job placement for youths in several states. Its goal is to not only provide employment skills and opportunities, but to also help develop important personal and social skills (Hamilton and McKinney, 1999). Research has shown that chronic exposure to poverty, drugs, and violence leads to hopelessness, despair, distrust—and delinquency. Thus, successful intervention strategies for neighborhood youth centers and job training programs should include: street outreach and referral; needs and interest assessments; supportive, personal relationships with adults; positive role models; peer group discussions; family interventions; neighborhood projects; education and job training; clear-cut program objectives; close attention to job placement; and long-term follow-up (Greene, 1993; Frey, 1999).

The Highfields Project

Not all sociologically oriented treatment and prevention programs involved such ambitious attempts at mobilizing and focusing community resources as the aforementioned programs. One of the classic small group treatment programs in a sociological framework was the Highfields Project begun in New Jersey in 1950.

The Highfields Project took boys who had been placed on probation by the court and assigned them to a facility where they lived, worked, and played in supervised small social groups. Viewing delinquency as a group phenomenon, the Highfields Project stressed guided group experiences, and the strengthening of conformity to social expectations of the group. The boys were allowed to go to town, attend movies, visit the drugstore soda fountain, go skating, and participate in other social activities, but they returned to the facility by a specified hour. The project was limited to 16- and 17-year-olds who were beyond the age of compulsory school attendance. The facility did not provide formal education, but stressed vocational development and focused upon providing work for the boys for which they were paid. The expectation was that after experiencing the short-term treatment program, the boys would be much less likely to participate in further delinquency upon their return to their communities.

H. Ashley Weeks (1958) evaluated the Highfields Project by comparing the success rate of boys who went through the program to that of boys who had committed similar offenses but who were sent to Annandale Farms, the New Jersey State Reformatory for males. Weeks addressed three basic research questions:

1. Did delinquents who participated in the program show lower recidivism rates than boys in other kinds of programs?
2. Did delinquents in the program change their attitudes, values, and beliefs about their families, the law, and their perspectives on life?
3. Did delinquents in the program change their basic personalities or the behavior through which they demonstrated their personalities?

These youths defined as "at risk" learn woodworking skills at a youth corps training center.

In answer to the first question, recidivism rates were lower for the Highfields participants, but not dramatically. The answer to the second and third questions was "No" (Weeks, 1958). Still, the project was viewed as having been effective with a large number of the boys.

The Provo Experiment

The Provo Experiment was begun in 1956 in Provo, Utah. It was based upon the Subcultural and Differential Association Theories of delinquency (see Chapters 6 and 7). The Provo Experiment insisted that delinquency is acquired from social groups and the only way to treat it is in a group context.

Habitual juvenile offenders between the ages of 15 and 17 were assigned to the Provo Experiment, which utilized the Pinehills Center for many of its activities. Boys lived at home, but participated in various group programs at the center during the day. The program was based upon the assumption that when boys are around other boys, peer pressure becomes the primary motivation for behavior. The Provo Experiment attempted to capitalize upon that peer influence by putting the boys into social situations in which pressure from within the group would lead to conformity to social norms. The experiment attempted to make conventional and delinquent alternatives clear to the participants; lead delinquents to question the value and utility of delinquent activities; and help conventional alternatives appear more positive to the boys (Empey and Rabow, 1961).

There was no specified length of stay in the program. Emphasis was placed upon developing good working habits and seeking to find meaningful employment for the boys in the community. Overall, Lamar Empey and Jerome Rabow (1961) viewed the Provo Experiment as successful. They suggested that changing the boys' attitudes and values toward work, while they experienced group encouragement and support for conformity to conventional norms, helped reintegrate them into the community in a way that was likely to reduce further involvement in delinquency.

While the Provo Experiment gained a great deal of attention in the sociological literature, the program was not widely adopted or followed in other areas. In many ways, the apparent success may have been related to the particular social circumstances of the Provo community. The strong Mormon emphasis upon conformity may have influenced the youths who participated in the program. In other words, juveniles raised in the Mormon tradition, although adjudicated delinquent, may have reacted differently and been more responsive to the programs offered in the experiment than would youths from the inner city slums of Detroit, Chicago, or other major cities.

The Millcreek Youth Correctional Facility

The Millcreek Youth Correctional Facility for serious offenders, located in Ogden, Utah, emphasizes social responsibility in its rehabilitation efforts. The maximum security facility houses approximately 60 of the most dangerous and violent juvenile offenders in Utah (NBC News, 1987). Although monitored by closed-circuit television, kept behind locked doors, and surrounded by a high fence, the youths are encouraged and rewarded for contributing to the social group and environment to which they belong. Group counseling, intense social interaction with positive role models (workers and counselors in the facility), and positive reinforcement seem to make dramatic changes in the youths' behavior after release. When Barry Krisberg studied the Millcreek program, he found that released youths had fewer arrests, and, if arrested, had committed less serious offenses (NBC News, 1987).

The Paint Creek Youth Center

The Paint Creek Youth Center in Bainbridge, Ohio, is an example of a cooperative effort funded by state, federal, and private sources that serves up to 34 males convicted of first or second-degree felonies. It focuses on developing occupational, independent living, and social skills while providing drug and alcohol counseling, and teaching problem-solving techniques, values clarification, victim awareness, anger management, personal hygiene, and human sexuality (OJJDP, 1988). A follow-up study on former residents of the Paint Creek facility showed disappointing results, however, with self-report delinquency data indicating virtually no difference between boys who had been through the program and those who had not (Greenwood and Rand, 1993). The famous Boys Town established by Father Edward Flanagan in Nebraska in 1917, however, reportedly still enjoys moderate success carrying out a similar agenda (Santoli, 1992).

Project New Pride

Project New Pride began in Denver, Colorado in 1973, and has since been copied across the United States. The project's goal is to reintegrate hard-core juvenile offenders between the ages of 14 and 17 back into the community so they can become productive family members, students, and workers. Each juvenile who participates in the year-long project is intensively involved in alternative schooling, counseling, and job training for a six-month period and then slowly reintegrated into the community over the following six months, during which they are expected to attend school and work at a job.

Project New Pride also offers counseling to the families of the juveniles who participate in the program. Like other community correctional programs, the success rate of Project New Pride is difficult to determine, but it is considered to be a cost-effective approach to juvenile corrections, usually costing approximately one-fifth the expense of housing a juvenile offender in an institution (Project New Pride, 1985).

Mentoring Programs

An innovative approach to delinquency prevention that has been around for quite some time, but increased in popularity during the 1990s, is mentoring. There are numerous mentoring programs across the United States. While they vary in their specific approaches, all share the common element of targeting "at risk" children—those from single-parent and low-income families, and providing them with positive adult role models (mentors). **Mentoring programs** typically *use adult volunteers who commit a certain amount of time each week (2–6 hours) to work one-on-one with a youngster to encourage academic, personal, social, athletic, and artistic development in an effort to prevent delinquency.* These programs are cost-effective, and have been shown to improve school attendance and performance, reduce antisocial behavior (e.g., smoking, alcohol, and drug abuse), and otherwise discourage and decrease involvement in delinquent activities (Grossman and Garry, 1997).

Big Brothers/Big Sisters is one of the oldest and best known mentoring programs and served as a model for the federal **JU**venile **M**entoring **P**rogram (JUMP) created in 1992 and administered by the Office of Juvenile Justice and Delinquency Prevention (OJJDP). Congress authorized $19 million to fund JUMP, and in 1994–95 OJJDP created 41 mentoring programs that in their first year served over 2,000 at-risk youths in 25 states. Volunteer mentors include police officers, firefighters, school teachers, senior citizens, and business people. A two-year evaluation of the program indicated that mentored youths were less likely than members of a matched control group to skip school, use drugs or alcohol, get in fights, or be involved in vandalism or other delinquent acts. Moreover, the mentored youths reported improved relationships with their parents and peers (Grossman and Garry, 1997).

Mentoring programs reflect cooperative efforts among juveniles, parents, and adult volunteers to help disadvantaged youths in an effort to prevent juvenile delinquency. Other programs reflect similar efforts and combine schools, churches, and other agencies in an effort to mobilize entire communities for delinquency prevention.

Other Programs

Numerous other delinquency prevention programs based upon sociological underpinnings have been developed throughout the United States and in some other countries (see Box 16-2). A delinquency prevention program in an economically depressed urban community was based upon elements from both biological and social environmental theories of delinquency (Bass and Mandell, 1982). This program attempted to unify existing social agencies into a cooperative network intended to strengthen social ties between juveniles and social institutions, and to encourage nondelinquent behavior.

A community-based program was developed in North Carolina to provide additional educational, vocational, and social opportunities for juveniles. A study by the Governor's Advocacy Council (1983) indicated general satisfaction with the program among juvenile justice officials, school officials, and program practitioners.

Bruce Berg (1984) described an interesting program for juveniles tried in an eastern correctional facility which followed social scientific theory in delinquency prevention. This program included the clinical sociological technique of **sociodrama,** *a method involving role playing, intergroup relations, and collective ideologies.* This program, run by inmates, was judged highly successful because of its flexibility, cost-effectiveness, and positive impact upon the participants.

David Farrington (1985) explored the issue of delinquency prevention in the 1980s, and concluded that attempting to change basic social institutions (such as family, schools, and church), along with focusing on individuals, is a worthwhile effort. Similarly, Thomas Gullotta and Gerald Adams (1982) indicated that delinquency prevention must integrate theory and practice. They cited education, competency promotion, community organization, and natural caregiving as being the four important tools in delinquency prevention. A project in Louisiana designed to facilitate reentry into the community by adjudicated delinquents incorporated many of those elements into its program (Behre et al., 1982). San Diego developed a system-wide strategy to reduce delinquency which involved cooperation among social services, criminal justice agencies, and other community organizations. It involved consistent, early intervention for even minor offenses with the implementation of graduated sanctions based on offense history and the nature of the offense. A two-year assessment of the program indicated that it was successful in reducing juvenile crime (Pennell et al., 1990).

Increasingly, the family is recognized as an important component in the treatment and prevention of delinquency. Brown (1983:13) provided a list of 21 family approaches to delinquency prevention. This list included some pragmatic strategies such as agreeing upon and following rules of conduct, spending more time together, and helping the child with homework. It also included some more abstract and subjective suggestions such as creating a more stable family environment, developing healthy family relationships, and parents setting a good example through their own behavior.

The emphasis on educational strategies for resocialization is present in numerous delinquency prevention programs. Farrington (1985) pointed to the school as potentially making meaningful contributions to the delinquency prevention effort. Murray Thomas and Paul Murray (1983) proposed that many children do not know enough about the law to make informed judgments about their behavior and the potential legal consequences of law violation. They proposed that schools should pursue strategies designed to better educate students about the law and its impact on their behavior, and get youths interested in the law before it gets interested in them. This is now being done in many schools across the country. For example, in one community, a 10-week course on Street Law is taught at night at the local high school by local attorneys (Horst, 1987). The course teaches criminal law and the consequences of its violation by youthful offenders. It was designed to reduce the number of juvenile complaints prosecuted in the juvenile court and to "influence youngsters to stay out of trouble with the law" (Horst, 1987:1).

While there is a lack of consensus as how best to attempt to prevent delinquency, a common trend in juvenile justice has been toward the deinstitutionalization of juveniles and diversion from the juvenile justice system. Consequently, communities and their various agencies are viewed as playing an important role in delinquency prevention.

Mobilizing the Community to Prevent Delinquency

Various forms of community involvement have arisen in recent years to combat delinquency and street crimes. Most forms of community involvement are encouraged as long as they stop short of **vigilantism**—*people taking the law into their own hands.* Law enforcement officials publicly tend to view vigilantism negatively while occasionally unofficially sanctioning it in its milder forms. The reaction of the general public is harder to assess, but at least in some cases, groups and individuals have been publicly applauded for their actions against alleged criminals and delinquents.

Crimestoppers and Hotlines

Another form of crime and delinquency prevention involves Crimestoppers, Crime Hotlines, and various other programs that encourage citizens to call a particular phone number through which they can provide anonymous tips about various crimes in the area. If the information leads to the arrest and/or conviction of persons involved in a particular crime, some type of monetary reward usually is offered. These programs have become extremely popular, and virtually every large community, and many small ones, sponsor such a program. Local newspapers and radio stations often participate in advertising the program and helping to fund the rewards, and local television stations often provide "reenacts" of crimes while urging viewers to call the "hotline" if they have any information relating to the crimes.

These programs are somewhat similar to the Neighborhood Watch programs discussed in the next section, except that they do not involve citizens becoming actively involved in crime prevention, or being involved in neighborhood patrols. Rather, the programs rely upon *private citizens informing upon one another.* Hence, we have coined the term **pseudovigilantism** to describe this phenomenon. Vigilantism involves citizens actively taking the law into their own hands because they feel the state to be unable or unwilling to enforce the law. Crimestoppers, on the other hand, involves private citizens aiding the state in its law enforcement efforts. This is also the intent of the Neighborhood Watch programs; hence they operate from the same philosophical stance. Yet, the Neighborhood Watch programs demand actual community involvement in the law enforcement process, and in some cases, some citizens become far too involved to suit the police. The "hotline" programs merely involve the sharing of information. A 1986 study of the success of the Crimestoppers and similar programs indicated that community participation in these types of programs is minimal. Two groups seem most likely to participate: the business community, and criminals themselves who may provide information about crimes committed by their associates (Rosenbaum et al., 1986:3). Nevertheless Rosenbaum et al. (1986) found that Crimestoppers was a very cost-effective method of social control in that the anonymous tips leading to the solution of previously unsolved crimes (usually property offenses) generally led to the recovery of goods which far exceeded the cost of the monetary awards for the information.

Neighborhood Watch and Youth Crime Watch

Neighborhood Watch programs have been developed in virtually every community. These programs are approved by the police and involve citizens joining together to reduce crime in their neighborhoods. These programs primarily are aimed at reducing burglary, vandalism, and other property offenses, many of which involve juvenile offenders. Representatives from the police department usually meet with interested members of the neighborhood and conduct a brief training session on how to reduce property crimes by better protecting their homes with various locks and alarms, and more importantly, how to be more observant. Residents are encouraged to watch each other's homes and to call the police if they notice any unusual or suspicious behavior in the neighborhood. Signs usually are posted in the neighborhood declaring that it participates in the watch program and that the police will be called. In some cases, however, local communities have formed neighborhood patrols armed with walkie-talkies, and occasionally guns, who sometimes attempt to apprehend suspected offenders and make citizens' arrests. In the latter case, a certain amount of neovigilantism is clearly involved.

Youth Crime Watch is a specialized version of Neighborhood Crime Watch that was organized when adults realized that youth volunteers often knew far more about what was going on in neighborhoods than did the adults. Youth Crime Watch focuses on good citizenship and involves far more than simply watching for criminal activities in neighborhoods. Youth Crime Watch programs receive funding from a national nonprofit organization to: provide drug and crime prevention education, establish youth patrols, create mentoring programs, provide conflict resolution training, establish community networks and partnerships, and send youths to the annual National Youth Crime Prevention Conference (Jones, 1999).

Guardian Angels

One of the better known examples of **neovigilantism**—private citizens taking on the role of law enforcers—in recent years is the Guardian Angels. Founded in New York City in 1979 by Curtis Sliwa, this group of young adults and teenagers operates as self-appointed organized patrols of the streets, alleys, and subways of many larger cities. What began as a group with just 13 members by 1982 had over 2,000 members in 41 cities (*Time,*1982:21). In 1987 the Guardian Angels claimed to have a membership of "over 5,000 in 67 American, Canadian, and Mexican cities," and today, the International Alliance of Guardian Angels has chapters in virtually every major city throughout the United States, Canada, Mexico, and the European continent. They have their own web-site and even have a special chapter known as "Cyber Angels" that promote safety over the Internet.

Outfitted in their distinctive red berets, the Angels go out on patrol to reduce many of the street crimes in which juveniles are likely to participate. Members of the Guardian Angels contend they are merely exercising their rights as private citizens and acting within the law as civilian extensions of the police force.

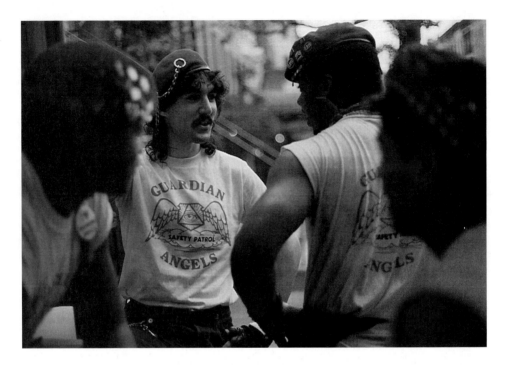

Although their efforts are not always met with enthusiasm by local police, members of the Guardian Angels patrol streets, sidewalks, and public transportation facilities in most large urban areas in an effort to discourage the sale and use of illegal drugs and related crimes.

Many law enforcement officials view the Guardian Angels in a different light, seeing them as vigilantes who hamper official law enforcement and could be potentially dangerous. When speaking on college campuses, the Sliwas vehemently deny that the Guardian Angels are vigilantes, preferring to refer to them as simply "concerned citizens." However, in their own literature they describe their efforts in their "war against drugs" in the following way:

> *Increasingly, we are being called upon by frustrated residents and small business owners to assist them in reclaiming their streets from the drug dealers. We have mounted major anti-drug and crackdowns on crack campaigns in Los Angeles, West Palm Beach, Florida and 42nd Street/Times Square in New York.*

In the same pamphlet, they estimated that their patrols had made over 800 citizens' arrests and that their presence had deterred countless other crimes. Thus, their actions clearly fit the definition of vigilantism. Where the Guardian Angels differ from most other forms of vigilantism and neovigilantism is that while they patrol, apprehend, and arrest, they do not routinely mete out punishment to their captives. Instead, they detain the alleged offenders until legal authorities arrive to take them into custody.

S.H.O.D.I.

An interesting and extremely controversial program in Ventura, California, Colorado Springs, Colorado, and Jacksonville, Florida is called S.H.O.D.I. (Serious Habitual Offender Drug Involved). Consistent with the assumptions of Control Theory, i.e., if an individual's inner containment is not strong enough to prevent deviance, societal measures of outer containment must be imposed, S.H.O.D.I. concentrates on monitoring the behavior of known juvenile offenders. Using computers, law enforcement personnel study arrest records to pinpoint the serious and habitual juvenile offenders in a particular area. Once identified, their names are placed on a list which is circulated to all law enforcement officers. If stopped, even for the most minor violation, these youths are arrested and taken to the police station. Social workers called "trackers" are assigned to these youths to monitor their behavior 24 hours a day if necessary. The trackers check to ensure that the youths are not violating curfew, skipping school, using drugs or alcohol, or committing any other infractions. While some of the youths' attorneys complain that the program amounts to little more than police harassment and unfair labeling of their clients, law enforcement officials are convinced that it is an effective way to reduce juvenile delinquent activities (NBC News, 1987).

Gang Intervention Programs

The increased gang activities of the late 1980s spawned numerous delinquency prevention programs. Along with the increased efforts of law enforcement personnel to thwart the illegal drug trafficking and increased violence among juvenile gangs, other groups formed to help rid their neighborhoods of gangs and their activities. One such group called "Mothers Against Gangs" was organized to focus increased media attention on the problem of teenaged gangs and their victims, in much the same way that MADD (Mothers Against Drunk Driving) did with the problem of drunk driving.

Other communities have decided that uniting mothers against gangs may be an important first step, but is not enough. Orange County, California has developed a community-wide antigang program that includes monthly meetings of law enforcement officials, school counselors, parents, and gang counselors in an effort to provide night and weekend activities for teenagers as an alternative to becoming involved in gangs. Costa Mesa converted a former junior high school into a teen center and also utilizes YMCA, school, and church facilities to provide meaningful activities for teens (Ramirez, 1994). New York City offers similar programs and includes conflict resolution as part of its program encouraging teenagers to sign contracts that they will not resort to violence when they have disagreements with their peers (Minton, 1995). And Fort Worth, Texas initiated a controversial program where the city hired six known gang leaders to work with the police department as gang counselors, prepared to intervene and negotiate peace between rival gangs, discourage recruitment of new members, and dissuade violence (Douglas and Martin 1994; Floyd, 1994).

Community-based gang intervention programs are highly controversial, and very little research has been conducted to evaluate their effectiveness. One program, however, has been systematically evaluated, and apparently has been effective in reducing gang membership and violence. *Neutral Zone,* a program developed in Mountlake Terrace, Washington, and replicated in several other Washington communities, offers already gang-affiliated and potential gang members attractive and safe recreational and social activities as alternatives to running with their gangs on Friday and Saturday nights. Data collected from direct observation, interviews, and official crime statistics indicate that the program has been successful in reducing gang activities and other delinquency (Thurman et al., 1996).

Evaluation of Delinquency Treatment and Prevention Strategies

Throughout this chapter we have summarized evaluative studies of various delinquency treatment and prevention strategies where they are available. One of the frustrating aspects of delinquency prevention and treatment, however, is the lack of systematic research on both the short-term and long-term effects of most programs (*Law Enforcement News,* 1997). Moreover, when research on the effectiveness of treatment and prevention programs is conducted, the results are often mixed. If we review the research that has been conducted, however, some general trends and patterns can be discerned.

Research indicates that the medical model that dominates many of the delinquency treatment programs—especially those related to alcohol and drug abuse—is inadequate because it focuses on the individual and symptoms rather than causes of problems, ignoring the larger social context in which the delinquency occurs. Many of the sociologically based prevention programs, however, have met with moderate success. In general those programs that have focused on involving entire communities and the important institutions within which juveniles interact on a daily basis—family, school, church, neighborhood, etc.,—have met with the most success. Moreover, the most successful strategies have been those where parents, businesses, social agencies, school officials, and law enforcement agencies have combined efforts to reduce, control, and prevent delinquency. Still, in the end, when two very important questions are posed—"Do treatment and prevention strategies work?" and "Do you get what you pay for?"—unfortunately the most accurate answer is: "Not necessarily" (*Law Enforcement News,* 1997). This prompts us to urge a dramatic "rethinking" of the delinquency problem in the next and final chapter of the book.

SUMMARY

This chapter examined the treatment and prevention ideologies in juvenile corrections and described some of the specific treatment and prevention strategies that have been used for juvenile delinquents. Clearly, traditional delinquency treatment and prevention programs have been dominated by the medical model and psychiatric approach. Hakeem (1957–58) indicated that the psychiatric approach focuses upon predelinquency, its causes, symptoms, and cures, and that while the psychiatric approach carries great prestige, its lofty status is not deserved. He charged that it is based on very little empirical verification and that the labeling of children as predelinquent is arbitrary and sometimes even

whimsical. He urged that sociologists should turn to their own concepts and theories to develop programs for the treatment and prevention of delinquency. Likewise, the sociologist and criminologist Donald Cressey (1955) lamented that when dealing with corrections, even sociologists often have ignored sociological theories and reform techniques. He insisted that delinquents are products of social interaction and any attempt to reform them must focus upon social groups and group processes.

We then reviewed some of the treatment and prevention programs which have incorporated sociological theory into their strategies. Some of the classic delinquency programs were discussed and the evaluations of their relative strengths and weaknesses presented.

Recent trends in preventing and treating delinquents have turned toward community involvement. Evaluations of these various programs have produced mixed conclusions.

While it is important for society to develop new and innovative approaches to dealing with delinquents and delinquency, it is equally important that its members not get caught up in what Finckenauer (1982) called the "panacea phenomenon." As he pointed out, the search for a "cure-all" persists because of two rather naive and simplistic ideas: "doism" and "newism." "Doism" is the "...belief that it is better to do something than nothing," and "newism" is the "...appeal of approaches or programs because they are new" (Finckenauer, 1982:27).

From the sociological perspective, it is unrealistic to assume that society can eliminate a problem such as juvenile delinquency. Rather, social control, treatment, and prevention programs should be aimed at reducing the number of deviant acts, and, more importantly, at re-

ducing their negative social impact. Many of the programs described in this chapter have shown evidence of success, while others have been much less effective. Delinquency is such a complex phenomenon that any attempt to control, treat, or prevent it must take its complexity into account. As Hurley (1985:68) indicated, "There is no field of knowledge that does not apply to delinquency, barring perhaps Plate Tectonics." Similarly, Sheldon Rose and Jeffrey Edleson (1987:xiii) argued for the "multi-method approach" to dealing with delinquency which "draws upon problem-solving techniques, the modeling sequence, and an operant, cognitive change, relaxation, socio-recreational, small-group, relational, and extra-group methods of intervention."

In keeping with the theme of this book, it is our contention that juvenile delinquency is inherently social in nature and that any meaningful attempts to deal with it will have to approach it within the social context in which it occurs. In Chapter 17 we explore a sociological approach to rethinking the problem of juvenile delinquency.

Concept Integration

Questions and Topics for Study and Discussion

1. Explain the treatment ideology in juvenile corrections. What are some of its strengths? What are some of its weaknesses?
2. Explain the prevention ideology in juvenile corrections. What are some of its strengths? What are some of its weaknesses? How can this ideology be implemented from a sociological perspective?
3. Summarize some of the major treatment programs for juvenile delinquents in the United States. What are the major weaknesses of these programs? How might they be improved to overcome those weaknesses?

4. Summarize some of the major prevention programs for juvenile delinquents in the United States. What are the major weaknesses of these programs? How might they be improved to overcome those weaknesses?
5. How has the sociological perspective been applied to delinquency treatment and prevention programs? Devise a hypothetical plan utilizing sociological concepts for your own community which could treat and prevent delinquency.

References

Bass, S. A., and Mandell, F. 1982. Building networks in urban settings: An approach to delinquency prevention. *New England Journal of Human Services* 2 (Summer):20–25.

Behre, C., Edwards, D., and Femming, C. 1982. Assessment of the effectiveness of a juvenile transitional

center for facilitating re-entry. *Journal of Offender Counseling, Services, and Rehabilitation* 6 (Spring):61–72.

Berg, B. L. 1984. Inmates as clinical sociologists: The use of sociodrama in a nontraditional delinquency prevention program. *Journal of Offender Therapy and Comparative Criminology* 28 (September): 117–124.

Berne, E. 1961. *Transactional analysis in psychotherapy.* New York: Grove. 1964. ———. *Games people play.* New York: Grove.

Brown, W. K. 1983. *What parents should know about juvenile delinquency and juvenile justice.* York, PA: William Gladden Foundation.

Cloward, R., and Ohlin, L. E. 1961. *Delinquency and opportunity.* Glencoe, IL: Free Press.

Cole, P. Z., and Hafsten, J. W. 1978. Probation supervision revisited: Responsibility training. *Journal of Juvenile and Family Courts* 29 (February):53–58.

Cressey, D. R. 1955. Changing criminals: The application of the theory of differential association. *American Journal of Sociology* 61 (September):116–120.

Douglas, J., Jr., and Martin, R. S. 1994. Some who have felt gang wrath favor hiring plan. *Fort Worth Star Telegram,* May 15:1; 17.

Empey, L. T., and Rabow, J. 1961. The Provo experiment in delinquency rehabilitation. *American Sociological Review* 26 (October):679–695.

Farrington, D. P. 1985. Delinquency prevention in the 1980s. *Journal of Adolescence* 8 (March): 3–16.

Finckenauer, J. O. 1982. *Scared straight! and the panacea phenomenon.* Englewood Cliffs, NJ: Prentice-Hall.

Floyd, J. 1994. FW blasted for plan to pay gang leaders. *Dallas Morning News,* May 12:1A; 15A.

Frey, H. E. 1999. Employment and training for Court-Involved Youth: An Overview. *OJJDP Fact Sheet* 102 (April):1–2.

Glasser, W. 1965. *Reality therapy.* New York: Harper & Row.

Governor's Advocacy Council. 1983. Opening doors for children: A study of the North Carolina community-based alternative program. Governor's Advocacy Council on Children and Youth, Raleigh, NC. Chicago: John Howard Society.

Greenberg, N. 1990. How college students can help delinquents. *Journal of Criminal Justice* 18 (1):55–63.

Greenwood, P. W., and Rand, S. T. 1993. Evaluation of the Paint Creek Youth Center: A residential program for serious delinquents. *Criminology* 31 (May):263–279.

Greene, M. B. 1993. Chronic exposure to violence and poverty: Interventions that work for youth. *Crime & Delinquency* 39 (January):106–124.

Grossman, J. B., and Garry, E. M. 1997. Mentoring—A proven delinquency prevention strategy. *Juvenile*

Justice Bulletin (April). Washington, DC: U.S. Dept. of Justice, Office of Juvenile Justice and Delinquency Prevention.

Gullotta, T. P., and Adams, G. R. 1982. Minimizing juvenile delinquency: Implications for prevention programs. *Journal of Early Adolescence* 2 (Summer):105–117.

Hakeem, M. 1957–58. A critique of the psychiatric approach to the prevention of delinquency. *Social Problems* 5 (Winter):194–206.

Hamilton, R., and McKinney, K. 1999. Job Training for Juveniles: Project CRAFT. *OJJDP Fact Sheet* 116 (August):1–2.

Harris, T. A. 1969. *I'm OK—You're OK.* New York: Harper & Row.

Heeren, J., and Schicor, D. 1984. Mass media and delinquency prevention: The case of "Scared Straight." *Deviant Behavior* 5 (1–4):375–386.

Higgins, P. S. 1978. Evaluation and case study of a school-based delinquency prevention program. *Evaluation Quarterly* 2 (May):215–235.

Horst, N. 1987. Young Emporia offenders offered an alternative. *Emporia Gazette,* March 30:1.

Hurley, D. 1985. Arresting delinquency. *Psychology Today* March:63–68.

Jesness, C. F. 1975. Comparative effectiveness of behavior modification and transactional analysis programs for delinquents. *Journal of Consulting and Clinical Psychology* 43 (December):758–779.

Johnson, B. D., and Goldberg, R. T. 1982. Vocational and social rehabilitation of delinquents: A study of experimentals and controls. *Journal of Offender Counseling Services and Rehabilitation* 6 (Spring): 43–60.

Jones, V. M. 1999. Youth Crime Watch of America. *Youth in Action* 2 (January):1–2.

Karchmer, C. L. 1984. Young arsonists. *Society* 22 (November/December):78–83.

Kobrin, S. 1959. The Chicago Area Project—25 year assessment. *Annals of the American Academy of Political and Social Science* 322 (March):20–29.

Law Enforcement News. 1997. Do you get what you pay for?: With CJ efforts, not necessarily. *Law Enforcement News* 23 (May):1; 18.

Liazos, A. 1974. Class oppression: The function of juvenile justice. *Insurgent Sociologist* 5:2–24.

Miller, W. B. 1962. The impact of a "total community" delinquency control project. *Social Problems* 10 (Fall):168–191.

Minton, L. 1995. Tough teens talk about a program that works. *Parade,* January 8:4.

Mobilization for Youth. 1961. *A proposal for the prevention and control of delinquency by expanding opportunities.* New York: Mobilization for Youth, Inc.

NBC News. 1987. Crime, punishment, and kids. *NBC News Special* July 26.

OJJDP. 1988. A private-sector corrections program for juveniles: Paint Creek Youth Center. Pittsburgh: Office of Juvenile Justice and Delinquency Prevention, U.S. Department of Justice.

OJJDP. 2000. Youth in Action. Want to Resolve a Dispute: Try Mediation. Washington, DC: U.S. Department of Justice.

Phillips, E. L., Phillips, E., Fixsen, D., and Wolf, M. 1971. Achievement place: Modification of the behaviors of predelinquent boys within a token economy. *Journal of Applied Behavior Analysis* 4 (Spring):45–59.

Pennell, S., Curtis, C., and Scheck, D. C. 1990. Controlling juvenile delinquency: An evaluation of an interagency strategy. *Crime & Delinquency* 36 (April):257–275.

Project New Pride. 1985. *Project New Pride.* Washington, DC: U.S. Government Printing Office.

Ramirez, D., Jr. 1994. Orange County suburb gives teens alternative to gangs. *Fort Worth Star Telegram,* March 6:A8.

Remington, C. 1982. Restitution can work for serious offenders. *Change: A Juvenile Justice Quarterly* 5 (2):9–10.

Robin, G. D. 1969. Anti-poverty programs and delinquency. *Journal of Criminal Law, Criminology, and Police Science* 60 (Fall):323–331.

Robison, J., and Smith, G. 1971. The effectiveness of correctional programs. *Crime and Delinquency* 17 (January):67–80.

Rose, S. D., and Edleson, J. L. 1987. *Working with children and adolescents in groups.* San Francisco: Jossey-Bass.

Rosenbaum, D. P., Lurigio, A. J., and Lavrakas, P. J. 1986. *Crimestoppers*—A national evaluation. Washington, DC: National Institute of Justice.

Rutherford, R. B., Jr. 1975. Establishing behavioral contracts with delinquent adolescents. *Federal Probation* 39 (March):28–32.

Santoli, A. 1992. Why Boys Town still works. *Parade Magazine* (February 9):20–21.

Schlossman, S., and Sedlak, M. 1983. The Chicago Area Project revisited. *Crime and Delinquency* 29 (July):398–462.

Shaw, C. R., and McKay, H. D. 1942. *Juvenile delinquency and urban areas.* Chicago: University of Chicago Press.

Skinner, B. F. 1971. *Beyond freedom and dignity.* New York: Knopf.

Sykes, G., and Matza, D. 1957. Techniques of neutralization: A theory of delinquency. *American Sociological Review* 22 (December):664–670.

Thomas, M. R., and Murray, P. V. 1983. Get kids interested in the law before the law gets interested in them. *Instructor* 92 (April):62–67.

Thurman, Q. C., Giacomazzi, A. L., Reisig, M. D., and Mueller, D. G. 1996. Community-based gang prevention and intervention: An evaluation of the neutral zone. *Crime & Delinquency* 42 (April):279–295.

Time. 1982. Guardian Angels' growing pains. *Time* (January):21.

Toby, J. 1965. An evaluation of early identification and intensive treatment programs for predelinquents. *Social Problems* 13 (Fall):160–175.

Towberman, D. B. 1992. National survey of juvenile needs assessment. *Crime & Delinquency* 38 (April): 230–238.

Velasquez, J. S., and Lyle, C. G. 1985. Day versus residential treatment for juvenile offenders: The impact of program evaluation. *Child Welfare* 64 (March-April):145–156.

Weeks, H. A. 1958. *Youthful offenders at Highfields.* Ann Arbor: University of Michigan Press.

17 RETHINKING THE DELINQUENCY PROBLEM

Reading Objectives

The reading of this chapter will help you achieve the following objectives:

1. Briefly review the social nature of juvenile delinquency and the social processes involved in defining, treating, controlling, and preventing this social problem.
2. Summarize some of the major recommendations that have been made for rethinking the problem of juvenile delinquency.
3. Reexamine various social values, norms, laws, institutions, policies, and issues associated with juvenile delinquency.
4. Explore some imaginative and innovative ways of creating meaningful social change to help alleviate some of the social conditions which contribute to juvenile delinquency.
5. Explore the redefinition of juvenile delinquency.

Introduction

In this final chapter, we underscore again the social nature of juvenile delinquency and outline some suggestions and recommendations to help alleviate the problem. Many of these suggestions have come from leading professionals in the fields of law, criminology, social work, and the social and behavioral sciences and some are uniquely ours. Some of the recommendations have been attempted and implemented, at least partially, and others have been routinely ignored.

We have reached the point where most textbooks on juvenile delinquency, or any other social problem for that matter, usually come to a conclusion. The ending is often highlighted by a typically nebulous summation—something to the effect of "now that we have defined, explored, and examined the nature of the problem, further research is needed in the areas that we have suggested in order to provide a more thorough understanding,…" As Haskell and Yablonsky (1978:543) noted:

> *Sociologists are often reluctant to make recommendations for changes in the law,…the criminal justice system, or in correctional policies. The prevailing attitude…is that sociologists should maintain scientific objectivity in their studies, report the results of their research, and leave the conclusions to be drawn by others.*

Perhaps it is the nature of our traditional scientific training that makes many sociologists reluctant to make suggestions for intervention strategies. Or perhaps it stems from the fact that sociologists are essentially theoreticians and not practitioners. From a pragmatic standpoint, it may be that it is much easier to discern and describe the nature of a problem than it is to suggest ways of dealing with it. Whatever the case, one of the most frustrating experiences for students of sociology has been the tendency for sociologists to eagerly participate in the exploration, discussion, and critique of social issues, only to rapidly retreat from any meaningful attempt to resolve them. We get excellent marks for asking probing questions, but seldom generate substantial answers. Our own backgrounds and experiences sorely tempt us to do the same thing. However, we agree with the assertion that "sociologists with years of experience in the field of delinquency should freely present their opinions and recommendations, even though many of their assertions are not based on firm empirical evidence" (Haskell and Yablonsky, 1978:544). For it is also an intrinsic part of our established perspective to exercise a *sociological imagination* (Mills, 1959) in which we seek to apply knowledge and expertise in creative and innovative problem-solving ways.

We should first acknowledge that not everybody believes that meaningful social changes are necessary in order to handle juvenile delinquency. There are those of the "traditional approach," who believe that all that is needed to curb delinquency is stricter rules, better law enforcement, and harsher punishments. This "get tough on crime/delinquency" attitude surfaces from time to time, as the social and cultural pendulum swings from the more liberal to the more conservative to the reactionary. We suggest, however, that any meaningful approach to the social problem of delinquency must go beyond the mere "tightening" of social control on youths. Rather, large-scale changes in cultural attitudes, values, and beliefs, along with changes in social institutions and practices, are necessary if the challenge of effectively dealing with juvenile delinquency is to be met. We challenge the reader to approach the chapter with an open mind and to explore the possibilities for social change presented herein.

The Social Nature of Juvenile Delinquency

Adolescence is a social product that reflects the dominant attitudes, values, and beliefs of American culture. Largely as a result of urbanization and industrialization, Americans created the concept of adolescence and its accompanying normative expectations in an effort to differentiate and regulate the social status, role, and legal treatment of people in this category from adult members of society. One of the results was the prolongation of the period of transition from childhood to adulthood. Another was the creation of a new form of social deviance—juvenile delinquency.

Prolonging the transition from childhood to adulthood in urban industrial America has been functional in many ways. For example, it has extended the length of time spent on formal education, delayed entry into the work force, delayed marriage (which in turn has had positive effects on reducing birthrates), and extended the period of time available for anticipatory socialization into future adult roles. On the other hand, it also has had some negative consequences. One of these is the *marginality* experienced by individuals who have biologically and physiologically matured into young adulthood, while socially and legally being denied access to meaningful adult roles.

Paul Goodman (1962), in *Growing Up Absurd,* laid the philosophical foundation for understanding the unique problems experienced by U.S. youths. He pointed out that a youth subculture forms, in part, in response to the difficulty of growing up in a society that forces adult values upon juveniles who are not allowed to fully participate in the social system. As Frank Musgrove (1965) pointed out, the creation of adolescence, and the fact that youths automatically experience social "limbo," denies them the opportunity to acquire the basic skills, knowledge, and other attributes required in adult life. The marginal status arising from this temporary "no man's land," between child and adult, undoubtedly contributes to adolescent deviance.

How to react to the social deviance of youths has been extremely problematic for American society. Ideologically floundering among the divergent philosophies of protecting, treating, rehabilitating, and punishing juveniles for their misbehavior, policies and programs have been developed which have attempted to do one or another, or all simultaneously. While there have been numerous individual successes, overall the result has been well over a century of indecisive and ineffective efforts toward alleviating the problem of juvenile delinquency.

A major element of the problem has stemmed from the inability or reluctance on the part of many to recognize and understand its social dimensions. Often viewed apart from its social context, delinquency has been approached as a discrete problem to be studied, analyzed, and treated, The consequence has been disjointed efforts at control and prevention aimed at specific individuals, or, in some cases, when viewed more sociologically, at families, neighborhoods, gangs, and communities. The vast majority of these efforts, however, have ignored the broader societal context of juvenile delinquency almost entirely.

In harmony with this idea of changing the social milieu in order to reduce crime, delinquency, and other forms of deviant behavior, criminologists, sociologists, and behavioral scientists generally welcomed the urban renewal projects of the 1960s and 1970s. These projects cleared massive slum areas to make way for new apartment complexes and expanding central business districts. Endorsement of the projects was based upon the inaccurate hypothesis that slums have little or no social organization, and the premature conclusion that the lack of strong local social organization was responsible for the high incidence of crime and delinquency in such areas. It was assumed that environmental manipulation such as razing old tenements and clearing out urban blight would strike at a fundamental cause of juvenile delinquency and other social problems.

Unfortunately, the sociological lessons learned from classic studies such as William F. Whyte's *Street Corner Society* (1943) and Elliot Leibow's *Tally's Corner* (1964) were ignored. These works clearly indicated that while social organization in urban slums was different from that experienced by middle class society, it was far from nonexistent. The traditional urban renewal projects that ruptured social networks and the sense of community exemplify the failure to comprehend or incorporate the social dynamics of a neighborhood in dealing with social problems such as juvenile delinquency.

In a 1967 Presidential Task Force Report, Virginia Burns and Leonard Stern (1967) pointed out the multifaceted nature of juvenile delinquency, and warned that the problem cannot be resolved through small or simple programs. Rather, they suggested that what was needed was a comprehensive effort to change the social system which produces conditions and strains conducive to the development of juvenile delinquency and other forms of youthful antisocial behavior. Unfortunately, an assessment of the impact of the Task Force Report 25 years later indicates that little progress has been made, and that many of the suggestions for social reform in that report have been largely ignored (Conley, 1994).

We agree with Burns and Stern's assessment that a problem as complex as delinquency cannot be resolved through Band-Aid types of programs that treat symptoms rather than basic causes. In fact, we contend that if the social problem of juvenile delinquency is to be realistically approached, nothing short of major social and cultural change is necessary. This change must go beyond projects or programs aimed at individual delinquents, their families, and neighborhoods.

The Office of Juvenile Justice and Delinquency Prevention (1979) also acknowledged the significance of social reform in dealing with delinquency. It totally rejected delinquency prevention programs based upon delinquents' proposed biological differences, personality differences, or learning disabilities. It also rejected all programs based upon early identification and intervention which used criteria such as personality tests, socioeconomic status, broken or intact homes, or the criminal histories of parents. The accompanying risks of labeling and self-fulfilling prophecy were viewed as far outweighing any potential benefits of those programs. The Office of Juvenile Justice and Delinquency Prevention (1979) insisted that the programs with the most likelihood of producing long-lasting benefits were those that focus upon organizational change, especially those that utilize the school as one of the critical institutions for implementing social change.

From a sociological perspective, juvenile delinquency, like any other social problem, is inherently social in nature. From the cultural values which undergird the social norms defining delinquency, to the peers, parents, teachers, police, juvenile courts, and correctional institutions which react, reinforce, and respond to it, the social dimensions are ever-present. Consequently, if society is to deal effectively with the problem of juvenile delinquency, its members must evaluate the problem in its broadest and most fundamental social context. This necessitates totally *rethinking the problem of delinquency*—its definition, its social causes, social context, and its social consequences. In our view, this process of rethinking the problem necessitates eliminating or at least reducing the social and legal marginality experienced by juveniles. It also should include standardizing juvenile codes (or eliminating them altogether), decriminalizing status offenses, revising juvenile courts, and modifying juvenile corrections. Further, such an effort must include strengthening the family institution, changing the educational system to provide improved socialization, and totally redefining the concept of juvenile delinquency.

Eliminating the Marginal Status of Juveniles

The marginal status of youths and the ambiguous normative expectations associated with their social positions may significantly weaken their social bonds with larger society. As social control theorists point out, the weaker the social bond the stronger the likelihood of norm violation. It has been argued that one of the most significant steps toward delinquency reduction would be to provide youths with more meaningful roles and enhanced status in society. For example, Haskell and Yablonsky (1978:546) indicated that society should "remove blocks to adult status," especially in regard to the legal and illegal discrimination in employment faced by youths. Roy Lotz et al. (1985:353) pointed out the importance of integrating youths into activities and decision making in the larger society:

> *Quite simply, many youths do not feel that they belong to, or make any difference to, the communities where they live. And persons who behave irresponsibly may do so, in part, because they have few opportunities to be responsible.*

This position is confounded by the phenomenon of rapid social change in today's society. It is no longer easy to predict what the future will be as technology further impacts upon society, culture, and lifestyle. As Kenneth Keniston (1968) noted, it is virtually impossible for today's youths to foresee their future places in society, because rapid social change confounds our ability to predict the future of society.

Nevertheless, there are at least two ways society could reduce or possibly eliminate the marginal status of adolescence and the resulting alienation and norm violation of today's youths. First would be to establish meaningful rites of passage into adulthood near the onset of puberty. Second is to accompany those rites of passage with innovative and appropriate social expectations and opportunities to participate in important decision-making social roles.

Rites of Passage

Throughout the life course, individuals move through a series of age-related phases or stages of development. Theoretically, the **life course** refers to *the successive role and status changes that each person occupies in society as a consequence of growing older.* Arnold Van Gennep ([1908] 1960) was one of the first to conceive of life as a series of passages or transitions from one stage to another and from one biological phase and social status to another. "Life is forever dynamic and anticipatory since there are always new thresholds to cross" (Van Gennep, [1908] 1960:189) and new adjustments to make. These adjustments are both biological and social, for while physical aging may be perceived as solely a biological/physiological process, how a person is viewed and treated at any particular age is based on sociocultural definitions. The life course is graphically illustrated in Figure 17-1.

You will note in Figure 17-1 that the upper horizontal line depicts the life course as the individual develops through the biological stages of childhood, adulthood, and old age. Each of these three stages is set apart and clearly delimited by the physiological events of birth, puberty, menopause (medical science indicates that males may also experience a form of menopause), and death.

In many small and preliterate societies these natural events closely parallel the simple sequence of social roles and statuses that are imputed to people during their lifetimes. For example, in American Samoa, puberty is a time of family and community celebration and ceremony as children quickly and easily leave childhood behind and take on the rights and responsibilities of adulthood (Mead, 1928). Later, as an individual's physical strength and reproductive powers decrease, public acknowledgment and ceremony again implement the transition from adult worker to an honored social role associated with advanced age. Van Gennep ([1908] 1960) called these ceremonies linking age changes and other biological phenomena with changes in social status **"rites of passage."** Wendall Oswalt (1986:106)

FIGURE 17-1   The Life Course

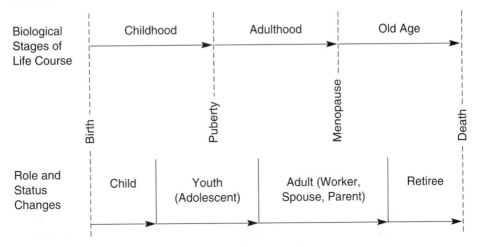

Source: Based on Arnold Van Gennep. *The Rites of Passage* (translated by Monika B. Vizedom and Gabriel L. Caffee). Chicago: University of Chicago Press, 1960 [1908].

defined a **rite of passage** as *"ceremonial recognition of a major change in social status, one that will alter permanently a person's relationship with members of the greater community."*

In contemporary U.S. society, we practice several ceremonies which serve as symbolic passage rituals. For example, christening and baptismal ceremonies, high school graduation exercises, college commencements, wedding ceremonies, retirement parties, and funerals all serve to ritualize and formalize the transition from one life stage and social status to another. However, many of these ritual events have little or no relationship to the biological stages of the life course. Again referring to Figure 17-1, the lower horizontal line represents the sequence of different roles and status positions that most persons experience in contemporary American society. In contrast to the societies referred to earlier, in which the transition from childhood to adulthood is easy and natural, there is a rather uneven "fit" between many of the biological stages and the different social roles and status positions one is expected to occupy. Especially problematic is the artificial social stage of adolescence which cuts across the two naturally occurring biological life stages of childhood and young adulthood.

Passage ceremonies closely associated with puberty are much more likely to exist in preliterate and preindustrial societies than industrial societies like ours (Oswalt, 1986). However, social rituals held near the time of puberty are not unheard of in contemporary U.S. society. For example, the "coming out" party of the upper class debutante marks her entry into adult society. Many middle class and lower class families provide their own version of this ceremony by giving their daughters a "sweet sixteen" birthday party. Still, these rituals come substantially after puberty or the biological onset of adulthood.

In our society, Jews probably provide the most clearcut rite of passage which most closely approximates the biological transition from childhood to adulthood. A *bar mitzvah* is held on the Jewish boy's thirteenth birthday and publicly acknowledges his assumption of adult religious responsibilities and duties. Although not as widely practiced, a similar

High school graduation is an important rite of passage in the lives of most teenagers that symbolically marks the transition from childhood to adulthood in American society. Yet, most high school graduates are still under the age of majority and do not enjoy many of the rights and privileges of adulthood, adding to a sense of marginality that can lead to delinquency.

ceremony, the *bat mitzvah,* often is observed for Jewish girls. Interestingly, several researchers have indicated that juvenile delinquency rates among Jews is much lower than among other ethnic groups (e.g.; Kvaraceus, 1945; Deardorff, 1955; Austin, 1977).

Why not develop and encourage meaningful social rituals to symbolize the rite of passage from childhood to adulthood which roughly coincides with the onset of puberty for all American youths? Surely such rituals and experiences are possible for an imaginative and creative society such as ours. Because of the pluralistic nature of American society, different racial, ethnic, religious, and social class groups could devise their own ceremonies which would be meaningful to them. For example, since many Jews already observe such a practice, there would be no need for them to change their ceremony. For other groups, the rite of passage need not have a religious connotation. A secular ceremony focusing upon rights and duties of adult citizenship or some similar topic would suffice. The significance would reside in the symbolic aspects of the ceremony which would signify to all that the young person participating in it was leaving childhood and entering adulthood. In order for such a ceremony to be successful, it would have to be institutionalized and internalized by everyone as being one of the most important rituals in our society. This ceremony could become a time of familial and community celebration and a time of fulfillment and achievement for youths. We have clearcut rites of passage to ease and announce the transition between other stages of the life course, for example, weddings, graduation exercises, and funerals. However, our culture includes no such standard or widely recognized device for moving our maturing children into adulthood. Why not?

Meaningful Social Participation

In a Presidential Task Force Report on delinquency prevention, it was emphasized that there is a strong need to involve young people in a much more meaningful and responsible way in the affairs of society that affect them (Burns and Stern, 1967; Conley, 1994). The Juvenile Justice Standards Project (1977:2) also insisted that juveniles "should have the right to decide on actions affecting their lives and freedom, unless found incapable of making reasoned decisions." Currently, adolescence is perceived by many as a time of irresponsibility, confusion, and financial dependency, yet many older teenagers are eager to assume the responsibility of young adulthood (Klein, 1990).

The Youth Development and Delinquency Prevention Administration (1972:28–30) specifically addressed the problem of lack of meaningful social roles on the part of adolescents and suggested the following principles:

1. Delinquent behavior in the young has as its most general cause their exclusion from socially acceptable, responsible, and therefore personally gratifying roles.

2. Roles are made available to the young by the institutions in which they participate.

3. With respect to the problem of delinquency, the critical matter in institutional role allocation is the acquisition of roles imparting to the individual a legitimate identity.

4. Since roles are a product of institutional design and procedure, and since obstruction to a favorable course of youth development arises from failure to provide roles creating legitimate identity, a rational strategy of delinquency reduction and control must address the task of institutional change.

5. Among the institutions significant in the lives of young persons during the period of maximum vulnerability to delinquency and/or withdrawal, the school is of central importance.

6. The process through which illegitimate identities are formed and a commitment to delinquent activity arises among adolescents is best understood by contrast with the formation and maintenance of legitimate identity by adults.

7. The tie of the young person to the school as his "institutional home" is maintained and reinforced by (a) the direct rewards of approval for valued academic and social performance; and (b) the indirect rewards of a credible promise of a desirable occupational future.

There is no reason, other than cultural tradition, why juveniles cannot occupy more meaningful social roles which more thoroughly integrate them into larger society. For example, in Ramona, California, a group of youngsters formed Kidco, a successful corporation headed by a 12-year-old boy. The company, comprised entirely of children between 9 and 14 years of age, developed a secret formula for exterminating gophers. Unfortunately, their thriving business was shut down and criminal sanctions were threatened by the state government, because they did not have a license to do extermination work—a license for which applicants must be at least 18 years of age! The corporate head of Kidco, Dickie Cessna, summarized their dilemma:

> *We do not think it is fair...because we are just some little kids who want to do a good job killing gophers and selling manure instead of being out with a gang getting in dutch. Still we seem to be in trouble all the time thanks to some dumb laws (The Daily Tidings, 1977:3).*

If a meaningful rite of passage is developed which signifies the movement into adult status, why not accompany that movement with the rights, responsibilities, and duties typically associated with adulthood? Mentoring programs such as those discussed in Chapter 16 could be widely developed to link youths with positive role models who could help them learn to fulfill social responsibilities and enhance their self-esteem. Young adults could serve on juries (especially in cases involving other young adults). Where communities have experimented with teen courts, the results have been quite positive, reducing overcrowded juvenile courts' loads and providing teenagers with opportunities to learn and use adult values and life skills (Godwin, 1996). The National Youth Network, established in 1997, is an example of how young people between the ages of 14 and 21 have demonstrated that they can team up to help prevent and solve youth problems if given a chance (Gruber, 1998). Youths in this program unite with each other and adults to distribute information, advocate youth involvement in positive community activities, and to promote policies and programs that prevent crime and delinquency. Youths also should be allowed to compete for jobs for which their physical strength, educational background and training qualify them, and serve on school, community, state, and even national commissions, boards, and committees under the direction of older encouraging adults. It particularly makes sense to allow students to serve on local school boards. Some examples of meaningful participation on the part of youths are described in Box 17-1.

In 1971, the Twenty-sixth Amendment was added to the U.S. Constitution which changed federal voting laws to allow 18-year-olds to vote. This change primarily came about in response to the complaint that young men aged 18 and over were being drafted to serve in military combat in Vietnam, but were not allowed to participate in the political process. Lowering the voting age to 18 was opposed by some, but was considered to be a step in the right direction by most. Perhaps it was not a large enough step. Should the voting age be lowered even further? In some states, the legal age of criminal majority is as low as 15 or 16 years of age. In many states, juvenile courts can relinquish jurisdiction of juveniles below that age to adult courts where they are held accountable for their criminal actions, especially in the case of serious felonies such as homicide. There are inmates on "death row" for criminal offenses they committed while only 15 or 16 years of age. Clearly, in those cases, the individuals were considered legally responsible for their actions, and held accountable in the same way as adults. In less dramatic fashion, most states issue drivers' licenses to 16-year-olds (and some states offer permits or licenses to 14- and 15-year-olds),

BOX 17-1 Concept Application

Meaningful Social Participation for Youths

Item: In the summer of 1978, a police officer in Menlo Park, California, recruited 10 teenagers to take responsibility for abandoned homes in or near their neighborhoods. The teenagers, called Junior Housing Inspectors, were paid $50 per week to guard the houses and prevent what had become an endless series of very expensive break-ins and vandalism. The result was a dramatic decrease in the vandalism, a new sense of community pride, and a grant which brought federal money into the community to provide jobs for responsible hard-working youths who needed employment.

Item: In Clovis, New Mexico, teenagers sit on juries to hear the cases of first-time juvenile offenders. They make recommendations to the judge regarding the adjudication and disposition of the cases. The program helped alleviate court crowding and is considered a success.

Item: In Danville, California, just east of San Francisco, Youth Court meets regularly to hear cases regarding youths accused of committing misdemeanors such as vandalism, marijuana possession, consumption or possession of alcohol, and petty theft. A practicing attorney serves as judge, but all other principal roles-attorneys, clerks, and jurors are filled by teenagers. Typical sentences involve community service, restitution, and maintenance of good grades in school. In over 200 cases heard before the court by 1990, only two involved repeat offenders.

Item: In Odessa, Texas, Teen Court was developed to hear cases of defendants between the ages of 10 and 16 charged with traffic violations and misdemeanors such as public intoxication, shoplifting, running away, vandalism, and disorderly conduct. Six teenage jurors make a recommendation for sentencing to a retired district judge who presides over the court. If the youth successfully completes the sentence, all charges are dismissed and no criminal record is maintained.

Item: In Lockesburg, Arkansas, a 13-year-old was elected to serve on the City Park Committee. His membership was not an honorary position. Rather, he served as a full-fledged active member. During the summer months he devoted a great deal of time to working at the park. During the school year, he attended all meetings of the committee and worked weekends on park responsibilities.

What do all these items share in common? They all represent social situations in which teenagers have been treated as responsible citizens. Each refers to actual cases in which individuals legally considered minors–"adolescents" or "juveniles"–have been judged to be mature enough to be held accountable for their actions in the same manner as adults.

These items indicate that treating teenagers as adults is not totally unheard of in American society. Doubtless, there are numerous other specific examples which could be included here. However, that is not the norm. Typically, people under the age of majority are not granted the rights or the responsibilities commonly associated with adulthood.

Without question, treating teenagers as adults has mixed consequences. If society believes in trial by a jury of one's peers, teenagers should sit on juries. If society believes in policing its neighborhoods, teenagers may be recruited for the job. And, if society believes that it is just to execute its murderers, teenagers may be executed.

On the other hand, if society insists on treating teenagers as something other than adults, it can resign itself to innumerable social problems, not the least of which is juvenile delinquency. The choices are difficult, but they eventually must be made.

* * * *

Using your sociological imagination, can you think of other meaningful ways in which teenagers could take on adult responsibilities and fulfill meaningful statuses and roles in American society?

and hold them accountable for obeying traffic laws in the same manner as adults. We know that juveniles aged 14, 15, and 16 are physically capable of performing many adult functions. Their exclusion from meaningful adult roles usually is based on what is perceived as their emotional and psychological immaturity rather than their lack of physical abilities.

Perhaps this so-called *emotional and psychological immaturity* is nothing more than **social retardation.** People in this age group are caught in the social paradox in which they are physically capable (and in some cases even physically superior) of performing virtually any of the roles occupied by their parents and other adults; yet, they are socially and legally prohibited from fulfilling that potentiality. Why? At least, we could eliminate the stereotype that all youths are disqualified and treat full societal participation as an individual matter. American society has moved in that direction at the other end of the life course by eliminating mandatory retirement at age 65.

Good judgment, social responsibility, and commitment to meaningful social roles do not magically occur when a person reaches a particular chronological age. Rather, individuals must learn them through effective socialization and the observation of exemplary role models. In addition, we learn to participate in meaningful social roles through actual experience in occupying them. Within the family, church, and school, juveniles must be provided greater access to full participation in social decision-making processes. Conformity to social norms probably would be more likely if juveniles participated in the norm-creating and norm-interpreting processes. As Schur (1973:167–168) commented, "There is some evidence that the most potent deterrent to delinquency lies in bonds of attachment to conventional society." Attachment to conventional society would no doubt be enhanced if juveniles were more realistically and meaningfully allowed to participate in it.

Standardization or Elimination of Juvenile Codes

Juvenile law is statutory law. That means that each state legislature establishes the juvenile code for its state through the passing of statutes. It is possible that 50 different states may have fifty different juvenile codes. Theoretically, this is also true for criminal codes which are created through the statutory process. However, steps have been taken to standardize criminal codes across the United States. For example, the Federal Bureau of Investigation, which compiles official crime data for all 50 states, the District of Columbia, and Puerto Rico in its annual *Uniform Crime Reports,* sets forth standard definitions for criminal offenses. While state legislatures enact their own criminal statutes, most have simply reiterated the definitions for specific criminal offenses set forth by the FBI. Consequently the definitions of murder, forcible rape, aggravated assault, robbery, burglary, larceny-theft, auto theft, and arson are remarkably similar from state to state. While states may vary in what they classify as **misdemeanors**—*less serious crimes usually punishable by fine and/ or imprisonment for less than a year,* as opposed to **felonies**—*more serious crimes punishable by fine and/or imprisonment for more than a year,* the fact that all of these acts are classified as **criminal** to some degree standardizes the legal codes.

Much of the dilemma in defining delinquency stems from the lack of standardization of juvenile codes. One way to resolve this problem would be to standardize juvenile codes across the country by establishing uniform minimum and maximum ages for the jurisdiction of the juvenile court, perhaps ages 7 to 16. Sixteen might be the logical age cut-off between juvenile and adult, since, as Regnery (1985:1) noted, 16-year-old boys commit crimes at a higher rate than any other single age group, and "these are criminals who happen to be young, not children who happen to commit crimes." The remaining question would be whether there should be any circumstances under which an individual under the maximum age of jurisdiction should be remanded to the adult criminal court. If juvenile courts and juvenile corrections were significantly changed, this might not be as significant an issue as it is today. We discuss some possible revisions later in this chapter.

Once the age of jurisdiction is uniformly established, juvenile delinquency should be more clearly defined. Steven Cox and John Conrad (1996:12) pointed out:

> *A basic difficulty with legal definitions of delinquency is that they differ from time to time and from place to place, An act that is delinquent at one time and in one place may not be delinquent at another time or in another place.*

Most of the problems related to inconsistency in juvenile codes are associated with the age of jurisdiction of the juvenile court and that part of the definition which concludes that delinquency is *any act adjudicated as delinquent by a juvenile court.* One way to clarify the definition would be to limit the extent of delinquency to those acts which would be criminal if committed by adults. Thus, juvenile courts would deal only with criminal behavior committed by juveniles. This would eliminate the time, energy, and effort currently focused upon juveniles who commit status offenses.

Another possible option for solving the problem of unstandardized juvenile codes would be to eliminate them altogether. If a meaningful rite of passage from childhood to adulthood were established which eliminated the marginal status of adolescence, it might be sufficient to simply treat those who have been granted adult status as *adults.* This would mean that those considered children would essentially be relieved of legal responsibility for law violating behavior (much of this legal responsibility could be transferred to their parents), and those considered adults would be held fully legally responsible for their actions. As Jay Albanese (1993:14) pointed out:

> *The underlying issue here is that the age of majority is arbitrary. There is no magic that occurs at age eighteen that makes one a responsible adult. In fact, we all know some young people who are mature and responsible at age fifteen, and those that are still trying at age twenty-one....*
>
> *An alternative is to abolish the age of majority... Instead all crime suspects, regardless of age, would be tried at a fact-finding hearing where some combination of punishment and/or treatment would be determined by a judge after a complete investigation of the suspect's background. This punishment and/or treatment would be administered regardless of age. It would hopefully be gauged to the type of offense, offender's needs, maturity, skill level, and the safety of the community.*

As previously mentioned, this type of change would require dramatic alteration of present cultural and social attitudes, values, and beliefs.

Decriminalization of Status Offenses

If the decision is made that states should retain separate juvenile codes, those codes should be as precise as adult criminal statutes. Schur (1973:169) recommended that "juvenile statutes should spell out very clearly just what kinds of behavior are legally proscribed, and should set explicit penalties for such violations (with perhaps some limited range of alternatives available to sentencing judges)." One way to do that would be to eliminate all status offenses. This does *not* mean that norms regulating adolescent behavior would be eliminated. Instead, these norms would be informal in nature, and their violation would be dealt with socially, rather than legally. Parents, school officials, clergy, and social workers would enforce these norms and impose sanctions, rather than the police, court officials, and correctional officers. This would limit juvenile delinquency to *only* those acts which would be criminal if committed by adults.

It is evident that a very small number of youths account for an unusually large proportion of all serious juvenile crime. Longitudinal studies of large birth cohorts over a period of time have found that the assumption that most offenders progress through a delinquent career pattern from less serious to more serious offenses is highly questionable (e.g., Wolfgang et al., 1972). Rather, a fairly small number of persistent *chronic* juvenile offenders tend to continue a career of crime into adulthood, committing more serious offenses as they get older (Wolfgang et al., 1987). Steven Lab (1984) found that the vast majority of his subjects were involved in victimless crimes and status offenses, such as truants, runaways, beer drinkers, and curfew violators, and that over two-thirds (67 percent) ceased their delinquency before the fourth offense, regardless of whether or not they were apprehended and legally processed. Presently, those juveniles must be handled by the same court which handles abused, neglected, and dependent children, as well as muggers, robbers, rapists, and murderers. In an attempt to be "all things to all people," the juvenile court has been widely criticized as a failure.

The decriminalization of status offenses would greatly reduce the caseload of juvenile courts. This would allow court personnel, judges, social workers, police, and others who work with juveniles to concentrate their efforts on serious juvenile offenders.

There appears to be widespread support for the decriminalization of status offenses. The Juvenile Justice Standards Project (1977) recommended that all status offenses be removed from juvenile court jurisdiction. Charles Logan and Sharla Rausch (1985) concluded that deinstitutionalization of status offenders is pointless unless it is accompanied by decriminalization of status offenses. Some states have indeed decriminalized status offenses. In those states, the behaviors are no longer considered law violations, and juveniles who engage in those behaviors are referred to child protective services as opposed to law enforcement and court personnel (Snyder and Sickmund, 1999). This is not to say that the behaviors currently categorized as status offenses are not problematic, nor that they should be totally ignored. Rather, the point is that they need not be treated as *legal* problems. Truancy is essentially a school problem. Running away is a family problem. Many of the status offenses represent social problems that violate adult values about what is appropriate behavior for youngsters. If the prohibited behaviors are genuinely considered harmful or problematic, there is no reason why they cannot be handled by appropriate social agencies, family courts, departments of public welfare, and institutions outside the criminal justice system. Families, schools, churches, and social agencies in the community that have relinquished responsibility for youth to the legal system could reassert their significance in the socialization process.

Revision of the Juvenile Court

The juvenile court has received widespread criticism from a variety of sources. These criticisms have ranged from assertions that the court is too lenient to claims that it is too harsh;

from concerns about its devastating impact on youngsters who come before it, to the shocking realization that to many juveniles it is little more than a joke. Regardless of one's particular philosophical perspective, it appears almost unanimous that the juvenile justice system, most notably the juvenile court, is in serious need of revision.

Just as juvenile delinquency is part and product of the society which has created it, so is the juvenile court. Any attempt to revise the juvenile court must consider the social milieu in which it operates. As Krisberg and Austin (1978:569) noted:

> *To state the obvious—the juvenile justice system operates within society. Its efforts and consequences are circumscribed and guided by the social arrangements of that particular historical, material, and cultural context which is society.*

In Chapter 14, we suggested the future juvenile court should include: limited jurisdiction, full implementation of due process, competent professional judges in every court, adequate and trained court personnel, and wider availability of a variety of dispositional alternatives. Here, we briefly expand on those recommendations.

Limited Jurisdiction

In our view, the juvenile court should not attempt to be all things to all people. By spreading itself so thinly, the court is proving itself woefully inadequate much of the time. The jurisdiction of the juvenile court should be limited to persons under the age of majority who have committed acts which violate criminal laws that would bring them before a criminal court if they were adults.

Much of what is brought to the attention of the juvenile court probably could be handled better through other courts, nonlegal channels, other agencies, or, possibly, even be ignored. Child abuse and neglect are serious problems and cannot be ignored. But should the same court which handles youthful murderers, rapists, robbers, and burglars attempt to deal with these? We think not. We contend that abused, neglected, and dependent children classified as in need of supervision should be handled in family courts rather than juvenile courts. This would accentuate the fact that these juveniles are *victims* and *not offenders*. Likewise, while status offenses such as truancy, smoking, and drinking may need attention, it is not necessary to deal with them in the same way (or even in the same court) as serious criminal offenses.

It should be noted, however, that despite the arguments for the elimination of status offenses from juvenile court jurisdiction, there still are people who strongly believe they should be retained as a function of the juvenile court. These arguments tend to focus on the lack of alternatives for handling such problems, and the belief that families, schools, and other social agencies need the official support of the legal system to effectively deal with the types of problems identified as status offenses (Myren, 1988). While acknowledging that the behaviors associated with status offenses are problematic, we believe that the streamlining of the juvenile court's jurisdiction is necessary. Consequently, we contend that status offenses should be removed from the juvenile courts, and problems associated with those behaviors be addressed by other social agencies and institutions such as the family, school, church, welfare departments, counseling services, and others. These revisions would substantially limit the jurisdiction of the juvenile court, reduce its caseload, and allow it to focus its attention on dealing with youthful criminal offenders.

In order to facilitate these types of changes in the juvenile courts, a number of juvenile statutes, criminal statutes, social attitudes, and values would have to be significantly revised. Two very important changes which would help streamline the juvenile court in limiting its jurisdiction would involve the standardization of juvenile laws within each state and across the nation, and developing a standard age limit which legally distinguishes juveniles from adults in all 50 states.

Due Process

Once the juvenile court is limited to dealing with criminal law violations, the full constitutional and legal rights of all who appear before it must be ensured (Krisberg and Austin, 1993). Schur (1973:168) insisted that "the juvenile justice system should concern itself less with the problems of so-called 'delinquents,' and more with dispensing justice." Limited due process has made its way into the juvenile court through important U.S. Supreme Court decisions, and an increasing number of juveniles are represented by attorneys when they appear before the court. Currently, however, the juvenile court is not a criminal court in which a clearcut adversarial relationship exists between the state and the accused. Consequently, all the rights guaranteed to an adult criminal offender are not necessarily granted to a juvenile who may have committed the same offense. This should be changed.

If the court's jurisdiction were limited as we have suggested, only juveniles who have allegedly committed criminal acts would appear before the court, and a judicial adversary relationship clearly would exist. The youth would be charged with violating a criminal statute. Though the case would be handled in a special court designed for such a purpose, all the basic rights of due process accorded the suspected adult criminal should also be available to the youthful offender. The right to know the charges, have counsel present during questioning and at the hearing, and the presumption of innocence until proven otherwise should be necessary components of the revised juvenile court. The rights to not testify against oneself, trial by jury, and open access to records also should be included. Naturally, the right to appeal decisions should exist. The specific details of implementation would have to be worked out in each state (e.g., would the jury consist of adults; or of the literal peers of the accused—other juveniles?), but the complete application of due process should be an intrinsic part of the court proceeding.

Professional Judges and Court Personnel

The role of the juvenile judge is critical, and, if the juvenile court is to be successful, this role must be filled by the most competent people available. Yet, in most states, juvenile judges are either elected by the people or appointed by governmental officials. This is not to imply that they are incompetent, but that the criteria for selection have less to do with legal and professional training than with political activity and party loyalty. In a report by the President's Commission on Law Enforcement and Administration of Justice (1967:6–7), a survey indicated that one-half of all juvenile judges did not have a college degree; one-fifth had received no college education at all; and one-fifth were not members of the bar. Steven Cox and John Conrad (1996) lamented that while many juvenile judges clearly have the best interests of juveniles at heart, far too many show unfamiliarity with juvenile codes.

The judge in a juvenile court should at least have a degree in law, be a member of the bar, be knowledgeable about juvenile statutes, and have some experience in legal proceedings. Further, some training in or at least familiarity with the areas of early childhood development, sociology, and adolescent psychology would be beneficial.

In addition to the judge, other well-trained court personnel and consultants should be available in order to effectively carry out the mission of the juvenile court (i.e., protect the juvenile while also protecting society). The specific types of professionals might vary in different courts, but would probably include social workers, psychologists, and paralegal professionals who would be responsible for background checks, social investigations, and prehearing screening. Regardless of the specific make-up of the court personnel, the judge should have all the necessary professionals to call upon in order to best decide a case. This would require total community support in addition to the hiring of persons for that specific purpose.

Dispositional Alternatives

The availability of wider dispositional alternatives also would necessitate large-scale community support. Often juvenile judges have no choices other than the extremes of incarceration in a maximum security institution, or outright release. Other alternatives should be available such as placement in foster homes, treatment centers, community youth projects, youth shelters, and hospitals. In most states, these options exist in theory, but in some states, not in practice. The lack of availability of qualified foster parents, lack of proper diagnostic and treatment centers, and the insufficient funding common in most states have severely limited dispositional alternatives available to the juvenile judge. Most communities could be offering many more placements than are now being offered.

In Chapter 16 we described some of the treatment and prevention programs that ha.e been developed and tried in various parts of the country. It is imperative that those programs which have been successful be supported, and it is important for sociologists, criminologists, social workers, juvenile justice officials, and community leaders to develop creative and innovative programs so that juvenile judges have a wide variety of dispositional alternatives.

Other Revisions

In 1977, a special conference on Juvenile Justice Standards convened in Washington, DC. Members of that conference concluded their meetings with the following recommendations for revising juvenile courts:

1. *Status offenses should be removed from juvenile court jurisdiction.*
2. *Visibility and accountability of decision making should replace unrestrained discretion and closed proceedings.*
3. *Juveniles should have the right to decide on actions affecting their lives and freedom, unless found incapable of making reasoned decisions.*
4. *Role of parents in juvenile proceedings should be redefined, especially when there is potential conflict between the interests of the juvenile and the parents.*

> 5. *Limitation should be imposed on detention, treatment, or other intervention prior to adjudication and disposition.*
> 6. *Strict criteria should be established for waiver of juvenile court jurisdiction to regulate transfer of juveniles to adult criminal court (Juvenile Justice Standards Project, 1977:2).*

More recently, Ira Schwartz (1989) proposed an agenda for juvenile court revision which concluded that the *parens patriae* model of the juvenile court should be discarded. He indicated that delinquency proceedings should be opened to the public and the media so that they are subjected to the same scrutiny and accountability as criminal courts. Overall, Schwartz emphasized that the structure and quality of juvenile courts needed serious improvement, and that the number one priority of the courts should be dispensing justice.

Numerous scholars have made similar recommendations in an attempt to salvage the juvenile justice system and allow it to regain (or gain for the first time, its most severe critics might contend) its credibility. Others contend that the juvenile court and the juvenile justice system that it represents should not be changed, but abolished altogether (see Box 17-2). Hirschi and Gottfredson (1993), for example, argue that separating offenders on the basis of age is arbitrary and that one justice system for all would be better than two. Interestingly, however, they argue that of the two existing systems, the juvenile model is superior to the adult courts (Hirschi and Gottfredson, 1993).

Modification of Juvenile Corrections

Regardless of whether the juvenile court is kept as is, substantially revised, or eliminated altogether, there remains a need to dramatically modify juvenile corrections. Two necessary changes in juvenile corrections would begin with the disposition (or sentencing) phase of the correctional process. It has been suggested that juvenile sentencing should be **determinate** in nature, and **proportionate** to the seriousness of the offense (Juvenile Justice Standards Project, 1977; Mahler, 1977).

Determinate sentencing refers to *a disposition which specifies a definite period of time for the individual to be incarcerated, on probation, or otherwise supervised by the state.* In other words, rather than placing a juvenile under the auspices of an institution or court officer for an indefinite period of time, the length of sentence would be clearly delineated (e.g., 1 year, 2 years, or until the age of majority). This would eliminate the unreasonable power and unlimited discretion of probation officers, institution supervisors, and others who determine how long a juvenile is to remain under court supervision.

Proportionate sentencing simply means that *the severity of dispositions should be equivalent to the seriousness of the offense committed.* A major problem with juvenile corrections has stemmed from the inappropriateness and inconsistencies of sentences imposed upon juvenile offenders. One reads with horror of a 16-year-old juvenile being sent to a detention facility for a period of 18 months for committing homicide, while another youth aged 13 is remanded to an institution for the remainder of his minority (5 years) for shoplifting. Remember, the case which stimulated the landmark *Gault Decision* involved a young boy who allegedly made an obscene phone call, and was sent to a detention facility

BOX 17-2 Controversial Issue

Should Juvenile Courts Be Abolished?

Frustration over the juvenile court's inability to effectively handle serious juvenile offenders has prompted many of its critics to call for its abolition. Francis McCarthy (1977) contended that the legal concept of delinquency began to die with the Gault decision of 1967, and indicated that subsequent attempts to reformulate the legal concept of delinquency have failed. He concluded that delinquency jurisdiction should be removed from the juvenile court and be reverted to the criminal courts where the highly valued interests of society as well as the rights of juveniles can be protected more fully. Prominent criminologist Ernest van den Haag forcefully underscored that notion when he asserted:

> *I would abolish tomorrow all juvenile courts because they have been a terrible failure. I believe that anyone over thirteen should be dealt with in the adult court. (Cited in Bartollas, 1985:111.)*

Others added their voices to those calling for abolition of the juvenile court in contending that the rights of juveniles and social justice would be better served if youthful offenders were processed through adult criminal courts (e.g., Feld, 1993; 1999). Acknowledging that most juvenile offenses are misdemeanors in nature, many urge that even in cases for nonserious offenses it is important that the basic legal principles of criminal court be followed. Most of the calls for abolition of separate juvenile courts are accompanied by a push for decriminalization of status offenses and standardization of legal statutes governing juveniles' behavior. Since all cases brought against juveniles would then involve acts which would be crimes if committed by adults, the criminal court is viewed as the appropriate legal vehicle for their disposition. Many of the advocates for abolition believe that while juveniles should be tried in adult courts, it is still important to separate youthful offenders from adult criminals in correctional settings. Very few advocate incarcerating juveniles in adult prisons, although public opinion polls clearly show that a majority of Americans favor youthful felons being treated as adults

(Schwartz, et al., 1993). Rather than promoting a "get tough on juvenile crime" philosophy, the juvenile court abolition movement represents more of a movement to guarantee legal due process for juveniles accused of crimes.

Others contend that the move to abolish juvenile courts is misguided, and that while the implementation of juvenile justice has been seriously flawed, the philosophy behind it is not. Diane Dwyer and Roger McNally (1987), for example, insist that the *parens patriae* roots of the juvenile court were a response to important necessary legal reforms, and that to dismantle the juvenile court system would be a grave mistake. They argue that transferring youths to criminal courts would not solve any problems other than to express a lack of confidence in the present concept of juvenile justice. In their view, the abolition of juvenile courts would only lead to more problems as misdirected juveniles would be thrust into an already overburdened and equally ineffective adult criminal justice system. Instead of dismantling juvenile courts, they call for a reaffirmation of the basic protective and rehabilitative philosophy of the court and significant reforms to aid in its fulfillment of its original mission of preventing juvenile delinquents from becoming adult criminals.

Former juvenile court judge, H. Ted Rubin, a vocal critic of juvenile courts, echoed the sentiments of those in favor of reform over abolition. Despite its many flaws and shortcomings, Rubin (1979) believes that a separate system of juvenile justice should be retained. He calls for a major overhaul of juvenile courts which would include the elimination of status offenses, prohibition of the right of waiver of counsel, more accountability for juvenile court personnel (especially judges), and emphasis on due process and judicial fairness in handling juvenile cases.

The debate over whether juvenile courts should be retained or abolished continues. It calls attention to one important area of common consensus regarding juvenile courts, however, and that is the agreement that they are not functioning effectively at present.

Continued

BOX 17-2 *Continued*

Sources

Bartollas, Clemens. *Juvenile delinquency.* New York: Wiley, 1985.
Dwyer, Diane C., and McNally, Roger B. "Juvenile justice: Reform, retain, and reaffirm," *Federal Probation* 51 (September), 1987:47–51.
Feld, Barry C. "Juvenile (in) justice and the criminal court alternative." *Crime & Delinquency* 39 (October), 1993:403–424.
———. Bad Kids: Race and the Transformation of the Juvenile Court. New York: Oxford University Press, 1999.
McCarthy, Francis B. "Should juvenile delinquency be abolished?" *Crime and Delinquency* 23 (April), 1977:196–203.
Rubin, H. Ted. "Retain the juvenile court?" *Crime and Delinquency* 25 (July), 1979:281–298.
Schwartz, Ira M., Guo Shenyang, and John J. Kerbs. "The impact of demographic variables on public opinion regarding juvenile justice: Implications for public policy." *Crime & Delinquency* 39 (January), 1993:5–28.

---

for the remainder of his minority (6 years), whereas an adult would have received a maximum punishment of a $50 fine and/or 60 days in jail for the same offense. Mahler (1977) pointed out that in most states, juvenile dispositions are indeterminate and *not* related to the seriousness of the offense. He contended that juveniles should know where they are going, why they are going there, and for how long. Further, he suggested that a Case Assessment Bureau should be established to assess the gravity of the offense committed, and to prevent courts from imposing sanctions that are inordinately lenient or harsh.

If juvenile court dispositions are to be effective, there must be a wide range of dispositional alternatives available to the court. For juveniles who have committed serious criminal offenses, some type of maximum security correctional facility is necessary (Lundman, 1993). The message must be sent out to youthful hoodlums who terrorize innocent citizens that they cannot hide behind their juvenile status. Cox and Conrad (1996) suggested that those juveniles who commit predatory offenses may have to be institutionalized for the good of society. However, they warned that "the 'out-of-sight, out-of-mind' attitude should be eliminated through the use of programs designed to increase community contact as soon as possible" (Cox and Conrad, 1996:178).

In addition to maximum security facilities, there should be medium and minimum security institutions for less serious offenders. These centers also could be used to help ease the transition of even the most serious offenders back into the community prior to their release. Those incarcerated in the maximum security facility could be transferred to a medium security institution after a period of time, and if they successfully adapt to the increased freedom and responsibility there, they could eventually be transferred to a minimum security facility before being completely released. Thus, the offender would gradually experience increased freedom and responsibility while still under supervision. As Cox and Conrad (1996) indicated, assignment to these various facilities should not be made on a random basis or for convenience of vacancy or transfer. Rather, the seriousness of offense, prior offense record, age, and other pertinent factors should be taken into consideration in developing standard criteria for gradual return to the larger society.

This plan would necessitate major changes in existing juvenile institutions, and the creation of many new facilities. In addition to institutions, a number of smaller community treatment programs need to be implemented (Ferdinand, 1991). Neighborhood and community correctional approaches should be applied to less serious offenses and community treatment programs such as halfway houses, work furlough, probation, and closely supervised parole need to be expanded. This has been attempted in many areas, but, unfortunately, economic policies often severely limit the amount of federal and state funds available to finance such programs.

Schwartz (1989) suggested that juvenile institutions should be closed entirely. He lamented that juvenile correctional facilities are primarily custodial in nature, promote future criminal careers, experience high recidivism rates, and have no place in an enlightened juvenile justice system.

Closing juvenile correctional institutions indeed represents a workable approach to the problem, especially if the decision were made to eliminate separate juvenile codes and to abolish the juvenile court. Under such a plan, juveniles who currently are institutionalized for status offenses would be handled outside the legal system by other social agencies. Those who committed criminal acts would be handled by the adult criminal court system. If convicted of a crime, they would be sentenced as adults. This does not necessarily mean that they should be placed in adult jails and prisons as they presently exist. It might be that society would like to establish age-graded correctional institutions and want to separate criminal offenders on the basis of age. For example, separate correctional institutions could be created for offenders ranging from 16 to 25 years of age, while other facilities could house those between the ages of 26 and 45. Still another institution could be designed to house offenders aged 46 and older.

Another possible approach to the corrections dilemma might be to segregate offenders by types of offense, and to separate first-time offenders from recidivists. This would address problems faced today in both juvenile and adult corrections, in that relatively nonserious first-time offenders now often must be housed in the same facilities (and sometimes even in the same cells) with hardened repeat offenders. Most 16-year-old nonviolent offenders share more in common with the 36-year-old property criminal than with the 16-year-old robber, rapist, or murderer. Type of offense and prior criminal record might be more logical criteria for institutional segregation than mere chronological age.

A final suggestion related to juvenile corrections would be to minimize the stigma associated with adjudication and disposition. Along with being determinate and proportionate, sentences should also be finite. In other words, once a juvenile (or adult) is released from a correctional facility, or some other disposition (e.g., probation), the individual's "debt to society" should be erased. Haskell and Yablonsky (1978:557) recommended "amnesty upon completion of sentence" pointing out that once juveniles (and adults) have completed their restitution, it should be over. They suggested that arrest and sentencing records should not be publicly available, thus avoiding the stigma which denies equal access to schools, jobs, and other social activities.

Many researchers recommend more community-based delinquency correctional and prevention programs (e.g., Burns and Stern, 1967; Winslow, 1973; Haskell and Yablonsky, 1978; Krisberg and Austin, 1978; Schwartz, 1989; Ferdinand, 1991; Regoli and Hewitt, 1991; Cox and Conrad, 1996). However, not all communities have equal resources to provide adequate programs. Krisberg and Austin (1978:574) pointed out that the separation of delinquency prevention from basic human needs creates a false distinction, and insisted, "Reducing crime, improving the quality of education, promoting mental health, and supporting family life are several sides to a common, if complex, human service enterprise."

Acknowledging the social nature of delinquency, they pointed out that delinquency research indicates that we should encourage the full healthy development of all youths, stating:

> *Local centers…could offer educational and counseling programs in…health, nutrition, mental health, welfare, parent-effectiveness, and employment. Staffed by community people and professionals, neighborhood-based service centers could provide a vehicle for community organization efforts such as public forums on delinquency and related problems. (Krisberg and Austin, 1978:575)*

Strengthening the Family

Over the past two decades, perhaps no social institution has been paid more political "lip service" and yet more thoroughly ignored than the family. We learned in Chapters 7 and 9 that a strong social bond with the family is one of the most effective insulators against delinquent behavior. Also, in Chapter 9, we explored some ways in which the family can be involved in delinquency prevention. In this chapter we emphasize that in addition to the many social, legal, and judicial changes we have suggested, the process of rethinking the problem of delinquency must also involve strategies for strengthening the family.

When we suggest strengthening the family, we are not referring to the hollow political rhetoric of promoting "traditional family values." This popular phrase often serves as a thinly veiled slur toward everything from dual-career couples, to same-sex couples, single-parent, and even poor families, and urges a return to some mythical idyllic family of the past as portrayed by the media in *Leave it to Beaver* and *Father Knows Best*. Such nostalgia may

Research indicates that a close-knit family may play an important role in the prevention of juvenile delinquency.

be comforting, but in the twenty-first century, it is hardly practical or desirable. Rather, we suggest that meaningful social changes must be made to accommodate and reinforce the importance of the entire spectrum of families as they exist in today's real world—dual career, single-parent, same-sex, blended, stepfamilies, and others. These changes should include but not be limited to:

- adequate and affordable day care for working couples with children and single parents;
- paid maternity and paternity leave;
- family leave days for parents of both sexes for children's illnesses, parent-teacher conferences, to attend school functions, sporting events, etc.;
- adequate and affordable health care and health insurance for all families;
- equitable pay for women;
- access to affordable education, job training, and vocational counseling for all;
- educational, counseling, legal, and support services for families that suffer domestic violence;
- support services for families where a juvenile has broken the law;
- social, moral, financial, and legal accountability of parents for the whereabouts and activities of their minor children.

The family is the primary agent of socialization and the first line of societal defense against juvenile delinquency. If we are serious in our efforts to reduce and prevent delinquent activities, our efforts must begin with strengthening the family. Some states are now holding parents of delinquent children accountable for the actions of their minor children (e.g., truancy, property damage, etc.,), but few if any provide social, financial, or legal resources to families to deal with these troubled youths. If we are to meaningfully rethink the problem of delinquency, we must provide the resources necessary for families to successfully raise children, and then hold them accountable to do so. This involves rethinking all aspects of society and creating a cooperative effort among all social institutions. In that light, we turn to education.

Changing the Educational System

Earlier in this chapter we emphasized the importance of providing meaningful social roles for juveniles which give them greater decision-making power, especially in areas which affect their lives. With the possible exception of the family, no social institution more directly influences the lives of young Americans than the educational system. In our opinion, if meaningful social change is to come about in an effort to reduce the problems currently associated with juvenile delinquency, the schools will need to play a very significant role.

In Chapter 10, we explored the social arena of the school and its relationship to juvenile delinquency and delinquency prevention. At the end of that chapter we suggested ways in which the schools might take a more active role in delinquency prevention. Those suggestions included: less emphasis upon identifying and labeling "predelinquents"; reeducating and resocializing parents, teachers, and students to the problems associated with the success-failure philosophy of the schools; a wider range of tolerance of nonserious rule violations by students; and reducing some of the bureaucratization of the educational process.

Again, we must recognize the social context in which the schools exist and operate. Substantive changes in the educational process must be accompanied by widespread changes in the attitudes, values, and norms surrounding it. Since the Industrial Revolution, schools have tended to be modeled after the factory. Students entering the system are essentially viewed as "raw materials" to be shaped, formed, and molded into "finished products" upon graduation. The factory model revolutionized education, but not all of its results have been positive. The blue-ribbon panel of experts which produced the highly touted study *A Nation at Risk* (U.S. National Commission on Excellence in Education, 1983) enumerated some of the major problems related to education in America. Even that study, however, did not seriously question the attitudes, values, and norms which provide the foundation for the educational system. Rather, it primarily lamented declining test scores, lack of basic skills, and the failure of the teaching profession to retain the "best and the brightest." While these are significant issues, they do not address the broader scope of the problem.

The schools are one of the most important elements in reducing the problems of delinquency, but dramatic changes need to be made in the educational system. For instance, Krisberg and Austin (1978:575) insisted that education must be more broadly defined with an expanded curriculum and a modified idea "…about who should be involved in the learning process and where education takes place." They suggested broader community involvement in all aspects of the schools.

In our view, broader community involvement should also include more meaningful participation on the part of juveniles. One of the ways to provide youths with more access to the power structure in education would be to include students on local school boards. This would give them direct input on budget, personnel, and curriculum decisions as well as enhance their identity and status as role models for other youths.

Most colleges and universities allow a degree of student participation in campus government. Students serve on committees, have a student government association, and usually participate in the evaluation of their professors. These same procedures generally have not been incorporated at the high school or lower levels. Why not? We are not advocating turning the schools over to the students. Rather, we are suggesting that students should be included in the decision-making process in the school system. J. David Hawkins and Joseph Weis (1980) also viewed the school as one of the potentially most effective sources of delinquency control. They suggested more thorough and broader vocational training, alternative education opportunities, education in civil and criminal law, and more student input into educational programs. We anticipate that more student input might lead to a stronger commitment by students to the common educational endeavor and objective. Such participation would help develop leadership and analytical skills needed for problem solving. Moreover, participation in policymaking and administrative tasks would sensitize students to a broader perspective on many of the problems faced by schools.

Another change to be explored for the public schools is the elimination of compulsory school attendance laws. School attendance is important as a democratic society demands an educated citizenry. Yet many youths feel totally alienated, and experience nothing but frustration and failure in school. When truants are tracked down by police, processed as delinquent, and then forcibly brought back to school, it is not likely that positive educational results will occur. Once a person has undergone the rite of passage we have suggested denoting the transition into adulthood, the decision to attend school or drop out should rest

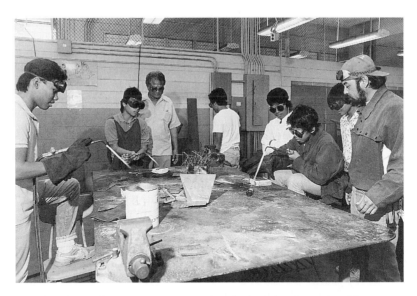

In rethinking delinquency, more vocational educational opportunities should be provided to youths who choose not to pursue a college education.

with that person. If alternative vocational and training programs are made available, the stigma of dropping out of school could be greatly reduced. Those desiring to stay in school and further their formal academic education would not be hampered by having to share limited educational resources with those who really do not want to partake of them. Similarly, this should greatly reduce the vandalism and violence in the public schools from those who are "imprisoned" there against their will.

Redefining Juvenile Delinquency

The recommendations made in this chapter amount to nothing short of a total redefinition of the concept of juvenile delinquency. In our view, this redefining process is long overdue, and essential if society is genuinely interested in reducing the problems associated with delinquency. In general, this redefinition must reflect a serious assessment by societal members as to what youthful behavior can and cannot be tolerated. Frederick Howlett (1973:492) insisted that "the community clearly must redefine its limits of acceptable behavior." Our current laws prohibit many behaviors which society is willing to allow, and in fact, routinely does allow for many. Curfew violation, premarital sexual activities, smoking, truancy, and other status offenses are routinely ignored by some parents, teachers, and law enforcement officials. On the other hand, on occasion, the full force of the justice system may be exercised upon a youth who commits any one of these offenses. Such hypocrisy and random or selective enforcement helps create general disrespect toward the law and the legal process.

Narrowing the definition of delinquency as we have suggested would help reduce the problems of hypocrisy and disrespect. Only those behaviors that are considered beyond toleration by the larger society should be classified as illegal or delinquent. Schur (1973:154) suggested this approach in his concept of *radical nonintervention,* explaining:

> *Basically, radical nonintervention implies policies that accommodate society to the widest possible diversity of behaviors and attitudes, rather than forcing as many individuals as possible to "adjust" to supposedly common societal standards (Schur, 1973:154).*

The basic principle of radical non-intervention is *"leave the kids alone wherever possible"* [italics in the original] (Schur, 1973:155). At the same time, we suggest that society must seek consensus on some basic non-negotiable standards of behavior. Those activities that do not seriously threaten the social order would be tolerated; however, those that were deemed beyond the range of tolerance by the larger society would be swiftly and appropriately sanctioned.

We have presented two possible ways in which society can broaden its range of tolerance and reduce some of the problems of juvenile delinquency. One solution is to redefine delinquency so as to standardize juvenile codes and eliminate status offenses. This standardization would include clearly specifying both the minimum and the maximum ages for juvenile court jurisdiction while retaining a sociological perspective on delinquency. Hence, the revised definition of delinquency would be: *all acts committed by individuals between the ages of 7 and 16 (or possibly 14) which would be considered criminal if committed by an adult, place the youth in the delinquent/criminal role, and result in society regarding the juvenile as intolerably deviant.* This new definition alone would resolve some of the problems of delinquency, especially those related to the ambiguity of its meaning. In order for this definition to be effective, however, it would need to be accompanied by some of the widespread modifications and revisions we have suggested in the operation of the juvenile court, and in juvenile corrections. This more concise and narrower definition would greatly reduce the quantity of what is considered delinquency, and allow available resources to be redirected in a more effective way toward implementing some of the proposed revisions in the court and correctional system. While the social problem of juvenile delinquency would not be eliminated, it would be significantly reduced. Further, the remaining juvenile delinquency which occurred could be handled more effectively.

A second, and perhaps more controversial way to approach the redefinition of juvenile delinquency, would be to "define it out of existence." You may remember from Chapter 2, we pointed out that sociologists view deviance as a natural consequence of the normative system of society. When norms are created, so is deviance. Thus, society cannot hope to eliminate deviance, but must continually seek methods for effectively controlling it and minimizing its negative impacts upon its members. Consequently, defining juvenile delinquency out of existence will not actually eliminate the behaviors that currently constitute delinquency. Youngsters would still skip school, run away from home, steal, and even rape and murder. However, while redefining delinquency would not eliminate those behaviors, it would dramatically change our reactions to them. Truancy and running away from home would not be illegal acts. Consequently, they would be ignored by the criminal justice system—not ignored by society—but ignored by the legal system. Stealing, raping, and killing, on the other hand, would be crimes—not delinquent acts—but crimes, and society would still react with justified indignation.

This second alternative would require the most dramatic social changes. Undoubtedly, society would not want to invoke full legal sanctions upon children just because they had reached the age of 7. Instead, children aged 7 would be considered just that—**children.** Children would not be held legally accountable for their actions until they had gone through a formal rite of passage initiating them into adulthood. While this initiation is often directly associated with the onset of puberty in many societies, it could be adjusted to fit society's consensually agreed-upon age. The rite of passage could be conducted at the age of 14, 15, or 16. From that point on, the individual would be accorded full adult status in society with all the normative expectations associated with adulthood—*rights* as well as *responsibilities.* Thus, any criminal violations would be handled through criminal courts.

There is ample research evidence to suggest that the midteens would be a logical point for legally differentiating between children and adults. For example, Barry Glassner et al. (1983) found that many youths sharply reduced their involvement in illegal activities after age 16. When asked, respondents indicated that they believed that there was a much greater probability of their being adjudicated as an adult, and actually going to prison if arrested after age 16. These findings indicated that being held legally accountable for their actions as adults had a highly specific deterrent effect on the subjects. Similarly, numerous studies suggest that many juveniles apparently "grow out" of their delinquency somewhere in their midteens (Wolfgang, et al., 1972; Lab, 1984), and official data indicate that both property and violent offenders tend to peak at about ages 16 and 17 (*FBI Uniform Crime Reports,* 1999).

This **spontaneous remission,** or *"aging out" phenomenon whereby juveniles at some point reach a level of maturity where they spontaneously reduce, and eventually even eliminate their involvement in law-violating behavior* may be partially explained by at least three well-known theories. *Maturation Theory* contends that juveniles may "grow out" of their delinquency (see Chapter 4). *Life Cycle Theory* contends that as youths progress through the life cycle and assume more conventional roles such as spouse, employee, and others, their values, attitudes, and beliefs are directed toward conformity and away from law violation (Rand, 1987). *Neutralization Theory* can also help explain this process as it contends that delinquents internalize the dominant social norms and are, for the most part, committed to them, but through a variety of circumstances may "drift" into delinquency if they can successfully rationalize or "neutralize" their deviance (Sykes and Matza, 1957; 1964). As a youth ages and becomes more mature, he or she is likely to become more committed to conventional norms, making it more difficult to rationalize deviant behavior (Thompson, 1994).

That being the case, perhaps lowering the age of legal accountability to 14 would achieve the same purpose. Youths would know that at age 14 they would socially and legally become adults. This might provide the same type of deterrent effect. In harmony with this idea, we know that, generally, young people in our society are reaching puberty at a younger age each generation. Therefore, rite of passage into adult social status would tend to approximate the biological onset of adulthood.

We concur with Jerome Stumphauzer's (1986) point that it is important to recognize and reinforce nondelinquency. Unfortunately, most of our attention is focused on punishing delinquents, not on rewarding nondelinquents. More public recognition of conforming and desired behavior by youths could serve to positively reinforce law abiding behavior.

We do not presume to know which direction society should take on this matter. Nor do we presume that these two possible directions in redefining delinquency are the only alternatives.

We do believe, however, that it is essential that there be a careful and innovative rethinking of the delinquency problem by our entire society.

This would entail vigorous new directions in research and theory construction to develop theories which can be *applied* by public policy makers and practitioners. More attention must be focused upon social conformity as offering fresh insights into deviant and delinquent behavior. Most researchers and theorists have focused upon the more sensational and interesting deviants, almost to the exclusion of the vast majority of youngsters not involved in serious offenses.

Another dimension to our call for new research and theory emphasizes the need for genuine interdisciplinary studies. Sociologists can hardly continue to ignore the accumulating etiological insights from other disciplines. Likewise, other disciplines must not ignore the important contributions of sociology toward explaining and controlling juvenile delinquency.

SUMMARY

The best way to summarize this chapter is to present a list of suggestions and/or recommendations for possible changes that would alter the way Americans view young people, juvenile misconduct, and youthful crime. The goals of these changes would be to more effectively deal with the social problem of juvenile delinquency, and to reduce and/or eliminate its negative impact upon society. Toward those ends, we suggest the following:

1. Delinquency is a social product and therefore must be viewed in its broadest sociological context. This requires societal members to seriously examine the values, attitudes, beliefs, and norms which surround the concept of juvenile delinquency.

2. Reduce or eliminate the marginal status of adolescence. This most effectively could be accomplished by establishing a meaningful rite of passage from childhood to adulthood which roughly coincides with or shortly follows the onset of puberty.

3. Provide meaningful social roles for individuals who have completed the rite of passage into adulthood. Eliminate barriers to reasonable employment based solely on age, and allow full participation in meaningful social roles and decision-making processes.

4. Standardize (or possibly eliminate) juvenile codes. If separate juvenile codes are maintained, there should be a uniform minimum and maximum age of juvenile court jurisdiction across the United States. Similarly, the definition of delinquency should be standardized, simplified, and clarified.

5. Decriminalize status offenses. Legal codes should narrow the concept of delinquency to include only those actions which would be crimes if committed by adults.

6. Revise (or possibly eliminate) the juvenile court system. If separate juvenile courts are maintained, they must be staffed with a wide variety of highly trained specialists. At the very least, all juveniles should be guaranteed the same access to full due process of law as are adults.

7. Modify juvenile corrections. Incorporate determinate and proportionate sentencing into the disposition phase of juvenile justice. Segregate first-time offenders from repeat offenders and nonviolent offenders from violent offenders. Create minimum, medium, and maximum security institutions with emphasis upon community participation in the correctional process, and successful reintegration into the community as the ultimate goal.

8. Remove the stigma attached to having gone through the juvenile and/or criminal justice system. Punishment for law violations should be finite. Once sanctions have been exercised, societal response to the deviance should end and the youth should be allowed and encouraged to resume his or her life.

9. Strengthen the family by making a wide range of changes that provide social, financial, and legal support for the adequate raising of children, and then hold parents accountable for the whereabouts and activities of their minor children.

10. Change the educational system. Deemphasize the process of identifying "problem children" and "predelinquents." Eliminate the success-failure philosophy which dominates education. Recog-

nize the importance of vocational and technical education as well as traditional academic pursuits, and remove the stigma currently associated with many of those nonacademic programs. Eliminate the "factory model" philosophy of education. Create stronger ties between the community and the schools, and allow students to participate in the decision-making processes in their schools.

11. Redefine juvenile delinquency. Either: (a) standardize, clarify, and narrow the definition of delinquency to include only those acts that society clearly cannot and should not tolerate from youths; or (b) eliminate the concept of juvenile delinquency altogether by lowering the age of legal responsibility so that parents would be held legally responsible for law violations of children under the cutoff age, and youthful offenders over that age would be legally handled as adult criminals.

12. Apply new sociological and interdisciplinary approaches to research and theoretical explanations of youthful conformity and deviance. And, apply sociological and interdisciplinary theories to public policy and social practice.

The implementation of some or all of these suggestions would alter dramatically the way our society views juvenile delinquency. Many of the negative consequences of delinquency would be diminished, and perhaps some would even be eliminated. However, it would not eliminate youthful misconduct and law-violating behavior. While youthful deviance might be reduced through implementation of our ideas, as long as we have social norms, we will have social deviance. No society can exist without norms. Therefore, deviance is inherently a part of every society. On the other hand, the way in which society chooses to define and react to deviance can be changed. Perhaps it is time that we do just that in regard to juvenile delinquency.

Concept Integration

Questions and Topics for Study and Discussion

1. Why is it important to view juvenile delinquency within a social context? What dominant values, attitudes, beliefs, and norms surround the concept of delinquency? What social changes would have to occur for society's concept of juvenile delinquency to be significantly altered?

2. Should separate juvenile codes be retained? If not, why not? If so, should they be standardized? Should they be reinforced? Why? Why not? What revisions would you recommend?

3. Do you favor the elimination of status offenses? Why? Why not?

4. Should a separate juvenile court be retained? If not, why not? If so, what modifications should be made in the present juvenile justice system? How might the juvenile court be modified to more effectively deal with the problem of delinquency?

5. What changes would you recommend in the present educational system in an effort to reduce the alienation of youths and lessen or prevent youthful misconduct and law violation?

6. Do you favor redefining the concept of juvenile delinquency? Or legally eliminating the concept altogether? If redefined, what should be the new definition? If eliminated, how would you handle the problems which now constitute delinquency?

7. What rites of passage presently function in American society to ease the transition from childhood to adulthood? Can you think of any new ones which might make this transition easier and possibly alleviate some of the problems faced by today's youths?

References

Albanese, J. S. 1993. *Dealing with delinquency: The future of juvenile justice* (2nd ed.). Chicago: Nelson-Hall.

Austin, R. 1977. Religion and crime control. Unpublished paper presented at the Conference of American Society of Criminology in Atlanta, GA.

Bartollas, C. 1985. *Juvenile delinquency.* New York: John Wiley.

Boyd, N. 1980. The circularity of punishment and treatment: Some notes on the legal response to juvenile delinquency. *Canadian Journal of Family Law* 3 (4):419–438.

Burns, V., and Stern, L. 1967. The prevention of juvenile delinquency. In *Task Force Report: Juvenile Delinquency and Youth Crime.* President's Commission on Law Enforcement and Administration. Washington, DC: U.S. Government Printing Office, Appendix S, pp. 361–364.

Conley, J. A. (Ed.). 1994. *The 1967 President's Crime Commission Report: Its impact 25 years later.* Cincinnati: Anderson.

Cox, S. M., and Conrad, J. J. 1996. *Juvenile justice: A guide to practice and theory* (4th ed.). Dubuque, IA: Brown and Benchmark.

Deardorff, N. R. 1955. The religio-cultural background of New York City's population. *Milbank Quarterly* 33 (April):152–160.

FBI Uniform Crime Reports. 1999. *Crime in the United States: Uniform Crime Reports—1998.* Washington, DC: U.S. Government Printing Office.

Ferdinand, T. N. 1991. History overtakes the juvenile justice system. *Crime and Delinquency* 37 (April):204–224.

Glassner, B., Ksander, M., Berg, B., and Johnson, B. D. 1983. A note on the deterrent effect of juvenile vs. adult jurisdiction. *Social Problems* 31 (December): 219–221.

Godwin, T. M. 1996. A guide for implementing teen court programs. *Office of Juvenile Justice and Delinquency Prevention, Fact Sheet #45* (August) Washington, DC: U.S. Dept. of Justice.

Goodman, P. 1962. *Growing up absurd: Problems of youth in the organized society.* New York: Random House.

Gruber, P. 1998. The National youth network. *Youth in Action* 1 (March):1–2.

Haskell, M. R., and Yablonsky, L. 1978. *Juvenile delinquency* (2nd ed.). Chicago: Rand McNally.

Hawkins, J. D., and Weis, J. G. 1980. *The social developmental model: An integrated approach to delinquency prevention.* Seattle: Center for Law and Justice, University of Washington.

Hirschi, T., and Gottfredson, M. 1993. Rethinking the juvenile justice system. *Crime and Delinquency* 39 (April):262–271.

Howlett, F. W. 1973. Is the Youth Service Bureau all it's cracked up to be? *Crime and Delinquency* 91 (October):485–492.

Juvenile Justice Standards Project. 1977. *Juvenile justice standards.* Washington, DC: National Conference on the Proposed IJA/ABA Juvenile Justice Standards, October 30–November 3.

Keniston, K. 1968. *Young radicals: Notes on committed youth.* New York: Harcourt, Brace and World.

Klein, H. 1990. Adolescence, youth, and young adulthood: Rethinking current conceptualizations of life stage. *Youth & Society* 21 (June):446–471.

Krisberg, B., and Austin, J. (Eds.). 1978. *The children of Ishmael: Critical perspectives on juvenile justice.* Palo Alto, CA: Mayfield.

———. 1993. *Reinventing juvenile justice.* Newbury Park, CA: Sage.

Kvaraceus, W. 1945. *Juvenile delinquency and the school.* Yonkers: World Book.

Lab, S. P. 1984. Patterns in juvenile misbehavior. *Crime and Delinquency* 30 (April):293–308.

Liebow, E. 1967. *Tally's corner: A study of Negro street-corner men.* Boston: Little, Brown.

Logan, C. H., and Rausch, S. P. 1985. Why deinstitutionalizing status offenders is pointless. *Crime and Delinquency* 31 (October):501–517.

Lotz, R., Poole, E. D., and Regoli, R. M. 1985. *Juvenile delinquency and juvenile justice.* New York: Random House.

Lundman, R. 1993. *Prevention and control of juvenile delinquency* (2nd ed.). New York: Oxford University Press.

Mahler, J. M. 1977. *Rational approach to the reality of juvenile crime in America.* Rockville, MD: National Institute of Justice.

McCarthy, F. B. 1977. Should juvenile delinquency be abolished? *Crime and Delinquency* 23 (April): 196–203.

Mead, M. 1928. *Growing up in Samoa.* New York: LW Morrow.

Mills, C. W. 1959. *The sociological imagination.* New York: Oxford University Press.

Morris, N., and Hawkins, G. 1970. *The honest politician's guide to crime control.* Chicago: University of Chicago Press.

Musgrove, F. 1965. *Youth and the social order.* Bloomington: Indiana University Press.

Myren, R. A. 1988. *Law and justice: An introduction.* Belmont, CA: Wadsworth.

National Advisory Committee for Juvenile Justice and Delinquency Prevention. 1984. *Serious juvenile crime: A redirected federal effort.* Washington, DC: U.S. Government Printing Office.

Office of Juvenile Justice and Delinquency Prevention. 1979. *Delinquency prevention: Theories and strategies.* Washington, DC: Law Enforcement Assistance Administration, U.S. Department of Justice.

Oswalt, W. H. 1986. *Life cycles and lifeways: An introduction to cultural anthropology.* Palo Alto, CA: Mayfield.

Regnery, A. S. 1985. Getting away with murder: Why the juvenile justice system needs an overhaul. *Policy Review* 34 (Fall):1–4.

Regoli, R. M., and Hewitt, J. D. 1991. *Delinquency in society: A child-centered approach.* New York: McGraw-Hill.

Schur, E. M. 1973. *Radical non-intervention: Rethinking the delinquency problem.* Englewood Cliffs, NJ: Prentice-Hall.

Schwartz, I. M. 1989. *(In)justice for juveniles. Rethinking the best interests of the child.* Lexington, MA: Lexington Books.

Sipila, J. 1985. Community structure and deviant behavior among adolescents. *Youth and Society* 16 (June):471–497.

Snyder, H. N., and Sickmund, M. 1999. Juvenile Offenders and Victims: 1999 National Report. Washington, DC: Office of Juvenile and Delinquency Prevention.

Stumphauzer, J. S. 1986. *Helping delinquents change: A treatment manual of social learning approaches.* New York: Haworth Press.

The Daily Tidings. 1977. Kid corporation is in trouble again. *Daily Tidings,* Ashland, Oregon, November 3, 1977:3.

Thompson, W. E. 1994. Spontaneous Remission. In *Encyclopedia of Criminology.* New York: MacMillan.

U.S. National Commission on Excellence in Education. 1983. *A nation at risk.* Washington, DC: U.S. Government Printing Office.

Van Gennep, A. [1908] 1960. *The rights of passage* (Trans. M. B. Vizedom, and G. L. Caffee). Chicago: University of Chicago Press.

Whyte, W. F. 1943. *Street corner society: The social structure of an urban slum.* Chicago: University of Chicago Press.

Winslow, R. H. (Ed.). 1973. *Juvenile delinquency in a free society* (2nd ed.). Encino, CA: Dickenson.

Wolfgang, M. E., Figlio, R. M., and Sellin, T. 1972. *Delinquency in a birth cohort.* Chicago: University of Chicago Press.

Wolfgang, M. E., Thornberry, T. P., and Figlio, R. M. 1987. *From boy to man, from delinquency to crime.* Chicago: University of Chicago Press.

Youth Development and Delinquency Prevention Administration. 1972. *Delinquency prevention through youth development.* Youth Development and Delinquency Prevention Administration Pub. no. (SRS) 73–26013. Washington, DC: U.S. Government Printing Office (May):28–30.

GLOSSARY

Achieved Status   A status position and level of prestige earned through personal effort that is usually based on educational level, occupation, and income.

Act   Conduct or behavior that violates a norm and is legally classified as juvenile delinquency.

Actor   The one who acts; the juvenile whose role performance is identified as delinquent.

Adjudication   The judgment stage of the juvenile court hearing. Essentially, a juvenile can be adjudicated delinquent, in need of supervision, or neglected, or the case can be dismissed.

Adolescence   An artificial stage of the life course in U.S. society between childhood and adulthood in which youths are automatically consigned. Adolescents generally have marginal social status and identity, uncertain roles, and little power or meaningful participation in society.

Adolescent Identity Crisis   The role confusion common among U.S. youth as they make the transition from childhood to adulthood.

Aftercare   Juvenile parole. Supervised release of a juvenile who must adhere to a set of court-imposed guidelines and periodically report to an officer of the court. Used *after* institutionalization.

Age-crime Curve   The tendency for crime to be committed during an offenders youth and to decline as his/her age advances.

Aggravated Assault   One of the FBI Crime Index Offenses. An unlawful attack upon another for the purpose of inflicting bodily injury.

Anomie   A concept originally developed by Durkheim suggesting a condition of normative confusion or "normlessness" in a society, group, or some persons. The concept (as a general theory of deviance) was expanded by Robert Merton, who said that anomic individuals, frustrated in achieving culturally approved success goals, may turn to illegitimate means of achievement.

Arena   A public place where individuals or groups are pitted against each other in struggles to determine dominance and often survival.

Arena Behavior   A struggle for status and territory.

Argot   Specialized slang or jargon of a particular subculture that promotes group unity and provides a sense of boundary maintenance.

Arson   One of the FBI Crime Index Offenses. Any willful or malicious burning or attempt to burn a dwelling house, public building, motor vehicle, aircraft, or personal property of another.

Ascribed Status   A status position or level of prestige assigned (usually at birth) to an individual based upon certain social criteria such as race, sex, and parents' social status.

Atavism   A concept developed by Cesare Lombroso of the Positive School of Criminology. He argued that there is a "born criminal" whose body structure and antisocial behavior reflect an underlying atavism—an earlier, more primitive stage of human evolution.

Audience   The members of the social group or society that reacts to the actor and the act and determines if juvenile delinquency has been committed.

Bar mitzvah   A social and religious ceremony that functions as a rite of passage to mark the transition of the 13-year-old Jewish male from childhood to adulthood.

Bat mitzvah   A social and religious ceremony that functions as a rite of passage to mark the transition of the 13-year-old Jewish female from childhood to adulthood.

Behavior Modification   Treatment strategy that uses positive reinforcement to encourage desired behavior and negative reinforcement to dissuade undesired behavior.

Birth Order   Order of one's birth relative to siblings—that is, first-born, middle, baby.

Breed v. Jones, 1975   U.S. Supreme Court case, which ruled that the double jeopardy doctrine (cannot be tried twice for the same offense) applied to juveniles.

Broken Home   Refers to family where one of the parents is not present in the home on a permanent basis.

Bureaucracy   A structured organization characterized by a hierarchy of authority; an elaborate system of rules and regulations; where people are treated as "cases" rather than individuals; and where a clearcut career pattern exists for those working within the bureaucracy.

Burglary   One of the FBI Crime Index Offenses. The unlawful entry of a structure to commit a felony or theft.

Chicago Area Project   Delinquency prevention program developed in Chicago by University of Chicago sociologists, which was based upon an ecological approach to juvenile delinquency. "High delinquency" areas were targeted for programs run by local residents to help deter and prevent juvenile delinquency.

Child Savers   Group of concerned clergymen, social workers, and other social reformers during the nineteenth century who embraced the "rehabilitative ideal" for juvenile offenders. Their view that delinquents were products of heredity and brutal urban environments used the "medical model" approach to juvenile delinquency.

Clique   A small group within the youth subculture.

Community Policing   Policing that emphasizes cooperative efforts between the police and other members of the community.

Composite Delinquent Profile   Based upon official sources of delinquency data, it is possible to develop a composite picture of the "typical" delinquent as male, urban, lower class, from a broken home, etc. However, the composite profile produced by these "correlates of delinquency" may be more stereotypical than typical.

Compulsive Masculinity   Exaggerated masculinity, or overemphasis of "manly" traits; believed by some to be caused by the absence of the father from the home.

Concentric Zone Theory   A model suggested by Ernest Burgess to depict the concentric pattern of specialized urban land usages and population groupings as they were spatially distributed and organized around the central core of Chicago. Zone II, comprised of slums occupied by transitory, impoverished immigrant groups, was considered by Burgess to be especially conducive to crime and other social problems.

Conduct Disorder   A term used by the American Psychiatric Association to describe the behavior of adolescents who manifest a repetitive pattern of actions that violates the rights of others and major conduct norms.

Conflict-Oriented Gang   In the absence of both legitimate and illegitimate role models, these youths practice predatory violence and intra-gang warfare.

Conformity   Behavior that is in harmony with the dominant normative standards of a social group to which one belongs; normative behavior.

Constitutional Typology   A classification scheme of body types that often identifies certain traits of character and personality as corresponding with each body type. A mid-twentieth century version of biological determinism.

Containment Theory   A Social Control Theory contributed by Walter Reckless that conceptualizes a double line of defense protecting society against delinquency and other forms of deviance from important norms.

Correlates of Delinquency   The statistical correlation or association of certain demographic and social characteristics and factors with delinquent behavior. The data and data gathering methodologies that support such correlations have been the subjects of extensive debate among scholars.

Counterculture   A subculture which rejects the overall attitudes, values, beliefs, and norms of the larger culture and replaces them with an alternative normative system which conflicts with the larger culture.

Crime-Oriented Gang   A youth gang with adult criminal models and committed to such activities as theft, fraud, and extortion.

Crime-Prevention Role of Police   Police acting as social workers helping juveniles stay out of situations which may lead to delinquency.

Criminal or Delinquent Subculture   A subculture that manifests such extreme and negative nonconformity to the normative system of the larger society that its members are generally viewed as antisocial. Its members violate laws as a result of membership in the subculture.

Cross-Cultural   A concept incorporated in the content and format of this book to facilitate comparisons of the laws, etiology, treatment strategies, and other dimensions of the national experience with juvenile delinquency in selected countries with those prevalent in the United States.

Cultural Relativity   The principle that behavior must be evaluated for conformity or deviance within the cultural context of the specific social group in which the questionable behavior occurred.

Cultural Transmission Theories   A group of delinquency theories that share the underlying assumption that the twentieth-century industrialization and urbanization of the United States generated an urban mosaic of ethnic, religious, political, and social class subcultures—each promulgating and endorsing its own standards of conduct.

Culture   The shared and learned beliefs, values, attitudes, traditions, normative expectations, and other forms of knowledge that are passed on from one generation to the next within a society.

Culture Conflict   A concept well stated by Thorsten Sellin, who pointed to the abrasive contact between the diverse values, norms, and practices of subgroups within a heterogeneous population, or such culture conflicts between various ethnic minorities, with the dominant culture of the larger society being the seedbed of much crime and delinquency.

Decriminalization of Status Offenses   A reform of the Juvenile Justice System that would remove truancy, running away, and other so-called juvenile status offenses from the codified state and local laws and from the jurisdiction of juvenile courts.

Defense Attorney   Represents the juvenile in juvenile court.

Deinstitutionalization   Avoiding the placement of juveniles into correctional institutions.

Delinquency and Drift   A variation of Control Theory developed by David Matza who argues that some ordinarily conforming youths are occasionally unleashed from constraining norms and thus are temporarily free to "drift" into delinquent behavior.

Delinquency and Opportunity   An expansion of Merton's Anomie Theory of Deviance applied to juvenile delinquency by Richard Cloward and Lloyd Ohlin. They contend that many lower class youth not only have differential opportunities for success through legitimate means, but also differential opportunities for achievement through illegitimate means. The kind of illegal opportunities available in a given area, according to Cloward and Ohlin, will determine the kind of gang activity that will emerge: crime-oriented, conflict-oriented, or retreatist/drug-oriented.

Delinquent Acts as Symptoms   A fundamental premise of the psychogenic approach to explaining and treating delinquency is that such misbehaviors are overt manifestations of hidden stress or maladjustment.

Delinquent Gang   A group of associating youths with identifiable leaders, organization, and territory, whose lifestyle includes a propensity to engage in collective illegal conduct.

Detention Facilities   Places used to detain or hold juveniles who are awaiting a hearing in juvenile court.

Determinate Sentencing   A court disposition which specifies a definite period of time for an individual offender to be incarcerated, on probation, or otherwise supervised by the state.

Deterrence Theory   A contemporary offshoot of the Classical School of Criminological Thought which takes the position that stern and prompt punishment will successfully discourage many juvenile and adult offenders from repeating their illegal conduct.

Developmental Career   The theoretical view of the longitudinal process that results in the fully developed deviant career. This model suggests that there is a developmental history behind the deviant and his or her behavior that involves gradual change in values, attitude, and conduct over time.

Deviant Behavior   Conduct that is perceived by society as violating established and widely respected normative expectations for behavior.

Deviant Subculture   Any subgroup that deviates markedly from the generally accepted values, norms, and behavioral expectations of the dominant culture.

Dietary Deficiencies   This line of inquiry regarding delinquency causation suggests that inadequate nutrition or allergic food reactions can lead to biochemical imbalance and subsequently to hyperactivity and misconduct.

Differential Association Theory   A Social Learning Theory developed by Edwin Sutherland that presents a logical sequence through which criminal behavior is learned through primary contact with criminal elements present in one's environment.

Differential Identification   An expansion of the Theory of Differential Association by Daniel Glaser who emphasized the extent to which the potential offender identifies with criminal or delinquent role models.

Differential Reinforcement   A Learning Theory spin-off from Differential Association by Ronald Akers who suggests that juveniles may be discouraged from repeated misbehavior by punishment or negative social response. On the other hand, some juveniles may continue to pursue delinquent activities because they have received some form of positive reinforcement.

Disposition   Stage of the juvenile court hearing where the judge decides what to do with the juvenile before the court. Roughly equivalent to the sentencing stage in adult criminal court.

District Attorney   Represents the state in juvenile court cases; prosecutes the case.

Diversion   Process of using alternatives for juveniles to remove them from the formal juvenile justice system.

Double Failure   A concept suggested by Richard Cloward and Lloyd Ohlin (See *Delinquency and Opportunity*) to describe a youth who fails to achieve material success and enhance social status through legitimate *and* illegitimate means.

Due Process   Constitutional safeguards designed to protect persons accused of law-violating behavior. These safeguards must be followed before individuals can be deprived of life, liberty, or property.

Due Process Court   Juvenile court characterized by high task differentiation, decentralized authority, high discretion for court services staff. This court routinely handles status offenders and has low formalization.

Dyad   A social group comprised of two persons.

Dyslexia   A brain malfunction whereby visual signs are scrambled, resulting in a learning disability. This malfunction has hypothesized linkage with delinquent behavior.

Ectomorph   A body type in William Sheldon's constitutional typology. He described the type as having a lean and fragile build and possessing a sensitive and introspective personality.

Ego   One of the three dimensions of the personality theoretically identified by Freud. The ego in Freud's model is that part of the personality or self that serves as the unifying and pragmatic arbitrator between the impulsive and primal id and the socially sensitive and idealistic superego.

Ego Diffusion   A concept suggested by Erik Erikson to describe the confusion and inconsistency of ethics, roles, and behavior that characterize many adolescents as they seek self-identity and adult status.

Ego Ideal   A personality, character, or image to which a person may aspire or fantasize.

Ego Identity   According to Erikson, "A persistent sameness within oneself and a consistent sharing of some essential character with others." This "ego identity" is acquired during the formative adolescent years as the youth matures.

Electroencephalogram   A recording of the summated electrical activity of the neurons in the human brain. It has been found that variations in these brain-wave patterns accompany certain forms of brain abnormalities and different levels of alertness. It has been hypothesized that chronic criminals may also have distinctive EEG patterns.

Electroencephalograph   An electronic test with medical applications that measures the frequency and pattern of brain waves. The EEG has been administered to a number of deviant personalities and criminals on the premise that their brains emit abnormal frequencies. Fragmentary findings are only tenuous and inconclusive.

Endomorph   A body type in William Sheldon's constitutional typology that he described as having a soft, rotund physical build and a self-indulgent, jolly personality.

Ethnicity   The national and cultural background of a particular group.

Etiology   The study of the cause(s) of an event, phenomenon, or behavior.

Extended Family   Family where more than two generations live under one roof and cooperate in the economic, social, and psychological support of the family.

"Fag Bashing"   Derogatory slang used by youths to describe the beating up (aggravated assault) of homosexuals by male juveniles. Often accompanied by robbery.

Family of Orientation   Term sociologists use to refer to family of origin.

Family of Origin   The family in which a child is socialized; usually consists of parents and children.

FBI Uniform Crime Report Index   Often referred to as the "Index Offenses." The first eight crime categories of the *FBI Uniform Crime Reports,* because of their seriousness, frequency of occurrence, and likelihood of being reported to the police are known as Index Offenses. The first four are often grouped together as "Violent Crimes" directed against persons. The second four are also often treated as a subcategory and are known as "Property Crimes," nonviolent crimes directed against property.

FBI Uniform Crime Reports   Annual compilations of the numbers and types of crimes committed in the United States. The reports are based on arrest data collected from a nationwide reporting network of law-enforcement agencies and are tabulated by age, race, sex, place of residence, and other traits of those arrested. The system is designed to measure the extent, fluctuation, distribution, and nature of serious crime in the United States.

Felony   A more serious crime punishable by fine and/or imprisonment for more than a year.

Female Auxiliary   A branch of male gangs comprised of girlfriends, sisters, groupies, and other females who identify with the male gang.

Filtering Process   Process whereby police and juvenile courts use their discretion to informally handle or "filter out" juveniles from the criminal justice system, based upon a variety of subjective criteria.

Folkways   Informal agreements or understandings among the members of society about what is considered appropriate and inappropriate behavior.

Forcible Rape   One of the FBI Crime Index Offenses. The carnal knowledge of a female forcibly and against her will.

Free Association   A basic psychoanalytical technique in which the patient is encouraged to spontaneously say whatever comes to mind on the assumption that such expressions are more likely to come from the unconscious part of the mind.

Frustration-Aggression Hypothesis   Individuals unable to reach desired goals become frustrated, and this frustration is manifested by aggressive behavior.

Furman v. Georgia, 1972   U.S. Supreme Court Case which ruled that capital punishment constituted "cruel and unusual punishment" and violated the eighth amendment to the U.S. Constitution.

Gang   A group of persons assembled and acting or working together.

Gang Cluster   Several age-graded male subgroups plus a female auxiliary that are formally or informally affiliated or allied for some practical and mutual advantage.

Gang Rape   A group or multiple rape of a single victim.

Gault Decision   A 1967 decision by the U.S. Supreme Court that reversed the lower court adjudication of 15-year-old Gerald Gault on grounds that the youth did not receive his constitutional rights. For the first time, limited due process was formally granted to America's minors.

Gemeinschaft   According to Toennies' theoretical continuum, a community characterized by a smaller population, less complex division of labor, and dominated by primary face-to-face interaction and informal social control.

General Theory of Deviance   A precise and testable statement of the relationship between variables that is broad enough so as to offer causal explanation for a variety of deviant behaviors (for example, Merton's Theory of Anomie). As yet, no General Theory of Delinquency has been developed.

Gesellschaft   According to Toennies' theoretical continuum, a community characterized by a larger population, a complex division of labor, secondary social relationships, and formal social control.

Graffiti   The distinctive language/symbolism of street gangs that is scrawled in public places to identify gang territories and members, and to challenge rivals.

Group Context of Delinquency   A major sociological emphasis in the study of delinquency, since the majority of such conduct is committed by social groupings of varying size, purpose, and organization. Thus, the group becomes the unit of analysis.

Group Homes   Facilities where juveniles live in a dormitory-type setting under adult supervision. Youths are generally allowed limited participation in the community, going to school or work for part of the day.

Guardian Angels   Group of young adults and teenagers who operate as self-appointed "patrols" of the streets, sidewalks, and subways of many American cities, making citizens' arrests of suspected law violators.

Hate Crimes   Crimes directed at people because of their race, ethnicity, religion, sexual orientation, or some other physical or cultural characteristic that sets them apart from the perpetrator.

High Delinquency Area   Clifford Shaw's and Henry McKay's term for a particular neighborhood or district (ordinarily in a large city) characterized by a very high incidence of juvenile crime and a local subculture that encourages such behavior.

Highfields Project   Small group-treatment program designed for boys in a New Jersey correctional facility. Aimed at strengthening conformity within a group under supervision that would later make readjustment to home, school, and community normative expectations easier.

House Arrest   A program where youths are confined to their homes and closely supervised by their parents. Routine unannounced visits or phone calls are made by a probation officer.

House of Refuge   Established in 1825, in New York City, to provide separate correctional facilities for children between the ages of 7 and 14 who had been convicted of crimes.

Hyperkinesis   A frenetic activity and excitement found by some researchers to have unusually high incidence among the delinquent children in their studies. Often referred to as "hyperactivity."

Id   That dimension of the human personality represented in Freud's model as a set of primitive, self-centered impulses and demands.

Ideal Type   A conceptual model expressed in a pure and exaggerated form. The core characteristics of a community, an individual, or a pattern of human conduct. This "ideal" abstraction, while hypothetical, may serve as a useful reference point for observations of social phenomena in actual reality.

Informal Social Control   Methods of social constraint applied by societal members which include gossip, ridicule, humor, ostracism, and peer pressure.

Initiation Rituals   Some gangs subject new or aspiring members to special ceremonies, hazings, ordeals, or other requirements in order to demonstrate courage, commitment, and worthiness for membership.

Inner Containment   The result of successful socialization and internalization of social norms that enables the individual to exercise affective self-control in resisting temptations to deviate.

In Re Gault, 1967   U.S. Supreme Court case which granted limited rights of due process to juveniles, including: the right to counsel; the right to face and cross-examine witnesses; the right to refuse to answer self-incriminating questions; the right to a transcript of the proceedings; and the right to appeal juvenile court decisions.

In Re Holmes, 1954   U.S. Supreme Court case which upheld the concept that the basic constitutional rights of due process afforded adult criminal offenders did not apply to the juvenile court, since an adversary relationship did not exist between the state and the juvenile.

In Re Winship, 1970   U.S. Supreme Court case in which the court ruled that "proof beyond a reasonable doubt" also applied to juvenile cases.

Instrumental Theory   An innovative approach to explaining juvenile delinquency by the radical theorists Herman and Julia Schwendinger (See Chapter 7). The Schwendingers' main thesis is that the parents' social class is not the most important variable in determining the delinquency potential for adolescents. Rather, they argue, the youth's relative status position among other teenagers is the best predictor of delinquency. Illegal conduct, to the juvenile involved, can be "instrumental"—that is, serving as a vehicle for attaining social identity with his or her particular subgroup.

Intact Home   Refers to family where both parents are present in the home on a permanent basis.

Intake   Initial stage of juvenile court proceeding. Petition is read, a court services officer is assigned to the case to conduct a social background investigation, and decisions are made regarding waiver, detention, and other matters.

Integrative Theories   The contemporary efforts of scholars to synthesize elements of major theories of deviant and delinquent behavior into general theories with enhanced explanatory power.

Intelligence Quotient (IQ)   The ratio of a person's Mental Age to his/her Chronological Age. Fifty years ago, psychologists popularized the IQ Tests on the assumption that they could identify mental defectives and link their "measured mental capacities" with an inclination to delinquent behavior. In recent years the validity and predictive ability of IQ Tests have been strongly challenged.

Interventionist Court   Handles a high rate of cases judicially and has a high commitment rate.

Joyriding   Theft of an automobile simply for the fun of driving it around for a while. Most common form of juvenile auto theft.

Juvenile   Any person in American society under the legal age of majority.

Juvenile Code   Statutes or laws that are formally codified and applied by a state legislature to those juveniles within state boundaries and jurisdiction.

Juvenile Court Referral   A case of law violation involving a juvenile offender that is referred or assigned to a juvenile court for disposition or adjudication.

Juvenile Courts   Judicial tribunals established to deal with the special cases of young people (usually between ages 7 and 18).

Juvenile Delinquency (Synthesized Definition)   All acts committed by individuals between the ages of 7 and 16 (or possibly 14) that would be considered criminal if committed by an adult; that place the juvenile in the delinquent/criminal role; and that result in society regarding the juvenile as dangerously deviant.

Juvenile Officers   Police officers who receive special training in child development, adolescent psychology, sociology, and counseling, in order to better equip themselves to handle the unique problems associated with policing juveniles.

Juvenilization of Poverty   It has been projected that, in the near future, one of every five adolescents will live at or below the poverty level. A number of social scientists contend that such impoverishment is related to increasing violence and other social problems among American youths.

Kent v. United States, 1966   U.S. Supreme Court decision that ruled that before a juvenile court can waive its jurisdiction a hearing must be held.

Labeling Theory   A sociological explanation of juvenile delinquency that focuses on the interaction between the actor and the societal audience that evaluates behavior and thereby imputes a social identity or label to the individual.

Larceny-Theft   One of the FBI Crime Index Offenses. The unlawful taking, carrying, leading, or riding away of property from the possession of another.

Latchkey Children   School-aged children of working parent(s) who return home from school to an empty house and are unsupervised for a period of time.

Law Enforcement Role of Police   Police concentrating on arresting juveniles who have committed crimes.

Legal Definition of Delinquency   Any act that, if committed by an adult, would be a crime. Involves an age boundary between juvenile and adult offenders.

Life Course   The successive role and status changes that each person occupies in society as a consequence of growing older.

Loco Parentis   Parental role toward juveniles.

Looking-Glass Self   A term coined by Charles H. Cooley to describe the process through which an individual's self-evaluation and self-identity reflect how he or she perceives and adopts societal evaluations and expectations.

Lower Class Focal Concerns   Six basic values of trouble, toughness, smartness, excitement, fate, and autonomy that Walter Miller felt are intrinsic to the lower class and that, when acted out by lower class males, place them in nonconforming opposition to dominant middle class values and behavioral expectations.

Macrosociology (also macroscopic sociology)   Focuses on large-scale social units such as large groups, organizations, cultures, and societies.

Mala in se   Acts that are considered inherently evil, such as murder and rape.

Mala prohibita   Acts that are considered evil only because they are prohibited, such as status offenses by minors.

Malevolent Vandalism   The vicious and malevolent destruction of property, as opposed to the more common thoughtless vandalism where the primary motive is fun.

Marginal Persons   Those immigrants, outsiders, members of racial or ethnic groups, and other persons of "marginal" and uncertain social status who are on the untenable periphery of mainstream society, or whose commitment and identity are fragmented because they are caught between two conflicting cultures and societies. The condition of social marginality.

Mass Media   Any form of information outlet designed to communicate a standardized message to large masses of individuals simultaneously (e.g., newspapers, magazines, radio, television, and movies).

Maturation Effect   The theoretical idea, supported by considerable evidence, that young people typically seem to mature or "grow out" of their deviant behavior in time—without stern societal sanctions (See *Spontaneous Remission*).

McKiever v. Pennsylvania, 1971   U.S. Supreme Court case in which the court ruled that juveniles do not have the right to a trial by jury.

Medical Model   Views crime/delinquency as a social pathology analogous to physical illness. Delinquency is viewed like an "illness" with identifiable "symptoms" needing diagnosis and treatment.

Meidung   Edict used by the Old Order Amish that invokes the practice of "shunning" those who have violated the dictates of their religion.

Mens Rea   The concept of "evil mind" or criminal intent. Refers to one's ability to understand right from wrong, and to understand the consequences of one's actions. In criminal law, a youth must be at least seven years old to be considered capable of mens rea.

Mentoring Programs   Uses adult volunteers who commit a certain amount of time each week to work one-on-one with a youngster to encourage academic, personal, social, athletic, and artistic developments in an effort to prevent delinquency.

Mesomorph   A body build in William Sheldon's constitutional typology that he described as muscular and strong and as having an impulsive and energetic personality that predisposes this individual, more than other types, to delinquent behavior.

Microsociology (also microscopic sociology)   Studies small social units such as individuals and small groups and their interaction.

Mid-City Project   Delinquency prevention program in Boston directed at the community, families, and gangs. Based upon the assumption that the roots of delinquency were to be found in the social environment.

Middle Class Gangs   A number of studies indicate that delinquent youth gangs are not exclusively a lower class phenomenon. While locale, purpose, organization, style and type of misconduct, and societal perception and response may vary significantly from their better-known, lower class counterpart, the existence and danger of middle class gangs is well documented.

Minimalistic Court   Handles a low proportion of its cases judicially with a low commitment rate.

Minnesota Youth Advocate Program   School-based delinquency prevention program in Minnesota that attempted to help institutionalized juvenile delinquents more successfully readjust to school and community upon their release.

Miranda v. Arizona, 1966   U.S. Supreme Court decision which ruled that adults must be informed of their constitutional rights at the time of arrest in order for any of their testimony to be used as evidence in court.

Mirandize   To advise a suspect of his or her legal rights based on the U.S. Supreme Court case of *Miranda v. Arizona.*

Misdemeanor   A less serious crime usually punishable by fine and/or imprisonment for less than a year.

Mobilization for Youth   Delinquency prevention program developed in Manhattan based upon Cloward's and Ohlin's Theory of Differential Opportunities in slum areas of major cities. Attempted to open up legitimate opportunity structures through school, businesses, government, and other social institutions and agencies.

Modes of Individual Adaptive Behavior   A typology developed by Robert Merton of six possible responses of individuals to the anomic juxtaposition of culturally approved goals and the institutionalized means of achievement:

I. Conformity: One who accepts both traditional goals and approved means.

II. Innovation: One who accepts traditional, cultural success goals but whose sense of anomic frustration leads to innovative, illegal means of reaching those goals.

III. Ritualism: This person realizes that the idealized, cultural goals are unreachable but continues to strive in the socially expected ways.

IV. Retreatism: This person, in response to anomie-generating circumstances, abandons both the culturally approved success goals and the institutionalized means of hard work for attaining those objectives.

V. Rebellion: This malcontent, disillusioned with traditional goals and means, substitutes new objectives and new methods for achievement.

Moral Devlopment Theories   Explanatory constructs, principally conceived by Jean Piaget and Lawrence Kohlberg, that depict human cognitive and moral development occurring on a typology of successive stages. An etiological extension of these theories has suggested that criminals and delinquents seem to function at lower, more sensory and selfish levels of moral development.

Mores   The more important, formal, and seriously enforced norms of a society. Mores are generally perceived as vital to the cohesion and survival of society.

Motor-Vehicle Theft   One of the FBI Crime Index Offenses. The theft or attempted theft of a motor vehicle.

Mules   Individuals who transport narcotics or other illegal substances for drug dealers.

Murder and Non-negligent Manslaughter   One of the FBI Crime Index Offenses. The willful killing of one human being by another.

National Juvenile Court Statistical Reporting System Program   The National Center for Juvenile Justice and Delinquency Prevention in the U.S. Department of Justice collects data from a nationwide network of participating juvenile courts and publishes annual summaries of juvenile court caseloads. The data are tabulated by age, race, sex, and type of offense or need of the children and youths appearing before the courts.

Near Group   A theoretical contribution by Lewis Yablonsky who maintained that most delinquent gangs are midway on a group-mob continuum and are structurally neither groups nor mobs. He described the gang as a "near group" in organization, membership, quality of leadership, and other traits.

Neighborhood Watch   Citizen groups in neighborhoods who watch for criminal/delinquent activities and report any suspicious individuals to the police.

Neighborhood Youth Corps   Delinquency prevention and treatment program designed to provide vocational training and better work opportunities for disadvantaged and delinquent youths.

Neoclassical Position   A modified version of the Classical theorists that recognized that not all persons were equally rational and personally responsible for their behavior.

Neovigilantism   Renewed wave of vigilantism—private citizens taking on the role of law enforcers.

Neurological Abnormality   A mental impairment induced by disease or injury that has been linked by psychiatric research with some forms of aberrant and even occasional antisocial behavior.

Norms   The rules, standards, laws, customs, and beliefs that regulate human behavior and social interaction for a society or social group.

Nuclear Family   Family where two generations or less live under one roof and cooperate in the economic, social, and psychological support of the family.

Ostracism   The experience of being expelled from a social group.

Outer Containment   The formal laws and law enforcement agencies—external to the individual—that restrain most members of society from serious norm violation.

Parens Patriae   The legal concept from British Common Law that established the King (or the state) as the "ultimate parent"; provides legal basis for the state to intervene on behalf of children.

Paternalistic Court   Handles a low rate of cases judicially but has a high commitment rate.

Personality   The unique organization of relatively stable psychological traits possessed by an individual, as revealed by one's interaction with others in his or her environment.

Personality Trait   A distinguishing feature, quality, or disposition of mind or character.

Petition   Official statement filed by police, parents, school officials, or some other adult which contains the important facts relevant to why the juvenile should appear before the juvenile court.

Phrenology   An early nineteenth-century notion of Joseph Gall who speculated that traits of personality and character and concomitant behavioral proclivities are housed in separate portions of the brain and can be revealed by the scientific study of the bumps and irregularities of the skull.

PLACE   Program developed at Syracuse University where youthful first-time offenders attend a 90-minute class session in which they are involved in role-playing, mock trials, and discussions on the juvenile justice system and causes of delinquency.

Play Group   The natural and spontaneous neighborhood play group of urban youngsters was first identified by Frederick Thrasher as the informal and innocuous beginning of the evolution of the predatory, antisocial street gang.

Police Discretion   The wide latitude police officers have in deciding how to handle juvenile offenders.

Positive School of Criminology   A late nineteenth-century view of criminal behavior based on biological determinism. Lombroso and others believed that predatory, antisocial behavior is genetically programmed in some individuals who, as physical manifestations of an earlier phase of our evolutionary past, are irresistibly attracted to crime.

Post-Traumatic Stress Disorder   Negative psychological and social repercussions from emotional or physical assault or abuse.

Predelinquency   An early, preliminary stage of personality development that, according to some psychologists and psychiatrists, precedes full development of the delinquent personality and identity.

Predelinquent   Based upon the "medical model" is a youth who exhibits "symptoms" thought to be associated with juvenile delinquency.

Prescriptive Norms   Rules or laws that "prescribe" certain kinds of behavior as appropriate or desirable; societal "thou shalts."

Prevention Ideology   Based upon the "medical model" approach to delinquency, this strategy attempts to identify "symptoms" of delinquency and "treat" them in order to prevent the delinquency before it occurs.

Primary Deviation   An initial, impulsive, or experimental act of deviance (or perhaps several such acts) in which the individual does not internalize a permanent nonconforming role and self-concept.

Proactive Strategies   Programs designed to identify and eliminate delinquency before it occurs.

Probation   First established in Boston in 1841, a form of supervised release where a juvenile delinquent is allowed to remain free, but must adhere to a strict set of guidelines imposed by the court. The juvenile must also periodically report to an officer of the court. Used *instead* of institutionalization.

Profit Motive   An economic rationale for gang activities focused on the pursuit of financial gain, as in the marketing of illegal drugs and car thefts.

Projective Test   Psychogenic test designed to elicit the unconscious feelings and "projections" of patients by exposing them to unstructured and unidentifiable stimuli.

Proportionate Sentencing   A judicial concept and principle meaning that the severity of dispositions should be roughly equivalent to the seriousness of the offense committed.

Proscriptive Norms   Rules or laws that "prohibit" certain kinds of behavior as inappropriate or undesirable; societal "thou shalt nots."

Provo Experiment   Delinquency rehabilitation and treatment strategy based upon theory of differential association. Used in a facility for habitual delinquent offenders in Provo, Utah.

"Pseudo-vigilantism."   Term coined by the authors to refer to activities such as "crimestoppers," crime "hot-lines," and other programs where individuals do not actually enforce the laws, but anonymously call law-enforcement officials with "tips" regarding criminal/delinquent activities. If these "tips" lead to arrests, the citizens usually receive some type of monetary reward.

Psychiatry   A medical specialty concerned with the diagnosis, treatment, and prevention of disordered or "abnormal" behavior.

Psychoanalysis   Various techniques developed and implemented by psychologists and psychiatrists for probing and examining the unconscious forces, motives, and problems behind human behavior.

Psychogenic Approach   An eclectic and generic term denoting the common ground shared by psychology and psychiatry as they seek to understand and explain human behavior in general and delinquency in particular.

Psychology   A behavioral science that investigates and associates mental processes with behavior.

Psychopath (Sociopath)   A severely "flawed personality" in that the individual has not internalized some major values and norms of society. Thus, the psychopath does not differentiate right from wrong in the typical way and feels little guilt over misdeeds or compassion for his or her victims.

Racial Group   One of several human groupings that are classified according to observable physical differences, such as skin color, facial features, and hair texture.

Radical Theory   A body of sociological etiology that accounts for adult crime and juvenile delinquency as a precipitate of conflict between social classes as their vested interests and values clash, and as law enforcement is differentially applied to the social classes.

Reactive Strategies   Programs designed to intervene and treat a youth after delinquency has occurred.

Reactive Subculture   A set of post-World War II theories that shared the view of lower class youth gangs as being a hostile, subcultural response to middle class cultural values and goals that have been imposed on all of society.

Reactive Subculture Responses   Several sociological theorists (e.g., Cloward and Ohlin, and Cohen) have described lower class street gangs as viable subcultures with distinctive values, norms, and behavioral practices. These theorists often explained delinquent gang behavior as an alienated re-action to the dominant culture of the middle class. Albert Cohen, for example, saw three possible responses of lower class boys as they recognize and seek to cope with their disadvantages:
1. College-Boy Response: Youths in this category seek upward social class mobility.
2. Corner-Boy Response: This type withdraws into a disenchanted, alienated subculture of lower class youths.
3. Delinquent-Boy Response: The banding together of delinquent youths in a gang whose behavior reflects values that are antithetical to the middle class.

Reality Therapy   Treatment strategy that attempts to make the offender take responsibility for his or her actions. Based upon the writings of William Glasser.

Referral   Process whereby a juvenile's name is given to the juvenile court.

Reformatory   A correctional facility designed to discipline and rehabilitate rather than punish juvenile offenders.

Rehabilitative Ideal   Emphasizes the temporary and reversible nature of delinquency if remedial measures are applied early enough.

Reliability   A fundamental research and methodological objective. A measure can be assumed to have reliability when it yields the same data or results upon replication of the measuring or data-gathering procedure by other investigators.

Restitution   The offender is required to compensate the victim(s) for losses related to the offense.

Restorative Justice Model   Focuses on accountability, restitution, and community involvement in the corrections process.

Retreatist-Oriented Gang   This juvenile group, in the face of their double failure at achieving success in legitimate avenues of success and in attaining proficiency in traditional criminal activities, symbolically retreats into drug abuse and illicit sexual activities.

Reverse Certification   In some states a youth who is over the age of sixteen and has committed what would be a felony for an adult will automatically stand trial as an adult unless he or she is "reverse certified" to be treated as a juvenile.

Rite of Passage   Symbolic ritual marking the transition from one social role and status to another; one that permanently alters a person's relationship with members of the greater community.

Ritualistic Court   Handles a high proportion of cases judicially with a low rate of commitment.

Robbery   One of the FBI Crime Index Offenses. The taking or attempting to take anything of value from the care, custody, or control of a person or persons by force or threat of force or violence and/or by putting the victim in fear.

Role   The behavioral performance expected of a person who holds a certain status in the social group or society.

Role Conflict   The fulfillment of one role necessitates the violation of another.

Role Definition of Delinquency   Behavior by an individual who sustains a consistent pattern of delinquency over a long period of time and whose life and identity are organized around such deviant behavior.

Role Modeling   The learning of social roles from observation, imitation, and the identification with those who occupy those roles.

Role Strain   The set of expectations accompanying one role (i.e., law enforcement officer) may be at odds with fulfilling the expectations of another role (i.e., a concerned adult acting on behalf of a child in trouble).

Rorschach Ink-Blot Test   One of the projective tests designed to elicit deep, often camouflaged feelings, motives, and needs. The Ink-Blot Test is comprised of a series of nondescript, ink-drop patterns that, since they portray nothing known or prelearned for which there is a predetermined response, are assumed to draw from the subject those hidden, sublimated emotions and drives.

Runaways   Juveniles who voluntarily leave their homes.

Sanctions   Methods by which norms are enforced. Can be either informal or formal; positive or negative.

Scared Straight!   Program begun by inmates at Rahway State Prison where juvenile offenders spend part of a day at Rahway being shown the more brutal side of life inside a maximum-security prison.

Schall v. Martin, 1984   U.S. Supreme Court case that ruled youths could be held without bail if they were being held for their own protection or the protection of society.

Screening Device   The schools act to "screen out" members of society based upon educational credentials (e.g., diplomas, degrees, etc.), as well as willingness to conform to and internalize dominant attitudes, values, beliefs, and norms.

Secondary Deviation   An emergent, repetitive pattern of deviant behavior as an individual's self-concept is altered and the deviant role is assumed.

Self-Fulfilling Prophecy   Defining a situation or person in a certain way and then acting as if the definition is real may in fact cause the situation or person to become as defined. In schools, labels are applied to students, and they are treated as if the labels are meaningful; consequently students may fulfill the role expectations associated with the label.

Self-Report Study   The survey of a part of a population regarding their participation in illegal activity. If the subjects are randomly selected, findings may be generalized to a larger population. If responses are made anonymously this approach is useful in measuring undetected and unreported delinquency.

Shock Incarceration   A short prison stay designed to shock the youth and to impress upon him or her the seriousness of the problem and potential consequences of further delinquency (see *Shock Probation*).

Shock Probation   A short prison stay designed to shock the youth and to impress upon him or her the seriousness of the problem and potential consequences of further delinquency (see *Shock Incarceration*).

SHODI (Serious Habitual Offenders Drug Involved)   A program used in California, Colorado, and Florida, which uses the computer to identify serious habitual juvenile offenders. When confronted by the police for even the most minor offense, they are immediately arrested and officially processed. The program attempts to maintain awareness of the whereabouts of all known serious habitual offenders.

Short-Term Hedonism   A practical and simple conclusion by some students of delinquency phenomena that much juvenile misbehavior is little more than spontaneous adventuring in pursuit of immediate pleasure.

Situational Prostitutes   Prostitutes who enter the profession temporarily due to specific social circumstances.

Social Bond   Extent to which a youth feels an "attachment" to basic social institutions like the family and school. Believed by Hirschi and others to increase conformity to the conventional norms of society.

Social Bond Theory   A Social Control Theory put forward by Travis Hirschi who depicted the juvenile delinquent as lacking sufficient "social bond" to the basic values and expected behaviors of society. He detailed four elements of social bonding that must be effectively activated in early childhood in order to elicit conformity: Attachment, Commitment, Involvement, and Belief.

Social Capital   A reservoir of resilience in some individuals that enables them to resist the allure of potentially damaging associates and activities. Social capital is acquired initially through nurturing, intergenerational relationship within one's family of origin.

Social Class   Social position (status) based upon occupation, education, and income.

Social Conflict   The viewpoint of Marx, Dahrendorf, and other "conflict theorists" that the origin of many prevailing social norms can be traced to the unscrupulous efforts of the capitalist class to control and exploit the less powerful working classes.

Social Consensus   The viewpoint of Weber, Durkheim, and other theorists that the source of our dominant social norms has deep cultural roots as the members of society, from generation to generation, organize themselves to meet certain basic survival prerequisites. Over time, traditional ways of fulfilling these societal needs become institutionalized.

Social Contract   The voluntary abdication of a measure of personal autonomy and submission to group norms in exchange for enhanced security supplied by a dominant power structure and hierarchy over the social collectivity.

Social Control   Those aspects of society and culture that are designed to reduce the incidence of juvenile delinquency and to minimize its negative impact upon the members of society.

Social Control Theories   In contrast to other groups of sociological theories, Social Control Theories approach the etiology of delinquency by asking "What causes conformity?" The underlying assumption is that youthful behavior cannot and should not be superficially dichotomized into "delinquent" and "nondelinquent."

Social Disability   A concept suggested by James Short and Fred Strodtbeck to describe the lack of interpersonal skills, social assurance, knowledge of the job market, and sophistication in relations with girls that characterize most delinquent gang members.

Social Imperative   The intrinsic and compelling need of all social creatures—including humans—to interact with and relate to others of the same species.

Social Interaction   The dynamic process of communication and relationships between humans that are necessary for the physical and emotional health, development, and survival of individuals and groups.

Social Interdependence   The symbiotic network of relationships and mutual aid that characterizes successfully functioning and enduring human societies and communities.

Socialization   The process whereby individuals learn and internalize the attitudes, values, and behaviors appropriate to persons functioning as members of a society or social group. This shared knowledge or culture content of a social group or society is transmitted to successive generations.

Social Learning Theories   A group of sociological theories founded on the assumption that deviant and delinquent behavior can be explained as the product of socialization.

Social Network   A fundamental sociological concept used to summarize and explain the interconnected, formal, and informal array of relationships among individual members of society. It follows that human behavior can hardly be conceived of in isolation—without social causes or impacts traceable to others.

Social Organization   The generally recognized and accepted pattern or structure of instrumental leadership and behavior utilized by a social group in achieving its objectives.

Social Problem   An objective, observable, and verifiable condition within a society that common consensus agrees is a threatening problem, requiring concerted remedial action and about which it is felt something can be done.

Social Role   A set of behavioral expectations that accompany a particular status.

Social Status   An individual's prestige position in relation to others in the social group or society.

Social Strain Theories   The theoretical explanations of deviance and delinquency grouped together in this category share the underlying assumption that nonconforming behavior arises out of social circumstances in which individuals or groups experience normative confusion or disruption. This normative confusion has a special application to ethnic or social class minorities under pressure from dominant groups or classes.

Social Structure Hypotheses   The popularized premises underlying many programs and policies designed to alleviate social problems. For example, many concluded that poverty is caused by structural features of capitalism. Following this reasoning, it is society that must change, not individuals. Applications to crime and delinquency have been made by several radical theorists.

Societal Response Definition of Delinquency   The members of the juvenile's social group or society comprise an "audience" that must perceive and judge the behavior in question as delinquent.

Society   The general term for people living in social interdependence in a particular geographic area who socially interact and share a common culture.

Sociobiology   A newly developing area of inquiry and study that maintains that social behavior of all species is a product of evolutionary history and genetics. This involves temperament, personality traits, and physical characteristics as each member of a social species unconsciously musters all its resources to protect the gene pool and insure propagation and species survival. While the implications of such hypotheses for deviant and delinquent behavior are numerous and profound, there has been little empirical support thus far.

Sociolegal Definition of Delinquency   Those actions that are illegal for juveniles, that place the juvenile in the delinquent role, and that result in society regarding the juvenile as delinquent.

Sociological Imagination   The application of sociological knowledge and expertise in creative and innovative problem-solving ways.

Sociological Perspective   The observation, analysis, and explanation of human behavior and social phenomena—including juvenile delinquency—that rests upon a careful consideration of the social context or environment in which the behavior or phenomenon occurs.

Sociology   The scientific quest to discover, explain, and predict the patterned social behaviors within human groups and between groups and individuals.

Solitary Delinquent   A significant minority of all juvenile offenses are committed by individuals acting alone. This does not negate their direct and indirect relationships with numerous others who are affected by the illegal behavior.

Spontaneous Remission   The "aging out" phenomenon whereby juveniles at some point reach a level of maturity where they spontaneously reduce, and eventually even eliminate, their involvement in law-violating behavior. (See *Maturation Effect*).

Spotter   Member of automobile theft ring who "spots" or locates automobiles for theft.

Status   The prestige position of a person in relation to other persons in the social group or society.

Status Offenses   Acts considered illegal for juveniles because of their minority status. These acts are not against the law if committed by adults (e.g., smoking, drinking or possessing alcohol, truancy, or running away from home).

Street Corner Society   A book by William Whyte that takes its title from the informal but highly viable form of social organization in slum neighborhoods.

Street Kids   Juveniles who have left home (either voluntarily or involuntarily) for life on the streets and sidewalks of cities.

Street People   Bag ladies, chronically unemployed, vagrants, and others among the homeless who inhabit the streets and sidewalks of cities.

Subculture   A smaller group within a culture that shares most of the elements of the larger culture, but has some unique attitudes, values, beliefs, and norms that distinguish it from the larger culture.

Subterranean Value System   A point made by Gresham Sykes and David Matza in maintaining that delinquents often justify their misdeeds as only transient since they actually subscribe to temporarily "subterranean" adult values of propriety.

"Subway Vigilante"   Bernhard Goetz, the individual who shot four youths who allegedly attempted to rob him on a New York subway.

Superego   An antithetical or opposite force in the personality that restrains the impulsive id. One of the three personality components in Freud's model.

Swarm   An overwhelming and intimidating group of gang members who suddenly invade commercial stores and private homes to loot and assault vulnerable occupants.

Techniques of Neutralization   According to Gresham Sykes and David Matza, many juveniles are able to reduce or neutralize the negative impacts of delinquent behavior such as feelings of personal guilt by extending a set of psychological defense mechanisms. These justifications for deviance are: Denial of Responsibility; Denial of Injury; Denial of the Victim; Condemnation of the Condemners; and Appeal to Higher Loyalties.

Theory   A general statement that accurately relates cause-and-effect variables in order to explain events or behavior.

Throwaways   Juveniles who are driven from their homes by their parents or untenable living conditions.

Total Institution   Term used by Erving Goffman to describe a place where individuals live, work, recreate, and socially interact in an environment isolated from larger society over a long period of time.

TOUGHLOVE   Program for parents of "troubled youths." Over 1,500 chapters nationwide where parents meet and provide mutual support as they work out strategies for confronting and dealing with their teenaged children in order to reduce and eliminate their delinquent behavior.

Tracking   Educational strategy where students are grouped according to intelligence as measured by standardized tests, academic performance, and other criteria.

Traditional Court   Juvenile court characterized by low task differentiation, centralized authority, low discretion for court services staff, routine handling of status offenders, and low formalization.

Training Schools   Long-term facilities for housing juvenile offenders (comparable to adult prisons).

Transactional Analysis   Treatment strategy which views delinquency as a result of an underdeveloped ego-state. Treatment attempts to move offender to an "I'm OK, you're OK" life position.

Treatment Ideology   Follows the rehabilitative ideal of the juvenile court; tends to view delinquency as a result of an individual pathology.

Triad   A group of three persons engaged in social interaction.

Truancy   "Skipping school"—missing school without the knowledge or consent of parents or guardians— a status offense.

Turf   The geographical area or neighborhood dominated by an urban street gang in the struggle with other groups for identity, status, and territory.

Typology   A classification system that organizes a diversity of information or objects into predetermined and orderly categories. For example, Ferdinand's Typology of Delinquency has three main types and nine subcategories.

Unconscious   A subterranean mental reservoir of unfulfilled needs, desires, and feelings accumulated throughout life and not ordinarily available to conscious thought.

Validity   A fundamental research and methodological objective. A research operation or statistical measure has validity when it in fact measures whatever it is designed or intended to measure. A finding or conclusion is said to be valid if it accurately reflects factual evidence.

Values   Beliefs and ideas that are held in high esteem by a particular group; includes attitudes about what is right and wrong.

Victimization Survey   Data-collecting efforts that focus on the victims and their recollections of the crime, circumstances, and the offenders.

Vigilante   An unauthorized individual who attempts to enforce the law and administer punishment to law violators.

VisionQuest   Rehabilitation program for hard-core juvenile delinquents who are put through a series of physical challenges in the wilderness. These experiences act as a "rite of passage," geared toward building a more positive self-concept and more mature outlook on life.

Vocational Prostitutes   Prostitutes who enter the profession as a career.

Voluntary Control   Self-imposed social constraint.

Waiver   Decision made by a juvenile judge during the intake procedure to declare a juvenile an "adult" and remand her or him to adult criminal court.

Wilding   Slang term created to describe the activities of bands of bored youths on the street who prowl, assault, rob, and rape for "something to do."

Working Mother   The mother is employed outside the home.

XYY Hypothesis   A chromosomal abnormality has been tentatively linked to criminal aggression in some mates. However, research on imprisoned criminals with an extra gene carrying chromosome Y has had methodological shortcomings, and findings are very inconsistent.

Youth Service Bureaus   Established in local communities to divert youthful offenders from the juvenile justice system.

Youth Subculture   The unique attitudes, values, beliefs, and behavioral practices that distinguish a subculture, loosely comprised of all youths ranging in age from early adolescence through the late teens and early twenties.

Zero Tolerance   School policies that prohibit the possession, use, sale, or supply of any type of weapon, alcohol, or illegal drug on school premises or at any school-related functions.

NAME INDEX

Italic page numbers refer to pages on which bibliographic references will be found.

SUBJECT INDEX